These Ragged Edges

The David J. Weber Series in the New Borderlands History
Andrew R. Graybill and Benjamin H. Johnson, editors

The study of borderlands—places where different peoples meet and no one polity reigns supreme—is undergoing a renaissance. The David J. Weber Series in the New Borderlands History publishes works from both established and emerging scholars that examine borderlands from the precontact era to the present. The series explores contested boundaries and the intercultural dynamics surrounding them and includes projects covering a wide range of time and space within North America and beyond, including both Atlantic and Pacific worlds.

Published with support provided by the William P. Clements Center for Southwest Studies at Southern Methodist University in Dallas, Texas.

These Ragged Edges

Histories of Violence along the U.S.-Mexico Border

Edited by
ANDREW J. TORGET
GERARDO GURZA-LAVALLE

The University of North Carolina Press
Chapel Hill

© 2022 The University of North Carolina Press
All rights reserved

Set in Minion Pro by Westchester Publishing Services
Manufactured in the United States of America

The University of North Carolina Press has been a member of the
Green Press Initiative since 2003.

Library of Congress Cataloging-in-Publication Data is available at
https://lccn.loc.gov/2022007375.

ISBN 978-1-4696-6838-3 (cloth: alk. paper)
ISBN 978-1-4696-6839-0 (pbk.: alk. paper)
ISBN 978-1-4696-6840-6 (ebook)

Cover illustration: Carol M. Highsmith, *Humble Cemetery in the Tiny Pima County,
Arizona, Community of Quijotoa, near the Mexican Border* (Carol M. Highsmith
Archive, Library of Congress Prints and Photographs Division,
LC-DIG-highsm-49675).

For Andrew Graybill, Sherry Smith, Ruth Ann Elmore,
and Chuck Grench, who made this possible

Contents

Figures, Graphs, Map, and Tables

Acknowledgments

The William P. Clements Center for Southwest Studies at Southern Methodist University has been the foundational support for this project. A powerful incubator for scholarship on borders and borderlands, the Clements Center sponsors symposia every year on important topics in borderlands history. During the spring of 2012, the editors of this volume began a conversation with Andrew R. Graybill, the Center's director, Sherry L. Smith, then the Center's co-director, and Ruth Ann Elmore, the Center's assistant director, about the possibility of putting together an international symposium focused on the history of violence along the U.S.-Mexico border. Andrew, Sherry, and Ruth Ann immediately offered their deep support for the project and its vision of fostering a cross-border conversation between scholars in both the United States and Mexico. We could not know at the outset how enduring and steadfast that support would prove to be, which we needed throughout the intricate planning and execution of two international symposia and the long road that followed as we brought this volume to completion. We are grateful beyond words.

Within Mexico, we were lucky to have the ideal partner in the Instituto de Investigaciones Dr. José Maria Luis Mora. The Instituto Mora hosted the initial paper workshops and a public event in Mexico City, allowing everyone involved in the project to begin our work in the midst of a truly transnational exchange. We are deeply indebted to Luis Jáuregui, then the director of the Instituto, for his enthusiastic support of the symposium and project.

We are tremendously fortunate to have worked with the University of North Carolina Press from the very beginning. Our original editor, Chuck Grench, has been a steadfast champion of the project who came to our symposiums in both Mexico City and Dallas, listened to endless paper workshops, and offered sage advice on shaping the volume for which we are exceedingly grateful. When Chuck retired, we were fortunate to bring the volume to print with Debbie Gershenowitz, and we are indebted to the many talented people at UNC Press who helped transform the manuscript into this book. Andrew Graybill and Benjamin Johnson brought the volume into the David J. Weber Series in the New Borderlands History, and we could not have asked for better series editors.

Along the way, innumerable people have supported and strengthened this work. We are deeply grateful to Marcela Terrazas for her participation in both symposiums, for her invaluable input during the paper workshops, and for being a steadfast friend to the project from beginning to end. We benefited greatly from conversations with Luis García, David Romo, Alfredo Corchado, Ian Grillo, Dianne Solís, and Neil Foley. Insights provided by anonymous readers for UNC Press sharpened the collected essays throughout. More than anyone, the contributors to this volume have continually shaped and reshaped our understanding of the border and its tangled past. One of the singular joys of this project has been the opportunity to work closely with so many talented scholars who care deeply about the intersections between the peoples and histories of Mexico and the United States.

Our greatest debts are to our families for their unwavering support throughout the remarkably long journey this project required.

Andrew J. Torget and Gerardo Gurza-Lavalle

These Ragged Edges

Figure 0.1 Movie poster for *Contrabando y Traición*, 1977. Courtesy of Arturo Martínez.

Introduction

The Problem of Violence along the U.S.-Mexico Border

ANDREW J. TORGET AND GERARDO GURZA-LAVALLE

The long border between the United States and Mexico has earned an enduring reputation as a site of brutal violence. During the past twenty years in particular, the carnage of the Drug Wars—fueled by the international movement
of narcotics and vast sums of money—has burned into the consciousness of
both countries an abiding image of the U.S.-Mexico border as a place of endemic bloodshed. Stories of brutal killings, beheadings, mass graves, and the
murder of innocent men and women became numbingly commonplace in
newspapers and magazines as journalists documented the rapid escalation of
violence among cartels competing for dominance in the growing border drug
trade during the early 2000s. In 2010, during a spike in cross-cartel killings,
CBS News dubbed Ciudad Juárez (sister city to El Paso across the Rio Grande)
the "murder capital of the world."[1] Journalists working on both sides of the
border began publishing best-selling books—such as Charles Bowden's *Murder City*, Ioan Grillo's *El Narco*, and Alfredo Corchado's *Midnight in Mexico*—
that offered deeper dives into drug-related mayhem along the border than
any newspaper column could provide.[2] During that same period, a rising tide
of migrants and refugees (often fleeing violence within their home countries)
made their way from Central America and Mexico into the United States, generating their own headlines when they crossed the same porous border that
had become a war zone between cartels and government forces.[3] News coverage of these cross-border movements of migrants helped to magnify widespread perceptions that had already been forged by the Drug Wars: that the
U.S.-Mexico border was a poorly regulated, chaotic, and deeply dangerous
place. Indeed, anyone paying attention to news coverage of the U.S.-Mexico
border during the past several decades has had to wade through seemingly
endless stories of borderland chaos and brutality.

Such imagery has bled into popular culture within the United States, shaping worldwide imaginations of this international border. During the 1990s,
the cartoonish violence of the *El Mariachi* and *Desperado* films (both of which
followed a Mexican musician in his shoot-'em-up quest for revenge against
the drug lord who murdered his girlfriend) launched the career of filmmaker
Robert Rodriguez. Acclaimed novelist Cormac McCarthy offered a far darker,

grittier vision of the border in his 2005 novel *No Country for Old Men*, the story of a borderland drug deal gone awry and the never-ending carnage that followed in its wake. Adapted into a movie in 2007, *No Country for Old Men* won four Academy Awards, including Best Picture, for its portrayal of a drug-ravaged landscape where people find themselves trapped within inescapable cycles of violence that both surrounds and defines them. Philipp Meyer built upon that grim model in his award-winning 2013 novel *The Son*, which follows three generations of a single family in South Texas where their lives and fortunes are united by an unbroken legacy of brutal violence that weaves across two centuries of life in these contested lands. Adapted into a mini-series, *The Son* joined a growing chorus of popular works during the past two decades—ranging from the movie *Traffic* in 2000 to the hugely popular TV series *Breaking Bad* from 2008 to 2013—where violence is portrayed as the unavoidable birthright of the U.S.-Mexico border.

A similar perception has emerged within Mexico. For much of the twentieth century, most Mexicans—particularly those who lived in Mexico City, the cultural, financial, and political center of the country—regarded the nation's northern frontier primarily as the site of seedy border towns like Tijuana and Cuidad Juárez (which catered to American tourists looking to escape restrictive U.S. vice laws) rather than as a place of violence. That largely nonthreatening image, however, began to shift during the 1970s, as drug trafficking—and news coverage of it—increased significantly along the U.S.-Mexico border. Mexican filmmakers, in response, began producing movies focused on the violent adventures of borderland drug dealers. Films such as *Contrabando y Traición* (1977) and *La Banda del Carro Rojo* (1978) hoped to reach broad audiences by offering highly romanticized takes on the lives of cartel bosses and their gangs, threading elaborate shootout scenes between lurid tales of romance and betrayal in telenovela style. These movies often portrayed drug dealers in a sympathetic light, as anti-government rebels or quasi-folk heroes, and some featured ballads celebrating narco-bosses and their bloody lifestyles.[4] Although these films were typically low-budget, low-quality productions, they nonetheless found eager audiences on both sides of the border during the 1970s, 1980s, and 1990s. The dramatic escalation of drug-related violence during the early 2000s fed directly into these images, hardening perceptions within Mexico about the border as a violent place.[5] Because so much of the cartel-related bloodshed took place on the Mexican side of the border, the Drug Wars became a constant fixture within Mexican news media. Popular perceptions within Mexico about the border thus began to merge with those in the United States during the early twenty-first century, as both Mexicans and Americans found themselves deluged with news reports on borderland killings at the same moment that Hollywood-produced films like *No Country for Old Men* and *Sicario* played to sellout crowds in both countries.

Within all these visions, whether in contemporary news or popular culture, there is often a timeless quality to modern depictions of violence along the border: the characters involved may change, but brutality seems to be the constant backdrop. In large measure because the Drug Wars have continued across multiple decades, bloodshed has come to be a defining aspect of how Mexicans and Americans think about the border between their countries. One powerful result has been the creation of a stubborn perception within the United States (and, to a lesser extent, within Mexico) of the border as a place that surely has *always* been inescapably violent. Much of this comes from the very human tendency to read the present back into the past: if border violence appears so intractable in the modern era, why would that have been different decades or even centuries earlier? From this perspective, violence can appear as an essential and almost predestined part of the border, as natural to the territory as the landscape itself.

Near the end of the film version of *No Country for Old Men*, a weary Sheriff Ed Tom Bell visits the ramshackle home of his uncle Ellis, where Bell confesses to feeling "over-matched" by the brutality that surrounds him. Rather than console Bell, Ellis replies with a parable of sorts: the story of how a relative of theirs was shot and left to die on his own front porch in 1909. "What you got ain't nothin' new," Ellis concludes. "This country is hard on people." According to Ellis, violence always has—and therefore always will—curse this borderland region. "You can't stop what's coming," he warns.

This book offers a different viewpoint. We do not believe that the U.S.-Mexico border is either destined or cursed to be a violent place. Nor do we believe that bloodshed is an inevitable result of the inequalities between the United States and Mexico that come crashing together in this tumultuous region. We believe, instead, that every episode of borderland violence has its roots within a particular historical context (that is, a specific set of circumstances tied to a certain time and place) and therefore the rapid evolution of conditions along the U.S.-Mexico border during the past two centuries has directly shaped the ebb and flow of conflict within the region. Everything, in other words, depends on context. The Drug Wars of the early twenty-first century, for example, emerged from far different circumstances than those that gave rise to the violence of the Mexican Revolution during the early twentieth century. The bloodshed of Comanche cross-border raiding during the nineteenth century sprang from very different conditions than the violence directed against Latin American migrants smuggling their way into the United States during the early twenty-first century. Violence, therefore, has emerged along the U.S.-Mexico border during particular historical moments because of specific and evolving circumstances in the region, rather than simply being an essential and unavoidable fact of life in the territory during the past two hundred years.

At the same time, we also recognize that the U.S.-Mexico border does possess a particularly violent past. Although it would be hard to quantify such comparisons, the international boundary between the United States and Mexico has witnessed far more large-scale conflicts during the past two centuries (such as the U.S.-Mexico War, the Mexican Revolution, and the modern Drug Wars) than has the line between the United States and Canada.[6] A similar comparison can be made with Mexico's southern border with Guatemala, which has experienced its own share of violence over the years but not on the same scale as Mexico's northern border.[7] The broad differences between these three major North American borders during the past two hundred years serve as a powerful reminder that international boundaries do not, by themselves, necessitate regular cycles of conflict or violence. At the same time, the fact that the history of the U.S.-Mexico border does stand out as particularly violent among the three suggests that there must be reasons why conditions along this boundary have more frequently fostered violence than other borders on the continent. This is not to say that violence has been a constant force within the region. Despite its popular image, the U.S.-Mexico border has enjoyed periods of calm and peace during the last two centuries. Yet the U.S.-Mexico boundary has also witnessed numerous periods of remarkable brutality during that same timeframe, reinforcing modern perceptions in the United States and Mexico that violence is somehow an immutable part of the nature of this border.

Some factors that have fomented violence in the region can be traced to broad forces shaping the development of both nations. In its most elemental sense, the U.S.-Mexico border has been the primary point of overlap between rapidly evolving conditions in each country during the last two hundred years. Broad structural forces shaping and reshaping the daily realities facing people in both nations could, and often did, come crashing into one another along the border. It was, for example, the place where the expanding power of the U.S. economy during the last two hundred years exercised its most tangible, and sometimes destructive, influences on the more impoverished and extractive economy of Mexico. The rapid growth of U.S. territory and population during the nineteenth century offered powerful economic rewards for those who dared to smuggle cattle and goods across the U.S.-Mexico border. Similar market forces helped to shape the cross-border movement of drugs, weapons, and people throughout the twentieth and twenty-first centuries. The proximity of American markets to Mexican territories has, as a result, provided long-term incentives for smuggling along the border, one of numerous ways that economic forces shaping North America have exercised particularly powerful influences along the line.

Other broad developments in both nations have played central roles in defining realities along this shared line. The border has been the place, for example, that often revealed both the grand ambitions and severe limits of political power in Washington, D.C., and Mexico City, as politicians in each country attempted to shape the development of their side of the border and, in the process, their nation's relationship to the other. Such political measures have taken innumerable forms during the past two centuries, ranging from the presence of military forces along the border to evolving national policies about migration and trade. And each of these measures has helped to continually reshape conditions along the U.S.-Mexico line and thus the lives of the people who lived there. Even the disparate ways that the history between the United States and Mexico has been remembered in each country—such as how the legacies of the U.S. conquest of the modern American Southwest shaped racial and ethnic identities and their portrayal in popular culture— has molded the lived experience along the border. Indeed, the very ways that people of varying backgrounds have imagined each other over the years has, in turn, informed how they interacted with one another, particularly in moments of tension. None of these broad structural forces—whether economic, political, cultural, or otherwise—began at the border, yet the border is the place where those forces from both countries come crashing into one another. And it is in those overlaps between the structural forces in the United States and Mexico and the unique and local conditions of the border itself, which have shaped the evolution of daily realities along this shared line, that we find the waxing and waning of border violence during the past two hundred years.

The boundary between the United States and Mexico, then, offers a remarkable window through which to examine the history of violence in North America. It is a border whose modern image is one of endemic violence—defined by the scourge of drug-related bloodshed. Yet it is also a border whose long history has seen tremendous change and variation, allowing us to examine how shifting circumstances on the ground have affected the evolution of violence in the region over several centuries. It is a place, in other words, where we can ask far-reaching questions: How has violence along the U.S.-Mexico border changed during the boundary's two-hundred-year history? What role has the border itself played in fostering or suppressing violence during that time period, and has that role changed as conditions in the region have shifted? Are there common threads woven across the nineteenth, twentieth, and twenty-first centuries—specific conditions in the region that have persisted across time—that helped make this territory a more frequent site of violence than other international borders on the continent? Indeed, what can we learn about violence in North America if we examine the long history of conflict along the U.S.-Mexico border?

This book is an attempt to begin grappling with such questions by examining various moments of borderland violence from the early nineteenth century through the modern day. The central goal is to historicize those moments of conflict, revealing both what has changed and what has remained consistent about border violence over the years. By diving deeply into episodes of violence, the essays in this volume each provide a case study of the relationship between violence and the border during particular historical contexts. The result is a series of deep treatments of both the roots and consequences of border violence across numerous eras. By stacking these studies side-by-side, something even more valuable emerges from the collection: a broader vision of the evolution of violence along the U.S.-Mexico border over the course of the past two hundred years.

This volume began as a series of conversations among scholars at two international symposiums held during the fall of 2015 and spring of 2016. During the mid-2010s, the Clements Center for Southwest Studies at Southern Methodist University formed a partnership with the Instituto Mora of Mexico City, with each institution committing to sponsor and host a series of discussions among researchers studying violence along the U.S.-Mexico border. The driving idea behind the partnership was the same as this volume: to bring together leading scholars in the field for a series of discussions that could begin contextualizing the long history of violence along the border. At the same time, the Clements Center and the Instituto Mora shared another goal for the project. Because we believed that understanding the history of violence in the region would require examining both sides of the border, we decided that we needed to structure the symposiums as a series of transnational dialogues. Our plan was to bring together scholars from both the United States and Mexico in hopes of combining insights, perspectives, and experiences culled from both the northern and southern sides of the international boundary. In framing the symposiums this way, we hoped to create conversations that would be truly transnational—rather than dominated by one particular side—which could, in turn, broaden and deepen the perspectives of contributors from both sides of the border. The result, we hoped, would be a series of essays and discussions that would bring together the best of modern scholarship on the topic while also fostering an ongoing dialogue between U.S. and Mexican scholars about their shared border.

Collectively stretching from the twilight of Spanish power in colonial Mexico through the modern Drug Wars, each essay in this volume investigates distinct episodes, moments, or themes related to violence along or connected to the U.S.-Mexico border. The charge for each contributor was to dive deeply into those moments, eras, and issues in order to examine how violence emerged within particular sets of circumstances. In so doing, each essay shares a common interest in untangling the situational logic behind those moments and restoring the context of the era and specific conditions that produced conflict.

Focusing on situational logic, in turn, allows each essay to engage the great variability of violence. Violence, of course, comes in innumerable forms—it can be physical, emotional, economic, political, and everything in between. It does not even have to take place in order to be powerful, as the mere threat or possibility of violence often feels as real and terrifying as any other form. Throughout both symposiums, we collectively discussed what each of us meant by "violence" and came up with a basic definition that could encompass the breadth of the collective essays: we consider violence to be damage— whether real or threatened—to humans and property. Within that broad window, however, each of the essays engages the concept of violence on their own terms, exploring the great variability of borderland conflicts within the distinct contexts that produced them. As a result, the chapters that follow do not attempt to fit each of their engagements with violence into a single defining form—they instead embrace both the complexity and wide variation of violence as it played out on the ground along the U.S.-Mexico border.[8]

Focusing deeply on particular moments, eras, and themes also meant that we never intended to provide a comprehensive history of violence along the border. Although that would be an important and noble undertaking, such a project would require a far different approach in order to focus on breadth of coverage rather than depth of investigation. As such, there are numerous moments of border violence that we do not address in this volume simply because we could not include everything. Some of these include well-known moments of martial violence between the United States and Mexico that have received sustained attention from other historians, such as the U.S.-Mexico War of 1846–48 or Pancho Villa's 1916 raid on Columbus, New Mexico, and the Pershing Expedition that followed.[9] Some subjects that we could not address are far less well-known to the public but have nonetheless received important and sustained attention from other scholars, such as the exploitation of ethnic Chinese in the United States and Mexico, the lives of both enslaved and free African Americans along the border, and the use of violence in the exploitation of working-class Mexicans in both countries.[10] Similarly, there is a growing and powerful literature on the borderland abuse of women that reveals the horrific depths of gendered violence in human trafficking and sexual exploitation. In particular, pathbreaking work has emerged during the last several decades on femicides along the U.S.-Mexico border, particularly in Ciudad Juárez, Chihuahua, where untold thousands of women have been brutally murdered during the last three decades, even as official authorities at all levels have continually failed to act.[11] And yet, as many historians have documented, law enforcement officials—at the national, state, and local levels—have played powerful roles in fostering this and other forms of violence on both sides of the border through prison systems and border enforcement agencies, such as the Border Patrol and Immigration and Naturalization Service within the United States and police forces and the federal army within Mexico.[12]

All of these are deeply important subjects that deserve sustained scholarly treatments, and we do not mean to imply that any subject not included here is somehow less important than the topics we do address. But since we knew that we could not address everything, we sought instead to collect a series of particular moments of violence that allowed deep treatments of how the evolution of both broad structures and local conditions could foster and suppress border violence at different moments. We sought out essays, therefore, that could overlap in meaningful ways, whether in themes, in approaches, or sometimes by engaging a singular topic from multiple perspectives, which we could put into conversations with one another as we searched for insights into the ebbs and flows of violence along the border during the past two centuries.

For similar reasons, we did not attempt to cover all the geography of the U.S.-Mexico border in equal measure. As borderland scholars know so well, there is almost no end to the tremendous variety of histories, experiences, and episodes of violence that have played out across the nearly 2,000-mile-long line that divides the United States and Mexico. Although the essays that follow touch on all sections of the border—ranging from Texas, New Mexico, Arizona, and California to Tamaulipas, Nuevo León, Coahuila, Chihuahua, Sonora, and Baja California—we also knew that we could not account for all portions of that enormous space in equal fullness. And because we sought out contributions that could overlap thematically over such a long period of time, the essays in this volume tend to engage the eastern half of the border more frequently than the western half. Part of that reflects our decision to begin the volume during the twilight of Spain's presence in Mexico, as the eastern half of what would become the border emerged as the far more populated region during much of the nineteenth century. Another part reflects what historian Rachel St. John observed in her history of the western half of the U.S.-Mexico border: there has been, for a variety of reasons, much more scholarship produced on the eastern half than the western half, which sometimes provided us more opportunities to bring together scholars around overlaps in their work.[13] We also did not want the contributors to limit the reach of their work solely to the territories that run parallel to the international line, and thus several essays roam well beyond the border as they trace the power, influence, and implications of borderland violence as far north as Nebraska and as far south as Central America.

Throughout the project, we remained aware that our decision to focus on violence came with its own risks. One that emerged during our conversations in both Mexico City and Dallas was a concern that by focusing on moments of violence, even to contextualize and historicize them, the resulting book would, by necessity, be full of essays about violence, which might thereby contribute to overemphasizing the influence and presence of violence along the U.S.-Mexico border. In other words, stacking treatments of border violence alongside one another has the potential, if only through sheer volume, to reinforce perceptions that violence is an endemic and natural aspect of this borderland region. We openly acknowledge that challenge. Our intention, however, is precisely the opposite: we hope that providing a more historicized understanding of violence along the U.S.-Mexico border will, instead, contribute to an understanding of violence in the region that is more grounded in the evolution of conditions along the border. Indeed, this is one reason we do not seek to be comprehensive in our coverage of either topics or geography: we did not want to give the false impression that violence has been a constant feature of the border's long history. As borderlands scholars know so well, the U.S.-Mexico border has enjoyed periods of peace—and even during periods of great upheaval along particular portions, numerous other sections of the border often remained unscathed. Although we wrestled with this, we ultimately concluded that the benefits of curating a series of deep examinations of borderland violence outweighed the risks of those collective treatments unintentionally reinforcing the very stereotypes we hope to undermine.

Indeed, we accept that risk because we believe the chapters in this volume make important contributions to a rapidly expanding literature that seeks to create a more contextualized and historicized vision of borderland violence. Some of the most important recent works in borderlands history have focused specifically on the power and legacies of violence in the region. Our understanding of the eighteenth- and nineteenth-century U.S.-Mexico borderlands, for example, has been reshaped in recent years by Ned Blackhawk's *Violence over the Land*, Cuauhtémoc Velasco Ávila's *La Frontera étnica en el Noreste Novohispano*, Pekka Hämäläinen's *The Comanche Empire*, Sara Ortelli's *Trama de una Guerra Conveniente*, Brian DeLay's *War of a Thousand*

Deserts, Karl Jacoby's *Shadows at Dawn*, José Marcos Medina Bustos and Esther Padilla Calderón's *Violencia Interétnica en la Frontera Norte Novohispana y Mexicana*, and Lance Blyth's *Chiricahua and Janos*, all of which used the lens of violence as windows into the evolution of these territories.[14] Ana María Alonso's *Thread of Blood*, Héctor Aguilar Camín's *La Frontera Nómada*, Benjamin Johnson's *Revolution in Texas*, Charles Harris and Luis Sadler's *The Plan de San Diego*, Timothy Dunn's *The Militarization of the U.S.-Mexico Border*, Howard Campbell's *Drug War Zone*, Wil Pansters's edited collection *Violence, Coercion, and State-Making in Twentieth-Century Mexico*, and Jason De León's *The Land of Open Graves* have done the same for our understanding of the place of violence along the border during the twentieth and twenty-first centuries.[15] As work on the territories along the shared edges of the United States and Mexico continues to mature as a "borderlands" field, the role of violence in the evolution of the region has become a powerful lens through which to understand this history.[16]

––––––––

The essays in this volume are organized into three parts, each of which roughly correspond to eras of violence along the border. Part 1, "Livestock, Markets, and Guns," examines the period from the early 1800s through the 1870s, when smuggling—primarily livestock theft—served as a primary catalyst for igniting violence in the borderlands.

As Alberto Barrera-Enderle and Andrew Torget show in their essay, the violence that emerged during the 1810s along the edge between New Spain and the United States had deep roots in the long history of Spain's failures to occupy and control the territories that would become northeastern Mexico. Throughout the eighteenth century, the territory had remained fiercely contested between interloping Spaniards and the numerous independent Indian groups who lived in and controlled most of the region. The Spaniards who did eke out a life along the border often did so in the shadow of violent raids by nearby Indian nations. At the same time, these Spaniards also found themselves perpetually isolated from the rest of New Spain, as the centralized trading system embraced by royal authorities (which required all trade to flow through Veracruz and Mexico City) ensured that Spaniards living on the northeastern frontier often could not get access to even the most basic necessities. Smuggling along the U.S. border, as a result, emerged as a survival tactic for local Spaniards by the early nineteenth century. Yet it was two major shifts during the 1810s that increased both smuggling and violence to unprecedented levels. The first shift came with the outbreak of the Mexican War for Independence, which brought tremendous bloodshed to Texas and forced hundreds of Spaniards into exile as refugees in U.S.-held Louisiana. The second shift came with the massive expansion of markets in the southwestern United States when the "cotton revolution" of the 1810s brought insatiable new demands for horses. The combination of these two events dramatically increased the incentives for all peoples living along this border—particularly independent Indians in search of livestock—to engage in smuggling and, as a result, drastically amplified violence in the region on the eve of Mexico's independence.

Even as Mexico became independent, Indian raids of Mexican settlements for livestock to sell to the United States continued in full fury. Mexico's national government proved unable to stop the incursions, and each of the northern states of Mexico lacked the resources to shield their settlements from raids. Anglo-Americans, meanwhile, continued to migrate into the regions along the U.S.-Mexico border, which further expanded the markets—and thus incentives—for dealing in stolen livestock. As a result, at the conclusion of the U.S.-Mexico War, the government of Mexico insisted that the United States assume responsibility for preventing further raids across the newly redefined U.S.-Mexico border by independent Indian nations, an agreement enshrined in Article 11 of the Treaty of Guadalupe-Hidalgo.

What changed after the treaty? Joaquín Rivaya-Martínez tackles this question in an essay drawing on ethnohistorical perspectives to explain the logic behind Comanche predatory incursions into Mexico. Rivaya-Martínez argues that the incentives for and the intensity of Indian raids across northern Mexico remained largely stable during both the periods preceding and following the U.S.-Mexico War. Despite its pledge in Article 11, the United States made little effort to enforce that promise, and in any case, the U.S. Army lacked both the resources and the personnel necessary to carry it out. Because Texas had retained control of its public lands when it joined the United States, the U.S. government also had little capacity to force the Texas state government to comply with Article 11. Incentives for Comanche raiding continued to grow during the decades that followed the 1820s, as herds of bison dwindled on the Texas and New Mexico plains at the same time that Americans began pouring into the newly expanded U.S. Southwest. The combination of those two forces ensured that Indian raids of Mexican territory—which were poorly defended yet relatively rich in livestock—remained highly profitable. At the same time, expanding Anglo-American populations in the region also made firearms more easily accessible to Indian raiders—a reality that persisted even after the war. A weak presence of both the United States and Mexico governments along the border, combined with an expanding supply of firearms and a highly profitable market for stolen livestock, kept strong incentives for violence along the U.S.-Mexico border during the years following the Treaty of Guadalupe-Hidalgo.

Lance Blyth focuses on how violence played out on the ground among cattle rustlers working on both sides of the U.S.-Mexico border. Blyth suggests that violence in the borderlands became more pervasive after 1848, arguing that the creation of the new boundary between the United States and Mexico created new incentives for both cattle rustling and violence. The ineffectiveness of government authorities on either side of the international line during the mid-1800s made it difficult to protect herds, and the ability of rustlers to slip easily from one side of the border to the other (much as the Comanches did) helped to shield them from prosecution. Just as important, the borderline also disrupted social networks that had previously served to repress violence. Before the U.S.-Mexico War, ties of friendship, kinship, and social obligation had often bound communities across Anglo-American and Mexican settlements which, while not preventing violence completely, had suppressed cycles of vengeance and retaliation that otherwise could go on for years. The establishment of the new U.S.-Mexico border in 1848, however, severed many of these ties and relationships, which led to escalating cycles of violence. The continued weakness of both the U.S. and Mexican governments in the region, in turn, did nothing to stop the bloodshed.

Part 2, "State Power in Transition," focuses on the evolving role of governments in fostering and suppressing the use of violence along the U.S.-Mexico boundary during the second half of the nineteenth century. Both the United States and Mexico attempted to increase their presence along the border during these crucial decades, and each sought—though never fully succeeding—to exert more control over the uses of violence in the region. During the early part of this period, the still-anemic state structures on both sides of the border contributed to outbreaks of violence because both Mexico and the United States proved largely ineffective at policing the territory. By the late 1800s, however, the presence of both governments had increased, which allowed them both to exert expanded influence over border violence.

Miguel Ángel González Quiroga explores a manifestation of state weakness in episodes of what he calls "cooperative violence." In examining the Federalist War of 1840 and the Cortina War of 1859, González Quiroga observes the formation of unlikely alliances and collaborations between Mexicans and Anglo-Americans who joined forces to use violence toward mutual ends. Although each conflict arose from different circumstances and played out in disparate ways, both took place against a backdrop of state weakness, and they provide insight into the shifting identities and the ambiguous sense of national allegiance of many people living along the border during this period. When it was in their mutual interest, Anglo-Americans and Mexicans could form interethnic alliances to use violence to attain goals that, if not completely shared, were at least compatible. These alliances also reveal that—at least in certain contexts—ethnicity and race did not always predetermine who would use violence against whom, and that the use of violence in transethnic partnerships could bridge alliances across the border.

Alice Baumgartner offers a different interpretation of the Cortina War, arguing that the conflict marked a turning point along the border when the informal mechanisms that had previously been effective in keeping violence in check on both banks of the Rio Grande strained and broke. Alliances of cooperative violence did not work anymore, she argues, because questions of Cortina's nationality became a defining issue for the Texas and U.S. governments. If Cortina were merely a troublesome U.S. citizen, then his uprising could be handled by local authorities. If, however, Cortina were instead a Mexican national invading American soil, the revolt then posed a much more significant threat that, in turn, demanded a more vigorous response from the U.S. government. In a borderlands space of shifting and ambiguous identities, questions of citizenship and loyalty had become increasingly important as the United States weighed how to respond to the uprising. In this, Baumgartner agrees with an argument also made by Blyth: state weakness did not necessarily have to give way to endemic violence, so long as the informal social networks and ad hoc agreements that brought together communities and local authorities on both sides of the river could collaborate in the suppression of violence. Yet in the Cortina revolt, these local arrangements no longer sufficed when border violence became "nationalized" and the response to it therefore became a matter for state and national authorities.

Timothy Bowman focuses on this "nationalization" phenomenon of border violence, exploring how both Mexico City and Washington, D.C., shifted their perceptions about the border during the period from 1848 to 1875, as each country sought to suppress violence and crime along their shared border. Much of the impetus for that more assertive presence came from those living along the line, as citizens on both sides recognized the dreadful toll that violence associated with cattle theft and Indian raids had wrought in their lives. A stronger state could, they hoped, provide greater stability in the region by cataloguing and suppressing local conflict. In response, the United States created the Robb Commission and Mexico City created the Comisión Pesquisidora, both of which were charged with investigating the history, causes, and costs of border violence on their citizens. The reports, in turn, reveal the growing interest of both the U.S. and Mexican governments in expanding their influence on the use of violence along the border (usually blaming the other side for conflict), as well as the limits of those aspirations during the era.

Gabriel Martínez-Serna offers a deep look at this process of state growth in an essay that focuses on the evolution of state-level security within Nuevo León, which shifted from a militia composed of local citizens intended to fend off Indian raids into a "new security architecture" of the Mexican state by the late 1890s. The centerpiece of this new security apparatus was a more disciplined, centralized, and state-funded police force, which joined with the new federal rural police—known as the *Rurales*—to guard the state and the border area. Powerful economic growth and new technologies in the region, such as railroads and telegraphs, contributed to the growing power of these new state-run police forces, which could exert for the Mexican government a more powerful presence along the border toward fighting banditry and repressing those who opposed the regime of Porfirio Diaz.

Part 3, "Violence at the Turn of the Century," focuses on the transition that took place during the 1890s and early twentieth century when the line dividing the United States and Mexico became more defined in practice as populations grew on both sides of the border. Growing towns, a denser network of communications, and an expanding Mexican-origin population in southern Texas increased ethnic tensions as well as competition for land and resources.

Against this backdrop, Brandon Morgan analyzes the uprising of Santana Pérez in Chihuahua in 1893–94, when the centralizing and modernizing dynamics of the Porfiriato were in full swing. With a small band of armed men, Pérez raided the customs house of Palomas on the Chihuahua–New Mexico border, with the apparent aim of sparking a broad uprising against Mexico's national government. A seasoned Apache fighter, Pérez had originally been on the side of the federal army in the suppression of a previous revolt at Tomóchic. The brutality of government repression at Tomóchic, and its sequel at Santo Tomás, however, moved Pérez and his followers to condemn the tyranny of the federal government and take up arms against it. Morgan focuses on the discursive war Mexican officials waged in diplomatic dispatches and newspapers to deny legitimacy to the rebels and portray them as mere bandits. Pérez and his followers, by contrast, succeeded in obtaining favorable coverage in American newspapers, which lent credibility to the revolutionary aims of the revolt. The revolt and the discursive war that surrounded it reveal that the Mexican state had no monopoly on the use of violence on its side of the international border, which people such as Pérez used to resist the efforts at capitalist development and political centralization in the region by the Porfirio Diaz regime.

Indeed, as the twentieth century dawned, outbreaks of violence often involved communities that spanned the border. Sonia Hernández analyzes the case of Gregorio Cortez, a Mexican leaseholder in Karnes County, Texas, who shot and killed the county sheriff in 1901 in an act of self-defense. While attempting to flee, Cortez also clashed with other law enforcement officers, leading Texas to charge him with the murder of three sheriffs by the time he was finally captured and jailed. While imprisoned and awaiting trial, Cortez found himself the target of an attempted lynching, and his ordeal reveals how powerfully ethnic tensions played into the ways that state authorities along the border used violence and sanctioned the use of vigilante "justice" during the early twentieth century. At the same time, Cortez's proximity to Mexico also provided him access to ethnic social networks that transcended the border and offered him a measure of protection, as an "unlikely transnational alliance" of ethnic Mexicans from southern Texas and northeastern Mexico pooled their resources for the legal defense of Cortez. Hernández thus shows how conditions along the U.S.-Mexico border during the early twentieth century could both stoke ethnic tensions that led to violence and foster transnational networks and relations that could, simultaneously, mitigate violence.

Gregorio Cortez was lucky: he not only escaped a lynching but also received a pardon from the governor and was released after spending ten years in prison. Many other Mexicans, however, perished at the hands of lynching mobs throughout the nineteenth and early twentieth centuries. In a broader approach to the lynching of persons of Mexican descent, William Carrigan and Clive Webb agree with Hernández on the power of ethnic tensions to provoke incidents of extralegal justice. Based on a thorough analysis of more than three hundred documented cases of lynching of ethnic Mexicans in the United States from 1848 until 1928, Carrigan and Webb identified three spikes of such violence over the course of eighty years. The first two spikes, during the 1850s and the 1870s, respectively, coincided with periods during which Mexican immigration to the United States and competition for resources rose considerably, leading to racial friction and bursts of extralegal executions. The border itself played an important role in triggering this behavior. Especially in the Lower Rio Grande Valley, lynching often emerged as a response to fears that supposed perpetrators might seek haven on the Mexican side of the line; it was also a desirable choice for those unwilling to wait for the due process of law. Carrigan and Webb thus posit a correlation of violence with scarce resources, a growing population of Mexican descent (and/or its movement back and forth across the border), and concerns about law and order. The third spike in lynching episodes took place during the Mexican Revolution, especially between 1915 and 1919, when raids related to the Plan de San Diego unleashed a wave of extralegal executions of Mexicans.

Alan Knight's essay focuses on the relationship between the border and political violence during the Mexican Revolution. Mexico's civil conflict spilled across the U.S.-Mexico line during the mid-to-late 1910s, as a shift toward irregular warfare in the struggle led to a series of raids and counterraids that culminated in the Plan de San Diego in southern Texas and, more famously, Pancho Villa's attack on Columbus, New Mexico. From the beginning, Knight argues, the border proved essential to the revolutionary struggle as *norteños* (people from northern Mexico) found themselves in the vanguard of the fight and relied on the advantages their proximity to the international boundary could provide. Being close to the border—and thus far from central Mexico—made it easier for norteños to defy federal authority, and they tapped into a long tradition of norteño military culture that derived, in part, from the long history of violent clashes with Indians along the border. More important, revolutionary norteños could use the border as a line of refuge and safe haven, much as the Comanches of the mid-nineteenth century had used it, as well as a source for badly needed military supplies that would allow them to continue their fight.

Part 4, "Drugs and Migrants," addresses the two subjects most readily associated by the public today with border violence—drug trafficking and illegal migration—by offering long-view historical perspectives on each. For much of the twentieth century, both the movement of undocumented migrants and the smuggling of drugs across the U.S.-Mexico line took place without much violence. That began to shift, however, when the governments of the United States and Mexico increased their efforts to control the transnational movement of people and drugs, which led, in turn, to increasingly complex adaptations by smugglers that bred expanded violence on each side.

Santiago Guerra traces the evolution of the drug trade across the twentieth century, from its early small-scale structure to the massive and complex organizations that control it today. Before the 1940s, families living along the northern edge of the U.S.-Mexico border engaged in smuggling primarily as a means for supplementing their meager farming incomes, relying on their intimate knowledge of the local terrain to avoid detection. But as the U.S. and Mexican governments increased their efforts to curtail such trafficking during the post–World War II era, both the economic rewards of the trade and the violence associated with it increased. The steady militarization of the border during the last few decades of the twentieth century accelerated that process, as small and familial organizations came to be supplanted in the drug trade by complex criminal corporations that could afford the rising costs—and increased violence—associated with drug smuggling. As Guerra explains, this has created a vicious cycle: increased policing of the border, ironically, fostered more violence among drug cartels, which, in turn, has only increased the desire within both Mexican and the United States for greater law enforcement along the border.

Elaine Carey and José Carlos Cisneros provide an important and often ignored perspective on the subject of drug trafficking: the role and experience of women in the trade. Stories of how professional traders have used women as "mules" are well known, but the historical role of women as cartel bosses and high-level operatives is far less understood. By delving deeply into the lives of a few of these women, Carey and Cisneros show that women were not always the victims of male bosses but that some entered the trade as the result of a rational decision: in a world of poverty and lack of opportunities, compounded by gender inequality, the drug trade could offer women the chance to make a good living and to control their own lives. Carey and Cisneros agree with Guerra on the central role that families played in the early trade. Indeed, they emphasize how women relied on family networks to run their organizations, a trait of female-run organizations that has remained remarkably consistent from the 1950s through the present day. Carey and Cisneros also suggest that women in the trade behave somewhat differently than their male counterparts: women tend to be less prone to resort to violence, even if that has not shielded them personally from bloodshed.

Finally, Alejandra Díaz de León closes the volume with an essay about the relationship between violence and border enforcement against illegal immigration. In the years before the U.S. Immigration Reform and Control Act (IRCA) of 1986, it was relatively easy for Mexican and Central American migrants to cross into the United States without documentation. IRCA, however, greatly increased policing and restrictions on movement along the border. Those restrictions, in turn, pushed the flow of migration into more remote, desolate, and dangerous portions of the border. The result was a steep rise in the number of migrant deaths and greater vulnerability of the migrants to extortion, kidnapping, forced recruitment, and other abuses in the hands of operatives of criminal organizations and agents of the border patrol. Migrants from Central America (who traverse Mexico on their way to the United States) have become even more vulnerable since the early 1990s, when the Mexican government began cooperating with the United States to halt these movements, subjecting Central Americans to similar problems and exploitation in both countries. As such, violence associated with the U.S.-Mexico boundary spreads well beyond the border itself—reaching as far south as Mexico's line with Guatemala.

Studying the history of the U.S.-Mexico border means acknowledging the tremendous diversity of peoples, geographies, events, and experiences that have played out during the past two centuries along this two-thousand-mile international boundary. As the essays in this collection document in vivid detail, violence has also scarred this land in innumerable ways across those great spans of time and space. Stacked alongside one another, the essays also point toward common threads woven throughout these histories of border violence.

Economic inequalities between the United States and Mexico have long fostered powerful incentives for illicit movements across the border. The rapid growth of markets in the United States during the nineteenth and twentieth centuries, for example, promised lucrative rewards to smugglers willing to flout regulations and restrictions on both sides of the boundary. For most of the nineteenth century, much of that smuggling centered on cattle and horses. During the twentieth century, the trade's center shifted toward contraband drugs and migrants as U.S. market demands changed. Yet questions of whether and how violence would accompany those illegal movements often pivoted on local circumstances and evolving conditions. The lack of any sustained governmental presence along the border during much of the nineteenth century, for instance, made it difficult for ranchers to protect their herds, which led to increased livestock theft that was, in turn, sometimes accompanied by violence that tended to be episodic, often retaliatory, and usually quite localized. The rapid expansion of governmental presence along the border during the twentieth century, however, led to a very different set of conditions that could foster violence. Efforts to regulate various drugs and narcotics within the United States during the second half of the twentieth century increased both the difficulty and the profitability of such contraband trade, which led to sustained episodes of violence between competing drug suppliers and the governmental agencies that sought to suppress them. As the specific circumstances surrounding border smuggling shifted dramatically over time, so too did the conditions that produced associated violence at particular moments and places along the border.

One of the broader threads of the collection is the documentation of the rise of state power during the past two centuries. Sustained efforts by both the United States and Mexico to increase their position and influence along the border began during the latter half of the nineteenth century, in part as efforts to control and monopolize the use of violence along the border. Yet the increased role of government agents and the accompanied militarization of the border during the twentieth and early twenty-first centuries failed to impose enduring control on the use of violence in the region. The expansion of state power on the border has, instead, increased both the legal consequences and the economic rewards for those who would defy federal regulations, which has, in turn, increased the violence associated with the transnational drug trade and human smuggling operations. That shift during the last half century suggests that economic disparities between the United States and Mexico have proven far more powerful than state agencies or governmental policies in shaping borderland realities.

Conditions along the border itself also mattered enormously, as this region has never been merely the farthest extension of the United States or Mexico and their respective governments. The sheer distance of the border from both Washington, D.C., and Mexico City, for example, allowed people in the region more power and ability to defy state authorities and government agencies. Comanche and other independent Indian nations used that distance and the international boundary itself as a shield during much of the nineteenth century against the efforts of Mexican authorities to pursue them for cross-border raiding. Mexican rebels during the Revolution of the 1910s crossed the border regularly for similar reasons and found similar advantages, albeit under wildly different circumstances. On a smaller scale, individuals accused of crimes or transgressions—ranging from those who became famous, such as Juan Cortina, to everyday men and women—often fled across the border in order to escape prosecution by authorities or the wrath of their neighbors and the violence that could result. The border, in that sense, has long held the power to protect people and suppress violence by offering asylum. Yet, at the same time, fears that suspected criminals might try to escape justice by crossing the border also led to spikes in extralegal lynching during the late 1800s and early 1900s, demonstrating that circumstances with the potential to suppress violence in certain moments could also, in other moments, foster it.

A persistent thread throughout the collection is that communities and relationships along the border mattered in determining the use or suppression of violence in the region. Social networks, community relationships, personal friendships, and ad hoc agreements that spanned the international boundary often empowered people who lived near this line to work together toward either the suppression or exploitation of violence in their communities. Whether it was regulating cross-border cattle rustling during the nineteenth century or coordinating familial networks for the drug trade during the twentieth century, transnational relationships had the power at different moments to amplify or mitigate certain kinds of violence when it was in the mutual interest of different members of those communities to do so. But when those cross-border relationships and alliances broke down because of shifting events or evolving circumstances, the ability of local communities to regulate violence could—and often did—break down just as quickly. The people who lived along the border, in other words, proved to be their own powerful forces in shaping the day-to-day realities of life in the region, even as they also had to cope with the pervasive influence of other forces and agendas being imposed on the border territories from across the rest of Mexico and the United States.

Perhaps the thread most deeply woven throughout the essays is that the rapid shifting of conditions along the border played some of the most powerful roles in shaping the ebb and flow of violence within the region. Comanche raids across the border during the 1840s, for example, may have relied on similar structures as the cross-border movement of Mexican rebels during the 1910s, but the specific conditions fostering those movements, and the violence they produced, proved very different from one another. Whereas Comanches raided in response to the dwindling of buffalo herds and the steady movement of Anglo-Americans into the Southwest, Mexican rebels of the 1910s used the border to support strategic war planning and as a reliable depot for military supplies so necessary to continue their fight. In a similar way, the smuggling associated with livestock in the nineteenth century and the drug trade of the twentieth and twenty-first centuries both exploited broad gaps between market demands and governmental policies, yet the circumstances fostering violence in each situation nonetheless proved quite different. Livestock rustling often happened in the absence of reliable law enforcement and spiked during the mid-nineteenth century because the sudden redrawing of the borderline in 1848 disrupted many of the Anglo-Mexican social alliances that had previously served to suppress such crime and violence. The drug trade, by contrast, remained small-scale and largely violence free for most of the first half of the twentieth century, until expanded policing at the border rapidly increased both the danger and profitability of the trade—and thus the violence that came with it. In each of these, it was the shifting of particular circumstances along the border that set into motion specific conditions that could, in different moments, either foster or suppress violence.

Today we live with the legacies of those histories, which have helped to shape the border into its modern form. The Drug Wars of the twenty-first century that so define contemporary conceptions of the border did not emerge from a vacuum or as the latest iteration of a conflict that has always existed. The modern fights between cartels and law-enforcement agencies emerged instead because of the confluence of specific economic forces, governmental policies, and local conditions that converged during the last half century along the U.S.-Mexico boundary. It was not always this way and, as the essays in this volume document, the long history of violence along the border is one of constantly shifting conditions in the region. And shifts are, indeed, continuing to happen. The border today is more militarized than at any other point in its history, as pieces of border wall erected by the United States create new ragged edges intended to separate the two nations. These walls are not the inevitable culmination of the past two centuries, nor are the widespread feelings of unease that so many Americans and Mexicans harbor about the border as an inherently dangerous and violent place. A deeper understanding of the long history of violence along the border will, we hope, contribute to a more powerful and usable understanding of our particular moment today and its tangled relationship to the past.

Notes

1. Barry Petersen, "Juarez, Mexico—Murder Capital of the World," cbsnews.com, August 12, 2010, http://www.cbsnews.com/news/juarez-mexico-murder-capital-of-the-world/.

2. Ioan Grillo, *El Narco: Inside Mexico's Criminal Insurgency* (London: Bloomsbury, 2012); Alfredo Corchado, *Midnight in Mexico: A Reporter's Journey through a Country's Descent into Darkness* (New York: Penguin Books, 2013); Charles Bowden, *Murder City: Ciudad Juárez and the Global Economy's New Killing Fields* (New York: Nation Books, 2010).

3. These migrants have often themselves become the victims of drug-related border violence. See, for example, the murder of seventy-two Central American migrants in Tamaulipas in 2010 by the Zeta cartel: "Survivor Tells of Escape from Mexican Massacre in Which 72 Were Left Dead," *The Guardian*, August 25, 2010, https://www.theguardian.com /world/2010/aug/25/mexico-massacre-central-american-migrants.

4. Norma Iglesias-Prieto, "Trascendiendo límites: La frontera México–Estados Unidos en el cine," *Forum for Interamerican Research* 3, no. 2 (November 2010), http:// interamerica.de/, and David R. Maciel, "La frontera cinematográfica," in *Nuestra frontera norte*, ed. Patricia Galeana (México, Archivo General de la Nación, 1999). For a comparison of drug-trade bosses and social bandits, see Alan Knight, "Narco Violence and the State in Modern Mexico," in *Violence, Coercion, and State-Making in Twentieth-Century Mexico: The Other Half of the Centaur*, ed. Wil Pansters (Stanford, CA: Stanford University Press, 2012), 115–34. Juan Villoro has argued that narco-*corridos* romanticize drug-related violence and have bestowed "pedigrí artístico al negocio de vivir matando." See his "'¡Qué manera de perder!' Violencia y narcotráfico en México," *Words without Borders: The Online Magazine for International Literature*, March 2012, https://www.wordswithoutborders .org/.

5. Popular perceptions within Mexico were also affected by an expanding body of fictional literature that engaged themes of drug-related violence. See María Eugenia de la O and Elmer Mendoza, "Narcotráfico y Literatura," *Desacatos* 38 (January–April 2012): 193–99. For a debate on the quality and validity of narco-literature, see Rafael Lemus, "Balas de Salva," *Letras Libres* no. 81 (September 30, 2005), http://www.*letraslibres*.com/mexico/balas -salva; and Eduardo Antonio Parra, "Norte, Narcotráfico y Literatura," *Letras Libres* no. 82 (October 31, 2005), https://letraslibres.com/revista-mexico/norte-narcotrafico-y -literatura/.

6. Although there is a broad literature on the history of the U.S.-Canada border, the history of conflict along that border has become the subject of increasing scholarly attention. See, for example, Alan Taylor, *The Divided Ground: Indians, Settlers, and the Northern Borderland of the American Revolution* (New York: Knopf, 2006); Andrew R. Graybill, *Policing the Great Plains: Rangers, Mounties, and the North American Frontier, 1875–1910* (Lincoln: University of Nebraska Press, 2007); Benjamin H. Johnson and Andrew R. Graybill, eds., *Bridging National Borders in North America: Transnational and Comparative Histories* (Durham, NC: Duke University Press, 2010).

7. On the history of the Mexico-Guatemala border and violence along that border, see Manuel Ángel Castillo, Mónica Toussaint Ribot, Mario Vázquez Olivera, *Espacios Diversos, Historia en Común. México, Guatemala y Belice: La Construcción de una Frontera* (México: Secretaría de Relaciones Exteriores, 2006); Jan de Vos, *Las Fronteras de la Frontera Sur:*

Reseña de los Proyectos de Expansión que figuraron la Frontera entre México y Centroamérica (Villahermosa: Universidad Juárez Autónoma de Tabasco/Centro de Investigaciones y Estudios Superiores de Antropología Social, 1993); Luis G. Zorrilla, *Relaciones de México con la República de Centroamérica y con Guatemala* (México: Porrúa, 1984).

8. For broad discussions of violence, both contemporary and in history, see Randall Collins, *Violence: A Micro-Sociological Theory* (Princeton, NJ: Princeton University Press, 2008) and Steven Pinker, *The Better Angels of Our Nature: The Decline of Violence in History and Its Causes* (London: Penguin, 2011).

9. The literature on the U.S.-Mexico War, and violence associated with it, is vast. Some recent examples of scholarship that focus on moments of violence as interpretive lenses include Amy Greenberg, *A Wicked War: Polk, Clay, Lincoln and the 1846 U.S. Invasion of Mexico* (New York: Knopf, 2012) and Peter Guardino, *The Dead March: A History of the Mexican-American War* (Cambridge, MA: Harvard University Press, 2017). For the war on the border states of Mexico, see Laura Herrera Serna (coord.), *México en Guerra (1846–1848): Perspectivas regionales* (México: Consejo Nacional para la Cultura y las Artes, 1997); Josefina Zoraida Vázquez, *México al tiempo de su guerra con los Estados Unidos (1846–1848)* (México: Secretaría de Relaciones Exteriores/Colegio de México/Fondo de Cultura Económica, 1997). On Villa's famous raid and the U.S. military response, see Friedrich Katz, *The Life and Times of Pancho Villa* (Stanford, CA: Stanford University Press, 1998); Ana María Alonso, "U.S. Military Intervention, Revolutionary Mobilization and Popular Ideology in the Chihuahuan Sierra, 1916–1917," in *Rural Revolt in Mexico: U.S. Intervention and the Domain of Subaltern Politics*, ed. Daniel Nugent (Durham, NC: Duke University Press, 1998), 207–238; Eileen Welsome, *The General and the Jaguar: Pershing's Hunt for Pancho Villa—A True Story of Revolution and Revenge* (Lincoln: Bison Books, 2007).

10. For anti-Chinese violence along the U.S.-Mexico border in the nineteenth-century United States, see Stacey L. Smith, *Freedom's Frontier: California and the Struggle over Unfree Labor, Emancipation, and Reconstruction* (Chapel Hill: University of North Carolina Press, 2013). For violence against ethnic Chinese in Mexico during the twentieth century, see José Jorge Gómez Izquierdo, *El movimiento antichino en México, 1871–1934: Problemas del racismo y del nacionalismo durante la Revolución Mexicana* (México: Instituto Nacional de Antropología e Historia, 1991) and Julia Maria Schiavone Camacho, *Chinese Mexicans: Transpacific Migration and the Search for a Homeland, 1910–1960* (Chapel Hill: University of North Carolina Press, 2012). On free and enslaved African Americans on both sides of the border, as well as working-class Mexican laborers, see James David Nichols, *The Limits of Liberty: Mobility and the Making of the Eastern U.S.-Mexico Border* (Lincoln: University of Nebraska Press, 2018); María Camila Díaz Casas, "'In Mexico You Could Be Free, They Didn't Care What Color You Was': Afrodescendientes, esclavitud y libertad en la frontera entre México y Estados Unidos, 1821–1865," PhD diss., Historia y Etnohistoria, Escuela Nacional de Antropología e Historia, 2018; Omar S. Valerio-Jiménez, *River of Hope: Forging Identity and Nation in the Rio Grande Borderlands* (Durham, NC: Duke University Press, 2013). For the exploitation of working-class Mexican laborers in South Texas during the twentieth century, see Juan Mora Torres, *The Making of the Mexican Border: The State, Capitalism, and Society in Nuevo León, 1848–1910* (Austin: University of Texas Press, 2001); John Weber, *From South Texas to the Nation: The Exploitation of Mexican Labor in the Twentieth Century* (Chapel Hill: University of North Carolina Press, 2015).

11. See, for example, Julia Monárrez Fragoso, "Serial Sexual Femicide in Ciudad Juárez: 1993–2001," *Debate Feminista*, 13th ed., vol. 25, April 2002: 279–305; Diana Washington Valdez, *The Killing Fields: Harvest of Women* (Los Angeles: Peace and the Border, 2006); Alicia Gaspar de Alba and Georgina Guzmán, eds., *Making a Killing: Femicide, Free Trade, and La Frontera* (Austin: University of Texas Press, 2010); Katherine Pantaleo, "Gendered Violence: An Analysis of the Maquiladora Murders," *International Criminal Justice Review* 20, no. 4 (2010): 349–65; Sergio González Rodríguez, *The Femicide Machine* (Los Angeles: Semiotext(e): 2012); Susan Tiano and Moira Murphy-Aguilar, eds., *Borderline Slavery: Mexico, United States, and the Human Trade* (London: Routledge, 2012); Dan Werb, *City of Omens: A Search for the Missing Women of the Borderlands* (New York: Bloomsbury, 2019). On femicide in a broad perspective, see Jill Radford and Diana E. H. Russell, eds., *Femicide: The Politics of Woman Killing* (Buckingham: Open University Press, 1992).

12. On violence in the prison system along the U.S. side of the U.S.-Mexico border, see Kelly Lytle Hernandez, *City of Inmates: Conquest, Rebellion, and the Rise of Human Caging in Los Angeles, 1771–1965* (Chapel Hill: University of North Carolina Press, 2017) and Robert Chase, *We Are Not Slaves: State Violence, Coerced Labor, and Prisoners' Rights in Postwar America* (Chapel Hill: University of North Carolina Press, 2020). On the U.S. Immigration and Naturalization Service, see S. Deborah Kang, *The INS on the Line: Making Immigration Law on the U.S.-Mexico Border, 1917–1954* (New York: Oxford University Press, 2017). On the U.S. border patrol, see Kelly Lytle Hernandez, *Migra!: A History of the U.S. Border Patrol* (Berkeley: University of California Press, 2010). On immigration policy in both the United States and Mexico, and specifically their effects on the border itself, see Julian Lim, *Porous Borders: Multiracial Migrations and the Law in the U.S.-Mexico Borderlands* (Chapel Hill: University of North Carolina Press, 2017).

13. Rachel St. John, *A Line in the Sand: A History of the Western U.S.-Mexico Border* (Princeton, NJ: Princeton University Press, 2011), 209n2.

14. Ned Blackhawk, *Violence over the Land: Indians and Empires in the Early American West* (Cambridge, MA: Harvard University Press, 2006); Cuauhtémoc Velasco Ávila, *La Frontera étnica en el Noreste Novohispano: Los Comanches entre 1800–1841* (México, Centro de Investigaciones y Estudios Superiores de Antropología Social, 2012); Pekka Hämäläinen, *The Comanche Empire* (New Haven, CT: Yale University Press, 2008); Sara Ortelli, *Trama de una Guerra Conveniente: Nueva Vizcaya y la Sombra de los Apaches, 1748–1790* (México: El Colegio de México, 2007); Brian DeLay, *War of a Thousand Deserts: Indian Raids and the U.S.-Mexican War* (New Haven, CT: Yale University Press, 2008); Karl Jacoby, *Shadows at Dawn: An Apache Massacre and the Violence of History* (New York: Penguin, 2008); José Marcos Medina Bustos y Esther Padilla Calderón, eds., *Violencia Interétnica en la Frontera Norte Novohispana y Mexicana* (Hermosillo: El Colegio de Sonora/El Colegio de Michoacán/Universidad Autónoma de Baja California, 2015); Lance Blyth, *Chiricahua and Janos: Communities of Violence in the Southwestern Borderlands, 1680–1880* (Lincoln: University of Nebraska Press, 2012). The literature on violence and the U.S.-Mexico borderlands is rapidly expanding. As examples, see also Luis Aboites, "Poder político y 'bárbaros' en Chihuahua hacia 1854," *Secuencia* 19 (1991): 19–32; Víctor Orozco, *Las guerras indias en la historia de Chihuahua: Primeras fases* (México: CONACULTA, 1992); Isidro Vizcaya Canales, *Tierra de guerra viva: Incursiones de indios y otros conflictos en el noreste de México durante el siglo XIX, 1821–1885* (Monterrey: Academia de Investigación Humanística, 2001); James Brooks, *Captives and Cousins: Slavery, Kinship, and Community*

in the Southwest Borderlands (Chapel Hill: University of North Carolina Press, 2002); Mark Santiago, *The Jar of Severed Hands: Spanish Deportation of Apache Prisoners of War, 1770–1810* (Norman: University of Oklahoma Press, 2011); Elliott Young, *Catarino Garza's Revolt on the Texas-Mexico Border* (Durham, NC: Duke University Press, 2004).

15. Ana María Alonso, *Thread of Blood: Colonialism, Revolution, and Gender on Mexico's Northern Frontier* (Tucson: University of Arizona Press, 1995); Héctor Aguilar Camín, *La Frontera Nómada: Sonora y la Revolución Mexicana* (México, Siglo XXI, 1981); Benjamin H. Johnson, *Revolution in Texas: How a Forgotten Rebellion and Its Bloody Suppression Turned Mexicans into Americans* (New Haven, CT: Yale University Press, 2003); Charles H. Harris and Luis R. Sadler, *The Plan de San Diego: Tejano Rebellion, Mexican Intrigue* (Lincoln: University of Nebraska Press, 2013); Timothy Dunn, *The Militarization of the U.S.-Mexico Border, 1978–1992: Low-Intensity Conflict Doctrine Comes Home* (Austin: University of Texas Press, 1995); Howard Campbell, *Drug War Zone: Frontline Dispatches from the Streets of El Paso and Juarez* (Austin: University of Texas Press, 2009); Wil Pansters, ed., *Violence, Coercion, and State-Making in Twentieth-Century Mexico: The Other Half of the Centaur* (Stanford, CA: Stanford University Press, 2012); Jason De León, *The Land of Open Graves: Living and Dying on the Migrant Trail* (Berkeley: University of California Press, 2015). As more examples, see also Clarence C. Clendenen, *Blood on the Border: The United States Army and the Mexican Irregulars* (Toronto: Macmillan, 1969); W. Dirk Raat, *Revoltosos: Mexico's Rebels in the United States, 1903–1923* (College Station: Texas A & M University Press, 1981); Linda Hall and Don Coerver, *Revolution on the Border: The United States and Mexico, 1910–1920* (Albuquerque: University of New Mexico Press, 1988); Friedrich Katz, *The Life and Times of Pancho Villa* (Stanford, CA: Stanford University Press, 1998); Charles H. Harris and Luis R. Sadler, *The Texas Rangers and the Mexican Revolution: The Bloodiest Decade, 1910–20* (Albuquerque: University of New Mexico Press, 2004). There is also a large and growing literature focused on contemporary violence associated with drug smuggling.

16. Within the United States, the concept of "borderlands" has become a broadly embraced lens for historical investigation over the course of most of the last hundred years. For a sense of the evolution of "borderlands" as an interpretive lens for U.S. scholarship, particularly on the regions that connect to the U.S.-Mexico border, see Herbert Bolton, "The Epic of Greater America," *American Historical Review* 38, no. 3 (April 1933): 448–74; David J. Weber, "Turner, the Boltonians, and the Borderlands," *American Historical Review* 91 (February 1986): 66–81; Jeremy Adelman and Stephen Aron, "From Borderlands to Borders: Empires, Nation-States, and the Peoples in between in North American History," *American Historical Review* 104 (June 1999): 814–41; Sam Truett and Elliott Young, "Making Transnational History: Nations, Regions, and Borderlands," in *Continental Crossroads: Remapping U.S.-Mexico Borderlands History* (Durham, NC: Duke University Press, 2004), 1–32; Pekka Hämäläinen and Samuel Truett, "On Borderlands," *Journal of American History* 98 (September 2011): 338–61. Within Mexico, however, scholarship on the northern states—much less the border itself—long remained peripheral to work that focused instead on the development of the nation-state, with the center of the country (rather than the borders) at the heart of that narrative. That began to shift during the late 1960s, as historiography in Mexico began to emphasize the marked regional diversity of the nation and more work began to emerge on northern Mexico's role in the Mexican Revolution and the Indigenous peoples of the region. For discussions of these trends, see Barry Carr, "Las Pecu-

liaridades del Norte Mexicano, 1880–1927: Ensayo de Interpretación," *Historia Mexicana* 22, no. 3 (January–March 1973): 320–46; David C. Bailey, "Revisionism and the Recent Historiography of the Mexican Revolution," *Hispanic American Historical Review* 58, no. 1 (February 1978): 73–74; David Piñera Ramírez, *Historiografía de la Frontera Norte de México: Balance y Metas de Investigación* (Tijuana: Universidad Autónoma de Baja California, 1990); Thomas Benjamin, "Regionalizing the Revolution: The Many Mexicos in Revolutionary Historiography," in *Provinces of the Revolution: Essays on Regional Mexican History*, ed. Benjamin and Wasserman (Albuquerque: University of New Mexico Press, 1995), 319–57; Cuauhtémoc Velasco, "Historiografía de un Territorio Perdido," *Historias* 40 (April–September 1998): 21–27; Alan Knight, "Patterns and Prescriptions in Mexican Historiography," *Bulletin of Latin American Research* 25, no. 3 (July 2006): 340–66.

PART I

Livestock, Markets, and Guns

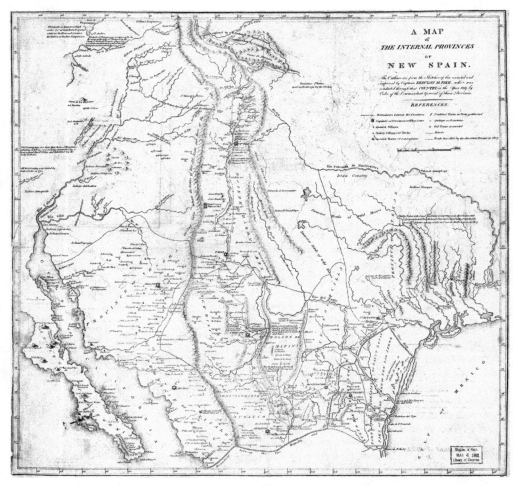

Figure 1.1 "A Map of the Internal Provinces of New Spain" by Zebulon Pike, 1807. Courtesy of the U.S. Library of Congress.

Chapter 1

Smuggling and Violence in the Northern Borderlands of New Spain, 1810–1821

ALBERTO BARRERA-ENDERLE AND ANDREW J. TORGET

In early 1820, a Spanish military detachment arrested nineteen-year-old Cornelio Lozoya near the border between Texas and Louisiana, as Lozoya awaited the delivery of more than a hundred mules and horses that his *patrón* had bargained from nearby Comanches. Lozoya's hazardous journey to that moment provides a revealing window into the violent realities of life along New Spain's northeastern borderlands during the twilight of Spain's presence in the region. Lozoya's saga began in 1813, when, during the Mexican War for Independence, he had to flee his home in San Antonio to avoid being killed by the soldiers of José Joaquín de Arredondo. Arredondo had arrived in the region at the head of a nearly two-thousand-man-strong royalist army bent on destroying a rebellion that had burned through Texas as part of Mexico's struggle for independence. After decimating a rebel army just south of San Antonio, Arredondo unleashed a merciless campaign of scorched-earth retribution against all Spaniards in the region suspected of supporting the rebels. Imprisoning hundreds of men, women, and children in San Antonio, Arredondo executed any Spaniards accused of disloyalty and seized their homes and property for the crown. He also sent his cavalry in pursuit of anyone who dared to run in an attempt to escape his wrath.[1]

Like hundreds of his neighbors, Lozoya suddenly found himself fleeing eastward along a barely visible road in a desperate bid to save his own life, until he finally crossed the international boundary into the United States, where he sought refuge in the state of Louisiana. Lozoya settled in the town of Natchitoches, where, to survive, he soon became the servant of a fellow Spanish refugee, Ignacio Góngora. Having lost nearly everything to Arredondo's wrath, Góngora and Lozoya began supporting themselves by turning to smuggling. Illegally transporting horses and mules from Spanish Texas into the United States, they discovered, paid quite well. And so the two men began new lives centered on evading Spanish military authorities in Texas as they traveled in secret across the border in order to trade U.S.-made goods to Indian nations in New Spain for horses and mules, which they then smuggled back into the United States to be sold to merchants in Louisiana. It was a highly risky operation, one that depended on evading the Spanish military and constantly risked attack by other Indians or rogue bands of fellow smugglers. After several lucky years, Lozoya was finally discovered and arrested by Spanish authorities. He stood accused of trespassing the border illegally and trading with Comanches and other independent Indian nations in contravention of royal decrees.[2]

Although records of Lozoya's ultimate fate have been lost, his experiences shine a light on the devastating violence that overtook Spain's northeastern borderlands during the last decade of Spain's rule in the region and how that devastation, in turn, fostered increased smuggling along the U.S.-Spanish border. Even before Arredondo arrived with his army, Spanish settlements in the region had long endured isolation from the rest of New Spain that made the marginalized and economically underdeveloped territory a haven for such illegal commerce. Yet the violence of the Mexican War of Independence and the simultaneous rapid growth of markets in neighboring Louisiana combined to greatly expand both smuggling and violence in the northern borderlands of New Spain. As Lozoya and so many of his fellow Spaniards experienced, the widespread violence of the 1810s that made him a refugee also put him into such dire economic circumstances that smuggling became deeply attractive. In order to understand the interconnected nature of violence and smuggling in the region, we need to understand the peculiar historic configuration of the northern frontier of New Spain and the role that it played within the broader economic system of the Spanish empire.

"Settling" the Northeastern Frontier of New Spain

For the whole of its existence, the northeastern frontier of New Spain was a remote territory that maintained weak ties to the political center of the viceroyalty in Mexico City. Although Spanish authorities had claimed sovereignty over that vast frontier region since the late sixteenth century, in practice the territory remained largely Indian country and a place where violent conflicts between Spaniards and independent Indians defined the daily existence of Spanish settlements in the region.

When Spain began venturing into these far-northern territories, it was largely to support and protect its ongoing—and highly profitable—mining operations in central Mexico. The colonization of what would become the territories of Coahuila and Nuevo León, for example, was the result of Spaniards moving northward at the end of the sixteenth century in search of lands and Indians needed to meet the rising demands for both materiel and labor in the more-southernly mining regions of Zacatecas and surrounding areas. The colonization of Texas and Tamaulipas (then known as Nuevo Santander) began later, during the eighteenth century, but was also an effort to defend these same interests of central New Spain, in this case by creating a distant buffer that would prevent the French or English from establishing a presence too close to the wealth coming out of colonial Mexico (which, Spanish officials feared, foreign powers might use to raid silver shipments or even attack the mines themselves). Populating Texas and Tamaulipas, then, would serve the same purpose for Spain as colonizing Coahuila and Nuevo León: they were all meant to support the mineral wealth coming out of colonial Mexico that enriched the Spanish Crown.[3]

Yet these settlements never prospered as Spanish authorities had hoped. The general lack of mineral wealth in New Spain's far north made the region an unattractive territory for Spanish settlers, leaving those settlements perpetually underpopulated.[4] The anemic Spanish population in the region, in turn, left those same settlements perpetually vulnerable to raids and violent resistance by the independent Indian nations who controlled most of the territory and found they could easily raid these distant Spanish outposts. Bloody clashes between Spaniards and Indians became painfully commonplace along this northern frontier, preventing the Spanish monarchy from consolidating its authority over the vast territory. Missions established in the region failed to transform local Indians into stalwart Spanish allies, and forts erected in the territory remained perennially undermanned. The colonization of northern New Spain was shaped, then, by both the geographical conditions of the territory and the fierce and violent resistance of the seminomadic Indians who inhabited it. The far-northern frontier, therefore, was not a region forged by Spanish power but was instead the product of complex and often violent encounters between Spaniards and various Indians in the region.[5]

By the end of the eighteenth century, Spanish authorities had resorted to making regular offers of gifts—tribute, really—to the territory's more powerful Indian nations in exchange for promises of peace for Spanish settlements. The strategy worked for a short time as Spanish authorities achieved a precarious peace in the region at the dawn of the nineteenth century. The change in tactics also represented a strategic shift in the political agenda of Spain, as the empire moved away from exploring new territories in order to focus more energy on consolidating and protecting its northern border against both Indian raids and threats from encroaching foreign powers.[6]

Yet the success of the tribute strategy proved to be short-lived as the fragile peace it bought began to unravel during the early nineteenth century under the pressure of two events. First, Spain's sale of Louisiana to the United States in 1803 meant that gifts used to pacify Indian tribes now had to be hauled overland from the much more distant—and therefore unreliable—Mexico City rather than be imported from nearby New Orleans, a shift that produced major disruptions in the flow of tribute goods to local Indians that had briefly bought peace. Second, the outbreak of the Mexican War for Independence in 1810 further exacerbated this problem when insurgents cut off roads, and therefore commercial connections, between New Spain's northern frontier and the central provinces from which these goods were now shipped.[7] The outbreak of the war, moreover, forced viceregal authorities in Mexico City to focus their attention on pacifying the insurgency rather than on attempts to continue pacifying the northern frontier, and so almost no sustained effort was made to restore shipments of tribute goods to the far-northern frontier.

The Louisiana Purchase also cut off the Spaniards who lived in northeastern New Spain from access to the New Orleans markets, with painful consequences. The Spanish frontier had always played a supportive role within the colonial economic system of New Spain and the few Spanish settlers who lived in the northern provinces supported themselves largely by exporting various products (such as lead, tallow, wheat, wool, salt, and livestock) that could sustain more profitable regions of the empire. Raising livestock was perhaps the economic activity that most closely tied the northeast with the rest of New Spain.[8] Yet no local industry, not even livestock, proved very profitable, in large measure because severe geographical isolation made it almost impossible for any local industry to develop. Being so distant from the legal markets in the center of New Spain, with almost no adequate roads to connect to them, meant that any goods shipped in either direction between the hinterland and Mexico City invariably became far more expensive because of exorbitant shipping costs and the heavy taxes Spain levied on such shipments.

To make matters worse, the mercantilist system adopted by the Spanish Crown during the sixteenth century, which restricted trade to certain ports and privileged a small number of merchants, contributed mightily to the slow economic growth of the northeastern frontier of New Spain.[9] In New Spain, this centralized economic system centered on the port of Veracruz, which served as the only port licensed to receive goods from and ship cargo to Spain or other international destinations.[10] Along with a privileged sector of politically connected merchants from Mexico City, Veracruz profited handsomely from the arrangement and exercised a near monopoly over the entire commerce of New Spain. Spaniards living along the far-northern hinterlands, as a result, were forbidden from importing directly from any other ports along their coast and thus had to rely on the onerous and tremendously expensive delivery of goods hauled overland from Veracruz to places as far away as Texas.[11] Likewise, any Spaniards living along the northern frontier who wanted to sell goods in the colonial market had to offer products at rates far below their actual value, lest exorbitant freight fees and shipping duties price them out of the market. The unsurprising result was that all along the Spanish frontier even the most basic commodities either were in drastically short supply at hyperinflated prices or were simply not available at all.

In order to cope, most Spaniards living along the frontier took advantage of their geographic proximity to American markets in Louisiana, which were forbidden by the Spanish Crown but nonetheless offered all manner of commodities at a fraction of the price. The incentives for traversing the border in order to procure goods in New Orleans at rock-bottom prices were simply too great, and the needs of isolated Spanish settlements in this far-flung region simply too much, for most local Spaniards to resist. Although smuggling had long been a frequent practice along the northeastern frontier of New Spain, the industry reached new heights during the early nineteenth century.

These shifts also brought renewed violence between local Indians and Spaniards. Because the ending of legal access to New Orleans effectively ended the Spanish gifting policy, independent Indians resumed their violent raiding of settlements in northeastern New Spain. Indians launched regular raids that stole livestock—mainly horses and mules—which they then traded to Anglo-American merchants in the nearby United States in exchange for American-made goods to replace Spanish tribute payments. These horses were then sold by American merchants to buyers in Louisiana and other regions of the southern United States, where demand for livestock from northern New Spain proved nearly insatiable. Soon thousands of horses were being smuggled each month from New Spain into the United States.[12] As a result, the 1810s witnessed the strengthening of economic linkages between northeastern New Spain and the southern United States that would only increase over time and, in turn, would also foster conditions for rapidly increased violence within the region. To a great extent, this violence would revolve around expanded livestock theft and violent raids of Spanish settlements by independent Indians to secure horses for trading with the Americans, all underwritten by the persistent inability of Spain's weak government in the region to do anything about it.

In chapter 2 of this volume, Joaquín Rivaya-Martínez chronicles violence wrought by incursions of Comanches across the northern frontier during the first decades of postcolonial Mexico. Lance Blyth and Tim Bowman analyze the growth of transnational violence fueled by cattle theft and the role of weak nation-states along the border during the second half of the nineteenth century. In large measure, many of the underlying structures that generated these moments of violence in the U.S.-Mexico borderlands throughout the nineteenth century had their origins in the 1810s when the War for Independence in New Spain and the economic pressure that nearby U.S. markets wrought on Texas combined to shatter the fragile hold the Spanish Crown had established on the region by the end of the eighteenth century.

War for Independence and the Insurgency in Northeastern New Spain

The outbreak of the Mexican War for Independence would vastly increase violence along the border between the United States and New Spain, and in the process, create even more incentives for transnational smuggling in the region. Unlike many other regions of New Spain, most of the northeastern territories—with the crucial exception of Texas—were not the scenes of great battles during the War for Independence. Early in 1811, insurgents briefly controlled Coahuila and Nuevo León. This was not, however, the result of rebel military victories. Rather, political leaders of both provinces had simply decided to pass—along with most of their troops—to the insurgent side in order to avoid bloodshed. Most of the local population avoided participating in the military struggle, and when rebel leaders Miguel Hidalgo and Ignacio Allende were arrested and later executed, both provinces then returned peacefully to the royalist side. The situation was similar in Nuevo Santander, except that this province experienced a second wave of the insurgency in 1817 when the liberal Spaniard Xavier Mina landed on the coast of the province with the aim of making Mexico independent of Spain. In spite of this, the insurgency of Nuevo Santander also proved fleeting and did not enjoy widespread popular support.[13]

Unlike Coahuila, Nuevo León, and Nuevo Santander, Texas experienced far greater support for the insurgency. By 1810, this province remained one of the most extensive yet least populated territories of New Spain, with only about 4,500 non-Indian inhabitants. Most of these were people who made their living raising livestock, and they concentrated in only three villages: San Antonio de Béxar, La Bahía (later named Goliad), and Nacogdoches.[14] In January 1811, when news of the surrender of the royalist armies of Coahuila, Nuevo León, and Tamaulipas arrived in Texas, Captain Juan Bautista de las Casas convinced royalist troops stationed in San Antonio to follow the example of their neighbors in Coahuila and Nuevo León and rebel. De las Casas and his supporters arrested both the governor of the province and the local military commander.[15] Yet enthusiasm among these rebels quickly waned as support for the insurgent cause failed to materialize from central Mexico and, instead, news arrived of rebels in other provinces suffering military defeats at the hands of royalist forces. Local Spaniards soon organized themselves into a counterrebellion and overthrew de las Casas, thereby realigning Texas with the royalist army.[16]

A year later, a new and much bloodier insurgent movement shook Texas. This rebellion was organized by José Bernardo Gutiérrez de Lara, a native of the province of Nuevo Santander. Unlike insurgent movements that occurred throughout the rest of New Spain, this rebellion emerged because of the specific dynamics and complex characteristics of New Spain's far-northern frontier. Both its composition (consisting of a mixture of Spaniards, Anglo-Americans, and Indians) and its goals (to legalize and establish commercial links between the northeast frontier of New Spain and the United States, in addition to freeing Mexico from Spanish rule) denote its particular borderlands and transnational origins.[17]

This rebellion, indeed, began as a mixture of Spaniards and Americans. Gutiérrez traveled to the United States to negotiate the support of the U.S. government for the Mexican insurgent cause. In meetings with U.S. officials in Washington, D.C., Gutiérrez asked for military support for Mexican rebels and, at the same time, made offers to the United States that suggest one of his driving objectives was to foster the economic integration of both Texas and northeastern New Spain with Louisiana and the southwestern United States.[18] Although the U.S. government refused to support the rebellion openly, the Americans also did nothing to impede Gutiérrez's later efforts to organize an invasion of Texas. Gutiérrez then joined forces in Louisiana with an American named Augustus Magee, and together they recruited 150 volunteers (almost all Anglo-Americans) for a rebel invasion of Texas.[19] In what became known as the Gutiérrez-Magee expedition, this "Northern Republican Army" entered Texas in August 1812 and immediately captured Nacogdoches. The invaders encountered no resistance but rather were cheered by local Spaniards who hoped that Gutiérrez represented the end of Spanish commercial restrictions and the beginning of newly legalized trade with the markets of the United States.[20] The invaders then made their way westward and, after picking up more Spanish recruits and Indian allies, captured San Antonio in April 1813 and imprisoned the royalist governor, Manuel de Salcedo, and the royalist commander of the local troops, Simón de Herrera. Within three days of marching into San Antonio, the rebels put both Salcedo and Herrera to death as they completed their bloody capture of Texas.[21]

Although the Gutiérrez-Magee invasion began like the rest of the insurgencies in New Spain—as a struggle for local political autonomy from Spanish rule—it also emerged as a broad response among locals to the specific needs of the northeastern frontier, a region severely affected by the commercial restrictions of the Spanish Crown. Most Spaniards in Texas believed that economic exchange with American markets in neighboring Louisiana would benefit them by providing them access to cheaper and more diverse commodities and that the rebellion might lead to legalized trade between the regions. At the same time, the Anglo-Americans who joined the Gutiérrez-Magee expedition apparently expected that they would be rewarded with lands in Texas that would then become all the more valuable when the region became more directly integrated into the world economy through open trade with Louisiana. In other words, all these actors longed to legitimate and legalize the transnational and transcultural commercial exchanges between north-eastern New Spain and the southwestern United States that were already happening illegally along the border. And they proved willing to use violence to achieve those goals.

Texan attempts to rebel against colonial authorities thus largely erupted from an interest among locals in capitalizing on the economic opportunities offered by the borderlands economy, which put the territory in contrast with other Spanish provinces in the region. This helps to explain why elites in other neighboring provinces did not also embrace armed rebellion, despite having the same complaints as the Texans about Spanish colonial policies. Coahuila, Nuevo León, and Tamaulipas had not experienced the same level of integration with the U.S. and Atlantic economies as Spaniards in Texas. Their economic activities were also far more diverse than those in Texas, and these provinces did not suffer quite as greatly from geographical isolation from New Spain's economic and political core as Texas did. The negative effects of the restrictive Spanish commercial system, in other words, were less painful and the presence of state authority was more pronounced in Coahuila, Nuevo León, and Tamaulipas than in Texas. As a result, the insurgency enjoyed broader—and more violent—support in Texas than it did in the rest of north-eastern New Spain.[22]

Following the capture of San Antonio by the Gutiérrez-Magee rebels, the viceroy in Mexico City dispatched a royalist officer named José Joaquín de Arredondo with orders to retake the region from the rebellion and restore royal authority in Texas. Arredondo quickly assembled an army of 1,800 soldiers and marched for Texas, where his reassertion of the Crown's control over the region would bring both a bloody new wave of violence to the territory and severe repercussions for all Spaniards living in Texas. When Arredondo's forces drew near San Antonio, the rebel army marched out to meet him, and the two forces ran headlong into one another along the banks of the Medina River on August 18, 1813. The battle that ensued turned into a one-sided slaughter as royalist troops killed at least 1,300 of the 1,400 rebels in what remains the bloodiest battle ever to take place in Texas.[23] Arredondo's quick victory marked the end of the insurgency in Texas, but it inaugurated a long period of violent retribution for the Spanish Crown.

Following his victory at Medina, Arredondo unleashed a campaign of un-relenting terror against the Spaniards in Texas, whom he considered traitors to New Spain. Arredondo's soldiers imprisoned hundreds of people in San Antonio, where they executed several hundred men and forced local women to feed and entertain the royal troops. Many hundreds more local Spaniards, such as Cornelio Lozoya, ran eastward in desperate attempts to save their own lives. Whether or not they had collaborated with the insurgency, these local Spaniards often had no choice but to flee if they hoped to live. Escaping alongside Lozoya was Cayetano Villarreal, a native of Tamaulipas who had emigrated to San Antonio in 1808 and supported himself as a tailor before the rebellion. As royalist troops approached San Antonio, Villarreal heard that "Arredondo would punish everyone alike, regardless of whether they had been supporters" of the rebellion, and so he fled with his family as quickly as he could, until eventually he managed to reach Natchitoches, Louisiana. Like his neighbor Lozoya, Villarreal suddenly found himself living as an exile in the southwestern United States. And like Lozoya, Villarreal soon turned to smuggling livestock from northern New Spain into U.S. territory as a means for supporting himself and his family, until, years later, he was also finally captured and arrested by Spanish authorities.[24]

Not all Spaniards fleeing eastward were as lucky as Lozoya and Villarreal to make it to safety in U.S.-held Louisiana. To hunt down those who had escaped, Arredondo dispatched a cavalry unit under the command of Ignacio Elizondo to ride hard eastward in pursuit of refugees. Elizondo's men captured more than two hundred fleeing Spaniards along the banks of the Trinity River, where they killed seventy-one men and then set the rest on a forced march westward to face the Crown's judgment. When these prisoners arrived back in San Antonio, Arredondo ordered the execution of all the men and had their bodies hung for months in the main plaza. Anyone even suspected of having collaborated with the insurgency had their lands, homes, and property confiscated without trial by Arredondo's troops. In the end, Arredondo's brutal repression successfully reclaimed Texas for the Crown.[25] But it also badly weakened an already anemic Spanish presence in the region, which undermined what little power Spaniards in the territory had to withstand the raiding of Comanches and other independent Indian nations. And it drove hundreds of Spaniards into U.S. territory, many of whom turned to a newly expanded trade in smuggling livestock across the international border as a means for survival.

Smuggling along the U.S.–New Spain Border

In chapter 12 of this book, Santiago Guerra demonstrates how drug trafficking developed in the U.S.-Mexico borderlands during the early decades of the twentieth century. Guerra underscores how prohibition and high demand for drugs in the United States made drug contraband both highly desirable and profitable. More than one hundred years before, smugglers along the border had similar reasons to get involved in a similar illegal trade focused on other commodities.

Contraband trade first emerged in earnest in northeastern New Spain during the last decades of the eighteenth century. By the dawn of the nineteenth century, this illegal trade commonly involved Spaniards (both rich and poor), mission and pacified Indians, independent Indians, Anglo-Americans, and Frenchmen. The northeastern territories of New Spain constituted an immense area that served simultaneously as a cultural borderland (because it was a place where Spaniards and dozens of Indian nations of different cultural origins lived together outside the reach of Spanish royal authority) and a political border after Louisiana passed to the United States in 1804. The geographic position of the region, coupled with its marginality within the Spanish colonial economic system, forced its inhabitants to resort to smuggling in order to survive. Typically this entailed Spanish settlers from the far-northern provinces traveling overland to Louisiana in order to exchange furs, hides, and cattle for premade and hard-to-acquire goods available in U.S. markets like New Orleans—such as firearms, gunpowder, and tobacco—that would be secretly brought back into New Spain.[26] Although Spanish authorities in Mexico City or Madrid wanted their northeastern border to divide people based on political distinctions, what actually existed at the local level was a borderland that united and connected different ethnoracial communities along common interests based in trade.[27]

These cross-cultural trade alliances, developed during the first decade of the nineteenth century, would become even more important during the second decade. Some inhabitants of northeastern New Spain had cultivated personal connections and relationships with particular Comanches or representatives of other Indian nations during the early 1800s specifically for trade purposes, creating what historian James Brooks has called "border communities of interest."[28] Comanches might arrive at villages in northern New Spain loaded with products obtained from Anglo-American traders, with dried meat and hides of bison, and sometimes with captives (Hispanics, Indians, or Anglo-Americans), all available for trade. In exchange, Spaniards in the region usually offered fabrics, tobacco, knives, and other goods made from metal, all products highly valued by Comanches.[29] For some of the Spaniards who found themselves driven out of Texas in the aftermath of Arredondo's reclaiming of the region, those associations with Comanche and other Indian groups forged during the early 1800s would serve during the 1810s as their basis for engaging in the thriving business of horse smuggling along the U.S.-Spanish border. Francisco Ruíz, for example, had lived in San Antonio until the Gutiérrez-Magee expedition forced him to flee to Louisiana. Once in exile, Ruíz then set about rebuilding his life by using his connections among the Comanche to put himself at the center of smuggling horses into U.S. territory—which he did so successfully that it eventually drew the worried attention of the Spanish governor of Texas.[30] Other exiled Spaniards in Louisiana did the same, as the large-scale smuggling networks that emerged during the 1810s built upon smaller-scale networks that had been forged during the preceding decade.

At that same moment, a new development in the southern United States drastically increased the demand for horses on the U.S. side of the border. Following the close of the War of 1812, British industrialists undertook a rapid transformation of their textile industry by moving toward producing cotton cloth as a more durable, comfortable, and profitable alternative to wool. To make that possible, British factory owners put out advertisements promising to pay top rates for as much raw cotton as suppliers could send them, which led to the global price for cotton to double—rising from 15 cents to 30 cents per pound—during 1815. This unprecedented rise in cotton prices then set off a massive migration of Americans into the Mississippi River valley, where they hoped to establish cotton farms and plantations that could capitalize on the region's rich soils, long growing season, and ready access to the international markets through New Orleans. Hundreds of thousands of Americans poured into the territories that would become Alabama, Mississippi, and Louisiana during the five years that followed, and by 1820 the combined population of those three U.S. states topped 370,000 people. Cotton production in the region immediately soared, and by 1820 the United States had surpassed India to become the leading producer of cotton in the world.[31]

The result was that a third of a million Americans moved into the regions alongside the U.S. border with New Spain at precisely the same moment that the violence of the Mexican War for Independence drove hundreds of Spaniards into exile in Louisiana. That meant that massively expanded markets were now suddenly available to Spaniards in U.S. territory. Even more important, the farm and plantation districts these Americans established in Alabama, Mississippi, and Louisiana had created insatiable new demands for horses that persistently outstripped the supply available in the United States. Horses, it turned out, were absolutely vital to the ongoing development of these new American cotton districts because draft animals were indispensable to the work of plowing the fields, powering the cotton gins that cleaned the crops, and hauling goods to and from New Orleans. The cotton revolution remaking the southwestern United States, in other words, depended on horses, and there simply were not enough to keep up with demand. American traders, as a result, began making their way into northern New Spain in a desperate search for some way to supply the ravenous demand for horses emerging in the southwestern United States.[32] When that explosive new market demand in the United States crashed into devolving conditions of northeastern New Spain during the late 1810s, the result was a massive spike in both smuggling and associated violence in the region.

It was a particular combination of factors, then, that brought smuggling and violence to new heights along the U.S.–New Spain border during the 1810s. First, the enduring economic isolation of the region had already established informal networks of smuggling that helped to sustain the local economy and communities. Second, the Mexican War for Independence, in all its horrific violence, then pushed local Spaniards in Texas into even more precarious circumstances, either as desperately poor settlers in Texas or as exiled refugees in Louisiana. For both groups struggling in the aftermath of Arredondo's bloody reclaiming of the region, smuggling became a matter of survival. Third, at that same moment, the explosive expansion of markets in the southwestern United States due to the cotton revolution meant that demand—and thus rewards—for smuggling livestock from New Spain into the United States had never been higher than it was during the late 1810s. In response to all of this, Spaniards on both sides of the border threw themselves headlong into the rapidly expanding smuggling economy in Texas, while independent Indians launched devastating new raids against the territory's Spanish settlements in search of horses to sell to American markets.

Local authorities recognized what was happening and begged Mexico City to legalize trade between northeastern New Spain and the southwestern United States. Doing so, they argued, would bring broad economic benefits for the Spanish side of the border and would, in turn, reduce violence by eliminating the need for smuggling in the region. Melchor Núñez de Esquivel, one of the most experienced local administrators in Nuevo León, recommended that royal authorities authorize the four provinces of northeastern New Spain to export livestock legally to Louisiana. His reasoning was both simple and compelling: such exports to the United States would drastically improve the local economic situation, bringing broad improvements in all aspects of life in the region.[33] Unfortunately for Esquivel and other local officials, the commander of northeastern New Spain, Joaquín de Arredondo, opposed such a change. Arredondo was in favor of loosening some of the existing restrictions on trade in the territory, and he openly acknowledged that illegal trade in livestock was a major catalyst for violence in northeastern New Spain. Yet Arredondo also feared that legalizing livestock trade to the United States would only encourage even more contraband trade and thereby incite independent Indians to increase their raiding of Spanish villages and ranches.

He advised the Crown against such a move, and no exemption was ever granted by Spanish authorities.[34]

With Spain's restrictions remaining in place, Anglo-Americans continued to venture into the region illegally in search of livestock, which led to regular clashes with local Spanish soldiers. William Finely, for example, was arrested in 1819 by a Spanish military contingent near Nacogdoches, where they found Finely illegally transporting a cargo (including silk scarves, cotton clothes, premade fishing lines and hooks, tobacco, and bolts of quality blue cloth) that the American planned to use in trade with local Indians in exchange for horses. In a similar manner, an Anglo-American farmer named Abraham Leeds was arrested while transporting a set of blankets that he hoped to trade to Indians in exchange for a cow. Nathaniel Shields was captured on his way back to his native Tennessee while driving a herd of thirty horses and mules that he had bartered from Indians in Texas. David Long and Alexander Colhane were both arrested in Texas after buying more than twenty horses and mules that they intended to resell back in Louisiana. As these Americans encountered Spanish soldiers, they often found themselves quite vulnerable. Levi King, a native from Massachusetts, traveled to Nacogdoches during this period in order to trade for horses and mules, but was captured on his way back to the United States by a group of Spanish soldiers who then stole his small herd of five horses and a mule.[35] The highly unregulated nature of trade along the border not only made smuggling possible but also left smugglers themselves open to being victimized.

Indeed, violence accompanied these smuggling operations in various forms. Often smugglers found themselves robbed and attacked as they made their way toward Louisiana while laden with valuable goods or livestock. Benito Pariente and his servants, for example, hoped to smuggle a herd of 169 mules into Louisiana that they had somehow secured near Monterrey. But along the Atacosito road, they encountered a group of Anglo-Americans who assaulted them, tied up Pariente's men, and stole the herd.[36] Extortion was another threat that bedeviled smugglers in the region, usually when military officials extorted smugglers they had captured. In March 1819, for example, a smuggler named Salvador Carrasco was arrested for illegally transporting goods from the United States into the La Bahía village on Matagorda Bay in Texas. In his official statement to Spanish authorities, Carrasco explained that he had been smuggling goods into the area for a long time with the open knowledge of—and under duress from—the local lieutenant in La Bahía, Juan de Castañeda. Lieutenant Castañeda had apparently discovered Carrasco's smuggling and then blackmailed Carrasco into giving him a regular cut of the illegal merchandise whenever it arrived in the village, which Castañeda later sold to his soldiers at a massive profit.[37]

The overwhelming proportion of violence associated with smuggling during the 1810s came in the form of increased Indian raids against ranches and settlements in the four provinces of northeastern New Spain. The same market forces that enticed Anglo-Americans and Spaniards to cross the border in search of livestock also drove independent Indians in the region to raid Spanish settlements for horses they could sell to American traders. Throughout the 1810s, Comanches, Apaches, and other groups launched massive raids on Spanish ranches and villages across Texas and the northern portions of Nuevo León, Coahuila, and Nuevo Santander.[38] Several important Spanish political and military leaders in the territory, such as Simón de Herrera, Juan Antonio Padilla, and Gaspar López all agreed that the presence of Anglo-Americans in the region was responsible for rapidly increasing levels of local violence because they incited the Indians to steal in order to trade with them and obtain the goods that the Spanish could no longer provide.[39] Ramón Díaz de Bustamante reported in May 1810 that Comanches continued to harass the area of Laredo, where they had recently stolen 260 horses. During that raid, the Comanches had killed two Spaniards—scalping one man and cutting off his genitals—and severely injured two others.[40] These raids would continue in relentless wave after wave until, by 1819, more than 80 percent of the Spanish ranches around Laredo had been abandoned in the wake of Indian violence from Texas.[41]

Joaquín de Arredondo referred to the year of 1813—the same year as his bloody reclaiming of Texas from the rebels—as particularly heavy with Indian raids.[42] The Lipan Apaches, for example, repeatedly raided the northernmost town in Nuevo León, Lampazos, for several weeks in November 1813. Local authorities reported that Apaches raided a ranch near the town, where the invaders killed three Spanish ranchers and captured two others as they stole livestock. The next day, these same Apaches then killed another Spaniard and assaulted an additional four ranchers, although those particular four somehow managed to escape. A few days later, a band of Apaches attacked two brothers tending livestock in the area. The Apaches stole the herd and kidnapped one of the brothers as the other hid in a nearby river.[43] In the village of Vallecillo, Nuevo León, Apaches became so bold in their raids that they attacked the mayor's hacienda, where they stole all his horses and mules after killing several of his workers.[44]

Even Joaquín de Arredondo came to understand that the violence he had brought to Texas had pushed the surviving population of northeastern New Spain into a tighter embrace of smuggling. In a report that he sent to Spain in late 1814, Arredondo explained that it was impossible to contain smuggling in northeastern New Spain because of rampant shortages of goods due to the official commercial monopoly exercised by Veracruz traders in New Spain that so badly constricted commercial transactions along the northern frontier. Local Spaniards resorted to smuggling, Arredondo explained, because it was 400 percent cheaper for them to buy goods obtained illegally from Louisiana than to buy anything hauled in legally from the state-approved Veracruz route. Likewise, the stark scarcity of almost every commodity imaginable in these northern borderlands pushed locals to search in illegal markets for things they needed and wanted. As Arredondo detailed in his report, the violence of suppressing the Gutiérrez-Magee expedition had exacerbated these problems and led to even more smuggling, which meant that the provinces of northeastern New Spain could contribute nothing to the revenue of the Spanish empire.[45] What the region had become, instead, was an incubator for horse smuggling and all the mayhem that entailed.

Such violence continued to wash over northeastern New Spain throughout the decade. In April 1819, a band of independent Indians assaulted the Pantano Ranch located between Sabinas and Vallecillo in Nuevo León, where they killed a Spaniard and stole two hundred horses.[46] A few days later, sixteen Indians raided Agualeguas, Nuevo León, where the Indians assaulted local Spaniards, stole horses, and captured a man named Manuel García. This raiding party then assaulted the San Xavier Ranch, where they stole more horses and captured eight more people, including the ranch owner's three sons. The Indians then made their way to the nearby Punteagudo Ranch, owned by a man named Valentin Longoria, where they stabbed Longoria's wife to death, killed Longoria's son, and captured his son's wife and three children. Soon afterward, a Spanish military detachment arrived and confronted the raiders. Because the Indians were outnumbered by Spanish troops, they released seventeen captives and fled with some of the horses they had stolen. When two of the former captives were later questioned, they testified that the band of Indians had comprised ten Apaches, four Comanches, and two Indians from the mission in Laredo. By the late 1810s, then, it was not only independent Indians but also "pacified" Indians who participated in these illegal activities, and their mutual interest in raiding Spaniards for horses to sell to Americans had created some remarkable pan-tribal alliances in the region.[47]

Although livestock smuggling may have relied on interethnic and cross-cultural cooperation—a topic discussed in more detail in this volume in chapter 4 by Miguel Ángel González Quiroga—it was nonetheless marked during this period primarily by violence. In chapter 2, Joaquín Rivaya-Martínez will demonstrate that this thread of violence did not end with the birth of Independent Mexico. Indeed, during the decades that followed, Indian raids into northern Mexico not only continued but increased because the factors that fostered those raids during the 1810s would persist and even expand in influence.

———

The violence that emerged along the U.S.–New Spain border between 1810 and 1821 had deep roots. Even as late as 1810, the region remained a territory fiercely contested between the Spanish Crown and the many independent Indian nations who controlled most of the territory. Indeed, the northeastern frontier was scarcely populated by Spaniards, and their settlements remained weakly linked to the political and economic cores of New Spain. This vast and remote region of New Spain thus suffered from endemic poverty as local Spanish settlements remained painfully underdeveloped. Most of the Spaniards who lived in the region, particularly the handful of local elites, blamed the Spanish Crown's heavy-handed trade restrictions for these enduring challenges that made daily life so difficult for Spaniards of the northeastern frontier.

The Mexican War for Independence and the economic boom in the southwestern United States during the 1810s aggravated these long-standing problems. First, the Mexican insurgency paralyzed legal trade within most of New Spain (which pushed independent Indians to resume raiding Spanish settlements when the gifting policy failed) and drastically increased both the price and scarcity of most commodities along the remote northern frontier. Second, the simultaneous cotton boom in the southwestern United States created massive and insatiable new markets along the edge of northeastern New Spain, which seemed to offer a solution for both Indians and Spaniards seeking goods that were available nowhere else. The currency for these exchanges became livestock due to massive demands for draft animals in the southwestern United States, which fueled the rapid increase in both smuggling and associated border violence during this period.

Smuggling functioned along this border largely because of, rather than in spite of, the ethnic diversity of its participants, as independent Indians, Spaniards, Anglo-Americans, and Frenchmen converged in this borderlands territory to negotiate and trade with one another. Although violence was a constant element in borderlands daily life, so too were the interethnic alliances between these different actors that made such illicit trade possible. In that, the border became an escape valve during this era for the people of northeastern New Spain, as it provided them with a badly needed connection—through the United States—to the global economy and thereby access to commodities they both needed and wanted. The forces that made that possible, the weakness of the Spanish state and the economic power of the southwestern United States, would continue to serve as catalysts for violence in the region during the decades to come.

Notes

1. For a detailed narrative of Arredondo's violent campaign in Texas, see Bradley Folsom, *Arredondo: Last Spanish Ruler of Texas and Northeastern New Spain* (Norman: University of Oklahoma Press, 2017), 95–108.

2. All information about Cornelio Lozoya and his trial comes from Archivo General de la Nación (hereafter, AGN), *Provincias Internas*, vol. 187, exp. 12, folios 291–97.

3. New Spain's northern frontier was a vast territory. In this essay, we focus on the northeastern region that included Texas, Coahuila, Nuevo León, and Tamaulipas. At the end of the Spanish colonial era, this region was called the Eastern Interior Provinces. Nuevo León was known as Nuevo Reino de León and Tamaulipas was known as Nuevo Santander. For the sake of modern readers, we use the modern names for these Mexican states throughout the text.

4. François Chevalier, *Land and Society in Colonial Mexico* (Berkeley: University of California Press, 1963), 181.

5. There is a burgeoning historiography that highlights how American Indian resistance prevented Spain (and then Mexico) from effectively controlling these territories. Some of the best examples of this historiographical trend are Pekka Hämäläinen, *The Comanche Empire* (New Haven, CT: Yale University Press, 2009), 1–18; Brian DeLay, *War of a Thousand Deserts: Indian Raids and the U.S.-Mexican War* (New Haven, CT: Yale University Press, 2009), 9–31; Juliana Barr, *Peace Came in the Form of a Woman: Indians and Spaniards in the Texas Borderlands* (Chapel Hill: University of North Carolina Press, 2007); Isidro Vizcaya Canales, *Tierra de guerra viva: Incursiones de indios y otros conflictos en el noreste de México durante el siglo XIX, 1821–1885* (Monterrey: Academia de Investigaciones, 2001); Cecilia Sheridan-Prieto, "¿Rebelión o resistencia? Tierra de guerra en el noreste novohispano," in *Las ciudades y la guerra, 1750–1898*, ed. Salvador Broseta, Carmen Corona, Manuel Chust, et al. (Castelló: Universitat Jaume I, 2002), 19–47; Martha Rodríguez, *Historias de resistencia y exterminio: Los indios de Coahuila durante el siglo XIX* (México: Centro de Investigaciones y Estudios Superiores de Antropología Social/Instituto Nacional Indigenista, 1995); Sara Ortelli, *Trama de una guerra conveniente: Nueva Vizcaya y la sombra de los apaches (1748–1790)* (México: El Colegio de México, 2007); David M. Vignes, *Incursiones de indios al noreste en el México independiente, 1821–1885* (Monterrey: Archivo General del Estado de Nuevo León, 1995); David B. Adams, "Embattled Borderland: Northern Nuevo León and the Indios Bárbaros, 1686–1870," *Southwestern Historical Quarterly* 95, no. 2 (October 1991): 205–20; Susan Deeds, *Defiance and Deference in Mexico's Colonial North: Indians under Spanish Rule in Nueva Vizcaya* (Austin: University of Texas Press, 2003).

6. Cuauhtémoc Velasco Ávila, *La frontera étnica en el noreste mexicano: Los comanches entre 1800–1841* (México: Centro de Investigaciones y Estudios Superiores de Antropología Social, 2012), 134; Cuauhtémoc Velasco Ávila, *Pacificar o negociar: Los acuerdos de paz con apaches y comanches en las Provincias Internas de Nueva España* (México: Instituto Nacional de Antropología e Historia, 2015), 27.

7. Velasco, *Frontera*, 147.

8. Manuel Miño Grijalva, *El mundo novohispano: Población, ciudades y economía, siglos XVII y XVIII* (México: Fondo de Cultura Económica/El Colegio de México, 2001), 245–56. See also Antonio Peña Guajardo, *La economía novohispana y la élite local del Nuevo Reino*

de León en la primera mitad del siglo XVIII (Monterrey: Fondo Estatal para la Cultura y las Artes de Nuevo León, 2005).

9. For a more detailed discussion of Spain's mercantilist system, see Matilde Souto Mantecón, "Creación y disolución de los consulados de comercio de la Nueva España," in *Revista Complutense de Historia de América* 32 (2006): 19–39 and the entry "Consulado," also written by Matilde Souto Mantencón, in *Diccionario de la Independencia de México*, ed. Alfredo Ávila, Virginia Guedea, and Ana Carolina Ibarra (México: Universidad Nacional Autónoma de México, 2010), 320–23.

10. Although the Spanish Crown liberated some trade restrictions and authorized the creation of some new ports during the late eighteenth and early nineteenth centuries, the changes made almost no difference in the lived experience of northeastern New Spain. See, for example, Mario Trujillo Bolio, *El péndulo marítimo-mercantil en el Atlántico novohispano (1798–1825): Comercio libre, circuitos de intercambio, exportación e importación* (México: CIESAS/Universidad de Cádiz, 2009).

11. Octavio Herrera Pérez, *La zona libre: Excepción fiscal y conformación histórica de la frontera norte de México* (México: Secretaría de Relaciones Exteriores, 2004), 34–35.

12. Andrew J. Torget, *Seeds of Empire: Cotton, Slavery and the Transformation of the Texas Borderlands, 1800–1850* (Chapel Hill: University of North Carolina Press, 2015), 34–42; Dan Flores, "Bringing Home All the Pretty Horses: The Horse Trade and the Early American West, 1775–1825," *Montana: The Magazine of Western History* 58, no. 2 (Summer 2008): 18.

13. For a detailed narrative about the insurgency in Coahuila, Nuevo León, and Nuevo Santander, see Isidro Vizcaya Canales, *En los albores de la independencia: Las Provincias Internas de Oriente durante la insurrección de Miguel Hidalgo y Costilla, 1810–1811* (Monterrey: Fondo Editorial Nuevo León, 2005); Laura Gutiérrez, "El prolongado ocaso de un estado y la gestación de otro," in *Breve historia de Coahuila*, ed. María Elena Santoscoy (México: Fondo de Cultura Económica/El Colegio de México, 2000), 93–202; Catherine Andrews and Jesús Hernández Jaimes, "La lucha por la supervivencia: El impacto de la insurgencia en el Nuevo Santander, 1810–1821," in *La independencia en el septentrión de la Nueva España: Provincias Internas e intendencias norteñas* (México: UNAM, Instituto de Investigaciones Históricas, 2010).

14. Vizcaya Canales, *Albores*, 175. For a description of Texas in 1809, see Nettie Lee Benson, "A Governor's Report on Texas in 1809," *Southwestern Historical Quarterly* 71, no. 4 (April 1968): 603–15.

15. Martín González de la Vara, "La lucha por la independencia mexicana en Texas," in *La independencia en el septentrión de la Nueva España: Provincias Internas e intendencias norteñas*, ed. Ana Carolina Ibarra (México: Universidad Nacional Autónoma de México, 2010), 85.

16. Raúl A. Ramos, *Beyond the Alamo: Forging Mexican Ethnicity in San Antonio, 1821–1861* (Chapel Hill: University of North Carolina Press, 2008), 32.

17. González de la Vara, "La lucha," 102–3.

18. J. C. A. Stagg, *Borderlines in Borderlands: James Madison and the Spanish-American Frontier, 1776–1821* (New Haven, CT: Yale University Press, 2009), 143; David E. Narrett, "José Bernardo Gutiérrez de Lara: Caudillo of the Mexican Republic in Texas," *Southwestern Historical Quarterly* 106, no. 2 (October 2002): 202.

19. Virginia Guedea, "Autonomía e independencia en la provincia de Texas: La Junta de Gobierno de San Antonio de Béjar, 1813," in *La independencia de México y el proceso autono-*

mista novohispano, 1808–1824 (México: Universidad Nacional Autónoma de México/ Instituto de Investigaciones Doctor José María Luis Mora, 2001), 151–54.

20. Narrett, "José Bernardo Gutiérrez de Lara," 209.

21. González de la Vara, "La lucha," 92.

22. Barrera Enderle, "Contrabando y liberalismo: La transformación de la cultura política en la Provincias Internas de Oriente, 1808–1821" (PhD diss., University of California at Irvine, 2013).

23. For a thorough account of the Battle of Medina, see Folsom, *Arredondo*, 81–94.

24. AGN, Provincias Internas, vol. 187, exp. 15, folios 321–27.

25. Folsom, *Arredondo*, 95–101.

26. Matthew Babcock, "Roots of Independence: Transcultural Trade in the Texas-Louisiana Borderlands," *Ethnohistory* 60, no. 2 (Spring 2013): 250.

27. For discussions about the differences between "border" and "borderlands," see Elliot Young, *Catarino Garza's Revolution on the Texas-Mexico Border* (Durham, NC: Duke University Press, 2004), 7; Jeremy Adelman and Stephen Aron, "From Borderlands to Borders: Empire, Nation-States, and the Peoples in between in North American History," *American Historical Review* 104 (June 1999): 814–41.

28. James F. Brooks, "'This Evil Extends Especially to the Feminine Sex': Captivity and Identity in New Mexico, 1700–1846," *Feminist Studies* 22 (1996): 280.

29. DeLay, *War of a Thousand Deserts*, 58.

30. Torget, *Seeds of Empire*, 41.

31. Torget, *Seeds of Empire*, 34–36.

32. Torget, *Seeds of Empire*, 36–42.

33. Melchor Núñez de Esquivel, "Sobre el estado actual de las Provincias Internas de Oriente," in *Monopolio y corrupción: 1814*, ed. Héctor Jaime Treviño Villarreal (Monterrey: Archivo General del Estado de Nuevo León, 1989), 36–39.

34. Archivo General de Indias (hereafter, AGI), Audiencia de Guadalajara, Signatura 297, *Sobre el estado de guerra y auxilios necesarios para el desarrollo de las Provincias Internas de Oriente*, Monterrey, September 7, 1814.

35. AGN, Provincias Internas, vol. 187, exp. 7, folios 211–48; exp. 8, folios 249–66.

36. AGN, Provincias Internas, vol. 187, exp. 10, folios 275–86.

37. AGN, Provincias Internas, vol. 252, exp. 9, folios 112–14, Monterrey, March 31, 1819.

38. Torget, *Seeds of Empire*, 34–42; Hämäläinen, *Comanche Empire*, 149.

39. Velasco, *Frontera*, 148–54.

40. AGN, Provincias Internas, vol. 201, exp. 2, folios 105–10.

41. Jack Jackson, *Los Mesteños: Spanish Ranching in Texas, 1721–1821* (College Station: Texas A&M University Press, 1986), 550.

42. Joaquín de Arredondo to Benito Armiñán, Béxar, January 31, 1814, Bexar Archives, University of Texas, Austin, Texas, roll 53: 508, quoted in Velasco Ávila, *Frontera*, 154.

43. Archivo Histórico Municipal de Monterrey (hereafter, AHMM), Correspondencia, vol. 1, exp. 21, folio 2, Lampazos, September 8, 1813.

44. AHMM, Correspondencia, vol. 1, exp. 38, s/f, Vallecillo, December 11, 1813.

45. AGI, Audiencia de Guadalajara, Signatura 297, *Sobre el estado de guerra y auxilios necesarios para el desarrollo de las Provincias Internas de Oriente*, Monterrey, September 7, 1814.

46. AGN, Provincias Internas, vol. 252, exp. 4, folios 77–79.

47. AGN, Provincias Internas, vol. 252, exp. 4, folios 80–89, Monterrey, April 3, 1819.

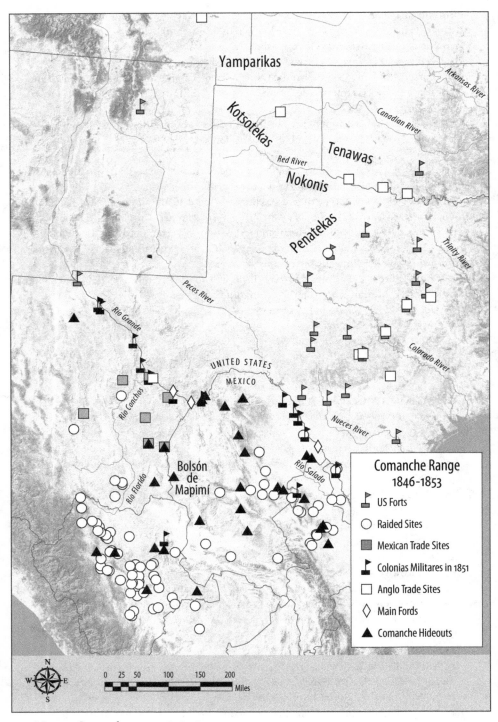

Map 2.1 Comanche range, 1846–1853

Chapter 2

Trespassers in the Land of Plenty

Comanche Raiding across the U.S.-Mexico Border, 1846–1853

JOAQUÍN RIVAYA-MARTÍNEZ

Prior to 1875, when the U.S. Army coerced the last free-roving Comanche bands into settling on a reservation in Indian Territory (today's Oklahoma), Comanche raiding parties, including sometimes Kiowas, Plains Apaches, and other allies, harassed today's northern Mexico and Texas relentlessly, destroying lives and property, and taking away livestock, captives, and other plunder. Comanche forays caused so much devastation and anxiety on both sides of the Rio Grande that the "fearsome" Comanche has become a myth of Homeric proportions in the collective memory of communities north and south of the border. Comanches have normally been portrayed in folklore, literature, and film as one-dimensional characters defined by fierceness, incarnating the archetype of the evil savage. Even scholars have sometimes contributed to perpetuate that unfortunate stereotype by taking for granted, exaggerating, or failing to contextualize Comanche violence. Such representations project the distorted view that Comanches were *always and inherently* aggressive, whether by nature or by culture.[1] This essay is an attempt to divest Comanches of that legendary aura by using an ethnohistorical perspective to understand their actions. At the same time, it contributes to the study of violence in the U.S.-Mexico border by offering a multifaceted answer to two central questions: why did Comanche raids occur, and who benefited from them?

This essay focuses on the years 1846 to 1853, the decisive period when the boundary line separating the United States and Mexico acquired its current delineation.[2] In December 1845, the United States annexed Texas, inheriting the Lone Star Republic's claim to Mexican lands south and west, which triggered the U.S.-Mexican War of 1846–48. The 1848 Treaty of Guadalupe Hidalgo brought an end to the conflict, validating a massive transfer of Mexico's territory to its northern neighbor, and sanctioning the U.S. commitment to impede incursions into Mexico from north of the border. The frontier acquired its present configuration in 1853 through the Gadsden Treaty, as the United States acquired additional territory from the southern republic, this time by purchase. That same treaty freed the United States of its obligation to prevent U.S.-based Indian raids into Mexico.

Even though raiding cost Comanches a high death toll, they continued to beleaguer Mexico year after year.[3] It would be tempting to blame such obstinacy on their aggressiveness. In fact, many contemporaries saw it that way—some still do.[4] Yet Comanches' bellicosity is not enough to explain the scale of their forays south of the Rio Grande in the 1840s and 1850s. Comanche incursions into Mexico between 1846 and 1853 did not differ dramatically from what happened immediately before and after those years. This is particularly puzzling if one considers the turbulent relations between Mexico and the United States, and the significant political, economic, and demographic transformations that occurred on both sides of the border during that period, as well as the tremendous mortality that successive epidemics of smallpox and cholera caused among Comanches and their allies in 1848 and 1849. The apparent continuity in raiding patterns at a time when the U.S.-Mexico borderlands and the Comanches' own world were changing drastically deserves a finespun explanation.

By contextualizing Comanche forays into Mexico between 1846 and 1853 through an ethnohistorical perspective, this essay offers a more nuanced interpretation of the raiders' motivations and actions, explaining the violence unleashed south of the border not as an end, but rather as an instrument to reach other goals. In this, I diverge from Brian DeLay's interpretation that "violence was less an inevitable by-product of raiding than an important goal in its own right."[5] As we shall see, Comanche incursions responded to cultural factors, as well as to a complex range of changing political, economic, and environmental circumstances that also enticed Comanches to trade or enter peace agreements. While Comanches' cultural schemas encouraged raiding, the magnitude of their incursions into Mexico had more immediate causes: Euro-American encroachment on the Comanchería; the gradual decline of the bison population; the enormous demand for equines north of the border; northern Mexico's wealth in horses and relative vulnerability; the very nature of the border region, most of which remained a sparsely populated, remote, and untamed wilderness; the absence or ineffectiveness of the state (both Mexico and the United States) along the border; and Washington's relative lack of jurisdiction in Texas. The combination of these factors made raiding Mexico a desirable, feasible, and profitable undertaking, luring in Comanches and their allies.

I interpret the forays as undertakings by Comanche individuals and groups seeking prestige and wealth, operating often in conjunction but autonomously, sometimes under tremendous pressure themselves, who tried to make the most of the changing circumstances of the frontier, but without any discernible unified or long-term political agenda. Despite our common emphasis on environmental and economic factors, I fundamentally disagree with

Hämäläinen's interpretation that Comanche raiding into Mexico was the result of a systematic imperial project of "a population of twenty to thirty thousand."[6] (There probably were no more than twelve thousand Comanches in 1846, and their population was severely reduced by the epidemics of 1848 and 1849.)[7]

DeLay's emphasis on vengeance as a causal explanation for Comanches' major campaigns south of the Rio Grande is not entirely persuasive.[8] Comanche revenge parties could be indeed large, sometimes incorporating warriors from multiple groups. However, they typically fulfilled their goal as soon as they inflicted on the enemy a number of losses proportionate to the number of dead Comanches they had set forth to avenge. Often, the taking of a single enemy scalp triggered the return of the party.[9] Most Comanche operations in Mexico were essentially about plundering, specifically about stealing horses and mules.[10] Although a rhetoric of revenge sometimes served mourners to enlist large contingents, even the largest bodies of Comanches and their allies usually split into multiple groups operating autonomously under their respective leaders once on Mexican soil. Indeed, parties were made and unmade rather fluidly. Even though raiders often gathered at their Mexican hideouts, typically, they moved around as a body only for protection or when facing a large enemy force.

In the middle decades of the nineteenth century, Comanches (*Nʉmʉnʉʉ* in their language) and their allies often spent long periods south of the Rio Grande, where they triggered tremendous security crises. Parties of up to several hundred warriors ranged over the vast territory that lies between the Western Sierra Madre and the Gulf of Mexico, encompassing much of Chihuahua, Coahuila, Nuevo León, Tamaulipas, Durango, Zacatecas, and San Luis Potosí. That immense region was dotted by an abundance of livestock-rich but poorly defended ranches and haciendas, Comanches' preferred targets, while topography and climate combined to create the ideal scenery for raiders to strike and retreat stealthily and elude potential pursuers. Comanches operated frequently from strongholds in the remote Bolsón de Mapimí, establishing sometimes temporary base camps in craggy sierras beyond its periphery, from where they could harass the surrounding country advantageously.[11]

The Bolsón de Mapimí is an endorheic basin (an interior drainage in which surface water does not reach the sea) of about eighty thousand square miles that spreads over eastern Chihuahua, western Coahuila, and northeastern Durango. With an average height of some three thousand feet, the Bolsón is a plateau scarred by a multitude of gullies and ravines and crossed by numerous mountain ranges. Despite its arid climate, it contains abundant seasonal ponds and permanent water holes, as well as several lakes.[12] In the mid-nineteenth century, the Bolsón was largely uninhabited—like today. Comanches often established base camps in Bolsón sierras that offered springs, pasture, and timber. In the relative safety of those hideouts, warriors could make arrows and heal their wounds between forays, and people and beasts could rest and become stronger before Comanches initiated the return trip. Besides, the rugged topography and the aridity of the Bolsón permitted the retreating raiders to evade or ambush chasing Mexican parties relatively easily. Thus, this uneven and barren highland became the Comanches' main bastion south of the Rio Grande.[13]

Comanches were not the first Indigenous people to raid today's northern Mexico. Throughout the colonial period, numerous groups of diverse size and ethnicity engaged in a poaching economy in northern New Spain—a practice that would persist in the region into the late nineteenth century (see chapter 3 by Lance Blyth and chapter 6 by Timothy Bowman in this volume). Tobosos, Salineros, Acoclames, Apaches, and other independent or apostate Indians, as well as assorted Hispanic renegades, raided the settlements of Nueva Vizcaya, Coahuila, and Nuevo León.[14] After Mexico's independence from Spain in 1821, the economic, political, and military disarray of the new republic favored an upsurge in the forays that Lipan Apaches, Comanches, Wichitas, and other independent Indians based north of the Rio Grande launched south of that river. The wars for Mexico's independence and the civil conflicts that succeeded it cost the new state a heavy toll in both human lives and wealth (see Alberto Barrera-Enderle and Andrew Torget's chapter 1 in this volume), keeping the Mexican treasury in dire straits. The Mexican government was unable to maintain the presidio system and continue the policy of diplomatic gifting that had been the cornerstone of the Spanish Crown's defensive strategy for northern New Spain in the late colonial period. Northern Mexico's vulnerability was further compounded after 1836 by the negligence (or lack of interest) of the Texan (and, later, American) authorities to prevent "their" Indians from campaigning south of the border. Moreover, the growing political and territorial factionalism within the Mexican republic often undermined interregional cooperation and prevented the central government from making quick decisions. All of this hindered Mexican attempts to organize an effective defense against Indian forays and punish the aggressors, which might have deterred them from further attacks.[15] Thus, the problems Mexican officials faced in the mid-nineteenth century were in some ways similar to those faced by their predecessors in the previous two centuries. The magnitude of the forays launched by Comanches and their allies south of the Rio Grande during that period was, however, unparalleled.

Prior to Mexico's independence, Comanche raids on Euro-American settlements normally involved parties of fewer than one hundred warriors, and circumscribed almost exclusively to the areas of San Antonio and La Bahía (today's Goliad), in Texas, and to a one-hundred-mile-or-so-wide corridor along the Rio Grande, east of its confluence with Devils River. Between 1816 and 1822, however, a strategic alliance with the Lipan Apaches facilitated the southern Comanches access to a much larger extension of northern Mexico, as members of both groups raided together often.[16] Comanches acquired thus an invaluable knowledge of the Mexican north from their ancestral enemies. They would benefit from, and expand on, that knowledge for decades.[17]

Comanches extended their raiding hinterland to Chihuahua in 1825, and began to launch major forays there in 1833.[18] The magnitude of Comanche expeditions continued to grow over the 1830s, reaching an unprecedented breadth in the 1840s and 1850s. At the time, Comanches constituted a rank society characterized by a martial ethos and a political economy that fostered aggressiveness toward their enemies and munificence toward their own. The subsistence of these inveterate nomads depended largely on foraging, while raiding and trading were important ways of gaining affluence and social esteem. Any prestigious warrior could organize and lead a foray, sometimes using a discourse of revenge to mobilize support. Individual performance offered Comanche men the possibility to gain wealth and status through success on the warpath, courage on the battleground, and generosity in the redistribution of plunder. These features influenced decisively the organization and execution of Comanche raids.[19]

Comanches' way of life and political culture made reaching agreements with them tricky. Always on the move, their vast geographic spread and lack of political integration, along with their loose, noncoercive form of leadership, created all sorts of problems to Mexican and American diplomats. The *Numunuu* were politically divided into several divisions, each of which generally acted independently in matters of war and peace. To a lesser extent, the same can be said of the multiple bands integrating each division. Around 1850, five major Comanche divisions occupied the plains between the Arkansas River and the Texas Hill Country (see map 2.1). The Penatekas, the southernmost division, had constant intercourse with the Indian agent in Texas, whose communications with the Nokonis and Tenawas (aka "middle Comanches") were much more erratic, and often through the intermediation of the former. The northernmost division, the Yamparikas, interacted little with the Upper Arkansas agent, whereas the Kotsotekas, the closest to New Mexico, had but sporadic contacts with American authorities.

Even though Comanche subgroups cooperated often, particular divisions and bands operated autonomously. In February 1848, after a series of incidents between Nʉmʉnʉʉ warriors and Texans, Mopechucope (Old Owl), the main Penateka leader, informed Robert Neighbors, federal Indian agent for the Lone Star State, that "the depredations" had been committed by a party of Tenawas and Nokonis "who had been on a foray in Mexico," as well as "a small portion" of the Penatekas "over whom he could exercise no control." According to Mopechucope, when the Tenawa and Nokoni raiders arrived at the Penateka camp with a drove of stolen horses, the local chiefs "immediately took possession of the stolen property for the purpose of returning them to their owners." Once the Tenawa leaders learned what had happened, however, "they sent their warriors out to steal more, saying, 'they wanted to see how long before the old chiefs of the Pe-ne-ta-kees would get tired of returning stolen horses.' Several parties immediately started down" and began poaching horses again.[20]

Comanche headmen led largely by persuasion, generally lacking the authority to compel others to abide by their designs. Occasionally, a highly prestigious leader rose to prominence extending his influence to other bands within his division, or even beyond. Most of the time, however, a headman's influence was limited to his own band, and only for as long as his following was willing to echo his advice. As in Mopechucope's case above, Comanche leaders could not always restrain their warriors. If individuals or factions dissented from a leader, they just broke away from their old band, joining another or establishing a new one.[21] Thus, Americans and Mexicans found it extremely difficult to deal with all divisions at once, negotiate with a single interlocutor, or achieve firm, long-lasting treaties that bound all or even a majority of the Nʉmʉnʉʉ. For instance, in early October 1850, Agent John Rollins recriminated Comanche leaders Buffalo Hump and Shanaco for "their many thefts and occasional murders" from which "it had been inferred that they had abandoned the treaty of 1846, and determined to be hostile." Buffalo Hump replied that "his people had been on the Rio Grande occasionally in small numbers, in company with other Indians, *against his wishes and in violation of his express orders* [emphasis added]," contending "that he and his people *generally* were friends—*truly so* [original emphasis]; but that they had bad men among them, whom they could not control, and he hoped the innocent would not be made to suffer in common with the guilty."[22]

Despite their lack of political cohesion, Comanche warriors often invited and enlisted volunteers from other bands and divisions, as well as non-Comanches, to partake in their predatory incursions. In January 1848, for instance, Neighbors reported that large numbers of northern Comanches, Kiowas, and Apaches were then gathering on the headwaters of the Brazos and counseling with the Penatekas with the "avowed intention . . . to make preparation for a descent upon the northern provinces of Mexico, Chihuahua, and others, early in the spring . . . proposing to unite and send several thousand warriors."[23] A Kiowa pictographic calendar reflects the frequent presence of Kiowas south of the Rio Grande between 1834 and 1859, including references to forays in the winters of 1850–51 and 1853–54.[24] Irrespective of their size and composition, Comanche raiding parties trespassed into Mexico with a common purpose: to obtain livestock and other plunder, including, sometimes, people.

Comanche raiders abducted women and children frequently. Captives played key roles in Comanche political economy and interethnic relations. As coerced laborers, abductees herded livestock, broke horses, and performed all sorts of physically demanding tasks and domestic chores. Some captives served their captors as interpreters and intermediaries with their ancestral people. Notably, the Nʉmʉnʉʉ incorporated abductees through adoption, marriage, and cooptation relatively often. Comanches used to adopt the infants they seized right away, whereas they enslaved older captives or held them in a state of semi-incorporation. Slavery was not hereditary, though, and captives typically received a gradually more benign treatment as long as they behaved according to their captors' expectations and became acculturated. That nineteenth-century Nʉmʉnʉʉ took the overwhelming majority of their captives south of the Rio Grande speaks to the centrality of the Mexican raids in their political economy.[25]

Since captives were privileged witnesses of Comanche pre-reservation life, their testimonies shed light on the nature of Comanche violence south of the border. Such was the case, for instance, of the deposition obtained in 1873 by Mexican authorities from a neighbor of Candela, Coahuila, named Jesús Ibarra. According to Jesús, in August 1851, when he was ten or eleven years old, Comanche and Kiowa raiders killed his brother Desiderio and kidnapped him at a field in the outskirts of Candela, slaying two more men in their retreat. The raiding party consisted of forty warriors and five women. Shortly, one of the warriors and two of the women broke off from the main group, taking Jesús to an *aguaje* (watering place) at the Cerro de Pájaros Azules, about one day away from Candela, while the others headed for Nuevo León via Bustamante. After ten or twelve days, the departed raiders returned from the "interior villages" with some three hundred horses and mules. The animals had been hurried so badly that they exhausted the water of two streams as soon as they arrived at the hideout. The Indians allowed four days for the beasts to recover. Then the Comanches left along the Río Salado toward the Rio Grande, whereas the Kiowas moved northward, leaving the Sierra de Santa Rosa on their left, and crossed the border above Piedras Negras, near a place called Resurrección.[26]

As the previous story illustrates, despite the frequent abductions of Mexican women and children, stealing equines was the primary objective of the raiders.[27] By the 1840s, the Numunuu had been an equestrian people for about a century and a half. They depended on horses for hunting, trading, and raiding. Mules and horses served them as pack animals. Individually owned equines indexed their proprietors' prosperity and status, and gifts of horses and mules enhanced one's prestige and political influence. Equines were also the main commodity in Comanche commercial transactions, as well as the primary target of raids by and on Comanches. Furthermore, the Numunuu ate equines in times of scarcity. Comanche herds also suffered frequent losses to enemy raiders, extreme winter conditions, and droughts, which were relatively common in the Comanchería. Indeed, paleoclimatic evidence indicates "a period of remarkably sustained drought and low streamflow" in an area of the high plains centered in eastern Colorado between roughly 1845 and 1856.[28]

Similarly, over the course of the nineteenth century, the steady disappearance of the bison from the Comanchería increased the dependence of the Numunuu on equines for their subsistence.[29] The unusually dry spell of 1845–56, which was particularly severe in 1845–48, 1851, and 1855–56, may have significantly accelerated the decline of the bison population on the southern plains.[30] As early as June 22, 1847, Agent Neighbors reported to the commissioner of Indian Affairs (hereafter, just "commissioner") that he had found some of the southern Comanche bands "very destitute of clothing." In some instances, he added, "they find it difficult to subsist by hunting," doing so "to a great degree upon horses and mules."[31] Similarly, in September 1853, Neighbors found the southern Numunuu, "with a very scanty subsistence, and no adequate means of procuring the necessaries of life" other than "the small quantity of provisions given them at the several military stations on the line, and the sale of the few [sic] horses they steal from Mexico." Their leaders, he wrote, "appear to be willing to discontinue the incursions, provided they can find any other means of subsisting."[32]

Even though the Numunuu raised their own livestock and captured wild horses, their constant internal demand for, and increasing dependence on, equines compelled them to raid other peoples. As early as 1818–19, Comanches reportedly stole "not less than 10,000" horses a year from settlements across northern New Spain.[33] In the following decades, the possibility of selling stolen horses and mules to a miscellaneous and changing assortment of commercial partners on both sides of the Rio Grande became a paramount enticement for their Mexican campaigns.

Between 1846 and 1853, Comanches traded much of the plunder acquired south of the Rio Grande to merchants operating from U.S. soil. Exchanges with neighboring Wichita-speaking groups, traditional Comanche allies, occurred all year round. Similarly, Indigenous and Hispanic dealers from northeastern New Mexico, the so-called Comancheros, penetrated the Comanchería often to supply the southern plains' nomads with produce, iron tools, beads, and other trinkets in exchange for hides, bison products, and livestock—often stolen in Old Mexico.[34]

While Comanche commerce with New Mexicans and Wichita speakers dated back to the eighteenth century, Anglo-American traders did not begin dealing significantly with Comanches until the 1800s. During the years preceding the U.S.-Mexico War, however, trade with Anglo merchants and Indians living along the eastern rim of the Comanchería became increasingly vital to the economy of the *Numunuu* and their allies, as those new trade partners could supply larger quantities of a wider variety of articles than Comancheros could, including much-coveted firearms and ammunition. Other than hides, the bulk of the Comanche trade consisted of stolen equines and, to a lesser extent, captives, acquired mostly in Mexico.

At the outbreak of the U.S.-Mexico War, Comanches and their allies used to trade much of their Mexican plunder at a series of posts established by American companies in the northern and eastern periphery of the Comanchería after 1820.[35] Perhaps paradoxically, European immigration into Texas resulted in the expansion of the Comanches' commercial network. On May 7, 1847, the Penatekas and the German colonists of the Fisher-Miller land grant in Central Texas ratified a peace treaty in Fredericksburg that created an additional venue for Comanches' plunder on the southern edge of their territory.[36] Some Comanche bands incorporated visits to the trading houses and the German settlements into their seasonal patterns of mobility. According to Macedonio Perales, a captive from San Buenaventura, Coahuila, who lived with the Comanches between 1849 and 1851, his captors used to visit two trading posts located respectively in "Los Pedernales" (probably the small German settlement by that name that existed at the time some seven miles southwest of Fredericksburg, Texas) and "near the Colorado River."[37]

U.S. Indian agents dealing with the independent natives of the West habitually operated from or near trading posts along the frontier. Such was the case of Robert Neighbors, who, from 1847 to 1854, routinely dealt with the southern Comanches from Torrey's Trading House on Tehuacana Creek (in today's McLennan County, Texas).[38] Similarly, between 1847 and 1849, Agent Thomas Fitzpatrick interacted normally with the northern Comanches from Bent's Fort on the Upper Arkansas (in today's southeastern Colorado).[39] Indian agents were thus well aware of the Comanche cycle of plunder south of the border and trade north of it.

American and Indian merchants sometimes became influential diplomatic intermediaries and couriers between U.S. authorities and the *Numunuu*, keeping Indian agents up to date on Comanche campaigns south of the border. In September 1848, for instance, Neighbors informed the commissioner that a party of Delawares working for trader George Barnard had "arrived direct from the Comanche village, and brought in the talks of the principal Comanche chiefs," as well as news that "most of the Comanche warriors are now on a foray in Mexico, and are doing much damage," returning "constantly with large numbers of horses, mules and prisoners."[40]

The *Numunuu* also sold much of their plunder to other Indians living east of the Comanchería. This commerce was partly an unexpected by-product of the U.S. policies toward Indians. Around 1830, natives removed to Indian Territory and Kansas from the eastern United States began to compete with the southern plains' nomads over the natural resources of the region. Soon, the settlements of the so-called Five Civilized Tribes and other displaced groups became preferred targets of Comanche raiders. In due time, though, small trading parties of Shawnees, Delawares, Kickapoos, and others became regular visitors to Comanche camps. Sometimes, these native partners accompanied Comanches in their forays.[41] In the 1840s, even traditional enemies of the *Numunuu* such as Osages and Pawnees became integrated into the former's commercial orbit.

All of those Indians channeled horses and mules stolen in Mexico and elsewhere into American markets while providing wealth- and prestige-thirsty Comanche warriors with the commodities they most coveted to continue raiding: firearms and ammunition.[42] On October 29, 1847, Agent Thomas Harvey complained to the commissioner that "when the Pawnees received guns at their annuity payment, they traded them to the Comanches." Similarly, the Osages, in the fall, used to acquire "a large number of guns for their winter hunt," which they bartered "in the summer with the Comanches and other southwestern tribes for mules."[43]

Despite recurrent objections from diverse Indian agents, the inability or unwillingness of the U.S. government to interrupt the ongoing trade between the *Numunuu* and their sedentary Indigenous neighbors to the east induced Comanches to keep up with their forays. As Harvey had done the previous year, on September 1, 1848, John Richardson, U.S. agent for the Osages, protested that his wards had "been on the most intimate relations with the Comanches for a number of years, meeting them every season in the prairie for the purpose of trade." Osages typically sold to Comanches guns, blankets, powder, lead, and other merchandise obtained from American traders, "and for a gun costing them at home twenty dollars, they . . . generally received one or two mules, worth to them on their return from forty to sixty dollars." In the spring of 1847 alone, Osages bartered goods worth $24,000 to Comanches, in exchange for "near fifteen hundred head of mules, worth at that time sixty thousand dollars." The trade was equally profitable for the *Numunuu*, who "taking their guns into Mexico" obtained "profits equally as great."[44]

Unsurprisingly, U.S.-based merchants of diverse extraction encouraged Comanches, sometimes overtly, to raid Mexico (and even Texas) to keep the flow of plunder. According to a captive named Francisco Treviño, for instance, Comanche raids south of the border acquired a "stronger intensity" after the independence of Texas, as Texans themselves encouraged the Indians to invade Mexico.[45]

Comanche commerce north of the Rio Grande grew steadily from 1821 to 1848, when a fatal smallpox outbreak spread among the southern plains' nomads, followed in 1849 by an even deadlier cholera epidemic.[46] The successive scourges cost the *Numunuu* and their neighbors many lives, causing such mayhem that they brought about the dismantling of most trading posts in and near the Comanchería. By then, however, the *Numunuu* and their allies had established additional commercial partnerships south of the Rio Grande.

By the mid-nineteenth century, a series of settlements in northeastern Chihuahua had become central to the Comanche trade. In 1854, runaway captive Macario Leal, a native of Laredo who had just spent seven years among the Comanches, declared to Nuevo León authorities that his captors used to sell much of their plunder at San Carlos (today's Manuel Benavides), their trade extending also to Presidio del Norte (today's Manuel Ojinaga), Coyame, and Chihuahua City, all of them in the state of Chihuahua, as well as to New Mexico, in exchange for firearms, ammunition, and food supplies that permitted them to continue with their forays.[47] German traveler Julius Fröbel considered *norteños* (the inhabitants of Presidio del Norte) "the allies, spies, powder purveyors . . . receivers and buyers of stolen goods" of the "Texan Comanches." In the words of U.S. Army officer and border surveyor William H. Emory, Comanches made "San Carlos a depôt [*sic*] of arms in their annual excursions into Mexico."[48] Leal agreed that Comanches acquired spearpoints and rifles at San Carlos but also in New Mexico and along the "Colorado River."[49] Comanche testimonies corroborate the importance of the trade in Mexico, where a horse could be exchanged for goods worth "ten to twenty dollars."[50]

Comanche trade networks were far more complex than is often assumed. According to Pablo López, a twenty-year-old captive who spent about ten years among the *Numunuu* before he "surrendered unconditionally" to the Mexicans at the battle of the Espíritu Santo Canyon, in southern Chihuahua, on February 13, 1854, Comanches used to sell livestock in Chihuahua City to José Cordero, the governor of Chihuahua himself! In the course of the aforementioned battle, Mexican forces killed two neighbors from San Carlos and one from El Norte who were visiting the Comanche camp to trade. Another ten neighbors from San Carlos del Coyame and Santa Teresa (today's El Grito, in the municipality of Camargo, Chihuahua) had left the encampment the day prior to the attack. According to López, all of these people were in the habit of visiting the Comanches to obtain livestock in exchange for "powder and provisions," selling the animals later on to "ten Americans located at the Álamo Chapo."[51] López's testimony illuminates the hitherto unexplained presence of non-Indians in Comanche parties south of the Rio Grande—by no means a rare occurrence. Not only did Euro-American traders encourage Comanche raids but also sometimes accompanied or visited the raiders in their Mexican sojourns to facilitate the dealings. In this way, Comanche warriors could spend more time pillaging, their plunder augmented, and so did the merchants' profits.

Meaningfully, there seems to be a correlation between the intensity and scale of Comanche raids into Mexico and the demand for horses and mules in American markets. Overall, that demand grew exponentially with the surge of the cotton industry in the U.S. South in the 1810s and the opening of the Santa Fe Trail in 1821, climaxing during the California Gold Rush of 1849–51, and decreasing gradually afterward. As Thomas Kavanagh has noted, the peak in the need for equines north of the border coincided with a height in Comanche campaigns south of it.[52]

The unprecedented demand for equines north of the border turned the livestock-rich but relatively vulnerable regions of northern Mexico into a "land of plenty" in Comanche eyes, and helps explain why so many raiders took the risks of venturing into areas so far removed from the Comanchería so often. Indeed, Comanche trespassers benefited from Mexico's endemic political, social, and economic instability, which hindered the ability of northern Mexicans to defend themselves, and the central government's capacity to provide military support to the vast but thinly inhabited northern third of the country.[53]

Comanche forays into Mexico reflect the intruders' understanding of geopolitics. Indeed, raiders shrewdly took advantage of every favorable conjuncture created by the volatile relations between Mexico and the United States, and Mexico's regional disarray. Sometimes, the Numunuu and their allies arranged ad hoc truces and even forged alliances with local or state authorities to sell their plunder or secure their safety in a region while they continued marauding elsewhere. The geographic scope of the incursions changed as the national borders of Mexico, Texas, and the United States shifted over time. Raiders exploited the rivalry between Mexico and the United States, which prevented Mexican forces from chasing them north of the border. The raiders also adapted their itineraries as new settlements were founded and military contingents deployed along the frontier, as well as to maximize their opportunities to trade their Mexican spoils.[54] Thus, after ca. 1840, the largest parties normally crossed the Rio Grande between its confluence with the Pecos and the old Presidio del Norte, preferring the fords along the Big Bend region, especially the crossings of Lajitas and Chisos, due to the relative absence of U.S. military forces in the area, and the proximity of San Carlos, Presidio del Norte, and other Mexican populations whose inhabitants were particularly prone to buy the marauders' plunder.[55]

Dispossession of land and resources also compelled Comanches and their allies to raid. The relentless Anglo-American intrusion into the Comanchería gained momentum with the independence of Texas in 1836. A seemingly ever-growing number of settlers kept pushing the frontier north and west, encroaching on Comanche territory and resources, and scaring away the game. Nomads tend to be less territorial than sedentary peoples. Notions such as "territory" or "homeland" cannot be translated into Comanche.[56] And yet, by the late 1830s, Comanches had become remarkably territorial, taking advantage of every opportunity to spell out what parts of the country they claimed as their own, and the issue of a clearly established borderline between Comanches and others gained prominence in diplomatic negotiations.[57] By the mid-1840s the spoliation had become a primary concern to the *Numunuu*, particularly to the southern bands, whose representatives complained about it at every encounter with the Texans. While the plains bison population declined, increasing numbers of livestock at relatively nearby and unprotected frontier settlements constituted an alluring temptation to Comanche raiders. The massive waves of immigrants received by Texas after 1845, and the corresponding advance of the frontier, resulted in a growing market for equines and other Mexican spoils increasingly nearer the Comanchería, as the overall Euro-American population in Texas skyrocketed from 125,000 people in 1845 to 212,592 in 1850.

When the U.S.-Mexico War broke out in May 1846, Comanches and their allies kept raiding south of the Rio Grande as part of their yearly economic cycle. As Brian DeLay has shown, the numerous raids launched by Comanches and other Texas- or U.S.-based independent Indians in the 1830s and 1840s contributed decisively to the Mexican defeat.[58] According to DeLay, the forays brought about the abandonment of ranches and haciendas as well as an overall population loss in northern Mexico, damaging its economy and leaving the region at the mercy of the intruding army. The failure of Mexico's central government to recognize the raids as a threat to the stability of the republic, poor coordination between local, regional, and national authorities, and the meagerness of their reaction to the *invasiones de bárbaros* (U.S.-based independent Indians' invasions) augmented the animosity between Mexican factions, fed the federalist attitudes of many Mexicans, and brewed the collaborationism of some northerners confident that the U.S.

invaders would bring an end to the endemic violence. Such hope was likely inspired by instances of interethnic and transnational cooperation that occurred in the region since the 1830s (see González-Quiroga's chapter 4 in this volume).

Reports from Indian agents and other sources produced north of the border suggest that the scope of Comanche raids into Mexico did not decrease during the war. Considering Comanches' obligation to avenge the killing of one's relatives by enemies, suffering deaths in Mexico at the hands of the occupying American forces may actually have functioned as an additional enticement, rather than a deterrent, prompting larger mobilizations of warriors.[59] That was the case after an encounter between Indian raiders and the First Missouri Mounted Volunteers resulted in several Comanche casualties in southern Coahuila in May 1847.[60] On September 14 of that year, Agent Neighbors reported that "the principal war chief of the Camanches, Buffalo Hump," was "still in Mexico, on a foray, with from six to eight hundred warriors," intent on visiting Chihuahua, Parras de la Fuente, "and surrounding country; on his return to attack some of the towns on the Rio Grande, probably San Fernando [today's Zaragoza, Coahuila], or its vicinity. One of his avowed intentions," the agent wrote, "is revenge for the defeat of a party of Camanches, near Parros [sic], by the Missouri volunteers."[61] Thirteen days later, Neighbors met in council with representatives from diverse Texas-based Indigenous peoples. Over 2,200 natives gathered for the occasion, partly allured by the expectation of diplomatic gifts. The agent noticed, however, that the Southern Comanche contingent was disproportionately small, owing to Buffalo Hump being still "on a foray in Mexico with most of the warriors."[62] Their alleged intention to take revenge notwithstanding, the Nʉmʉnʉʉ returned from that expedition, as usual, with a large drove of horses and mules, along with some captives.[63]

On February 29, 1848, the Mexican government agreed to an armistice with the occupying Americans in Mexico City that would later be ratified by local authorities in diverse parts of the country. Article 14 of the armistice stipulated that American commanding officers in northern Mexico would use "all their influence" to prevent incursions from the bárbaros and avoid their robberies and extortions. It also specified that Mexican forces would be allowed to "gather, confront, and chase" the Indians "even within the lines occupied by the American troops."[64] Such an extreme measure clearly indicates that the raids continued unabated.

The Treaty of Guadalupe Hidalgo of February 2, 1848, signaled the end of the U.S.-Mexico War, sanctioned Mexico's loss of the northernmost third or so of its territory to the United States, and established the Rio Grande from El Paso to its mouth as the new de jure border between both countries. Article 11 of the treaty stipulated that the American government would try by all means to avert the incursions of U.S.-based Indians south of the border, prevent any trade in Mexican plunder, and ransom any Mexican captives who might turn up north of the border.[65] In the following years, the U.S. Army established a series of garrisons near the lower Rio Grande, some of them in regions traditionally crossed by the *Numunuu* during their Mexican forays. Thus came into being, for instance, Fort McIntosh and Fort Duncan in 1849, and Fort Clark in 1852.[66] And yet Comanches and their allies continued their incursions into Mexico, traveling along new routes, and crossing habitually the Rio Grande at the more remote fords near the Chihuahua-Coahuila border.[67] As early as November 1848, Commissioner Medill called, in vain, for additional laws that would enable the United States to carry out Article 11 of the Treaty of Guadalupe Hidalgo.[68]

Between 1849 and 1853, engagements between Comanches and U.S. regular soldiers were relatively rare in Texas, occurring mostly in the area between the Nueces River and the Rio Grande.[69] The lack of a significant military presence in West Texas, however, permitted Comanches and their allies to cross into Mexico by the Big Bend fords unopposed.

At the same time, Northern Mexico suffered a debilitating lack of troops. According to a report prepared in December 1851 by the Mexican Ministry of War, there existed at the time eighteen military colonies in charge of guarding the northern frontier, twelve of which were located along the stretch of the Rio Grande Basin that the Comanches and their allies used to cross, between El Paso and the Gulf of Mexico. Altogether, these twelve colonies amounted to just 850 men, officers and troopers included.[70] The enormous distances that separated most of these outposts permitted the Comanches to cross the Rio Grande at diverse points between Aguaverde and Nuevo Laredo and invade Mexico without hindrance. By the same token, the *milicias cívicas* (local militias) were often undermanned, insufficiently trained, and poorly supplied with firearms and ammunition, so they could not compensate for the scant presence of the regular army along the frontier. Despite the efforts of regional leaders such as Santiago Vidaurri in Nuevo León, the so-called Ejército del Norte would not come to fruition until 1855.[71]

To make things worse, the unique status of the Lone Star State within the Union undermined the ability of the U.S. federal government to implement Article 11 of the Treaty of Guadalupe Hidalgo. Commissioner Medill, echoing the reports of the Texas Indian agent, complained year after year about the "peculiar situation" of the natives in the new state, and "the anomalous character of their relations to the general government."[72] As he put it in his 1848 report, "Texas, on coming into the Union, expressly reserved the right to, and exclusive jurisdiction over, all the vacant and unappropriated lands lying within her limits. The existing laws regulating trade and intercourse with the Indians . . . never having been expressly extended over Texas, are not believed to be in force in that State." One undesired outcome of that situation, he wrote, was that "the duties of the agent have thus far been confined to such persuasive influences as he could bring to bear during his intercourse with the chiefs of the different tribes."[73] As late as September 1853, Neighbors still complained that "the appropriation for Indian purposes in the State of Texas" was "not at all commensurate with the extent of territory occupied by the Indians, and the number of Indians to be provided for," comparing unfavorably "with the provisions made for other States and Territories."[74]

While the U.S. government procrastinated, the *Numunuu* and their allies continued raiding south of the border, as their incentives to raid persisted, horse-rich northern Mexico remained vulnerable, and Americans proved unable or unwilling to prevent it. News regarding Indian incursions grew exponentially in the official publications of Mexico's northern states after the U.S.-Mexico War. U.S. Indian agents were aware of the crescendo, sometimes through their wards' explicit acknowledgment, and sometimes as direct witnesses. Neighbors, for instance, came across a Comanche party bound for Mexico on the banks of Brady's Creek on April 5, 1849, during a trip to El Paso.[75]

On July 27, 1853, Comanches, Kiowas, and Plains Apaches signed a treaty with the U.S. government at Fort Atkinson, in what would soon become Kansas Territory. Through Article 5 of the agreement, the Indians committed themselves to put an end to their Mexican campaigns. In a puzzling twist, however, the same article also stipulated that Comanches and their allies would restore any Mexican captives that they might take thereafter, and "make proper and just compensation for any wrongs" that they might inflict upon Mexicans from that point on.[76] Such a bewildering contradiction suggests that the Americans had little trust in the pacifist professions of the natives—or in the leaders' ability to restrain their warriors.

Just as in past agreements, the Fort Atkinson Treaty did not involve all Comanche bands: Yamparikas, Kotsotekas, and Penatekas "were there *en masse,* together with delegations from some of those more remote from the lines of travel."[77] The agreement was only reached "after a most protracted negotiation" that lasted several days, "and not without some hesitation on the part of one or two of the more southern bands of the Comanches." According to Agent Fitzpatrick, the main difficulty during the negotiations concerned the U.S. call for "a cessation of all hostilities against the neighboring provinces of Mexico, and the restoration of prisoners hereafter captured." Once the agreement was reached, Comanches and Kiowas sent runners "off to the south to recall all the war parties that had recently started in that direction." They also asked "for letters of safe conduct for one or two of their chiefs, who departed at once, and alone, for the neighboring States of Mexico, in order to confirm friendly relations there, and to give assurance to the authorities of Coahuila, Chihuahua, and New Mexico, that they were no longer enemies." These developments convinced an optimistic Fitzpatrick that the Indians "were sincere in their professions; and that thus the obligations of the government of the United States, under the eleventh article of the treaty with the republic of Mexico, will be carried out, so far as is at present practicable."[78]

Regardless, the Fort Atkinson Treaty did little to alleviate the dire situation of Mexico's north. On September 16, 1853, Neighbors reported that during a recent visit to the southern *Numunuu*, "a number of the warriors were absent," and he "was informed by the chiefs that there were considerable bodies of the Comanches then in Mexico."

Neighbors believed that "the only policy likely to effect any permanent good" with regard to the southern Comanches would be "procuring the necessary land, &c." for their "permanent settlement." The agent further believed that, properly subsidized, such policy was "the only practicable one by which" his wards could "be induced to abandon their forays into Mexico."[79] Neighbors's vision would eventually come to fruition in 1854, when part of the southern *Numunuu* moved to a reservation on the Clear Fork of the Brazos. The ephemeral reservation was soon vacated, however, hampered by interferences from hostile off-reservation nomads, as well as by the racist antagonism and mistrust of influential Anglo settlers and politicians.

Paradoxically, on December 30, 1853, within a half-decade of the end of the U.S.-Mexico War, and only five months after the Treaty of Fort Atkinson, Article 3 of the Gadsden Treaty between Mexico and the U.S. abrogated Article 11 of the Treaty of Guadalupe Hidalgo.[80] In any case, the situation would not change much in the following years. On September 27, 1854, John Whitfield, who had replaced Fitzpatrick as the agent for the Upper Arkansas tribes, reported that Comanches and Kiowas had "faithfully complied with their treaty stipulations, save one," denying "ever having consented not to war on Mexicans" as they purportedly had "no other place to get their horses and mules from."[81]

As Neighbors repeatedly complained, the U.S. forces deployed along the frontier were simply not enough to put an end to the forays. Despite the Indians' professions of friendship, the agent complained, they committed "many depredations to and from Mexico," rendering all the "roads leading towards the Rio Grande unsafe to travelers."[82]

Eventually, the establishment of Fort Davis in 1854, Fort Lancaster in 1855, and especially Fort Stockton at Comanche Springs in 1859, all of them situated in water-scant regions that southward-bound Comanche parties used to frequent, significantly hindered the ability of the *Numunuu* and their allies to launch major expeditions into Mexico.[83] In the following years, despite the

Comanches' gradual loss of military might and the strengthening of the U.S. military presence along the frontier, the *Numunuu* and their allies remained invulnerable in their high plains' strongholds and continued marauding, albeit on a smaller scale, and mostly north of the border. Defeating the warlike nomads in their remote and harsh environment would take the U.S. another two decades.

Only the Red River War of 1874–75, when large military contingents including abundant cavalry launched a sustained winter offensive into the heart of the Comanchería, mercilessly destroying Comanche horses and other property, did the most recalcitrant Comanche bands accept to enter a reservation.[84] By then, Americans had become significantly more knowledgeable about the southern plains than they were two decades earlier, and the settled frontier and the line of military forts had moved closer to the Comanche heartland— two important factors facilitating the logistics of the campaign. At the same time, a stronger, more experienced U.S. Army, hardened by the Civil War and successive Indian conflicts, had at its disposal more sophisticated weapons and equipment. Most importantly, the *Numunuu* and to a lesser extent their native allies had been severely weakened by successive epidemics and continuous warfare, the southern plains bison was on the verge of extinction, and the Mexican campaigns had already entered the realm of Comanche memory.

———

All in all, by historicizing Comanche raids into Mexico between 1846 and 1853 through an ethnohistorical perspective, we have shown that, rather than merely the inevitable by-product of a bellicose culture, those raids were the result of specific historical circumstances. While Comanches' martial ethos encouraged raiding, the magnitude of their forays into Mexico depended on a variety of factors, including the harshness and remoteness of the borderlands setting, environmental processes and conjunctures such as the 1845–56 drought on the high plains, the gradual decline of the bison, or the 1848–49 epidemics, and enticing political and economic scenarios north and south of the Rio Grande, including the westward advance of Euro-American settlement, Indian removal, the ongoing U.S.-Mexico rivalry, the sustained demand for horses, and new market opportunities.

Much of the spoils obtained by Comanche raiders in Mexico flowed across an intricate commercial matrix toward various markets on both sides of the Rio Grande. At every node, merchants of diverse ethnic and geographic origins made a profit by selling horses, mules, and other commodities plundered south of the border. Thus, Comanche forays into Mexico constituted a highly profitable business for many non-Comanches.

Bilateral treaties between Mexico and the United States, boundary shifts, Indian policies, military strategies, and other decisions dictated from Washington and Mexico City created new challenges and opportunities for the people living on both sides of the border. Most significantly, the relative inability of the two states to enforce jurisdictions and laws across the Rio Grande borderlands created a favorable environment for the multiethnic and international assortment of individuals and groups who benefited from the forays. The breadth of Comanche raiding into Mexico between 1846 and 1853 must therefore be understood within this broader, continental framework. That Comanches and their allies continued launching successful forays into Mexico (and Texas) in the wake of the U.S.-Mexico War challenges Jeremy Adelman and Stephen Aron's thesis that "the American and French revolutions . . . put Indian peoples on the permanent defensive," showing instead that at least some Native Americans retained their capacity for initiative, as well as their ability to use the frontier in their favor even after the establishment of the U.S. hegemony in North America.[85]

Notes

Research resulting in this chapter was funded by the University of California Institute for Mexico and the United States (UC MEXUS), the Philips Fund, the Newberry Library, the Wenner-Gren Foundation for Anthropological Research, Mexico's SEP-Conacyt (CB 2015-01 n. 250624), the UCLA Institute of American Cultures, and Texas State University. This essay also benefited from the diligence and advice of the staff at the different repositories where I conducted my research. Jesús Ávila Ávila and the late Artemio Benavides Hinojosa at the Archivo General del Estado de Nuevo León, Margarita Domínguez Martínez at the Archivo Histórico Municipal de Monterrey, Francisco Rodríguez and Alfonso Vázquez Sotelo at the Archivo General del Estado de Coahuila proved particularly helpful. Finally, I am deeply indebted to my Comanche consultants, particularly to the late Carney Saupitty Sr. and the late Ray Niedo, as well as colleague historian Carlos Valdés, for their generous help. I would also like to thank all the participants in the two symposia out of which this book came into being who gave me feedback on earlier versions of this essay, especially Sherry Smith, Miguel Ángel González Quiroga, Lance Blyth, Andrew Torget, Gerardo Gurza, J. Gabriel Martínez Serna, Alan Knight, Alice Baumgartner, Alberto Barrera Enderle, Andrew Graybill, Tim Bowman, Sonia Hernández, William Carrigan, and Elaine Carey.

1. For a recent example, see S. C. Gwynne, *Empire of the Summer Moon: Quanah Parker and the Rise and Fall of the Comanches, the Most Powerful Indian Tribe in American History* (New York: Scribner, 2010), 43–46.

2. Thus, the present work takes over the story of Plains Indians' raids south of the Rio Grande approximately where Brian DeLay's pathbreaking work stops. DeLay, *War of a Thousand Deserts: Indian Raids and the U.S.-Mexican War* (New Haven, CT: Yale University Press, 2008).

3. On raid-related casualties and their effect on Comanche population decline, see Joaquín Rivaya-Martínez, "A Different Look at Native American Depopulation: Comanche Raiding, Captive Taking, and Population Decline," *Ethnohistory* 61, no. 3 (2014): 391–418.

4. See, for instance, E. A. Graves, [Letter to Mannypenny], Southern Apache Agency, Dona Ana, New Mexico, June 8, 1854, *Annual Report of the Commissioner of Indian Affairs for the Year 1854*, 180. As to modern authors, see, for instance, Gwynne, *Empire of the Summer Moon*, 43–46.

5. DeLay, *War of a Thousand Deserts*, 118.

6. According to Hämäläinen, a "strategic intention . . . to decrease the possibility of punitive campaigns into Comanchería" led to the expansion of the raids. Hämäläinen, *Comanche Empire* (New Haven, CT: Yale University Press, 2008), 221.

7. See Rivaya-Martínez, "Different Look," 393.

8. DeLay, *War of a Thousand Deserts*, 115–18.

9. Thomas W. Kavanagh, comp. and ed., *Comanche Ethnography: Field Notes of E. Adamson Hoebel, Waldo R. Wedel, Gustav G. Carlson, and Robert H. Lowie* (Lincoln: University of Nebraska Press, 2008), 154, 223–24.

10. Rivaya-Martínez, "Different Look," 395, 398–400.

11. There is an ample bibliography on Comanche incursions into Mexico. The most thorough scholarly works published in recent years are DeLay, *War of a Thousand Deserts*; Isidro Vizcaya Canales, *Tierra de guerra viva: Incursiones de indios y otros conflictos en el noreste de México durante el siglo XIX, 1821–1885* (Monterrey: Academia de Investigación Humanística, A. C., 2001); Cuauhtémoc Velasco Ávila, *La frontera étnica en el noreste mexicano: Los comanches entre 1800–1841* (México: CIESAS, INAH, 2012).

12. Chantal Cramaussel, "El Bolsón de Mapimí: un hábitat indígena en la época colonial," in *Caminos y vertientes del septentrión mexicano, homenaje a Ignacio del Río*, ed. José Enrique Covarrubias and Patricia Osante (México: Universidad Nacional Autónoma de México, forthcoming), 167–88; C. Montaña, ed., *Estudio integrado de los recursos vegetación, suelo y agua en la Reserva de la Biosfera de Mapimí* (México: Instituto de Ecología, 1988).

13. That is not to say, as Hämäläinen argues, that Comanches turned the Bolsón into "a permanent, self-sustaining colony." See Hämäläinen, *Comanche Empire*, 224.

14. The historiography on the subject is enormous, including Sara Ortelli, *Trama de una guerra conveniente: Nueva Vizcaya y la sombra de los apaches (1748–1790)* (México: El Colegio de México, 2007); Chantal Cramaussel, *Poblar la frontera: La provincia de Santa Bárbara en Nueva Vizcaya durante los siglos XVI y XVII* (Zamora: El Colegio de Michoacán, 2006); Susan M. Deeds, *Defiance and Deference in Mexico's Colonial North: Indians under Spanish Rule in Nueva Vizcaya* (Austin: University of Texas Press, 2003); Cecilia Sheridan, *Anónimos y desterrados. La contienda por el "sitio que llaman Quauyla", siglos XVI–XVIII* (México: CIESAS, Miguel Ángel Porrúa, 2000); Carlos Manuel Valdés, *Los bárbaros, el rey, la iglesia: Los nómadas del noreste novohispano frente al Estado español* (Saltillo: Universidad Autónoma de Coahuila, 2017); as well as the many relevant essays in Marie-Areti Hers et al., eds., *Nómadas y sedentarios en el norte de México: Homenaje a Beatriz Braniff* (México: Universidad Nacional Autónoma de México, 2000).

15. Cuauhtémoc Velasco Ávila, "La amenaza comanche en la frontera mexicana, 1800–1841" (PhD diss., Universidad Nacional Autónoma de México, 1998), 59–138; DeLay, *War of a Thousand Deserts*, 90–138; Max L. Moorhead, *The Presidio: Bastion of the Spanish Bor-*

derlands (Norman: University of Oklahoma Press, 1991), 111–14; Rupert N. Richardson, *The Comanche Barrier to South Plains Settlement* (Austin: Eakin, 1996), 97–105.

16. Jean Louis Berlandier, *The Indians of Texas in 1830*, ed. John C. Ewers, trans. Patricia Reading Leclerq (Washington, DC: Smithsonian Institution Press, 1969), 75, 132.

17. Berlandier, *Indians of Texas*, 122–23; William B. Griffen, *Utmost Good Faith: Patterns of Apache-Mexican Hostilities in Northern Chihuahua Border Warfare, 1821–1848* (Albuquerque: University of New Mexico Press, 1988), 141–42.

18. Berlandier, *Indians of Texas*, 75, 132–33; Velasco Ávila, "La amenaza comanche," 112–232.

19. Thomas W. Kavanagh, *Comanche Political History: An Ethnohistorical Perspective, 1706–1875* (Lincoln: University of Nebraska Press, 1996; repr., 1999), 28–35, 48–51, 60–61; Kavanagh, *Comanche Ethnography*, 43, 56–59, 63, 137, 152–56, 166, 215, 236, 240, 326, 333, 358–59; José Francisco Ruiz, "Relación . . . [facsimile; n.d.]," in *Report on the Indian Tribes of Texas in 1828*, ed. John C. Ewers (New Haven, CT: Yale University Library, 1972); Ernest Wallace, "David G. Burnet's Letters Describing the Comanche Indians," *West Texas Historical Association Year Book* 30 (1954): 131–34; Carney Saupitty Sr., interview with author, Apache, Oklahoma, July 14, 2005; Ray Niedo, interview with author, Indiahoma, Oklahoma, July 15, 2005.

20. Robert S. Neighbors, *Report of R. S. Neighbors, esq., special agent for Texas Indians, from 20th January to 2d March, 1848* [to William Medill], United States Special Indian Agency, Trading Post, No. 2, March 2, 1848, *Annual Report of the Commissioner of Indian Affairs for the Year 1848*, 577. I follow the spellings and translations of Comanche names proposed in Kavanagh, *Comanche Political History*.

21. On Comanche political culture, see Kavanagh, *Comanche Political History*, 28–62.

22. John H. Rollins, Austin, November 2, 1850, *Annual Report of the Commissioner of Indian Affairs for the Year 1850*, 113.

23. Robert S. Neighbors, [Letter to William Medill], United States Special Indian Agency, January 20, 1848, *Annual Report of the Commissioner of Indian Affairs for the Year 1848*, 574.

24. James Mooney, *Calendar History of the Kiowa Indians* (Washington, DC: Smithsonian Institution Press, 1898; repr., 1979), 269–306.

25. Joaquín Rivaya-Martínez, "Becoming Comanches: Patterns of Captive Incorporation into Comanche Kinship Networks, 1820–1875," in *On the Borders of Love and Power: Families and Kinship in the Intercultural American Southwest*, ed. David Adams and Crista DeLuzio (Berkeley: University of California Press, 2012), 47–70. On Comanche captives, see Daniel J. Gelo and Scott Zesch, "'Every Day Seemed to be a Holiday': The Captivity of Bianca Babb," *Southwestern Historical Quarterly* 107, no. 1 (2003): 35–49; Michael L. Tate, "Comanche Captives: People between Two Worlds," *Chronicles of Oklahoma* 72, no. 3 (1994): 228–63; James F. Brooks, *Captives and Cousins: Slavery, Kinship, and Community in the Southwest Borderlands* (Chapel Hill: University of North Carolina Press, 2002), 59–79, 160–207, esp. 180–93; DeLay, *War of a Thousand Deserts*, 90–95; Hämäläinen, *Comanche Empire*, 250–59; Rivaya-Martínez, "Different Look."

26. Jesús Ibarra, Declaración ante la Comisión Pesquisidora de la Frontera del Norte, Candela, Coahuila, June 28, 1873, Archivo Histórico de la Secretaría de Relaciones Exteriores (hereafter, AHSRE) L-E-1589: 282v–288. Translations from Spanish into English are the author's.

27. For Hämäläinen, Comanche demand for slaves was one of the main enticements for the raids. Hämäläinen, *Comanche Empire*, 223, 250–53, 302. Contrary to his view that

Comanches launched "slave raids," the taking of captives was largely a by-product of the quest for equines. I explore this issue in depth in Rivaya-Martínez, "Different Look." Brian DeLay has also pointed out that horses were more important than captives in motivating raids. See DeLay, *War of a Thousand Deserts*, 90, 95–98.

28. Connie A. Woodhouse, Jeffrey J. Lukas, and Peter M. Brown, "Drought in the Western Great Plains, 1845–56: Impacts and Implications," *Bulletin of the American Meteorological Society* 83, no. 10 (2002): 1485–93; Edwin R. Sweeney, *Prelude to the Dust Bowl: Drought in the Nineteenth-Century Southern Plains* (Norman: University of Oklahoma Press, 2016), 53–56.

29. On the progressive decline of the bison population on the Great Plains, its causes, and its effects on the Indigenous peoples in the region, see Douglas Bamforth, *Ecology and Human Organization on the Great Plains* (New York: Plenum, 1988); Dan L. Flores, "Bison Ecology and Bison Diplomacy: The Southern Plains from 1800 to 1850," *Journal of American History* 78, no. 2 (1991): 465–85; Pekka Hämäläinen, "The First Phase of Destruction: Killing the Southern Plains Buffalo, 1790–1840," *Great Plains Quarterly* 21 (2001): esp. 110–11; Andrew C. Isenberg, *The Destruction of the Bison: An Environmental History, 1750–1920* (Cambridge: Cambridge University Press, 2000); Elliot West, *The Way to the West: Essays on the Central Plains* (Albuquerque: University of New Mexico Press, 1995), 51–83.

30. Woodhouse, Lukas, and Brown, "Drought in the Western Great Plains," 1489–90.

31. Robert S. Neighbors, [Letter to W. Medill], Torrey's Trading House, June 22, 1847, *Annual Report of the Commissioner of Indian Affairs for the Year 1847*, 176.

32. Neighbors, [Letter to George W. Manypenny], San Antonio, September 16, 1853, *Annual Report of the Commissioner of Indian Affairs for the Year 1853*, 186.

33. Wallace, "Burnet's Letters," 132.

34. On Comancheros, see J. Evetts Haley, "The Comanchero Trade," *Southwestern Historical Quarterly* 38, no. 3 (1935): 157–76; Charles L. Kenner, *History of New Mexican-Plains Indian Relations* (Norman: University of Oklahoma Press, 1969); Frances Levine, "Economic Perspectives on the Comanchero Trade," in *Farmers, Hunters, and Colonists. Interaction between the Southwest and the Southern Plains*, ed. Katherine A. Spielmann (Tucson: University of Arizona Press, 1991), 155–70; Thomas Merlan, and Frances Levine, "Comanchero: José Piedad Tafoya, 1834–1913," *New Mexico Historical Review* 81, no. 1 (2006): 36–65.

35. H. Allen Anderson, "Adobe Walls, Texas," *Handbook of Texas Online*, accessed April 17, 2017, http://www.tshaonline.org/handbook/online/articles/AA/hra10.html; Henry C. Armbruster, "Torrey Trading Houses," *Handbook of Texas Online*, accessed January 12, 2010, http://www.tshaonline.org/handbook/online/articles/TT/dft2.html; Morris L. Britton, "Coffee's Station," *Handbook of Texas Online* accessed July 13, 2015, http://www.tshaonline.org/handbook/online/articles/CC/dfc1.html; Kavanagh, *Comanche Political History*, 284–85; John Willingham, "Barnard, George," *Handbook of Texas Online*, accessed July 13, 2015, http://www.tshaonline.org/handbook/online/articles/fba68.

36. On Comanche-German relations, see Kenneth F. Neighbours, "The German-Comanche Treaty of 1847," *Texana* 2, no. 4 (1964): 311–22; Daniel J. Gelo and Christopher J. Wickham, *Comanches and Germans on the Texas Frontier: The Ethnology of Heinrich Berghaus* (College Station: Texas A&M University Press, 2017).

37. Macedonio Perales, Declaración ante la Comisión Pesquisidora de la Frontera del Norte, San Buenaventura, Coahuila, octubre 8, 1873, AHSRE, L-E-1589: 366v–67.

38. On Neighbors, see Kenneth F. Neighbours, *Robert Simpson Neighbors and the Texas Frontier, 1836–1859* (Waco, TX: Texian, 1975).

39. On Fitzpatrick, see Leroy R. Hafen, "Thomas Fitzpatrick and the First Indian Agency of the Upper Platte and Arkansas," *Mississippi Valley Historical Review* 15, no. 3 (1928): 374–84.

40. Neighbors, [Letter to William Medill], U.S. Special Indian Agency, Torrey's Trading Post, September 14, 1848, 595.

41. On September 18, 1847, for instance, Agent Fitzpatrick reported that Comanches and Kiowas had "gone south" in the company of "some of our Missouri frontier Indians; either Delawares or Osages, or both." Thomas Fitzpatrick, [Letter to Thomas H. Harvey], Bent's Ford, Arkansas River, September 18, 1847, *Annual Report of the Commissioner of Indian Affairs for the Year 1847*, 245–46.

42. On the relations between Comanches and other Plains nomads and the sedentary groups of Indian Territory, see David La Vere, *Contrary Neighbors: Southern Plains and Removed Indians in Indian Territory* (Norman: University of Oklahoma Press, 2000).

43. Thos. H. Harvey, [Letter to W. Medill], Fort Leavenworth Agency, October 29, 1847, *Annual Report of the Commissioner of Indian Affairs for the Year 1847*, 103.

44. John M. Richardson, [Letter to Samuel M. Rutherford], Office U.S. Sub-Agency Great and Little Osage Indians, September 1, 1848, *Annual Report of the Commissioner of Indian Affairs for the Year 1848*, 541–42.

45. Francisco Treviño, Declaración ante la Comisión Pesquisidora de la Frontera del Norte, Hacienda de las Hermanas, Coahuila, septiembre 21, 1873, AHSRE, L-E-1589: 355v–59v.

46. On the effects of Old World-imported epidemic diseases on Comanche population, see Joaquín Rivaya-Martínez, "Incidencia de la viruela y otras enfermedades epidémicas en la trayectoria histórico-demográfica de los indios comanches, 1706–1875," in *El impacto demográfico de la viruela: De la época colonial al siglo XX*, ed. Chantal Cramaussel and David Carbajal López (Zamora, Michoacán: El Colegio de Michoacán, 2010), 63–80; Rivaya-Martínez "Comanche Raiding," 393, 400–402, 409–10.

47. Macario Leal, Felipe N. de Alcalde, and Juan N. Marichalar, Declaración de Macario Leal, Monterrey, mayo 12, 1854, Archivo Histórico Municipal de Monterrey, Principal 3, 7. For an English translation and a thorough discussion of Macario Leal's rich testimony on his captivity, see Rivaya-Martínez, "Captivity of Macario Leal."

48. Julius Fröbel, *Seven Years Travel in Central America, Northern Mexico, and the Far West of the United States* (London: Richard Bentley, 1859), 408; W. H. Emory, *Report of the United States and Mexican Boundary Survey, Made under the Direction of the Secretary of the Interior* (Washington, DC: Government Printing Office, 1858), 86.

49. Leal, Alcalde, and Marichalar, Declaración.

50. According to Herman Asenap, in Kavanagh, *Comanche Ethnography*, 33.

51. José Andrés Luján, [Letter dated February 15, 1854, to the secretario del gobierno del Departamento de Chihuahua], Jiménez, *El Registro Oficial: Periódico del Gobierno del Departamento de Durango*, n1152, March 10, 1854, 2–4.

52. Kavanagh, *Comanche Political History*, 381; Kavanagh, "Comanche," in *Handbook of North American Indians*, ed. William C. Sturtevant (Washington, DC: Smithsonian Institution, 2001), 888; Andrew Torget, *Seeds of Empire: Cotton, Slavery, and the Transformation of the Texas Borderlands, 1800–1850* (Chapel Hill: University of North Carolina Press, 2015), 36–42.

53. On northern Mexico's vulnerability to U.S.-based raiders, see, for instance, DeLay, *War of a Thousand Deserts*, 141–93; Velasco Ávila, *La frontera étnica*, 173–206.

54. Treviño, Declaración, septiembre 21, 1873.

55. On Comanche trails, see Joaquín Rivaya-Martínez, "Tras la huella de los bárbaros: Itinerarios comanches a través de México, 1821–1875," in *Los caminos transversales: La geografía histórica olvidada de México*, ed. Chantal Cramaussel (Zamora, Michoacán: El Colegio de Michoacán, Universidad Juárez del Estado de Durango, 2016), 189–216.

56. Daniel J. Gelo, "The Comanche Landscape: Concepts and Context," *Panhandle-Plains Historical Review* 83 (2011): 7.

57. See, for instance, R. A. Irion, Report to Sam Houston, Houston, March 14, 1838, in Dorman H. Winfrey and James M. Day, eds., *The Indian Papers of Texas and the Southwest, 1825–1916* (Austin: Texas State Historical Association, 1995), vol. 1, 42–45.

58. DeLay, *War of a Thousand Deserts*.

59. DeLay considers vengeance a paramount factor in the organization of large Comanche campaigns into Mexico; see DeLay, *War of a Thousand Deserts*, 114–38.

60. Winstron Groom, *Kearny's March: The Epic Creation of the American West, 1846–1847* (New York: Vintage, 2011), 238–39.

61. Neighbors, [Letter to W. Medill], Torrey's Trading House, September 14, 1847, 182.

62. Neighbors, [Letter to W. Medill], October 12, 1847, 184.

63. Richardson, *Comanche Barrier*, 98–99. According to Kavanagh, *Comanche Political History*, 306, Potsanaquahip (Buffalo Hump) and twenty-five "principal warriors and under-captains" returning from Mexico with "many horses, mules, and a number of prisoners" stopped at the Torreys' trading house in December 1847.

64. "Convenio militar para la suspensión provisional de las hostilidades," *El Órgano Oficial del Gobierno del Estado de Nuevo León* 1, no. 1 (April 6, 1848), 3–4.

65. "Treaty of Guadalupe Hidalgo; February 2, 1848," Lillian Goldman Law Library, accessed July 20, 2015, http://avalon.law.yale.edu/19th_century/guadhida.asp.

66. Ben E. Pingenot, "Fort Clark," *Handbook of Texas Online*, accessed January 12, 2010, http://www.tshaonline.org/handbook/online/articles/FF/qbf10.html; Pingenot, "Fort Duncan," *Handbook of Texas Online*, accessed January 12, 2010, http://www.tshaonline.org/handbook/online/articles/FF/qbf17.html; Garna L. Christian, "Fort McIntosh," *Handbook of Texas Online*, http://www.tshaonline.org/handbook/online/articles/FF/qbf35.html; Gary C. Anderson, *The Conquest of Texas: Ethnic Cleansing in the Promised Land, 1820–1875* (Norman: University of Oklahoma Press, 2005), 246–58.

67. Rivaya-Martínez, "Captivity of Macario Leal," 383–84. On Comanche trails north and especially south of the Rio Grande, see Rivaya-Martínez, "Tras la huella de los bárbaros."

68. William Medill, *Report of the Commissioner of Indian Affairs* [to W. L. Marcy], War Department, Office of Indian Affairs, November 30, 1848, *Annual Report of the Commissioner of Indian Affairs for the Year 1848*, 408.

69. See Thomas T. Smith, *The Old Army in Texas: A Research Guide to the U.S. Army in Nineteenth Century Texas* (Austin: Texas State Historical Association, 2000), 135–39.

70. Manuel Robles, "Memoria del Ministerio de la Guerra.- 1852. Colonias Militares de la Frontera," in *Documentos interesantes sobre colonización*, ed. Vicente E. Manero (México: Imprenta de la V. e Hijos de Murguía, 1878), 28–36; Vizcaya Canales, *Tierra de guerra viva*, 185–94.

71. See Luis Alberto García, *Guerra y frontera: El ejército del norte entre 1855 y 1858* (Monterrey: Fondo Editorial Nuevo León, 2006); Luis Medina Peña, *Los bárbaros del Norte: Guardia Nacional y política en Nuevo León, Siglo XIX* (México: Fondo de Cultura Económica, 2014). For later developments, see J. Gabriel Martínez Serna's contribution to this volume in chapter 7.

72. Medill, *Report of the Commissioner of Indian Affairs* [to W. L. Marcy], War Department, Office of Indian Affairs, November 30, 1848, 408.

73. Medill to Marcy, *Report of the Commissioner of Indian Affairs*, November 30, 1848, 408.

74. Neighbors, [Letter to George W. Manypenny], San Antonio, September 16, 1853, 189.

75. Cited in Neighbours, *Robert Simpson Neighbors*, 74.

76. "Treaty with the Comanche, Kiowa, and Apache, 1853," in *Indian Affairs: Laws and Treaties*, ed. Charles J. Kappler (Washington, DC: Government Printing Office, 1904), 601.

77. Thomas Fitzpatrick, [Letter to A. Cumming], Saint Louis, Missouri, November 19, 1853, *Annual Report of the Commissioner of Indian Affairs for the Year 1853*, 123–25.

78. Fitzpatrick to Cumming, *Report of the Commissioner of Indian Affairs*, November 19, 1953, 123–25.

79. Fitzpatrick to Cumming, *Report of the Commissioner of Indian Affairs*, November 19, 1953, 187–88.

80. "Gadsden Purchase Treaty: December 30, 1853," Lillian Goldman Law Library, accessed July 20, 2015, http://avalon.law.yale.edu/19th_century/mx1853.asp.

81. John W. Whitfield, [Letter to A. Cumming], Westport, Missouri, September 27, 1854, *Annual Report of the Commissioner of Indian Affairs for the Year 1854*, 91.

82. Robert S. Neighbors, [Letter to George W. Mannypenny], San Antonio, Texas, September 16, 1854, *Annual Report of the Commissioner of Indian Affairs for the Year 1854*, 158.

83. Douglas C. McChristian, "Fort Davis," *Texas Handbook Online*, accessed January 12, 2010, http://www.tshaonline.org/handbook/online/articles/FF/qbf15.html; John W. Clark Jr., "Fort Lancaster," *Texas Handbook Online*, accessed January 12, 2010, http://www.tshaonline.org/handbook/online/articles/FF/qbf30.html; Ernest Wallace, "Fort Stockton," *Texas Handbook Online*, accessed January 12, 2010, http://www.tshaonline.org/handbook/online/articles/FF/hff2.html.

84. On the Red River War, see Wilbur S. Nye, *Plains Indian Raiders: The Final Phases of Warfare from the Arkansas to the Red River* (Norman: University of Oklahoma Press, 1968); Nye, *Carbine and Lance: The Story of Old Fort Sill* (Norman: University of Oklahoma Press, 1969); J. Brett Cruse, *Battles of the Red River War: Archeological Perspectives on the Indian Campaign of 1874* (College Station: Texas A&M University Press, 2008).

85. Jeremy Adelman and Stephen Aron, "From Borderlands to Borders: Empires, Nation-States, and the Peoples in Between in North American History," *American Historical Review* 104, no. 3 (1999): 839.

Figure 3.1 "Cattle Raid on the Texas Border," *Harper's Weekly*, January 31, 1874.
Courtesy U.S. Library of Congress.

Chapter 3

Theft and Violence in the Lower Rio Grande Borderlands, 1866–1876

LANCE R. BLYTH

Many of the essays in this book clearly demonstrate that livestock theft and violence were a near-constant in the borderlands from the beginning to the middle of the nineteenth century. Alberto Barrera-Enderle and Andrew Torget showed linkages between the smuggling of horses and cattle from Spanish Texas to American Louisiana and a vulnerability to insurgent violence. Joaquín Rivaya-Martínez demonstrated the importance of horses, and horse raiding, to the Comanches. Tim Bowman illustrated how concern over the killing for cattle drove both Mexico and the United States to take a stronger interest in their shared border, as Alice Baumgartner detailed one specific episode of transnational violence, one that began with a falling out over stolen livestock.

Yet in the years between 1866 and 1876, violence in the U.S.-Mexico borderlands on either side of the river called Río Bravo del Norte in Mexico, Rio Grande in the U.S., downriver from Laredo–Nuevo Laredo became, in the words of Miguel Ángel González-Quiroga, "particularly hellish." It was, as local historian Mary Amberson recorded, "one of the most terrifying periods" in the history of the region. There is evidence to suggest it was a very violent period in the borderlands. In Cameron County, Texas, near the mouth of the river along the Gulf Coast, grand jury indictments for violent incidents during this time increased nearly tenfold in annual frequency and fivefold in total, supporting the idea that Rio Grande borderlanders were "familiar with violent death."[1]

In search of an explanation of why this should be so, U.S. officials believed the growth in violence was "synonymous" with "the growth of cattle-stealing." Again, evidence from Cameron County suggests livestock theft increased in the years following 1866 with indictments for cattle stealing again growing almost tenfold. On the other side of the border in the Mexican state of Nuevo León, nearly one-third of the cases heard by the Supreme Court of the State during 1868 and 1869 were for horse stealing.[2] (Also see graph 5.1 in Alice Baumgartner's chapter.) While scholars have linked livestock theft with violence, the role of the border in the local logic of borderland violence remains obscure. Ultimately the border existed as a site of division: splitting markets, providing sanctuary, inhibiting law enforcement, and diminishing social controls. This increased the opportunity for theft and the potential for violence. As the border became a site for cooperation, particularly between the military forces of both sides, it closed the space for theft, ultimately limiting violence.

––––––––

From the Spanish colonization as Las Villas del Norte in the eighteenth century, the heat, rocky terrain, long grasses, and dense scrub, or chaparral, of the region across both sides of the river made it well suited for pastoral production and little else. In 1872, American authorities described the lower Rio Grande as "one vast prairie" used for the "raising of beef-cattle" and "the breeding of horses." Isolated ranchos, with *casas de sillar* (fortified stone houses), outbuildings, and corrals, along with associated pasturage and watering sites, were thus scattered across the landscape, often many miles apart. The vast majority of the rancheros were ethnic Mexicans, either Mexican nationals on the right bank of the river or Mexican citizens of the United States and Texas on the left, *mexicanos* as they likely thought of themselves, many of whom were related in one form or another. American ranchers constituted a distinct minority, with only a few owning ranchos along the Rio Grande; they were mainly clustered along the Nueces River, farther into Texas. Most of the rancheros were small-scale stock raisers, with at most several hundred head of cattle or horses, but a few had several thousand head. The largest herd held by a mexicano ranchero in 1870 was that of Pedro Longoria of Cameron County, who ran 4,400 cattle, 700 horses, and 200 head of mules, oxen, sheep, and swine, on 12,015 acres.[3]

There were a few large-scale stock raisers, sometimes referred to as *hacendados*, whose vast herds and large tracts dominated their smaller ranchero neighbors. On the Mexican side of the border was General Juan Nepomuceno Cortina, a *caudillo fronterizo* (borderer chieftain) who clashed with Texan and U.S. authorities in 1859 and 1861, as Alice Baumgartner showed, before fighting with the Mexican Liberals against the Conservatives and their French allies. He returned to the borderlands in September 1870 as military commander of the Line of the Río Bravo and began to aggressively acquire ranchos, ultimately owning twenty, and beef contracts within Mexico and for Spanish Cuba. On the other side of the border was Richard King, river pilot, steamboat impresario, and large-scale rancher. He too steadily bought up ranches, particularly along the Nueces River at the outer edge of the borderlands, beginning with the 15,500-acre Hacienda de Santa Gertrudis in 1853 and by 1871 owned some twenty ranches and their associated *fierros* (branding irons).[4]

Cortina and King invested in large-scale production as there was a near-insatiable demand for borderland livestock after 1865. The stockyards of western Kansas provided the single greatest market for Texas cattle. In 1867, Texan stockmen drove only 35,000 head northward, but by 1872, the number had increased tenfold, to 350,000. Cattle were also in great demand within the borderlands; the city of Matamoros consumed over 17,000 head a year by 1872. Further, cattle were not just valuable on the hoof. Their hides were "of more value and commanding importance" than any other item of commerce in the borderlands, as hide prices doubled on the international market in the years between 1862 and 1872. Hundreds of thousands of raw hides left the Gulf Coast ports in the borderlands to feed this demand. Galveston's export of hides almost doubled from 205,000 in 1867 to 407,000 in 1871, while Matamoros exported over 100,000 hides between August 1871 and January 1873. Finally, as stock-raising used, and wore out, large numbers of mounts—vaqueros (cowboys) required a string of six or more—horses were in continual demand.[5]

While rancheros knew that their cattle, hides, and horses were quite valuable, they realized that they were quite vulnerable to misappropriation—unintentional or otherwise—and outright theft. Livestock vulnerability was directly tied to practices of livestock raising. Rancheros, without the materials or capital for fencing, allowed their stock to roam, claiming ownership with distinctive brands and ear-markings. Cattle often wandered great distances in search of forage, water, or shelter from inclement weather. The Cameron County inspector of hides and animals examined a herd of over two hundred head seized from rustlers in June 1875. He was only able to determine the ownership, from brands and ear-marks, of less than half. Thirty-five rancheros in seven Texas counties owned 102 head: seventeen mexicanos, three Mexicans—including the Brownsville consul Manuel Treviño—and fifteen Americans. Most of the herd's brands and marks were unrecognizable, unknown, or nonexistent and many animals either were feral or had wandered into the region. Horses, while kept closer to the ranch house, still often shared pasture with other caballadas (horse herds). So cattle and horses regularly became intermingled in the borderlands. Once or twice a year, rancheros gathered their livestock, sorted out those belonging to other ranchos, castrated, and branded any unmarked animals and calves or colts following a cow or mare with their brand. Branding complete, a ranchero would then separate out the stock he wished to trail to market, typically four-year-old steers. Such a herd, and its herders, could easily spend several weeks, if not several months, on the trail.[6]

There were several ways a ranchero could lose livestock in this process. First off, an unscrupulous ranchero could easily drive off and sell any cattle that were not his, simply by claiming he had a bill of sale or by marking out the existing brand and burning his own onto the animal. The farther the cattle were driven, especially out of state, the easier this was to accomplish. One instance occurred when sixty-six head of cattle were sold and the seller's brand was on only four of them. Further, it was very easy for a ranchero to lose hides to anyone mounted and armed with a gun and a knife. These "peelers," as they were called on the U.S. side of the border, worked at night, shooting an animal and skinning it before it was even dead, leaving the carcass to rot, often with a calf bawling in distress alongside. A Brownsville paper in 1873 reported "thousands" of cattle were being flayed "daily," certainly an exaggeration but one that provides an understanding into how rancheros felt about the problem. Finally, a stockman intent on adding to his own herd could brand a calf following a cow with a different brand, especially if the stockman did not recognize the brand or felt the rightful owner would not be able to claim restitution. Richard King was often accused of doing exactly this to neighboring ranches, sending his men into their pastures, rounding up their cattle, and branding their calves with his brand.[7]

Rancheros had few options when they discovered such theft or misappropriation had occurred. Neither side of the border had a functioning police force "sufficient to pursue" robbers, and what law enforcement there was, was often days away from a rancho. So, rancheros had to rely upon cooperation to police themselves. Some of the larger American ranchers, including King, utilized lawyers and the law to do so, exchanging powers of attorney to allow anyone of their number who detected theft to work to recover the livestock, regardless if it was theirs or not. Smaller Mexican, mexicano, and American rancheros did not have access to such means and instead had to rely on their reputation—especially their reputation as someone who was not to be stolen from and would use violence to rectify the situation—to defend themselves against theft, unintentional or otherwise.[8]

In this light, it is easier to understand why cross-border theft so enraged rancheros. Once the rustlers were on the other side of the border, rancheros believed they were safe. The livestock they had taken was lost, since rancheros of both nations had no faith in the authorities of the other to recover their property or to stop the thieves. As Tim Bowman demonstrated, citizens of both nations did not trust the government of the other. Mexicans believed that it was "useless to appeal to the authorities in Texas for justice against the thieves and traders in stolen animals," as "corrupt public functionaries in Texas protected the thieves and abetted stealing in Mexico." American and mexicano stock raisers felt that Mexican authorities "not only tolerated this system of plunder, so long carried on by Mexican citizens on the property and interests of citizens of Texas, but have encouraged the thieves." Keeping Cortina, "protector of the lawless bands," in command in the north showed, "on the part of the Mexican authorities, a wanton disregard of the authority of this Government and the rights of its citizens."[9]

Rancheros and ranchers were painfully aware of their vulnerability. Their herds of cattle and horses represented the "hard labor of years." As most rancheros were small-scale raisers, with only a few hundred head, they faced the possibility they could be wiped out in a single night by rustlers. For larger stock raisers a loss of livestock, while not as devastating, would unquestionably be an affront and possibly an advertisement to future thieves of their vulnerability. Not only could they lose all they had, rancheros knew they had little recourse for recovery, especially if the rustlers drove the stock across the border. So, when Antonio Tijerina learned rustlers had gathered a herd of cattle on his rancho near Brownsville in February 1872, he sent word to his neighbors and set off in pursuit. He followed the trail across the river to Matamoros and found the thieves selling some of the cattle to Dionisio Cárdenas, a cattle dealer and butcher, and later a city official, who apparently refused to return any cattle to Tijerina.[10]

In such a situation, where a ranchero like Tijerina was at economic risk to rustlers and the organs of the state could neither prevent nor punish theft, all he had to defend his herds was his reputation as someone who would use violence. So, unable to recover his cattle from Cárdenas, Tijerina, now joined by a number of his neighbors and friends, sought out the rest of his stolen stock, locating them at another dealer's corrals. But, when the rustlers fired upon him, Tijerina and his party charged the thieves, guns presumably blazing, scattered them, and recovered the cattle. Yet this was not the only case of rancheros demonstrating their willingness to use violence to defend their herds, and by extension, their reputations. In 1870, Francisco Martínez discovered a band of rustlers at the Rancho Saino in Texas, crossing cattle into Mexico. Making his escape, Martínez went to a neighboring ranch, raised a party of men, and attacked the rustlers, recapturing forty-two head, but over one hundred were already in Mexico and were not recovered. Yet, the violence was not always so direct, with rancheros resorting to lynching, a form of deterrence and retaliation discussed in William Carrigan and Clive Webb's essay in chapter 10 of this volume. Sometime in 1872, outside Brownsville, Texas, rancheros captured and hung Pancho Blanco and Cipriano Guerrero from a mesquite tree, both men long known, a local paper announced, as "robbers of great notoriety." The rancheros left Blanco's and Guerrero's bodies swaying in the wind as a warning. Don Antonio Palacios did much the same in the same year, raising a party of men on Rancho Concepcion in Duval County, Texas, pursuing a rustler band, recovering the cattle, and hanging Hypólito Vela, one of the suspected rustlers.[11]

―――――――

The demonstrated willingness of rancheros to use violence to defend their herds—and ensure their reputations as people who would use violence to defend their herds—placed rustlers into something of a bind. While cattle thieves took great precautions to conceal their illicit activities and, more likely than not, had no wish to do violence or inflict harm upon rancheros, the rancheros' readiness to do violence to them meant the only sensible action for the rustlers, when confronted with a potential threat, was to use violence, preferably first, to protect themselves. (This logic of "kill or be killed, even if you don't want to kill" is sometimes called a "Hobbesian trap.") It was thus a best practice in the borderlands to shoot first when discovered on a cattle raid, lest one be shot. At the stock corrals outside Matamoros in February 1872, the rustlers who stole Antonio Tijerina's cattle clearly took this logic to heart and fired upon Tijerina and his party first. Thus, as U.S. officials noted, rustlers were "not specifically seeking to murder" but would "nevertheless at any time take life without remorse." Much of this ability and willingness to do violence, to kill, was a product of the skills needed for stock-raising in the borderlands.[12]

Vaqueros, the mounted rural workers of the cattle economy, carried out most of the labor on a rancho—gathering, herding, branding, castrating, skinning, butchering, fence-building, trailing—often organized into *corridas* (small parties), under a *caporal* (leader) and his *segundo* (second), who took their instructions from a *mayordomo* (foreman). As this labor was necessary, at best, only twice a year, vaqueros plied their trade among a circle of ranchos belonging to relatives and friends, *primos* and *compadres*, often on both sides of the border. This work provided a specific set of skills—regular practice working in small teams, habitual subordination to leaders, excellent horsemanship, expertise with tools such as knives and lassos that were weapons, intense knowledge of the terrain, and the experience of spending weeks and months living in the outdoors, in the chaparral, or on the trail—that made borderlanders a natural light cavalry force.[13]

Indeed, in the decade prior to 1866, both the national and local states in Mexico and the United States made great use of the military abilities of borderland vaqueros, who proved unforgiving of their enemies. Santiago Vidaurri organized the Army of the North to fight on the Liberal side during the War of the Reform in 1858. Drawn primarily from the local militias of Coahuila and Nuevo León, the Army of the North, four-fifths of which were cavalry troops, was regularly accused of "savagery" by its Conservative opponents, often due to the refusal of norteños to take prisoners. During the U.S. Civil

War, Confederate Texas enlisted thousands of mexicanos, primarily into the 33rd Texas Cavalry under the command of Colonel Santos Benavides of Laredo, who also expressed an unwillingness to accept surrenders. Along with quasi-official forces like that led by Octaviano Zapata as discussed by Tim Bowman in chapter 6 of this volume, nearly one thousand mexicanos stood by the Union, most serving in the 2nd U.S. Texas Cavalry. An officer named Cárdenas served in the 2nd Texas, moved to Mexico after the war, and led a raid into Texas at the end of 1874, pursued closely by the African American soldiers of the 9th U.S. Cavalry.[14]

Even with the end of the wars, borderland vaqueros did not lose their military capacity. When revolution threatened at Monterrey, Mexico, in October 1871, General Cortina quickly organized a cavalry corps, the Fieles de Cortina, soon followed by another, the Exploradores, composed of "adventurers" from both sides of the border. Further, vaqueros served as the rural police along the Mexican border, mobilized by an *encargado* (one in charge) appointed at each rancho. Across the river, American and mexicano vaqueros joined short-term, often ninety-day, "minute companies" authorized by the State of Texas, including Warren Wallace's Nueces County company and that of Refugio Benavides in Laredo, formed during the summer of 1874. Given the vast military experience of vaqueros, it is not surprising to find them using this experience as rustlers. At the Rancho Florida on March 4, 1872, a force of rustlers picketed the roads and threw out a line of skirmishers to cover the crossing of stolen cattle. The assumption was that the rustlers were in fact a unit of Mexican soldiers. While this is uncertain, it is quite probable that more than a few of the rustlers at the Rancho Florida that March day had served in the militaries and paramilitaries on both sides of the border.[15]

For rustlers, lethal physical force was not an aberration in their everyday lives as vaqueros, but a work tool. Much like the gauchos of the Uruguayan-Brazilian borderland at the same time, vaqueros had a "habit of slaughter" developed from the conditions of their work with potentially dangerous, semiferal cattle in rough terrain: roping and jerking a cow down with a lasso, as it gasped for air; burning calves with branding irons as they bellowed in fear and pain; cutting the testicles from young bulls; shooting their horse as it struggled to rise, screaming, from a broken leg or trailing intestines after being gored by a bull; slitting an animal's throat, hanging it kicking, blurting, and bleeding to die, hacking the raw body apart for meat to feed the rancho; or skinning a cow as it lay jerking from a pistol shot to the head, the blood still spurting. Military service would only exacerbate this "habit," turning it on fellow humans, as the light cavalry warfare based on the slashing raid deep into enemy territory that vaqueros excelled at simply "had no place for prisoners." Thus, in pursuit of cattle and horse theft or thieves, vaqueros or "cow-boys"-turned-rustlers or -pursuers would kill to ensure their survival and success.[16]

Rustler parties were transnational, opportunistic, with a fluid, often overlapping, membership, though kinship ties and bonds of friendship appear to have been central. Mexican authorities identified a corrida led by the brothers Pedro and Longinos Lugo, natives of San Carlos, Tamaulipas, who had reportedly committed a murder in their youth and fled to Texas. Pedro returned in 1871 and served in the Mexican 7th Regiment of Cavalry from February to August "when he deserted, mounted and armed." He joined with his brother back in Texas, and they settled with their families at the Rancho Las Tranquilas near Brownsville on the U.S. bank of the river. From there, the Lugo brothers led a corrida of rustlers who gathered "whenever an opportunity presented itself to commit robbery on either side of the river." American officials received reports of a rustler band led by Andres and Hermengildo Holguín that operated from ranchos along a sixty-mile stretch of the Mexican bank. Their party reportedly included, among others, Captain Sabas García of the Mexican Army and Cortina's forces, the Perales brothers, and the Lugo brothers, apparently in their spare time.[17]

Rustler corridas, such as those led by the brothers Lugo or Holguín, gathered for their expeditions at ranchos on the other side of the river and the border. After crossing, they split into several small bands of a few men each and penetrated several days into the interior of the country. On reaching their targeted pasturage, perhaps spotted by one of their number while working for a local rancho, the rustlers would rendezvous and gather a herd of livestock. Then, usually under the cover of night, they would run the animals fifty or sixty miles to the river, to a designated crossing point, where corrals, often owned by a *primo* or *compadre*, channeled the stock down and into the river, while allies on the other side assisted in the crossing. The whole time the rustlers were across the border, they knew they were at risk for the whole country turning out against them. So they were quite cautious to cover their movements, sometimes placing guards on homes along their return route, to prevent any knowledge of their presence from getting out. The passage of upwards of several hundred running, bellowing cattle and whooping, hollering rustlers was impossible to mask, as was their crossing of the river, so at these times, when the rustlers were at their most vulnerable, they simply killed to prevent any information from getting to authorities.[18]

This is why rustlers killed Edward Cleveland in 1869, the Hidalgo County sheriff reported, as Cleveland came upon a band of rustlers near the river driving a herd of stolen and cattle, who shot him "to prevent him from giving any information to civil authorities." A party of hide-peelers in 1872 killed Blas Hinojosa, since he refused to join them and to "prevent him from giving information to the authorities." They also killed a Catholic priest who apparently attempted to intervene on Hinojosa's behalf. On March 23, 1875, Alexander Morel, a mexicano "raised on the river," was on his way to his brother Victor's rancho when he came across a band of rustlers, driving cattle to the river. A number of the rustlers recognized Alexander, and he apparently them, and so they took him prisoner, tied him up, and then shot him to death, "to prevent his giving of information." His killers later bragged of the deed in Reynosa, Mexico, saying where Victor could find his brother's body. A month later, George Hill, a Civil War veteran of the Fourth Wisconsin Cavalry, was out looking for horses near his Rancho Tio Cano, when he too surprised a band of rustlers pushing a herd of stolen cattle to the banks of the Rio Grande. They shot Hill four times and took his saddle, bridle, and rope and presumably the horse they were attached to, along with Hill's pistol and all his clothes except his bloodstained shirt. As the adjutant general of Texas noted, rustlers would apparently "kill anyone" and "many have been killed for no other reason than they knew too much." But, in the rustlers' logic of violence, these killings helped to ensure they would not be killed.[19]

As they patrolled along the river, mounted customs inspectors were another target of rustler violence. On December 18, 1869, attackers crossed the border to the house of Mary C. Clark in Clarksville, Texas, at the mouth of the Rio Grande, where they killed Inspectors Hammond and Phelp, and wounded Inspector Ryan. Rustlers crossing cattle into Mexico at Rancho Las Cuevas in March 1871 fired upon Inspectors Albert Dean and T. J. Handy. The inspectors caught them with thirty to fifty head across the border, another ten to twenty in the river, and only five or six on the left bank. A band of cattle thieves and hide-peelers working the border downriver from Rio Grande City, Starr County, regularly fired upon inspectors in early 1875. On January 18, Inspector Dean, having survived the 1871 shoot-out, along with Joseph Dunn, stopped a party of vaqueros who had just crossed the border. Their "outfit," particularly their rawhide lariats "and other paraphernalia of the cattle-thief," possibly branding irons or skinning knives, caught the inspectors' attention and "indicated the objective of their visit." Fearing arrest, or worse, the vaqueros yanked Winchester carbines from their saddle scabbards and opened fire. Dean and Dunn survived this scrape, but the rustlers were not finished. On April 22, someone fired upon Dunn and fellow inspector G. W. Lowe from the chaparral in the same area. The bullet grazed Lowe, "cutting through his clothing across his chest." Both Lowe and Dunn searched for their assailant, but to no avail.[20]

Having established a reputation as men who would kill, rustlers also used the threat of violence to deter local inhabitants from reporting their presence or identifying them to officials, maintaining the mobility so necessary for their raids and the anonymity needed for their survival. When caught driving a herd of stolen cattle in the open, too far from the river to make a run for the border, rustlers would simply abandon it and ride away, often unchallenged, as it was a "common sight to see" corridas of vaqueros, armed, mounted, and going about their business in the borderlands. If confronted, they could easily claim to be working for some distant rancho, be out looking for or selling livestock, or be on their way to visit friends and relatives in Mexico or Texas. The peripatetic nature of cattle work meant all such claims were quite plausible. If authorities took the suspected rustlers to a nearby rancho, the inhabitants would confirm their tales, possibly more out of fear than friendship. According to one Texan, the threat of violence by rustlers had "thoroughly cowed" the local population.[21]

One segment of the population rustlers particularly wished to deter were those rancheros "prominent in hunting those raiders down or organizing parties to pursue them." Rustlers would let it be known via public statements of "We will kill that man within a week" or sending word by a friend that they would kill the ranchero if they found him at his rancho. Yet these threats were plausible only if the rustlers demonstrated their willingness and ability to kill. So rustlers killed Hypólito Mendiola in the summer of 1874 on his ranch near Laredo. The minute company under Refugio Benavides pursued Mendiola's killers, but only managed to wound and capture one, while the rest escaped across the border. On December 1, 1874, Carlos Danache, a ranchero in Cameron County who had "been active in pursuit" of rustlers, received word from a party of thieves encamped on his ranch that "they would be pleased to see him." Danache raised a force from his vaqueros, kin, friends, and neighbors and went to the camp the next morning, but the rustlers had left, leaving the mutilated body of a mexicano hanging from a tree as a warning to Danache. Many rancheros were not as fortunate as Danache during 1875, as it was reported rustlers killed somewhere between eight and fifteen, including Alejo Garza in July. Rustlers even made an attempt to kill Richard King on the night of July 31, 1872, as he traveled to testify to the U.S. commissioners in Brownsville. King's coach was crossing the San Fernando Creek near Corpus Christi when a lively fusillade rang out, some thirty to forty shots. King survived unscathed, but bullets struck his traveling companion, killing him.[22]

Rustlers also targeted others who made themselves "obnoxious." This included vaqueros, increasingly used from the early 1870s, to guard the rancho and to watch for herds of cattle being driven to the river and dispatched to the outer reaches of a rancho's range to keep an eye on livestock. An 1873 livestock raid in the upper reaches of the Rio Grande borderlands, in Webb and Duval Counties, killed twenty-four Mexican and mexicano "herdsmen," wounding another fifteen. The raiders made off with seventy-five to one hundred horses and scattered the rest of the stock across the countryside. Rustlers, in June 1875, fired on Francisco Fuente's vaqueros to drive "them out of the range," placing the livestock "at the mercy of the invaders." Then, presumably, the rustlers could round up cattle without fear of detection, interruption, or attack.[23]

But as rancheros guarded their ranchos more closely and kept a better eye on their livestock, cattle theft and hide peeling became more difficult. So many rustlers turned to robbing the small stores, post offices, and customs houses that dotted the borderlands. However, the rustlers' logic of violence remained; they were taking property, property that would be defended by violence, thus necessitating violence to take. So on May 9, 1874, a band of twenty-five to thirty men attacked the store at Rancho Peñescal southwest of Corpus Christi, killing the two owners and two others before looting the place. Pursuers later caught and hung one of the thieves, identified by the hat he wore taken from the store. Raiders in such instances knew they had to shoot first; otherwise, as in the case of a storekeeper in Duval County named Roach, who was forewarned of an attack in August 1874 and who "made a successful defense," they could be killed. Later that year, on November 3, thieves robbed the store of George E. Blaine at Rancho Los Olmos. Blaine put up no fight, so no lives were initially lost, but the raiders then determined to kill Blaine, likely lest he identify them. However, the arrival of an armed rescue party caused the party to flee. J. L. Fulton, owner of a store, and his assistant, Mauricio Villanueva, were not as fortunate, as a band of ten to twelve thieves killed both in February 1875. On April 19, 1875, twelve raiders crossed the border from Guerrero, Mexico, to Carrizo, Zapata County, Texas, entered the store of Dr. D. D. Lovell, killed him, and took several thousand dollars in cash and goods. Finally, a party attacked the store of Dionisio Garza, a mexicano, in Zapata City in January 1876, killing him and his family, before robbing the store.[24]

The logic of violence associated with livestock theft and theft in general was by no means unique to the U.S.-Mexico borderlands, as livestock theft is endemic among herding peoples worldwide. In such situations, particularly in those where law enforcement is weak, differently enforced, or nonexistent, the primary form of the law is the feud, and herding societies are preponderantly feuding societies. The feud threatens or directs retaliatory violence against an attacker and his kin, his associates, and his larger residential and social groupings—village, clan, tribe—in the hope that these social networks will pressure the original attacker to make compensation, will deter further attacks, or will deescalate the situation. Practices such as the use of arbitrators and prohibitions against killing anyone not involved in the feud, for example, seek to limit its spread and work to bring an end, or at least an abeyance, to the violence.[25]

In the U.S.-Mexico borderlands, however, the presence of the border frustrated "the peace in the feud." The border, once crossed, ensured rustlers a degree of anonymity. Uncertainty about who had committed the theft and violence made it difficult to determine their social networks, upon which the feud would bring pressure. Further, the border limited the power of these relations, as it divided what had previously been the whole of *Las Villas del Norte* (northern towns), fragmenting families into Mexican and Texan branches. While these families still had extensive interconnections, legal national boundaries circumscribed social relations, economic associations, and matrimonial alliances, diminishing kin coherence. The diminution of cross-border social control and ambiguity about the attacker's identity made it difficult for families and associates to exert pressures that could limit further violence. Lastly, any act of vengeance across the border to enforce the strictures of the feud was illegal, while demands for compensation were all too often unenforceable on the other side of the national line.[26] As Alice Baumgartner's discussion of Cortina's failed attempt to feud with Adolphus Glavecke shows (in chapter 5 of this volume), frustrated by the border, violent feuds along the lower Rio Grande spread outward to target national identity, taking on aspects of an exterminatory ethnic conflict or eliminatory race war.

From the American point of view, Mexicans exhibited "a violent antipathy to the gringos, or Americans" and seemed to "cultivate and foment all the hostility they can against 'los Yankees,'" to the extent that they thought "the killing of a Texan something to be proud of." Rustlers, it was reported, believed they "had a right to do as they pleased over there [across the border], as that country belonged to Mexico." A Mr. Alexander was murdered, so the idea went, "simply because he was an American." Americans, Mexicans protested, committed crimes and outrages against Mexicans and mexicanos in Texas. Texan authorities did admit that "a considerable element" of Americans in the borderlands thought "the killing of a Mexican no crime," as exhibited by several Texans who killed a mexicano as "he would not go and play the fiddle for them." Captain Wallace's 1874 minute company exhibited "bloody-thirsty instincts" against Mexicans and mexicanos during its ninety-day tour. Mexicanos were caught in the middle, targeted by all sides, as thieves were "punished in a summary manner . . . without distinction of nationality." Further, Mexicans threatened to drive out or kill "the Americanized Mexicans," apparently mexicanos who worked with the Americans, along with the Americans.[27]

Into this maelstrom rode two corridas in late March 1875. Organized on the Mexican side of the border, the parties crossed over separately and rendezvoused twenty miles from Corpus Christi in Texas, far into the United States. The raiders commenced operations on March 26, taking the usual precautions of killing anyone who might give their presence away, including stabbing two Americans to death and hanging two mexicanos. They sacked the ranch house of Frank Page. They attacked the store owned by Samuel H. Frank, where the attackers killed a mexicano who refused to accompany them. The raiders ambushed passers-by at Frank's store, taking some twenty prisoners, before driving them "before them like sheep" to Thomas Noakes's store, which they burned down, after having lost one of their number. Continuing on, they released their prisoners, fought off an American attack, killing one, and then drove two wagons "filled with plunder" toward the border. On the night of April 2, they surrounded the border town of Roma, Texas, aiming to sack the place, but the presence of a company of U.S. troops deterred them. Upon crossing the border back into Mexico, local authorities arrested eight of the men and dispatched them to Matamoros. There the U.S. consul prepared to present testimony, but en route, the prisoners were diverted to Monterey, deeper in the interior and harder for American witnesses to reach.[28]

With the attackers removed beyond the border, American retaliation fell, predictably, upon those Mexicans and mexicanos who may or may not have been accomplices, or who may or may not have been involved in cattle theft and hide peeling. American "cow boys," including "Red" Dunn, who had earlier served in Wallace's company, and some mexicano vaqueros, among them Jesús Segura, formerly of Cortina's forces, formed a minute company under T. Hines Clark. Clark's company conducted repeated expeditions to the south of the Nueces River valley, into the region known as "The Sands," where they killed mexicanos and Mexicans indiscriminately and burned houses, ranch buildings, and stores. Minute companies in every county from the Nueces to the Rio Grande, as the Texan adjutant general would later report, "banded together with object of stopping the killing of cattle for the hides, but have themselves committed the greater crimes of murder and arson."[29]

The raid and retaliations forced Texas state authorities to act. Yet, Adjutant General W. M. Steele had a long-held conviction, only reinforced by the actions of Wallace's company the year prior, "of the impropriety of organizing a local force whenever there is a question of local interest involved." So, Company A, Washington County Volunteer Militia, recruited far from the borderlands, mustered into state service on April 1 and its captain, Leander H. McNelly, ordered to proceed to Corpus Christi the next day. It took several weeks for the company to reach the Nueces valley, much to the increasing concern of the local sheriff. But when he did arrive in late April, McNelly determined American armed bands had caused much of the recent outrages and saw to their disbandment, including Clark's company. After taking several more weeks to acquaint himself with the region and equip the forty men of his company, McNelly made his way to the border in late May. Once there, he began to take actions that undercut the rustler logic of violence.[30]

Rustlers used violence to ensure the anonymity and mobility necessary to conduct successful cattle theft, secure in the knowledge they could avoid retaliation by crossing the border. McNelly struck at this by establishing a network of informers in those ranchos where rustlers organized, planned, and delivered their cattle, and harshly interrogating, torture if you will, suspects for information. Jesús Sandoval, a mexicano member of McNelly's company, had many enemies on the other side of the border who said he was "Americanized and consequently a criminal—a traitor to Mexico." Sandoval was therefore quite willing to torment his tormentors, throwing a loop around their neck, stringing them from a tree limb, asphyxiating them until they agreed to tell what they knew.[31] (As noted earlier, the use of a rope to choke animals into compliance was a regular vaquero practice.)

McNelly was quite willing to act upon his intelligence, openly attacking rustlers at Palo Alto prairie on June 12, 1875, killing all twelve and losing one militiaman. The use of violence by rustlers was less useful to ensure success when they were outnumbered and attacked by a paramilitary force. During the night of November 18–19, McNelly and his company crossed the border in pursuit of stolen cattle purportedly heading for Juan Flores's Rancho Las Cuevas. The Texans attacked the wrong ranch and were forced back to the right bank of the Rio Grande. Despite being outnumbered and the intervention of both local Mexican and U.S. military authorities, McNelly refused to leave Mexico for several days before finally withdrawing and accepting the token return of sixty-five cattle.[32] McNelly's use of violence across the border signaled that rustlers would have to carefully consider their use of violence, as the border was now less of a sanctuary than it had been previously.

McNelly's actions did not end the problem of theft and violence in the borderlands, and his company remained employed. On December 28, 1875, a scouting party discovered a slaughtering site for stolen cattle, likely to harvest their hides, not their beef. The sergeant leading the patrol arrested the ranchero, who attempted to bribe him. Later, perhaps as a consequence, the ranchero was reported as "tried to escape and was killed in the attempt." At the end of January 1876, members of McNelly's company tried, unsuccessfully, to find the trail of a remuda (group) of stolen horses. But, one of their number would later remember, "the bandit business had fallen off to almost nothing" and the company "had an easy winter." This ease continued into the spring, for it was not until May 17, 1876, five miles from Edinburg, that the company saw action, surprising four rustlers crossing stolen cattle over the border. They attacked, killing two, badly wounded one, and recovered seven head of cattle and six horses with equipment.[33]

McNelly may have given rustlers some pause, but his few tens of rangers could not have stopped a concerted effort at theft or violence by the several hundred or several thousand potential rustlers in the borderlands. By the spring of 1876, however, many of these were otherwise engaged, since as Miguel Ángel González-Quiroga showed, cattle thieves made ready borderland revolutionaries. In March, Mexican general Porfirio Díaz crossed the Rio Grande from Texas, rebelling in support of the Plan of Tuxtepec. He made great use of the military capacity of the borderlanders, mustering nearly two thousand men from villages and ranchos along both sides of the border. Cortina, returned from a short exile in Mexico City, raised battalions of Fieles, Rifleros, Carabineros, and Exploradores from among his ranchos and supporters. With this brigade, Cortina maintained a loose siege of Matamoros for most of the year. Not only did Díaz's invasion recruit many potential rustlers into its ranks, those who did not join were likely deterred by a countryside swarming with armed and mounted men who looked askance at other armed and mounted men.[34]

While Díaz's rebellion "and the enlistment of some of the turbulent element of Tamaulipas under his banner, caused a lull in the raids," it was only a lull. By March 1877, the American military commander on the border was complaining of "depredations recently committed by marauding parties of Indians and Mexicans from the neighboring Republic of Mexico," dating back to the previous October. Despairing that the new government of President Porfirio Díaz would do nothing to stop these raids, the American president ordered General Edward O. C. Ord to "invite such cooperation on the part of the local Mexican authorities," while informing them that a failure to do so would "render necessary the occasional crossing of the border by our troops." In response to the increased American interest in the border, and fearing another invasion, the Mexican government ordered General Gerónimo Treviño to take his northern division to the border and prevent any crossing of the river by American troops, while pursuing any robbers who were fleeing from, or attempting to flee to, Mexico.[35]

Neither general, however, wished to start a war. Within days of Treviño's orders, Ord visited him in Mexico "conferring upon the manner of preventing the depredations made for robbery," while Treviño reciprocated, visiting Ord in Texas. (During one of these visits, Treviño met Roberta Augusta, Ord's daughter, whom he would eventually marry on July 20, 1880.) Both commanders came to a "good understanding . . . regarding prompt action to suppress marauding and the co-operation of our troops on both sides of the river in necessary pursuit," without the need for American troops to enter Mexico. By the spring of 1878, the U.S. Congress noted "the attention of the President and of Congress" had been "given to the precarious condition of our people on the border, the number of our troops stationed there has been increased, and better measures of defense inaugurated." As Tim Bowman discussed in chapter 6 of this volume, the violence associated with theft forced the United States to attempt to control its own border, eventually causing a Mexican response to do the same, primarily by regularizing state security forces as shown by J. Gabriel Martínez-Serna.[36]

The border as a site of cooperation between U.S. and Mexican forces from the later 1870s, vice division, effectively disarmed the Hobbesian trap of kill-or-be-killed. Rancheros and local officials could appeal to army officers for support, and they to their counterparts, increasing faith in the national governments on both sides of the border. This reduced the ranchero need for, and reliance on, violent self-help to maintain their property. This lessened their threat to rustlers. If rancheros were less likely to do violence to them, rustlers were far less likely to use violence to protect themselves, lessening the threat of violence to rancheros. Further, with all the troops in the borderlands, violence was even less useful than before, due to all the armed and organized men able to pursue the rustlers or interdict them. Finally, the border ceased to serve as a guaranteed sanctuary as Mexico and the United States began to cooperate legally, practicing extradition and extraterritoriality enforcement in the borderlands. All of this did not end livestock theft—herding and rustling go hand-in-hand to the present-day—but it did reduce the violence.[37]

Economic developments in the borderlands further undercut the rustler logic of violence as the border came to serve as a legal conduit for the cattle trade. Stock-raising became a national industry on both sides of the border, with the United States becoming the world's largest cattle producer and Mexico becoming the primary exporter of cattle to the United States. In Texas, the decade after 1875 saw a cattle boom that consolidated large ranches, with increasingly American owners, although mexicano rancheros also benefited. These large-scale ranchers then had the capital to fence their pastures, enclosing the previously open range, ensuring greater property security. Economic, legal, and military cooperation at the border thus shrank the opportunities for theft and its attendant violence in the borderlands. The violence associated with cattle theft entered the realm of memory and romance. The *corridos* (ballads) that emerged in the 1870s, many about theft and violence, exhibited in the words of James Brooks, both "the beauty and the terror of the borderlands" and of the border.[38]

Notes

1. Miguel Ángel González-Quiroga, "Conflict and Cooperation in the Making of Texas-Mexico Border Society, 1840–1880," in *Bridging National Borders in North America: Transnational and Comparative Histories*, ed. Benjamin H. Johnson and Andrew R. Graybill (Durham, NC: Duke University Press, 2010), 33–58, first quote p. 38; Mary Margaret McAllen Amberson, et al., *I Would Rather Sleep in Texas: A History of the Lower Rio Grande Valley and the People of the Santa Anita Grant* (Austin: Texas State Historical Association, 2003), 313, (second quote); *Report of the United States Commission to Texas, December 10, 1872* (Washington, DC: Government Printing Office, 1872), 34 (third quote), 63 (hereafter, RUSC).

2. RUSC, 34 (quote), 63; *Comisión pesquisidora de la frontera del norte, 1873* (New York: Baker & Goodwin, 1875), 17 (hereafter, CP). In my thoughts on theft and violence, I am indebted to the essay by James F. Brooks, "Served Well by Plunder: *La Gran Ladronería* and Producers of History Astride the Río Grande," *American Quarterly* 52 (2000): 23–58.

3. Andrés Tijerina, *Tejano Empire: Life on the South Texas Ranchos* (College Station: Texas A&M University Press, 1998); RUSC, 3 (quote); Armando C. Alonzo, *Tejano Legacy: Rancheros and Settlers in South Texas, 1734–1900* (Albuquerque: University of New Mexico Press, 1998), 183–226.

4. Jerry Thompson, *Cortina: Defending the Mexican Name in Texas* (College Station: Texas A&M Press, 2007); Tom Lea, *The King Ranch* (Boston: Little, Brown, 1957).

5. Joseph G. McCoy, *Historic Sketches of the Cattle Trade of the West and Southwest* (Kansas City, MO: Ramsey, Millet & Hudson, 1874), 106, 267; CP, 44, 94, 97, 101; RUSC, 19 (quote). Many of the Mexican claims to the joint U.S.-Mexican claims commission between 1868 and 1874 were for stolen horses. See Martaelena Negrete Salas, "La frontera texana y el abigeato 1848–1872," *Historia Mexicana* 31 (1981): 79–100. Also see graph 5.1 in of this volume for the increase in livestock value, especially after 1865.

6. RUSC, 3–5; *Texas Frontier Troubles* (H.R., 44th Cong., 1st Sess., Rep. No. 343, February 29, 1876), 84–86 (hereafter, TFT); Tijerina, *Tejano Empire*, 58–63.

7. CP, 47–65, 105.

8. CP, 39, 124 (quote); RUSC, 5.

9. RUSC, 8–9, 22–31 (quotes pp. 22–23); CP, 11–21, 33–41 (quotes pp. 34, 38).

10. RUSC 5 (quote), 14. For the connections between herd vulnerability and a willingness to do violence, see Richard E. Nisbett and Dov Cohen, *Culture of Honor: The Psychology of Violence in the South* (Boulder, CO: Westview, 1996), 4–7.

11. RUSC, 11, 14; CP, 108; *Depredations on the Frontiers of Texas* (H.R., 43d Cong., 1st Sess., Exec. Doc. No. 257, May 26, 1874), 6 (hereafter, DFT); Nisbett and Cohen, *Culture of Honor*, 4–5.

12. RUSC, 34 (quote). For a discussion of the Hobbesian trap, see Steven Pinker, *The Blank Slate: The Modern Denial of Human Nature* (New York: Penguin Books, 2002), 322–24.

13. Tijerina, *Tejano Empire*, 45–57, 59–63; TFT, 10, 13; Silvio R. Duncan Baretta and John Markoff, "Civilization and Barbarism: Cattle Frontiers in Latin America," *Comparative Studies in Society and History* 20 (1978): 587–620, esp. 604.

14. Luis García, "Cultural Adaptations on Borderlands War: The Mexican Northern Army during the War of Reforma," paper presented to the Western Historical Association

2012 meeting, Denver, CO; Jerry D. Thompson, *Vaqueros in Blue & Grey* (Austin, TX: State House Press, 2002); James W. Daddysman, "Zapata, Octaviano," *Handbook of Texas Online*, published by the Texas State Historical Association, accessed October 1, 2015, http://www.tshaonline.org/handbook/online/articles/fza12; TFT, 62.

15. TFT, 11–12, 162; CP, 154–56 (quote p. 154); RUSC, 15.

16. John Charles Chasteen, "Violence for Show: Knife Dueling on a Nineteenth-Century Cattle Frontier," in *The Problem of Order in Changing Societies: Essays on Crime and Policing in Argentina and Uruguay*, ed. Lyman L. Johnson (Albuquerque: University of New Mexico Press, 1990), 47–64 (quotes pp. 48 and 50).

17. CP, 84–85, 114, 156 (quotes p. 85); RUSC, 17.

18. RUSC, 9; TFT, 33, 37.

19. *Report of the Secretary of War* (House of Representatives, 44th Cong., 1st Sess., Exec. Doc.1, pt. 2, 1875), 100, 102, 110 (hereafter, RSW); TFT, 53, 122, 126.

20. RUSC, 37, 12; TFT xxi (first quotes), 134 (last quote).

21. TFT, 9 (first quote), 25; RSW, 103 (second quote).

22. TFT, xii (first and second quotes), xxi (third and fourth quotes), 9–10, 51, 97, 106; RUSC, 35–35, 37.

23. TFT, 10, 51, 126 (quotes).

24. TFT, xviii–xxi, 10, 43, 51 (quote), 54; RSW, 110.

25. Nisbett and Cohen, *Culture of Honor*, 6–7; Max Gluckman, "The Peace in the Feud," *Past and Present* 8 (1955): 1–14. For examples of herding and feuding societies, see Jacob Black-Michaud, *Cohesive Force: Feud in the Mediterranean and the Middle East* (Oxford: Blackwell, 1975); and Christopher Boehm, *Blood Revenge: The Anthropology of Feuding in Montenegro and Other Tribal Societies* (Lawrence: University Press of Kansas, 1984).

26. Gluckman, "Peace in the Feud"; Omar S. Valerio-Jiménez, *River of Hope: Forging Identity and Nation in the Rio Grande Borderlands* (Durham, NC: Duke University Press, 2013). In interior Texas, where the border was not a factor, "great outbursts of the feuding spirit were part of the aftermath of the Civil War." See C. L. Sonnichsen, "Feuds," *Handbook of Texas Online*, published by the Texas State Historical Association, accessed July 14, 2015, http://www.tshaonline.org/handbook/online/articles/jgf01.

27. TFT, xi (ninth quote), 13 (first quote), 26 (fourth quote), 36 (second quote), 84 (tenth quote), 98 (fifth quote), 121 (sixth quote), 122 (third and eighth quotes), 124 (seventh quote).

28. TFT, xix–xx, 121–22; Leopold Morris, "The Mexican Raid of 1875 on Corpus Christi," *Quarterly of the Texas State Historical Association* 4 (1900): 128–39; William Hager, "The Nuecestown Raid of 1875: A Border Incident," *Arizona and the West* 3 (1959): 258–70.

29. Cynthia E. Orozco, "Nuecestown Raid of 1875," *Handbook of Texas Online*, published by the Texas State Historical Association, accessed December 29, 2014, http://www.tshaonline.org/handbook/online/articles/jcnnt; J. B. (Red) John Dunn, *Perilous Trails of Texas* (Dallas, TX: Southwest, 1932), 96–106; TFT, 57, 123 (quote).

30. TFT, 122 (quote); Walter Prescott Webb, *The Texas Rangers: A Century of Frontier Defense* (New York: Houghton Mifflin, 1935), 238–39; Robert M. Utely, *Lone Star Justice: The First Century of the Texas Rangers* (New York: Oxford University Press, 2002), 160–61; Mike Cox, *The Texas Rangers*, Vol. 1, *Wearing the Cinco Peso, 1821–1900* (New York: Forge Books, 2008), 244–47.

31. TFT, 8–9, 83–84 (quote); Webb, *Texas Rangers*, 242–43.

32. Webb, *Texas Rangers*, 239–41, 255–78; Utely, *Lone Star Justice*, 164–67; Cox, *Texas Rangers*, 251–54.

33. *Special Report of the Adjutant-General of the State of Texas, September 1884* (Austin: E. W. Swindells, State Printer, 1884), 43 (quotes); George Durham, *Taming the Nueces Strip: The Story of McNelly's Rangers* (Austin: University of Texas Press, 1962), 134; Andrew R. Graybill, *Policing the Great Plains: Rangers, Mounties, and the North American Frontier, 1875–1910* (Lincoln: University of Nebraska Press, 2007), 91–97.

34. Laurens Ballard Perry, *Juárez and Díaz: Machine Politics in Mexico* (DeKalb: Northern Illinois University Press, 1978), 203–31; Richard Blaine McCornack, "Porfirio Díaz en la frontera texana, 1875–1877," *Historia Mexicana* 5 (1956): 373–410; Thompson, *Cortina*, 230–34, 298n81.

35. J. Fred Rippy, *The United States and Mexico* (New York: Alfred A. Knopf, 1926), 294; *Relations of the United States with Mexico* (H.R., 45th Cong., 2d Sess., Rep. No. 701, April 25, 1878), 235–36, 241–43 (hereafter, RUSM).

36. RUSM, 263–64, vii; "An International Wedding," *New York Times*, July 25, 1880; Robert D. Gregg, *The Influence of Border Troubles on Relations between the United States and Mexico* (Baltimore: John Hopkins University Press, 1937), 48–64; Alice L. Baumgartner, "The Line of Positive Safety: Borders and Boundaries in the Rio Grande Valley, 1848–1880," *Journal of American History* 101 (2015): 1106–22, esp. 1117–20.

37. Pinker, *Blank Slate*, 330–31, discusses how "adjudication by an armed authority" is the best means to reduce violence; the legal aspects are covered in Daniel S. Margolies, *Spaces of Law in American Foreign Relations: Extradition and Extraterritoriality in the Borderlands and Beyond, 1877–1898* (Athens: University of Georgia Press, 2011), esp. 1–94; for the present-day Julián Aguilar and Miles Hutson, "Cattle Theft Still a Modern-Day Problem in Texas," the *Texas Tribune*, October 28, 2015, reported that in 2014, 5,325 head of livestock were stolen in Texas, worth $4.89 million, but few crossed into Mexico, due to border security measures.

38. David Montejano *Anglos and Mexicans in the Making of Texas, 1836–1986* (Austin: University of Texas Press, 1987), 50–74; Alonzo, *Tejano Legacy*, 196–226; Maria-Aparecida Lopes and Paolo Riguzzi, "Borders, Trade, and Politics: Exchange between the United States and Mexican Cattle Industries," *Hispanic American Historical Review* 92 (2012): 603–35; Gregg, *Influence of Border Troubles*, 81–145; Brooks, "Served Well by Plunder," 47–50 (quote p. 50).

PART II

State Power in Transition

Figure 4.1 Juan Nepomuceno Cortina. From *Frank Leslie's Illustrated Newspaper*, April 9, 1864. Courtesy U.S. Library of Congress.

Chapter 4

Cooperative Violence on the Rio Grande Frontier, 1830–1880

MIGUEL ÁNGEL GONZÁLEZ-QUIROGA

In the last days of October 1851, the sleepy town of Cerralvo, Nuevo León, came suddenly to life. It became a battleground in a revolt for local autonomy led by José María Carbajal against the Mexican government.[1] Carbajal was defeated by government forces led by General Antonio María Jáuregui, and his movement eventually disintegrated. Beyond the causes and consequences of the revolt, a revealing aspect of the conflict was on display in Cerralvo. I refer to the composition of the forces that faced each other. Carbajal's force was made up of Mexicans and Anglos, while Jáuregui's unit included Mexicans, Seminole Indians, and Blacks. The episode offers important insights on the nature of violence in the U.S.-Mexico borderlands. Alliances among diverse racial groups were more common than most histories would have us believe. They occurred frequently throughout the nineteenth century, when it is supposed that most of the conflict was caused by racial and ethnic antagonism and pitted Anglos against Mexicans.[2] For the sake of brevity, these alliances will be referred to as cooperative violence, which does not refer to random acts involving a few individuals, but conspicuous cases of cooperation that involved large numbers of people and had a significant impact in and beyond the border region.

These alliances began early. In 1813, several hundred Mexicans led by José Bernardo Gutiérrez de Lara and a large group of Anglos headed by Augustus Magee joined to fight royalist forces in Texas during the struggle for Mexican independence. In 1835 during the siege of Bexar, which was part of the movement for Texas independence, Mexicans fought alongside the Texans against the Mexican government. In 1839–40, a sizable group of Anglo-Texans joined their neighbors of Tamaulipas, Coahuila, and Nuevo León in their revolt against that same government in a federalist uprising led by Antonio Canales. In the early 1850s, an alliance of Brownsville merchants, Texas filibusters, and Mexican federalists headed by José María Carbajal again made war on the Mexican government, a revolt that included the episode cited above. Later in that same decade, Santiago Vidaurri received Anglo-American support for his conquest of regional power in Northeast Mexico and for his participation in the War of Reform. Despite national and ethnic differences, throughout the 1850s, military men on both sides of the border often worked together to combat Indian raiders. During the 1860s, the Civil War in the United States and the War of French Intervention in Mexico provided many opportunities for cooperation as some four thousand Mexicans enlisted in the Confederate and Union armies and a like number of Anglos marched to Mexico to fight for Juárez or Maximilian. In his rise to power, Porfirio Díaz obtained refuge in Brownsville and economic support from Texas merchants to topple the government of Sebastián Lerdo de Tejada. Finally, the pacification of the border at the end of the 1870s was brought about by the determined policy of both nations, but also by the cooperation on the ground of U.S. forces led by General E. O. C. Ord and Mexican troops headed by General Gerónimo Treviño.[3]

My aim is to explore two events that occurred in the Texas-Mexico border region that involved the alliance of mostly Anglos and Mexicans acting in concert against a common enemy or in favor of a common cause. These episodes are the Federalist War of 1839–40 and the Cortina War of 1859. These events, referred to as "wars" in American accounts and merely as "revolts" in Mexican versions, were chosen because they reflect, better than most, the broad range of reasons that borderlanders had for banding together. In the Cortina Revolt the allies shared the same objective, while in the Federalist War they had divergent goals that converged at a particular moment. These two events disclose the possibilities and limits of cooperative violence: one turned out badly, though not necessarily for all the participants, and the other, with external support, essentially achieved its intended outcome. One occurred before and the other after the existence of a formal border. Both of these events raise the same basic questions: How and why did these alliances occur? Who were the protagonists and what were their motivations and objectives? How did these conflicts evolve and what lessons do they offer? Finally, what role did the border play in these events?

The Federalist War in Northeast Mexico followed a pattern of revolts that swept the country in the late 1830s. People in the provinces were angry. The centralist wave that swept Mexico in the mid-1830s and culminated in the Constitution of the Seven Laws in 1836 "upset the operational system of the former states [now departments], leaving them without funds and affecting the interests of local commercial and bureaucratic elites."[4] Governors would now be designated by the central government, protectionist policies were reinforced, and state militias, which were considered bastions of federalism, were abolished. Regional elites that had grown accustomed to relative autonomy under federalist governments now felt threatened.[5] The *vecinos* of the Northeast had two additional and powerful reasons to rebel against the central government. They were forced to endure commercial policies that punished local merchants and consumers with onerous tariffs and prohibitions, and they suffered the incessant violation of their territory and destruction of their lives and property at the hands of Comanche and Apache raiders who swept down from the southern plains of the United States. The government in Mexico City, mired in political chaos, seemed oblivious to their plight.

Federalist movements erupted in Jalisco, Sinaloa, Sonora, Tamaulipas, and Yucatán. The one that erupted in Northeast Mexico may be considered an extension of the revolt that broke out in Tampico in October 1838. On November 5, Antonio Canales, a lawyer and former deputy of the Tamaulipas state government, seconded that revolt in the border town of Guerrero. The movement was centered on the Villas del Norte, the towns on the margins of the Rio Grande from Matamoros to Laredo.[6] It differed from other federalist uprisings because its location allowed the rebels to turn to Texas for support. A virtual Who's Who of the political and economic elite of the region directed the uprising. Tamaulipas was represented by Antonio Canales, Juan Nepomuceno Molano, Jesús Cárdenas, José María Carbajal, Basilio Benavides of Laredo, and Antonio Zapata of Guerrero. From Nuevo León, there was support from liberal leaders such as Manuel María de Llano and Pedro Lemus. Francisco Vidaurri, a former governor, was the leading figure from Coahuila. His nephew, Santiago Vidaurri, destined to become one of Mexico's strongest regional caudillos in the 1850s, gained his federalist credentials during this conflict. Joining this group from outside the region was Juan Pablo Anaya, a former minister of war in Mexico, fluent in English, who had served in the war for Mexican independence and fought with Andrew Jackson in the Battle of New Orleans in 1815. The movement found support among all classes, including merchants and rural people of the region.[7]

Personal and family issues were involved in the movement. Some of its leaders were linked by marriage: Molano was a brother-in-law of Canales; Carbajal's son, José María, was married to a daughter of Canales. One historian has noted that "the federalist leadership was a family clan, and dominated politics in Tamaulipas long after the revolt had been quelled."[8] Several of the participants claimed that they had suffered the loss of their property. Canales declared that his land on the Rio Grande had been confiscated. Anaya too had suffered confiscations, and Antonio Zapata complained of his financial ruin. All blamed the Mexican government and its centralist policies.[9]

The leaders of the revolt justified their actions and expressed their aims. Antonio Canales wrote that the *fronterizos*, the inhabitants of the frontier, were making use of their "inalienable right . . . to secure the common happiness which is the end of [every] organized society."[10] Jesús Cárdenas dispensed with the flowery language, declaring that they rose up in "defense of their liberty, property and interests."[11] Other leaders such as Juan Pablo Anaya and Manuel María de Llano blamed centralism and called for a return to the Constitution of

1824. In a circular to the people of Nuevo León, de Llano pilloried the national government for imposing onerous taxes, paralyzing industry and commerce, and allowing Indians to run riot throughout the northern provinces.[12]

The revolt lasted two years, from November 1838 to November 1840, and covered an area that included South Texas and Northeast Mexico, though all of the battles were fought below the Rio Grande. The federalists won some early victories, taking the cities of Monterrey and Saltillo in the spring of 1839, but by the summer, the central government had concluded the so-called Pastry War with France and turned its attention to suppressing the revolt. Monterrey and Saltillo were retaken, and the rebels appeared to be contained in the region bordering the Rio Grande. That is when Juan Pablo Anaya arrived in the region and was immediately commissioned to travel to Texas to obtain arms and men to bolster the federalist cause.[13]

In September 1839, Anaya traveled to Houston, then the capital of Texas, and began recruiting volunteers. He found a receptive climate and was able to obtain resources and recruit men for the federalists. What drove Texans to risk their lives in a foreign adventure? They shared an ideological affinity for federalism and disdain for centralism. Some Texans desired a republic in northern Mexico to serve as a buffer between Texas and her hostile neighbor. Others sought an alliance with the federalists to combat the Indians.[14] Practical or economic considerations were probably more important. It was reported in the *Colorado Gazette* that volunteers would be rewarded with "a bounty of half a league of land" and exclusive rights to the spoils of war.[15] It is not surprising that many of the enlistees were not imbued with idealism. Some had served the Texas government as rangers or soldiers and had been mustered out. They were hit hard by the Panic of 1837 and were drawn by the prospect of receiving land and money.[16] Many "had been the very cattle thieves or so-called cowboys that had preyed on the Mexican cattle herds that ranged the ranches on the north bank of the Rio Grande."[17] Historian Sam Haynes captured the logic of many of these men: "For twenty-five dollars a month and a share of the spoils, they temporarily put aside their hatred of Mexicans."[18]

The relations between the Texas volunteers and the federalist leaders were complex. They can best be illustrated by the experiences of two men: Antonio Canales and Antonio Zapata. Canales had leadership qualities, but was disliked and distrusted by the Texans. They dismissed his military capability after he abandoned the attack on Matamoros and when they observed his reticence to enter the field of battle at El Cántaro. Zapata, in contrast, gained their admiration and respect for his fearlessness in battle and his willingness to share hardships with his men. Zapata was a mulatto, but the race-conscious Texans overlooked this because of his courage and military prowess. They named a county in South Texas in his honor after the conflict.[19]

More than two hundred Texans enlisted and chose as their leaders Colonels Reuben Ross and Samuel W. Jordan, two men with military experience. Also joining the movement were several dozen Carrizo Indians. It is not clear why the Carrizos chose to fight alongside the federalists. However, they had been integrated decades earlier into Spanish and later Mexican society; they spoke Spanish, practiced Catholicism, and suffered the same problems as other fronterizos, including Comanche raids. The new recruits gave the federalists an injection of vitality, which was evident in their defeat of the local militia of Guerrero on October 1, 1839. Two days later, near the town of Mier, they won a resounding victory in the battle of El Cántaro, defeating a force of five hundred centralist troops led by General Francisco González Pavón.[20]

An occurrence at Guerrero is worth mentioning because it became a prevailing theme of the federalist revolt. An old warrior from the war of Mexican independence, Bernardo Gutiérrez de Lara, tried to defend the town but was defeated and taken prisoner. Antonio Canales ordered his execution, but Reuben Ross intervened to save his life when he learned that Gutiérrez de Lara and his uncle had fought together in Texas three decades earlier. Although Ross saved his life, Gutiérrez de Lara recognized that the presence of Texans was fatal to the movement. He reproached Canales for enlisting Texans to make war on Mexicans. This would become the predominant narrative of centralist political and military authorities against the federalists.[21]

The federalist resurgence was short-lived. At the head of a thousand men, Antonio Canales marched to Monterrey. He did not know that Mariano Arista, newly appointed commander of the army in Nuevo León and Coahuila, had arrived at the Nuevo León capital with a force of about 1,600 troops. The two men exchanged letters. Canales called on Arista to leave Monterrey and fight in the open. In an angry reply, Arista reproached Canales for causing destruction to the region and for "bringing strangers to thrust a dagger into his Mexican compatriots."[22]

After an unsuccessful attempt to take Monterrey and in the face of superior forces, Canales retreated toward the border. Early in January 1840, at Guerrero he was reunited with Antonio Zapata and Francisco Vidaurri, who had been defeated by a centralist force in Coahuila. These setbacks did not deter them. With other federalist leaders, they crossed the border and in a convention, established a governing structure for an administrative unit that they called the Frontera del Norte de la República Mexicana. Jesús Cárdenas, a Reynosa lawyer, was chosen as president with Canales as commander of the federalist army.[23] It was widely believed in Texas that this action was a separatist movement with the intention of creating a Republic of the Rio Grande. Perhaps that is what Antonio Canales wanted the Texans to believe in order to continue receiving their support.[24]

The military fortunes of the federalists continued to flounder. At Santa Rita de Morelos in Coahuila, their most charismatic leader, Antonio Zapata, was captured along with about twenty-three men, half of whom were Texans. Canales and a force of about four hundred men attempted to rescue Zapata but were defeated badly on March 24. Arista offered Zapata amnesty if he renounced his loyalty to the federalist cause, but the proud soldier refused. The centralist general had Zapata executed and his head cut off and placed on a pole opposite his house in Guerrero as a lesson to those who rebelled against authority.[25]

The federalists once again sought salvation in Texas. Their principal leaders, Canales, Cárdenas, and Carbajal, were received warmly in San Antonio, Victoria, and Refugio. Samuel A. Maverick, mayor of San Antonio, endorsed their movement; Samuel G. Powell provided a loan of about $3,000 for their cause. Merchants of South Texas, many of whom had traded in Mexico, were eager to provide weapons and provisions to the federalists. Supporters in Texas such as Cornelius Van Ness and Juan N. Seguín obtained an audience for Canales with Mirabeau B. Lamar. The Texas president was publicly noncommittal but probably supported the rebels in a discreet way. Seguín wrote in his memoirs that Lamar provided him with arms for the federalists and encouraged him to aid them in recruiting Texans.[26]

The appeal of the federalists to Texans for help raises the question of their loyalty to Mexico. Mexican officials familiar with the border region were certain that fronterizos had better relations with the Americans than with their own government in Mexico City. This was the tenor of the letter that General José Urrea sent to the deposed vice president, Valentín Gómez Farías. Urrea was convinced that Mexico could lose her northern provinces because the vecinos shared with the Americans "relations and sympathies," which made them susceptible to separatist movements.[27] Another military man, Francisco Mejía, was convinced that fronterizos had "an exaggerated sympathy for the United States and Texas." He declared: "They do not care about our nationality, but only about getting whatever they are after."[28] Urrea and Mejía exaggerated the affinity of norteños to their northern neighbor, but it is true that they had an ambivalent attitude toward the nation. Their loyalties were mainly to their families and their region. They drew closer or strayed farther from the nation in accordance with their particular interests. They aligned with the national government when it worked to resolve their problems and needs, but withheld their support when their needs were ignored.

By summer, Canales was on the Nueces River with a force of about three hundred Mexican rancheros, eighty Carrizo Indians, and 140 Anglo-Texans. With this new infusion of support, the federalists tried to reinvigorate their movement. They seriously underestimated their centralist rival, Mariano

Arista. The wily general had been waging not only a military but a propaganda campaign against the federalists. In a broadside published in local newspapers, he exhorted the vecinos to help him repel a reprehensible enemy composed of Texans, who were thieves and assassins; Indians, who were brutal savages; and Mexican federalists, who were dupes and traitors pursuing selfish interests. Arista also made it a point to respect the property of the inhabitants, something the federalists, especially their Texan allies, were loath to do.[29]

The federalists crossed the Rio Grande and divided their force into two columns, one headed by Canales bound for Monterrey and one led jointly by Juan Molano and Samuel Jordan, which headed toward Ciudad Victoria in the interior of Tamaulipas. This latter force, composed of about 250 men, half of them Texans, had no difficulty in taking Victoria, as it was not heavily fortified. However, their victory ended not in joy but recrimination, marred by a dispute between Molano and Jordan due to the conduct of the Texans. This rowdy group, led by the unstable Jordan, insisted on abusing and despoiling the population of the towns through which they passed. Molano knew that this would alienate the people against them and play into the hands of Arista. He expressed his views in the Matamoros newspaper, *El Ancla*, writing that he could not consent to the Texans' behavior because it would be "to make war against his own country."[30]

Arista surely was informed of Molano's views and took advantage of the situation to drive a wedge between the rebel leader and the Texans. He invited him to abandon the movement and offered him and his troops amnesty. Molano accepted and on the eve of the attack on Saltillo decided to join the centralists and fight the Texans. Jordan's group of Texans were greatly outnumbered and had to retreat toward the Rio Grande. Their harrowing escape through centralist-infested country was facilitated by more than thirty Texas-Mexican volunteers sent by Juan N. Seguín.[31] While this was occurring, Canales and his column faced superior forces and had to abandon their march to Monterrey and return to Camargo. Aware of Molano's defection and the anger of the Texans, Canales realized that he could no longer seek refuge above the Rio Grande. Arista recognized his predicament and offered a conciliatory end to the conflict. The rebel leader accepted and in a sign of unity, he and Arista entered Monterrey on November 10, 1840. The Federalist War ended amid music and cheering crowds in the Nuevo León capital.[32]

Twenty years passed, years of important changes in the lower Rio Grande. The war between the United States and Mexico (1846–48) raised a permanent boundary between the two countries. Invisible but no less profound was another barrier that developed between Anglos and Mexicans on the Texas side of the river. Acquisitive Anglo merchants, ranchers, and lawyers began to arrive in greater numbers and to acquire the property of Mexicans, by fair means or foul. Their disrespectful attitude toward Mexican property and customs was mirrored in other parts of the state. The 1850s was not a good time for Mexicans in Texas. They were persecuted and expelled from some communities for their supposed or real support of runaway slaves, for their competition with Anglos for jobs, or simply for being Mexicans, whom many Anglos considered an inferior race. Some of these tensions were felt in Brownsville and its surrounding region. Anglos took possession of political and economic power, often in tandem with members of the Mexican landed elite. Middle- and lower-class Mexicans—rancheros and peons—were on the losing side of an increasingly oppressive system.[33]

These class and racial differences were temporarily subordinated by a regional prosperity fueled by commerce with northern Mexico. Much of that trade passed through Brownsville and Matamoros, across the river. One observer of the period, John Salmon (Rip) Ford, wrote that the "quantity of goods entering by way of Brazos de Santiago and the mouth of the Río Grande was enormous. They represented $10,000,000 a year and sometimes $14,000,000 a year."[34] Another observer, John L. Haynes, reported that stock buyers from as far away as Missouri, Illinois, Kentucky, and Tennessee came to Brownsville "to buy the cheap stock of the coast and of the neighboring republic." In a twelve-month period ending in October 1859, he reported that "at least thirty thousand horses and three hundred thousand head of sheep" had been sold.[35] This prosperity was put at risk in early 1859, when General David E. Twiggs decided to remove the troops stationed at Fort Brown. Twiggs sent those troops to other frontier forts where Indian depredations were intense and deadly. Haynes expressed the concern of many merchants and producers of the region, calling the move "hasty and inconsiderate." To complicate matters, the Rio Grande region was not a priority for the United States or Mexico. In late 1859, the former was distracted by John Brown's attack on Harpers Ferry, Virginia, while the latter was in the throes of a bitter civil war and without an effective government.[36]

Before daybreak on September 28, 1859, the people of Brownsville were awakened by gunfire and shouts of "Viva Mexico" and "Mueran los gringos." A group of about seventy Mexicans, led by Juan Nepomuceno Cortina, raided the town in search of several Anglos whom Cortina accused of robbing or committing abuses against the Mexican population. When the firing stopped, three Anglos whom Cortina considered enemies and two Mexicans, all citizens of Brownsville, lay dead. Of the two Mexicans who died, one was probably hit by a stray bullet and the other was killed defending an Anglo friend.[37] Cortina, or Cheno as he was known on both sides of the border, did not occupy the town. At sunrise, Brownsville authorities issued a frantic call for help to their counterparts in Matamoros. That same morning, José María Carbajal, who had fought against the Mexican government in three wars, crossed the river to parley with Cortina. He was joined by other prominent Matamoros leaders, and together they convinced Cortina to withdraw his forces immediately. Cheno marched his troops to Rancho del Carmen, the property of his mother upriver from Brownsville. That evening he received another delegation from Matamoros that also included customs collector Frank W. Latham. Cortina agreed not to attack Brownsville again unless provoked, but he insisted on exacting vengeance on his enemies. The delegation left thinking that Brownsville was still in danger.[38]

Assistance from Matamoros went beyond these negotiations with Cortina. On the same day of the raid, Brownsville sheriff J. G. Brown called on the commander of the military garrison at Matamoros, Joaquín Arguelles, to send help. Arguelles promptly complied, sending arms and men to the threatened town.[39] On September 30, José María Carbajal crossed the river at the head of fifty Mexican troops of the Tamaulipas National Guard. Historian Jerry Thompson captures the scene: "Several citizens watched in awe as Mexican soldiers crossed the Rio Grande to protect United States citizens from an irregular army of Mexicans led by a man [Cortina] who considered himself a United States citizen."[40]

Who was this scourge named Cortina and what led him to rebel? Originally from Camargo, Tamaulipas, Cheno's family owned land on the north bank of the Rio Grande in the region around Brownsville. It was there that he grew up. He served Mexico in its war with the United States but returned to South Texas, where he got into trouble for stealing cattle and allegedly killing a man. He was accused by his detractors of being a thief and a murderer, and there were indictments against him since 1850, but he was never arrested, presumably because of his support among the Mexican population, which was a vast majority in Cameron County.[41] Unlike his brothers, who accommodated easily into the new social order, Cheno defied a system that allowed corrupt judges and politicians to twist the law and despoil Mexicans of their property. He felt that he was chosen by Providence to break the chains that enslaved the Mexican people and "fight against [their] enemies."[42]

The Cortina Revolt was fueled by personal and social grievances. Cheno was convinced that his mother had been pressured to cede a large portion of her land that ended up in the possession of Charles Stillman, one of Brownsville's most powerful merchants. Cortina considered that his mother was cheated out of her property and that Adolphus Glavecke, his bitter enemy, had played a major role. On July 13, 1859, Cortina witnessed the beating of a former employee by Marshal Robert Shears and he reacted violently, shooting the law officer. Another indictment for his arrest for attempted murder was handed down by a grand jury.[43]

These personal issues mirrored a broader pattern of Mexican resentment at the abuse and the loss of their land that accompanied the establishment of Anglo domination in South Texas. These grievances were expressed in fiery rhetoric in two public proclamations issued by Cortina, one on September 30 and the other on November 23, 1859. He described the avaricious men who had descended on the Rio Grande as "flocks of vampires in the guise of men" who perpetrated or permitted the abuse of the Mexican inhabitants. To his countrymen he declared: "Many of you have been robbed of your property, incarcerated, chased, murdered and hunted like wild beasts." The three Anglos who died in the attack on Brownsville, declared Cortina, deserved their fate because of their crimes against the Mexican people.[44]

The loss of Mexican land deserved Cortina's most scathing attack. He condemned a "secret conclave" of corrupt judges, politicians, and lawyers that had formed "for the sole purpose of despoiling the Mexicans of their lands and usurp[ing] them afterwards." He singled out Adolphus Glavecke, who as deputy sheriff "in collusion with the said lawyers, has spread terror among the unwary, making them believe that he will hang the Mexicans and burn their ranches . . . that by this means he might compel them to abandon the country, and thus accomplish their object." To these men, he thundered: "Our personal enemies shall not possess our lands until they have fattened it with their own gore."[45]

The objectives of the movement were also manifested in the two proclamations. Cheno made it clear that his revolt was not meant to harm innocent people. He regretted deeply the death of two innocent Mexicans in the Brownsville raid. He stressed his respect for all civilians, Anglo and Mexican, and stated that this was demonstrated when he refused to allow his men to sack the town. He insisted on paying for the provisions required by his men and punished them harshly for robbing or abusing the population. His main object was "to chastise the villainy of our enemies, which heretofore has gone unpunished."[46] Other vague objectives were expressed in the second proclamation. One was the creation of a society to work for "the improvement of the unhappy condition" of the Mexican population, and the other was a strange call for governor-elect Sam Houston to "give us legal protection within the limits of his powers."[47]

Throughout October and November, the residents of Brownsville lived in fear of another attack, as Cortina, in a menacing posture, hovered nearby at his mother's ranch. They made frantic calls to the state and national governments to send troops to defend the town. When Cortina's right-hand man, Tomás Cabrera, was captured, Cheno ordered Cabrera be released or Cheno would attack the town again. An improvised militia was formed in Brownsville that called itself the "Brownsville Tigers." It included about twenty Anglos led by William B. Thompson and some forty "poorly armed Mexican rancheros" commanded by Antonio Portillo. This force was joined by seventy-five troops from the Tamaulipas National Guard that had come over from Matamoros. On October 24, the two units attacked Rancho del Carmen and were decisively defeated.[48]

A body of Texas Rangers led by William G. Tobin arrived in Brownsville on November 10 and promptly escalated the conflict by hanging Tomás Cabrera. Cortina promised swift retribution. What followed was a series of deadly attacks by both sides, as the Rangers committed abuses against all the Mexicans they could find, including those who had nothing to do with Cortina. The struggle was evolving from a personal feud into a larger conflict between Anglos and Mexicans. In a series of clashes on November 22 and 23, Cortina's force decisively defeated Tobin's Rangers.[49]

These defeats and the continuing threat of another attack on Brownsville raised the fears of the Anglo population as fevered letter writers and a militant Texas press generated wildly exaggerated accounts of the conflict. One typical example is that of Gilbert Kingsbury, the Brownsville postmaster, whose letter, written under the pseudonym of F. F. Fenn, was published by a San Antonio newspaper. He wrote that Cortina's force numbered between 500 and 1,200 men and declared that almost all the Mexicans of the region supported the rebel in what was clearly becoming "a war of races."[50] The *Brownsville Flag* published an affidavit by two residents of Corpus Christi who were convinced that "the entire Mexican population on both sides of the Rio Grande are up in arms, advancing upon us to murder every white inhabitant and to reconquer our country as far as the Colorado river."[51]

The Mexican press lampooned these reports as ridiculous but was convinced that they contained a sinister aspect: create conditions that would justify making a war on Mexico for the purpose of annexing more of her territory. A Mexico City newspaper quoted the *New York Times*, which also dismissed reports coming out of Texas: "Mexican territory will be violated, our influence in Mexico gravely compromised and our national honor tarnished by a foolish act, bereft of common sense if it wasn't promoted by the desire to provoke an unjust and useless war against our neighbor republic."[52]

These press reports brought to the fore important issues that were being discussed throughout the region. One involved the nature of the conflict: whether it was strictly a Texas problem or if it was a broader issue between Mexico and the United States. Of crucial importance was Cortina's nationality and that of his followers. Some sources, particularly in the Texas press, took note of the fact that a Mexican flag was raised over Rancho del Carmen and insisted that Cortina was a Mexican national and the Mexican government was responsible for his actions. This too was scorched by Mexican newspapers. The most vocal, *La Sociedad*, declared that it was not certain whether the Mexican flag was used, but the accusation only served to justify making claims against Mexico for damages caused by Cortina, or worse, to find a "pretext to invade and militarily occupy our northern provinces." It reminded its readers that Cortina "confessed being a U. S. citizen without the least intention of changing his nationality."[53]

Another important issue was the attitude of the inhabitants toward Cortina and his revolt. It should be pointed out that the vast majority of the population of the region was Mexican. In Brownsville, wrote Israel B. Bigelow, editor of the *American Flag*, out of a population of about 2,500 there were no more than "one hundred and fifty male persons who speak the English language." He considered that there were "not more than fifty Mexicans whose interests and feelings [were] sufficiently identified with [the Anglo population] to cause them to join in the defense of the city." There is no doubt that most of the Mexican population identified with a movement that sought to combat the abuses of the Anglo minority and to restore their dignity. This support only grew when the Rangers arrived and began committing outrages against all Mexicans, irrespective of their loyalties.[54] Testimonials abound with respect to the massive support that Cortina enjoyed among the Mexican population on both sides of the border. This became evident when a Brownsville Committee for Public Safety sought volunteers in Cameron and Hidalgo counties to defend Brownsville. Few came. A force of some thirty Mexicans was recruited by William Neale, whose son was killed in the Brownsville raid. These were placed under the command of Justo Treviño, but they refused to participate in the battle of October 25 because they did not want to fight against Cortina.[55]

Some Texas Mexicans did participate against Cheno. It is estimated that between forty and sixty fought against Cortina under the leadership of Antonio Portillo. Other Texas Mexicans whose interests were firmly tied to the new order also opposed Cortina. Among them were Francisco Yturria, one of the most prominent merchants and landowners of Brownsville and Sabas Cavazos, Cortina's half-brother.[56] However, the most important source of support for Brownsville in its fight against Cortina came from Matamoros. This was recognized by the mayor of Brownsville, Stephen Powers, and by a grand jury of leading citizens. The latter praised "the activity and zeal with which the authorities of the State of Tamaulipas, and especially the city of Matamoras [sic], both civil and military, attempted to rescue the city of Brownsville." Cortina himself expressed disappointment that the authorities of Matamoros had sent troops against him.[57]

An extensive report by the U.S. Appraiser General's Office in New Orleans pointed out that Matamoros "apparently sympathized with the citizens of Brownsville; not only inviting the women and children of the town to remain over there, but furnished a company of their infantry to repel any attack Cortinas might make on the town." However, it recognized that Matamoros was a refuge for Cortina, who was often seen there without being molested by Mexican authorities. This provoked distrust in Brownsville, whose citizens were also apprehensive about the Tamaulipas National Guard in their midst. At one point Guard troops returned to Matamoros and another eyewitness stated that their departure came as a "relief [to] most of our people, who had great dread of them, fearing them to be more likely to turn against us than otherwise." He concluded: "We are over a bed of burning coals and wholly at the mercy of the people of Matamoras [sic]."[58] Another Brownsville citizen implied that it was unmanly to rely on Mexicans for their safety: "We feel somewhat humiliated at the necessity of calling on the Mexican authorities for protection."[59]

The support provided by Matamoros was the best argument of the Mexican press against charges that Cortina's revolt was orchestrated from Mexico.[60] *La Sociedad* declared that the only interference by Mexican authorities was that of "sending an armed force to aid the Americans at their request." It correctly noted that the U.S. government had abandoned the border region and Mexican authorities were compelled to do what that government could not do. The newspaper once again quoted the *New York Times* to make its point: "Mexico, whose soldiers have been the only defense of our countrymen . . . has performed its duty loyally and more so in coming to the aid of American citizens." The editorial concluded: "When even U. S. newspapers express themselves [in this manner], it seems unnecessary that the Mexican press continue to insist on the absence of responsibility of our country in Cortina's depredations."[61]

In mid-November, after many appeals from South Texas, the U.S. government decided to send troops. Major Samuel P. Heintzelman was chosen to lead three companies to suppress the revolt. He arrived in Brownsville on December 6 and promptly sought out José María Carbajal for intelligence on Cortina's force. Contrary to exaggerated reports, Carbajal believed that Cortina's force numbered about two hundred. Heintzelman felt confident that his 165 troops, joined by 125 Rangers, and a great superiority in arms were sufficient to go after the rebel chief. His force set out in search of Cortina and engaged in a series of skirmishes with the rebels, who avoided meeting Heintzelman's force in open battle. At this point both *Cortinistas* and Rangers proceeded to plunder and destroy many of the ranches upriver from Brownsville. The Rangers were particularly brutal, burning and looting all property suspected of belonging to sympathizers of Cortina. Heintzelman later wrote: "The whole country from Brownsville to Rio Grande City, one hundred and twenty miles, and back to the Arroyo Colorado, has been laid to waste."[62] On the foggy morning of December 27, 1859, the two forces met outside Rio Grande City. After bitter fighting, Cortina's small army, which now numbered about five hundred soldiers, was decisively defeated. Jerry Thompson writes: "Many of the rusty muskets of the Cortinistas proved to be no match for the regulars' Sharp's rifles." As he fled across the river, Cortina lamented the loss of between sixty and two hundred men and the complete disarticulation of his movement.[63]

During the first two months of 1860, the conflict degenerated into a guerrilla war as small bands of Cortinistas carried out attacks on the north bank of the Rio Grande and Rangers continued to lay waste to Mexican ranches on the Texas side and crossed the river at will to attack Mexicans on the south bank. Meanwhile, in the Texas capital, newly elected governor Sam Houston sought to use the crisis on the Rio Grande as an excuse to invade Mexico. Duff Green, an agent of the U.S. government, talked extensively with Houston and was convinced that the hero of San Jacinto wanted to establish a protectorate in northern Mexico, win the support of the southern states, and propel himself into national politics with a view toward vying for the presidency. Houston sent two men to the border to report to him directly. One of these was Angel Navarro, graduate of Harvard and son of José Antonio Navarro, one of three Mexicans who signed Texas's Declaration of Independence and probably the most respected Mexican in the state. Angel Navarro wrote that Mexican depredations would continue unless the United States occupied "a sufficient portion of the border sections of Mexico." He also believed that "the Mexican people, as a mass, are hoping for a deliverance from anarchy, and would rejoice in the establishment of a stable form of government which would protect their lives and property and give them peace." His impressions coincided with Houston's expansionist policy and reinforced the governor's ambitious plan.[64]

However, the crisis was being defused as other actors entered the scene. General Guadalupe García assumed command of Mexican military forces on the border and expressed to both Heintzelman and Navarro that his government had given him orders to cooperate with American authorities in apprehending Cortina and putting a stop to the depredations committed by his followers. Both men were skeptical. Navarro wrote to Houston that García would not move against Cheno because the rebel chief had the sympathy of "a large majority of the Mexicans, and those in power."[65] Meanwhile, authorities in Washington took a more aggressive approach in the matter. Secretary of War John B. Floyd wrote to Governor Houston that "an officer of great discretion and ability has been dispatched to take command of the department of Texas." Colonel Robert E. Lee, who would soon lead the Confederate Army in the U.S. Civil War, was given precise instructions: "The most vigorous measures for the capture of Cortinas and his band will be resorted to, and if necessary, the secretary of War directs that they be pursued beyond the limits of the United States."[66]

Lee's orders, which resembled the infamous Ord Order of 1877 that almost provoked a war between Mexico and the United States, became moot when

Cortina suddenly abandoned the border region. The rebel leader marched south to participate in Mexico's War of Reform on the side of Benito Juárez. The army command at San Antonio, Texas, reported this fact to Washington in mid-March 1860, adding that the Cortina Revolt had apparently ended. This effectively torpedoed Houston's plan (not to speak of his political ambitions) to invade northern Mexico with U.S. government support.[67]

Authorities in Washington were informed of events on the Rio Grande through various sources. One of these was Colonel Harvey Brown, who during two weeks conducted interviews throughout the region. In a dispatch and a later report, Brown provides one of the most lucid expositions of the event known as the Cortina War. He wrote that the revolt was "commenced by Texans, and carried on (vainly) by and between them." Cortina and most of his followers, wrote Brown, were native Texans: "Few, if any, Mexicans from the opposite side took part in the disturbances."[68] The revolt, according to Brown, had been "greatly exaggerated, never approached the dignity of a war, but was, in its commencement and continuance, a mere raid." He advised Washington to consider the reports of newspapers and "anonymous letter-writers . . . with the greatest caution," as they were "put in circulation by persons interested in fomenting trouble."[69]

One of Brown's recommendations was with respect to the Rangers: "The removal of the Texan volunteers," he wrote, was necessary because of the "great and reciprocal animosity [that subsists] between them and the Mexicans." This suggestion was apparently put into practice. By July, an American military official reported that with the decrease in raids and the departure of the Rangers, the frontier was "perfectly quiet."[70]

––––––––

This study reveals two examples of cooperation between Anglo-Texans and Mexicans in violent events that occurred in the border region. In the Federalist War, the alliance was essentially a marriage of convenience, as each group sought to use the other to achieve its particular ends. Each side sought its own self-interest, but these differing interests converged at an opportune time and place. Federalist leaders in Northeast Mexico declared war on their government because they felt threatened by centralist policies that affected their interests. Moreover, they wanted greater regional autonomy, flexible commercial policies, and resources to combat Indian predators. They sought alliances with Anglo-Texans, who had their own reasons for joining the revolt. A few genuinely believed in federalism; others sought to separate a part of Mexico to create an independent republic that would serve as a buffer between Texas and Mexico. The majority of the Anglos who participated were adventurers interested only in plunder and the spoils that came with it.

Like the federalist uprising, the Cortina Revolt was motivated by a combination of personal and collective grievances. Cortina considered himself a victim of land-grabbing Anglos, and he sought personal revenge as well as vindication for all Mexicans. Many of his followers, who fought for their dignity, also felt victimized by the small Anglo minority that took power on the lower Rio Grande after the U.S.-Mexican War. Some of his followers, who only joined the movement for plunder, no doubt resembled the Anglo-Texans in the earlier Federalist War.

Most of the Mexican population north and south of the border sympathized with Cortina, but a small group of Texas Mexicans allied with the Anglo population to suppress the revolt. They were joined by soldiers of the Tamaulipas National Guard sent from Matamoros. Most of the Texas Mexicans who confronted Cortina were either merchants or property owners who had vested interest in the system and who felt that the revolt endangered the peace and prosperity of the region, of which they were beneficiaries. The Mexican soldiers from Matamoros were simply following orders from military and civil authorities who were fearful that an escalation of the conflict would destabilize the region and serve as a pretext for another invasion of Mexico. Given Cortina's level of support, it is clear that only an outside force could have suppressed the revolt. This was borne out when the U.S. Army and a group of Texas Rangers defeated Cortina in battle and disarticulated his movement.[71]

A comparison of the two events reveals differences as well as similarities. The first basic difference is that the Federalist War was a revolt of Mexicans from Mexico, while the Cortina Revolt mainly involved Texas Mexicans. In the first, cooperative violence was used by rebels, while in the second, to fight rebels. Finally, in the federalist revolt, the Anglo and Mexican allies were fighting against a common enemy, the Mexican government, while in the Cortina uprising, Anglo-Texans and their Mexican allies were fighting for a common cause: to maintain peace in the region.

There are also similarities. In both events, the majority of the people was passive and refused to take sides. Most of the inhabitants of towns and ranchos in Northeast Mexico had nothing to do with the Federalist War but suffered the depredations of the federalists and the demands of the centralists. In the Cortina Revolt, most of the Mexican population on the Texas side of the border also suffered, more so at the hands of the Texas Rangers than from the raids of the Cortinistas. In both conflicts, the allies joined not from a spirit of friendship or solidarity but due to self-interest. Another interesting similarity is that the press of both countries, more so in the case of the Cortina Revolt, was mobilized to support or condemn one or the other of the protagonists. The question of identity was important in both revolts. In the Federalist War, General Mariano Arista successfully portrayed the rebels as traitors of the nation, devoid of patriotism for bringing Texans to make war on Mexico. In the Cortina Revolt, the Anglo-Texan press refused to consider Cortina as a native Texan and a U.S. citizen and pictured him as an alien outsider making war on their country.[72] Although identity was important, race was not an impediment to cooperation. Texans rode willingly alongside Antonio Zapata, the Mexican Mulatto, because they shared a common objective. Mexican authorities and much of the population opposed the Texans not because they were white, but because they were Texans. In the Cortina Revolt, when Brownsville Anglos asked for reinforcements from Matamoros, they did not demand "whites only."

A final similarity is that both conflicts reveal the possibilities and limitations of cooperative violence. In the earlier event, the federalists lost the war, but their leaders, including Antonio Canales and Jesús Cárdenas, used the Texans to gain leverage against the Mexican government. By blandishing the Texas sword, they were able to gain concessions. When the fighting ended, they were welcomed back to the fold and their families retained positions of power for many generations. Similarly, the Texans gained by breathing life into a movement that kept the Mexican government tied down fighting a regional revolt, allowing them to buy time to consolidate their freedom.[73] The Anglo-Mexican alliance in the Cortina Revolt was perhaps sufficient to stay Cortina's hand for a short time, but it became evident that a greater force was necessary to crush his movement.

What role did the border play in the episodes of violence and, in particular, in promoting cooperative violence? It is my belief that the principal cause of violence was the competition among different groups for the resources of the region: land, livestock, salt, and others. But there were contributing factors. The region's remoteness from the centers of power in Washington and Mexico City facilitated the violence because there was an absence of government authority during a large part of the century, as the essays of Tim Bowman in chapter 6 and Lance Blyth in chapter 3 of this volume point out. The border served as a refuge for rebels, Indian raiders, and lawless men because they could carry out their activities on one side of the boundary and escape punishment by crossing to the other side. This recourse was used by Cortina and other rebels throughout the century and into the twentieth century, especially during the Mexican Revolution, as Alan Knight points out in his essay in chapter 11. Indian raids in Northeast Mexico were a harrowing reality throughout most of the century. These were motivated essentially by a market logic, as Joaquín Rivaya-Martínez points out in his essay in chapter 2, but that did not render the violence that they perpetrated any less destructive. The border also stoked the desires of ambitious men who had annexation of part of Mexico as their goal. This too was manifested by politicians and the press during both episodes.

The border was a good breeding ground for cooperative violence because it was a middle ground where different racial and ethnic groups came together. The lower Rio Grande saw the confluence of Mexicans, Anglo-Americans, Europeans, Native Americans, and African Americans. They found common ground in many diverse activities, especially in commerce, and it is logical to suppose that one of their many interactions would be in the realm of violence. Moreover, most of the fronterizos, with the possible exception of government officials and the clergy, identified more closely with their region than with the nation. They were driven more by pragmatism than by ideology or national sentiments. These considerations facilitated their acceptance of alliances with diverse groups.

Thus, the border set the stage for cooperation and interethnic alliances in acts of violence. On that stage, border residents joined to face a common problem or enemy or to fight for a common cause. A problem common to Anglo and Mexican border residents was the Indian raids that disrupted their lives and destroyed their property. This menace played a role in both of the events analyzed in this chapter. One of the reasons that the federalists went to war against their government in 1839 was because of its failure to protect them. And one of the objectives of federalists and Texans was to join together to fight off Indian attacks. During the Cortina Revolt, Indian raids on the Texas western frontier obligated the transfer of military forces away from the lower Rio Grande, which facilitated Cortina's insurgency. Both Anglo-Texans and Mexican federalists, for diverse reasons, considered the Mexican government as their enemy and together made war on that government. The Federalist War of 1839–40 is a good example of that kind of alliance, as was the Carbajal Revolt of 1851, though on a smaller scale. An example of cooperation in pursuit of a common goal is the Cortina Revolt, where the Anglo citizens of Brownsville and the Mexican authorities of Tamaulipas joined together to suppress the rebels because they threatened the peace of the region, which was essential to commerce and prosperity.

From the foregoing, it is clear that the border region was a propitious place for cooperative violence. However, this observation is not limited to the nineteenth century. The work of drug and human traffickers in today's border region necessarily involves cooperation between persons of various ethnic groups, and the efforts to stop them also necessitate cooperation by law enforcement agents from both sides of the border.[74]

Notes

1. The Carbajal Revolt was known in Texas as the Merchants' War because it had the backing of Brownsville merchants, and in Mexico as the "Plan de la Loba." For an account of the revolt, see Joseph Chance, *Jose Maria De Jesus Carbajal: The Life and Times of a*

Mexican Revolutionary (San Antonio, TX: Trinity University Press, 2006). For differing accounts of the battle, see "Later from Mexico," *San Antonio Ledger,* January 15, 1852, 1; and *Telegraph and Texas Register,* January 16, 1852, 2.

2. Many studies have focused on racial animosity as a source of conflict between Anglos and Mexicans. The following are a few examples: Michael L. Collins, *Texas Devils: Rangers and Regulars on the Lower Rio Grande, 1846–1861* (Norman: University of Oklahoma Press); Arnoldo De León, *They Called them Greasers: Anglo Attitudes toward Mexicans in Texas, 1821–1900* (Austin: University of Texas Press, 1983); Neil Foley, *The White Scourge: Mexicans, Blacks, and Poor Whites in Texas Cotton Culture* (Berkeley: University of California Press, 1997); Oscar J. Martínez, *Troublesome Border* (Tucson: University of Arizona Press, 1988); John C. Rayburn and Virginia Kemp Rayburn, eds., *Century of Conflict 1821–1913: Incidents in the Lives of William Neale and William A. Neale, Early Settlers in South Texas* (Waco, TX: Texian Press, 1966); and Andrés Tijerina, *Tejanos and Texas under the Mexican Flag, 1821–1836* (College Station: Texas A&M University Press, 1994).

3. Many other examples could be cited. The Salt War at San Elizario in 1877 and the Fort Grant Massacre in Arizona in 1871 both featured multiethnic alliances. See Paul Cool, *Salt Warriors: Insurgency on the Rio Grande* (College Station: Texas A&M University Press, 2008); and Karl Jacoby, *Shadows at Dawn: An Apache Massacre and the Violence of History* (New York: Penguin Books, 2008). A strong argument can be made that the border was largely pacified by the beginning of the 1880s. Indian raids were largely eliminated as hostile tribes were decimated or consigned to reservations. An enclosure movement in South Texas spearheaded by Mifflin Kenedy and Richard King made rustling more difficult. The railroad permitted the rapid mobilization of troops to the border to suppress violent episodes. And both governments expressed a willingness to work together, as shown by the rescission of the Ord Order in 1880 and an agreement in 1882 allowing reciprocal crossings of the border in pursuit of predators.

4. Josefina Zoraida Vázquez, *La supuesta Republica del Rio Grande,* 2nd ed. (Ciudad Victoria: Instituto de Investigaciones Históricas, Universidad Autónoma de Tamaulipas, 1995), 6.

5. Luis Medina Peña, *Los bárbaros del norte: Guardia Nacional y política en Nuevo León, siglo XIX* (México, D.F.: Fondo de Cultura Económica; Centro de Investigación y Docencia Económicas, 2014), 91; Josefina Zoraida Vázquez, "The Texas Question in Mexican Politics, 1836–1845," *Southwestern Historical Quarterly* 89, no. 3 (1986): 313. A Mexico City newspaper editorialized that in the northern states there was a preference for federalism and the government would do well to return a measure of sovereignty to the departments: "If the notable men of the capital insist in maintaining the essence of centralism. . . . The spirit of the people will rebel and the torch of discord will cover the territory of the republic." "Interior," *El Cosmopolita,* March 14, 1840, 2–3.

6. These were Matamoros, Reynosa, Camargo, Mier, Guerrero, and Laredo. With the exception of Laredo, these were located on the right bank, or Mexican side of the river.

7. Stanley C. Green, "The Texas Revolution and the Rio Grande Border," *The Texas Revolution on the Rio Grande: Bi-National Conference Proceedings,* March 25, 2005 (San Antonio: Daughters of the Republic of Texas Library at the Alamo, 2005), 63; Octavio Herrera, *El norte de Tamaulipas y la conformación de la frontera México–Estados Unidos, 1835–1855* (Ciudad Victoria: El Colegio de Tamaulipas, 2003), 36–37; Vázquez, "Texas Question," 322; Medina Peña, *Bárbaros del norte,* 181.

8. Joseph B. Ridout, "'An Anti-national Disorder': Antonio Canales and Northeastern Mexico, 1836–1852" (master's thesis, University of Texas at Austin, 1994), 60.

9. Lindheim, *Republic of the Rio Grande*, 1; Ridout, "Anti-national Disorder," 53–54.

10. Quoted in Green, "Texas Revolution," 64.

11. *Correo del Río Bravo del Norte*, February 16, 1840, 1.

12. Circular, March 4, 1839, wallet 12, no. 19, Pablo Salce Arredondo Collection, Benson Latin American Collection, University of Texas at Austin (hereafter, PSA, BLAC, UTA); Horace V. Harrison, "Los federalistas mexicanos de 1839–40 y sus tanteos diplomáticos en Texas," *Historia Mexicana* 6, no. 3 (1957): 338–39.

13. Joseph M. Nance, *After San Jacinto: The Texas-Mexican Frontier, 1836–1841* (Austin: University of Texas Press, 1963), 152, 160–61, 168.

14. Harrison, "Los federalistas mexicanos," 336–37, 341; Ridout, "'Anti-national Disorder," 76, 100–101; Vito Alessio Robles, *Coahuila y Texas desde la consumación de la independencia hasta el Tratado de Paz de Guadalupe Hidalgo*, 2 vols. (México: Talleres Gráficos de la Nación, 1945), 2:207.

15. Quoted in Nance, *After San Jacinto*, 302.

16. Chance, *Jose Maria De Jesus Carbajal*, 49, 53.

17. Juan José Gallegos, "'Last Drop of My Blood:' Col. Antonio Zapata: A Life and Times on Mexico's Rio Grande Frontier, 1797–1840" (master's thesis, University of Houston, 2005), 120.

18. Sam W. Haynes, *Soldiers of Misfortune: The Somervell and Mier Expeditions* (Austin: University of Texas Press, 1997), 44.

19. Gallegos, "'Last Drop of My Blood,'" 44, 131, 198; Nance, *After San Jacinto*, 227; Green, "Texas Revolution," 64.

20. This battle is known in Texas as Alcantra. Alessio Robles, *Coahuila y Texas*, 2:216; Milton Lindheim, *The Republic of the Rio Grande. Texans in Mexico, 1839–40* (Waco, TX: W. M. Morrison, 1964), 2, 14; Nance, *After San Jacinto*, 218–19, 227–29; Ridout, "Anti-national Disorder," 64.

21. Nance, *After San Jacinto*, 219.

22. Nance, *After San Jacinto*, 219; *Semanario Político*, January 3, 1840, p. 2 quote.

23. Nance, *After San Jacinto*, 251, 252; *Correo del Río Bravo del Norte*, February 16, 1840, 1.

24. This is the belief of Herrera, *El norte de Tamaulipas*, 33n. Although there is a museum in Laredo, Texas, dedicated to the Republic of the Rio Grande and many Texans and some Mexicans believe that it really existed, historians are not agreed on the subject. Among those who believe it existed are David M. Vigness, "The Republic of the Rio Grande: An Example of Separatism in Northern Mexico" (PhD diss., University of Texas at Austin, 1951); Nance, *After San Jacinto*; Lindheim, *Republic of the Rio Grande*; and Ridout, "Anti-national Disorder." Among those who believe that it only existed in the minds of Anglo-Texans are Vázquez, *La supuesta República*; Gallegos, "'Last Drop of My Blood'"; and Herrera, *El norte de Tamaulipas*.

25. Nance, *After San Jacinto*, 249–67; *Telegraph and Texas Register*, April 29, 1840, 3.

26. Nance, *After San Jacinto*, 206, 281, 288, 328; Hobart Huson, *Refugio: A Comprehensive History of Refugio County from Aboriginal Times to 1953*, 2 vols. (Woodsboro, TX: Rooke Foundation, 1953), 1:441–42, 444; Lindheim, *Republic of the Rio Grande*, 6.

27. Urrea to Gómez Farías, April 6, 1840, #625, folder 47a, Gómez Farías Papers (hereafter, GFP), BLAC, UTA. A Mexico City newspaper wrote that there was genuine hatred in

the northern provinces against Mexico City. See "Interior," *El Cosmopolita*, March 14, 1840, 2–3.

28. Quoted in Herrera, *El norte de Tamaulipas*, 71. The nature of the border region fostered attitudes contrary to nationalism. Historian Andrés Reséndez affirms: "The isolation and hardship of the frontier fostered a remarkable openness toward outsiders." Historian David Weber states that the "isolation and distance from the nation's core assured . . . a measure of independence and protection from retaliation by the central government." See Reséndez, *Changing National Identities at the Frontier: Texas and New Mexico, 1800–1850* (Cambridge: Cambridge University Press, 2005), 125; Weber, *Mexican Frontier*, 280.

29. Broadside, Arista to residents of Saltillo, December 12, 1839, #943, Mexican Imprints from the Streeter Collection, Mary and Jeff Bell Library, Texas A&M University–Corpus Christi (hereafter, MI, SC, BL, TA&MCC), microfilm reel 15; Nance, *After San Jacinto*, 308.

30. Quoted in Nance, *After San Jacinto*, 308, 337 quote. Jordan was prone to violence. One historian reports that on one occasion he tried to kill Sam Houston with an axe and eventually committed suicide. See Ridout, "Anti-national Disorder," 69.

31. Nance, *After San Jacinto*, 343 353–60; Lindheim, *Republic of the Rio Grande*, 8.

32. Juan Fidel Zorrilla, Maribel Miró Flaquer, and Octavio Herrera Pérez, *Tamaulipas, una historia compartida, 1810–1921*, 2 vols. (Ciudad Victoria, Tamaulipas: Instituto de Investigaciones Históricas, Universidad Autónoma de Tamaulipas, 1993), 1:115; Alcance al *Semanario Político*, November 12, 1840; Nance, *After San Jacinto*, 347, 362, 364, 370, 373–74.

33. This hostile environment is depicted in David Montejano, *Anglos and Mexicans in the Making of Texas, 1836–1986* (Austin: University of Texas Press, 1986) and Arnoldo DeLeón, *Mexican Americans in Texas, a Brief History* (Arlington Heights, IL: Harlan Davidson, 1993), among other works.

34. John Salmon Ford, *Rip Ford's Texas* (Austin: University of Texas Press, 1987), 460.

35. Hayes to Hemphill, October 1, 1859, "Difficulties on the Frontier," 27.

36. Twiggs to Thomas, January 13, 1859, and Citizens of Brownsville to Governor Runnels, October 2, 1859, in "Difficulties on Southwestern Frontier: Message from the President of the United States, Communicating, in Compliance with a Resolution of the House, Information in Reference to the Difficulties on the Southwestern Frontier," H.R., 36th Cong., 1st Sess. Exec. Doc. No. 52 ([Digital Version] https://scholarship.rice.edu/jsp/xml/1911/22069 /1/aa00333.tei.html), 5, 22.

37. A succinct account of the raid is provided by Jerry Thompson, *Cortina, Defending the Mexican Name in Texas* (College Station: Texas A&M University Press, 2007), 39–45.

38. Thompson, *Cortina*, 44, 46. See also "Mas sobre los sucesos de Brownsville," *La Sociedad*, October 28, 1859, 3; Latham to Twiggs, September 28, 1859, "Difficulties on the Frontier," 32. Carbajal had sided with the Texans in their war of independence; he was one of the leaders of the Federalist War; and he led his own revolt, *El Plan de la Loba*, against the Mexican government in 1851.

39. Brown to Arguelles and Arguelles to Brown, September 28, 1859, Arguelles to Governor of the State, September 29 and October 3, 1859 and February 20, 1860, 1-15-1683 (1877), Fondo de Gaveta, Archivo Histórico de la Secretaría de Relaciones Exteriores, (hereafter, FG, AHSRE).

40. Thompson, *Cortina*, 48. See also "Mas sobre los sucesos de Brownsville," *La Sociedad*, October 28, 1859, 3; Brownsville citizens to Runnels, October 2, 1859, "Difficulties on the Frontier," 22.

41. Gilberto López y Rivas, "Cortina y el conflicto fronterizo entre Estados Unidos y México," in *Tamaulipas, textos de su historia, 1810–1921*, ed. Juan Fidel Zorrilla, Maribel Miró Flaquer, and Octavio Herrera Pérez (México D.F.: Instituto Mora; Ciudad Victoria: Gobierno del Estado de Tamaulipas, 1990), 1:334; Report of A. Navarro to Gov. Sam Houston, February 15, 1860, "Difficulties on the Frontier," 120, 123, 125.

42. López y Rivas, "Cortina," 334–35; Proclamation of November 23, 1859, "Difficulties on the Frontier," 81–82.

43. Thompson, *Cortina*, 25, 32, 37, 39.

44. Proclamation of Juan N. Cortina, November 23, 1859, and September 23, 1859, "Difficulties on the Frontier," 70, 80, 81. A report by W. J. Reyburn lent substance to this latter assertion by Cortina. He wrote that the men killed, William Peter Neale, George Morris, and Robert L. Johnson, had all been accused of shooting Mexicans, but had never faced punishment. See Reyburn Report in Hatch to Floyd, November 22, 1859, "Difficulties on the Frontier," 65.

45. Proclamation of Juan N. Cortina, September 23, 1859, "Difficulties on the Frontier," 71, 72.

46. Proclamation of Juan N. Cortina, September 30, 1859, "Difficulties on the Frontier," 70 (quote), 71; López y Rivas, "Cortina," 336–38.

47. Proclamation of Juan N. Cortina, November 23, 1859, "Difficulties on the Frontier," 82.

48. Thompson, *Cortina*, 53–54. Another account states that Portillo led a force of about sixty Mexicans. See Mary Margaret McAllen Amberson, James A. McAllen, and Margaret H. McAllen, *I Would Rather Sleep in Texas: A History of the Lower Rio Grande Valley and the People of the Santa Anita Land Grant* (Austin: Texas State Historical Association, 2003), 167.

49. Thompson, *Cortina*, 63, 64, 65.

50. "Latest from the Rio Grande," *San Antonio Ledger and Texan*, December 10, 1859, 1; Thompson, *Cortina*, 59–60.

51. Affidavit of William D. Thomas and Nathaniel White, November 6, 1859, "Difficulties on the Frontier," 50.

52. "Editorial: Los sucesos de Brownsville con relación a México," *La Sociedad*, January 4, 1860, 1.

53. "Editorial: Los sucesos de Brownsville con relación a México," *La Sociedad*, January 4, 1860, 1. Even a superficial reading of Cortina's pronouncements reveals that he considered himself a U.S. citizen. He was living on the U.S. side of the border when the war between the United States and Mexico ended, and by the Treaty of Guadalupe Hidalgo those who chose to stay became U.S. citizens. Cortina stayed. With respect to his followers, a report at the end of the conflict concluded that the majority of the Mexicans who attacked Brownsville were U.S. citizens. See Thompson, *Cortina*, 45, 49; Lee to Adjutant General, March 6, 1860, "Difficulties on the Frontier," 136.

54. "Editor's News," October 23, 1859, *American Flag*, in "Difficulties on the Frontier," 47 quote; Thompson, *Cortina*, 89.

55. López y Rivas ("Cortina," 339) alludes to the many letters and reports found in the government document "Difficulties on the Frontier" that stressed the theme of overwhelming Mexican support for Cortina. Thompson, *Cortina*, 51, 56, 57.

56. Thompson, *Cortina*, 48, 53; Amberson, McAllen, and McAllen, *I Would Rather Sleep in Texas*, 167; Ford, *Rip Ford's Texas*, 264–65; John M. Hart, *Revolutionary Mexico: The Coming and Process of the Mexican Revolution* (Berkeley: University of California Press, 1987), 115.

57. Powers and others to President Buchanan, and Report of the Grand Jury, "Difficulties on the Frontier," 75–76, 93 quote. Cortina's protest at the intervention of Matamoros is found in his Proclamation of September 23, 72.

58. See Reyburn Report in Hatch to Floyd, November 22, 1859, "Difficulties on the Frontier," 67–68 first quote; "Special correspondence of the Picayune," October 10, 1859, in "Difficulties on the Frontier," 40 second quote.

59. Quoted in Chance, *Jose Maria De Jesus Carbajal*, 170.

60. A persistent accusation was that the conservative party led by Miguel Miramón was providing arms and resources to the rebels. See, for example, Hale to Floyd and Twiggs to Floyd, "Difficulties on the Frontier," 43, 58.

61. "Editorial. Los sucesos de Brownsville," *La Sociedad*, January 4, 1860, 1.

62. Quoted in Thompson, *Cortina*, 72–74, 77 quote.

63. Thompson, *Cortina*, 79 quote, 80. See also reports by Heintzelman and Seawell to Adjutant General, December 27, 1859 and January 5, 1860, "Difficulties on the Frontier," 98–99.

64. Navarro to Houston, January 31, 1860, "Difficulties on the Frontier," 117–18; Thompson, *Cortina*, 92–93.

65. Thompson, *Cortina*, 82; Navarro to Houston, February 15, 1860, "Difficulties on the Frontier," 122 quote.

66. Floyd to Houston, February 28 and Adjutant General to Lee, February 24, 1860, "Difficulties on the Frontier," 133–34.

67. Thompson, *Cortina*, 91–92.

68. Brown dispatch included in a report from Lee to War Department, "Difficulties on the Frontier," 136–37.

69. Brown report, "Difficulties on the Frontier," 147.

70. Brown report, "Difficulties on the Frontier," 147; Thompson, *Cortina*, 94.

71. Some Texas Mexicans outside the border region also opposed Cortina, among them, the prominent Navarro family of San Antonio. On his mission for Sam Houston, Angel Navarro carried a letter from his father addressed to Cortina. José Antonio Navarro exhorted him to seek justice without violence and reminded him that not all Anglos were like those who had wronged him. See Thompson, *Cortina*, 88. Ironically, several years later, during the U.S. Civil War, Angel Navarro sought to live in Mexico, tired of the racist abuse of Confederate authorities in Texas.

72. The question of identity in the border region is eloquently addressed by Andrés Reséndez. He argues that borderlanders had to decide on their loyalties with many "contradictory forces swirling around them." These "identity choices almost always follow[ed] a situational logic. A person was not a mission Indian *or* a Mexican, a black slave in Mexico *or* an American, a foreign-born colonist *or* a Texan, but could be either depending on who was asking"; Reséndez, *Changing National Identities*, 3.

73. Herrera, *El norte de Tamaulipas*, 42; Nance, *After San Jacinto*, 172.

74. See, for example, the essays by Alejandra Díaz de León in chapter 14 and Santiago I. Guerra in chapter 12 in this book.

"PROCLAMA"
DEL CIUDADANO
NEPOMUCENO CORTINAS!

J. NEPOMUCENO CORTINAS á las habitantes del Estado de Texas y con especialidad á los de la ciudad de Brownsville.

CONCIUDADANOS: Un suceso de grave importancia en el cual me ha cabido en suerte figurar como actor principal desde la madrugada del dia 28 del que fina, os tiene suspensos y temerosos tal vez de sus consecuencias y progreso...

[...]

JUAN NEPOMUCENO CORTINAS.
Rancho del Cármen en el Condado de Cameron á 30 de Sbre. de 1859.

Chapter 5

Citizenship, Violence, and the Cortina War

ALICE L. BAUMGARTNER

At the close of the Independence Day celebrations in Matamoros, musicians shouldered their instruments and partygoers traipsed unsteadily home while Juan Nepomuceno Cortina loaded his gun.[1] By the early morning hours of September 28, 1859, Cortina was riding at the head of a small band across the Rio Grande. Charging through the streets of Brownsville, Texas, he and his men shot five of their enemies and set a dozen prisoners free from the city jail.[2] The attack on Brownsville was the opening salvo of what became known as the Cortina War. In response, Americans and Mexicans participated in what, in chapter 4 of this volume, Miguel Ángel González Quiroga calls "cooperative violence." At the invitation of the authorities in Brownsville, several of the leading citizens of Matamoros negotiated with Cortina, and the Matamoros militia crossed the river to fight alongside their Anglo counterparts. They did so, according to González, because it furthered their self-interest. To keep peace on the border—a matter of mutual concern to local merchants—the residents of Brownsville joined forces with their Mexican neighbors.

From González's arguments, it might be surmised that cooperation would arise when disorder broke out and halt when peace was restored. But such a verdict fails to explain why cooperation grew strained in the months following Cortina's raid. Even as the *cortinistas* continued to pose a threat on the Rio Grande, Major Samuel P. Heintzelman rebuffed General Guadalupe García's offers to cooperate; Colonel Harvey Brown commented on the "great and reciprocal animosity" between Mexicans and the Texas Rangers; and the U.S. government issued orders to General Robert E. Lee to pursue Cortina "beyond the limits of the United States"—with or without permission from his Mexican counterparts. Keeping the peace might have remained important to both sides, but cooperation was no longer deemed essential to that goal. To account for this dramatic shift, we must examine what Anglos and Mexicans themselves understood to be in their best interest. This chapter argues that the decision to cooperate depended on whether Texans defined Cortina as an American or a foreigner.[3]

As soon as news of Cortina's attack was keyed into telegraphs and dispatched across the wires, Americans argued over who Cortina was and, by extension, why he had attacked Brownsville.[4] Was he a "naturalized American citizen," seeking vengeance against his enemies, or a foreigner waging war against the United States?[5] Historians have dismissed the dispute over Cortina's citizenship as another example of the racism against which he purportedly took up arms because Cortina met the citizenship requirements outlined in the Treaty of Guadalupe Hidalgo.[6] But this view overlooks the fact that the provisions of the treaty relating to the ceded territory did not apply to the former Republic of Texas.[7] Instead, the state constitution set the legal standards of citizenship.

Rather than simply an expression of pervasive racism, Cortina's disputed status was part of a larger debate over citizenship in Texas that can help to explain why violence breaks out across borders and how it comes to assume such great importance beyond the borderlands. This makes for a complicated story, so some signposting is in order. After the Mexican-American War, the citizenship of Tejanos was unclear—an uncertainty that fostered cooperation. As livestock prices soared, along with the incentives to rustle, cooperative violence helped authorities on both sides of the Rio Grande to maintain order.[8] That violence *enforces* the law might seem paradoxical, because the law is often seen as restraining violence. But behind every law, as legal scholars have pointed out, is the threat of violence—the sheriff's sale, the penitentiary, the gallows.[9] During the 1850s, it was cooperative violence that kept the peace on both sides of the Rio Grande, including the early weeks of the Cortina War.

Debates over Cortina's citizenship came to undermine the networks upon which cooperative violence depended. Defining Cortina as a foreigner ensured the arrival of state and national forces that were neither able nor willing to reactivate them. If Cortina were a Mexican invader, how could a Mexican military force be expected to help suppress his raids? These kinds of questions persisted after the war ended. By the time that Cortina returned to the Rio Grande as the general of the Army of the North, rustling had gone so unchecked that it threatened to start another war between Mexico and the United States. Because these rustlers were seen as foreign invaders, their crimes attracted more attention than similar episodes of violence in the interior of the United States. As in the case of Santana Pérez's revolt that Brandon Morgan describes in chapter 8 of this volume, narratives about violence, often more than the number of victims, determine whether the conflict is seen as legitimate or illegitimate, noteworthy or forgettable.

As the members of the U.S.-Mexico Boundary Commission unpacked their chronometers and theodolites, marking pins and plumb bobs in El Paso, the Texas judiciary found itself tasked with a different kind of division between citizens of Mexico and the United States.[10] Some Tejanos claimed citizenship under the Treaty of Guadalupe Hidalgo, which guaranteed political rights to

"Mexicans now established in territories previously belonging to Mexico."[11] Although the Mexican authorities understood this provision to include Texas, the U.S. government disagreed. In 1855, the U.S. Supreme Court ruled that the treaty did not refer to Texas, whose independence the government had recognized long before the outbreak of hostilities with Mexico.[12] Unlike Mexicans in Arizona, New Mexico, and California, Tejanos could not claim U.S. citizenship under the Treaty of Guadalupe Hidalgo.[13]

Instead, Tejanos were subject to state law. The Constitution of the Republic of Texas, and later, the state constitution, extended citizenship to "all persons, (Africans, the descendants of Africans, and Indians excepted,) who were residing in Texas on the day of the Declaration of Independence." Although the state legislature regularly granted land to Tejanos who proved continual residence or military service, the constitution stated that those who fled the state "for the purpose of evading participation" in the Revolution forfeited citizenship and its attendant rights.[14] The difficulty of parsing intentions from actions, however, meant that those who left Texas during the Revolution would not lose their citizenship until "incurred and adjudged by some proceeding"—in other words, by a trial court.[15] Absent an adjudication, these individuals occupied a liminal status, having neither secured nor forfeited U.S. citizenship.

In most of the state, this uncertainty made Tejanos particularly susceptible to violence. One man traveled north of the Arroyo Colorado to inspect his family's ranch but was instead tied to a wagon wheel and whipped, nearly to death, by a gang suspected to be in the employ of the land grabbers.[16] The municipal councils of Seguin, Bastrop, and Austin expelled Mexicans from their city limits, as did the counties of Uvalde, Matagorda, and Colorado.[17] In 1857, Anglo freighters, wearing masks fashioned from gunnysacks, robbed and murdered their Mexican competitors in a "nasty racial outbreak."[18] This violence was possible because Anglo-Texans represented a majority, desirable because it furthered their economic ascendance by helping them to secure Tejanos' land, and justifiable because Tejanos' inclusion in American society was already suspect.

But the circumstances were different in South Texas. The valley's sand and loam would not become tillable soil until the advent of irrigation and dry farming techniques. The proximity of the border meant that Anglos could turn greater profits as merchants and smugglers than as planters and landowners.[19] Moreover, Tejanos constituted a majority of the population, and this demographic advantage gave them considerable clout. Although rarely winning election to state office—a record that stands testament to racism in *other* parts of Texas—Tejanos served as election judges, jury foremen, road overseers, and special commissioners.[20] Even humble Tejanos learned to petition the state government—for the establishment of favorable county boundaries and against the disenfranchisement of voters.[21] Anglo men married Tejano women and formed business partnerships with Tejano men.[22] As historians Armando Alonzo and David Montejano have shown, the region south of the Nueces did not experience the oppression of other parts of Texas because neither Anglos nor Tejanos could dominate the other by force.[23] The region was a middle ground, created not only by necessity but by the relationships that crossed the border.[24]

The uncertainty of Tejanos' citizenship made them into ideal intermediaries between local authorities in Mexico and the United States. Deputy Collector L. H. Box of Edinburgh contacted his Tejano neighbors when livestock stolen from Mexico turned up in town.[25] On April 17, 1851, the first constitutional judge of Reynosa wrote to the justice of the peace in Edinburg, "asking that he help C. Juan Cantú who was crossing to the other bank in order to pursue a pack of mules that had been robbed."[26] The justice of the peace in Edinburg might have complied with the request from the judge in Reynosa because, in addition to their official duties, both men were merchants. Their business dealings no doubt brought them together from time to time, giving rise to a familiarity that would have made their official requests easier to make and fulfill.[27]

Assistance was not limited to the exchange of information. Mexican militiamen routinely fought alongside their American counterparts against rustlers. On June 15, 1858, Judge F. F. George from Rosario, Texas, caught two men who worked at a nearby ranch crossing the river with livestock stolen from Mexico.[28] Finding himself outnumbered, George returned to the ranch several hours later with more men only to meet a volley of gunfire.[29] Gravely injured, George wrote to his friend Dr. Ramón Jiménez of Salado, Texas, to ask the authorities at Reynosa, Mexico, for reinforcements. "Bring everyone you can, and come as quick as you can, because my life is in danger," he wrote.[30] Jiménez did as his friend instructed, and the militiamen from Reynosa helped George and his men to capture the thieves.[31] If the foundation of this cooperation was trust, forged through business and family connections that bound both sides of the border together, the linchpin of these local relationships was Tejanos like Dr. Ramón Jimenez of Salado, Texas, who secured reinforcements from Reynosa for the beleaguered F. F. George.

After the Mexican-American War, the requirements for citizenship in Texas were uncertain. While the courts deliberated over which laws applied—the Treaty of Guadalupe Hidalgo or the state constitution—the jurisdictional uncertainty raised doubts about which authorities were responsible for restraining those who thieved and murdered in the Rio Grande valley.[32] Even after the courts decided that the Treaty of Guadalupe Hidalgo did not apply to Texas, it remained difficult for Tejanos to prove that they were citizens under the state law. But this uncertainty made it easier for local authorities to cooperate with their counterparts across the border. Despite the soaring price of livestock, the cooperation between authorities in Mexico and the United States helped to keep rustlers in check. Indeed, the border was so quiet that Brevet Major-General D. E. Twiggs, commander of the Military Department of Texas, recommended that the army abandon its outposts on the Rio Grande in order to do what they were supposed to be doing, which was fight Indians and other marauders.[33] The posts were expensive—and unnecessary. A soldier stationed at Fort Brown complained that his company had done "no big fighting."[34] By the early months of 1859, the troops were gone.

On September 30, two days after the attack on Brownsville, Cortina issued a *pronunciamiento*.[35] His reason for seizing Brownsville was to seek justice against a "secret conclave" of Americans, organizing for the "sole purpose of despoiling the Mexicans of their lands" and stripping them of "the longed-for boon of liberty." Cortina went on to explain that his quarrel was not with the American people—he himself claimed U.S. citizenship—but with a very small number of Brownsville residents.[36] The recently reconstituted Committee of Public Safety responded to the raid as it had to every other disturbance on the Rio Grande: by activating local networks of cooperative violence. On the same day that Cortina issued his *pronunciamiento*, the committee sent a dispatch to Matamoros, addressed to General José María Jesús Carbajal, the commander of Mexico's military forces in Tamaulipas, and Carbajal replied by sending fifty militiamen. At the end of October, General Carbajal sent another infantry regiment and a four-pound howitzer from Matamoros to Brownsville. After their defeat in a battle at Cortina's ranch, Governor Andrés Treviño of Tamaulipas ordered the Matamoros militia to "assist as much as possible the authorities of Brownsville to repulse the aggressions of Cortinas [sic] and his men and to maintain the public peace."[37]

But the Committee of Public Safety never asked for assistance from the Mexican authorities again. The citizens of Brownsville began to place Cortina in a different category than the lawbreakers who had crossed the border in the previous decade. After Cortina's predawn raid, the residents of Brownsville were on edge, and so they fashioned narratives to help make sense of their panic.[38] Some compared the *cortinistas* to Indians. "We are being warred upon by atrocious savages who would as soon beat out the brains of an infant as shoot an undoubted spy," opined the *New Orleans Daily True Delta*.[39] John Hemphill, a U.S. senator from Texas, compared the "ravages of the marauders"

to the "hostilities of the savage."[40] To Somers Kinney, a resident of Brownsville, Cortina was a "Christian Comanche."[41]

Contemporary events suggested another comparison. On October 16, not
even three weeks after Cortina attacked Brownsville, John Brown and eighteen men seized the arsenal at Harpers Ferry, Virginia. Federal troops under
Brevet Colonel Robert E. Lee did not recapture the arsenal until October 18.[42]
The raid on Harpers Ferry raised the specter of a John Brown–like rebellion
in South Texas. "What great difference is there between the outlawry of Opos-
sum Brown, or whatever his name is, and that of Juan Nepomuceno Cortina?" wondered the *New Orleans Daily Picayune*.[43] The *San Antonio Daily
Herald* was even more explicit, attributing the Cortina War to "an organized
system of fanatics of the John Brown stamp, deliberately planned, and executed with a fiendish adroitness."[44] As Texas legislator John L. Haynes
lamented, "Cortina and John Brown got inextricably mixed up."[45] Texans
worried that nonslaveholders would join Cortina's ranks. Rumors circulated
that Cortina intended to ally with the Seminole Indians and the fugitive slaves
who lived alongside them at a military colony in Coahuila.[46] On the eve of
the Civil War, Americans' fear of racial violence verged on hysteria.

A third explanation was that Cortina was a foreigner.[47] Stephen Powers, a
lawyer in Brownsville, scoffed that Cortina "pretends to the rights of American citizenship," but "he takes refuge in Matamoros, he issues his threats there,
he collects his men there."[48] Four of the leading citizens of Brownsville told
Governor Hardin Runnels: "To make him a citizen (his parents being aliens)
he should have resided here (and have been of age) six months before the acceptance of the constitution of Texas by the Congress of the U.S." But, they
argued, "neither *he, nor any of his men*" met these criteria.[49] Two months after
the attack on Brownsville, a grand jury in Cameron County refused to charge
Cortina with treason against his country because no man who shouted "Viva
la República Mexicana!" and who attempted to raise "the flag of Mexico upon
the flag staff" of Fort Brown could be an American citizen. The jurors concluded "without hesitation that the entry upon the city of Brownsville on the
28th of September 1859 was an invasion of American territory by armed Mexicans under the Mexican flag with hostile intentions against the constitutional authorities of the State and Country."[50]

This argument was compelling for two reasons. First, it suited the interests of the state authorities and local merchants who stood to profit from the
return of the U.S. Army. To maintain a military presence in the Lower Valley, the government paid $990,957.10 in contracts, salaries, wages, and other
costs in 1855 and $635,322.77 in 1856. At least some of that money went toward
the local purchase of food and supplies, which the merchants of Brownsville

eagerly provided. Although exact figures are lacking, the state legislator and merchant John L. Haynes of Rio Grande City estimated that by the 1850s, the trade between Brownsville merchants and the U.S. Army amounted to several million dollars.[51] The U.S. Army was a boon to the frontier economy. If Cortina's raid were a foreign invasion, then the U.S. Army would have every reason to return to Brownsville.

Second, this argument was convincing even to those who would not materially benefit because of the uncertainty of Cortina's legal status under state law. Born in Camargo, Tamaulipas, Cortina lived in Matamoros after Texas declared independence and served as a scout under General Pedro Ampudia in the Mexican-American War. By 1850, he had returned to Texas, appearing on that year's census as a resident of Cameron County.[52] Having neither secured nor forfeited U.S. citizenship, Cortina occupied an uncertain status—an uncertainty that gave credibility to the claim that he was a foreigner. Soon it was not just a few men in Brownsville claiming that Cortina was a Mexican citizen. On February 13, 1860, Governor Sam Houston urged Secretary of War John S. Floyd to do something. "The territory of Texas has been invaded," Houston exclaimed.[53] The *New York Times* described the governor as being in a "slightly excited" condition.[54] But the rhetorical shift is telling: Cortina was not a neighbor, guilty of murder, but a foreigner, bent on destruction.

This shift is important, because it raised doubts in Texas about the forces coming from Mexico to help. If Cortina were Mexican, and supported by, as some argued, the "Church party" of Mexico, how could the Matamoros militia be trusted?[55] Over the course of their two stays in Brownsville, the Mexican forces had raised suspicions—and hackles. One citizen feared that they were "more likely to turn against us than otherwise."[56] The Texas journalist George Wilkins Kendall opined, "[How] humiliating it must be to the survivors of the gallant force, which in 1846 defended Fort Brown with such stubborn heroism, to see the day when a Mexican force is called from across the Rio Grande to guard the very spot."[57] Cooperation was giving way to distrust. The consequences of this shift were profound.

If Cortina were a foreign invader, his raid ceased to be a local matter, amenable to local remedies. The Rio Grande, as "a national boundary," required "national defence."[58] Troops from as far away as Kansas and Virginia marched toward Texas. On November 10, Captain William Gerard Tobin arrived in Brownsville, sixteen days after leaving San Antonio with sixty rangers and a commission from Governor Hardin Richard Runnels. The governor had instructed them to arrest anyone "charged with the murder of peaceable citizens" but also to "be prudent."[59] But the night after arriving in Brownsville,

Tobin's rangers lynched Tomás Cabrera, a sixty-year-old *cortinista* lieutenant.[60] They torched the farms and ranches of landowners known to support Cortina, stealing the cattle, horses, and swine that escaped the flames. Rather than cooperate with Mexican forces, Tobin's rangers blamed them for Cortina's success. "The sympathies of many of [the] border inhabitants of Mexican origin on both sides of the river are with Cortina," Tobin wrote.[61] Ranger captain John S. "Rip" Ford reported that Mexicans supplied him with food, weapons, and information about the Americans' whereabouts.[62]

The Texas Rangers did not care to cooperate with their Mexican counterparts—and neither did the three army regiments that arrived in Brownsville on December 6, 1859 under the command of Major Samuel P. Heintzelman. Lacking any personal relationships that might facilitate an ad hoc arrangement for crossing the border, Heintzelman and his Mexican counterpart General Guadalupe Garcia met in January to discuss a formal agreement. Heintzelman nixed Garcia's proposal to allow either army to cross the border in pursuit of bandits. But when Garcia tipped the Americans to Cortina's whereabouts, Heintzelman sent his men and some rangers across the Rio Grande, without the permission of Mexico's military authorities, and proceeded to mistakenly attack the Matamoros National Guard. (The Americans subsequently asserted that the militiamen were in cahoots with Cortina.)[63]

By the time that Robert E. Lee took command of the U.S. Army on the Rio Grande, the Mexican authorities were skeptical of the Americans' intentions. On April 3, 1860, Colonel Lee penned a letter to the governor of Tamaulipas, Andrés Treviño, asking him to "break up and disperse the bands of banditti which have . . . sought protection within the Mexican territory."[64] Governor Treviño, who, five months earlier, ordered the utmost cooperation with the authorities of Brownsville, referred Lee's request to the "federal executive," as it was "of an international character."[65] The local systems of cooperative violence were grinding to a halt.

If violence was a collective action problem, remedied by cross-border cooperation, this shift represented what game theorists term a defection. Historians have ignored the arguments justifying this defection, on the assumption that Cortina's citizenship could brook no serious debate. But because the U.S. Supreme Court ruled that the Treaty of Guadalupe Hidalgo did not apply to Texas, Cortina's citizenship status was, in fact, uncertain. A trial court might have clarified matters, but so too did the violence that began in the early morning hours of September 28, 1859. Defining Cortina as a foreigner undermined local networks of cooperative violence that had helped to maintain order on the Rio Grande since the Treaty of Guadalupe Hidalgo. If Cortina were a foreign invader, the authorities at Brownsville could not plausibly appeal to their counterparts in Matamoros for assistance. As Texans cast Cortina as a foreigner, a local matter became a national outrage. The state and national forces that were sent to turn back the invasion had neither the inclination nor the contacts to activate the networks of cooperative violence that might have contained the conflict. "It will be a long time before the ill-feeling engendered by this outcome can be allayed," Colonel Heintzelman predicted.[66] Indeed, this tension would never be completely eased—not even after Cortina escaped to the Burgos Mountains, the Texas Rangers returned home, and the Rio Grande became, in the words of one American officer, "perfectly quiet."[67]

————

After fighting in the French Intervention—first for Benito Juárez and then briefly for Maximilian—Cortina returned to the Rio Grande as general of the Army of the North. No one questioned his citizenship. If he had once claimed U.S. citizenship, he now cast his lot with Mexico. Almost as soon as he arrived in northern Mexico, his men, smartly dressed in their uniforms, were spotted driving cattle across the Rio Grande.[68] A soldier in the Mexican Army reported that Cortina had sent him and his regiment to guard the crossing of over two hundred stolen beeves from Texas.[69] "Since the arrival of General Juan N. Cortina and his troops upon the frontier, the marauding has increased tenfold," complained Lieutenant Colonel A. McCook.[70]

If Texans blamed Cortina for the Cattle Wars, historians fault larger economic trends.[71] After the U.S. Civil War, a steer that cost only five dollars in Brownsville sold for thirty-six in St. Louis.[72] An entrepreneur named Joseph McCoy saw the "great disparity of Texas values and northern prices" as an opportunity to turn a profit. In 1867, he built a stockyard at the head of the Kansas-Pacific Railroad and started to ship Texas longhorns north. As the demand for cattle increased, so too did the incentives to steal them from Mexico.[73] But economic factors alone cannot explain the increase in crime and the attendant surge in violence. Although livestock prices were increasing, they were not as high in real terms as in the 1850s (graph 5.1). Why did Mexicans and Texans cooperate to stop the mounting violence in the 1850s but not in the 1870s?

Norteños and Texans did not cooperate because local networks, already strained from the Cortina War, were continuing to break down. The vital link between Anglos and Mexicans, after all, was the Tejano elite. L. H. Box helped Mexicans recover their stolen livestock because of his business dealings with Tejanos in Edinburg. The authorities of Reynosa sent reinforcements to Judge F. F. George at the request of the Tejano Ramón Jiménez. But Tejanos found their position in South Texas slipping by the 1870s. A combination of

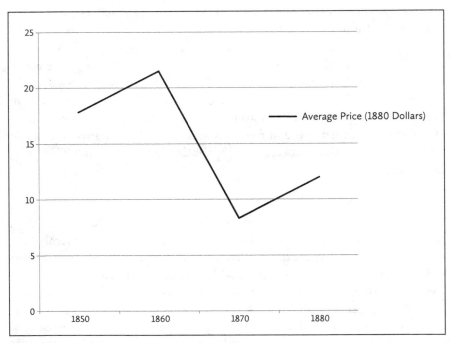

Graph 5.1 The price of cattle in 1880 dollars, 1850–1880

Using county data from the Agricultural Censuses, I divided the value of livestock (both live and slaughtered) by the number of livestock (defined as horses, oxen, cows, and other) to calculate average price. I then adjusted these prices for inflation using Scott Derks's *The Value of a Dollar* (for 1850–1870) and Robert Shiller's *Irrational Exuberance* (for 1871–1880). For data, see Texas, Census of 1850, http://usda.mannlib.cornell.edu/usda/AgCensus Images/1850 /1850a-20.pdf; Agriculture of the United States in 1860, Part III, http://usda.mannlib.cornell .edu/usda/AgCensusImages/1860/1860b-07.pdf; Table 4, General Tables of Agriculture, Census of 1870, http://usda.mannlib.cornell.edu/usda/ AgCensusImages/1870/1870c-04.pdf; Clarence W. Gordon, "Report on Cattle, Sheep, and Swine" (Washington, DC: U.S. Government Printing Office, 1880), 22; Statistics of Agriculture, Tables 8 and 9, Agricultural Census of 1880.

burdensome taxation, costly litigation, and an economic depression that followed the Panic of 1873 forced many to sell their lands and move elsewhere.[74] Stripped of land and status, Tejanos no longer served as the linchpin of the cooperative networks that had once spanned the Rio Grande.

As cooperation decreased, each side blamed the other for acting in bad faith. Mexicans wondered how a mere band of criminals could escape punishment from the U.S. government. The U.S. Consul in Piedras Negras reported that "the Mexican government and the people in general here think that such things could not occur on the American side if these parties were not protected by the authorities."[75] Americans were equally suspicious of their neighbors. Texas Ranger captain L. H. McNelly testified before Congress that the Mexicans "could bring together a force which would overpower five hundred armed men" at "any time within twenty-four hours," but never did so to stop rustlers.[76] "We, Americans, living in this county, live all the time in dread," said Deputy-Collector L. H. Box. He had given up notifying Mexicans if their stolen livestock turned up in Edinburg, because he feared for his life.[77] Given the difficulties of convicting rustlers after the fact—the accused party could simply claim to have purchased the livestock, ignorant of its unlawful provenance—the elimination of these informal arrangements between Mexican and Texan officials spelled the end for the most effective means of catching rustlers: chasing them across the Rio Grande in hot pursuit.

Transnational crime went increasingly unchecked as a result. Ranchers gave up on pursuing their stolen livestock across the Rio Grande. Celio Díaz, a stock raiser from Gigedo, testified that it was "useless" to try to recover rustled animals by legal means.[78] Texan authorities did not know as many of their neighbors across the border and as a result, required "deposits and other proofs which are difficult to produce" when they claimed their livestock.[79] In February 1869, rustlers stole five horses and a mule from Rancho de los Conales near Montemorelos, Nuevo León. Their owner was Francisco Zepeda Cavazos, one of the men who had previously recovered his stolen livestock with the help of L. H. Box, the customs collector of Edinburg. Now, when Zepeda found one of the horses outside Edinburg, the sheriff would not return Zepeda's horse without "a certification that he had not sold the animals." By the time Zepeda presented the required document to the sheriff, the horse was gone.[80]

The mounting disorder did not immediately draw the attention of the U.S. government and the larger public.[81] The U.S. Army would defend against Indians and foreign invaders, but the state authorities were tasked with policing criminals, and the rustlers under Cortina seemed to occupy the last category. Texans continued to insist that their foes were more than petty criminals, using the same arguments that they had perfected after his attack on Brownsville in 1859. "The men engaged in this work are Mexicans, well mounted, carrying fire-arms of the most approved pattern, and not infrequently belong to the regular army of Mexico," reported one official.[82] Inspector-General N. H. Davis insisted that their aims were more grandiose than rustling livestock. "These Mexicans openly boast that they can and yet will, clean out the Americans south of the Nueces River," Davis wrote to his superiors. "They are fast doing it; they claim this country is theirs."[83] The citizens of Brownsville claimed that "the people between the Nueces and the Rio Grande" had suffered at the hands of "Mexican marauders" for too long. This was a "depredatory war," and it demanded a federal response.[84]

The citizenship of the marauders was important because it would determine which authorities were responsible for stopping them. "It is because each state or nation has undertaken to restrain its people from making war on the people of its neighbors that the law of nations forbids an armed force from entering the territory of another," Governor Richard Coke pontificated.[85] The solution was not greater cooperation. If the Mexican government could not restrain its citizens from crossing into Texas, Americans believed that they had the right not to join forces with the Mexican Army but to do the job for them. Impatient to put an end to the raids, Governor Richard Coke ordered the Texas Rangers to pursue rustlers into Mexico—with or without permission from the Mexican government.

Now the authorities in Washington took note of the violence in the Rio Grande valley, not because they saw the rustlers as foreign invaders but because Texans' response to these incursions threatened to start another war with Mexico—a war that the United States could ill afford. As cooperation between local authorities grew strained, and the national governments failed to negotiate an agreement to take the place of these arrangements, the result was disorder. In the absence of cooperation, local forces were ineffective. The "well-known animosity existing on the border between the two races" made them unsuited to the task, explained the commander of the Department of Texas, General E. O. C. Ord. Only "well-disciplined regulars" could prevent another war.[86] The commanding officer of Fort Brown came to the same conclusion, warning that the cattle raids in Texas "may lead to a predatory war on either side or [sic] the river, eventually producing a conflict between the two nations."[87]

The solution to the violence of the Cattle Wars was not greater cooperation, as González's theory would predict, but a stronger presence of the national government on the U.S.-Mexico border. The local interests that might have encouraged cooperation did not triumph for two reasons. First, the networks of cooperation had broken down. Second, foreign criminals now seemed to merit national attention, not because they represented an invasion but because they might cause one. In a process similar to that described by Brandon Morgan, the narratives about violence mattered as much as, if not more than, the number of casualties in determining whether the U.S. government would take action. In 1859, the authorities in Washington tried to understand the reasons that Cortina attacked Brownsville, in order to determine whether the conflict was "a matter involving local laws and interests" or one that "pertained to the honor or interests" of the United States.[88] By the end of the Cattle Wars, however, any crime committed by an alien deserved a national response, for it might provoke an international war. Foreignness had become a proxy for intention.

———

"Cortina is simply a creation," General William Tecumseh Sherman testified before the Senate in 1877.[89] This essay has traced how Cortina's creation, first as a foreign invader and later as a foreigner who might cause an invasion, undermined the cooperation that seemed to serve the interests of both Mexicans and Americans. Crucial to this story is the question of citizenship. After Cortina attacked Brownsville in the early morning hours of September 28, 1859, the local authorities activated the networks of cooperative violence that had helped to maintain order on the Rio Grande during the 1850s. Meanwhile, the residents of Brownsville cast Cortina as a foreign invader—a move that undermined the logic of local cooperation. If Cortina were hoisting a Mexican flag over his camp, how could the Matamoros militiamen be trusted to repulse him? This rhetoric also ensured the arrival of state and national forces on the Rio Grande. These soldiers were more numerous and, in some instances, better trained and equipped, but their commanders proved unwilling and unable to participate in the cooperative violence that might have ended the conflict faster and more effectively. "The Rangers were burning all— friends and foes," Heintzelman reported.[90]

By casting Cortina as a foreigner, Texans eventually made him into one. When Cortina returned to the Rio Grande in 1870, he wore the uniform of a Mexican military commander. As Tejanos like Cortina left South Texas, local networks of cooperative violence disintegrated. The result was a "saturnalia of crime, violence, and rapine."[91] If the federal government defended against foreign invaders, and the state authorities were tasked with policing criminals, who was responsible for foreign criminals, like the rustlers acting on Cortina's orders? Texans used the same rhetorical moves as they had in the wake of his attack on Brownsville. They argued that though he did not fight pitched battles, his intentions were nonetheless bellicose: to return the Nueces Strip to Mexico. What convinced the federal authorities to intervene, however, was that this transnational crime might provoke a war between Mexico and the United States. By this logic, any foreigner, whether a petty criminal or a uniformed soldier, was a potential concern of the national government.

This essay draws three broader conclusions. First, it seeks to move beyond the question of whether Cortina exploited widespread prejudice for his own gain or whether he sincerely sought to remedy it. To argue that racism prompted the Cortina War and continued unchanged after it is to cast racism as static, ignoring the ways in which its violence is rendered legitimate: by drawing distinctions between Mexicans and Americans. Second, this chapter reminds us that although cooperation is a regular feature of the U.S.-Mexico borderlands, these alliances—who joins them and to what end—are variable. Such shifts are crucial, because they help us to see that violence, far from being endemic to the region, results when these networks of cooperative violence are disrupted. Third, and relatedly, this argument suggests that the U.S.-Mexico border is not always more dangerous than other regions, like Los Angeles or Chicago.[92] But it has gained a reputation for violence because these episodes have come to be seen as issues of national security in a way that a shooting in an inner city does not. From 1850 to 1864, the homicide rate in Los Angeles was 209 per one hundred thousand residents—a number comparable to that of Ciudad Juárez more recently.[93] But the U.S. government did not dispatch commissioners to southern California. Nor were the lurid reports of murder in the *Los Angeles Star* reprinted in newspapers across the United States. This was a fact that the Committee on Military Affairs recognized during its investigation of the Cattle Wars. "Historically, is the number of people killed in that region any greater than the number killed in any of our western mining Territories during the same space of time?" a senator asked, trying to understand the scale of the violence. "No," General Sherman responded. "I think not."[94]

Notes

1. From 1837 to 1855, Mexicans officially celebrated independence on two separate occasions: September 16, the day that Hidalgo issued his call to arms, and September 27, when Iturbide and his Army of the Three Guarantees marched into Mexico City. See Robert H. Duncan, "Embracing a Suitable Past: Independence Celebrations under Mexico's Second Empire, 1864–6," *Journal of Latin American Studies* 30, no. 2 (May 1998): 249–77. Jerry Thompson writes that independence had been rescheduled for "unknown reasons" but a likelier explanation is that this fiesta was to commemorate Iturbide's victory. Jerry Thompson, *Cortina: Defending the Mexican Name in Texas* (College Station: Texas A&M University Press, 2007), 39.

2. Arnoldo De León, *They Called Them Greasers: Anglo Attitudes toward Mexicans in Texas, 1821–1900* (Austin: University of Texas Press, 1983), 54.

3. For more on how culture can inform self-interest, see David R. Roediger, *The Wages of Whiteness: Race and the Making of the American Working Class* (New York: Verso, 1991); and Neil Foley, *The White Scourge: Mexicans, Blacks, and Poor Whites in Texas Cotton Culture* (Berkeley: University of California Press, 1997).

4. Robert Luther Thompson, *Wiring a Continent: The History of the Telegraph Industry in the United States, 1832–1866* (Princeton, NJ: Princeton University Press, 1947).

5. For "naturalized American citizen," see Mexican Consul in Brownsville to M. Treviño, Secretary of State, November 1, 1859, 4-1-5474, Archivo Histórico de la Secretaría de Relaciones Exteriores (hereafter, AHSRE). For similar rhetoric, see José Antonio Navarro to Juan N. Cortina, January 4, 1860, folder 36, box 2014/109-1, Records of the Governors, Samuel Houston, Texas State Archives (hereafter, TSA). For examples of Cortina being described as a foreigner, see E. H. Vontruss to Governor Hardin Richard Runnels, Vattana, Texas, Novem-

ber 16, 1859, folder 23, box 308, Hardin Richard Runnels Papers, TSA; Edward J. Davis, F. W. Latham, Stephen Powers, Robert B. Kingsury to Hardin Runnels, November 16, 1859, folder 23, box 308, Hardin Richard Runnels Papers, TSA; John S. Ford to Runnels, Goliad, November 22, 1859, folder 23, box 308, Hardin Richard Runnels Papers, TSA.

6. Charles William Goldfinch, "Juan N. Cortina, 1824–1892: A Re-Appraisal" (PhD diss., University of Chicago, 1949); Thompson, *Cortina*; De Leon, *They Called Them Greasers*, 54.

7. Opinion, delivered by Justice Campbell, John F. McKinney v. Manuel Saviego, and Pilar, His Wife, 29 US 235, Supreme Court of the United States (December Term 1855).

8. For another model of cross-border cooperation, see Peter J. Kastor, "'Motives of Peculiar Urgency': Local Diplomacy in Louisiana, 1803–1821," *William and Mary Quarterly* 58, no. 4 (October 2001): 819–48.

9. Robert M. Cover, "Violence and the Word" (1986), Faculty Scholarship Series, Paper 2708, http://digitalcommons.law.yale.edu/fss_papers/2708; Austin Sarat and Thomas R. Kearns, eds., *Law's Violence*, Amherst Series in Law, Jurisprudence, and Social Thought (Ann Arbor: University of Michigan Press, 1992).

10. Tamar Herzog, *Frontiers of Possession: Spain and Portugal in Europe and the Americas* (Cambridge, MA: Harvard University Press, 2015); Sheila McManus, *The Line Which Separates: Race, Gender, and the Making of the Alberta-Montana Borderlands* (Edmonton: University of Alberta Press, 2005); Jane T. Merritt, *At the Crossroads: Indians and Empires on a Mid-Atlantic Frontier, 1700–1763* (Williamsburg, VA: Omohundro Institute, 2003); Peter Sahlins, *Boundaries: The Making of France and Spain in the Pyrenees* (Berkeley: University of California Press, 1991).

11. Section 8, Treaty of Guadalupe Hidalgo.

12. Opinion, delivered by Justice Campbell, John F. McKinney v. Manuel Saviego, and Pilar, His Wife, 29 US 235, Supreme Court of the United States (December Term 1855).

13. This decision was particularly troublesome for those who lived on the strip of land between the Nueces River and the Rio Grande. Not until after the Treaty of Guadalupe Hidalgo did Texas exercise de facto jurisdiction over the Nueces Strip. As a result, lawyers made the case that the treaty did apply to the region, where there were "no civil officers . . . no tax collectors, no judges, no elections, no organized counties; in fact, no organized civil government" before 1848—an argument that would secure for Mexican residents the protections of the Treaty of Guadalupe Hidalgo. See De Baca v. U.S., U.S. Court of Claims, May 20, 1901, 37 Ct. Cl. 482, 1900 WL 1529.

14. Report of the Committee on Public Lands, December 15, 1859, *Journal of the Senate of Texas, 8th Legislature* (Austin, TX: John Marshall & Co., State Printers, 1860), 137; Constitution of the Republic of Texas (1836), General Provisions, sec. 10.

15. C. J. Wheeler, Majority Opinion, Eleazer Kilpatrick et al. v. Rosalia Sisneros et al., 23 Tex. 113, Texas Supreme Court. See also Hardy v. De Leon, 5 Tex. 211, Mcilwaine v. Coxe's Lessee, 4 Cranch 209; Swift v. Herrera, 9 Tex 263, Jones v. Montes, 15 Tex 351; Jones v. McMasters, 20 How. 8; Paul v. Perez, 7 Tex. 338 (1851); Texas v. De Casinova, 1 Tex. 401 (1848).

16. Thompson, *Cortina*, 32.

17. David Montejano, *Anglos and Mexicans in the Making of Texas* (Austin: University of Texas Press, 1987), 28–29; James David Nichols, "The Line of Liberty: Runaway Slaves and Fugitive Peons in the Texas-Mexico Borderlands," *Western Historical Quarterly* 44, no. 4 (2013): 424.

18. Thompson, *Cortina*, 35.

19. George T. Díaz, *Border Contraband: A History of Smuggling across the Rio Grande*, 1st ed. (Austin: University of Texas Press, 2015).

20. Armando C. Alonzo, *Tejano Legacy: Rancheros and Settlers in South Texas, 1734–1900* (Albuquerque: University of New Mexico Press, 1998), 124.

21. Alonzo, *Tejano Legacy*, 126.

22. Alonzo, *Tejano Legacy*, 131.

23. Montejano, *Anglos and Mexicans in the Making of Texas*, 50; Alonzo, *Tejano Legacy*, 283.

24. Richard White, *The Middle Ground: Indians, Empires, and Republics in the Great Lakes Region, 1650–1815* (Cambridge: Cambridge University Press, 2010). It is interesting to consider why the concept of a middle ground, so popular among other subfields of history, has not yet been incorporated into our understanding of South Texas.

25. Testimony of Francisco Cavazos, 1873, box 4, 7-12-20, AHSRE. For Box's contacts with the Tejano community, see Alonzo, *Tejano Legacy*, 131. For other examples of cross-border cooperation, see 2° Constitutional Judge to C. Antonio Rodriguez, July 10, 1848, AHSRE, 7-12-20, box 4; 2° Constitutional Judge to C. Eusebio Guajardo, July 14, 1848, AHSRE, 7-12-20, box 4; 1° Constitutional Judge to S. B. Baquelos, October 2, 1848, AHSRE, 7-12-20, box 4; 1° Constitutional Judge to Justice of the Peace of Edinburg, April 17, 1851, AHSRE, 7-12-20, box 2.

26. 1° Constitutional Judge to Justice of the Peace of Edinburg, April, 17, 1851, AHSRE, 7-12-20, box 2. For other examples of Tejanos or Mexicans traveling in Texas helping their Mexican neighbors, see Certification of F. Saunt Le Roy, Notary of Rio Grande City, September 5, 1851, "Acta verbal promovida por Dn Mariano Lozano, contra Valentin Guerra por el robo de una mula que vendió en Texas de la propiedad del primero," Suprema Tribunal de Justicia, Archivo General del Estado de Nuevo León (hereafter, AGENL).

27. For an example of authorities helping each other to defend against Indians, see Antonio Orteaga to Alcalde Sr 1 Constitucional de Múzquiz, June 30, 1860, folder 134, box 11, second chronology, Múzquiz Collection, Beinecke Library. For more on cooperation, see Alice Baumgartner, "'The Line of Positive Safety': Borders and Boundaries in the Rio Grande Valley, 1848–80," *Journal of American History* 101, no. 4 (March 2015): 1106–22.

28. Testimony of Trinidad Flores, AHSRE, 7-12-20, box 4.

29. Investigation of the Mayor of Reynosa, May 8, 1856, AHSRE, 7-12-20, box 4. Military Commander of Reynosa to Mayor of Reynosa, May 21, 1856, AHSRE, 7-12-20, box 4.

30. F. F. George to Dr. Ramón Jiménez, June 15, 1858, AHSRE, 7-12-20, box 4.

31. Ayuntamiento of Reynosa to Commander of the Line, June 18, 1858, AHSRE, 7-12-20, box 4.

32. For how overlapping jurisdictions or jurisdictional voids create unclear protocols in the borderlands, see Katrina Jagodinsky and Pablo Mitchell, eds., *Beyond the Borders of the Law: Critical Legal Histories of the North American West* (Lawrence: University Press of Kansas, 2018).

33. D. E. Twiggs to Assistant Adjutant General Thomas, September 8, 1857, Letters Sent by the Department of Texas, vol. 1, M1165, National Archives and Records Association (NARA).

34. John Work to G. W. Bauvleck, Esq., March 7, 1855, TSA, Texas Adjutant General Records (TAGR), folder 381–9.

35. Will Fowler, ed., *Forceful Negotiations: The Origins of the Pronunciamiento in Nineteenth-Century Mexico* (Lincoln: University of Nebraska Press, 2011).

36. "Proclamation: Juan Nepomuceno Cortina to the Inhabitants of the State of Texas, and Especially to Those of the City of Brownsville," 36th Cong., 1st Sess., 1860, H. Exec. Doc. 52, 71.

37. Andrés Treviño to Secretary of War, November 10, 1859, 481.3/7595, Archivo Histórico de la Secretaría de la Defensa Nacional (AHSDN).

38. John S. Ford to Governor Hardin Richard Runnels, June 2, 1858, Hardin Richard Runnels Papers, folder 7, box 308–27, TSA.

39. *New Orleans Daily True Delta*, December 10, 1859.

40. John Hemphill to the President, October 8, 1859, 36th Cong., 1st Sess., 1860, H. Exec. Doc. 52, 373.

41. *Corpus Christi Ranchero*, December 3, 1859.

42. For more on Brown's raid, see David S. Reynolds, *John Brown, Abolitionist: The Man Who Killed Slavery, Sparked the Civil War, and Seeded Civil Rights* (New York: Knopf, 2009); Tony Horowitz, *Midnight Rising: John Brown and the Raid That Sparked the Civil War* (New York: Henry Holt, 2011); Eugene L. Meyer, *Five for Freedom: The African American Soldiers in John Brown's Army* (Chicago: Chicago Review Press, 2018).

43. *New Orleans Daily Picayune*, November 20, 1859.

44. *San Antonio Daily Herald*, n.d.

45. *Austin Southern Intelligencer*, n.d.

46. John S. Ford to Governor Hardin Runnels, November 22, 1859, Hardin Runnels Papers, TSA; Leonardo Manio, Ayuntamiento de la Villa de Reynosa, to Jesus Botello, Jefatura Politica del Distrito del Norte de Tamaulipas, AHSRE, 4-1-5474, f. 127.

47. War Department to General Taylor, May 28, 1845, *Executive Documents*, 30th Cong., 1st Sess., H. Doc. No. 60, 79–80. See also Gary Clayton Anderson, *The Conquest of Texas: Ethnic Cleansing in the Promised Land, 1820–1875* (Norman: University of Oklahoma Press, 2005).

48. Stephen Power to President Buchanan, October 18, 1859, Letters Received by the Office of the Adjutant General, M567, R615, NARA. For other examples, see *Corpus Christi Ranchero*, January 5, 1861 and F. W. Latham to President James Buchanan, *Difficulties on Southwestern Frontier, Message from the President of the United States, Communicating, in Compliance with a Resolution of the House, Information in Reference to the Difficulties on the Southwestern Frontier*, 1860, United States, Congress, 36th Cong., 1st Sess., 1859–60, 74.

49. Edward Davis, F. W. Latham, Stephen Powers, Robert Kingsbury to Hardin Runnels, November 30, 1859, folder 23, box 308, Runnels Papers, TSA.

50. District Court, Cameron County, 12th Judicial District, November 14, 1859, TSA, Records of the Governors, Samuel Houston, 2014/109-1, folder 34. See also Report of Mr. Britton, Chairman of the Committee on the Militia, February 1, 1860, *Journal of the Senate of Texas, 8th Legislature* (Austin, TX: John Marshall & Co., State Printers, 1860), 419.

51. Alonzo, *Tejano Legacy*, 99–100.

52. Thompson, *Cortina*, 256.

53. "The Rio Grande Affair," *Navarro Express*, March 24, 1860.

54. "The Texan Frontier," *New York Times*, March 19, 1860.

55. John S. Ford to Hardin Richard Runnells, November 22, 1859, folder 23, box 308, Hardin Richard Runnels Papers, TSA.

56. "Cortina, the Leader, and His Character," October 10, 1859, *New Orleans Daily Picayune*, 39–40.

57. *New Orleans Daily Picayune*, November 20, 1859.

58. John L. Haynes to John Hemphill, U.S. Senate, October 18, 1859, Letters Received by the Office of the Adjutant General, microfilm, M567, R615, NARA.

59. Runnels to Tobin, October 13, 1859, folder 23, box 308, Hardin R. Runnels Papers, TSA.

60. Robert Utley, *Lone Star Justice: The First Century of the Texas Rangers* (New York: Berkley Books, 2003), 111.

61. Tobin to Runnels, November 27, 1859, Sam Houston Papers, folder 24, box 308, Hardin R. Runnels Papers, TSA.

62. Ford to Runnels, November 22, 1859, folder 23, box 308, Runnels Papers, TSA.

63. John Ford, *Rip Ford's Texas* (Austin: University of Texas Press, 2010), 295; George Stoneman and John S. Ford to C. W. Thomas, March 18, 1860, *Troubles on the Texas Frontier*, 36th Cong., 1st Sess., Exec. Doc. No. 81, 80–81.

64. John H. Jenkins, ed., *Robert E. Lee on the Rio Grande: The Correspondence of Robert E. Lee on the Texas Border, 1860* (Austin: Jenkins, 1988), 12–13.

65. Andrés Treviño to Col. R. E. Lee, April 15, 1860, Letters Received by the Adjutant General, microfilm, NARA.

66. Heintzelman to Lee, March 1, 1860, 36th Cong., 1st Sess., 1860, H. Exec. Doc. 52, 13.

67. Quoted in Thompson, *Cortina*, 96.

68. A. McCook, Lieut. Col. 10th Infantry, to Acting Assistant Adjutant General, Department of Texas, March 19, 1872, U.S. Commission to Texas, box 2, National Archives, College Park, MD.

69. Extracts from the report of the United States commissioners for inquiring into the depredations committed on the Texas frontiers, appointed under joint resolution of Congress, approved May 7, 1872, 42d Cong., 3d Sess., H. Exec. Doc. 39, 103.

70. A. McCook to, Thomas F. Wilson, August 2, 1871, *Report and Accompanying Documents*, 85.

71. See Martaelena Negrete Salas, "La frontera texana y el abigeato 1848–1872," *Historia Mexicana* 31 (1981): 88; Montejano, *Anglos and Mexicans in the Making of Texas*, 53.

72. Kristin Hoganson, "Meat in the Middle: Converging Borderlands in the U.S. Midwest, 1865–1900," *Journal of American History* 98, no. 4 (March 2012): 1042. James E. Sherow, *The Chisholm Trail: Joseph McCoy's Great Gamble* (Norman: University of Oklahoma Press, 2018), 39

73. Joseph McCoy, *Historic Sketch of the Cattle Trade of the West and Southwest* (Kansas City, MO: Ramsey, Millett, and Hudson, 1874), 40.

74. Montejano, *Anglos and Mexicans in the Making of Texas*, 55; Commander A. McCook of Fort Brown to Acting Adjutant General, April 4, 1872, National Archives, College Park, MD, U.S. Commission to Texas, Miscellaneous Records, RG 76, box 2, vol. 17.

75. US Commercial Agency at Piedras Negras to the Second Assistant Secretary of State, April 9, 1872, *Despatches from United States Consuls at Piedras Negras, Coahuila*, microfilm, U.S. State Department Records in the National Archives, Washington, DC: National Archives, 1868–1906.

76. Testimony of McNelly, January 24, 1876, *Report and Accompanying Documents*, 169.

77. *Report and Accompanying Documents*, vii.

78. Report of Municipal President Manuel Hernández, Gigedo, Coahuila, September 25, 1877, AGEC, FSXIX, C8, F9, E2, 4F.

79. Testimony of Casiano Martinez, Rancho de las Norias, AHSRE, 7-12-20, box 2.

80. Testimony of Francisco Zepeda Cavazos, AHSRE, 7-12-20, box 2.

81. The rates of violence in Los Angeles, for instance, were higher even than the (probably exaggerated) statistics from the Robb Commission suggest. See John Mack Faragher, *Eternity Street: Violence and Justice in Frontier Los Angeles* (New York: W. W. Norton, 2016).

82. Extracts from the report of the United States commissioners for inquiring into the depredations committed on the Texas frontiers, appointed under joint resolution of Congress, approved May 7, 1872, 42d Cong., 3d Sess. H. Exec. Doc. 39, 99.

83. Special report of Inspector-General N. H. Davis, United States Army San Antonio, Tex., May 14, 1875 to Inspector General R. B. Marcy, War Department Washington D.C., 44th Cong., 1st Sess., H. Rep. 343, P. 143, 134.

84. Official Copy of the Proceedings of a Meeting of the Citizens of Brownsville, August 16, 1872, box 2, U.S. Commission to Mexico, National Archives, College Park, MD.

85. Richard Coke to Attorney General Williams, n.d., *Report and Accompanying Documents,* 161.

86. "Report of Brigadier-General E.O.C. Ord," San Antonio, October 1, 1877, *Foreign Relations of the United States,* 79.

87. McCook to Wilson, August 2, 1871, 45th Cong., 2d Sess., Serial 1824, Rep. 701, 85–86.

88. "The Mexican Frontier," *New York Times,* March 9, 1860.

89. "Testimony Taken by the Committee on Military Affairs in Relation to the Texas Border Troubles" 45th Cong., 2d Sess., Misc. Doc. No. 64 (Washington, DC: Government Printing Office, 1878), 35.

90. Samuel P. Heintzelman Journals, December 16, 1859, quoted in Thompson, *Cortina,* 74.

91. "Report of the Grand Jury," March 25, 1872, *Report and Accompanying Documents,* 92.

92. Faragher, *Eternity Street.*

93. Faragher, *Eternity Street,* f. 263.

94. "Testimony Taken by the Committee on Military Affairs in Relation to the Texas Border Troubles" 45th Cong., 2d Sess., Misc. Doc. No. 64 (Washington, DC: Government Printing Office, 1878), 24.

Figure 6.1 "Mexican side, pontoon bridge over Rio Grande River," showing view into Matamoros, ca. 1866. Courtesy U.S. Library of Congress.

Chapter 6

Violence, Crime, and the Limitations of State Power in the U.S.-Mexico Borderlands, 1848–1875

TIMOTHY BOWMAN

In January of 1850, a thief from Mexico stole some property from Charles Stillman, a wealthy merchant from Brownsville, Texas, just north of the U.S.-Mexico border. Stillman responded by assembling a posse that traveled across the border the next day to the nearby Mexican village of Palmito Ranch. Upon arriving, Stillman's men gathered some of the locals together, tied them up, and whipped them until they confessed the perpetrator's identity. The victims gave up the name of Juan Chapa Guerra, who lived in the nearby village of Ranchito. Stillman's men found Chapa Guerra and dragged him back across the border to Texas, where they subsequently tortured and murdered him. Only after some time did Stillman and his men learn that they had lynched the wrong person: the perpetrator of the original crime was a Mexican named Juan Chapa *García*. Adding insult to injury, the murder went completely unpunished.[1]

Texas-Mexico border residents frequently complained of crime and violence—often, transborder crime—after the U.S.-Mexico border's establishment in 1848.[2] Crime most commonly took the form of livestock theft, but assaults and murders were not uncommon. Twenty-two years after Chapa Guerra's murder—on May 7, 1872, to be precise—a U.S. congressional commission appointed by President Ulysses S. Grant that included Thomas P. Robb of Georgia, as well as Richard H. Savage and Fabius J. Mead of Mississippi, arrived in Brownsville and began deposing American witnesses who had allegedly lost property to Mexican thieves.[3] In response to the "Robb Commission's" staggering claims—property damages, they argued, reached into the millions of dollars—President Sebastián Lerdo de Tejada of Mexico sent a group of officials north to the Mexico-Texas border in the fall of 1872; La Comisión Pesquisidora not only dismissed the Robb Commission's claims as extravagant but also produced a litany of its own claims relating to cattle thefts, assaults, and murders, all allegedly committed by Texans and American Indians in northern Mexico. The resulting drama led to increased calls for greater state presences in the form of military forces and greater border policing on both sides of the line.

The border's establishment in 1848 did not in itself give people a reason to be especially violent, but its appearance as a new geopolitical abstraction meant that border spaces could serve as a safe haven for people committing certain crimes due to the fact that local, municipal, or federal law could only properly be enforced on one side of the border or the other, barring extreme circumstances or perhaps extradition treaties. Border violence from 1848 to the 1870s is thus instructive for a multitude of reasons. While the tendency to think of the border in such dichotomous terms as "open or closed" might be easy or even natural, doing so runs the danger of blurring the very promise of borderlands history, itself: illuminating the human agency and lived experiences of people in borderlands spaces. As such, the arrival of both the Robb Commission and La Comisión Pesquisidora in the borderlands requires subjugation to the desires of borderlanders themselves. The commissioners represented each nation state at the border because Americans and Mexicans had, essentially, called for their presence through complaints about transborder crime and violence.

Ultimately, this essay makes two arguments: first, people on both sides of the border, themselves, called for greater state intervention as a potential solution to the problems of transborder crime and violence during the 1870s. Given that the logic of violence had changed due to the border's bifurcation of the region, people on both sides thus envisioned federal solutions to what had previously been local or regional problems. Second, the states' resulting presences in the Mexico-Texas border region never served as a "cure-all" for crime or violence in the Weberian sense of a state's responsibility to monopolize violence within its own territorial boundaries. Because of this, although the Mexican and U.S. federal governments expressed alarm at the seemingly commonplace nature of transborder crime and violence during the 1870s, the slipshod nature of states' ability to control modern borderlines meant that crossing the border to commit questionable acts can also be understood as demonstrations of agency that borderlanders expressed in contradistinction to state power. This is a significant lesson, given the cacophony of calls in the twentieth- and twenty-first-century U.S. political arenas for the federal government to "secure" the U.S.-Mexico border. The ultimate inability of each state to completely monopolize border violence after developing an increased consciousness of it during the 1870s shows that fully securing or closing the border is a historical anachronism at best, if not a complete fantasy.

At heart, the members of the two commissions served as interpreters of the past, not unlike professional historians, despite clearly suspect levels of objectivity. The "dueling commissions" of the 1870s are instructive regarding each nation's perceptions of the recent past in the borderlands (both at the regional and federal levels), perceptions of border violence among Mexicans and U.S. nationals, and Mexican and U.S. federal intervention into the borderlands. Interestingly, the members of the Comisión Pesquisidora sought a more direct federal introduction of certain useful mechanisms to "close" the borderline itself than did their U.S. counterparts. Mexico's government had three reasons for wanting a more policed border with Texas: first, it would stop Americans from committing acts of crime and violence against *norteños* (people living in northern Mexico); second, it would stop Native Americans from crossing the border and doing the same; and third, it would keep Mexican nationals from leaving the country and moving north of the border to work on American ranches, farms, and railroads, which was a fast-growing problem during the 1870s.[4] In an interesting historical flip, then, it was the Mexican government that dreamed of closing or monitoring the international border during this early period, while the U.S. federal government made no such promises. In fact, Americans in late-nineteenth-century South Texas who sought land, cattle, and perhaps most importantly, Mexican labor had little reason to want a closed border. The Texas state capital in Austin did, however, reconstitute the Texas Rangers to—in the words of one historian— "extend white hegemony to regions beyond Austin's control."[5] Border policing, from the Texas side, was thus also a necessary protection against violence from across the Rio Grande.

Studying violence across the Rio Grande during the nineteenth century also promises to push the field of borderlands history in new directions. In their seminal historiographical statement on the field in the *Journal of American History*, historians Samuel Truett and Pekka Hämäläinen argue that work on violence "has the potential to reconfigure the foundations of borderlands history." In their view, borderlands historians "have tended to equate borderlands with accommodation, asking how they revolved around conciliatory networks. New work on borderlands violence highlights different networks; by showing how violence can simultaneously divide, connect, break, and revitalize societies, it demonstrates how borderlands communities could be locked into long-standing relationships that endured despite—and at times because of—the violence."[6]

As this essay will show, those "long-standing relationships" that some borderlanders became locked into were as members of the Mexican or U.S. federal states. Some people in the 1870s Mexico-Texas borderlands, at least, became either *more* Mexican or *more* American specifically because of the region's endemic violence. Bloodshed clearly divided people in this shared transnational frontier space, but by the 1870s, calls for a policed border in turn led to a greater sense of belonging in either the American or Mexican national communities. In the process, frontier-style interactions between peoples of diverse backgrounds gave way to a modern borderline that divided two nation states—as well as two different peoples, Americans on one side and Mexicans on the other—more clearly.[7]

Federal Limitations and Disinterest in the Early U.S.-Mexico Borderlands

Both Mexico and the United States experienced long periods of massive disruption during the mid-nineteenth century—for Mexico, the War of the Reform and the French Intervention, and for the United States, the Civil War and Reconstruction eras—to the extent that neither nation could conceivably address the issue of controlling the border before the late nineteenth century. As historian Luis García notes, "informal agreements among regional forces" stretching across the new borderline effectively demonstrate the degree to which neither Mexico City nor Washington, D.C., could exert control over the Rio Grande borderlands during the mid-nineteenth century.[8] Mexico's first substantial act of governance in the region was the establishment of the Zona Libre in March of 1858—a six- to eight-mile-wide free-trade zone in Tamaulipas stretching from Matamoros on the coast to just west of Nuevo Laredo—which only further encouraged border crossing and transnational or transcultural blurring. Governor Ramón Guerra of Tamaulipas was the official who decreed the Zona Libre, which provides circumstantial evidence of the Mexican federal government's relative powerlessness in the borderlands during the late 1850s.[9]

Evidence from official records suggests that both the federal governments in Washington, D.C., and Mexico City gave scant attention to national control of their shared border spaces before the 1870s. The Ulysses S. Grant administration had a political ally in Austin, Texas, during this time period that might explain Grant's willingness to finally take the cries of South Texas borderlanders more seriously than he might otherwise have done—that person was the Radical Republican governor of Texas Edmund J. Davis, who led the state from 1870 to 1873.[10] Direct appeals to Grant from the people of South Texas increased during Davis's governorship. On August 28, 1872, George Davis of Brownsville wrote to Grant in order to "request the President of the United States to use the powers of our government . . . to repel or prevent the constant incursions upon our soil." Davis's letter came on the heels of numerous other outcries that spurred congressional action on the matter. Other appeals to Grant noted that 1872 was an election year, such as that of Joseph A. Haden and James A. Millican of Austin: "As the Fall election [is] approaching, we feel it our duty to confer with you in behalf of the voters of our section, as regards the Mexican depredations on our Frontier: to learn your views in regard to its protection. Every one is in favor of a war, and we think that by some decided action in the case, you could gain the majority in our State; as we know several who are willing to vote, and even canvas, for such a president."[11]

The fantasy of a Republican incumbent carrying deeply Confederate and Democratic Texas in the 1872 election aside, such entreaties exemplify that north of the Rio Grande, it was Texans who called for federal government action to nationalize and protect the border. Politically and geographically, the problem was remote to Grant and Washington, D.C. It would not even be until 1874, two years after the congressional investigations, that President Grant signed a bill authorizing the expenditure of $100,000 to build telegraph wires between a number of the U.S. Army bases in the region.[12] Clearly, the Texas-Mexico borderlands were still not of great concern to the U.S. federal government. The federal government had larger problems, such as the tumultuous reconstruction of the United States following the U.S. Civil War, which served as a distraction.

Arguably, Mexico experienced the first stirrings of modern nationalism with the 1854 Revolution of Ayulta and the subsequent period known as "The War of the Reform"—during which Mexican liberals overthrew Santa Anna, leading to the eventual establishment of the liberal Constitution of 1857—but in reality, by the 1870s the Mexican federal government had also only recently become concerned with the borderlands.[13] In other words, as in the case of South Texans, the maturing nation-state served yet only limited real-world benefits for *norteños*, if any at all. *Hacendados* in the northern states of Nuevo León and Coahuila had lost thousands of *peones* to Texas since the establishment of the borderline in 1848. "The institution of servants," noted one observer, "cannot be sustained." Furthermore, Antonio Moreno, a senator from the northern state of Sonora, which borders Arizona, noted during the late 1870s that "nobody changes nationalities to assume a worse condition, and it is very dangerous to see just beyond the conventional line prosperity and wealth, and on this side destitution and poverty."[14] Northerners' losses of laborers to the United States, combined with the issue of transborder violence, meant that the border posed a serious problem for the wealthy and well connected in northern Mexico, just like it did for their counterparts across the border in the South Texas. Otherwise, the Mexican federal government, just like the U.S. federal government, had little reason to be concerned with the territorial integrity of its northern borderlands spaces.

Indeed, as this essay will show, calls for nationalizing border territories after 1848 stemmed primarily from the periphery as opposed to the center. The periphery thus brought border issues into the consciousness of the cores of both nation-states. As time passed, each nation-state sought to work these desires to its respective advantages.

Killing for Cattle

Mexican officials hoped to ensure the protection of their national sovereignty during the negotiations that ended the U.S.-Mexico War in 1848. Considering the U.S. government's relative inability to control Native Americans north of the new boundary, the Mexican government pushed for the following language to be included in Article 11 of the Treaty of Guadalupe Hidalgo:

> Considering that a great part of the territories, which, by the present treaty, are to be comprehended for the future within the limits of the United States, is now occupied by savage tribes, who will hereafter be under the exclusive control of the Government of the United States, and whose incursions within the territory of Mexico would be prejudicial in the extreme, it is solemnly agreed that all such incursions shall be forcibly restrained by the Government of the United States whensoever this may be necessary; and that when they cannot be prevented, they shall be punished by the said Government, and satisfaction for the same shall be exacted all in the same way, and with equal diligence and energy, as if the same incursions were meditated or committed within its own territory, against its own citizens.[15]

Furthermore, the Mexican government also pursued the issue of crimes related to captive taking and cattle and property theft: "It shall not be lawful, under any pretext whatever, for any inhabitant of the United States to purchase or acquire any Mexican, or any foreigner residing in Mexico, who may have been captured by Indians inhabiting the territory of either of the two republics; nor to purchase or acquire horses, mules, cattle, or property of any kind, stolen within Mexican territory by such Indians."[16]

Given the inclusion of such language in the treaty as well as the treaty's ratification by the U.S. Senate, the Robb Commission clearly faced a double problem: not only did numerous Texans file claims against the Mexican government, but the U.S. government's past inability to uphold an international treaty threatened its diplomatic reliability. Binational problems appeared immediately in the borderlands' cattle industries.

Cattle had long been a staple of the northern Mexico and Texas economies. After the U.S. Civil War, the cattle business exploded in Texas. The war had severely curtailed Northerners' ability to get good beef. South Texas cattle ranches consequently grew exponentially larger during the late 1860s and 1870s as cowboys and vaqueros drove the herds north to railheads for shipment farther north and east. Cattle became exceptionally valuable commodities in the Texas-Mexico borderlands, practically overnight.[17]

Cattle theft was a local and regional problem that both the U.S. and Mexican federal governments could exploit in order to articulate a greater sense of territoriality in their shared border spaces. Without the U.S. cattle boom, binational squabbling over the border might not have become the major concern that it did by the 1870s. Both the Robb Commission and the Comisión

Pesquisidora recognized that widespread transborder cattle and livestock theft were thus relatively recent phenomena in the early 1870s. Members of the Comisión Pesquisidora argued that a cabal of cattle rustlers operated out of Brownsville as well as greater Cameron County in Texas. Thefts often occurred against Mexican nationals on Texas soil. Rarely a month went by in Cameron County when a Mexican citizen failed to complain to the nearby consul about property theft, oftentimes in the form of stolen cattle. In fact, from 1855 to 1872, no fewer than 198 individuals claimed of such wrongdoings committed against them by American citizens.[18] Clearly, then, although the high price of cattle would incentivize thefts after the U.S. Civil War, the Mexican commissioners were correct in noting that American citizens had targeted Mexicans for quite some time before the Texas cattle boom. Little deterrent existed for any Americans living along the border with Mexico to break the law.

Mexican officials had documentary evidence of Americans crossing into Mexico to steal cattle dating as far back as 1832, long before the establishment of the modern U.S.-Mexico borderline and even predating Texas's successful revolt against the Mexican federal government.[19] However, numerous norteños gave detailed testimony to the commissioners about losing cattle more recently. One such man was Juan Hinojosa, who in 1866 had for eighteen years resided in Nueces County, Texas. Hinojosa increasingly felt that the longer he resided in the state, the more serious the threats to his well-being became.[20] Hinojosa lost property that wound up in the hands of agents of the massive King Ranch. He soon learned how little control he had over his own affairs when every lawyer whom he approached in Corpus Christi refused to represent him out of fear of antagonizing the powerful Richard King. According to Hinojosa, this was normal. Mexicans living in Texas could find no legal recourse after having alleged wrongs committed against them by American citizens, thus necessitating his own eventual migration back across the border to Matamoros.[21]

Other reclamations speak to the complexities of borderlands politics and alliances. José Treviño owned a small ranch in Reynosa, Tamaulipas, in the years immediately following the U.S.-Mexico War. Sometime during the spring of 1852, Treviño claimed, the famed borderlands caudillo José Maria de Jesús Carbajal—a regional powerbroker who acted not only out of his own desire for material gain in Texas but oftentimes against the enforcement of centralized governmental power from either Mexico City or Washington, D.C.—crossed the border from Hidalgo County in Texas to attack Reynosa with a force of some two hundred men. Sometime during the roughly twenty-day attack, Carbajal and his men happened upon Treviño's ranch, where they seized eight threshing boards, ten cows, and five heifers. Treviño, who also lost a few other smaller items, valued his losses at 1,270 pesos, a substantial amount of property for a small rancher in northern Mexico at the time. Of course, since the commissioners hoped to have each nation address property losses that had occurred since the establishment of the U.S.-Mexico borderline, Treviño expected the U.S. government to repay him in full, despite two decades having passed.[22]

Conversely, Texans who gave testimony to the Robb Commission made countless claims pertaining to cattle theft moving in the opposite direction. Some of South Texas's largest proprietors historically grazed their cattle on the open range: this included the famous King and Kennedy families, the Hale and Parker Company, and T. Hines Clark. One of the initial problems that these large-scale cattle barons faced was the simple limitation of space in the borderlands. Large ranchers like the Kings and Kennedys whose cattle herds numbered between fifty thousand and seventy-five thousand head needed so much land to graze their herds—an area one hundred miles long and fifty miles wide—that they inevitably ran into problems with theft on either side of the border. Stolen head and hides inevitably dotted the region, in this case as far to the south as Monterrey, in Nuevo León.[23] Such massive business ventures existing in a region with little to no state presence were simply too big to be contained within the confines of the relatively newly determined U.S.-Mexico border; the temptation of crossing the border to make gains, illegally, at the expense of others was too strong for many in both the United States and Mexico to resist.

The American commissioners noted the singular uniqueness of the region in terms of individuals' propensity to commit crimes:

> The character and extent of the territory on which these depredations have been committed for so many years past offer facilities for the commission of crime to an extent not to be found in any other part of the country. Expeditions for the purpose of cattle stealing in Texas have generally been organized on the right bank of the Rio Grande, in the State of Tamaulipas, although not unfrequently, as a change of base, in the State of Coahuila. The men engaged in this work are Mexicans, well mounted, carrying fire-arms of the most approved pattern, and not unfrequently belong to the regular army of Mexico.[24]

Noting the state of lawlessness in the region indicated that these "facilities" might not otherwise have existed were it not for lack of state mechanisms to control people's bad behaviors. Interestingly, even the limited presence of the U.S. Army in the region did nothing to deter this alleged violence. As such, the relative lack of any greater state presence clearly left local people to their own devices.

Cattle stealing had allegedly gotten so bad for South Texas ranchers that by 1873 the region's cattle population had fallen to between 25 and 33 percent of its number immediately following the U.S. Civil War. Some thefts were indeed the fault of Mexican gangs that drove into Texas, sometimes as far as one hundred miles north of the Rio Grande. Thieves recrossed the border and then used Mexican ranches as rendezvous points to shift the cattle farther south into Mexico. Mexican authorities had not listened to the American press, according to the U.S. commissioners. The Mexican government's only alleged responsiveness came in its March 1872 recalling of General Juan Cortina, public enemy number one among Anglo South Texans following his famous raid on Brownsville in 1859 and the alleged ringleader of a large gang of transborder cattle thieves, from the northern border region. Cattle thefts up to that point, according to the Robb commissioners, totaled some $27.8 million in losses for Texas ranchers. The commissioners, who, unlike their Mexican counterparts, only worked in the vicinity of Brownsville and themselves did not cross the border, laid out 102 petitions and counted 354 witnesses, the vast majority of whom blamed Mexico and its allegedly weak government for the problem of Mexican cattle thefts. Notably, a number of historians have questioned the veracity of the Robb Commission's claims, due in large part to the limited scope of their methodology as well as the disparate power relationships that had developed between Anglo and Mexican ranchers in the region over the course of the previous few decades.[25]

Most Anglo South Texans indeed pointed all of the blame at Juan Cortina. Adolphus Glavecke, himself a large rancher in the region, reported to the commissioners that he warned General Carbajal—the same Carbajal who raided José Treviño's ranch above—of an impending attack the night before Cortina's raid on Brownsville in 1859. Carbajal, fearing that his standing as a military leader in South Texas would not quell Cortina's uprising, allegedly refused to stop him. Unsurprisingly, then, the first large-scale explosion of reports of stolen cattle from Texas all date back to 1859. Cortina virtually disappeared from Texans' accounts of cattle stealing again until the early 1870s, but numerous American eyewitness accounts told of alleged cattle thievery perpetrated by others during the intervening years. During one trip across the river, a man named W. D. Thomas allegedly saw Luis López, a known Mexican cattle thief, with one hundred head of stolen Texas cattle within a mile of Matamoros. López then sold the cattle to a local butcher named Carriola for the low price of $2 per head. When confronted by Thomas about his purchasing of stolen cattle, Carriola replied, "I bought them; I do not give a damn." Thomas also reported having knowledge of Carriola forwarding $20 to a man named Palacios to bring him twenty stolen beeves from Texas. Later during his trip, Thomas witnessed another man named Ensauldo driving four hundred to five hundred head of cattle near Matamoros. Ensauldo threatened to harm Thomas if he tried to stop him.[26]

The Robb Commission also relied on certain points of circumstantial evidence in order to make its charges that Mexican cattle thievery was a problem in the borderlands. Stolen Texas cattle could fetch roughly $1.50 to $7 per head on the Mexican side of the border, while to the north those same head fetched $12 to $15. Depressed cattle prices in northern Mexico allegedly stemmed from the long periods of political unrest that Mexico continuously experienced since it gained independence from Spain in 1821. Typically, a Mexican stock raiser could expect to receive about $5 per head. Evidence suggesting that cattle could be sold at a lower price indicated that much of the stock being sold in Mexico had to have been stolen. Furthermore, some South Texas ranchers noted that the estimated cost to themselves of raising a four-year-old steer that would later be sold for beef was about $7 per head. As such, it was simply impossible for anyone to sell a head of Texas cattle for less than $5 to $7 dollars unless the animal had been stolen. Corroborating testimony indicated to the commissioners that thousands of head of Texas cattle crossed the border each year. Justo López and Marco Sánchez noted that Texas had lost roughly sixty thousand head of cattle since the end of the U.S. Civil War in 1865. Rancher Thaddeus Rhodes testified to the commission that between 1868 and 1870, roughly three thousand head of cattle crossed the Rio Grande per month. For Rhodes, then, the figure of sixty thousand head lost since 1865 would be too low.[27]

Clearly, by the 1870s transborder cattle theft had become a major cause for concern not just for Texans and Mexicans living in the borderlands but also for the Mexican and U.S. federal governments, whether or not the figures provided by each commission were accurate. Many people believed that only a concerted state intervention into the region—perhaps in the form of increased border policing or greater federal controls enacted over commerce—could stem the flow of cattle either south or north across the border. Fortunately for the victims of transborder crime, when the Texas cattle boom ended during the 1880s, the impulse toward livestock theft across the border naturally dropped off.[28] Unfortunately, what seemed to continue unabated north of the border into the twentieth century was the mostly Anglo theft of Mexican and Tejano lands and other properties.[29] The borderlands would be rife with instability for some time.

Octaviano Zapata and the American State

Cattle theft was, in reality, only one of a host of problems that the porous nature of the early U.S.-Mexico borderline presented. The U.S. Civil War arrived in the borderlands in 1861, splitting people on both sides of the border into self-interested factions. Both the U.S. and Mexican governments were essentially powerless to control the newly drawn borderline, especially given the previously mentioned concurrent warring factions inside of both the United States and Mexico. This comes as little surprise, given that the federal governments could not, as has already been shown, control the simple movement of people across the borderline to commit thefts a decade later when the horrors of civil war had subsided. Nonetheless, the U.S. federal government still exerted some pressure along the borderline during the war, but it was largely able to do so by proxy through local actors. The importance of the 1860s was that the two federal states were relatively powerless to do anything other than manipulate on-the-ground violence in the region rather than exert any kind of a commanding presence. Naturally, when it came to the U.S. Civil War, the majority of Anglo-Texans north of the Rio Grande sided with the Confederates, as did some of their Tejano allies as well as Mexican merchants who benefited from the international cotton trade during the U.S. Civil War.[30] The Union, of course, also had supporters on both sides of the border.

Individual people did serve as stand-ins for these warring states (or in the case of the Confederacy, perhaps "proto-states"). One such person was Octaviano Zapata, who committed acts of violence on behalf of the Union government in lieu of the United States having any widespread power in the region. Government intervention by proxy thus bred even more violence in the borderlands rather than causing it to dissipate. Zapata's life would ultimately show how little concern states had for controlling border violence before the 1870s; in fact, the U.S. and Mexican federal states sometimes exacerbated transborder violence in order to attain some kind of benefit.

Zapata—a Union sympathizer like his better-known friend and compatriot Juan Cortina—was a constant irritant to Confederate South Texans. Little is known about his early life. He was born in northern Mexico and eventually came to own a small ranch in rural Zapata County, Texas, called El Clareño. In April of 1861, Captain Santos Benavides—a Confederate sympathizer and borderlands caudillo from Laredo, Texas—arrived in the vicinity of Zapata's ranch to quell tensions between local Confederates and Unionists. Benavides had pursued a Union sympathizer named Antonio Ochoa to El Clareño. A fight ensued, whereby several people were killed. Zapata and his family, fearing more violence, subsequently fled across the Rio Grande to the Mexican town of Guerrero. There, Zapata and a large group of followers committed themselves to opposing Confederate power along the border at any cost. Notably, the U.S. government immediately sought to take advantage of the situation—the United States paid Zapata and his men $200 per enlistment in his force, safely stationed in Mexico, with the express agreement that Zapata's force would occasionally cross the border to harass Confederate regulars.[31]

Zapata began conducting raids on both sides of the border after the fight at El Clareño, endearing himself to the dispossessed poor as well as to the Union Army. Zapata's activities helped tie down the Confederate Army on the western portion of the Texas-Mexico border, keeping them from moving back east to fight Union troops. By the end of 1861, the name "Octaviano Zapata" was well known throughout the region.[32] Nevertheless, like the problem of cattle theft, Zapata himself eventually became a problematic figure for both Mexican and American officials alike.

Several incidents in 1862 and 1863 were of particular interest to La Comisión Pesquisidora. Zapata and a large force of his men crossed into Texas twice in December of 1862. Early in the month, the raiders attacked a Confederate supply train; three weeks later they waylaid a train of three wagons escorted by five Confederate soldiers traveling from Fort Brown in Cameron County to Ringgold Barracks in Starr County, resulting in the deaths of all but one of the soldiers.[33] A group of Confederate soldiers retaliated that same month, crossing the border at Salinillas in search of the hated Zapata and his men. The troops advanced on Guerrero. According to several eyewitnesses, the soldiers killed three Mexicans, stole some horses and guns, and returned to Texas.[34] Confederate Texans, in their desire to rid themselves of the Zapata nuisance, had invaded Mexican sovereign space and, essentially, from the Mexican federal government's perspective, committed an act of war.

But northern Mexico, like South Texas, was still very much subject to regional rather than federal power. Things got particularly tense in 1863. In February of that year, Confederate general Hamilton P. Bee of Fort Brown and Governor Albino López of Tamaulipas reached an agreement whereby Confederate troops could now cross the border with official Tamaulipan consent in search of Zapata and his forces. Again, this was a sign of local actors taking on the role of the state in place of any real federal power in the region on either side of the border. The alcalde of Mier suggested Major Santos Benavides and his Thirty-Third Texas Cavalry—a nearly all-Tejano Confederate regiment—to do the job.[35] Benavides, of course, was a border caudillo with deep ties to Mexican powerbrokers as well as to powerful Anglos in Texas. López, however, also acted in the style of frontier *caudillismo* himself, reaching an international agreement between Tamaulipas and a foreign nation (the Confederacy) that could potentially have all sorts of diplomatic repercussions for the Mexican federal government. For the Mexican commissioners analyzing the incident a decade later, this was clearly not a valid agreement. To the commissioners, the events that followed the agreement constituted "invaciones de CC Americanos armados al territorio Mexico" (invasions of armed Confederate Americans of Mexican territory).[36]

Confederate activities against Zapata were truly a transnational affair. One resident of Rancho San Ygnacio, Texas, watched as Santos Benavides and his men crossed the border in pursuit of Zapata. Luciano Bernal recalled that on one occasion Benavides and his men killed an associate of Zapata's, rancher Jesús García Ramírez. Bernal and a number of other men subsequently joined forces with Zapata in August of 1863. The group reconvened at Mier, where they clashed with Santos Benavides's brother Refugio Benavides and lost some horses and arms to the Confederates, who later recrossed the border back into Texas.[37] A full-on border war between the Confederate States of America and Union-sympathizing Zapata and his men was underway.

The fight did not last long. One Mexican witness noted that in the fall of 1863, some forces "compuestas de Texanos y Americanos" (composed of Texans and Americans) crossed the border again. In response, Zapata's forces received reinforcements from local norteños. Macedonio Rodriguez of Mier, for example, joined them, due to the fact that his *patrón*, the aforementioned Jesús García Ramirez, had been killed. In August and September, Zapata's force encountered the Confederates while on patrol near Mier. The resulting conflict at a stream called Arroyo del Coronel with Benavides and eighty men from Texas left about eleven or twelve of Zapata's men killed before the Confederates moved back north across the border. In September, Santos Benavides and his brother Refugio once again crossed the border into Mexico and finally succeeded in killing Zapata, along with eight or nine of his men.[38]

Zapata's story is instructive in establishing the perceived challenges to state authority that individual transborder actors could embody during this tumultuous period. Zapata was a thorn in the side of Confederates as well as their ethnic-Mexican allies on both sides of the border. Interestingly, the Robb Commission never mentioned Zapata once in its report. The Comisión Pesquisidora, however, related the above tale in brief. The Mexican commissioners noted that Zapata was a threat to the sanctity of Mexican territoriality on multiple levels. First, and quite simply, to them, "Zapata . . . fué muerto en territorio de Méjico por una fuerza confederada, que invadió nuestro suelo con ese fin"(was killed in Mexican territory by a Confederate force, which had invaded our land to this end).[39] Simply put, Zapata's activities led to an invasion of Mexico by the Confederacy. Nevertheless, the Mexican commissioners' historical interpretation when looking back on the violence during the 1870s made clear that the U.S. federal government was also to blame for the violation of Mexican sovereignty as well as the later transborder violence after the U.S. Civil War had ended: "But it is easily perceived that the violation of neutrality of Mexican territory, the organizing of armed forces initiated or accomplished, the fact of constituting said territory into a basis of operations hostile to Texas, and the authorizing by the agents of the United States government of undisciplined forces to cross over to the American territory and carry hostilities to the Confederates, would necessarily give rise to loose habits amongst the inhabitants of the two frontiers, from which nothing but evil could result."[40]

————————

Thus, not only had the Confederacy invaded Mexico, but also the U.S. government had meddled in Mexican space and exacerbated the problem of border violence, contributing to the unrest that plagued the region during the late 1860s and early 1870s. In turn, these "loose habits" that the Mexican commissioners mentioned—or, people's propensity to commit acts of violence on both sides of the border—were, to the Mexican commissioners, primarily the fault of the Civil War American state, *not* the Confederacy nor the Mexican government.[41] Zapata's standing as a perpetrator of transborder violence begged questions of the role of state-level manipulation of mid-nineteenth-century border violence. In this case, one federal state had clearly acted against the greater good of international cooperation and territorial sovereignty.

Octaviano Zapata's brief career elucidates major issues related to governance and the international boundary. For Mexico, his activities illuminated manipulation of border violence by the U.S. government. Ironically, though, purposeful state intervention into the borderlands seemed to be the only salve to stop this gaping international wound by the 1870s. For the Mexican commissioners, it must have seemed as if chaos at the border might never end.

Native Americans and the "Border Problem"

Clearly, people's propensity for crossing borders had become a problem for each state almost immediately after 1848. Native Americans, like cattle theft as well as the violence-by-proxy of the U.S. Civil War years, also highlighted the immediate danger of relative statelessness in the borderlands. The Comisión Pesquisidora focused on the transborder Indian problem to a much greater degree than did the Robb Commission. To be sure, the number of nomadic or seminomadic groups native to northern Mexico that could potentially have raided into the United States remained relatively high.[42] But also Indian wars raged within the United States, making the problem of Indian violence a familiar one to many Americans.[43] Not only did numerous Indian nations resist U.S. western expansion, but many powerful groups such as the Comanches and the Apaches raided south into U.S. borderlands communities and deeper into northern Mexico for decades before the U.S. Civil War.[44]

The Robb Commission dealt with the problem of Indian violence in South Texas rather simplistically: the commissioners, in their final report, conflated

Indian raids from Mexico into Texas as being almost indistinct from Mexicans crossing the border to commit violent crimes. Numerous witnesses gave testimony. Thomas F. Wilson, then U.S. consul at Matamoros, reported a raid of Kickapoos thirty-five miles north of Laredo on a private ranch. Wilson noted that the Indians "disguised themselves as Mexicans" and robbed the ranch. Rancher Thaddeus Rhodes testified before the commission that "Carrizo Indians are noted cattle thieves. Rafael or Boca Chica, one of their chiefs, was a great thief." Similarly, in 1852, a band from Mexico raided the settlement of Edinburg in Hidalgo County, killing ten Americans.[45]

In fairness, the U.S. commissioners did note that Indian violence originating from Texas was not solely, or even largely, an issue stemming primarily from the openness of the international borderline. For example, one witness to the Robb Commission, Alexander M. Sanders, noted a raid by Comanches that killed several people at the small Gonzaleña Ranch as far back as 1838. More recently, Comanches had murdered Louis McGrath and his wife near their ranch in Laredo in 1858. The commissioners noted that "the extent and gravity of the reported disorders . . . and the continued outrages of Indians on the northern and north-western frontiers [of Texas], call for the most careful examination in the future, these remote regions being difficult of access."[46] Although the commissioners would go on to blame the Mexican government for its inability to stop Indian raids *into* Texas from Mexico, its examination here of North and particularly West Texas—the stronghold of Comanche and Plains Indian power—does indicate some conception of Indian violence as being part of a larger "frontier problem" rather than solely a transborder one. As such, evidence from the Robb Commission provides tangential reasoning behind conceptualizing the U.S.-Mexico border before 1870 as functioning more like a traditional zone of frontier interaction, much in the same way that regions in the nineteenth-century U.S. West functioned beyond the pale of control for the U.S. federal government. The State of Texas reacted similarly, creating and calling up "frontier defense battalions" in April of 1874 for the whole state. Only one of these "frontiers" was the U.S.-Mexico border; the rest were scattered throughout the northern, western, and central parts of the state. Ultimately, however, what one historian notes as a "strong current of white racism" led to locals pressuring the state to subjugate Indians, a task that fell directly onto the shoulders of the Texas Rangers.[47]

Conversely, the problem of transborder Indian violence from the United States into Mexico, noted the Mexican commissioners, was the direct result of decades of failed U.S. Indian policy in the American West and borderlands regions. Not only did the commissioners arrive at this conclusion themselves, but also such problems were apparent to many norteños at the time. Jesús Escobar y Armendáriz, a government official from Paso del Norte (later renamed Ciudad Juárez), commented on problems related to Indian violence in Chihuahua in early 1875. Escobar lamented Indian raids into Mexico, arguing that such incidents resulted from failed U.S. Indian policy, which did not provide reservation Indians with adequate resources on which to subsist. Escobar also insisted that Apaches, in particular, publicly sold animals and stolen goods with the willful knowledge of the American authorities. Escobar's solution to the problem lay in "la colonización de la zona fronteriza y la educación del pueblo," or, in the increased colonization of Mexican border spaces and the education of its people to problems such as transborder Indian raids. The violence had only gotten worse since 1848, Escobar argued, which left most Mexicans wondering why the affixing of the borderline at the Rio Grande should make life so difficult for Mexicans who lived nearby.[48]

Primary source records corroborate Escobar's claims. Between 1848 and 1852, 495 Indians are recorded as having crossed the border into Chihuahua alone, killing twenty-eight Mexicans and dragging two off into captivity. Interestingly, Indian raids into Chihuahua remained constant until 1864, when a sharp increase in raiding occurred. Between 1864 and 1874, observers recorded anywhere between 100 and 305 Indians crossing into Chihuahua annually on raids. Raiders killed only twenty-seven Mexicans during those ten years, however, taking none into captivity and leaving only five people with serious injuries. The real impetus behind the continued raids was clearly theft. Raiders took anywhere from 38 to 163 horses per year, 63–111 mules per year, 65–195 other animals per year, and about 18,000 sheep total for the entire decade. Anywhere from 65 to 329 local men went out in pursuit of Indian raiders per year, sometimes being gone for as long as two months at a time. Clearly, Escobar's argument was correct; although the Indians did not appear to have killing Mexicans as their primary target, it would be extremely difficult for a rancher in northern Chihuahua to make a living during the 1860s or 1870s because of such raids.[49]

Recent scholarship has added another level of complexity to this international problem. Historian Pekka Hämäläinen notes that the Comanches and their Plains Indian allies were, in fact, the preeminent power in the North American Southwest for the century stretching from 1750 to 1850. Furthermore, historian Brian DeLay argues that failed Mexican peace agreements with numerous Indian groups led to an outburst of Indian raiding across the borderlands during the 1820s and 1830s.[50] Although the Mexican commissioners may have been correct in noting the general failure of U.S. Indian policy, it is clear that Indian groups had long been the preeminent power in a region where both the United States and Mexican federal governments simply had not exerted any level of meaningful federal control.

Norteños who complained of Indian violence during the late 1840s and 1850s thus dealt with a problem that had been relatively common to the region for decades. People did not hesitate to call on the Mexican federal government for help. Recent scholarship has suggested that Mexican nationalism coalesced and became stronger due to Mexico's losses in the Texas Revolution of 1835–36 and the U.S.-Mexico War of 1846–48; as such, perceptions of a need for state intervention and control of the new border in the years immediately after the signing of the Treaty of Guadalupe Hidalgo point toward the emerging appeal of a national consciousness for norteños in relation to transborder problems with the United States.[51] For example, near the town of Cerralvo late one night in 1849, fourteen members of the Mexican National Guard found themselves engaged in combat with a group of Indians of roughly the same size.[52] Four guardsmen lost their lives during the combat, including the contingent's leader, Sergeant Don Antonio González. Rather than looking to American authorities to blame for their inability to stop the Indians from crossing into Mexico, however, the survivors complained that they had been insufficiently armed to take on such a force and thus petitioned the Mexican government for 200 pesos to arm themselves in order to stave off any further attacks. Consciousness of the lack of a U.S. state presence on the other side of the border was the farthest thing from these men's minds.[53]

Fighting against Indians was different from the other forms of crime of theft and wartime raids. Nonetheless, the inclusion of the so-called Indian problem for northern Mexicans in the *comisión*'s report pointed toward the same impulse for increased border security. Indeed, many norteños noted that the problem of transborder Indian violence was a problem that only Mexican federal intervention into the borderlands could solve. On February 6, 1849, the alcalde of Pesqueria Grande wrote a letter to the provincial governor of Nuevo León in Monterrey, begging that one hundred permanent troops be sent immediately in order to protect the town against Indian raids.[54] Such requests were undoubtedly common in the Mexican borderlands by the late 1840s and early 1850s. One local official lamented that the federal government was not able to protect the communities of Hidalgo, Pesqueria Grande, and Santa Catarina: "This community, esteemed sir, is a border state that has an immense uninhabited Northwest where Indians make their raids, running sometimes to Santa Catarina and is worthy of a considerable look by the supreme government."[55] The necessity of Mexican state intervention was, again, of paramount importance.

The Mexican National Guard was, in truth, the only answer that people had by the 1850s, but it was still largely ineffective in stopping raiding Indians from crossing the border into Mexico. Things were particularly bad in Nuevo León during the summer of 1850. In early June, an attack occurred at Canas, whereby the citizens of the town organized themselves and counterattacked. Nearby, the Indians stole mules from Jesús González and Manuel Villarreal, leaving both men injured and near death.[56] Thirty members of the

Mexican National Guard, led by Commander Diego González, were called up in late June of that year. The guardsmen stationed themselves at a known Indian crossing on the Rio Salado.[57] Their inability to quell the raids, however, shows that the well-intentioned National Guard was simply not enough to protect northern Mexican villages and towns. Locals eventually raised over 350 men from a smattering of communities across the northern frontier to defend the region, themselves.[58]

Locals might have resented the ineffectiveness of the Mexican federal government. In reality, norteños defending themselves would only have led to further resentment of and violence toward Indians who crossed the border from the United States, not unlike the many Americans in the U.S. West who resented and ultimately dehumanized Indians where the U.S. federal government simply had no ability to intervene in violent conflict. As such, Mexican communities arming themselves against Indians would only further destabilize an already violent region that neither the U.S. nor Mexican federal government could control. Violence and bloodshed in northern Mexico would continue to be an everyday occurrence, much as they were just north of the border in Texas.

But evidence suggests that some norteños' thinking on the subject changed over time. Locals responded in droves after the Comisión Pesquisidora released a call for testimonies from Mexicans who had fallen victim to Indian raids from across the border in the United States. A number of people came forward to make claims against the U.S. government. Guadalupe Hernández claimed thirty pesos in damages "por depredaciones de los bárbaros" (for depredations by the barbarous Indians). Casimira Sánchez claimed the more modest sum of ten pesos. Some *vecinos* filed petitions in groups, like Mariano Flores and a group of his neighbors and friends, who claimed 354 pesos in damages.[59]

Countless others from Nuevo León, Tamaulipas, Zacatecas, and San Luis Potosí came before the commissioners with claims that Indians from the United States had destroyed their property or murdered friends and family members. According to the Mexican commissioners, the total financial losses since 1848 were incalculable. The Mexican commissioners were also quick to argue that Americans were complicit in the raids. As they concluded: "The robberies and murders which have been the result of these depredations have been committed, not only by the Comanches and other northern tribes, but also by some American officials and private citizens, who instigate the savages to pillage, by purchasing from them stolen property with arms and ammunition, and who stimulate them by accompanying or guiding them on their expeditions."[60]

The commissioners furthered this argument by stating that proof could be found through the testimonies of Mexican citizens as well as through newspaper and documentary evidence from Texas. Also, the Comisión Pesquisidora considered U.S. Indian policy a general failure, which was an idea that even some Americans at the time did not hesitate to share.[61]

What the Mexican commissioners called for was greater federal intervention into Mexico's northern borderlands. Greater settlement of the sparsely settled northern frontier, more troops to guard the border against the United States, and greater regulation of transborder commerce and exchange between Mexicans and Americans might, according to the commissioners, bring an end to this rampant violence.[62] Ultimately, the commissioners wanted the Mexican government to effectively control the border, which by 1873 it had not yet done.

Ironically, the point became moot not long after the report's issuance. The conclusion of the Red River War that the U.S. Army carried out against the Comanches and their allies in the Texas Panhandle in 1874 effectively stopped Indian raids into Mexico from Texas. Similarly, the surrender of the Apache leader Geronimo farther west in Cochise County, Arizona, in 1886 ended the era of transborder Indian violence along the desert portions of the western U.S.-Mexico border altogether.[63] In both cases, the U.S. federal government had unwittingly addressed a borderlands problem by defeating nonstate Indian groups. Indian control of the U.S.-Mexico border and the ability to cross it freely had thus been subsumed by the U.S. federal government. One of the layers of problems related to violence and the new international borderline that had plagued the norteños in particular had finally eroded away.

――――――――

Was the U.S.-Mexico border particularly or especially violent? Perhaps not, although people's consciousness of it as an exploitable geopolitical entity after 1848 certainly brought problems related to the region's relative frontier statelessness vis-à-vis acts of violence to the fore. The border might have existed as something of an abstraction in the years following 1848, but it was an abstraction that clearly meant something to the people who lived along it. Although both the Mexican and U.S. federal governments seemed to want to effect change at the border, their primary concern was clearly the implementation of power and control in the borderlands. Each commission's interpretation of the past during this tumultuous early period in the border's history explains several important things about violence and the limitations of statecraft in borderlands regions. First, it indicates that when federal governments lack a discernible presence at the margins of modern nation states, people's perceptions of crime and violence as international problems grow. The everyday nature of private individuals crossing the border to commit acts of violence has been mitigated over the course of the twentieth century with the maturation of nation-states and their attendant propensity to further incorporate liminal spaces and to attempt to control borders. Of course, Mexico's monopoly over violence in its borderlands has been usurped in recent years by powerful drug cartels. Illegal border crossings and illicit economic activity also continue. Rather than these latter points being taken simply as evidence of a lack of state power, however, these phenomena exist at least in part due to human ingenuity and localized responses to increased state controls along the borderline.[64]

The two commissions of the 1870s blamed each opposing nation as being the cause of their shared border violence. Cattle theft had boomed because neither state exerted an effective ability to police criminal activities. Octaviano Zapata was an independent actor who was manipulated by the U.S. state in its effort to gain ultimate supremacy in the region during the U.S. Civil War. Finally, Native Americans augured a simple need for a military-style border security, which is the provenance of modern nation-states. Interestingly, other research has shown that this model for understanding violence, borders, and federal states works similarly in other borderlands spaces. Historian David Peterson del Mar argues that violence in the Oregon-Washington-British Columbia border region dissipated during the second half of the nineteenth century, as these regions by the 1890s "became more settled . . . and an ethos of self-restraint had eroded the combatant masculinity of previous generations. The law was more powerful" after a few decades had passed in the wake of the drawing of the 49th parallel as the borderline between the United States and Canada in 1846, "and more people expressed a willingness to follow its dictates."[65] Although Peterson del Mar does not specifically analyze people who crossed the U.S.-Canada border to commit crimes or acts of violence, his research clearly indicates that a greater state presence in the U.S.-Canada borderlands contributed to a general lessening of violence in the region. The state did not completely end violence, of course, nor did the presence of federal officials lead to complete governmental control of the U.S.-Canada border. Nevertheless, the increased presence of the Canadian and U.S. legal bureaucracies clearly served as a deterrent to *some* crime and violence. Mexican and U.S. borderlanders saw the state presence as the ultimate deterrent to problems along their shared border during the 1870s as well.

This period of Texas-Mexico border violence also shows the deep degree to which non-border-situated social and economic variables like the post–U.S. Civil War cattle industry as well as the end of the Indian Wars on the southern Great Plains served as stand-ins for federal control of shared border spaces. Additionally, Porfirio Díaz's quest for economic modernization and political control in the Mexican North during the late nineteenth century undoubtedly served as a temporary mitigating factor for transborder crime as well as briefly stemming the flow of Mexicans moving north in search of better jobs.[66] As such, much of the Mexican federal government's concern for controlling the border stemmed from the fiscal concerns of a newly growing and maturing nation state. Added to this was U.S. General E. O. C. Ord's order on June 1, 1877, which allowed U.S. troops to pursue Mexican cattle thieves south of the international borderline and served as temporary insurance that violence related to widespread property theft would dissipate after the 1870s (although this did increase tensions between the Mexican and U.S. federal governments for a short time). Nevertheless, the "Ord Order" did not address the root causes of border violence.[67] Nor did it appear early enough to act as a major deterrent to cattle theft.

Ultimately, the border's arrival in 1848 complicated people's lives in numerous ways. Some individuals used it to take advantage of one another, which in turn led to cries for state intervention that, over time, would contribute to life in the borderlands simply becoming more complicated than it had been before. Some borderlanders may have called for an increase in the two federal governments' presences on both sides of the line during the 1870s, but others would only continue to usurp federal authority along the border throughout the nineteenth and twentieth centuries in numerous ways. Complete governmental control of the U.S.-Mexico borderline remained (and still remains) impossible. The U.S.-Mexico borderline will always be heavily patrolled, but full state control of the border—by building border walls, enforcing immigration policy, or completely stopping transborder crime—will forever remain elusive. The U.S.-Mexico border is a creation of modern nation states, but, as this essay has shown, the border ultimately created *more* problems for both states related to simple questions of governance and enforcement of laws, rather than simply solving preexisting ones, like stopping transborder violence.

Much the same remains true today.

Notes

1. "Invasión por Norteamericanos al punto llamado el Ranchito y asesinato del Sr. Juan Chapa Guerra," documento diez, caja 5, Fondo Comisión Pesquisidora, Archivo Histórico de la Secretaria de Relaciones Exteriores, México, D.F. (hereafter, CP-AHSRE). For more on violence and cattle theft during this time period, see Lance Blyth's essay in chapter 3 in this volume.

2. By "crime," I simply mean the breaking of laws in the United States or in Mexico. "Violence" refers to a specific act of harm perpetrated on the body of one individual by another.

3. "Proclamation," Ulysses S. Grant, in *The Papers of Ulysses S. Grant*, ed. John Y. Simon (Carbondale: Southern Illinois University Press, 2000), 23:123 (hereafter, USGP).

4. "Report of the United States Commissioners to Texas, Appointed under Joint Resolution of Congress, Approved May 7, 1872" (Washington, DC: Government Printing Office, December 10, 1872), 40–41 (hereafter, RC); "Informes que en cumplimiento del decreto de 2 de octubre de 1872 rinde al Ejecutivo de la Unión: La comisión pesquisidora de la frontera del norte, sobre el desempeño de sus trabajos" (México, D.F.: Imprenta de Díaz de León y White, 1874), 118–24 (hereafter, CP); "Reports of the Committee of Investigation Sent in 1873 by the Mexican Government to the Frontier of Texas" (New York: Baker and Godwin, 1875), 401–4 (hereafter, CP-ENG).

5. Andrew R. Graybill, *Policing the Great Plains: Rangers, Mounties, and the North American Frontier, 1875–1910* (Lincoln: University of Nebraska Press, 2007), 15.

6. Samuel Truett and Pekka Hämäläinen, "On Borderlands," *Journal of American History* 98, no. 2 (September 2011): 351.

7. For more on this larger conceptual framework, see Jeremy Adelman and Stephen Aron, "From Borderlands to Borders: Empires, Nation-States, and the Peoples in between in North American History," *American Historical Review* 104, no. 3 (June 1999): 814–41.

8. Luis Alberto García, "Dominance in an Imagined Border: Santos Benavides and Santiago Vidaurri's Policing of the Rio Grande," in *Border Policing: A History of Enforcement and Evasion in North America*, ed. Holly M. Karibo and George T. Díaz (Austin: University of Texas Press, 2020), 43.

9. For more on the *zona libre*, see George T. Díaz, *Border Contraband: A History of Smuggling across the Rio Grande* (Austin: University of Texas Press, 2015), 30.

10. "Proclamation," USGP, 23:123–24.

11. "Proclamation," USGP, 23:125.

12. "To Congress," USGP, 25:114.

13. Miguel Ángel González-Quiroga, *War and Peace on the Rio Grande Frontier, 1830–1880* (Norman: University of Oklahoma Press, 2020), 102–6, 166–73.

14. Juan Mora-Torres, *The Making of the Mexican Border: The State, Capitalism, and Society in Nuevo León, 1848–1910* (Austin: University of Texas Press, 2001), 27–28. Both quotations on page 28.

15. "Treaty of Guadalupe Hidalgo, February 2, 1848," The Avalon Project, Yale Law School, accessed April 1, 2015, http://avalon.law.yale.edu/19th_century/guadhida.asp#art5.

16. "Treaty of Guadalupe Hidalgo."

17. Alice Baumgartner, "The Line of Positive Safety: Borders and Boundaries on the Rio Grande, 1848–1880," *Journal of American History* 101, no. 4 (March 2015): 1107, 1113, 1116. For more on cattle ranching in Texas during this time period more generally, see Daniel Kerr, "From Grass to Grain of Cows and Plows, Politics and Power," *Journal of the West* 50, no. 2 (2011): 38–50. For more on border violence and cattle theft, see Lance Blyth's essay in chapter 3 in this volume.

18. "Sobre la nacionalidad y domicilio de los abigeos," 1872, documento uno, caja cuatro, CP-AHSRE.

19. "Origen del robo de ganados—cantidades robadas antes de 1848 de México para Texas," documento dos, caja cuatro, CP-AHSRE.

20. For more on race in nineteenth-century South Texas, see David Montejano, *Anglos and Mexicans in the Making of Texas, 1836–1986* (Austin: University of Texas Press, 1987), 29, 37–38, 82–85. Notably, Montejano argues that racism in South Texas grew much worse after about 1880. For more, see 92.

21. "Reclamación de Don Juan Hinojosa," Enero 10, 1873, expediente uno, caja cuatro, CP-AHSRE.

22. "Reclamacion de Jesús Treviño," Marzo 16, 1873, expediente diez, caja cuatro, CP-AHSRE. For an interesting study of Carbajal, see Joseph Chance, *José María de Jesús Carbajal: The Life and Times of a Mexican Revolutionary* (San Antonio, TX: Trinity University Press, 2006).

23. RC, 5.

24. RC, 8.

25. RC, 2, 5–8. For more on Cortina, see Jerry Thompson, *Cortina: Defending the Mexican Name in Texas* (College Station: Texas A&M University Press, 2007); see also Alice Baumgartner's essay in chapter 5 in this volume.

26. RC, 10, 11, 29.

27. RC, 18.

28. For more on the Texas cattle industry, see Kerr, "From Grass to Grain"; for more on commerce in the region on both sides of the border, Alicia Dewey, *Pesos and Dollars: Entrepreneurs in the Texas-Mexico Borderlands, 1880–1940* (College Station: Texas A&M University Press, 2014); and Mario Cerutti, *Burguesía, capitales e industria en el norte de México: Monterrey y su ámbito regional (1850–1910)* (Monterrey: Facultad de Filosofía y Letras de la Universidad Autónoma de Nuevo León, 1992).

29. These issues are explored nicely in Benjamin H. Johnson, *Revolution in Texas: How a Forgotten Rebellion and Its Bloody Suppression Turned Mexicans into Americans* (New Haven, CT: Yale University Press, 2005).

30. For more on Confederate Tejanos, see Jerry Thompson, ed., *Tejanos in Gray: The Civil War Letters of Joseph Rafael de la Garza and Manuel Yturri* (College Station: Texas A&M University Press, 2011). For an interesting study of the borderlands between the Confederate States of America and Mexico, see Gerardo Gurza-Lavalle, *Una vecindad efímera: Los Estados Confederados de América y su política exterior hacia México, 1861–1865* (México, D.F.: Instituto de Investigaciones Dr. José María Luis Mora, 2001).

31. García, "Dominance in an Imagined Border," 53; González-Quiroga, *War and Peace on the Rio Grande Fronter, 1830–1880*, 221–23; James W. Daddysman, "ZAPATA, OCTAVIANO," *Handbook of Texas Online*, accessed June 19, 2015, http://www.tshaonline.org/handbook/online/articles/fza12, uploaded on June 15, 2010, Texas State Historical Association; and CP, 37–39.

32. Daddysman, "ZAPATA, OCTAVIANO."

33. Daddysman, "ZAPATA, OCTAVIANO."

34. "Sobre la invasion hecha en el Rancho Clareño por soldados Confederados en Agosto de 1863," cuaderno 19, expediente cinco, caja uno, CP-AHSRE.

35. Daddysman, "ZAPATA, OCTAVIANO."

36. "Sobre la invasion," CP-AHSRE.

37. "Sobre la invasion," CP-AHSRE.

38. "Sobre la invasion," CP-AHSRE.

39. CP, 38.

40. CP, 39.

41. CP, 39.

42. Historian José Angel Hernández argues that the Indigenous population of New Spain and later independent Mexico held steady at about 60 percent well into the nineteenth

century. For more, see José Angel Hernández, *Mexican American Colonization during the Nineteenth Century: A History of the U.S.-Mexico Borderlands* (Cambridge: Cambridge University Press, 2012), 40–41. Thus, it can be deduced the number of Indigenous peoples in northern Mexico from 1848 to 1873 must have remained relatively high.

43. For more, see Pekka Hämäläinen, *The Comanche Empire* (New Haven, CT: Yale University Press, 2008).

44. For more, see Brian DeLay, *War of a Thousand Deserts: Indian Raids and the U.S.-Mexican War* (New Haven, CT: Yale University Press, 2009). For a brief overview of transborder Indian violence in northeastern Mexico in particular during the period in question, see Isidro Vizcaya Canales, *Incursiones de indios al noreste en el México independiente, 1821–1885* (Monterrey: Archivo General de Nuevo León, 1995); for more on the Comanches and border violence, see Joaquín Rivaya-Martínez's essay in chapter 2 in this volume.

45. RC, 38.

46. RC, 2, 38.

47. General Order No. 1, Headquarters Frontier Battalion, Austin, May 7, 1874, folder 392-1, General Correspondence, May 1–15, 1874, box 401-392, Texas Adjutant General Department Records, Texas State Archives, Austin, Texas; and Graybill, *Policing the Great Plains*, 61.

48. Jesús Escobar y Armendáriz al Presidente de la comisión investigadora en Sonora y Chihuahua, Paso del Norte, Enero 2 de 1875, documento uno, caja dos, CP-AHSRE.

49. "Noticia de las incursiones de indios barbaros habidas en este distrito . . . ," Sebastian Vargas, Paso del Norte, Enero 5 de 1875, documento uno, caja dos, CP-AHSRE.

50. Hämäläinen, *Comanche Empire*; DeLay, *War of a Thousand Deserts*.

51. For more on the emergence of Mexican nationalism during this time period, see Will Fowler, "The Texan Revolution of 1835–1836 and Early Mexican Nationalism," in *Contested Empire: Rethinking the Texas Revolution*, ed. Sam W. Haynes and Gerald Saxon (College Station: Texas A&M University Press, 2015), 97–137. Luis García supports the idea that nationalism had failed to emerge among the people of northeastern Mexico prior to 1845. For more, see García, "Medieval Frontier," 237.

52. For a recent study of the Mexican National Guard and Indian fighting in the nineteenth-century Mexican North, see Luis Medina Peña, *Los bárbaros del norte: Guardia nacional y política en Nuevo León, siglo XIX* (México, D.F.: Fondo de Cultura Económica, 2014).

53. "Contiene constancias oficiales que manifiestan la accion continua y enérgica de las Autoridades de Nuevo León en la persecución de los indios desde 1848 hasta 1873," cuaderno quatro, caja uno, Convención de Reclamaciones, CP-AHSRE. Notably, however, certain members of Mexico's federal government might not have shared this reaction. Historian Brian DeLay writes that Mexico's minister to the United States endeavored to make sure that the United States policed its borders per Article 11 of the Treaty of Guadalupe Hidalgo, dubbing the article "'the only advantage' in the treaty that could compensate Mexico for its vast losses in the war." For more, see DeLay, *War of a Thousand Deserts*, xiii.

54. "Contiene constancias oficiales que manifiestan la accion continua y enérgica de las Autoridades de Nuevo León en la persecución de los indios desde 1848 hasta 1873," cuaderno quatro, caja uno, Convención de Reclamaciones, CP-AHSRE.

55. "Constancias oficiales que manifiestan la acción continua y enérgica," CP-AHSRE.

56. Patricio Guerra a Estimado Senor Gobernador de Estado del Nuevo Leon, June 2, 1850; Senor Alcalde de San Nicolas Hidalgo a Gobernador del Estado, June 4, 1850, both

copied by the Comisión Pesquisidora on August 8, 1873, cuaderno quatro, caja uno, Convención de Reclamaciones, CP-AHSRE.

57. Antonio Villarreal a Estimado Gobernador, June 27, 1850, copied by the Comisión Pesquisidora on August 8, 1873, cuaderno quatro, caja uno, Convención de Reclamaciones, CP-AHSRE.

58. Vital de la Garza a Estimado Gobernador del Estado, September 15, 1850, copied by the Comisión Pesquisidora on August 8, 1873, cuaderno quatro, caja uno, Convención de Reclamaciones, CP-AHSRE.

59. "Reclamaciones de México," caja uno, CP-AHSRE.

60. CP-ENG, 382–83.

61. CP-ENG, 382–83, 427–43. For a prominent American critique of U.S. Indian policy from the time period, see Helen Hunt Jackson, *A Century of Dishonor: A Sketch of the United States Government's Dealings with Some of the Indian Tribes* (Minneapolis: Ross and Haines, 1964). Jackson's book was originally published in 1881.

62. Jackson, *Century of Dishonor*, 442.

63. For more on the war that ended Comanche power in the U.S. Southwest, see Hämäläinen, *Comanche Empire*, 339, 340–41, 344; for the end of the Apache wars, see Katherine Benton Cohen, *Borderline Americans: Racial Division and Labor in the Arizona Borderlands* (Cambridge, MA: Harvard University Press, 2009), 5.

64. For more on illicit border trade, see Díaz, *Border Contraband*; and Chad Richardson and Michael J. Pisani, *The Informal and Underground Economy of the South Texas Border* (Austin: University of Texas Press, 2012).

65. David Peterson del Mar, *Beaten Down: A History of Interpersonal Violence in the West* (Seattle: University of Washington Press, 2002), 70.

66. For more, see Mora-Torres, *Making of the Mexican Border*, 52–165. This state control, of course, proved temporary and perhaps even illusory, as it came at the cost of alienating people in the northern Mexican countryside. For more on northern Mexico and border security during this time period, see Gabriel Martínez-Serna's essay in chapter 7 in this volume.

67. Miguel Ángel González-Quiroga, "Conflict and Cooperation in the Making of Texas-Mexico Border Society, 1840–1880," in *Bridging National Borders in North America: Transnational and Comparative Histories*, ed. Benjamin H. Johnson and Andrew Graybill (Durham, NC: Duke University Press, 2010), 38. According to historian Alice Baumgartner, the "Ord Order" merely legalized at the federal level what had already been common practice among borderlands law enforcement for some time. For more, see Baumgartner, "The Line of Positive Safety," 1119–20.

Figure 7.1 "Corporación del contrarresguardo para los estados de N. León y Tamaulipas," in Fondo Sandoval-Lagrange, Biblioteca de Colecciones Especiales Miguel de Cervantes Saavedra, Tecnológico de Monterrey.

Chapter 7

State-Construction and Industrial Development in the Transformation of State Violence in the Texas-Mexico Borderlands during the Early Porfiriato

J. GABRIEL MARTÍNEZ-SERNA

During the early phase of the Porfiriato the Mexican border state of Nuevo León saw a new security architecture built, which brought the political stability that allowed Monterrey's industrial takeoff in the last decade of the century. Previously, volunteer citizen militias were the main elements of local defenses and state-sanctioned violence, mostly conducted against Indians, American filibusters, highway bandits, and cattle rustlers. The militias were led by local military leaders who were also the region's dominant political figures. During the last quarter of the nineteenth century, these militias gave way to a patchwork of federal and state corps that focused on economic stability and the persecution of the regime's adversaries. These forces benefited from incipient industrialization in the form of modern communications and materiel, allowing the Díaz regime to cement a federal presence in the region and making it an emblematic case of state formation, economic development, and a new type of political violence.

In the sweltering summer heat of July 1874, the 9th Regiment of the National Guard quartered in Cerralvo mutinied and about thirty-five well-armed men rampaged through various nearby towns. Cerralvo was a strategic bulwark defending Monterrey against hostile Indian and cattle rustling incursions from across the Rio Grande and key for the defense of trade routes to Tamaulipas and Texas.[1] Local militias were summoned by the governor, and these soon clashed with the mutineers, who barricaded themselves in the nearby Sierra de Salinas. The governor summoned reinforcements and ordered them to "move violently against" the mutineers and coordinate their operations with the state Public Security force created by the state legislature the previous year. They "battered and defeated" the mutineers, killing some, taking others prisoner, and recuperating the arms and horses stolen from Cerralvo. The governor was particularly proud of the new state Public Security corps because it was its first campaign and it had taken years for it to be built, but payment for militias became a dispute between municipal and state governments, underscoring the chaotic and haphazard security arrangements.[2] The governor denied the municipality of San Nicolás Hidalgo their request to pay its rural police force, since such actions "deal with the security of private interests and the conservation of the public order, and both rural and urban police are obligated to such service, the latter paid for by the municipalities, [and] the former have as compensation for their occasional few days of service the complete exemption from any sort of taxes during that year."[3]

Thus, even though the motley collection of municipal rural forces equipped with outdated materiel had been instrumental in the suppression of the Cerralvo mutiny, the governor refused to pay for their service, citing old frontier practices of volunteer citizen militias. The security arrangement that put down the Cerralvo mutiny would undergo a dramatic transformation in the last quarter of the nineteenth century as the growing power of the central government manifested itself through a permanent armed federal presence in the region, making the years of suppression of the Cerralvo mutiny a watershed in the history of state-sanctioned violence in northeastern Mexico.

The haphazardly coordinated security forces used to put down the 1874 Cerralvo mutiny reflected the protean nature of the security framework in the borderlands and the difficulty the central governments had in confronting destabilizing episodes of cross-border violence during the years after the signing of the Treaty of Guadalupe Hidalgo in 1848. During the ensuing decades, neither nation-state was able to impose its will in the borderlands, and most cases of state-sanctioned violence were perpetrated by local authorities. The last quarter of the century was the historic pivot when Mexico's central government set the bases for a dramatic change in state-sanctioned violence in the borderlands that helped consolidate advances in economic development and state-building. In these years, under the dictatorship of Porfirio Díaz, Mexico achieved an unprecedented level of political stability and economic development, and a state-sanctioned violence previously consisting of local militias fighting Indians, filibusters, and cattle rustlers was replaced by security forces using industrial technology such as telegraphs, railroads, and modern military hardware. A surge of foreign investment in extractive industries in turn intertwined the economies of northern Mexico and the southern United States further together.[4] The waning of Indian raids, the eclipse of cattle fortunes, and an incipient industrialization set the stage for a new economy to accompany the new security architecture.[5]

The Porfirian regime was obsessed with developing the country's economy by opening it up to foreign investors. After independence followed a half century of political instability and economic stagnation, leaving little national capital for productive investment. To entice foreign capital, Díaz sought to bring order and stability to a country that had experienced continuous civil wars since its break from Spain. A more orderly and predictable political environment was needed, including a government that could enforce laws protecting capital. In the northeast, Díaz had to deal with locals well versed in the use of violence and a fiercely independent streak. "Taming" the northeastern borderlanders became a cornerstone of his national project.

Before the first election of Porfirio Díaz in 1876, the army and National Guard were the main pillars of Mexico's state security apparatus at the national level, with some regional variations. In the northeast, these institutions theoretically complemented the frontier militias controlled by regional caudillos who at will commanded local regiments of the National Guard or even entire divisions of an ostensibly federal army.[6]

Díaz was suspicious of northeastern caudillos in part because of his defeat in the Battle of Icamole in Nuevo León during the Tuxtepec Revolution of 1876 that paved the way to his election. Furthermore, military strongman Jerónimo Treviño and his ally General Francisco Naranjo were in ascendance in national politics during the Díaz interregnum of 1880 to 1884 (the only time between 1877 and the start of the Revolution of 1910 when Díaz was not president). These were the years of the presidency of the Tamaulipas general Manuel González, who appointed consecutively as his ministers of War and Marine the two Nuevo León generals (Treviño during 1881–82 and Naranjo from 1882 to 1884). Thus Díaz was deeply distrustful of these borderlanders and decided to send General Bernardo Reyes as military leader of the region but also as his personal representative—a situation the local elite quickly realized to its surprise. After centuries of dominating the region, their control of state-sanctioned violence was about to be usurped.

Jalisco native Reyes was appointed military leader of the Third Military Zone (which included all three northeastern states) and subsequently interim or constitutional governor of Nuevo León, which he ruled almost uninterruptedly for the next twenty-four years. Reyes craftily marginalized the Treviño and Naranjo political clique through patronage and the construction of a new security architecture mostly funded by the federal government.[7]

In the Mexican side of the border, the pillars of the emerging security architecture were the federal army, mounted police, a revamped custom guard, reorganized local state and municipal forces, and a sprawling network of spies, informers, and agents of the regime. Some of these structural and institutional innovations were to outlast the Díaz dictatorship and become the basis for the postrevolutionary security apparatus. The Mexican Army had an important but ultimately circumscribed role in the deployment of political violence when Díaz was in power.[8] Previously, it had generally sided with conservatives in repeated clashes with liberals and was a pillar of Santa Anna's last stint as president (1853–55).

After the fall of Santa Anna and the defeat of the conservatives, Santiago Vidaurri swore alliance to the new liberal regime and consolidated troops under his command as the "Northern Army," an ostensibly federal force funded by tariffs from the customs houses in the borders of the merged states of Coahuila and Nuevo León. With it, Vidaurri implemented his "Plan Restaurador de la Libertad," a local version of the Plan de Ayutla that had overthrown Santa Anna. Vidaurri replaced Santa Anna's ally General Ampudia and became the undisputed caudillo of the northeast.[9]

Vidaurri dominated the northeast through his iron grip of local militias and his "Army of the North," and after his fall and defeat by Juárez, Coahuila and Nuevo León were once again split, and that is when the Nuevo León politics were taken over by the Treviño and Naranjo political faction until the arrival of Reyes in 1885.[10]

In 1885, Díaz appointed Reyes as commander of the Third Military Zone, which included Coahuila, Nuevo León, and Tamaulipas and some of the most profitable customs houses in the country. Reyes displaced the network of Treviño and Naranjo and subsequently dominated the northeast in the name of the central government through his command of the federal army as well as his command of other federal security forces and local ones as the constitutional governor of Nuevo León. He always used a heavy hand when dealing with his gubernatorial counterparts in Coahuila and Tamaulipas.

In addition to the federal army, the other nominally national force during the middle of the century was the National Guard. In sheer numbers, it was almost four times as large as the army but lacked its professionalism, and as the episode at the beginning of this essay showed, discipline and allegiances to authorities were dubious.

It was not a standing army, and its equipment was often old and with no standardization of materiel and lacking qualified leaders and regiment discipline. Its objectives were limited to defending national sovereignty against foreign invasion "within their respective regions" and only when specifically summoned. Furthermore, its members lacked military immunity (*fuero militar*) that the army had. The 1842 law stipulated for the first time that it was the duty of every Mexican citizen to cooperate in the defense of the country and reestablishment of public order.[11]

The political turmoil and constitutional changes during the struggle against the United States' invasion changed the relationship between the National Guard and the federal army. Originally the National Guard was meant to be a complementary force to and not in direct competition with the army.[12] As a result of these constitutional changes, the relationship between armed citizens and the state was fundamentally transformed and would eventually undermine the rationale for the existence of frontier militias in the northeast.[13]

The National Guard and the army were sometimes in open conflict during political disputes. The latter tended to side with centralists and conservatives, whereas the former, composed of locals, usually sided with liberals and federalists. Politicians often tried to blur the lines to their advantage. For example, during his last stint as president under the conservative banner in 1853–55, Santa Anna tried to incorporate the best elements of the National Guard into the army and dissolve the rest, but local military leaders resisted, as was the case in the northeast.[14] Juárez himself was not above "innovating" and restructuring the National Guard when it served his cause.

There was no presence of the National Guard in Nuevo León prior to 1846, and after the collapse of local governments, for a while the security situation in northeast Mexico was tempered by the presence of U.S. troops stationed in Matamoros, Tampico, and Monterrey. But after these forces withdrew, chaos and violence returned with a vengeance as banditry and attacks on isolated settlements increased dramatically, and turmoil in Mexico City precluded the passage of any legislation regulating the corps, forcing locals to continue to rely on citizen militias.[15]

Benito Juárez advocated for the eradication of the "old vices" of the army and justified the existence of the National Guard as "one of the institutions which the national government will protect, because it understands that it too is a pillar of public liberties, and because of this, will attempt to promptly organize the most useful way of attaining this objective."[16] But his government never did. Once Maximilian's empire had crumbled and Juárez was secure in the peacetime presidency, he proceeded to demobilize the wartime army, reducing its size and transferring some of the National Guard's best regiments into a revamped federal army. In this way, some citizen militia became professional soldiers, and demobilized army units were then used as security forces in their respective states.[17] And this was perhaps the main reason for the falling out between President Juárez and local caudillo Santiago Vidaurri.

Throughout the presidencies of Juárez and Lerdo de Tejada, their administrations had been either too busy or too afraid of local strongmen to decree the standardization of the National Guard. This political vacuum left states with no common national standards. The legislature of Nuevo León, with the memory of the 1874 Cerralvo mutiny still fresh, on April 13, 1877 dissolved the National Guard in the state.[18] Governor Genaro Garza García claimed it simply did not exist in the state, "nor did any other force that could replace it in case it was needed, and were it not for the fact that currently most of the Northern Division of the Federal Army resides in the state, it would be impossible to secure order and public peace."[19] The last mention of the National Guard in the country's laws is in 1880.[20] After his return to power in 1884 and for the rest of his increasingly violent, autocratic, and repressive dictatorship, Díaz would never again use the National Guard and instead would lean on other security institutions, in particular the infamous Rurales (see below).

The professionalization of the army and the disappearance of the National Guard were only part of the reforms of the security apparatus of the Porfirian regime. At the end of his second term in office (1884–88) and with over two decades to go before the start of the Revolution of 1910, President Díaz gave a speech as he was preparing for his second consecutive reelection for the period 1888 to 1892. He boasted of over twelve years of peace and rising prosperity in his message to the nation:

> Much has been done in the organization of the police, both urban and rural: this last one distributed in regiments, not only in the Federal District but also in various states of the Federation, that keep a constant eye in the security of the roads, placing themselves in strategic places and acting in accordance to the police of the states, such that an individual's safety and security can be guaranteed. This situation, advantageous in all manners to the common good, has produced abroad a favorable opinion of us, to a great degree replacing the previous concerns based on our apparent social situations brought about by false rumors, and which were so pernicious to immigration attempts and relations with foreign powers.[21]

Díaz may have claimed that local police were important for keeping the peace, but it would be federal forces that became the main pillar of the new security architecture of the region.

The Rural Forces of the Federation (Fuerzas Rurales de la Federación, better known as simply "los Rurales") were mounted police that became the quintessential component of the Porfirian security apparatus and a symbol of the regime's violent and authoritarian nature and its idealization of a particular brand of macho masculinity. Some romanticized this mounted police as virile keepers of stability and order, but their arbitrary brutality became one of their hallmarks, especially toward the end of the Porfiriato.[22] By then, the wily dictator was using them as his political shock troops and as the main institutional counterbalance to the professional army.

Díaz did not create the Rurales but instead transformed them to suit his regime's needs. He took a protean institution with relatively little importance and over time shaped the corps into an effective tool of social control and political repression:

> The Rurales before Díaz . . . were insignificant and unsung. It was only after he had reorganized them and made them an integral and permanent part of the Porfirian system that their distinctive character developed. The Rurales during the presidencies of Juárez and Lerdo, though nominally federal police, did not appreciably differ in organization, duties, and effectiveness from the local bands of the 1840s and the 1850s.

It was Díaz who created "the Rurales" that became a symbol of Porfirian Mexico's "law and order" and "ruthlessness."[23]

As was the case with the National Guard, the immediate institutional origins of the Rurales came about in turbulent political times. The corps came into existence by a decree of President Juárez in May 6, 1861, initially consisting of four mounted regiments whose main duty was "the preservation of order on the highways of the nation." They were organized by and under the orders of the minister of war. A further three regiments were created by Juárez in 1866 and 1867, the waning days of the Second Mexican Empire.[24] To complement their capabilities, Juárez transferred *fuerzas volantes* (light cavalry) that had been part of the army. Another decree from Juárez in 1869 reassigned four regiments from the Ministry of War to the Ministry of the Interior, foreshadowing their future role as enforcers of the Díaz dictatorship.

Díaz began the restructuring of the security apparatus of the Mexican state because of an upsurge in banditry after his first election as president in late 1876.[25] Taking advantage of the public outcry over the climate of insecurity throughout the country, Díaz placed more regiments of Rurales under the direct command of the interior ministry to "guard highways and railroads and to persecute guerrilla bands and bandits." Among their duties were to be on the lookout for suspicious strangers that could potentially alter the social order, to keep them under constant surveillance while in their jurisdictions, and to notify neighboring authorities of a suspect's presence in their territories once they left their own. They were also mandated to help the federal army by serving as scouts or engaging in guerrilla fighting.[26] The evolution of the Rurales from a military corps to an indispensable political enforcer continued until the eve of the Revolution, by which time only two regiments remained under formal military commanders and the rest were controlled directly by the interior ministry.[27]

In 1880, comprehensive regulations governing the Rurales were standardized as chain of command, regiment cohesion, discipline, and uniforms and materiel were codified into law for the first time. Requirements for candidates were similar to those of local militias: a healthy male and citizen of good standing, able to read and write, aged between twenty and fifty, skillful in the use of a horse, and able to afford uniform, arms, and a horse on his own. Enlistment was for four-year periods. By the time Díaz retook the presidency from González in 1884, the Rurales had consolidated their presence in various regions. Most regiments were stationed in central Mexico, but Nuevo León was the only northern state where the Rurales were operating during the González presidency, where the X Corps patrolled the borderlands of northern Nuevo León, Coahuila, and Tamaulipas and the border with Texas.[28] Thus when Reyes arrived in the northeast in 1885, Nuevo León already had a regiment of Rurales under federal control to complement his control of the Third Army Zone.[29] But his consolidation of political power and state-sanctioned violence was only just beginning.

Another pillar of the emerging security architecture in the northern frontier was a renovated and expanded Customs Police (known as the Contrarresguardo Aduanal or Fiscal Gendarmerie). Contraband and smuggling had a long tradition in the borderlands going back to colonial times, but the move of the U.S.-Mexico border to the Rio Grande provided new opportunities. Tariffs had been an important source of income for Vidaurri, and both Juárez and later Díaz saw the establishment of a strong federal customs police in the northern border not only as a security guarantee against incursions from the United States by political adversaries and would-be revolutionaries, but also as a means of cutting off a source of revenue for regional political opponents.

The origin of the Contrarresguardo was in a project formulated during the Juárez presidency by Treasury minister Matías Romero. In 1869, he proposed its creation and deployment to the northern frontier, and in the following June the respective ordinances were passed. His successor Francisco Mejía issued new regulations for the northern frontier in 1872. Finally, in 1878 a new decree was issued regulating it in the Zona Libre.[30] In the northeast, the Contrarresguardo consisted of mounted "flying companies" that patrolled the Zona Libre with its headquarters in Monterrey, even though the city was outside the Zona Libre. (In fact, the city's merchants complained because they felt disadvantaged with respect to competitors outside Monterrey who continued benefiting from smuggling.)[31]

The Treviño and Naranjo political machine that dominated state politics was heavily dependent on income generated by its control of the countryside of northern Nuevo León, especially the Lampazos area, near the geographical nexus of the borders of Coahuila, Nuevo León, Tamaulipas, and Texas. Although no direct evidence links either Treviño or Naranjo as actively participating in contraband, tariffs and smuggling did allow their political machinery to flourish, though this antagonized Monterrey merchants for their alleged comparative disadvantage vis-à-vis merchants from Coahuila and Tamaulipas.[32] A strengthened Customs Police could only mean the weakening of the Treviño and Naranjo *cacicazgo* (political chiefdom).

Contraband had been a source of considerable profits for Monterrey merchants during the U.S. Civil War, but after the Contrarresguardo was reformed and strengthened by Díaz, they claimed it made them uncompetitive. Even as railroads, telegraphs, and proximity to the Texas economy were turning Monterrey into the preeminent northeastern economic hub, the city's merchants complained that it took just two hours to ship merchandise from Laredo to Monterrey in railroads, and in theory another two to get it from

Monterrey to Saltillo. But the Contrarresguardo in Monterrey could take days to process merchandise, thus giving smugglers in the Zona Libre an unfair advantage.[33] Cracks in the consensus emerged as some merchants began questioning the Treviñistas' hold over state politics, and this fissure in the local elite was the excuse Díaz and Reyes needed to hatch a plot to sideline Treviño and Naranjo and their political machinery in the state.

Shortly after taking office for the first time in 1877, Díaz appointed General Juan Vara as the new commander of the Contrarresguardo in the northeast.[34] Vara's orders were to set the force on a sustained and permanent standing through negotiations between federal dependencies and local authorities. For this purpose, in 1878 the Ministry of War ordered Vara to consolidate and liquidate old debts and formalize a monthly payment of 125 pesos from the federal treasury for the Twenty-Second Battalion of the Second Cavalry Corps and the Third Artillery Brigade that were to be permanently stationed in Monterrey.[35]

President Díaz replaced Vara a few months later with General Juan de Haro.[36] The new commander took to his duties enthusiastically. In October of that year, members of the Contrarresguardo violently entered a house in Linares searching for contraband. The terrified wife of the owner of the house did not resist, and after ransacking the residence, the troops simply left when they realized they had mistakenly raided the wrong house.[37] General Haro wrote to the governor apologizing for the mistake, but the incident foreshadowed troubling changes ahead.

Another example of the Contrarresguardo's role in the transformation of state-sanctioned violence in the northeastern borderlands occurred shortly afterward. General Haro was informed via a telegram from the treasury ministry in Mexico City that two Texans on a cattle-buying trip had been robbed at gunpoint in northern Nuevo León and that the reputed perpetrators were seven members of the Contrarresguardo. Haro asked his underlings in the municipality of General Bravo to conduct an inquiry to establish the facts and report back.[38] It was quickly established that the supposed members of the customs police were instead impostors that had been seizing merchandise on the roads of the northern part of the state at gunpoint. Although the law allowed citizens to seize contraband from suspected smugglers, they were obliged to immediately report and turn it over to the nearest office of the Contrarresguardo. Instead, the impostors kept the merchandise and when discovered, fled to the nearby area of Las Cuestas. General Haro was determined an example be made of the impostors so that such a "deplorable incident" would not be emulated by others.[39]

Despite efforts to professionalize the Contrarresguardo, discipline and morale were a constant problem, and as with the Rurales, coercion and arbitrary violence plagued the corps. Many of its members were prone to violence themselves, instead of supposedly keeping a lid on it. In May 1894, a member of the Flying Company stationed near the Hacienda Los Alamos reported being attacked after a friendly game of cards went awry. The *celador* (the lowest enlisted men of the customs police) claimed to have been wounded by an irate mob of hacienda workers. When the celador's superior arrived at the scene, he heard a gunshot and saw his underling bleeding on the ground next to his horse. The celador told him he was attacked without provocation by the hacienda workers after he had called them out as cheaters during a game of cards.[40] However, a follow-up report ascertained that it had instead been the celador who initiated the aggression: in a drunken stupor, he had first threatened the workers after losing a hand; subsequently he was disarmed by them, only for him to then go searching for another pistol and injuring himself as he tried to mount his horse in his impaired state.

Despite these incidents of violent misconduct against innocent civilians, the Contrarresguardo became another pillar of the new security architecture in the northeast complementing the X Corps of the Rurales, the regiments of the Third Army Zone, and supported by the state Security Force created in the wake of the Cerralvo 1874 uprising, as well as an urban police force created for Monterrey in the 1880s, and the remaining municipal rural militias (though these were increasingly an afterthought because of lack of discipline and antiquated materiel).[41] By centralizing political, military, and paramilitary power, Reyes became an effective political operator directing state-sanctioned violence in the service of the regime. For example, in 1901, Reyes sent a combined force of members from the Contrarresguardo and the X Corps of the Rurales to follow, engage, and ultimately dismantle a band of violent smugglers hiding in the Sierra de Mamulique halfway between Monterrey and the U.S border that had been disrupting trade with Texas.[42] Border controls were no longer in the hands of local grandees, but the modern forces of the federal government. Thus, the consolidation of the Díaz dictatorship and the institutional changes in the security forces he implemented improved dramatically the way in which the federal state projected its power in the northeast, but the regime was helped by modern technology such as railroads and the telegraph.

The official response to a couple of small uprisings in two municipalities in the central part of Nuevo León in 1884 illustrate the changing nature and role of state-sanctioned violence in the region. On October 1, 1884, locals gathered and attempted to force from office the local magistrate of Sabinas Hidalgo. When he refused, an armed posse entered his home and shot him in front of his family and afterward continued on a violent rampage. At dawn the next day, they attacked the local police force and overwhelmed it after eight hours of resistance; the rioters then took possession of the courthouse, destroyed its archive, and killed the judge's father as well as the town mayor.[43] New communication technologies notified the state government in Monterrey, and this resulted in a more rapid and efficient coordination and response of the various security corps than had been the case for the 1874 Cerralvo mutiny.

In his subsequent report to the state legislature, the governor stressed how the use of railroads and telegraphs had been crucial in summoning and jointly deploying the state security force and rural militias to quickly surround the town and keep the rioters from escaping. The men, horses, and materiel of the state security force were "transported in an express train that left this city at 11 o'clock at night and were on the outskirts of Sabinas by noon the next day" ready for combat. Railroads were also used to transport reinforcements from militias in other parts of the state. Within a couple of days over five hundred mounted men under arms were stationed in a perimeter outside Sabinas Hidalgo and ready to arrest or kill the rioters. Seeing they were numerically and materially outmatched, the rioters laid down their arms. Afterward the governor disbanded the joint forces, but as a precaution and warning, after establishing temporary municipal authorities, he changed the status of some of the state security forces into temporary municipal police and forced the municipality to pay the costs until proper order was restored. The governor claimed that the state's coffers paid for some of the "unexpected costs" of the uprisings but pointed out that it had promptly been put down thanks to the fact that neighboring municipalities deployed their militias under the joint command of the state government. Unlike his predecessor who had declined to reimburse the militias that had helped put down the Cerralvo episode of 1874, now the governor asked the state legislature to pay for these services by replacing with new equipment the weapons, horses, and saddles that were used or lost during the operations.[44]

By the end of the decade, the state security force became a permanent fixture of the states' budget. Indeed, the next year, Governor García asked the legislature to raise its numbers, which then consisted of twenty-five men and an officer.[45] Referring to this corps, he explained:

> The police, a force created for the prevention of crime and the apprehension of delinquents, is divided into urban and rural, depending on whether they serve within a community or outside of it. The urban does not really exist in the state except in the capital, because the rest of the state's municipalities, if there are any individuals who have such duties, it is only on a temporary basis, performing the said actions as the duties of a *vecino*, due to the fact that municipal coffers are so depleted that they cannot provide sufficient resources for the upkeep of a small security force.[46]

But it proved a considerable strain on Nuevo León's finances: it was the single largest item in the state budget, representing almost a third of general expenses. Even then, it was eclipsed by the costs of federal forces assigned to the region.[47] But Governor Reyes had by 1890 unparallel coercive power at his disposal, from federal, state, and municipal sources.

The final pillar of the Porfirian security apparatus in the northeast consisted of an unprecedented network of agents providing intelligence and engaging in propaganda, sabotage, physical and psychological intimidation, and even the assassination of enemies of the regime. Sometimes these activities even took place across the U.S. border with the tacit approval of Texas authorities. Ironically, this cooperative transnational violence brought about the final contours of the borders of the three northeastern Mexican states. And it was Reyes's obsession with maintaining his iron fist in the northeast and finally vanquishing intermittent interstate violence between citizens of the three border states that brought about the final and current borders between them.

Since colonial times, Nuevo León's northern border was disputed with Coahuila and Tamaulipas. Some interpretations claimed Nuevo León's northern border was the Salado River, a tributary of the Rio Grande about fifty kilometers to its south. Other interpretations of colonial grants had Nuevo León's border farther north on the Rio Grande and even the Nueces River. Whether Nuevo León had direct access to the Rio Grande was of paramount importance to Reyes's grip on power. Treaties between the United States and Mexico stipulated that only border governors could deal directly with their counterparts on the other side of the border to expedite extraditions of "problematic" persons without having to go through formal diplomatic channels in Washington and Mexico City, a process that could take months in the best of circumstances. Thus, it was vital for Reyes to make Nuevo León a formal border state.

The situation Reyes encountered on his arrival in the northeast in 1885 was evolving quickly. Between the Cerralvo uprising of 1878 and 1884, the last groups of Lipan Apaches had been eradicated, along with the menace of Texas filibusters. Furthermore, Monterrey had no municipal police force during these years because of a lack of funds, and in that year, postelection violence broke out in the municipalities of Galeana, Santiago, and Sabinas Hidalgo as a rival group contested the hegemony of the political machine headed by Treviño and Naranjo.[48]

In the 1885 Nuevo León gubernatorial elections, the opposition group headed by Lazaro Garza Ayala contested the elections against the Treviñista nominee. There was a minor incident in Bustamante before the elections, but postelection events provided the opportunity for Díaz to appoint Reyes as military leader and eventually insinuate himself in state politics. When the

Treviñistas won the elections, the opposition appealed to Díaz for federal intervention on their behalf. Díaz and Reyes pretended not to take sides in the conflict, while quietly operating for the opposition and undermining the Treviñistas. When the duly elected governor left for Mexico City to appeal directly to Díaz for help in the dispute, he left an unpopular and not very competent substitute governor in his place. Meanwhile, the opposition deployed a force of 150 armed and mounted men from Lampazos under local leader Manuel Rodriguez to march on the capital Monterrey, forcing the provisional governor to ask for special powers from the state legislature, which after doing so dissolved itself while the emergency passed. When the provisional governor foolishly left the state briefly, the opposition asked for federal intervention on the basis of a vacuum of constitutional authority in the state. This was quickly provided by Díaz, and Reyes was installed as interim governor for the remainder of the 1885–87 period. Within months, Reyes and Díaz had dismantled the political machine that had dominated the state since the fall of Vidaurri.[49] But Reyes was not done.

As an example of his extended powers that crossed local state boundaries, in 1886 Reyes dismantled a revolt in neighboring Tamaulipas. A small armed group, supported by newspaper publisher, doctor, and former Mexican military Ignacio Martínez, based in Laredo, tried to unsuccessfully foment a larger rebellion against the federal government. Although the revolt fizzled in large part because it never had good access to financial or military resources, Reyes was sufficiently worried that he sent armed troops through the railroad from Monterrey to Nuevo Laredo in order to reinforce the federal presence at the border.[50] Martínez would be assassinated in the streets of Laredo in 1891 by what is widely believed to be Reyes's associates, a brazen murder that radicalized the Mexican community in South Texas, while demonstrating just how much Reyes had expanded and consolidated federal power in the border region.

The murder of Martínez was the catalyzer for the Catarino Garza rebellion of later that year that posed the most serious threat to the regime in the borderlands. Writing years later about the Martínez murder, Catarino Garza expressed his anger at the degree of control Reyes had achieved:

On the 3d of February of 1891, in Laredo Texas, U.S.A.; he was assassinated in a cowardly and treacherous manner by two Mexican henchmen sent on horseback by the army under a Colonel Cerón, blind instrument of the executioner of the borderlands Bernardo Reyes, Governor of the State of Nuevo León. Known as "The Jackal" by the press, he performed the same role that [the governor of Veracruz] had done in his state, with the difference being that Reyes had to violate the territory of the United States to assassinate General and Doctor Ignacio Martínez.[51]

Garza fought the Díaz regime in Mexico as well as the Anglo establishment that dominated Texas's Democratic political machine until he was forced to flee to Central America, where he died while fighting in Panama in 1895.

Thus the period from Reyes's arrival in the northeast in 1885 to the exile of Catarino Garza in 1892 was crucial in the consolidation of the federal control over the northeast borderlands. Indeed, Garza's words and actions were the crucial last link in this institutional consolidation process by the regime. In the summer of 1888, an ethnic Mexican was detained and later shot by an Anglo customs guard in Starr county under the excuse that he attempted to flee.[52] The customs guard was reassigned to Brownsville, but tempers among the Mexican community in South Texas remained sufficiently raw that local newspapers kept clamoring for justice. Among those doing so were Catarino Garza, whose writings had upset the customs guard. While in Rio Grande City, he walked up to Catarino and shot him and a companion, before being chased out of town under fire from Garza supporters. But Garza's actions would have long-lasting repercussions in the very borders of the northeastern states. Reyes could not tolerate someone like Garza challenging his authority, but with Nuevo León lacking a formal border with Texas, his hands were tied by provisions in the various treaties between the Unites States and Mexico.

As late as 1888, Coahuila and Nuevo León were disputing jurisdiction over lands between the Rio Grande and the Salado River (with both governors even challenging each other to a fistfight). Relations between Nuevo León and Tamaulipas had also been fraught with tension, as many border communities such as Nuevo Laredo and Mier had more economic interaction and security cooperation with settlements from northern Nuevo León than with the Tamaulipas state government. In response to Garza's perceived threat, Reyes tried to resolve this conflict by making Nuevo León a formal border state with lands adjacent to the Rio Grande. With federal pressure, an "Arbitration Convention" was convened in Saltillo on June 28 of 1890, where Reyes chastised leaders from both states for letting this matter linger in the courts rather than come to a mutually agreed resolution through the executives and legislatures.[53]

Reyes forced the two state legislatures to an agreement that traded lands between the states, giving Candela to Coahuila but crucially giving Nuevo León a strip of land from the Salado River to the Rio Grande, thus finally making Reyes a formal border governor with the ability to deal directly with Texas authorities. The agreement was promptly approved at the federal congress in July 1892.[54] Reyes specifically stated in the state government December 1892 decree implementing the law that now "we can manage extraditions of dangerous prisoners that have committed serious crimes, without the intervention of the Ministry of Foreign Affairs" as stipulated in existing treaties.[55]

Reyes's actions betrayed his nervousness at the various attempted uprisings in the border region that culminated in the Garza rebellion of 1891–92. Earlier episodes included the capture of notorious smuggler Mariano Reséndez in Matamoros, the assassination of Ignacio Martínez in Laredo, and the Sandoval uprising in the Tamaulipas panhandle with the possible involvement of the Naranjo clan from Lampazos. Garza's uprising, then, helps to temper the traditional view of Díaz's dictatorship as a monolithic three and a half decades of oppression, rather than a steady buildup of a repressive state apparatus.[56]

Garza had been a target of the Coahuila government since 1886, when he started writing against the excesses of its governor José María Garza Galán. Reyes joined the Coahuila governor in his determination in having Garza extradited to Mexico, and even coopted some Texas state authorities to harass him there, including a stint in a county jail Garza did for libel and having his printing equipment confiscated.[57] But Reyes could not formally extradite him while Nuevo León was not officially a border state. This was all changed with the 1892 legal modifications.

Texas authorities at first refused to hand Garza over after Reyes specifically asked for his extradition. The existing treaty between both countries limited his ability to deal with his Texas counterparts.[58] With news of an upsurge in Garza's activities following Ignacio Martínez's assassination in February 1891 and conscious of a looming two-year judicial deadline for implementing the Arbitration Convention of 1890, Reyes expedited the process, and a border dispute that had been festering for decades was resolved within eight months. Nuevo León formally became a border state when it ceded the territory of Candela in the northwestern part of the state to Coahuila and the later ceded a territory between the Rio Grande and Salado Rivers that was incorporated into Nuevo León. After Congress authorized the changes at the federal level, Díaz signed the appropriate decree on December 13, 1892. The news arrived in Monterrey immediately, and just two days later, Reyes sent the state legislature a proposal for the founding of the settlement of Colombia in the territories ceded by Coahuila. The Nuevo León legislature approved it on December 16, and that very day, Reyes wrote a memorandum to the Ministry of Foreign Affairs asking them to formally communicate to the State Department that Nuevo León had become a border state and that this information be relayed to Texas authorities and its attorney general as soon as possible. Reyes wasted no time using his new powers: in his report to the legislature of 1895, he bragged about using them to extradite sixteen "revoltosos" from Texas in just two years.[59]

While Reyes was consolidating the Porfirian security state in the northeast, Monterrey's economy was being transformed by an avalanche of investments, a crucial historical pivot where the old land-owning and merchant elite that dominated the state became an emerging industrial class.[60] Incipient industrialization changed Monterrey from a sleepy backwater to a commercial hub and a budding economic powerhouse. While Reyes was busy building the new security architecture, in the economic sphere he made at least three concessions to expand public lighting in the city,[61] while others were issued for inner-city light trains[62] and for railroads connecting Monterrey to the southern parts of the state, central Mexico, and Texas.[63]

By the turn of the century, it was hard to recognize Nuevo León from what it had been during the Cerralvo uprising of 1874. Reyes had thoroughly reorganized the security architecture in the northeast and reoriented state-sanctioned violence to new objectives and purposes, while setting the basis for an economy based on breweries, smelting, steel mills, and glass factories. A final episode in 1903 illustrates this change and foreshadows the violence that would dominate Mexico's political system for rest of the century.

During the Porfiriato, April 2 became a national holiday celebrating the victory over the French in Puebla during the Second Empire. For the Nuevo León elections of 1903, a rival political group was contesting Reyes's stranglehold on local politics. In Monterrey, the civic celebrations of April 2 of 1903 coincided with an anti-reelection gathering under the banner of the "Unión Democrática" in the city's Alameda plaza a few blocks away from the main city square. A rival pro-government rally gathered in the plaza in front of the municipal government building to celebrate the festivities. After a series of speeches calling for the election of a new president, the opposition protesters marched toward the main square, but municipal and state forces were deployed in order to keep both sides from physically engaging. Despite this, a kerfuffle broke out, and after a few minutes of mayhem, gunfire erupted. Witnesses claimed the shots came from the direction of the city hall building. Regardless, the crowd scattered as police reinforcements arrived and started beating and arresting protesters. By the time the situation had calmed down, eight people were dead and dozens of pro-democracy activists arrested. The culprits for the deaths were never officially named or captured, but the violence fulfilled its purpose in intimidating political opponents: there would be no effective opposition to the Díaz regime in Nuevo León for the rest of the dictator's time in power.[64]

When seen in the context of state coercive capabilities, the political violence deployed by Reyes in 1903 was fundamentally different from the state-sanctioned violence that had dominated the region previously. From the Cerralvo uprising in 1874 to the Monterrey April 2 massacre of 1903, state-sanctioned violence had undergone a profound change in nature. It was now mostly of urban nature, and overtly political in nature, and now under the orders of a Machiavellian federal proconsul sent from Mexico City. Gone were the old military strongmen on horseback who had risen to prominence fighting Indians, foreign invasions, unwanted federal troops, or local political rebellions. In fact, the political violence of Monterrey's 1903 April 2 demonstrations has much more in common with the state-sanctioned violence deployed against opponents of the postrevolutionary single-party regime than it did with the state-sanctioned violence that had existed in the northeastern frontier for centuries.

Nuevo León was perhaps the most successful experiment of the Porfiriato's politics of security overhaul and economic development. The transformation and professionalization of the security apparatus swept away the last remnants of the citizen militias that had dominated the administration of state violence for centuries. After Reyes's arrival, the National Guard was gone and the rural militias had been mostly eclipsed and finally replaced by the federal army, the Rurales, and the Contrarresguardo. The central government thus gained control of the border in a way that had never been possible before, becoming the main purveyor of state-sanctioned violence. In Nuevo León, state construction, the delimitation of internal and international borders, and the industrial takeoff of Monterrey were all part of the same historical process.

Notes

1. *Cuerpos Rurales y de Seguridad*, caja 1 (1871–1915), exp. 2 ff1, Archivo General del Estado de Nuevo León (hereafter, AGENL); *Memoria que el gobierno del estado de Nuevo León presentó al soberano congreso del mismo, y que fue leída por el Secretario de despacho en la sesión del día 21 de Septiembre de 1874 sobre el estado de los ramos de la administración pública* (Monterrey: Imprenta del progreso, 1874), 8–9.

2. *Memoria* (Monterrey, 1874); *Cuerpos Rurales y de Seguridad*, caja 1, (1871–1915), Exp. 2, AGENL.

3. *Cuerpos Rurales y de Seguridad*, caja 1, (1871–1915), exp. 2, AGENL.

4. Barry Carr, "Las peculiaridades del norte mexicano, 1880–1927: Ensayo de interpretación," *Historia Mexicana* 22, no. 3 (January–March 1973): 325.

5. Juan Mora-Torres, *The Making of the Mexican Border: The State, Capitalism, and Society in Nuevo León, 1848–1910* (Austin: University of Texas Press, 2001), 38. Apaches and Comanches were not the only Indian "problem" in the Mexico-Texas borderlands. Other groups regularly crossed the border, though not always to raid or steal cattle. As late as 1868, Texas ranches close to the Rio Grande were being raided and Nuevo León, Coahuila, and Tamaulipas were expecting cross-border reprisals, and the inevitable Indian attacks farther south that would follow, as had happened previously. Another example were the Kickapoos residing in Coahuila, who were accused of raiding ranches in Texas. The next year, U.S. Army officers and Kickapoo leaders from the Indian Territories traveled to Coahuila to try to entice the rest of the tribe to live in the United States and rid Texas of transborder raids. Most of the Kickapoos acquiesced, but a few remain in Coahuila to this day. Isidro Vizcaya Canales, *Tierra de Guerra Viva: Incursiones de indios y otros conflictos en el*

noreste de México durante el siglo XIX, 1821–1885 (Monterrey: Academia de Investigaciones, 2001), 215–21.

6. An example was Santiago Vidaurri, an astute politician and a veteran of the Indian wars who consolidated power during the middle of the century by annexing Coahuila to Nuevo León for a few years. A competent administrator who built the institutional basis for the modern state of Nuevo León, Vidaurri took control and revamped the Army of the North, which was nominally under the control of the central government but in reality was commanded by him and funded through his control of the region's customs houses. Vidaurri was also a ruthless military commander capable of a brutality shocking to modern sensibilities, arguing the barbaric nature of the Lipan Apaches, and openly advocated genocide even though he acknowledged these were "unnatural and horrible deeds." As leader of Nuevo León and Coahuila in the wake of the U.S. Civil War, he had constant communication with the military authorities in Texas. Vizcaya Canales, *Tierra de Guerra Viva*, 185–88, 190, 201, 203, 207. For a rather hagiographic treatment of Vidaurri, see Artemio Benavides, *Santiago Vidaurri: Caudillo del noreste mexicano (1855–1864)* (Monterrey: Tusquets, 2012).

7. For the quick denouement of the Treviño and Naranjo *cacicazgo*, see E. V. Niemeyer Jr., "El Establecimiento del Porfirismo en la Frontera Noreste (1885–1889)," in *El General Bernardo Reyes*, trans. Juan Antonio Ayala (Monterrey: UANL, 1966), 33–50.

8. The army was one of the most enduring and influential institutions in nineteenth-century Mexico, but during his years in power, Díaz kept it purposefully small, relying instead on other institutions like the Rurales for maintaining his iron grip; see below for a discussion on this. For a look at the army in the early years of independence, see William DePalo Jr., *The Mexican Army, 1822–1852* (College Station: Texas A&M Press, 2004). For its evolving role in the northeast during the midcentury, see Luis Alberto García, *Guerra y frontera: El Ejército del Norte entre 1855 y 1858* (México: Fondo de Cultura Económica, 2007).

9. Hugo Valdés, *Fulguración y disolvencia de Santiago Vidaurri* (México: Secretaría de Cultura/INEHRM, 2017), 33–140; Hortencia Camacho Cervantes, *Fundaciones y asentamientos en Nuevo León, siglos XVIII y XIX: Cuatro villas en el norte* (Zuazua, N.L.: UANL/ Unidad Cultural Hacienda San Pedro, 1991); for the way in which Vidaurri organized this army and provided his power base, see García, *Guerra y frontera*. Vidaurri was only dislodged from his dominance of northeastern Mexico after he clashed with President Benito Juárez when the latter came to the northeast fleeing the conservatives' forces and their French allies during the Second Empire. Vidaurri even briefly entertained a possible alliance with the Southern Confederacy during the U.S. Civil War. But having twice chosen the losing side of two different civil wars, he was eventually caught and executed as a traitor.

10. Valdés, *Fulguración y disolvencia*, 237–354; Mora-Torres, *Making of the Mexican Border*.

11. Although the National Guard was constitutionally enshrined in the Constitution of 1824, only in 1842 was the first law passed regulating it, containing strong influences from the militias of the Cadiz Constitution of 1812 but also the citizen militias of the U.S. Constitution. Its main attributions were its temporality, regional focus, and reliance on voluntary service. José Manuel Villalpando César, *La evolución histórico-jurídica de la guardia nacional en México* (México: UNAM, 1991).

12. Villalpando César, *La evolución histórico-jurídica*, 1143.

13. Luis Medina Peña, *Los bárbaros del norte: Guardia nacional y política en Nuevo León, siglo XIX* (México: Fondo de Cultura Económica/CIDE, 2014), 92.

14. Villalpando César, *La evolución histórico-jurídica*, 1153.

15. Medina Peña, *Los bárbaros del norte*, 103.

16. Benito Juárez, *Justificación de las Leyes de Reforma* (México: UNAM, 1981), 93–94, quoted in Villalpando César, *La evolución histórico-jurídica*, 1155.

17. Villalpando César, *La evolución histórico-jurídica*, 1156.

18. *Memoria que el licenciado Genaro Garza García gobernador constitucional del estado de Nuevo León, presenta al Soberano Congreso del mismo, sobre el estado de los ramos de la administración pública* (Monterrey: Imprenta del Gobierno en Palacio, 1879), 26.

19. *Memoria que el licenciado Genaro Garza García*, 37.

20. Villalpando César, *La evolución histórico-jurídica*, 1157.

21. Porfirio Díaz, *Informe del C. General Porfirio Díaz Presidente de los Estados Unidos Mexicanos a sus compatriotas acerca de los actos de su administración en el periodo constitucional del 1ero de diciembre de 1884 a 30 de noviembre de 1888* (México: Imprenta de F. Diaz de León Suceros S.A., 1888), 29–30.

22. John W. Kitchen, "Some Considerations on the *Rurales* of Porfirian Mexico," *Journal of Inter-American Studies* 9, no. 3 (July 1967): 441–455; Paul Vanderwood, *Los rurales mexicanos* (México: Fondo de Cultura Económica, 2014), chaps. 2, 3, and 4.

23. Kitchen, "Some Considerations," 444.

24. Kitchen, "Some Considerations," 442.

25. Vanderwood, *Los rurales*, 57–59.

26. Kitchen, "Some Considerations," 446.

27. Kitchen, "Some Considerations," 445.

28. Secretaría de Gobernación *Memorias* (1884), "Cuerpos rurales de la federación: Documentos," 1–8, quoted in Kitchen, "Some Considerations," 446; see also the map on page 12 of Vanderwood, *Los rurales*, "Localización de los destacamentos de rurales en 1880–1884."

29. Even as he was reorganizing the Rurales, some private forces for large or remote haciendas were allowed to remain. Vanderwood, *Los rurales*, 59. This was the case for Evaristo Madero in Coahuila. It was perhaps fortuitous that a regiment of Rurales was stationed in Nuevo León during the 1880–84 presidency of González. Stationing federal forces by González and his two consecutive Nuevo León secretaries of war was looked on favorably by northeasterners, and it is doubtful that a federal presence would have been equally accepted had a non-northeasterner like Díaz ordered it.

30. The "Zona Libre" was a region with special status existing parallel to the Rio Grande and land borders of Chihuahua and New Mexico, Sonora and Arizona, and the Californias, but it did not extend beyond a few dozen miles from the border; Cuadro 43, "Principales leyes, decretos y reglamentos emitidos entre 1868 y 1910 en materia de política fiscal, de crédito público, de orden administrativo y en el campo de las monedas y los bancos," in Leonor Ludlow, Coord., *Los secretarios de hacienda y sus proyectos, 1821–1933* (México: UNAM, 2002) 2:211–13. Octavio Herrera, *La zona libre: Excepción fiscal y conformación histórica de la frontera norte de México* (México: Secretaría de Relaciones Exteriores, 2004).

31. "Dictamen que la comisión nombrada por la Cámara de Comercio de Monterrey para el estudio de 'La Zona Libre,' ha presentado á la misma, el que después de su aprobación se

acordó sea remitido a la Confederación Mercantil de la República" annex in *Informe Gob. Canuto.*

32. "Dictamen que la comisión nombrada por la Cámara de Comercio de Monterrey."

33. "Dictamen que la comisión nombrada por la Cámara de Comercio de Monterrey."

34. "Carta del comandante del Contrarresguardo de la frontera del norte al gobernador de Nuevo León," General Juan Vara, Monterrey, 12 de abril de 1877, *Ramo Gendarmería Fiscal (Contrarresguardo Aduanal)*, caja 2, 1876–1884, AGENL.

35. "Carta de Blas de Zambrano al gobernador de Nuevo León sobre la liquidación de adeudos del Contrarresguardo," Blas de Zambrano, Monterrey, junio 5, 1878, *Ramo Gendarmería Fiscal (Contrarresguardo Aduanal)*, caja 2, 1876–1884, AGENL.

36. "Carta del General Vara al Gobernador entregando su puesto a su sucesor," Juan de Vara, Monterrey, octubre 14 1878, *Ramo Gendarmería Fiscal (Contrarresguardo Aduanal)*, caja 2, 1876–1884, AGENL.

37. "Carta del General de Haro al Gobernador sobre un allanamiento cometido por empleados de la 5ª Sección del Contrarresguardo," Juan de Haro, Monterrey, 24 de octubre, 1878, *Ramo Gendarmería Fiscal (Contrarresguardo Aduanal)*, caja 2, 1876–1884, AGENL.

38. "Carta del General Haro al Gobernador sobre un asalto a extranjeros," Juan de Haro, Monterrey, 29 de noviembre 1878, *Ramo Gendarmería Fiscal (Contrarresguardo Aduanal)*, caja 2, 1876–1884, AGENL.

39. "Carta del General Haro al Gobernador para que castiguen a impostores haciéndose pasar por elementos del Contrarresguardo," Juan de Haro, Monterrey, 23 de diciembre 1878, *Ramo Gendarmería Fiscal (Contrarresguardo Aduanal)*, caja 2, 1876–1884, AGENL.

40. "Informe sobre lo ocurrido en la Hacienda El Alamo donde fue herido el celador," 21 de mayo de 1894, Monterrey, *Ramo Gendarmería Fiscal (Contrarresguardo Aduanal)*, caja 2, 1876–1884, AGENL.

41. *Periódico Oficial del Estado de Nuevo León*, Tuesday, April 7, 1885.

42. Vanderwood, *The Rurales*, 81.

43. *Memoria presentada por el Ciudadano Licenciado Canuto García, Gobernador Constitucional del Estado Libre y Soberano de Nuevo León sobre la situación que guarda cada uno de los ramos de la administración pública* (Monterrey: Imprenta del Gobierno en Palacio, 1885), no page number available. It is also notable that this report has for the first time whole annexes specifically dedicated to laud the work being done on "urban railroads" as well as rail lines connecting Monterrey to Linares and Hualahuises in the southern part of the state.

44. *Memoria presentada por el Ciudadano Licenciado Canuto García*, 36.

45. *Memoria presentada por el Ciudadano Licenciado Canuto García*, 39. Neighboring Coahuila embarked on a similar path as Nuevo León in restructuring its own security force, passing an 1878 law establishing a security corps with its "only and sole object to pursue lawbreakers, thieves, rustlers, kidnappers, murderers, and all other types of criminals." Like its Nuevo León counterpart, it was under the command of the governor and reported directly to him; "Reglamento para la organización de la fuerza de seguridad pública que conforme al acuerdo de la H. Legislatura del Estado del presente debe ponerse sobre las armas en el Distrito de Monclova," Saltillo, Febrero 1878, PM c121 e 40, Archivo Municipal de Saltillo.

46. *Memoria que el licenciado Genaro Garza García*, 26.

47. The budget for this "small force" was 15,000 pesos, in a year when the general state budget was 36,000 pesos; *Periódico Oficial del Estado de Nuevo León*, Monterrey, Friday, March 27, 1885. By comparison, that same year, the X Corps of the Rurales received from the federal government a sum that was more than six times that amount, and even this expense was but a fraction of the total spent by the federal government in establishing its authority in the northeast. The X Corps stationed in Nuevo León was given over 95,000 pesos, and the total budget for the Customs Police was over 650,000 pesos. This amount was larger than those given to the military colonies in Sonora, Chihuahua, Durango, and Coahuila during the same period.

48. Mora-Torres, *Making of the Mexican Border*, 75.

49. After that, Reyes ally Garza Ayala was governor from 1887 to 1889, but from that year until 1909, Reyes would be military leader and constitutional governor of Nuevo León, with interim governors taking his place during brief intervals when Reyes was out of the state. Mora-Torres, *Making of the Mexican Border*, 75–76.

50. An important difference between both cases was that in the case of Nuevo León, Reyes and Díaz took advantage of a local dispute to consolidate federal power, whereas the Tamaulipas revolt of 1886 was specifically directed against the Díaz regime; Elliott Young, *Catarino Garza's Revolution on the Texas-Mexico Border* (Durham, NC: Duke University Press, 2004), 63.

51. Catarino Garza, "La Era de Tuxtepec en México o sea Rusia en América," cited in Celso Garza Guajardo, *En busca de Catarino Garza* (Monterrey: UANL/Centro de Información de Historia Regional, 1989), 268.

52. It was the same excuse often used by security forces in Porfirian Mexico with the notorious Porfirian *Ley Fuga*, in which a prisoner is essentially executed under the justification that he was about to flee his captors.

53. Camacho Cervantes, *Fundaciones y asentamientos*, 194.

54. Camacho Cervantes, *Fundaciones y asentamientos*, 196.

55. Bernardo Reyes, "Fundamento a la Iniciativa del decreto 52 con fecha del 16 de diciembre de 1892," quoted in Camacho Cervantes, *Fundaciones y asentamientos*, 201.

56. See chap. 2, "Resisting the *Pax Porfiriana*," of Young, *Catarino Garza's Revolution*, and Camacho Cervantes, *Fundaciones y asentamientos*, chap. 5, "Bernardo Reyes y la disidencia antiporfirista de Catarino Garza."

57. Camacho Cervantes, *Fundaciones y asentamientos*, 202–3.

58. Signed on December 11, 1861, the "Treaty between the United States of America and the Republic of Mexico for the Extradition of Criminals" in its Articles 2 and 4 stipulated that the border states of both countries could extradite criminals directly; in all other cases, the petition had to go through the Foreign Ministry in Mexico City and the State Department in Washington. *The Avalon Project*, published by the Lillian Goldman Law Library, accessed on November 10, 2021, http://avalon.law.yale.edu/19th_century/mx1861a.asp.

59. *Memoria que el C. Gral. Bernardo Reyes, Governador Constitucional del Estado de Nuevo León presenta a la XXVIII Legislatura* (Monterrey, 1895), 72.

60. Mario Cerutti, *Burguesía y capitalismo en Monterrey (1850–1910)* (Monterrey: Fondo Editorial de Nuevo León, 2006), 13–46, and the first chapter of Michael Snodgrass, *Deference and Defiance in Monterrey: Workers, Paternalism, and Revolution in Mexico, 1890–1950* (Cambridge: Cambridge University Press, 2006). Mora-Torres, *Making of the Mexican Border*, passim.

61. *Sección Energía Electríca*, caja 1, 1888–1892, AGENL; Ramón Treviño writes to the governor asking him to authorize "the first company to put in place posts and cables for public lighting, for the first time in the city's history." Monterrey, December 3, 1888. An earlier attempt in 1882 had not borne fruit. That year, the Ayuntamiento and Randle & Hemenway, Stock, Real Estate, and Mining Brokers came up with the basis for a contract for establishing the first public lighting in Monterrey, but a few years later another proposal with a local entrepreneur came about. In 1889, another contract was made with a group of investors including a B. F. Larqué, Gaspar L. Blucher, and Blas Díaz Gutierrez to establish "more systems of public lighting, service for potable water, and a factory for making carbonic gas."

62. *Sección Comunicaciones, Tranvías, Luz y Fuerza Motriz*, caja 1, 1884–1890, *Concesión del gobierno del estado a la Compañia de Ferrocarriles Urbanos de Monterrey para construir una via de la Plaza Zaragoza a la Estación de Tren Monterrey-Golfo*, noviembre 8, 1889, AGENL.

63. Sección Comunicaciones, Ferrocarril y tranvías, caja 1, 1859–1963, 1888–1892, AGENL. Four different lines were being built in Monterrey or connecting it with Santiago, Linares, and Laredo.

64. *Ramo Secretaria General de Gobierno*, "Mitin Antireyista," caja 1, 1903 Expediente Único, Telegrama de Reyes a alcaldes y Secretario de Gobernación sobre los incidentes que ocurrieron tras la manifestación pacífica de ese día, Monterrey, abril 1903, AGENL.

PART III

Violence at the Turn of the Century

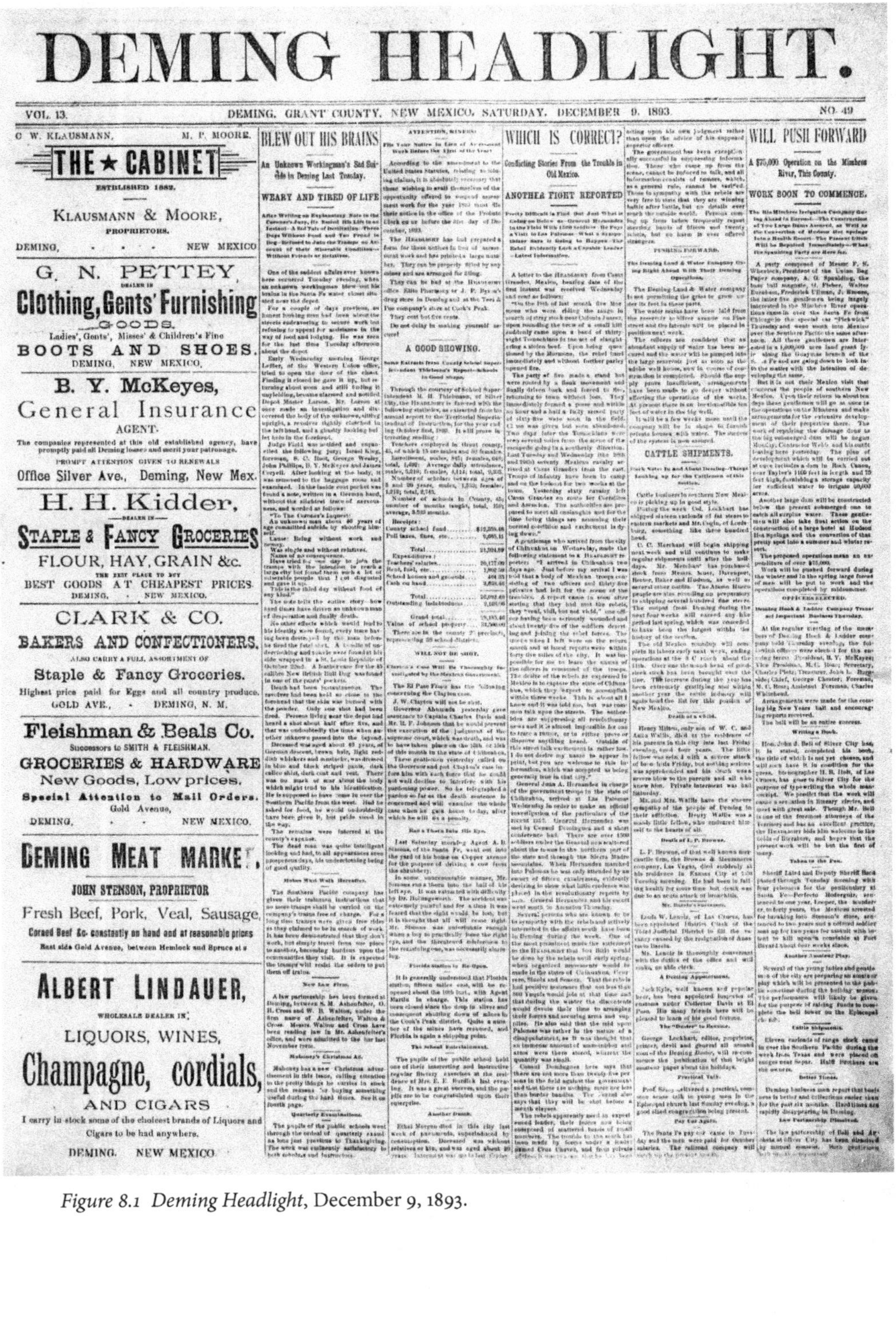

DEMING HEADLIGHT.

VOL. 13. DEMING, GRANT COUNTY, NEW MEXICO, SATURDAY, DECEMBER 9, 1893. NO. 49

C. W. KLAUSMANN, M. F. MOORE.

THE ★ CABINET

ESTABLISHED 1882.

KLAUSMANN & MOORE,

PROPRIETORS.

DEMING, - - - NEW MEXICO

G. N. PETTEY,

DEALER IN

Clothing, Gents' Furnishing GOODS.

Ladies', Gents', Misses' & Children's Fine

BOOTS AND SHOES.

DEMING, NEW MEXICO.

B. Y. McKeyes,

General Insurance

AGENT.

The companies represented at this old established agency, have promptly paid all Deming losses and merit your patronage.

PROMPT ATTENTION GIVEN TO RENEWALS

Office Silver Ave., Deming, New Mex.

H. H. Kidder,

DEALER IN

STAPLE & FANCY GROCERIES

FLOUR, HAY, GRAIN &c.

THE BEST PLACE TO BUY

BEST GOODS AT CHEAPEST PRICES

DEMING, NEW MEXICO.

CLARK & CO.

BAKERS AND CONFECTIONERS.

ALSO CARRY A FULL ASSORTMENT OF

Staple & Fancy Groceries.

Highest price paid for Eggs and all country produce.

GOLD AVE., - DEMING, N. M.

Fleishman & Beals Co.

Successors to SMITH & FLEISHMAN.

GROCERIES & HARDWARE

New Goods, Low prices.

Special Attention to Mail Orders.

Gold Avenue,

DEMING, - - NEW MEXICO.

DEMING MEAT MARKET.

JOHN STENSON, PROPRIETOR

Fresh Beef, Pork, Veal, Sausage,

Corned Beef &c. constantly on hand and at reasonable prices

East side Gold Avenue, between Hemlock and Spruce sts

ALBERT LINDAUER,

WHOLESALE DEALER IN

LIQUORS, WINES,

Champagne, cordials,

AND CIGARS

I carry in stock some of the choicest brands of Liquors and Cigars to be had anywhere.

DEMING. NEW MEXICO.

BLEW OUT HIS BRAINS

An Unknown Workingman's Sad Suicide in Deming Last Tuesday.

WEARY AND TIRED OF LIFE

ATTENTION, MINERS!

File Your Notice in Lieu of Assessment Work Before the First of the Year!

A GOOD SHOWING.

WHICH IS CORRECT?

Conflicting Stories From the Trouble in Old Mexico.

ANOTHER FIGHT REPORTED

PUSHING FORWARD.

CATTLE SHIPMENTS.

WILL PUSH FORWARD

A $75,000 Operation on the Mimbres River, This County.

WORK SOON TO COMMENCE.

OFFICERS ELECTED.

Figure 8.1 Deming Headlight, December 9, 1893.

Chapter 8

Avenging Tomóchic and Santo Tomás

Contested Narratives of Santana Pérez's Insurgency along the Chihuahua–New Mexico Border

BRANDON MORGAN

At 4:00 A.M. on November 8, 1893, Santana Pérez led a group of twenty-three well-armed men in a raid of the customs house in the tiny border town of Palomas, Chihuahua. The party surprised guards Lorenzo Muñoz and Mateo Muñoz Silva and forced them at gunpoint to hand over the store of arms and ammunition. Hearing the commotion, customs house administrator José S. Hernández and local residents rushed to aid the guards. All were overpowered, and in the commotion Rafael M. Pérez, another guard, was seriously wounded when one of the assailants shot his horse out from under him.

Stripped of their weapons, the guards, Administrator Hernández, and Cashier Agustín Lara offered little resistance as the party seized the keys to the safe and emptied its contents—only 203 pesos at the time. Despite the meager cache of supplies and funds, the insurgents considered the raid a success, according to Hernández. When Lara attempted to halt the raid by telling the perpetrators that they were committing a "grave outrage and they would be called into account for their misdeeds," they responded that "they deliberately intended to take Government funds with or without force wherever they could." In his report to his superiors in the Secretaría de Hacienda, Hernández noted the assailants' repeated claim that their actions were revolutionary in nature and that they hoped to foment a wide-ranging insurgency against the government of Porfirio Díaz. Hernández and his associates at the customs house, however, agreed that the party was composed of "bandits who used such ends as a pretext to commit their crimes."[1] Over the next few months, border-area newspaper editors, U.S. and Mexican diplomats, and the insurgents themselves struggled to define the nature of the attack. The conspirators issued revolutionary proclamations and continued their uprising in northwestern Chihuahua, while on the other side of the border, Deming (New Mexico) and El Paso newspaper editors challenged Mexican diplomats' efforts to characterize raid participants as mere robbers and bandits rather than as revolutionaries with a political agenda.

The discursive contest over the motivations and character of Pérez's forces illustrates the multiple and varied manifestations of violence centered on the

U.S.-Mexico border during the Porfiriato. Over the next five months, the insurgents, behind Santana Pérez, continued to issue proclamations and attract new supporters. Their movement inspired a violent reaction from Mexican military forces, while Mexican diplomats and border newspaper editors waged a war of words to shape the public narrative of the insurgency. With the exception of the group's several manifestos, borderlands editors and diplomats spoke in favor of Pérez and his supporters. Lacking a voice in the Mexican political system, Pérez's forces attempted to wield violence as a form of communication, but they quickly found that their message to the people of northwestern Chihuahua, and to the Mexican public more broadly, was subject to interpretation.[2]

Proximity to the border provided a convenient target that symbolized the power of the Mexican state (the remote customs house) and allowed the insurgents to use the international boundary as both a shield and a means of acquiring weapons and supplies. The meaning of the November 1893 attack was not self-evident, however. Efforts to quash the uprising militarily and control the story of the insurgents' motives show that the Pax Porfiriana was ensured through the Mexican state's ability to employ violence in a way that Porfirian political figures deemed legitimate, even as inhabitants of northwestern Chihuahua and the border region considered the Porfirian regime to be highly repressive and heavy-handed. As Timothy Bowman argues in chapter 6 in this volume, the U.S. and Mexican governments made great efforts to nationalize their respective sides of the border by establishing a monopoly on the legitimate use of violence in the latter half of the nineteenth century. The case of the Pérez insurgency shows that many inhabitants of the Chihuahua–New Mexico–Texas borderlands did not readily recognize state violence as legitimate, and they met military repression with raids and other bellicose actions of their own—a pattern similar to that outlined in Gabriel Martínez-Serna's chapter. Despite contemporary observers' hopes to the contrary, violence did not diminish even as state power in the border region grew. Instead, modern tools of diplomacy and the press channeled it into new forms.

Santana Pérez was the common thread that connected earlier bellicose flashpoints in Chihuahua at Tomóchic (1891–92) and the Santo Tomás massacre to the insurgency of 1893–94. From his home village of Yepómera in the Sierra Madre of the Guerrero District in western Chihuahua, he built a reputation as a fierce and able Apache fighter beginning in the early 1870s. According to legend, he was a humble agricultural laborer who took up arms when an Apache band kidnapped one of his young sons.[3] A ranchero of middling prosperity, he established himself in Guerrero's municipal leadership in the early 1880s but lost an election to serve as Temósachic's municipal president in 1892. At times, he supported Chihuahua's land, cattle, and banking baron, Luis Terrazas; on other occasions, he threw his regional influence behind governors that the Díaz administration imposed on Chihuahua. Pérez has been portrayed alternatively in scholarly histories as a "restless opportunist" whose pragmatism meant that "you could never tell which way he would point his rifle," or as a "highly regarded popular leader" who stood as a forerunner to famed generals of the Mexican Revolution like Francisco "Pancho" Villa.[4]

Following on-again-off-again support for the rebellion at Tomóchic, Pérez openly broke with the Porfirian regime and its auxiliaries in Chihuahua. That uprising began in the fall of 1891 when Cruz Chávez, a village leader and steward of the local chapel, took up arms against the Mexican state, declaring allegiance to the authority of God alone. Chávez's grievances against the government included his displacement in local leadership by figures with the support of Chihuahua's Porfirian-backed government, as well as his and his fellow villagers' loss of access to lands and resources that had been reallocated to foreign capitalists. Pérez headed a militia from the Guerrero district that was subordinated to General José María Rangel's federal troops during the effort to suppress Chávez's movement. Following a particularly troubling defeat at the hands of the Tomochitecos, Pérez was scapegoated for the loss. Rangel and others accused Pérez of traitorous actions ranging from a simple failure to support the *federales* to the charge that he ordered his men to fire on the federal troops from behind. The astute Pérez played various levels of authority off of one another, however, by appealing to Chihuahua governor Miguel Ahumada, with whom he cleared his name and reasserted his loyalty to the state. Still, by the final months of the conflict, Pérez realigned his allegiance and threw his support behind the insurgents at Tomóchic. When Rangel's troops massacred the final holdouts as they attempted to defend their position in the village chapel, however, Pérez was nowhere to be found. Cruz Chávez and his brother survived the assault along with four others. All were summarily executed on the morning of October 29, 1892.[5]

In the spring of 1893, Pérez participated in an uprising that federal forces brutally suppressed at the Chihuahua hamlet of Santo Tomás. Earlier, in 1889, Pérez had supported the rebellion of Celso Anaya, a fellow municipal leader in the Guerrero district who had been displaced by the Porfirian regime's official candidate. When that movement failed, Anaya and coconspirator Simón Amaya fled into New Mexico, reportedly taking up residence in Santa Fe and then in Pinos Altos. Although authorities in Chihuahua feared that a renewal of hostilities might come through the pair's organizing efforts north of the border, Anaya and Amaya launched their 1893 uprising not from New Mexico but from the village of Namiquipa. The *jefe politico* (political head) of Guerrero ordered Santana Pérez to raise a contingent to contest the insurgency, but he instead opted to join his former allies in their opposition to the government. Local authorities then charged him with insubordination, desertion of his duties, and siding with traitors. In early April, the insurgents took control of Temósachic and then occupied Santo Tomás with about 100 men. With the aid of local Apache-fighting legend Colonel Joaquín Terrazas, General Juan Hernández led between three hundred and five hundred men (reports vary) against the rebels. After a battle that spanned the better part of a week at the end of April 1893, Anaya and Amaya lay dead, their forces scattered into the nearby sierra. Hernández reported that eighty-two were killed during the course of battle; somehow Pérez survived the onslaught. By local accounts, Hernández and Terrazas's forces also sustained heavy casualties. Although not mentioned in the official accounts of the military expedition, residents of the Guerrero district reported that as a form of retaliation for their losses, after the battle "the victors at once proceeded to slaughter the women and children left in the town with no means of escape."[6]

The massacres at Tomóchic and Santo Tomás influenced Pérez's decision to openly declare his opposition to the government of Porfirio Díaz in the November 1893 raid on the Palomas Customs House. Pérez's coconspirator, Víctor L. Ochoa, printed proclamations distributed at Palomas in the weeks thereafter to underscore the insurgents' view that the current political and economic systems were tainted by "moral corruption and disorder." Ochoa was a U.S. citizen, the twenty-seven-year-old editor of the El Paso–area *Hispano Americano*. He had been born in Ojinaga, Chihuahua, but had relocated to West Texas, where he naturalized. From the U.S. side of the border, he expressed deep sympathies toward the Tomóchic and Santo Tomás movements. From his editorial post, he extolled the ideals of "democratic institutions and human equality" for his birth nation, and he considered Porfirio Díaz a despot who denied such important societal safeguards. Due to his efforts to promote Pérez's 1893–94 insurgency, the Mexican government targeted Ochoa for extradition and prosecution.[7] Together, both men's efforts, along with those of their supporters, illustrate the continuance of violence as a means of both constructing and contesting the economic, political, and social order along the New Mexico–Chihuahua border in the early 1890s.

Public and private forms of print, including newspapers and diplomatic dispatches, on both sides of the border constituted the forum through which the Palomas Customs House raid was broadcast and debated for months after the fact. The sustained coverage reflects the extent to which other parties attempted to revise and legitimate, or discount, the actions of Pérez and his compatriots. The revolutionaries continued to amass recruits and materiel for their struggle against the Díaz regime, advertised in proclamations issued in late 1893. In their statements, the few instances in which they spoke for themselves, they hailed the martyrs of Tomóchic and Santo Tomás to justify and provide inspiration for their movement. In response, Mexican consuls in

Deming and El Paso worked in tandem with Ambassador Matías Romero and Ignacio Mariscal, Secretario de Relaciones Exteriores, to suppress the "exaggerations" of the American press regarding the matter. At issue was the characterization of the perpetrators: they were acknowledged as "revolutionaries" in the U.S. borderlands press. Mexican officials worked to strip their actions of legitimacy by labeling them instead as "bandits."[8] Despite their attempt to utilize violence as a means of communicating their grievances against the Mexican state, the *revoltosos* were caught in the middle of a discursive battle between Mexican diplomats and newspapers in the borderlands on the U.S. side. It seems that Mexican officials were quickly able to control the version of the story reported in places like Mexico City and Ciudad Chihuahua but unable to directly do the same with the *El Paso Times* and the *Deming Headlight*.[9]

The tug-of-war over the narrative of the Palomas raid began immediately after the assailants had fled the customs house. Administrator Hernández filed a report mere hours after the assault that foreshadowed the official stance of the Mexican diplomatic corps on the rebels' self-declared political and social motives. Hernández submitted a second report later on the day of the raid in which he noted that the rebels had referred to themselves as "los pronunciados de Tomóchic."[10] The *Deming Headlight* referred to the insurrectionists as "Tomochian Indians." Due to the Tomóchic movement's association with Santa Teresa Urrea and various local folk saints on both sides of the border, the label carried the connotation of religious fanaticism. Although the forces that united behind Santana Pérez and Víctor L. Ochoa cited the memory of the martyrs of Tomóchic to emphasize the violent repression of the Porfirian regime, the use of the term by Mexican officials and the American press implied a type of religious zealotry and premodernism intended to deny the political legitimacy that the armed movement's leaders sought.[11] Although the *Headlight* (and the *El Paso Times*, as shown below) generally supported the insurgents, they still considered Pérez and his associates to be "backward" and ill-prepared to wage war with the Mexican state in many respects.

In the days following the attack, misinformation and anxiety ran through official Mexican communications and efforts to shape the story of the raid went into full gear. The Mexican consul in Deming, Adolfo L. Domínguez, learned of the raid shortly after it had occurred and immediately sent telegrams to officials in Ciudad Juárez and Ciudad Chihuahua and was soon the recipient of communications from Ambassador Matías Romero in Washington, D.C. Initial intelligence reports indicated that fifty armed men had surprised the guards at the customs house on the morning of November 8. Domínguez reported that during the raid the "bandits" mentioned that their next step would be to take the town of La Ascensión, although the mobilization of federal forces in northwestern Chihuahua forced them to take refuge in the Sierra Madre instead.[12] Even as Mexican diplomats initiated efforts to label the raid participants as "bandits," insurgents Macario Pacheco, Jesús Valera, and Valente García circulated their printed manifesto in La Ascensión and Janos prior to joining the others in the sierra in an attempt to contest the Porfirian state's discursive campaign not only with words but with arms.[13]

By November 9, press dispatches from Deming had circulated throughout the Southwest. José Zayas Guarneros, Mexican consul in El Paso, sent a dispatch to Romero on the 10th that highlighted his efforts to ensure that "the truth of what had happened" appear in the pages of the *El Paso Times* and *Herald*. Zayas warned that "because the American press, particularly in this place, tends always to exaggerate events of this type, to present them as a *revolution* in our Republic," he sought an immediate meeting with the editors of both papers so that he could revise their stories before they went to print. He was sorely disappointed, however, when he was unable to meet with the sleeping editor of the *Times*, Juan S. Hart, late on the night of November 9 to make his case before the morning daily was distributed.[14] The *Times* went to press, therefore, on November 10 with a story of the raid that had been relayed by its correspondent in Deming and that had not been doctored by Zayas.

The November 10 report on the Palomas raid echoed the *Headlight*'s labeling of the insurgents as "Los Tomochics," and declared that Santana Pérez led his group in an attempt to "begin another revolution in Mexico." Although it is difficult to surmise the exact reasoning for editors Edmund G. Ross and Hart's sympathies with the revoltosos, their earlier reporting on the Santo Tomás massacre provides some clues. The *Headlight* printed various stories between April and September that were reproduced in similar form in the *Times* and vice versa. The reports from Deming were based on testimonies from various residents of the region around Santo Tomás who had witnessed the violence of Mexican forces against anyone thought to have been in sympathy with Anaya, Amaya, and Pérez's challenge to state authority. On September 2, for example, the *Headlight* reported that "two Mexicans" had arrived in Deming with news that Mexican troops were still in pursuit of the Santo Tomás rebels and that a unit of *federales* had recently hanged ten people accused of sympathizing with their cause at the town of Cruces. In each of the reports, Ross, and then Hart, presented the claims from the informants as a scoop—they purported to have exclusive information about events in Chihuahua that the Mexican government worked hard to suppress. At the very least, it seems that journalistic acumen pushed them to publish reports that showed a group of underdogs attempting to challenge the far more powerful Mexican state in pursuit of social justice.[15] In doing so, both papers likened Pérez's November 1893 uprising to the events at Santo Tomás and Tomóchic, following a pattern that the insurgents themselves established in their manifestos.

Thwarted in his first attempt to revise the *Times* narrative of the raid, Zayas penned a letter to the editor of the *Herald*, which circulated in the afternoon. He informed the editor that the *Times* report was riddled with falsehoods relative to the attack and that the consulate in El Paso had received "datos verídicos" (true information). First and foremost, Zayas stated that the Palomas Customs House had been attacked by a group of armed robbers who were able to overpower the guards due to their superior numbers. They took cash and supplies and then moved on to look for "other offices where there might be money." In making this characterization of the events at Palomas on November 8, Zayas suggested in no uncertain terms that the robbery had no connection to a revolutionary movement. In fact, he railed against the *Times* piece already in circulation for its "anonymous libel, full of disrespectful characterizations of Mexico that were expressed in vulgar language with absolute ignorance." He levied these harsh charges precisely because the *Times* reported that the attack at Palomas signaled the beginning of another revolutionary movement in Chihuahua, in the spirit of Tomóchic and Santo Tomás. The *pronunciados* had issued a manifesto that outlined their grievances against the Porfirian regime and local *chihuahuense* authorities, but Zayas responded in his letter to the editor of the *Herald* that no such proclamation had been issued following the assault.[16] His claim came despite Consul Dominguez's inclusion of a copy of the manifesto in his November 9 report to the Secretaria de Relaciones Exteriores in Mexico City and reprints in the *Deming Headlight* in the days following the raid.[17]

The version of the proclamation that Domínguez attached to his report was a printed broadside, likely produced under the auspices of Víctor L. Ochoa in the El Paso area. The message was addressed to "Mexican soldiers," exhorting them to understand that they should not feel guilty for having been pressed into the service of Porfirio Díaz, who had violated their rights and who used them to "enslave" other members of Mexican society. The revolutionaries heralded the Constitution of 1857 as the document that "taught us to think like citizens and that elevates us to the status of free men." They further argued that "if the tyrant that pays you to kill us had governed by this Constitution," the pronunciados would not have taken up arms against the government. Their appeal ended on an especially poignant note: "You defend a man that enslaves you and looks only for his own aggrandizement. Down with tyrants! Long live the revolution and long live Tomóchi!"[18] The proclamation's tenor emphasized the problematic ways in which the Porfirian regime's centralization of power at the local level in Chihuahua had destabilized military organization and service, much as Gabriel Martínez-Serna has outlined for the Texas–Nuevo León region.

Below the proclamation, the revolutionaries added a postscript in which they described the massacre at Santo Tomás. According to their report, thirty-one people had been summarily executed in the days following the horrible destruction of the town. Of that number, only five or six were connected to the insurgency. The rest were innocent locals.[19] From the pronunciados' perspective, that massacre and the violent suppression of the insurgents at Tomóchic were intimately connected because they both stood as evidence of the brutality of the Mexican state against its own people in Chihuahua. Additionally, the revolutionaries argued that their statement was necessary because the story that had been published in Chihuahua's *Periódico Oficial* was "untrue and at the same time a deception." Their strategy was to appeal to those members of the federal army that had been impressed into service. Such was the pattern in northwestern Chihuahua where locals had been impressed into militia service at Guerrero to fight with federal forces against Cruz Chávez and his supporters in Tomóchic. In the aftermath of the Santo Tomás massacre, eighty men had been called into service at La Ascensión.[20] The proclamation was intended to appeal directly to the reality that recruits were not necessarily dedicated to the missions that they had been called to support, but neither did they wish to cross the Porfirian government. The revolutionaries pushed soldiers to recognize that the goals of the government for which they were fighting were unjust and that they were tearing apart innocent families. Finally, the manifesto indicated that the men who followed Pérez were not merely robbers or highwaymen; they were fighting to correct the grave injustices and violent reprisals perpetrated by the Mexican government in Chihuahua.[21] Subsequent proclamations published in the *El Paso Times* and circulated on the ground called for recruits to join Pérez's ranks with the guarantee of five dollars per day in payment, and reiterated grievances regarding the Díaz government's unjust impressment of men into military service.[22]

As the revolutionaries moved throughout northwestern Chihuahua (and into New Mexico by some accounts)[23] over the first half of November, Ambassador Romero worked through diplomatic channels to call attention to the conspirators' use of the border as a means of escaping capture and as a source of material support. In a November 12 report, Domínguez informed Romero that he knew the location where the "bandidos" gathered to plan the assault on the customs house and that he compiled a list that contained the names of the insurrectionists who had lived in the United States. To the names of Ochoa and Pérez, who had already been singled out as leaders, he added the names of Eleuterio Nevares, Luis Nevares, Jesús Mendoza, and Antonio Ybarra, all of whom had been residents of Santo Tomás prior to the April massacre. The first two, he indicated, had since lived at a ranch three miles south of Deming. Mendoza had taken up refuge in El Paso and Mimbres, New Mexico, and Ybarra in Silver City.[24] Three days later, in a letter to Secretary of State Walter Q. Gresham, Romero levied the charge that these men had violated neutrality laws and that U.S. officials had done nothing to prevent or prosecute such action. He also claimed that immediately following the Palomas raid, the insurrectionists had retreated "across the Rio Grande" to a refuge in the United States.[25]

Assigned by their military superiors to investigate Romero's accusations, First Lieutenant of the First Cavalry Oscar J. Brown and Adjutant Charles E. Dodge concluded that the uprising in Chihuahua posed no threat to Americans and that no violations of neutrality laws had taken place. Brown set up camp near Columbus, the New Mexico border town adjacent to Palomas, and interviewed as many Palomas residents as possible with the aid of Lieutenant Barber of the First Infantry, who served as interpreter. Based on reports of their interviews, locals from both sides of the New Mexico–Chihuahua border claimed that the insurgents had acted in a way "marked by great consideration for men engaged in lawless acts." They had provided a receipt for the money they had taken, and they left locals and American citizens in the area at peace due to their stated intention to avoid "interfering with anyone except Mexican officials." Their commitment to the cause of disrupting only Mexican government operations was further illustrated when they specifically took the horses and munitions of the customs house guards, "leaving better ones belonging to Americans." The rebels harassed only two Americans, injuring neither.[26]

Adjutant Charles E. Dodge concluded his separate tour of the area between Silver City and Deming on November 19 by interviewing Mexican consul Domínguez in Deming. Rather than emphasizing the insurrectionists' seeming restraint, Domínguez instead spoke of their continued efforts to raise recruits and materials north of the border. By his account, the insurgent leaders in southern New Mexico were Valente García and Macario Pacheco, who had raised a force of fifty to sixty men. He also reported that "a number of Mexicans, who were citizens of the United States, were then on their way to the border, well-armed, to join the Revolutionists in Mexico." The consul painted the region between Deming and Columbus as a place teeming with potential revolutionary forces, although Dodge claimed to have found no evidence to support such a characterization.[27] Together, Dodge's and Brown's reports suggest that the insurgents understood the value of the border to protect them from the Porfirian state, despite the Americans' unwillingness to characterize activities in New Mexico as a violation of neutrality laws.

Based on Dodge's and Brown's findings, Brigadier General Alexander McDonald McCook, commanding officer of the Department of the Colorado, which presided over southern New Mexico, concluded that Romero's accusations of neutrality violations were unfounded.[28] Judging from the types of questions they asked, however, the U.S. military investigators were more concerned with potential threats to U.S. citizens than with Romero's concerns about the transgression of neutrality laws. At the same time, to appease Romero, American military officials made known their intention to fortify the border as a shield against the possibility of neutrality violations and the flight of conspirators from Chihuahua into New Mexico or Texas. Romero's effort to leverage neutrality laws in the service of the Mexican state's campaign against the insurgents largely failed.

American newspaper reports regarding the insurrection seemed to multiply during the month of November 1893, even as Romero and Zayas continued their efforts to limit press coverage. Papers in places as distant as Albuquerque, Boise, Chicago, Boston, New York City, and Washington, D.C., printed dispatches from Deming and El Paso regarding the rebels' movements and commentary on their intentions. From their position in the borderlands, Editors Ross and Hart were able to influence the Associated Press dispatches relayed to other newspapers. Both maintained an attitude of sympathy to the insurgency but expressed concern that it was ill-advised. Hart in particular viewed it as a means of addressing injustices committed by the Mexican government against its own people.[29] Although the insurgents occasionally printed their own words in the *Headlight* and *Times*, both editors regularly spun the reports about their movements to emphasize the justice of their cause.

Reports of the insurgents' on-the-ground movements equally demonstrated that, as was the case for the discursive battle, information about physical conflicts was often based on rumor and peppered with commentary. A November 15 El Paso dispatch reprinted in various papers reported that Santana Pérez's forces had retaken the town of Palomas, causing "Mexicans and Americans alike" to flee across the border for refuge.[30] Reports issued the following day indicated that the revolutionaries had also taken control of La Ascensión and all "roads 100 miles the south." Estimates of the strength of the revolutionary force ranged from three hundred to six hundred men, depending on the dispatch, and one El Paso report indicated that General Neri of Guerrero State had also raised thirteen thousand men in support of the revolt in an attempt to imply a connection between anti-Díaz uprisings across Mexico—a connection that did not exist.[31] Such stories about the revolution were based on rumors and hearsay, including widely ranging estimates of the pronunciados' numbers, lending some credence to Mexican officials' allegations of sensationalism in the American press, much of which originated with Ross and Hart's reporting from the border.

Mexican sources corroborated the idea that the insurgency was gathering strength, however momentarily, even if the details of the revolutionaries' movements were exaggerated or uncertain. Throughout November, the revolutionaries made a circuit between Palomas, La Ascensión, and the Sierra Madre to the west of the two towns. The Ciudad Juárez telegraph officer reported that the revolutionaries had indeed retaken Palomas on November 15 and that their force was composed of "200 well-armed men." According to the *Deming Head-*

light, this time the customs house guards fled across the border "for safety and sought refuge in the house of A. O. Bailey at Columbus."[32] That same day, Chihuahua governor Miguel Ahumada relayed information from Domínguez that revolutionary forces had been planning their next moves near Deming on the American side of the border, suggesting U.S. military investigators' findings to be inaccurate. On November 17, Administrator Hernández wired Domínguez that the situation in and around Palomas was indefensible. The revolutionaries had camped at Boca Grande, to the south of Palomas, and "their number was on the rise," but federal reinforcements had not yet arrived to dislodge them from the town. Troops had been dispatched from Mexico City to support the customs guards and Gendarmería Fiscal forces from the area surrounding La Ascensión and Janos. According to Domínguez's reports, however, federal forces would not arrive at the border until November 21 at the earliest.[33]

In the meantime, local forces were dispatched to support the customs house guards at Palomas and also at La Ascensión, the rumored target of additional raids. Agents of the Secretaría de Hacienda and the Secretaría de Relaciones Exteriores ordered the local guards at both towns to hold their positions and make the best defense possible if attacked. Corporal Severo Trejo, an officer of the Gendarmería Fiscal headquartered at Janos, was ordered to Casas Grandes from his post near La Ascensión to raise volunteers to support the defense of the border customs posts. Although Trejo failed to convince the municipal president to support his request, on the night of November 17 "a Mormon, *vecino* of Colonia Juárez," arrived in town with the news that he and some of his fellow colonists had seen twenty-eight armed men in the hills surrounding the colony.[34] Upon receiving this report, the municipal president, with the support of the captain of the Fifteenth Regiment stationed at Casas Grandes, raised twenty-five soldiers and twenty-five armed civilians who marched through the night with Corporal Trejo and his Gendarmería Fiscal employees to reach Colonia Juárez. On November 18, Trejo met with Section President Henry Eyring to create a plan of action to protect the colony. Eyring informed Trejo that seven men from the colony, led by Orson Pratt Brown, had set out that morning to search once again for the revolutionaries. When the party located the band of insurrectionists, they were met with gunfire. The revolutionaries trapped six of the Mormons; Carl Nielson escaped to Colonia Juárez to raise reinforcements.[35]

Nielson reported that the "Tomoches," as the Mormon colonists called the rebels, had the party surrounded and had possibly killed them all. Although Trejo was ready and willing to accompany Nielson back to the scene of the battle, the civilian volunteers secretly returned to Casas Grandes, a move that Trejo characterized as "a desertion before the enemy." The commander of the small group of soldiers that had come from Casas Grandes also refused to join in the skirmish, arguing that he had received no orders to take such a course of action. Trejo and nine other members of the Gendarmería Fiscal were the only reinforcements that returned to the battlefield with Nielson. From the Mormons' perspective, the Mexican soldiers and civilians were an unorganized, superstitious bunch.[36] Yet, Mormon colonist Orson Pratt Brown's memories of the rebellion underscore its political nature. By his account, during his confrontation with three of the rebels, he accused them of being bandits and thieves. At this charge they became indignant, refuting his characterization by emphasizing that they had "another mission" that they intended to fulfill.[37] In the *Deming Headlight*'s report on the confrontation, Editor Ross indicated that the failure of local Mexican civilians to pursue the rebels was due to the fact that "at heart they were all in sympathy with the rebels."[38]

In mid-November, just as the revolutionaries had once again taken control of Palomas and forced the guards across the border, Romero issued a statement to the American press that downplayed their activity. Alongside the El Paso dispatch that acknowledged the rebels' capture of "500 horses, ammunition, camp stores and arms," the *New York Herald* also published Romero's statement that "the trouble is of small importance." According to the *Herald*, when asked about the activity along the New Mexico–Chihuahua border, Romero scoffed: "Why, there's no rebellion in Mexico. The papers give too much importance to the little disturbance a band of bandits is making for us along the border. They continue troublesome for the same reason that a few dozen Apache Indians were troublesome to this country. . . . They will eventually be surrounded and captured as the Apaches were, and if captured they would not be as mercifully dealt with as the Apaches."[39] Here, Romero sought to brand the insurrectionists as "uncivilized Indians" to erase any legitimacy that might be accredited to their movement. He did so in terms that Americans could directly relate to by claiming the rebellion was akin to the Apache wars that had raged along the border throughout the 1870s and 1880s.

The Deming and El Paso papers continued to report on the state of affairs in Chihuahua in a strikingly different light.[40] On November 25, the *Headlight* reported that all was quiet in the vicinity of Palomas and La Ascensión due to the fact that the revolutionaries "are very cautious and will not give battle to the troops unless everything is in their favor." The paper commented that the lull in combat had allowed regular business patterns to resume in Palomas but that the rebels, who numbered about two hundred men, boasted "that one decisive victory will increase their number to over one thousand men." Based on "private information" exclusive to the *Headlight*, the story also offered the news that "the leaders of the disturbance have even gone so far as to arrange for a provisional government and the circulation of money" in the event that they were able to "defeat federal forces definitively," another attempt by the border press to show that the government's version of events was tilted to deny legitimacy to the movement and justify the use of violence against its supporters. The story ended with the comment that Mormon colonists, as well as the town of La Ascensión, had actually escaped rumored rebel depredations. Still, the *Headlight* reported, "Consul Domingues [sic] expresses the opinion that all the trouble is over and that the rebels will be scattered and killed before Christmas."[41]

Juan S. Hart's *El Paso Times* continued to characterize the insurrection as a revolutionary movement, to the chagrin of Romero and Zayas, staunchly defending Santana Pérez's revolutionary credentials, arguing that he had long been a "respected and honored citizen and was never a robber in any sense of the term." The correspondent cited Pérez's faithful service in support of the Plan de Tuxtepec, the revolutionary initiative that brought Porfirio Díaz to power in 1876. Reportedly, Pérez "had been on the salary list of Diaz until about a year ago" when a federal commander unjustly accused him of failure to support the Mexican government in suppressing the Tomóchic rebellion. The *Times* concluded: "There is no doubt that Perez is a revolutionist, but he lacks the money and backing necessary to be a successful one."[42] Additionally, by late November Juárez consul Theodore Huston took Hart's side. On November 30, he submitted a report to the U.S. State Department in which he confirmed his belief that the insurrection was revolutionary in nature. Because of Zayas and Domínguez's early characterizations of the insurrection as nothing more than an attack by a group of "ordinary thieves," he initially failed to investigate the situation in any detail. Yet, reports from the Juárez military commander and the Palomas customs collector caused him to question the consul's accounts. Based on new information from those people closer to the pursuit of Pérez's band, he "formed the opinion that many of the followers of Pérez are the survivors of the Santo Tomás, Tomochic, and Guerrero revolts." Following the lead of Ross and Hart, Huston called the uprising "ill-advised" and asserted that it was most likely that the revolutionists would fail, as they had in the previous uprisings, "because of their lack of money and munitions."[43]

At about the same time, Pérez and his supporters attempted to inject their own voice into the transnational debate over the legitimacy of their actions. An interview between one of its correspondents and Macario Pacheco,[44] second in command to Santana Pérez, appeared in the November 28 El Paso Times and was reprinted in the December 1 New York Herald. Pacheco expressed faith in the growth of the revolutionary movement in Chihuahua, arguing that "it will not do for Diaz to throw dust in people's eyes by claiming that we are bandits. We are in a war for the purpose of overthrowing a despotism." Many of his statements echoed the initial proclamation issued by the group of twenty-three that raided the Palomas Customs House, and he also asserted the claim that "it is true we have had a battle with the regulars and we wiped them out.... We expect to have the regular forces desert and fight for freedom." This statement echoed the purpose outlined in the earlier proclamation—that regular Mexican soldiers wake up to the abuses of the Díaz regime and join the revolution. Despite Pacheco's assertion, his use of the future tense indicated that the rebels had yet to attract many soldiers to their cause. Pacheco dedicated much of the interview to setting the record straight on the idea that the revolt was based on either religious fanaticism or Indigenous grievances. As he put it, the revolutionaries' "principles have nothing to do with religion." Instead, their goal was to restore the spirit of the "republican constitution of '57." He also emphatically denied the charge that the revolutionaries were waging an "Indian war." He underscored that "if our war cry be 'Avenge Tomochic!' it is so because we remember the butchery that was made of a kindred town so dear to us by that despot, who tramples the laws of our country and her sons, as the whole world knows." These final assertions offered important clarification about the significance of Tomóchic for the revolutionaries themselves. Far from asserting religious fanaticism often associated with the Tomóchic rebellion, the rebels stood in solidarity with those slain by the Porfirian government to quash the dissent expressed by Cruz Chávez and his compatriots.[45]

The contest over the narrative of the raid reached a crescendo in December 1893, just after the publication of Pacheco's interview. Lending support to the ongoing assertions of editors Hart and Ross that the Mexican government had been suppressing all news of the revolutionaries' movements in Chihuahua, on December 5 Governor Miguel Ahumada issued an order that banned the circulation of the *El Paso Times* in the state of Chihuahua. Ahumada's action was taken under direction from Porfirio Díaz and Ambassador Romero. Significantly, the *Times* was the only El Paso newspaper prevented from circulating in the state; the *Herald* remained within the good graces of Mexican officials. According to Zayas, that paper (as well as the *El Paso Tribune*) consistently refuted *Times* reports on revolutionary movements in northern Chihuahua.[46] By mid-December, newspapers throughout the United States had followed the lead of the *Herald* and *Tribune*.[47] Although Consul Huston intervened to end the circulation ban within a month, the prohibition on the *Times* seems to have had its desired effect on reporting beyond the borderlands, and it highlights Hart's personal commitment to portraying the insurgency as a revolutionary movement.[48]

In the border region, dispatches from Deming and El Paso on continued violence in Chihuahua and clashes between the revolutionaries and federal forces helped to support the editors' counternarrative. On December 9 and 16, the *Deming Headlight* ran extended coverage of battles between Santana Pérez's forces and federal troops under the command of General Juan A. Hernández, the military chief Porfirio Díaz had called out of retirement to quash the uprising at Santo Tomás. The December 9 issue explained that Hernández marched into Palomas with a meager "escort of fifteen cavalrymen, evidently desiring to show that little credence was placed in the revolutionary reports by him." Consul Domínguez told the *Headlight*, "There are not more than twenty-five persons in the field against the government" who, he surmised, would "be shot before a month elapses." Although the official claims indicated the tide turning against the insurgency, Editor Ross noted, "The government has been especially successful in suppressing information," to the degree that many Mexican travelers in Deming refused to discuss the matter at all. Based on scant information from anonymous informants—a shaky source base—the *Headlight* reported that the revolutionaries planned to avoid engagements until the spring in order to build reinforcements and supplies for a new offensive. They were rumored to have the promise that eight hundred Yaqui people would join their ranks by that time.[49]

In its December 16 installment, the *Deming Headlight* underscored the claim that Mexican officials had been working to suppress information about the pronunciados in its account of a major engagement between Hernández's men and the rebels between Casas Grandes and Colonia Juárez. On the 13th, reports of the skirmish filtered into Palomas and were then relayed to Deming by "an American" who was in town at the time. Although the news was first recorded at the Palomas Customs House, Mexican officials reportedly had threatened locals with arrest should they convey the news to Americans. As a company of about six hundred federal forces searched for rebel strongholds in the Sierra Madre on the morning of the 12th, they unwittingly stumbled upon a band commanded by Santana Pérez himself. A battle between the two contingents raged for several hours. Fighting from a highly defensible position, the group of one hundred rebels purportedly killed between 150 and 300 federal soldiers, although they sustained twenty-five casualties of their own. Due to their losses, the revolutionaries were unable to press their advantage and instead retreated to their mountain hideouts.

The commentary in the *Headlight* emphasized the notion that Mexican officials had suppressed the battle's details so tightly that the number of federal forces present, as well as the number of casualties, could not be verified. Customs house officials did admit that twenty-five insurrectionists had been killed and that the *federales* had sustained serious losses, but they refused to provide any other information. The *Headlight*'s account compared this battle to the Santo Tomás massacre of the previous spring, news of which had been so vigorously suppressed by Mexican authorities that "an account of the battle never appeared in print." The report surmised that at Santo Tomás "eleven hundred soldiers were led into a narrow ravine and killed like sheep," yet even the most exaggerated estimates of the federal losses in April 1893 placed the number at eight hundred. Ironically, the Mexican government's heavy-handed approach toward the press provided space for such rampant speculation and exaggeration, and given the inflated casualty figures for Santo Tomás, it seems clear that Ross was happy to oblige. The piece in the *Headlight* concluded with the assertion that this report was more than mere rumor because the "battle has been confirmed at this office from three different sources and there is no reason to discredit a single particular."[50]

The *Dallas Morning News*, *New York Herald*, and *Daily Inter Ocean* (Chicago) initially reprinted the *Headlight*'s rendering of the battle, but within a few days they recanted and once again fell in line with the Mexican government's position. The *Dallas Morning News* ran a statement from Porfirio Díaz himself that affirmed calm and peaceful conditions throughout Chihuahua. Díaz downplayed the initial attack as the work of "some twenty-eight men from the American side of the Rio Grande" who assailed the "small settlement of Palomas, which numbers some ten or twelve shanties or jacales." Such claims reiterated the accusation that the insurrectionists had violated neutrality laws, and Díaz diminished the significance of Palomas itself. He even went so far as to claim, "There is no such man as Santana Pérez connected to this affair." All of the manifestos attributed to Pérez, by his account, were "of El Paso manufacture."[51] Sheriff F. B. Simmons of El Paso County echoed such sentiments and argued that "Mexican authorities understand the situation and they are not losing any rest."[52] By the end of December, the *New York Herald* printed a letter to the editor from Britton Davis, superintendent of the Corralitos ranching enterprise in northwestern Chihuahua. His letter completely disavowed any revolutionary activities in northwestern Chihuahua.[53]

Despite such public renunciations on both sides of the border, Mexican authorities in El Paso and Chihuahua actively pursued the arrest or extradition of Santana Pérez, Víctor L. Ochoa, Macario Pacheco, and other alleged perpetrators of the disturbance that began with the November 8 Las Palomas raid. In mid-November, Governor Ahumada alerted Consuls Zayas and Domínguez of Ochoa's role in the rebellion, and he suggested that they begin extradition proceedings. Ahumada also accused Ochoa of organizing armed bands of rebels at his home in Texas, along with printing the proclamations. Ochoa's status as an American citizen, however, complicated the situation for Mexican authorities. Working with Sheriff Simmons and U.S. federal marshals, Zayas secured Ochoa's arrest on November 30. U.S. federal judge Warner A. Gibbs, however, freed Ochoa on December 2 due to a lack of evidence in the case. Gibbs's decision infuriated Zayas, who claimed that he had provided more than enough evidence to support the extradition. Included with his reports on Ochoa's release, Zayas attached a copy of the December 3 *El Paso Times*. The front page ran a translation of the revolutionary proclamation that had been issued at the time of the Palomas raid. Zayas, however, characterized the manifesto as "a confused mixture of insults directed at our country and our head of state."[54]

By late December, news of the revolution in Chihuahua was no longer a staple of the border newspapers. The lack of military engagements meant that there was little to report. The rebels had settled into hiding in the Sierra Madre, and Mexican federal forces continued to search for them without result. Late January and early February 1894 saw a renewal of violence in the region near La Ascensión as the revolutionaries under Pérez, Pacheco, and Ochoa (now in Chihuahua) waged a more desperate guerrilla campaign against federal forces and regional recruits. Their bleak situation meant that efforts to control the story on all sides seemed to lose importance. The threat that the insurgency formerly posed to the Porfirian government had evidently dissipated.

The final blow came on February 8 when a group of insurgents under Pérez was nearly annihilated by federal forces forty miles south of Casas Grandes. As usual, information about the incident was tightly controlled and rumors and conjecture abounded. Details of the battle were carried to the Mormon colonies and in turn to Deming. The remaining insurgents had regrouped in small bands, hiding in the mountains south of Palomas. According to the report, they "recently concentrated for the purpose of meeting the troops." In the course of the battle, seventy-five revolutionaries and fifty soldiers were killed. Once again, Pérez somehow managed to escape.[55]

Only a few weeks later, Governor Ahumada issued a general amnesty for all "Mexican citizens that, since September 1892, have taken up arms against the constituted authorities." The only exceptions were Víctor Ochoa and Benigno Arbizo, due to their "status as foreigners."[56] The date hearkened back to the Tomóchic rebellion, drawing a connection between the earlier movement and the insurrection that began with the November 8, 1893 raid on the Palomas Customs House. The connection between the two movements was both symbolic and real. Santana Pérez fought on both sides of the Tomóchic uprising, aided the spring insurrection that ended at Santo Tomás, and led the most recent rebellion. For many inhabitants of northwestern Chihuahua, Tomóchic and Santo Tomás were symbols of the government oppression and violence that were manifested through both physical and legal means in the northwestern Chihuahua landscape. The second article of Ahumada's proclamation was also quite telling: the amnesty only applied to those who had committed "political crimes." The guilty parties were offered a period of two months during which they could turn themselves in to any state or municipal authority in Chihuahua. In the published amnesty offer, the governor himself admitted that the efforts of Pérez, Ochoa, and their supporters had been political in nature.[57]

In April of 1894, Santana Pérez and ten others "spontaneously presented themselves" before the governor to take advantage of the amnesty. According to the report in Chihuahua's *Periódico Oficial*, the men "expressed their great confidence in the Governor and delivered up not only their weapons, but also their unconditional service to the Government, shouting vivas to Gen. Porfirio Díaz, the Federal Government, the State, and Col. Miguel Ahumada."[58] The excitement with which Pérez and his associates surrendered surely was overstated.

Although failed, Santana Pérez's insurrection in 1893 and 1894 provides important context for the Tomóchic and Santo Tomás uprisings that preceded it. Despite the relative ease with which agents of the Mexican state were able to write off the earlier rebellions, Pérez's more complex relationship to the state highlights the Mexican government's attempt to stake a claim to the legitimate use of violence along the international boundary through manipulation of the public information outlets of the day. The Porfirian regime had to contend, however, with the competing narratives of the revolutionaries themselves and of sympathetic borderlands newspaper editors. Even with increasing capitalist development along the New Mexico–Chihuahua border, and the Texas–Nuevo León border as J. Gabriel Martínez-Serna shows in chapter 7 in this volume, the state did not naturally hold a monopoly on legitimate violence. It sought to assert that monopoly through military campaigns and calculated diplomatic and media efforts to discredit Pérez's insurgency.

Additionally, proximity to the U.S.-Mexico border provided opportunities for the revolutionaries to flee Mexican authorities. Ambassador Romero and consular agents were forced to negotiate with the U.S. State Department in order to pursue the insurgents in New Mexico and Texas, negotiations that emphasized the relative power imbalance between the neighboring nations. Both governments sent military reinforcements to the international line to solidify their claims to the borderlands. Although their specific plans and motives remain unclear, Pérez and associates' actions ostensibly targeted the legitimacy of Porfirian claims on order and progress in Mexico. In the case of modernization and capitalist development along the New Mexico–Chihuahua border in the late nineteenth century, "'progress' was the mother of rebellion."[59] In subsequent years, other rebellions targeted the Palomas customs house, and in the first decade of the twentieth century people in the Chihuahua border region—including an aging Santana Pérez—embraced the radical anti-Porfirian program of the Partido Liberal Mexicano. In 1910, agents of revolutionary Francisco Madero attempted to enlist Pérez to their cause. Only his advanced age prevented him from taking up arms in the struggle that became known as *La Revolución*.[60]

Notes

1. Report of José S. Hernández, Customs House Administrator, Las Palomas, Chihuahua, made to the Secretario de Hacienda Publica, Ignacio Mariscal, November 8, 1893, caja UI1351, expediente 1790, Fondo Hacienda Publica, Archivo General de la Nación, México, D.F. (hereafter, AGN). All translations were made by the author.

2. For more on the use of violence as communication, see José Angel Hernández, "Violence as Communication: The Revolt of La Ascensión, Chihuahua (1892)," *Landscapes of Violence* 2, no. 1 (2012): Article 6, accessed February 26, 2016, http://scholarworks.umass.edu/lov/vol2/iss1/6; and Hernández, *Mexican American Colonization during the Nineteenth Century: A History of the U.S.-Mexico Borderlands* (New York: Cambridge University Press, 2012), esp. chap. 7. The notion that violence is a tool of the powerless to express dissent is important, but as the Pérez insurgency illustrates, those who commit violence from a position of political weakness cannot control the ways in which the powerful interpret and assign meaning to their actions.

3. José Manuel Valenzuela Arce, *Entre la Magia y la Historia: Tradiciones, Mitos, y Leyendas de la Frontera* (Tijuana: El Colegio de la Frontera Norte, 2000), 72–73.

4. Paul J. Vanderwood, *Power of God against the Guns of Government: Religious Upheaval in Mexico at the Turn of the Nineteenth Century* (Stanford, CA: Stanford University Press, 1998), 121; Rubén Osorio, "*Villismo*: Nationalism and Popular Mobilization in Northern Mexico," in *Rural Revolt in Mexico and U.S. Intervention*, Monograph Series, 27, ed. Daniel Nugent (San Diego: Center for U.S.-Mexican Studies, University of California, San Diego, 1988), 150–51. See also Ana María Alonso, *Thread of Blood: Colonialism, Revolution, and Gender on Mexico's Northern Frontier* (Tucson: University of Arizona Press, 1995), 143; and Francisco R. Almada, *Resumen de Historia del Estado de Chihuahua* (México, D.F.: Libros Mexicanos, 1955), 348, 358.

5. Vanderwood, *Power of God*, 249–50, 257, 270; Alonso, *Thread of Blood*, 143, 183; and Osorio, "*Villismo*," 151. Osorio points out that by the first decade of the twentieth century, Pérez threw his support to the Magón brothers' Partido Liberal Mexicano. And "in 1910 Pérez declined an invitation to join the Madero movement . . . because of his advanced age" (151n6). For book-length treatments of the Tomóchic uprising and massacre, see Vanderwood, *Power of God*; Rubén Osorio, *Tomóchic en Llamas* (México, D.F.: Consejo Nacional para la Cultura y las Artes, 1995); and Jesús Vargas Valdez, ed., *Tomóchic: La Revolución Adelantada, Resistencia y Lucha de un Pueblo de Chihuahua con el Sistema Porfirista, 1891–1892*, 2 vols. (Cd. Juárez: Universidad Autónoma de Ciudad Juárez, 1994).

6. *Deming Headlight*, May 6 and June 3, 1893. Although the *Headlight* reported that "Simon Armalla" had been killed at "Santa Tomas," such misspellings (and mistranslations) of names from Spanish to English were common. The activities of this "Armalla" were the same as those attributed to Simón Amaya in official Mexican reports. See Rodolfo F. Acuña, *Corridors of Migration: The Odyssey of Mexican Laborers, 1600–1933* (Tucson: University of Arizona Press, 2007), 40–43; Osorio, "*Villismo*," 150–51, n4; Jesús Vargas Valdés, "Namiquipa, tierra de revolucionarios" *La Fragua de los Tiempos*, no. 826, August 9, 2009, Universidad Autónoma de Ciudad Juárez; and Aguilar, "Mayor Santana Pérez," 241–43.

7. Alonso, *Thread of Blood*, 183; Vanderwood, *Power of God*, 291–92; and Acuña, *Corridors of Migration*, 42–43. It is important to note that Vanderwood's skepticism toward Pérez's intentions and actions is also reflected in his portrayal of Ochoa. He considers Ochoa an opportunist who attempted to propel his own dreams of revolutionary grandeur by capitalizing on the memory of Tomóchic. As Vanderwood concludes of Ochoa's proclamations, "through his [Ochoa's] words we can see one of the ways in which rumors are planted and nurtured, how a real tragedy may be sifted for embers to spark other ambitions and embellished for political purposes" (291).

8. On the issue of labels and the social nature of movements labeled as "banditry," see Vanderwood, *Power of God*, 135–40; Gilbert M. Joseph, "On the Trail of Latin American

Bandits: A Reexamination of Peasant Resistance," *Latin American Research Review* 25, no. 3 (1990): 7–53, esp. 22; Hernández, *Mexican American Colonization during the Nineteenth Century*; and Hernández, "Violence as Communication."

9. Reports from *El Estado* (Chihuahua) reprinted in *Las Dos Repúblicas* (Mexico City) in November and December 1893 show that Porfirian officials dictated the characterization of the Palomas raid printed in those outlets. Specifically, see *Las Dos Repúblicas*, December 2, 1893. Additionally, an exchange between editors of *The Two Republics* (the English-language edition of the Mexico City paper) and the *El Paso Times* printed in the *Dallas Morning News*, November 27, 1893, provides a direct example of the Mexico City newspaper declaring the border reports of a legitimate revolution to be completely fabricated. Editor Juan S. Hart of the *El Paso Times* fired back that Pérez was a "revolutionist" and not a "bandit" as evidenced by his history as a law-abiding citizen of the Guerrero district in Chihuahua.

10. Report and Inventory of José S. Hernández, Customs House Administrator, Las Palomas, Chihuahua, made to the Secretario de Hacienda Publica, Ignacio Mariscal, November 8, 1893, caja UI1351, expediente 1790, Fondo Hacienda Publica, AGN.

11. Vanderwood, *Power of God*, 291–92; and Alonso, *Thread of Blood*, 183–84.

12. Telegram from Adolfo L. Domínguez to Ambassador Matías Romero, November 9, 1893, expediente 44-16-2 (I), Archivo Histórico Genaro Estrada, Secretaría de Relaciones Exteriores, México City, D.F. (hereafter, AHSRE).

13. Armando Ruiz Aguilar, "Mayor Santana Pérez, una semblanza," in Vargas Valdez, *Tomóchic*, 246.

14. Dispatch from José Zayas Guarneros to Ambassador Matías Romero, November 10, 1893, expediente 44-16-2 (II), AHSRE. Emphasis in original.

15. *El Paso Times*, November 10, 1893. Connections between the *Headlight* and the *Times* are also evident in the "Cullings of Deming" and "El Paso News" sections of each paper published regularly during the early 1890s. For the papers' earlier reporting on Santo Tomás, see *El Paso Times*, April 20, 1893, April 25, 1893, April 26, 1893, April 30, 1893, and June 25, 1893; and *Deming Headlight*, May 6, 1893, June 3, 1893, June 24, 1893, September 2, 1893, and November 11, 1893.

16. Letter from José Zayas Guarneros to the Editor of the *El Paso Herald*, Annex to Zayas's dispatch to Ambassador Matías Romero, November 16, 1893, expediente 44-16-2 (II), AHSRE.

17. See, for example, *Deming Headlight*, November 11 and 18, 1893; *New York Herald* (dispatches from Deming and El Paso), November 17, 1893; and *Santa Fe New Mexican*, 16 November 1893.

18. Annex to Telegram from Adolfo L. Domínguez to Ambassador Matías Romero, November 9, 1893, expediente 44-16-2 (I), AHSRE.

19. This report is quite muted compared with the report made in the June 24, 1893 *Deming Headlight*. The report in Deming seems geared to its American audience, cast in terms that would generate the greatest level of outrage. This proclamation, on the other hand, was intended to convince the soldiers that they were serving a tyrant, not to paint them as tyrannical themselves.

20. *Deming Headlight*, June 24, 1893.

21. For further analysis of the proclamation, as well as its appeal to support the kinship- and reciprocity-based traditional economy as opposed to the monetary-based capitalist one, see Alonso, *Thread of Blood*, 183. See also Vargas Valdés, "Namiquipa, tierra de revolucionarios."

22. *El Paso Times*, November 21 and December 3, 1893.

23. Ruiz Aguilar, "Mayor Santana Pérez," 243; and Report of Adolfo L. Domínguez to Matías Romero, November 12, 1893, expediente 44-16-2 (I), AHSRE. Reports of claims that the Mexican insurgents had organized in New Mexico were also printed in the *Santa Fe New Mexican*, November 21 and 23, 1893.

24. Domínguez to Romero, November 12, 1893, AHSRE; and Letter from Adolfo L Domínguez to José Zayas Guarneros, Mexican Consul at El Paso, Texas, November 16, 1893, expediente 44-16-2 (II), AHSRE.

25. Correspondence of General A. McDonald McCook, Commanding Officer of the Department of the Colorado: Report to the Adjutant General, November 29, 1893, tomo 417, Archivo Embajada de México en los Estados Unidos Americanos (hereafter, AEMEU), AHSRE. Romero and President Porfirio Díaz used "Rio Grande" as shorthand for the international border in their comments on Pérez's uprising, despite the reality that the insurgents were active near, and across, the desert border to the west of the Rio Grande.

26. Report of Oscar J. Brown, First Lieutenant, First Cavalry, to Brigadier General A. McDonald McCook, Commanding Officer, Department of the Colorado, November 20, 1893, tomo 417, AEMEU, AHSRE. The initial report of Administrator Hernández and his guards also reported that the revolutionaries had left a receipt for the $203 they took from the Customs House safe. See Report of José S. Hernández, Customs House Administrator, Las Palomas, Chihuahua, made to the Secretario de Hacienda Publica, Ignacio Mariscal, November 8, 1893, caja UI1351, expediente 1790, Fondo Hacienda Publica, AGN.

27. Report of Charles E. Dodge, Adjutant, to Brigadier General A. McDonald McCook, Commanding Officer, Department of the Colorado, included as an Annex to McCook's report to the Secretary of State, November 20, 1893, tomo 417, AEMEU, AHSRE.

28. Report of Alexander McDonald McCook, Brigadier General, Commanding Officer, Department of the Colorado, to the U.S. Adjutant General, November 29, 1893, tomo 417, AEMEU, AHSRE; Letter from Edwin F. Uhl, Acting U.S. Secretary of State to Matías Romero, January 9, 1894, tomo 432, AEMEU, AHSRE.

29. See, for example, Hart's editorials in the *El Paso Times*, November 16 and 26, 1893.

30. *Albuquerque Morning Democrat*; *Boston Daily Advertiser*; *Daily Inter Ocean* (Chicago); and *Idaho Statesman* (Boise), November 16, 1893.

31. *Deming Headlight*, November 18, 1893. For the November 16 El Paso dispatch, see *New York Herald-Tribune*; *Morning World-Herald* (Omaha); *Philadelphia Inquirer*; *Springfield* (MA) *Daily Republican*; and *The Sun* (Baltimore), November 17, 1893. For the report on General Neri and the rebel's control of the larger region surrounding Las Palomas and La Ascensión, see *New York Herald*, November 17, 1893.

32. *Deming Headlight*, November 18, 1893.

33. Telegram from C. Perales, Ciudad Juárez Telegraph Operator, to Secretario de Relaciones Exteriores, Ignacio Mariscal, November 15, 1893; Telegram from Miguel Ahumada to Secretario de Relaciones Exteriores, Ignacio Mariscal, November 15, 1893; Telegram from Adolfo L. Domínguez to Secretario de Relaciones Exteriores, Ignacio Mariscal, by way of Ciudad Juárez, November 17, 1893, expediente 44-16-2 (I), AHSRE; and Letter from Adolfo L Domínguez to José Zayas Guarneros, Mexican Consul at El Paso, Texas, November 16, 1893, expediente 44-16-2 (II), AHSRE.

34. Official Dispatch, from José Yves Limantour to V. Barrera, Commander of the 2nd Zone of the Gendarmería Fiscal, State of Chihuahua, November 17, 1893; and Telegram

from Vista Vevraumont to Secretario de Relaciones Exteriores, Ignacio Mariscal, November 18, 1893, caja UI1351, expediente 1790, Fondo Hacienda Publica, AGN.

35. Report of V. Barrera, Commander of 2nd Zone of the Gendarmería Fiscal, State of Chihuahua, to Secretario de Relaciones Exteriores, Ignacio Mariscal, December 2, 1893, caja UI1351, expediente 1790, Fondo Hacienda Publica, AGN; Thomas Cottam Romney, *The Mormon Colonies in Mexico* (Salt Lake City: University of Utah Press, 2005), 312–14; and "Memories of Orson Pratt Brown," Taylor Oden MacDonald Collection, 1857–1980, reel 1 (MS 9548), CHLA. See also Report of Section President Enrique [Henry] Eyring to Presidente Municipal de Distrito Bravos, October 6, 1893, Archivo Municipal de Ciudad Juárez [AMCJ], Microform copy, roll 72, part 2, reel 54, University Library, University of Texas at El Paso (UTEP).

36. "Memories of Orson Pratt Brown," Taylor Oden MacDonald Collection, 1857–1980, reel 1 (MS 9548), CHLA. The December 2, 1893 *Deming Headlight* published a story of the skirmish between Brown's party and the revolutionaries based on a letter from an unnamed Mormon in Colonia Juárez. The letter opined that "the action of the [Mexican] troops was cowardly in the extreme and that 'any old woman with a broom could have whipped the entire squad.'" See also Romney, *Mormon Colonies*, 314. Romney's work on the Mormon colonies presents the dual perspectives of an academically trained historian and a firsthand participant. He received a PhD in history under the direction of Herbert Eugene Bolton and included a personal account of the colonists' brush with the revolutionaries in November 1893 and his own role in the events that unfolded at that time.

37. "Memories of Orson Pratt Brown," Taylor Oden MacDonald Collection, 1857–1980, reel 1 (MS 9548), CHLA.

38. *Deming Headlight*, December 2, 1893.

39. *New York Herald*, November 18, 1893.

40. *El Paso Times*, November 26, November 28, and November 30, 1893.

41. *Deming Headlight*, November 25, 1893.

42. *El Paso Times*, November 26, 1893, repr. in *Dallas Morning News*, November 27, 1893. For the skirmish in Ciudad Guerrero between Pérez and Mexican federal forces, see Vanderwood, *Power of God*, 249–50.

43. State Department dispatch from Consul Theodore Huston, Ciudad Juárez, November 30, 1893, reel 5, Despatches from United States Consuls in Ciudad Juárez (Paso del Norte), 1850–1906, File Microcopy of Records in the National Archives, No. 184 (hereafter, Microcopy 184).

44. The *Herald* reported that Pacheco's name was "Nicario Pacho" and the *Times* spelled his name "Machario Pacho." Given the commonality of the misspelling of Spanish-language proper names in the American press, it seems likely that this was a misspelling of the name Macario Pacheco. Macario Pacheco was known by Mexican authorities in the region to have taken part in the Palomas raid. See Report of Charles E. Dodge, Adjutant, to Brigadier General A. McDonald McCook, Commanding Officer, Department of the Colorado, included as an Annex to McCook's report to the Secretary of State, November 20, 1893, tomo 417, AEMEU, AHSRE; and Report of José S. Hernández, Administrador de la Aduana de las Palomas, to Ignacio Mariscal, Secretario de Relaciones Exteriores, Caja UI1351, expediente 1790, Fondo Hacienda Publica, AGN.

45. *El Paso Times*, November 28, 1893; *New York Herald*, December 1, 1893. The fact that many observers in the borderlands and the Mexican diplomatic corps conceived of Tomóchic as "Indian" is ironic. Residents of Tomóchic, notably Cruz Chávez, pronounced a

mestizo identity through which they denigrated local Rarámuri (Tarahumara) people. See Vanderwood, *Power of God*, 24, 54.

46. Letter from José Zayas Guarneros to Ignacio Mariscal, Secretario de Relaciones Exteriores, December 3, 1893, expediente 44-16-2 (II), AHSRE.

47. *Dallas Morning News*, December 5 and 7, 1893; *New York Herald-Tribune*, December 6, 1893; *Salt Lake Weekly Tribune*, December 7, 1893; *Topeka Weekly Sentinel* (Kansas), December 7, 1893; and *Kalamazoo Gazette* (Michigan), December 9, 1893.

48. Letter from Juan S. Hart to Consul Theodore Huston, Ciudad Juárez, December 5, 1893, reel 5, Despatches from United States Consuls in Ciudad Juárez (Paso del Norte), 1850–1906, microcopy 184. Huston reported to Assistant Secretary of State Josiah Quincy that the actions against the *Times* seemed to be arbitrary and unjust. Yet, an unnamed State Department official responded that the suppression of the *Times* was within the purview of Mexico's rights as a sovereign state (correspondence also contained in reel 5).

49. On General Hernández, see Vanderwood, *Power of God*, 288–90. *Deming Headlight*, December 9, 1893; *Kalamazoo Gazette*, December 9, 1893; and *Daily Inter Ocean*, December 14, 1893.

50. *Deming Headlight*, December 16, 1893. The exaggeration of the Santo Tomás casualty count also calls into question the admittedly shaky figures for the federal forces in the December 12 battle. For more on the variation in casualty estimates, see Acuña, *Corridors of Migration*, 40–43; Osorio, "Villismo," 150–51, note 4; Vargas Valdés, "Namiquipa, tierra de revolucionarios"; and Aguilar, "Mayor Santana Pérez," 241–43.

51. *Dallas Morning News*, December 14 and 17, 1893; *New York Herald*, December 14, 1893; and *Daily Inter Ocean*, December 14, 1893.

52. *Dallas Morning News*, December 19, 1893.

53. *New York Herald*, December 29, 1893.

54. Telegrams and Dispatches from José Zayas Guarneros to Ignacio Mariscal, Secretario de Relaciones Exteriores, November 18, November 29, December 1, and December 3, 1893, expediente 9-5-16, AHSRE; *El Paso Times*, December 3, 1893; and *New York Times*, December 1, 1893.

55. *Deming Headlight*, February 17, 1894.

56. The amnesty order was printed in the Chihuahua *Periódico Oficial*, February 27, 1894. A copy of the order was included as an annex in Consul Huston's March 10, 1894 dispatch to Edwin F. Uhl, Assistant Secretary of State, reel 5, microcopy 184.

57. *Periódico Oficial*, February 27, 1894.

58. *Periódico Oficial* (Cd. Chihuahua), April 14, 1894. Interestingly, both the *Deming Headlight* and the accounts of Mormon colonists asserted the claim that it was, in fact, the colonists' pleas to Porfirio Díaz that resulted in the amnesty offer. See *Deming Headlight*, March 17, 1894; and "Memories of Orson Pratt Brown," Taylor Oden MacDonald Collection, 1857–1980, reel 1 (MS 9548), CHLA.

59. Alonso, *Thread of Blood*, 156.

60. Osorio, "Villismo," note 6 on 151 and Ramón Ramírez Tafoya, *Ascensión antes y después de la Revolución* (Chihuahua: Instituto Chihuahuense de Cultura, 2011), 73–85. For more on the prevalence of *La Revolución*, see Thomas Benjamin, *La Revolución: Mexico's Great Revolution as Memory, Myth, and History* (Austin: University of Texas Press, 2000), which outlines the ways in which the "Revolution with a capital letter" has come to define Mexican national identity to the present day.

Bolton & Mitchell, LAREDO, TEXAS.

Gregorio Cortez Killed sheriff Moris of Karnes Co Texas. Wednesday June 11th 1901. Killed sheriff Glover and constable Shand of Gonzales Co Texas June 13th 1901. Captured near Palofox about 50 miles above Laredo June 22nd, 1901 by Captain J. H. Rodgers of the State rangers and K.H. Merrem Inspector of Customs of Laredo Texas. Cortez was captured at a sheep ranch about 6 miles from the Rio Grande river. He was armed with two Colts 45 cal. six shooters but made no resistance. 1975/70-5237 5x4

Figure 9.1 "Gregorio Cortez, 1901." Courtesy of the Texas State Library and Archives Commission (Image 1975/070-5237).

Chapter 9

Por un compatriota

Gregorio Cortez, State-Sanctioned Violence, and the Forging of an Unlikely Alliance

SONIA HERNÁNDEZ

We lived . . . happily in the Tilmeyer [Thulemeyer] ranch . . . in Karnes County, my husband and four innocent children and I . . . when one day, on the 12th of June . . . the sheriff appeared . . .

—Leonor Díaz de Cortes, n.m.1901

The Mexicans resisted the officers, and the result was one Mexican shot to death, one hung, one wounded by a gunshot and one had his skull crushed by a rifle barrel. The Mexican was hung in an effort to make him divulge the whereabouts of Cortez.

—*Fort Worth Morning Register*, June 18, 1901

In 1901, *obreros* (factory workers) from the northern Mexican city of Monterrey received correspondence from fellow workers residing across the Rio Grande in Laredo, Texas. The letter was a plea for assistance on behalf of a fellow "*compatriota*." *Obreros* had gathered to discuss and take action on a recently transpired event that placed a heretofore-unknown Mexican migrant vaquero in the crossroads of two nations.[1] The *compatriota* and *fronterizo* Gregorio Cortez hailed from the outskirts of Matamoros, Tamaulipas, and as a young adult moved with his family to Central Texas during the 1880s.[2] The skilled worker had lost his brother, gone through a divorce, remarried, and escaped a lynching—all while in jail accused of the murder of three white Texas sheriffs. On that fateful twelfth day of June in 1901 at the Thulemeyer Ranch in Karnes County, miscommunication between Cortez, his brother Romaldo, and Sheriff Brack Morris and his translator Boone Choate led to the death of Cortez's brother and Sheriff Morris. Earlier that day, Karnes County authorities had been informed that a certain Gregorio Cortez had traded a horse and because he fit the description of "a medium-sized Mexican who had stolen a horse in Karnes County," Sheriff Morris, accompanied by Choate, had decided to visit the Cortez place and question the Mexican vaquero. Cortez's life and that of his family dramatically changed in the course of that afternoon. In a miscommunication due to sloppy Spanish translations, Sheriff Morris shot and killed Gregorio's brother Romaldo, and in self-defense, Gregorio Cortez fired back, fatally wounding the Texas sheriff. He then fled the scene. Soon, scores of Texas Rangers, local sheriffs, and vigilantes hunted Cortez. Eluding capture for more than a week, Cortez traversed central and southern Texas and managed to save himself from a lynching. The ordeal set off state-sanctioned violence on the ethnic Mexican community, yet it also served as the backdrop for the forging of an unlikely transnational alliance that rallied behind a fellow *compatriota*.

While what became known as the "Cortez Incident" has received scholarly attention in Texas and Chicano historiography, this unfortunate development has not been examined within the greater socioeconomic and political economy of the Mexican northern borderlands, particularly the period leading to and during the 1910 Mexican Revolution. This is surprising, given the intricate links between Texas, Tamaulipas, and Nuevo León as well as Cortez's own involvement in the Revolution.

Except for a brief section on Gregorio Cortez's participation in the Mexican Revolution in Américo Paredes's *With His Pistol in His Hand*, we know little about Cortez's connection to northern Mexico. New archival research in Mexico and Texas reveals another dimension to the Cortez incident. Retracing Cortez's manhunt and developments during and after his apprehension helps us to transnationally move this narrative beyond Central and South Texas. It also sheds light on the interactions among prominent Mexican and Tejano regional elites as well as working-class Mexicans and Mexican Americans negotiating on behalf of Cortez's defense. While "labor regimes and workers' movements have never been phenomena enclosed within national territories," what is noteworthy about this transnational alliance was that seemingly disconnected subjects—*obreros* and Tejano and Mexican regional elites—formed part of a greater regional web where they functioned as transnational cultural and political brokers despite differences in class and nationality.[3] While historians such as Neil Foley have argued that middle-class or affluent Tejanos aligned themselves with Anglo-Americans for societal acceptance and/or political reasons, the near-lynching attempt of Cortez reveals that violence and threat of violence could also trump sharp divisions of class. From a transnational perspective—that is, an analysis from a methodological, archival, and historiographical vantage point, the Cortez incident, as well as the subsequent cross-class alliance that emerged on Cortez's behalf, is a departure from this viewpoint, as it brought affluent and working-class Tejanos together. Thus, while members of the Mexican and Tejano elite could "distance themselves from the growing stigma associated with being considered a Mexican 'greaser' in the new social order of the southwestern United

States," as historian David Gutierrez has argued, it was also possible for middle-class or affluent Tejanos such as Francisco Chapa and Samuel Belden Jr. to align or partner with *obreros* and workers within and outside Texas; violence did not discriminate against social class, and alliances could help a member of the community remain alive.[4]

From a transnational perspective, one that goes beyond a Chicano or a Mexican or a Texas-based approach but takes these disciplinary fields as a whole, the near-lynching attempt of Cortez, the violence directed at ethnic Mexicans that emerged during his manhunt, and the cross-class, cross-national alliance that emerged provide a window into the complexities and contradictions of borderlands violence. At the turn of the twentieth century, in the midst of profound political and economic transformations and despite a steady decline of Tejano sociopolitical power, the borderlands environment provided room for resistance and collaboration. While Cortez "dodged the bullet" and was saved from a lynching, others were not so fortunate. Why was Cortez such an exception, and what was the nature of the borderlands at the turn of the twentieth century that provided such an allowance? Before examining the Cortez incident from a transnational vantage point, let us revisit what transformed a relatively unknown Mexican vaquero into both hero and villain.

A Brief Account of the Cortez Incident

In 1891, Gregorio Cortez married Leonor Díaz, a Tejana from Central Texas, and shortly thereafter he and his family as well as his brother Romaldo Cortez's family left Manor, Texas. They rented land from rancher Will A. Thulemeyer just outside of Kenedy and Karnes City and settled there.[5] Living in a county such as Karnes at the turn of the twentieth century was rough for Mexicans just as it was for African Americans. The town of Kenedy, which was about ten miles east of the Thulemeyer Ranch, was predominantly white—a mix of recent and more established German, Polish, and Czech immigrants. In nearby Karnes City, an 1877 report noted twelve organized communities with "ten white teachers and one colored teacher."[6] Boone Choate and Sheriff Brack Morris were among the well-known whites in that area. Choate had been asked to join Morris as the sheriff was to investigate and question Gregorio Cortez, regarding his recently acquired horse. Choate was tasked with accompanying Morris, since he "knew the Mexicans well," and Morris described him as capable of translating. The Mexican community was relatively small in Karnes and nearby Kenedy, and according to sources, Choate was well known in that community.[7] Choate's limited language skills, however, would have deadly consequences.

Morris and Choate approached the Cortez home on June 12, 1901, and via Choate, Morris asked Romaldo if Gregorio was in the house. Romaldo then called Gregorio, who walked toward his brother. As they faced Morris, Choate asked Cortez if he had traded a horse recently, or "que si había cambiado un caballo." Following standard Spanish gender distinction, Gregorio replied that he had not and made it clear that he had acquired a *yegua*—the Spanish translation for mare and, clearly, a word that was not in Choate's vocabulary. Choate did not misunderstand the meaning of *yegua*; what he heard was "no." Thus, the brief but fatal encounter occurred. Morris understood Gregorio Cortez's "no" as denying any involvement in a trade that led to acquiring a horse. Morris quickly reacted and asked Choate to inform Cortez that he would proceed to arrest him. Yet other Spanish words were uttered by Cortez that Choate did not understand at that moment—"no me pueden arrestar por nada," which Choate translated to "no one can arrest me." Instantly, Morris drew his gun, aimed, and hit Romaldo, and Cortez, seeing his brother on the floor, returned the fire, fatally shooting Morris.[8] Cortez eventually fled. He first headed north but soon turned south to head to Laredo to cross into Mexico.[9]

State-sanctioned Violence during the Search for Cortez

For almost two weeks, Texas Rangers, local sheriffs, and other law enforcement agents and volunteers hunted Cortez. Those suspected of aiding Cortez or his apparent "gang" were beaten, lynched, and left for others to see. The act signaled the power of the state and instilled fear in the Mexican-origin community. As the Cortez incident unfolded, Gonzales County sheriff Robert M. Glover rushed to seek information about Cortez from "the most likely source," the women in Cortez's family. Sheriff Glover questioned Cortez's mother, wife, and sister-in-law. Glover managed to question one of the Cortez women and "under pressure," the woman eventually spoke to Glover of Cortez's plans to flee. It was at that point that Glover, along with Gonzales County constable Henry Schnabel and other deputies, paid a visit to a Mexican farmer who was also Gregorio Cortez's friend and *compadre*, Martin Robledo. The Glover posse surrounded the Robledo home in pitch darkness, and soon thereafter, the fire exchange began. In a matter of hours, two officers died while Mrs. Robledo and a young boy who was living with the Robledos at the time, Ramón Rodríguez, were wounded. The media reported how "five Mexicans were captured," yet these included Mrs. Robledo, Mr. Robledo, the young Ramón, and two Robledo children. They were arrested given that Mr. Robledo was a close friend of Gregorio's.[10] The "capturing" and temporary "detainment" of Mrs. Robledo and her children worked to instill fear in the Mexican-origin community—the local officials' strategy to figure out Cortez's whereabouts. State agents instilled fear through detainment, despite no clear evidence that Mrs. Robledo and the children had assisted Cortez.

Like Ms. Robledo, Gregorio Cortez's wife, Leonor Díaz de Cortez, and her children were detained and remained in jail from June 12 through early October—nearly four months. She was not immediately released when Cortez was captured on June 22, and she remained in confinement separated from her older children. Mexicans assumed to be in cahoots with Cortez or who appeared suspicious were lynched and killed; just days before Cortez was finally detained, a group of Texas Rangers came across three Mexicans and arrested one of them while killing the other two.[11] Anyone who dared to protest the atrocities could be labeled a sympathizer and could likely face the same fate. Yet media outlets described those forming part of the chase as persistent and courageous. When former Ranger and retired Sheriff Will A. Wright died, Rio Grande valley newspapers lauded the old Ranger as a "hero" because he chased the "bandit" Cortez. It was Wright's "excellent woodsmanship and trailing ability [that were] at a premium."[12] The editorial boasted Wright's participation in a lynching he led in Wilson County.[13]

Such "courageous" men had encounters with "suspected bandits" who, in fact, were ordinary residents, yet because they were armed, state agents chasing Cortez considered them dangerous. It was quite common for men and women to not only own a rifle, pistol, or some type of weapon for self-defense but also carry it publicly in Texas. However, an armed Mexican appeared suspicious and in the eyes of the law could be dangerous. As the Cortez manhunt continued, Rangers encountered "armed Mexicans" near Belmont. One local newspaper reported, "The Mexicans resisted the officers, and the result was one Mexican shot to death, one hung, one wounded by a gunshot and one had his skull crushed by a rifle barrel. The Mexican was hung in an effort to make him divulge the whereabouts of Cortez."[14]

Cortez most likely fled because he knew how little his life was worth if he were captured (his fate likely to be a lynching). But authorities used his flight to spread fear among the Mexican-origin population and anyone who dared to aid him. The media sensationalized the ordeal and reported him as "leader of [a] bandit ring."[15] As the manhunt continued and the number of authorities chasing Cortez grew, so did media coverage. From local, to state, to national and international media outlets, the story of the infamous "bandit" occupied headlines. As authorities and vigilantes embarked on a statewide massive manhunt, local officials arrested Gregorio Cortez's brother Tomas, who worked in Manor, Texas. Authorities accused him of horse theft. The incident had been reported in Pleasanton, and despite scant evidence implicating Tomas, authorities detained and formally arrested him.[16]

The hunt for Cortez ended on June 22, 1901. A local *fronterizo*, Jesús González, locally known as "El Teco," spotted Cortez at Abrán de la Garza's sheep ranch near the Laredo coal mines and contacted authorities to inform them of Cortez's whereabouts. Captain J. H. Rogers, who camped a mere two hundred yards from the sheep ranch, along with former Ranger and *norteño* investor K. H. Merren, proceeded to apprehend Cortez.[17] Unlike the sensational reporting that claimed "if arrested . . . Cortez . . . as one of the most desperate men on the border . . . would fight with the gallows staring him in the face," Cortez did not resist arrest as Rogers and Merren surprised him while he rested in a small *jacal* (shack).[18] The *Dallas Morning News* reported on June 24, 1901, that if Rogers had arrived half an hour later "the man [Cortez] would have been safe on the south bank of the Rio Grande."[19] By the time Cortez was apprehended, nine ethnic Mexicans were killed and three were wounded.

Newspapers from around the nation reported the apprehension of Cortez by Captain Rogers. On the twenty-first of June, Laredo sheriff Ortiz, Rogers, and other Rangers escorted Cortez to San Antonio via the International and Great Northern Railroad.[20] Once detained in the old county jail, a mob, most of whom hailed from Kennedy, approached the jail and attempted to break into the premises with the goal of lynching Cortez.[21] Yet Sheriff F. M. Fly did not support lynch law. Fly prevented a three hundred–person mob from breaking into his jail to snatch Cortez. To disperse the mob, Sheriff Fly went as far as vowing to "deputize all those who were not shooting [and] arrest all those who had fired the shots."[22] Sheriff Fly assured the public, via statements to the local courts, that "there was no danger that the course of the law would be interfered with by the people of Gonzales country, who are confident that Cortez will be convicted and given the death penalty."[23] In the "lynching belt of Texas," which included Karnes County, "Mexicans live in terror and fear," the newspapers reported; even well-established newspapers such as the *San Antonio Express* and state officials lamented the fact that Cortez had not been lynched.[24] Cortez was quite lucky to have escaped a lynching. As Carrigan and Webb note in this volume, lynching victims were usually taken from jail cells. The lynching of ethnic Mexicans frequently took place near the jails and courtrooms, before formal justice could take place.[25] Even as late as 1922, historians have documented, in the Rio Grande valley town of Weslaco, a mob removed resident Elias Villarreal Zarate from the local jail and proceeded to lynch him.[26] To make matters worse, local judges often sided with law enforcement, sanctioning extralegal violence. Law enforcement agents themselves participated in lynching or other extralegal acts of violence.[27] How, then, could such state-protected practices come to an end? Given such state-honored practices, alliances were crucial to mitigate the violence. We now turn to the forging of a transnational political alliance, grounded on cross-border nationalistic rhetoric and a shared regional space, as one example of community response to such violence.

The political discussions and transnational business negotiations involving elites and merchants, as well as their interaction with workers alike, shed light on the way in which politically based transnational cooperation could be forged and could serve as a powerful tool to address state-sanctioned violence. The northern Mexican borderlands including southern Texas had witnessed some degree of cross-class collaboration dating back to the colonial period up through the Gilded Age and Porfiriato. The alliances among various class groups during the Vidaurri years and the Garzista rebellion and during the 1910 Mexican Revolution, as was the case with the Tamaulipas-based Carrera-Torres faction, serve as reminders of the possibilities, even if imperfect, of cross-class collaboration.[28] In the case of the Carrera-Torres faction and in the earlier Magonista collectives (followers of Ricardo Flores Magón), such cross-class alliances also witnessed cross-gender cooperation, albeit temporary and unequal. While no egalitarian society, as historiography has shown, the northern lands offered opportunities for cross-class and cross-racial alliances particularly in the face of increased Indigenous raids given the absence of dense population centers.

While violence was not and is not synonymous with borderlands sites (even those carved out in the aftermath of war), nor was war simply a consequence of borders, state-making *did often* involve violence. As scholar Monica Muñoz Martínez has pointed out, "state violence constituted the forms of state consolidation through the participation of state agents and local residents in the region," and such state-making was on full display in border states such as Tamaulipas and Texas.[29] Borders represent spaces that define the jurisdiction of nation-states. Consolidating those bordered lands represented a concerted effort that "symbol[ized] progress and modernity" that were crucial in the making of nation-states.[30] In this way, similar violence connected to state-making existed elsewhere, yet what made border-based violence unique in the period under examination was the way in which subjects associated with a different culture, religion, and language became integrated into mainstream society in the aftermath of a bloody, costly, and unpopular war.[31] By the 1870s, two decades after the end of the Mexican-American War, the population of non–ethnic Mexicans grew in the state, and so too did ideas of cultural and racial superiority that shaped the relationships between Mexican-origin peoples, Indigenous populations, and Euro-Americans or nonmestizo newcomers.[32] The borderlands that Cortez traversed were born out of violence, carved out after the Mexican-American War, and his unfortunate encounter with Texas authorities meant to protect him and his family remind us of the persistent "repercussions of the war [Mexican-American War]" and how long after 1848 "were still felt."[33] Mexicans in the ceded territories, now Mexican Americans, became U.S. subjects, although the question of citizenship and entitlement to its attendant rights remained major issues in the years to come. The question and role of race, citizenship, and belonging, as well as identity, always so tentative, were on public display during the Cortez years; the Cortez incident revealed, often through brutal ways, how a population that once held significant political and economic power was now not only perceived but treated in clearly second-class-citizen terms. This occurred despite the community's continued growth, particularly as Mexican immigrants arrived in Texas from Nuevo León, Tamaulipas, and San Luis Potosí.[34]

In 1901, border security involved the regional efforts of mounted inspectors, Mexican Rurales, Texas Rangers, and a mix of local authorities. Those in positions of authority charged to protect communities in the greater borderlands could both protect their respective members and inflict violence upon the very same communities. Violence could take the form of both non- and state-sanctioned physical violence, and as William Carrigan and Clive Webb have argued in chapter 10 in this same volume, racial violence was not a direct consequence of "frontier conditions . . . [or] the absence of a criminal justice system" but more so "the discriminatory manner in which it was enforced."[35] Further, as Lance Blyth and Brandon Morgan have also demonstrated, violence need not be manifested in physical ways and could have the same effect as violent rhetoric. The use of narratives and/or symbols could instill fear in communities, and this could result in deadly consequences.

Central and southern Texas as well as northeastern Mexico constituted a shared regional space with extensive sociopolitical, cultural, and economic ties—an *ámbito regional* (regional ambit) or *noreste extenso* (large northeast), to borrow from historians Mario Cerutti and Manuel Ceballos, respectively. While the border was not yet hard or in any sense fixed, it carried weight in the minds of people from a geopolitical perspective and not a cultural one. Tejano and Anglo communities in Texas knew there was a border, even if it was not heavily patrolled, and they maintained social, political, and economic ties. While episodes of violence disrupted people's lives, at the same time, these signaled community responses with transnational reach that directly shaped the contours of these *norteño-tejano* lands. Responses to violence also represented examples of transnational political cooperation that defied categories of class, gender, citizenship, and political affiliations.[36]

The late renowned cultural anthropologist Américo Paredes reclaimed Cortez, not only through the historical record and oral histories but through the recordings of various versions of the "Ballad of Gregorio Cortez." I build on Paredes's historical-ethnographic work and position Cortez's lived experience in this greater *noreste extenso*.[37] Repositioning the Cortez incident in this way fleshes out what border theorists Hastings Donnan and Thomas Wilson explain as transnationalism as people/sites "influenced by, and sometimes shar[ing] the values, ideas, customs and traditions of, their counterparts across the boundary line." And if culture is about power relations, examining violence in border culture, particularly in one of the most historically contested borderlands in the globe, sheds light on how episodes of violence shaped power relations and how these episodes inscribed particular meaning for particular groups of people. Thus, transnationalizing Cortez within the context of the *noreste extenso* repositions the interactions of Tejanos—elites and workers as well as *norteño* peoples—to help explain borderlands and borders as "meaning-making and meaning-carrying entities."[38] What did it *mean* to experience violence in the borderlands? And what were the implications of cross-class, cross-race collaboration in the borderlands to address such violence?

Violence was experienced differently, and such experiences hinged on an individual's race, ethnicity, gender, sexuality, language, religion, and class. Recourse for community members when confronted with violence varied. During the Cortez incident, ethnic Mexicans lost their lives at the hands of authorities for their apparent association with Cortez, mainly, that they *too* were of Mexican origin. And, as this essay reveals, they did not experience violence because state agents, such as the Texas Rangers, stubbornly adhered to "Ranger justice" popular in the nineteenth century, or because Rangers refused to enter the twentieth century, as some historians have claimed; Rangers inflicted violence on ethnic Mexicans because the state allowed it and often encouraged their actions.[39] While there was clearly an abuse of state power, such abuses could also lead to political transnational collaboration.

Unlikely Transnational Alliances? Norteño and Tejano Políticos, Workers, and Anti-Revolutionaries

The near-lynching of Cortez caused uproar and became the focal point of the Laredo workers in their appeals to Nuevo Laredo and Monterrey fellow *obreros*. Along the Texas-Mexico borderlands, residents learned about the incident and ensuing manhunt. The newspaper editor Pablo Cruz, who had publicly supported Starr County journalist Catarino Erasmo Garza and his plan to overthrow the Díaz regime in the 1880s, emerged as a strong public advocate of the Mexican-origin community. At the outbreak of the Cortez incident, Cruz rallied Mexican Americans and Mexicans on both sides of the Rio Grande in support of Cortez.[40] In the pages of *El Regidor*, Cruz blamed "poverty and inadequate legal representation" as "preventing *Tejanos* from receiving a fair trial as guaranteed by the American Constitution" in Texas and especially those outside the border region.[41] The Spanish language became a vehicle by which the Mexican-origin community protested violence during the postwar period and continued well into the first half of the twentieth century. The expansion of these media outlets allowed *norteños*, *vecinos* (denizens), or community members to keep abreast of news in the "*colonias mexicanas*" across the border in Texas. *Norteños* too learned about developments concerning their *compatriotas* in Texas through their own outlets including *La Voz de Nuevo León* and the *Periódico Oficial* from Monterrey. Thus, the expansion of Spanish-language newspapers operated by more affluent Mexicans and Tejanos aided in the forging of cross-class and cross-border alliances.[42]

As Cortez sat in several county (and later, state) jails, an elaborate political alliance transcending the geopolitical border, class, gender, and racial boundaries soon emerged. In their petition for their compatriot, the members of this alliance sought funds and emphasized Cortez's good fortune, as he had escaped a lynching, yet the workers knew that Cortez had been an exception. The Sociedad de Obreros from Laredo informed their *norteño* counterparts of the developments in Central Texas. Organizing the Comisión Organizadora Para Ayudar en su Defensa al Mexicano Gregorio Cortéz, the Sociedad and others reached out across national and state boundaries.[43] The Comisión had formed shortly after news broke of the manhunt, and the thought of hundreds of Texas Rangers, local sheriffs, and deputized civilians in pursuit of a fellow worker was compelling enough for the Laredo labor associations and those across the border in Nuevo Laredo to act quickly. As was the tradition since colonial times, *vecinos* came together and via the written word submitted petitions to community representatives for numerous causes. In this case, workers decided to petition the governor of Nuevo León directly. The plea came in the form of monetary assistance for Cortez's numerous legal appeals. Nuevo Laredo and Laredo workers had maintained ties with Monterrey obrero groups since the mid-nineteenth century.

In their petition to Nuevo León governor Bernardo Reyes, Laredo workers cited frustration with the "juez del condado (county judge) . . . who absolutely refused to extend the rights that [Cortez] was entitled to." The Comisión, with the help of other organizations, secured 902 signatures and pleaded with

Manuel Quiroz, Mexican ambassador in Washington, D.C., to intercede on behalf of Cortez.[44] While the practice of soliciting and providing mutual support for fellow workers was nothing new and was not seen as such a risky practice, signing a statement in favor of Cortez (in the eyes of authorities: in defense of a "bandit," "sheriff killer," and "ring leader") could present its own risks. Any Mexican who dared to challenge state- and non-state-sanctioned violence could lose his or her life over it. Further, that over fifty sheriffs from throughout Texas counties organized themselves "to kill that Mexican [Cortez]" was not a threat to be taken lightly.[45] As a response to such a daunting image, the Laredo workers insisted that Cortez "defended his life," leaving no doubt as to the willingness of Mexican people to defend themselves and by doing so "asserted the character of the Mexican people."[46] The workers' message was clear: the Mexican community had every right to defend itself—individually as in the case of Cortez or collectively, as the workers now proved through their organizing efforts.

The Sociedad de Obreros from Laredo petitioned Reyes to contribute to the defense fund to help pay for attorney fees. Representing the workers, Tejanos D. R. Davila and Emilio Flores reminded Reyes that "considerable funds" had already been contributed by "progressive governors" including those from Tamaulipas, Coahuila, Durango, Chihuahua, Zacatecas, Guanajuato, and the state of México for Cortez's defense. Appealing to Reyes's nationalist sentiment, the group insisted that they did so, "as their only wish was to help a fellow *mexicano* who found himself in disgrace, in foreign soil."[47] Further, the workers claimed that if Americans received protection from the Mexican government, while living and working in Mexico, then the state and federal government was obliged to extend those same protections to the "raza mexicana" (Mexican race) on the Texas side of the border.[48] The workers collaborated with Texas newspaper editor Pablo Cruz to raise funds, and, in turn Cruz contacted and hired Cortez's legal defense team.

While Américo Paredes and other scholars have argued that it was eventually either Cortez's "personal qualities as a man" that helped him convince Texas governor O. B. Colquitt to grant him a pardon or Tejano elite Francisco Chapa's influence, new research in Mexican and Texas archives points to yet other possibilities. The role of regional elites Samuel Belden Sr. and Belden Jr. of the Laredo-Monterrey–San Antonio corridor has not been examined and, as new research reveals, played a prominent role in Cortez's defense. While Chapa's activism on behalf of Cortez cannot be ruled out, it should, however, be examined as a larger, broader transnational effort with other well-known regional elite supporters of Cortez such as Belden and workers' participation.

Up to now, none of the writings about the Cortez incident have acknowledged the role of *norteño* regional elites such as the Beldens. Yet the Belden family was well known in northeastern Mexico, and since the late nineteenth century, Samuel Belden had entered in business partnerships with South Texas entrepreneur Charles Stillman from Cameron County as well as other merchants and regional elites. Belden had built his family's wealth from such business relationships and had profited from the business that he and Stillman engaged in, including the sale of almost the entire city of Brownsville, Texas.[49] The older member of the family, Franciso Belden, held economic interests in the burgeoning industrial capital of Monterrey. Francisco Belden acted as the representative of the Banco de Londres y México, and in the spring of 1898, Belden acted as intermediary for capitalist Thomas Braniff to establish a bank and associated agencies in Monterrey and Nuevo León towns.[50] Samuel Belden, while in San Antonio, maintained a political-economic relationship with regional elites and officials throughout Texas and the Mexican north.[51] The younger Samuel Jr., an attorney, joined Cortez's defense team composed of B. R. Abernathy and J. R. Woolen. Belden also had connections to an emerging anti-Díaz voice, Francisco I. Madero and his circle of influential *norteño latifundistas* from Nuevo León and Coahuila.[52]

Belden's influence extended well beyond the borders of San Antonio and Monterrey. He interceded on behalf of American Elliott C. Hull, who was acting manager of Rascón Manufacturing and Development Company of San Luís Potosí, the massive sugar complex that also encompassed acreages in southern Tamaulipas. Hull, just as many other Americans in Mexico and Mexican regional elites, was under siege as revolution broke out and was forced to abandon the premises without leaving funds to maintain the daily operation of the Hacienda Rascón. Safe in his downtown San Antonio office, Belden petitioned General Pablo Gonzáles, who now commanded the forces in Nuevo León, in mid-May 1914, asking him to protect Hull.[53] The Beldens' family influence in the region probably led to the "Mexicans of San Antonio making arrangements to engage counsel for him [Cortez]" after the court appointed B. R. Abernathy to defend Cortez.[54] In all likelihood, Belden's involvement in Cortez's defense coupled with the petitions to heads of state by workers and Cruz and Chapa's support, not Cortez's personality, all contributed to Cortez's release.

The influential Belden Sr. and his son had offered their loyalty and service to the Madero administration. As Cortez served his sixth year of his prison sentence in Huntsville, Belden Sr. urged Alfonso Madero to petition his brother, President Madero, to intercede on behalf of several Mexicans who had been detained and jailed in Texas prisons. Alfonso Madero also petitioned Federico (Roque) Gonzáles Garza, his brother's personal secretary in Mexico City. The detainees, accused of violating the neutrality laws in Laredo, according to Belden, deserved their freedom "because they helped us quite a bit in this past revolution."[55]

Belden also received support from the constitutionalist leader Venustiano Carranza, and it appears that Carranza himself asked Belden for political favors. Carranza, from nearby Coahuila, shared Belden and the Madero family's upbringing. Two months before Cortez's official pardon, Carranza wrote to Belden, informing him that the minister of the interior Jesús Acuña was to represent him in "several important matters," and he asked Belden if he could accompany Acuña as he met with Texas governor Oscar Colquitt in Austin.[56] Belden continued working on behalf of Carranza; when Pablo Gonzáles captured Mexico City for Carranza, Belden acted as Carranza's legal representative in Texas and communicated with Carranza via Acuña.[57]

Like Belden, Francisco A. Chapa, now a prominent Tejano merchant, originally from Matamoros, was a longtime supporter of Porfirio Díaz and Bernardo Reyes. He too was a Texas Ranger supporter and played a critical role in the transnational network of allies in the eventual release and pardon of Cortez. Chapa established a successful pharmacy that catered mostly to the Tejanos of the area.[58] He was a member of the governor's staff and lieutenant colonel in the Texas National Guard. Editor of *El Imparcial* of San Antonio, Chapa became known for his support of the Tejano community and, like Pablo Cruz, supported Cortez.[59] A close friend of Governor Colquitt, he used his political connections to plan and assist in counterrevolutions against the Francisco I. Madero administration.

Chapa's own identity as border Tejano elite and as someone in law enforcement was always a matter of negotiation, so as long as it satisfied his personal agenda. In historian Richard Ribb's estimation, Chapa had launched a "private war against revolutionaries."[60] Indeed, Chapa had solidified ties with conservative, *porfirista* officials since before the Cortez ordeal. He had maintained relationships with merchants, politicians, and community leaders. Yet Chapa also had maintained ties with *mutualistas* (organized workers) on both sides of the border, and in this way, he acted as a sort of transnational political and cultural broker.[61] The same authority figure that the Laredo workers had petitioned on behalf of Cortez, Bernardo Reyes, with Chapa's help, would plot to challenge Madero. While there was certainly a contradiction in the ideological positions of Chapa and those who were anti-Díaz, it is important to point out that even the more progressive of Tejanos, like the Laredo-based Idar family, defended Tejanos' right to choose whether or not to support the Mexican Revolution. In an editorial in the family newspaper, *La Crónica*, the Idars, including Clemente and Jovita Idar, reminded readers of their right to speak and think and argued that despite the call from the Texas governor to remain neutral from the current revolution raging in Mexico, "Mexicans and Mexican Americans have the right . . . to express any sympathies for the *maderista* cause or the *porfirista* cause." The editorial continued that Mexican Americans have "just as much right as Mexicans [in Mexico] to express our opinion and our sympathies as we please [como nos pegue la gana]."[62]

Tejanos such as Chapa found themselves in a hard place and quite frequently had to prove their worthiness and loyalty. When troops were sent to the border, Chapa reminded folks that "the people in the north need never fear the influence of border Mexican Americans," and he assured fellow authorities that if "there should be a war between Mexico and the United States, we Americans of Mexican blood would be found fighting for Uncle Sam."[63] Chapa negotiated his identity, and while he defended the state of Texas, the very institution that allowed the unjust and often unwarranted killing of ethnic Mexicans, he found himself working on behalf of a fellow *compatriota*. Ironically, Chapa, on multiple occasions, assisted Bernardo Reyes in counterrevolutions to oust progressives such as Francisco I. Madero.[64]

Other Tejanos including Miguel Quiroga, Miguel Lozano, and the Texas attorney R. F. Coon also worked with Chapa on addressing recent racist comments and discriminatory practices by prominent Texans including a well-known local pastor, Reverend Jones. Coon insisted that individuals such as Jones did not have an "honorable" place in society. Coon defended the Mexican-origin community by invoking their role as laborers, arguing that 95 percent of the fields in Texas were the result of Mexican labor.[65] Other Texas attorneys weighed in. Llano, Texas, lawyer Frederick Opp wrote to then governor of Texas Joseph D. Sayers protesting the indiscriminate violence toward Mexican-origin people during the hunt for Cortez. The *Dallas Morning News* reprinted the open letter.[66] "[The] respectable majority of Texas is looking to you [Gov. Sayers] for enforcement of the law against certain reckless bands that have recently scoured the southern portion of this state in search of Gregorio Cortez . . . [who in] said search ruthlessly slaughtered a number of innocent citizens of this State simply because they had the misfortune of being of the same blood as the alleged Mexican murderer."[67]

Just as the workers from Laredo and Nuevo Laredo had pointed to the difficulty and almost impossibility of a fair trial for any person of Mexican descent living in the United States, political elites, like Chapa, understood the delicate situation. After several trials in various Texas counties, Cortez finally, in the spring of 1904, found a bittersweet justice. The closing statements for Cortez's trial for the murder of Sheriff Morris were heard in Corpus Christi and took place on April 29, 1904. By this time, the trials had moved around the state numerous times so as to secure fairness in the process. San Antonio newspapers reported it was likely that Judge Stanley Welch, after evaluating the evidence, would call for an acquittal or a mistrial.[68] Finally, in the Corpus Christi trial, Judge Stanley Welch ruled in favor of Cortez. The excitement among the Mexican-origin community on both sides of the border was short-lived, however. Cortez awaited a third trial in Columbus, near San Antonio, for the murder of Glover and in 1904 was sentenced to fifty years in prison.[69] Notwithstanding the long sentence, the transnational political alliance worked in favor of Cortez, and in 1913, Governor Colquitt pardoned him.

Cortez as Counter-Revolucionario during the "Border Reign of Terror"

"El Asunto de Cortez," as the media put it, was "now history."[70] A pardon came in the summer of 1913, after Cortez served nine years in multiple jails and counties. Yet, the *asunto* or matter was not over. Cortez, in an ironic twist, instead of returning to Central or South Texas after serving time in prison, proceeded toward Nuevo Laredo, probably following the same route he took when he fled Karnes in 1901. Before heading to Nuevo Laredo, Cortez thanked supporters in Houston and Austin, as well as Governor Colquitt, and proceeded toward San Antonio. There, the "*colonia Mexicana*" congratulated him.[71] By July 1913, seven months had transpired since the assassination of Francisco Madero, when Cortez found himself fighting in Nuevo Laredo for the anti-Madero, pro-Díaz faction, now led by General Victoriano Huerta.[72] While hailed as a revolutionary hero in Mexican American historiography just as traditional Mexican historiography did for Francisco Villa, Cortez emerged as a counterrevolutionary fighting to bring back the old Porfirian regime.[73]

Cortez fought on behalf of Huerta during the period that historians have characterized as the "border reign of terror." Border residents witnessed one of the bloodiest decades in their lives during the 1915–19 period. As Alan Knight notes in chapter 11 in this volume, by 1915, the border witnessed pronounced violence with a series of cross-border raids. In the midst of state- and non-state-sanctioned violence conducted by Texas Rangers, local law enforcement, and vigilantes,[74] Cortez found himself in Nuevo Laredo. Once in Nuevo Laredo, Cortez joined the Huertista government forces soon after he produced papers proving he had recently been pardoned and was not some sort of Carranza spy. Matamoros was now in Carranza's hands as one of his generals, Lucio Blanco, captured Reynosa and Río Bravo. Carranza's circle, which now included former Cortez supporter Samuel Belden and other prominent regional elites from Nuevo León and Coahuila, ensured that border Huertista forces remain weak. When Huertista soldiers abandoned the Matamoros garrison and headed toward Brownsville, local border officials allowed these federal soldiers to head toward Nuevo Laredo to help defend the old border town. Yet local Brownsville officials allowed these recruits to cross through the Rio Grande valley so as to avoid running into Carrancistas from Reynosa and nearby towns. José M. Rodríguez, a Carranza ally from San Antonio, quickly assured Carranza that a letter of "protest" would soon reach Governor Colquitt's desk.[75] Despite this pro-federal/Huerta move, the Huertista stronghold along the border was short-lived.

Cortez fought on behalf of Huertistas in the battle to control Nuevo Laredo in May 15, 1914. Cortez commanded a group of Rurales—mounted men with the same reputation as the Rangers who chased him thirteen years prior. Carrancistas under General Jesús Carranza, however, easily took the city.[76] By mid-1914, local newspapers reported that approximately three hundred Huertista soldiers, given the lack of payment and the low morale, had crossed into Texas in search of agricultural work. Cortez's whereabouts between late May and the fall of that year are difficult to retrace. Many of the archival documents in Nuevo Laredo were burned during the military encounter in that town, according to historian Manuel Ceballos. There is no record in the state archives of Nuevo León to indicate Cortez fled to Monterrey, either. Local newspapers including the *Brownsville Herald* reported that several "ex-Huertistas" who now claimed allegiance to the Villista cause approached Reynosa in the fall of 1914 after the fall of Nuevo Laredo. U.S. colonel A. P. Blockson, who commanded a cavalry troop near Hidalgo, however, quickly arrested these supposed Villista converts and detained them in the Hidalgo County Jail.[77] What we do know is that after commanding the band of Rurales, Cortez found himself crossing through South Texas during the height of violence.[78] In either late 1915 or early 1916, Cortez crossed into Texas and eventually made his way farther north toward Manor, returning to his family's home.[79]

By the midyears of the Mexican Revolution, the border had witnessed great instability, the emergence of counterrevolutionary groups, and local uprisings such as the failed 1915 Plan de San Diego. It was also during this time that the number of ethnic Mexicans killed by vigilantes, Texas Rangers, and others reached great proportions.[80] As historian Benjamin Johnson has written, "The ongoing sights [of dead Mexicans lynching or shot in the back] were enough to convince any Tejano that there was no refuge in south Texas."[81] It seemed as if the "lynching belt" had moved farther south. It was in the midst of such violence, during what some media outlets of the period termed a "border reign of terror" or "orgy of bloodshed" during the 1915–19 period, that Cortez died.

On February 28, 1916, Cortez suffered an apparent heart attack, then in his forties, as he celebrated his third marriage, possibly to a fellow Mexicana, Esther Martínez from Big Springs, Texas.

As Cortez was laid to rest, the Revolution raged on. Carranza soon became the clear victor. His associate, Samuel Belden, who had played a critical role in Cortez's defense, by the end of 1916 found himself in New York and Washington compiling data on divorce laws of Texas and other states to share with Carranza as Mexico embarked on significant civil law reform.[82] Workers were on the verge of celebrating the beginning of labor reform as enacted in the 1917 Mexican constitution, and in Texas, a 1923 law mandated that the death penalty transfer to the state and out of the hands of county officials.[83] By the late 1920s, increased diplomatic pressure from Mexico helped to usher in a period of decline concerning lynching violence.[84]

The story of a "courageous" fellow *compatriota*, "with a pistol in his hand," captured in historical memory and *corridos*, resonated quite strongly with the Mexican community and may have given some kind of inspiration to those witnessing the rampant killing of ethnic Mexicans in South Texas between 1915 and 1919. Yet the man enshrined in song and memory as a *compatriota* had fought on behalf of the counterrevolution. There is or was no mention of him leading a band of federal *Rurales* in the songs. And no mention of the elaborate network of allies that had grown out of the near-lynching attempt of Cortez.[85] Cortez had not planned to challenge local sheriffs or the Texas Rangers. He knew that by allowing authorities to apprehend him, he would likely face death from a lynching. However, the developments thereafter paved the way for the forging of a political transnational alliance.

The Gregorio Cortez incident did not unfold in isolation. It was not simply an unfortunate event that transpired in Central Texas. It was connected to the decline of political and economic power of Tejanos; it involved the political and socioeconomic maneuverings of regional *norteño* elites and workers alike. While the scholarship has mostly credited Chapa for the release of Cortez, it was the concerted effort of Laredo, Nuevo Laredo, and Monterrey workers and Cruz, the Comisión Organizadora, Belden, and Chapa that laid the groundwork for releasing Cortez. While Cortez's pardon came at the expense of Mexican lives, the pardon resulted from an intimate, cross-border web of relations that emerged as the Cortez incident unfolded. Reexamining Cortez within the greater *noreste extenso*, transnationalizing his story, recasts the borderlands in new ways as it entered a new era of race relations that posed challenges and uncovers moments where unlikely alliances, even if temporary, offered some kind of hope to deal with moments of violence.

In 2015, the Texas Historical Commission approved and installed a marker in Karnes County recognizing Gregorio Cortez. Such marker, while symbolic, paves the way for a nuanced reckoning with past violence and a rewriting of history. Just as historical markers represent an effort by the state to acknowledge violence it sanctioned in past decades, attempts to connect stories across borders, both through binational archival research and from a transnational lens, help us situate episodes of violence that inscribed a particular meaning to life in the borderlands in the early twentieth century. It also uncovers possibilities of political collaboration as a way for transnational communities to respond to and address issues of violence. Lastly, it reveals how closely connected the histories of Tejanos, migrants, *obreros*, and regional elites on both sides of the border were and how together, all shaped the life of one *compatriota* and the region he traversed.

Notes

1. Correspondencia entre Obreros de Monterrey, Nuevo León y Sociedad Obreros de Laredo, Texas, October 12, 1901, Archivo Histórico del Estado de Nuevo León (hereafter, AGENL), Fondo: Trabajo, Asunto: Asociaciones, Organizaciones y Sindicatos, caja s.n. Depending on the source, Cortez sometimes appears with an *s*.

2. Cortez was born on June 22, 1875. To date, the best account of his life remains Américo Paredes, *With His Pistol in His Hand: a Border Ballad and Its Hero* (Austin: Texas University Press, 1958).

3. Donna Gabaccia, Franca Iacovetta, and Fraser Ottanelli, "Laboring across National Borders: Class, Gender, and Militancy in the Proletarian Mass Migrations," *International Labor and Working-Class History* 66, New Approaches to Global Labor History (Fall 2004): 55.

4. Neil Foley, *The White Scourge: Mexicans, Blacks, and Poor Whites in Texas Cotton Culture* (Berkeley: University of California, 1997); David Gutiérrez, "Migration, Emergent Ethnicity, and the 'Third Space': The Shifting Politics of Nationalism in Greater Mexico," *Journal of American History* 86, no. 2, Rethinking History and the Nation-State: Mexico and the United States as a Case Study: A Special Issue (September 1999): 481–517. For divergent views on the "whiteness debate," see, for example, Cynthia Orozco, *No Mexicans, Women, or Dogs Allowed: The Rise of the Mexican American Civil Rights Movement* (Austin: University of Texas Press, 2010); Carlos Blanton, "George I. Sánchez, Ideology, and Whiteness in the Making of the Mexican American Civil Rights Movement, 1930–1960," *Journal of Southern History* 72, no. 3 (August 2006): 569–604. Natalia Molina, *How Race Is Made in America: Immigration, Citizenship, and the Historical Power of Racial Scripts* (Berkeley: University of California Press, 2014).

5. "Sheriff Morris Killed," *Karnes County News* (Runge, Texas), 50th Anniversary Edition, 1937, SSM.

6. "Report"; I use the terms "white," "Anglo-American," and "Euro-American" to refer to individuals of non-Hispanic, non-Mexican origins and use them interchangeably.

7. Paredes, *With His Pistol in His Hand*, chap. 3, "The Man."

8. Crawling, the sheriff made his way a couple of yards outside of the home, but when fellow authorities found him, it was too late. Choate fled the scene to get help while Cortez

tended to his brother and soon would instruct his family to leave with the wounded Romaldo, as he knew he had to seek refuge. After some thirty-four hours had passed, he stopped in Belmont to rest and eat at a friend's house, about fifty-five miles from the town of Kenedy. He then headed toward his friend Martín Robledo's home nearby. There, shots were exchanged (what is curiously called the Battle of Belmont) in pitch darkness. Paredes, *With His Pistol in His Hand*, 67–71.

9. This is a brief summary of the incident which is now well known after the release of the film *The Ballad of Gregorio Cortez*, in great part based on Paredes's book *With His Pistol in His Hand*.

10. Paredes, *With His Pistol in His Hand*, 67–71; "The Battle of Belmont," *San Antonio Express*, June 16, 1901, 1; during one of Cortez's trials, the evidence presented indicated that one of Glover's own men had indeed fired, killing Glover.

11. "Had Running Fight: Detachment of Rangers Overtake Three Mexicans, Kill One, Capture Another," "Following a Trail North," "Scouring the Country," "Two Relatives Arrested," *Dallas Morning News*, June 19, 1901.

12. "Colorful Pioneer Valley Officer Dies Old Man's Death in His Bed," *Valley Sunday Star—Monitor Herald*, March 8, 1942.

13. "Colorful Pioneer Valley Officer Dies." Wilson County is just southeast of San Antonio and includes the towns of Floresville and Stockdale.

14. "Killed Mexicans: Posse Ran into Band of Armed Mexicans," *Fort Worth Morning Register*, June 18, 1901.

15. "Gregorio Cortez," *El Tiempo* (Las Cruces, New Mexico), July 13, 1901.

16. "Taken to Atascosa," *San Antonio Express*, June 28, 1901.

17. Paredes, *With His Pistol in His Hand*, 79. Paredes uses the spelling Merrem, while documents in the *Archivo Histórico del Estado de Tamaulipas* use Merren. In a 2003 publication on Captain John H. Rogers, historian Paul N. Spellman described Rogers as "one of the great Ranger captains of the next generation." *Captain John H. Rogers, Texas Ranger* (Denton: University of North Texas, 2003), 110.

18. "Seen Near Floresville," *Fort Worth Register*, June 18, 1901.

19. "Offered No Fight: The Man Supposed to be Sheriff Glover's Slayer Was Taken without Trouble," *Dallas Morning News*, June 24, 1901. Accompanying Rogers was K. H. Merren. A longtime-investor-turned-custom-agent, Merren held significant economic interests in Tamaulipas, as he owned the Hacienda La Victoria, acted as superintendent of the Mexico Realty Company, and held commercial agricultural interests in other parts of Mexico; Sonia Hernández, *Working Women into the Borderlands* (College Station: Texas A&M University Press, 2014), 90, 102; Richard Ribb, "La Rinchada: Revolution, Revenge, and the Rangers, 1910–1920," in *War along the Border: The Mexican Revolution and the Tejano Communities*, ed. Arnoldo De León (College Station: Texas A&M University Press, 2012), 62.

20. "Mexican Said to Have Confessed Her Murdered Morris," *Newark Daily Advocate* (Ohio), June 24, 1901, Special Collections, Sue & Radcliffe Killam Library, Laredo, Texas (hereafter, SC-SRKL); "Taken to San Antonio: The Prisoner Will Be Placed in Jail in That City," *Dallas Morning News*, June 24, 1901.

21. "Sheriff's Nerve Balked a Mob," *San Antonio Express* (published as the *Daily Express*), August 12, 1901.

22. "Sheriff's Nerve Balked a Mob."

23. "Sheriff's Nerve Balked a Mob."

24. The "lynching belt" reference comes from Paredes, *With His Pistol in His Hand*; "Sheriff's Nerve Balked a Mob."

25. William Carrigan and Clive Webb, *Forgotten Dead: Mob Violence against Mexicans in the United States, 1848–1928* (Oxford: Oxford University Press, 2013), 149; Richard Delgado, "The Law of the Noose: A History of Latino Lynching," *Harvard Civil Rights-Civil Liberties Law Review* 44 (2009): 302.

26. Carrigan and Webb, *Forgotten Dead*; see Appendix A entry "Nov. 11, 1922."

27. Benjamin H. Johnson, *Revolution in Texas: How a Forgotten Rebellion and Its Bloody Suppression Turned Mexicans into Americans* (New Haven, CT: Yale University Press, 2005). For an in-depth discussion of lynching of ethnic Mexicans in the greater Southwest, see William Carrigan and Clive Webb's essay in chapter 10 in this collection.

28. David Montejano, *Anglos and Mexicans in the Making of Texas* (Austin: University of Texas–Austin Press, 1987); Arnoldo De León, *The Tejano Community, 1836–1900* (Dallas: Southern Methodist University, 1997); Sonia Hernández, *Working Women into the Borderlands* (College Station: Texas A&M University, 2014); Elliott Young, *Catarino Garza's Revolution on the Texas-Mexico Border* (Durham, NC: Duke University Press, 2004); Elliott Young, "Imagining Alternative Modernities: Ignacio Martínez's Travel Narratives," in *Continental Crossroads: Remapping U.S.-Mexico Borderlands History*, ed. Samuel Truett and Elliott Young (Durham, NC: Duke University Press, 2004), 152.

29. Monica Muñoz Martínez, "Recuperating Histories of Violence in the Americas: Vernacular History Making on the US-Mexico Border," *American Quarterly* 66, no. 3 (September 2014): 662.

30. Muñoz Martínez, "Recuperating Histories"; Young, *Catarino Garza's Revolution*.

31. Martha Menchaca, *Constructing Race, Recovering History: The Indian, Black, and White Roots of Mexican Americans* (Austin: University of Texas Press, 2001); Arnoldo De León, *They Called Them Greasers: Anglo Attitudes toward Mexicans in Texas, 1821–1900* (Austin: University of Texas Press, 1983).

32. Arnoldo De León, *Mexican Americans in Texas: A Brief History*, 2nd ed. (Wheeling, IL: Harland Davidson, 1999), 49.

33. Raul Coronado, "Leaving Traces of Our Soul, of Who We Are: Tejana Writing in 1850s South Texas," keynote lecture delivered at NACCS-Tejas Foco Regional Conference, February 19, 2016, Lonestar College–Kingwood, Texas.

34. Juan Mora-Torres, *The Making of the Mexican Border: The State, Capitalism, and Society in Nuevo León, 1848–1910* (Austin: University of Texas–Austin Press, 2001); Miguel Angel González Quiroga, *Texas y el norte de México (1848–1880): Comercio, capitales y trabajadores en una economía de frontera* (México: Instituto Mora, 1999).

35. Carrigan and Webb, *Forgotten Dead*, 149.

36. Manuel Ceballos, "Tiempos y criterios de la conformación del Noreste Mexicano," in *El Noreste: Reflexiones*, coord. Isabel Ortega Ridaura (Monterrey: Fondo Editorial Nuevo León, 2006); Mario Cerutti, "Monterrey and Its *Ámbito Regional*, 1850–1910: Historical Context and Methodological Recommendations," in *Mexico's Regions: Comparative History and Development*, ed. Eric van Young (San Diego: Center for U. S.-Mexican Studies, UCSD, 1992), 145–65. Américo Paredes's concept of Greater Mexico could easily apply here as well; however, it is critical to incorporate research from Mexican archival repositories to better understand the greater political and socioeconomic context in which Tejanos

and Mexican-origin peoples found themselves, particularly as it involved political alliances; Américo Paredes, *Folklore and Culture on the Texas-Mexican Border* (Austin: University of Texas Press, 1993). Although there are questions of identity and identity formation as they relate to the concept of Greater Mexico, as David Gutiérrez points out, this essay will limit its focus on the political alliance that formed during the Cortez incident as a response to state-sanctioned violence. Gutiérrez, "Migration, Emergent Ethnicity," 485–86.

37. There is an extensive bibliography on the ballad of Gregorio Cortez in literary, cultural, and ethnomusicology and ethnography, and what follows is a selection of it. Américo Paredes, "El Corrido de José Mosqueda as an Example of Pattern in the Ballad," *Western Folklore* 17, no. 3 (July 1958): 154–62; Guillermo E. Hernández, "On the Paredes-Simmons Exchange and the Origins of the Corrido," *Western Folklore* 64, no. 1/2 (Winter–Spring, 2005), 65–82; Richard R. Flores, "The Corrido and the Emergence of Texas-Mexican Social Identity," *Journal of American Folklore* 105, no. 416 (Spring 1992): 166–82; José E. Limón, "Américo Paredes: Ballad Scholar (Phillips Barry Lecture, 2004)," *Journal of American Folklore* 120, no. 475 (Winter 2007): 3–18; María Herrera-Sobek, "Chicano Literary Folklore," in *Chicano Studies: A Multidisciplinary Approach*, ed. Eugene E. García, Francisco A. Lomelí, and Isidro D. Ortiz (New York: Teacher's College Press, Columbia, 1984), 151–70; Richard J. Mertz, "'No One Can Arrest Me': The Story of Gregorio Cortez," *Journal of South Texas* 1 (1974): 1–17; Aurelio González, "El Caballo y la Pistola: Motivos en el Corrido," *Revista de Literatura Populares* ño 1, núm. 1 (enero–junio, 2001): 94–114. Literature on Cortez before Paredes's publication focused mainly on labeling Cortez as a "bandit," justifying the near attempt of lynching and subsequent sentencing; see C. L. Patterson, *Sensational Texas Man-Hunt* (San Antonio, TX: Sid Murray & Sons Printers, 1939). While there have been more recent publications placing Cortez in a broader context of changing race relations in Texas, there are several works that maintain the idea of Cortez as bandit; see, for example, C. F. Eckhardt, *Tales of Bad Men, Bad Women, and Bad Places: Four Centuries of Texas Outlawry* (Lubbock: Texas Tech University Press, 1999). Closely related to this concept of *ambito regional* and the *noreste extenso* is Américo Paredes's Greater Mexico.

38. Hastings Donnan and Thomas M. Wilson, *Borders: Frontiers of Identity, Nation, and State* (Oxford: BERG, 2001), 4.

39. See, for example, Wesley Hall Looney, "The Texas Rangers in a Turbulent Era," master's thesis, Texas Tech University, 1971; more recent and more balanced treatments of the Rangers include Andrew R. Graybill, *Policing the Great Plains: Rangers, Mounties, and the North American Frontier, 1875–1910* (Lincoln: University of Nebraska Press, 2007); Benjamin H. Johnson, *Revolution in Texas*; and Richard Ribb, "La Rinchada."

40. Ana Luisa Martínez-Catsam, "Frontier Dissent: El Regidor, the Regime of Porfirio Díaz, and the Transborder Community," *Southwestern Historical Quarterly* 112, no. 4 (April 2009): 392; newspapers via the editors or editorial bodies were one way to obtain news and material goods from Mexico. See petition to obtain books on Ignacio Zaragoza for a Cinco de Mayo celebration planned by the Mexican-origin community in Oglesby, Texas, To Editor of Periódico Oficial (Nuevo León) from Comité Patriótico Mexicano, Oglesby, Texas, April 16,1900, AGENL, Fondo: Correspondencia producida por la administración pública estatal en su relación con la administración pública federal, Serie: Correspondencia Federal, Asunto: Correspondencia con el interior de Texas, caja 1, expediente

(1907–47); there are also numerous examples of ethnic Mexican resistance to state-sanctioned and non-state-sanctioned violence after the Cortez incident; see, for example, Miguel A. Levario, *Militarizing the Border: When Mexicans Became the Enemy* (College Station: Texas A&M University Press, 2012).

41. Martínez-Catsam, "Frontier Dissent."

42. "La emigración de obreros mexicanos es prejudicial a los mismos," Periódico Oficial reproduction of article from *La Voz de Nuevo León*, 30 de diciembre, 1904, tomo XXXIX num 105, Fondo: Ministerio de Gobernación, Asunto: Correspondencia, caja 21 (1902–6), expediente s.n., AGENL.

43. "Insaculación de Jurados para Juzgar a Cortéz," newspaper clipping from Karnes City, October 8, n.y., in Caso de Gregorio Cortez—Correspondencia entre Obreros de Monterrey, Nuevo León y Sociedad Obreros de Laredo, Texas, Fondo: Trabajo, Asunto: Asociaciones, Organizaciones y Sindicatos, AGENL.

44. To Governor Bernardo Reyes from "Sociedad de Obreros" Comisión Organizadora para Ayudar en su Defensa al Mexicano Gregorio Cortez, October 17, 1901, AGENL, Fondo: Trabajo Asunto: Asociaciones, Organizaciones y Sindicatos, caja. s.n.

45. "Insaculación de Jurados para Juzgar a Cortéz."

46. "Insaculación de Jurados para Juzgar a Cortéz"; the original quote is Cortez "defendió su vida dejando perfectamente sentada el concepto de la raza Mexicana."

47. To Governor Bernardo Reyes from "Sociedad de Obreros" Comisión Organizadora para Ayudar en su Defensa al Mexicano Gregorio Cortez, October 12, 1901, AGENL, Fondo: Trabajo Asunto: Asociaciones, Organizaciones y Sindicatos, caja. s.n.

48. To Governor Bernardo Reyes from "Sociedad de Obreros" Comisión Organizadora para Ayudar en su Defensa al Mexicano Gregorio Cortez, October 12, 1901, AGENL, Fondo: Trabajo Asunto: Asociaciones, Organizaciones y Sindicatos, caja. s.n.

49. John Mason Hart, *Empire and Revolution: The Americans in Mexico since the Civil War* (Berkeley: University of California Press, 2002), 23; Miguel Ángel González-Quiroga, "Conflict and Cooperation in the Making of Texas-Mexico Border Society, 1840–1880," in *Bridging National Borders in North America: Transnational and Comparative Histories*, ed. Benjamin H. Johnson and Andrew R. Graybill (Durham, NC: Duke University Press, 2010), 33–58; Alicia M. Dewey, *Pesos and Dollars Entrepreneurs in the Texas-Mexico Borderlands, 1880–1940* (College Station: Texas A&M University Press, 2014).

50. Licencia para Francisco Belden en representación de Thomas Braniff, Banco de Londres y México, AGENL, Fondo: Concesiones, caja 11, exp. 1, May 17, 1898.

51. R. E. Musquiz, El Paso, por Samuel Belden a Federico Gonzáles Garza, Chihuahua, Chih. June 16, 1914, CARSO, Fondo: Venustiano Carranza, Archivo del Primer Jefe del Ejército Constitucionalista 1889–1920, Carranza, no.CMXV.34.3346.1

52. George Burgess later joined counsel.

53. Gen. Pablo Gonzáles, Monterrey, from Samuel Belden, San Antonio, May 15, 1914, CARSO-LXVIII-1.15.2260.1; Hernandez, *Working Women*; Hart, *Empire and Revolution.*

54. "Counsel for Cortez," *Dallas Morning News*, July 10, 1901, SC-SRKL.

55. Federico (Roque) González Garza, Mexico City, from Alfonso Madero, Monterrey, April 9, 1912, CARSO, Carranza, CMXV.25.2457.1.

56. Samuel Belden, San Antonio, from Venustiano Carranza, Coahuila, May 17, 1914, CARSO-XXI.2.189.1.

57. "Mexico City Taken by Carranza Army," *Washington Post*, August 1, 1915, SC-SRKL; "Americans Are Jailed by Zapata," *Portsmouth Daily Times*, July 31, 1915, SC-SRKL. While later, in a 1939 publication, writer C. L. Patterson wrote that Colquitt had pardoned Cortez in exchange for "like treatment of a Texan by the Mexican Government," research does not substantiate such claim. Patterson, *Sensational Texas Man-Hunt* (San Antonio: Sid Murray & Sons Printers, 1939), 25.

58. Ribb, "La Rinchada," 59.

59. Ribb, "La Rinchada," 58.

60. Ribb, "La Rinchada," 65.

61. To Governor of Nuevo León from the Junta Patriótica Mexicana de las Sociedades Unidas, San Antonio, Texas (Unión Hidalgo, Gran Circulo de Obreros, Mutualista Mexicana, Club Mutualista Texas, & Club Atletico Unión), signed by Antonio P. Rivas, Francisco A. Chapa, Miguel González Dena, R. G. Scott, July 4, 1900, AGENL, Fondo: Correspondencia producida por la administración pública estatal en su relación con la administración pública federal, Serie: Correspondencia Federal, Asunto: Correspondencia con el interior de Texas, caja 1, expediente (1907–1947). There were other mutualistas in Brownsville that maintained communication with those from San Antonio and Monterrey; see Governor of Nuevo León from Sociedad Miguel Hidalgo y Costilla, Brownsville, July 1, 1900, AGENL, Fondo: Correspondencia producida por la administración pública estatal en su relación con la administración pública federal, Serie: Correspondencia Federal, Asunto: Correspondencia con el interior de Texas, caja 1, exp. (1907–1947).

62. "Derecho de Hablar," *La Crónica*, February 23, 1911, SC-SRKL.

63. "Many Mexicans Invade States, Says Starmont," *Des Moines News*, September 24, 1916, SC-SRKL.

64. Consul Jesse Johnson to Secretary of State, RDS, 812.00/2511, 2506, 2548; Consul Garrett to Secretary of State, December 19, 1911; RDS 812.00/2657, INS Records, reel 3, frame 0831, 0832, casefile 53108/71C. Soon, U.S. authorities caught up with Reyes and his border associates, including Webb County sheriff Amador Sanchez, and charged Reyes and his allies with violating the neutrality acts; see George Diaz, "Smugglers in Dangerous Times: Revolution and Communities in the Tejano Borderlands," in De León, *War along the Border*, 279–80.

65. "Se Expide Orden por el Gobernador de Texas para que no ayuden a los Revolucionarios de México," *La Crónica*, February 23, 1911, SC-SRKL; "Importante Carta," *La Crónica*, February 23, 1911, SC-SRKL.

66. "He Writes to Gov. Sayers: A Llano Lawyer Prefers Serious Charges for Investigation," *Dallas Morning News*, July 2, 1901, SC-SRKL).

67. "He Writes to Gov. Sayers: A Llano Lawyer Prefers Serious Charges for Investigation," *Dallas Morning News*, July 2, 1901.

68. "Cortez Trial Will Go to the Jury Tomorrow," *San Antonio Daily Light*, April 28, 1904, SC-SRKL.

69. "Gregorio Cortez Found Not Guilty," *San Antonio Express*, May 1, 1904.

70. "Picoteando," *La Prensa* (San Antonio), August 14, 1913, SC-SRKL.

71. "Picoteando," *La Prensa* (San Antonio), August 14, 1913, SC-SRKL.

72. "Libertad de Gregorio Cortez," *La Prensa*, San Antonio, July 24, 1913, SC-SRKL.

73. The bibliography on the Mexican Revolution of 1910 is quite lengthy. Of concern to issues along the border, see the two-volume work of Alan Knight, *The Mexican Revolution*

Vol. I&II (Lincoln: University of Nebraska Press, 1986); John Mason Hart, *Revolutionary Mexico: The Coming and Process of the Mexican Revolution* (Berkeley: University of California Press, 1987); Hart, *Empire and Revolution: The Americans in Mexico since the Civil War* (Berkeley: University of California Press, 2002); Frederick Katz, *The Secret War in Mexico: Europe, the United States and the Mexican Revolution* (Chicago: University of Chicago Press, 1983); De León, *War along the Border*; James Sandos, *Rebellion in the Borderlands* (Norman: Oklahoma University Press, 1988); and Johnson, *Revolution in Texas*.

74. The main primary source that documents the atrocities committed by the Texas Rangers and other members of law enforcement is the 1919 Canales Investigation. José Tomas "J. T." Canales called for an investigation of the Rangers that is more commonly known as the Canales Hearings. See Texas State Library and Archives Commission, Rangers and Outlaws, 1919 Ranger Investigation, https://www.tsl.texas.gov/treasures/law/index.html (last accessed on November 14, 2021). The transcript consists of three volumes; see research chapters based on evidence in the hearings among other sources in Sonia Hernández and John Morán González, eds., *Reverberations of Racial Violence: Critical Reflections on the History of the Border* (Austin: University of Texas Press, 2021).

75. To Venustiano Carranza (Piedras Negras) from José M. Rodríguez (San Antonio), June 9, 1913, CARSO-CMXV.33.3274.1-2.

76. INS Records, reel 5, frame 0088, casefile, 53108/71M; The records of the revolutionary battles in Nuevo Laredo were burned, and thus it has been difficult to secure archival material of the period from that municipal archive.

77. "Attack on Reynosa May Occur Early Wednesday," *Brownsville Herald*, November 30, 1914; "Band of Filibusters Cross River at Hidalgo," *Brownsville Herald*, December 1, 1914; and "Situation Quiet at Reynosa but Fight Expected," *Brownsville Herald*, December 2, 1914.

78. Paredes, *With His Pistol in His Hand*; famed writer Frank Dobie asserted in 1936 in *Riders of the Stars* that after Colquitt pardoned Cortez, he (Cortez) had become a "horse thief and was killed out near El Paso," yet there is no evidence indicating Cortez died in El Paso. *Port Arthur News*, 1936, SC-SRKL.

79. Paredes, *With His Pistol in His Hand*, 103.

80. Ribb, "La Rinchada," 75–79.

81. Johnson, *Revolution in Texas*, 118; see also Refusingtoforget.org, which Johnson and other scholars, including this author, have organized to mark the centennial of such border violence, much of it committed by the Texas Rangers.

82. "Belden to Mexico City," *San Antonio Light*, November 14, 1916, SC-SRKL.

83. Michael Ariens, *Lone Star Law: A Legal History of Texas* (Lubbock: Texas Tech University, 2011), 227–28. In 1919, Rep. José T. Canales called for a Texas Ranger investigation that led to the reorganization of the force; see Harold J. Weiss Jr., "The Texas Rangers Revisited: Old Themes and New Viewpoints," *Southwestern Historical Quarterly* 97, no. 4 (April 1994): 637. This would help to bring about a decrease in the number of extralegal lynching, in the opinion of historian Michael J. Pfeifer. See *Rough Justice: Lynching and American Society, 1874–1947* (Urbana: University of Illinois Press, 2004); see also various perspectives on lynching in the United States (mostly focused on African American lynching) in a special issue on lynching in the *Journal of American History*, December 2014.

84. See the essay by William Carrigan and Clive Webb in chapter 10 in this volume.

85. There was no mention either of Cortez's infidelity. I take up the issue of Leonor Díaz de Cortez, Gregorio Cortez's first wife, and the gendered dimensions of state violence in "Gendering Transnational State Violence: Intertwined Histories of Intrigue and Injustice along the U.S-Mexican Borderlands, 1900–1913" (article under review).

Figure 10.1 Portrait of Matías Romero upon presentation to the United States of America, 1863. Romero served as a diplomat for four decades, regularly protesting mob violence against Mexican nationals in the United States, finally achieving some limited success in the 1890s.

Chapter 10

Cycles of Lynching

The U.S.-Mexico Border and Mob Violence against Persons of Mexican Descent in the United States, 1848–1928

WILLIAM D. CARRIGAN AND CLIVE WEBB

On August 23, 1884, a gang of fifty or sixty masked men galloped on horseback after a Nebraska sheriff and his prisoner, identified as Luciano Padilla. The sheriff sought the Lincoln jail where he hoped his charge, a suspect in a sexual assault case, would be safe. The vigilantes, however, overtook him on the road. Five of the mob forcibly restrained the pleading sheriff as other men secured Padilla, a thirty-year-old Mexican national, who had been working at a laundry after his release following a previous criminal conviction from Nebraska's State Prison.

Padilla was a long way from Mexico, and we would know very little about him if he had not been killed. We do know that for some time before his initial arrest, he had lived in New Mexico. It was there that he was convicted, sentenced to the penitentiary, and sent to Nebraska's State Prison through a transfer program. When he was released, he found a local job in Lincoln. What Padilla's life and death demonstrate is the growing impact of Mexican immigration on parts of the United States far from the actual border. Well before the arrival of large numbers of Mexicans, individuals such as Padilla had already prompted those living far from the border to begin to formulate ideas and opinions about immigrants from Mexico. Padilla did not make a good impression.

The mob took Padilla to a creek several miles west of Lincoln, the spot where he allegedly had raped and stabbed a thirteen-year-old girl named Anna Grange. After giving Padilla time to pray, a dozen or so men that included a local postmaster, farmers, and shop owners hoisted the alleged rapist up with a rope provided by a local butcher, later described in an investigator's report as the "executioner-in-chief." Anna Grange's father reportedly placed the rope around Padilla's neck. Over the continued protests of a local judge and the sheriff, Padilla was then hanged. The mob dispersed. Reports indicate that the local population was in "sympathy" with the mob and believed that Padilla was a "ruffian" who deserved his fate. Despite identification by the sheriff, no charges were ever brought against any of the mob's leaders for Padilla's murder.[1]

The lynching of Luciano Padilla was only one of many similar cases in the United States in the nineteenth and early twentieth centuries. Scholarly estimates place the number of lynched Mexican nationals and American citizens of Mexican descent in the thousands, but historical records providing specific information about most of these cases no longer exist. Detailed and reliable information has only been documented in 547 cases. One of those of those cases is that of Luciano Padilla. Unlike most instances of anti-Mexican mob violence, however, Padilla's case did not end with decision of local officials that Padilla had died at the hands of parties unknown. Instead, his case drew the attention of Mexican diplomats in Washington and Mexico City. We will have more to say about that development later in the essay, but before then we will attempt to place Padilla's case in a broader context by analyzing all those cases in the inventory we have compiled of Mexican victims of mob violence.

From these data, it is clear that mob violence waxed and waned over the eight-decade period that began in 1848 with the conclusion of the U.S.-Mexican War and concluded in 1928 with the last known public lynching of a Mexican in Farmington, New Mexico. Several factors help to explain the many fluctuations in lynching patterns during this period, but we argue that the most important factor in explaining the cycles of anti-Mexican mob violence in the United States is the rise and fall of ethnic tension along the U.S.-Mexico border (even when that violence took place in areas far from the geographical borderline such as Nebraska). Such tensions, grounded in deep racial antipathy toward Mexicans, most often arose out of economic competition, but they also grew or declined based on the reactions of local, state, and federal officials to mob violence against Mexicans.

The Three Eras of Heightened Mob Violence against Persons of Mexican Descent

Mob violence against persons of Mexican descent in the United States did not follow the national timeline that typically describes the rise of lynching beginning in the 1830s, an escalation in mob violence after the Civil War, a peak in lynching at the turn of the twentieth century, and a slow decline that began after World War I and continued until the 1960s. By contrast, the chronology of anti-Mexican mob violence peaked at three different times (see Table 10.1), with each post-peak pattern being very different from the others. Not surprisingly, each surge in mob violence against Mexicans resident in the United States correlates roughly with increased movement back and forth over the border between the United States and Mexico.

Before proceeding to the specific eras of increased violence, there are important elements to understand related to the role that the Texas-Mexico

Table 10.1 Confirmed lynching of persons
of Mexican descent by period

Years	Number of lynchings	Lynchings per year
1849–51	12	4.0
1852–58	127	18.1
1859–72	63	4.5
1873–77	126	25.2
1878–83	60	10.0
1884–95	38	3.1
1896–1914	13	0.7
1915–19	103	20.6
1919–28	5	0.5

The authors have grouped the data after analysis of their year-by-year
inventory that they have compiled and published in William Carrigan
and Clive Webb, *Forgotten Dead: Mob Violence against Mexicans in the
United States, 1848–1928* (New York: Oxford University Press, 2013).
The data in this article reflect the most reliable of the data collected,
those that appear in Inventory A. The authors have compiled
information on over three hundred additional cases that are probably
lynchings of Mexicans between 1848 and 1928, but the information on
those cases is not included in the data analyzed in this essay. However,
the peak periods described in this essay are also found in these additional
cases. The totals for the three key periods are 1852–1858 (140 cases);
1873–1877 (31 cases); 1915–1919 (32 cases). The relatively greater number
of probable cases from the 1850s is likely attributable to the quality of the
surviving primary sources in this earlier era, which made it harder for
the authors to verify many of these early episodes.

border played in fostering mob violence and vigilantism. While there is something to be said for the argument that all borders are contested places that
allow opportunities for an escalation of conflict, the Texas-Mexico border
proved to be especially conducive to violence for several reasons. These factors
existed to one degree or another at other places along the U.S.-Mexico border but seemed to have been most powerful in the Lower Rio Grande Valley.

First among the specific factors at work was the perception of local populations of the value of crossing the border in order to escape legal punishment.
During key periods of the late nineteenth and early twentieth centuries, the
United States and Mexico either did not have an extradition treaty at all or had
one that was judged ineffective by those living along the border. This meant
that border residents, many of whom were concentrated in the nineteenth
century in the Lower Rio Grande Valley, believed that those who committed
crimes in one nation could reasonably hope to escape prosecution by escape
across the border. Both U.S. citizens and Mexican citizens took advantage of

this situation in the nineteenth and early twentieth centuries, which was made even more attractive by the sparsely settled nature of the territory on both sides of the border. Traditions of vigilantism, not surprisingly, can be found all over the world in places where criminals easily escape legal punishment.[2]

Second, and relatedly, the border heightened the traditional vigilante concern for delays in the punishment of prisoners. Vigilantes near the border were often particularly uncomfortable with even short delays in carrying out punishments of criminals because they worried about their captives escaping due to the poor quality of western jails and the proximity of the border. The result was a tendency of mobs to lynch Mexicans at the first opportunity.[3]

Third, the language barrier between the Spanish-speaking border population and investigating English-speaking authorities heightened appeals to summary justice near the border. For example, the inability to speak Spanish hampered the investigations of many Texas Rangers and made it more difficult for them to distinguish between law-abiding and law-breaking citizens. Such a problem might have been overcome by working closely with Spanish-speaking local sheriffs, but the Texas Rangers disliked working with Mexican sheriffs. Tragically, some preferred summary execution to overcoming this challenge.[4]

Fourth, increased immigration from Mexico contributed indirectly to rising tensions and violence in the Southwest. While the correlation between new arrivals from Mexico and increased mob violence is not perfect, it certainly must be counted as an important contextual factor. By comparing Table 10.2 (see below) with Table 10.1, one can see that decades of relatively rapid increase, such as the 1860s and the 1900s, were followed by periods of increased mob violence in the 1870s and the 1910s. Moreover, there is little doubt that the violence of the 1850s was greatly impacted by thousands of Mexican immigrants arriving in California, despite the fact that those arrivals were not captured in U.S. Census data. Just as revealingly, the relatively slow increase of the Mexican-born population in the late nineteenth century coincides with a low incidence of episodes of mob violence in the years before and after the turn of the century. There are exceptions, however, as the great influx of Mexican immigrants in the 1910s was followed by a decrease in the number of lynchings in the 1920s. Furthermore, there is no evidence that lynching tended to be located in areas most impacted by the influx of Mexican immigrants. Indeed, many of the places receiving the greatest number of new arrivals, such as San Antonio, hosted relatively few episodes of lynching. The impact of immigration was thus to raise tensions generally and not as a specific cause of particular episodes of mob violence.

All of these general fears of the border and their influence on vigilantism were heightened during periods when many Mexicans crossed back and forth across the border. While these factors apply to one degree to the entire U.S.-Mexico border, it is also clear that they were amplified along the Texas-Mexico

Table 10.2 Increase of Mexican-born population in the United States, 1850–1930

Year	No. of Mexican-born in United States	Percentage increase
1850	13,317	—
1860	27,466	106.2
1870	42,736	55.6
1880	69,399	62.4
1890	77,853	12.2
1900	103,393	32.8
1910	221,915	114.6
1920	486,418	119.2
1930	641,462	31.9

Campbell J. Gibson and Emily Lennon, "Historical Census Statistics on the Foreign-born Population of the United States: 1850–1990," Table 4, Washington, D.C.: U.S. Bureau of the Census, www.census.gov, Internet Release date: March 9, 1999.

border and even more dramatically in the Lower Rio Grande Valley. However, even in this region of most intense border tension, analysis of the historical context during the periods of peak lynching will show why violence along the border was not constant but flared at different times. This context is thus vital to connecting the border to the underlying factors promoting mob violence against Mexican nationals and U.S. citizens of Mexican descent.[5]

_____

The first explosion of anti-Mexican mob violence took place in the early and mid-1850s. There were two centers of this mob violence, California and Texas (see Table 10.3). Economic competition between Anglos and persons of Mexican descent played a key role in both places, but economic factors quickly became connected to political tensions relating to the meaning of the U.S.-Mexican War and the ability of Mexicans to cross the newly formed border.

Any discussion of the lynching of Mexicans in California must begin with the Gold Rush that followed President James Polk's late 1848 confirmation of the discovery of gold at Sutter's Mill earlier in the year. Hope for quick wealth quickly brought tens of thousands of immigrants from all over the world. To the frustration of Anglos eager for quick riches, some twenty-five thousand Mexicans migrated to the mining regions of California between 1848 and 1852.

To put this number in context, it is worth considering the population of California before American annexation. In 1845, the Mexican province of Alta California had been sparsely settled with an approximate population of only eight thousand Californios. At the same time, there were fewer than two thousand Anglos, mostly American immigrants. Both Californios and Anglos tended to be engaged in ranching and related agricultural activities that produced modest

Table 10.3 Confirmed lynching of persons
of Mexican descent by state, 1852–1858

State	Individuals lynched
California	88
Texas	28
New Mexico	11
Total	127

returns. The Indigenous population, historically hunters and gatherers, had been decreasing rapidly and numbered probably in the low thousands, a fraction of the estimated three hundred thousand that existed at the time of European contact. Thus, the arrival of thousands and thousands of gold miners, perhaps as many as three hundred thousand in total between 1848 and the mid-1850s, was both a demographic and economic revolution in California.

Many prospective Anglo goldseekers resented having to compete with Mexican immigrants. They typically believed that the recently concluded U.S.-Mexican War had stripped any rights that Mexicans had to the Southwest and that California and the Southwest were now for their use. Yet Mexicans arrived in the mines earlier than many Anglo prospectors and brought with them superior expertise and skills from the mines of northern Mexico. Most Anglos in the mines desired that the Mexicans return from whence they came, and some employed violence to encourage such an outcome. Not surprisingly, the violence escalated after 1851 as the Mexican population peaked, the mining became more difficult, and success in the goldfields became more elusive.

Violence and tension were evident before mob violence surged in 1852. In 1850, the California legislature had passed the "Foreign Miner's Tax" that was patently designed to limit access of Mexican and Chinese goldseekers to the mines. Thomas J. Green, chairman of the Finance Committee, in his recommendation of the act's passage warned that thousands of "the worst population of the Mexican and South American States" were either already arriving or planning to immigrate to California soon. These "convicts of Mexico" intended to "seek and possess themselves of the best places for gold digging" and "carry from our country immense treasure." The Mexicans, he concluded, were the practitioners of "vice and crime" and were "irredeemably lost to all social equality" with Anglos.[6]

With such rhetoric emanating from California's political leadership, one can hardly be surprised that deadly violence often emerged in the goldfields when Anglos confronted Mexican miners. In June 1852, mobs hanged first one and then a second Mexican near Jackson for the murder of a French miner. The *Sacramento Daily Union* noted that the first Mexican was hanged "amid demoniacal rejoicings, and a spice more of severity, than is usually administered by the barbaric code of Judge Lynch." According to the *Nevada Journal*, an Anglo man defended the second prisoner. He made a "clear and able" defense in a "forcible and eloquent" manner that "showed that there was not a particle of evidence—circumstantial or positive—to fix the crime upon the prisoner." Despite the man's efforts and "the moving pleadings of his anguished mother and sister," the Mexican was hanged and thus "ended the life of this unfortunate youth, who although he may have been guilty, certainly deserved the impartial trial which all have a right to expect in our land."[7]

Mobs connected the lynching of Mexicans to specific crimes, but there is no doubt that such violence was one element employed to force Mexicans from the goldfields. Violence was usually most fierce in the wake of a robbery or a murder that Americans blamed upon foreign miners. After an attack by Mexican outlaws at Phoenix Mill in 1853, for example, the "enraged people" tracked down and "disposed" of one band member. The violence, as was so often the case in such episodes, did not end there. A mob of three hundred organized to "burn the habitations of the Mexicans indiscriminately," take away their arms, and "give them all notice to quit."[8] Crimes committed by Mexicans were some of the justifications given for the expulsions of Mexicans along the Tuolumne River in the summer of 1850 and on the upper part of the Calaveras River in 1852.[9]

These episodes conformed to more general patterns in Gold Rush California. Anglo miners resented the presence of Mexican miners and took advantage of crimes allegedly committed by Mexicans to employ mob violence to intimidate and frighten all Mexicans into leaving the mines and returning to Mexico. Violence was greatest between 1852 and 1858 because those years were filled with much greater competition between gold miners and, consequently, much greater resentment against Mexicans. Moreover, Mexican resistance in the form of both violent self-defense and less defensible murderous reprisals had exacerbated tensions and accelerated the cycle of violence in the mid-1850s. The violence began to ebb only when thousands of Mexicans, in response to the combination of mining decline, legal discrimination, and mob intimidation, decided to leave California in the late 1850s.

California hosted more mobs than any other state or region during the 1850s, but Texas also experienced significant anti-Mexican mob violence during the same period. Like Alta California, Texas was a relatively sparsely settled part of Mexico in the early nineteenth century. Unlike California, however, U.S. immigrants began arriving in Texas in large numbers well before 1849. By the time of the War for Texas Independence in 1836, U.S.-born residents of Texas outnumbered Mexican-born residents approximately thirty thousand to eight thousand. In addition, the Anglos in Texas owned about five thousand slaves, another great difference from California. Indeed, the lure of cotton (and not gold) was the major driver in Anglo immigration.

Anglo perception of Mexicans was filtered through memories of having fought two wars with Mexico over the future of the region, but mob violence against Mexicans in Texas cannot be understood merely as an outgrowth of this history. To understand the cycles of mob violence against Tejanos, close attention to the role of the boundary line between Texas and Mexico is critical.

"The proximity of Texas to the Mexican border," noted a Texas historian, "made the escape of slaves a rather frequent occurrence."[10] In 1854, the U.S. minister to Mexico, James Gadsden, complained that the Mexican government was issuing "Cartas de Seguridad" with passports that allowed fugitive slaves to escape easily into the interior of Mexico. Gadsden "strongly admonished" Mexico that such actions encouraged slave flight and warned of "the increasing evil of Slaves thus encouraged to abscond from Texas."[11] Such protests had little practical impact and, as a result, Mexico became a haven for runaway slaves. One San Antonio newspaper reported that the land across the Rio Grande "has long been regarded by the Texas slave as his El Dorado for accumulation, his utopia for political rights, and his Paradise for happiness."[12] The Mexican government responded that Americans illegally crossed the border before the Civil War to recapture fugitive slaves.[13]

The failure of diplomatic efforts led some Texans to pursue extralegal methods. "Something should be done," one newspaper proclaimed in 1855, "to put a stop to the escape of negroes into Mexico. If the General Government cannot protect us, we should protect ourselves."[14] In Austin, Gonzáles, and other places, public meetings urged that all planters refuse to employ Mexican laborers because "a portion of the Mexican population in Western Texas aided" the escape of slaves.[15] When such actions were not satisfactory, some Texans pursued mob violence against Mexicans.

In 1856 and 1857, due to the alleged connection between Mexicans and slave resistance, three Texas counties—Colorado, Matagorda, and Bastrop—took the action of expelling all Mexicans.[16] The most well-known of these episodes is the one in Colorado County. On September 9, 1856, John H. Robson, H. A. Tatum, and J. H. Hicks of Colorado County sent a letter to a variety of newspapers in Texas with the heading "Contemplated Servile Rising in Texas." The writers discussed uncovering "a well-organized and systematized plan for the murder of our white population, with the exception of the young ladies, who were to be taken captives, and made the wives of the diabolical murderers of their parents and friends." The rebellion was set to begin late at night on September 6. The slaves, in groups ranging from two to ten, were to go to nearly every house in the county, kill the white men, plunder their homes, take "their horses and arms," and fight their way to a "free state," thought to be Mexico by the Vigilance Committee. The Vigilance Committee believed that two hundred slaves were involved in the conspiracy, and they punished all of these rebels with whippings so severe that two died from the lash. Three of the insurrection's leaders were hanged. According to the Vigilance Committee, the entire Mexican population of Colorado County "was implicated," and "they were arrested, and ordered to leave the county within five days, and never again to return, under the penalty of death."[17] The Colorado County plot was not the only one uncovered in 1856. Over the last three months of the year, authorities claimed to have discovered plans for three additional slave revolts in Texas. In October, in Lavaca County, a white man was given one hundred lashes after confessing to his role in a plot set for October 31 in which local slaves would rebel, kill their masters if necessary, and flee to Mexico.

One of the challenges of analyzing lynching is determining what motivated the mobs to do their work at particular times. While mobs almost always cited specific crimes as their justification, similar crimes at other times did not motivate lynching. Unstated motivations, such as jealousy over Mexican success in the goldfields or suspicion of Mexican aid to fugitive slaves, certainly played a key contributing role and help explain in part the cycles of mob violence in the American West.

———————

The second great period of anti-Mexican mob violence took place in the 1870s during a period of increased tension between Mexico and the United States over their shared border. Although the lynching of Mexicans in California continued, it was at a much lower rate due to the end of the Gold Rush period. Extralegal violence against Mexicans was greatest in Texas, but there was significant mob action in Arizona and New Mexico as well (see Table 10.4). As before, economic factors played a key role in animating lynchers, but there was an important political dimension to this era's violence, stemming from the end of the Civil War and the use of the border by both Mexican and Anglo outlaws.

Following the conclusion of the American Civil War in 1865, there was great financial incentive for livestock owners to transport their cattle to the North, whose economy not only had survived the Civil War but also was beginning a period of great economic growth and industrialization. The demand for beef dovetailed with several other factors, including the extension of railroad lines to the West, the invention of refrigerated rail cars, and the defeat of the Plains Indians. The result was a boom in Texas cattle prices and the establishment of regular cattle drives between Texas and railroad towns like Abilene, Kansas. The great increase in cattle prices spurred both legal and criminal activities all the way to the border with Mexico and beyond. The increased

Table 10.4 Confirmed list of persons of
Mexican descent lynched by state, 1873–1877

State	Individuals lynched
Texas	50
New Mexico	30
Arizona	21
California	13
Colorado	12
Total	126

criminality that came with the cattle boom, in particular, had great repercussions for the history of anti-Mexican mob violence.

In 1872, the *Goliad Guard* noted that "a company of Minute Men has been organized at Atascosa County to redress depredations made upon Texans by Mexican cattle thieves." The newspaper's editor heartily approved of this news, opining for the vigilantes to "Give em h—l, boys."[18] Two years later, the rhetoric had only grown more extreme. The *Brownsville Ranchero* recommended that citizens "turn out en masse" and hang "every man who cannot give a good account of himself, and raze to the ground every ranch known to harbor these villains who make cattle and horse stealing a business."[19]

Both Anglo and Mexican criminals utilized the U.S.-Mexico border to aid their escape from the respective authorities pursuing them. Mexicans raided American cattle and escaped southward, while Anglo cowboys raided Mexican cattle and fled northward. The result was greatly increased tension between Mexico and the United States in the 1870s, which was dangerous for those individuals of Mexican descent living in the United States. In 1876, the *Corpus Christi Gazette* urged that the United States should no "longer bear the repeated insults offered by the Mexican people" and claimed that "Mexico has insulted the United States by its refusal to cooperate in the suppression of the disorders existing along the line dividing Texas from her republic." The *Gazette* explained that Mexico has afforded "protection to outlaws, thieves and robbers, with property plundered from American citizens" and refused "to deliver them to justice."[20]

Political leaders in Texas echoed the rhetoric of newspapers such as the *Gazette*, and the combination was disastrous for many Mexicans living in South Texas. According to the *San Antonio Express*, Governor Richard Coke dispatched the Texas Rangers to the frontier "to kill Mexicans." Anglos living along the border, the newspaper continued "caught the inspiration emenating [*sic*] from the capital" and Mexicans in the region were "no longer safe upon the highways or outside of the towns," as "they will be shot down as if they were savages."[21]

While the impact of political conflict probably was not as great a factor as anger over cattle and horse theft, there is no doubt that political issues played a role in the high level of mob violence in the early 1870s. The period of Reconstruction after the Civil War was a violent era that witnessed the killing and intimidation of many former slaves. However, the Anglo majority also viewed Mexicans as politically dangerous. According to the *San Antonio Express*, "a majority of the Mexicans belonged to the Republican party" after the Civil War, which made them a target of public violence in the 1870s. The *Express* claimed that a rival paper, the *San Antonio Herald*, believed that Mexicans who served in the federal army were "Greasers" who murdered unarmed men in cold blood. The *Herald* urged their readers to show Mexicans "a revolver" and make them "run like a quarter-horse" for the border.[22]

Political and economic issues were also behind the most famous episodes of Anglo-Mexican violence in the 1870s, the San Elizario and El Paso Salt War. The conflict exploded after the arrival of Charles Howard, who sought to "redeem" West Texas from Republican rule and eventually clashed with local Mexican leader Louis Cardis over the region's salt flats. Howard attempted to claim ownership of the flats, while Cardis and the Mexican community demanded that the flats remain open to the community as had been the tradition. Violence soon erupted, with the Mexican population forming secret committees and acting in the vigilante tradition. Eventually, both Howard and Cardis were killed, along with probably twenty additional individuals. The Mexican vigilantes who killed Howard and three other Anglos fled to Mexico to escape retribution. The long-term result was not good for the Mexican population, which lost out both politically and economically. The county seat was moved from San Elizario to El Paso, which was also chosen as the destination for the railroad when it reached the region in 1883.

Texas was not the only place where violence between Anglos and Mexicans was high in the 1870s. Arizona and New Mexico also witnessed frequent bursts of vigilantism during this period, fueled in part by anger over border crossings. The federal government administered Arizona as part of the Territory of New Mexico until 1863, when it created two separate territories. Both territories remained sparsely settled throughout the nineteenth century, unlike Texas and California. In 1864, for example, Arizona probably only numbered about five thousand non–Native American residents. Ranching and agriculture were important in both territories, but a small mining economy emerged in Arizona, aided in part by the passing through of miners headed first to and then from California. Borders played an important role in the history of both territories. The Mexican border was obviously important, but so too was the eastern "border" with Texas. The arrival of Anglos from Texas in southern New

Mexico and southern Arizona introduced a group of Anglos with bitter racial prejudice against Mexicans.

It was the combination of Mexican use of the southern border with the influx of Texans from the east that generated some of the most devastating mob violence in Arizona and New Mexico in the 1870s. In 1872, a sheriff in Arizona approvingly reported to the territorial governor that the "hanging of that Mexican" put a "damper" on the Mexican outlaws who used the border to help aid their efforts to "rob and plunder."[23]

In New Mexico, a violent race war known as the Horrell War erupted when a group of Texans moved into the southeastern portion of the state. The Horrells were ranchers who had recently settled in New Mexico after fleeing Texas, where they had killed four officers of the pro-Republican State Police. They wasted little time in getting into trouble in New Mexico. Driven by the desire to avenge the murder of one of their family members, the Horrells took arbitrary action against all those of Mexican descent in the region. On December 20, 1873, the Horrells murdered four Mexicans at a dance in Lincoln; later that month, they lynched five Mexican freighters fifteen miles west of Roswell. The Horrells also intercepted and killed Severanio Apodaca while he was transporting a load of grain to a local mill. In all of these cases, the ethnic identity of the victim appears to have been the only reason why that person was killed.[24]

———

There was a slow decline of mob violence against Mexicans that began in the late 1870s and continued into the early twentieth century. While the lynching of African Americans in the South was rising, the lynching of Mexicans seemed to be on the road to extinction. The Mexican Revolution, however, unleashed a level of tension, fear, and anger along the U.S.-Mexico border in Texas that had not been seen since the U.S.-Mexican War of 1846–48. The result was the third and final era of extensive lynching of Mexicans.

The specific episode that sparked the rise of so much vigilantism was a series of raids led by Aniceto Pizaña and Luis de la Rosa that targeted the economic infrastructure and transport and communications networks of the Lower Rio Grande Valley and were part of a revolutionary plan to create a separate sovereign state in the American Southwest for persons of color. As Benjamin Johnson has demonstrated, the frustrations of the Mexican raiders stemmed from a combination of economic factors that had undermined the position of Mexicans vis-à-vis Anglos since the introduction of the railroad into the Lower Rio Grande Valley in 1904. The railroad, combined with the introduction of irrigation, made the lands of the region much more valuable but was a disaster for the region's Tejanos who saw their lands slip out of their hands when they were unable to pay the higher taxes or fell victim to other Anglo tactics designed to force land sales.[25]

Table 10.5 Confirmed lynching of persons of
Mexican descent by state, 1915–1919

State	Individuals lynched
Texas	98
All others	5

The raids unleashed a bloody torrent of retaliatory action. In a climate of intense paranoia, Anglos committed countless atrocities on Mexicans whom they mistakenly and sometimes willfully suspected of collusion with the insurrectionists. In September of 1915, three suspected Mexican raiders lodged in the San Benito jail were taken out in the middle of the night and lynched.[26] In October, vigilantes hanged four Mexicans for their role in the derailment of a train.[27]

Similar specific information, however, is lacking for most Mexicans killed during this period. According to the September 15, 1915 issue of the *San Antonio Express*, "the finding of dead bodies of Mexicans . . . has reached the point where it creates little or no interest." Virgil Lott, a newspaperman from South Texas, summed up the violence of the era years later: "How many lives were lost can not be estimated fairly for hundreds of Mexicans were killed who had no part in any of the uprisings, their bodies concealed in the thick underbrush and no report ever made by the perpetrators of these crimes."[28] Mexicans in South Texas refer to the years from 1915 to 1919 as the "Hora de Sangre" (Hour of Blood) because so many Mexicans died at the hands of vigilantes and Texas Rangers. Estimates of the number of Mexicans indiscriminately massacred by Anglos are in the thousands.

Cycles and Patterns in the History of Anti-Mexican Mob Violence

Analysis of the chronology of mob violence against Mexicans suggests a repeating cycle and pattern. Each of the three eras of peak violence was triggered by historical events, often related to economic competition that led to retributive violence that sparked one of the peak periods of mob violence. The three peak periods then developed a self-catalyzing character in which unpunished mob violence begat even more mob violence at an accelerating rate. The result was that each era culminated in the same manner: (1) one or more episodes of massive, mostly indiscriminate mob violence killed unknown numbers of Mexicans; (2) such tragedies led to diplomatic protest and negative media coverage; (3) this outside pressure, combined with self-reflection in some cases, convinced many in the Anglo majority that vigilantism had become too prevalent; and (4) the lynching of Mexicans declined with the collapse of public unity for the lynching of Mexicans.

———

As the Gold Rush reached the mid-1850s, violence between Anglos and Mexicans increased, fueled by disillusioned miners and episodes of retaliatory violence between the two groups. When local leaders did little, or even praised, vigilantes for their actions, mobs became increasingly bold. Two episodes illustrate this pattern. The first took place in August of 1855, when a mob of fifteen hundred gathered in response to a murderous raid on the town of Rancheria.[29] Thirty-six Mexicans were rounded up and held in a makeshift prison one mile from town. The vigilantes concluded that three of the Mexicans were guilty and should be hanged. The mob refused to be satisfied with the hanging of these three men. They ordered all Mexicans to leave before seven o'clock that night and then burned every Mexican house in the town, plus the dance hall. Some of the exiled Mexicans were murdered as they fled.[30] Other nearby towns decided to expel Mexicans as well. At half a dozen camps in the region, Mexicans were chased from the area and Mexican dwellings were burned and destroyed.[31] According to one newspaper, it was a "war of extermination" against Mexicans.[32] The second episode from California took place in 1857 after the murder of Los Angeles County sheriff James Barton. Retributive violence against Mexicans in southern California was fierce and indiscriminate. Posses swept through the area, hanging some Mexicans, beheading others. One of the vigilantes claimed to have hanged seventeen Mexicans in seventeen days.[33]

In Texas as well, the growing suspicion of and anger with Mexicans in the 1850s culminated in a bloody wave of vigilantism. During the summer of 1857, Anglo vigilantes, who consisted at least in part of working-class men who transported goods in the Texas interior, savagely attacked their Mexican competitors. These vigilantes not only destroyed property and disrupted business but also hanged or shot an unknown number of their rivals. Many of the killings took place in out-of-the-way places and the bodies of the Mexicans were never found. Goliad, however, was a center of violence because it lay en route from the Gulf Coast port of Indianola to San Antonio. John Linn, an Irish immigrant who had lived in Texas since 1829, later acknowledged in a memoir that the Anglo vigilantes were based in Goliad and that they "assassinated" a number of "innocent" Mexicans on the roads, sabotaged their carts, and then sold the goods they stole from their victims. Linn recalled that the "authorities of Goliad County seemed to regard the whole thing with supine indifference" and "made no efforts whatever either to suppress the crimes or to bring the criminals to justice."[34]

When the Mexican government learned of these hangings and murders, it opened an investigation and then filed several complaints with both Texas and the United States. On October 14, 1857, Mexican official Manuel Robles reported to Secretary of State Lewis Cass, "Committees of armed men have been organized for the exclusive purpose of hunting down Mexicans on the highway, spoiling them of their property, and putting them to death." Robles estimated the number of Mexicans killed at seventy-five. Furthermore, Robles noted that in San Antonio itself, "the residents of Mexican origin have been expelled." These families and others in the region fled for their lives to Mexico, crossing the river "in utter destitution and after suffering the hardships of a weary march on foot, compulsively undertaken for the salvation of their lives." Robles pointedly noted that these "families have been forced to abandon all the interests which they had at stake." He urged the United States to proceed with "every means" to "investigate the truth" and end the mistreatment of Mexicans because such a response is "demanded by justice, the law of nations, and the honor of the United States."[35] The lynching in and around Goliad of Mexicans stopped in late 1857 for a combination of reasons that included actions by state officials, increased criticism by area residents, and the creation of a new transportation route by Mexicans that avoided Goliad.

As with most complicated events, there were several factors behind the Cart War, including economic competition between Anglo and Mexican workers and simmering anger between the two groups that dated back to the Texas Revolution, but the specific context of the mid-1850s and rising tensions related to escaped slaves and the Mexican border was an important backdrop that emboldened some Anglos to begin a spree of mob violence that was unprecedented even for violent Texas.

––––––––

The period following the Cart War and the murderous violence of the Barton affair was followed by fifteen years of greatly diminished mob violence against Mexicans. Mob violence in California never returned to the level that it had during the Gold Rush, in part because some of the factors that led to the return of high levels of mob violence in Texas—the cattle boom of the 1870s and the Mexican Revolution of the early twentieth century—did not impact California as deeply. However, the much smaller Mexican population of California was also certainly a factor. Many Mexicans fled the state after the Gold Rush, and the Mexican population of California remained a fraction of that in Texas until the mid-twentieth century.

In Texas, where the Mexican population not only was larger but also owned significant and coveted property in the Lower Rio Grande Valley and elsewhere, the decline of mob violence was temporary. In late November 1873, a group of angry men intent on violence slipped on to the property of Toribio

Lozano in South Texas. Lozano was a successful rancher who owned property on both sides of the border and used his many lands for grazing sheep and other stock animals. He resided in Mexico most of the time but employed a large number of shepherds to tend his flocks in Texas. On December 4, 1873, authorities discovered the decaying bodies of seven Mexicans hanging near a creek several miles northwest of Corpus Christi. The hanging corpses were men from Lozano's ranch. Despite a lengthy investigation and the diplomatic intervention of Mexican officials, Texas authorities claimed that they could not discover the identities of the murderers.[36]

The men who lynched Lozano's shepherds left no records of their motives, but the desire for Lozano's land, as the men would have been certain of the profit that could be made on livestock during the cattle boom, was probably a factor. In any event, this act of unpunished mob violence was followed by dozens of others in the next several years. Tensions grew extremely high and culminated in a murderous rampage against Mexicans.

On July 25, 1877, a band of Mexican raiders reportedly murdered a farmer named Lee Rabb in Nueces County, Texas. In retaliation, a mob of Anglos went on a murderous spree against Mexicans in the region with very little investigation into whether or not they were involved in the Rabb murder. During an investigation the following year by the Committee on Military Affairs, a local man named Julius Tucker testified that men living in "that country" gathered and "banded together and killed quite a number of innocent Mexicans" which he estimated at "not less than forty." Tucker noted that the Mexicans were killed in Texas "on the ranches, roads, and wherever they were found" and that they were men who owned property in the region. He claimed that no official report of the murders was ever made, though it "was a well-known fact in our country."[37]

While Texas furnished the greatest number of Mexican victims, similar patterns on a smaller scale can be found in New Mexico and Arizona in the 1870s. The Horrell War discussed earlier is a good example of violent individuals emboldened to even greater levels of violence by the general climate of anti-Mexican feeling in the 1870s. In Arizona, in 1871, a Spanish-language newspaper titled *La Balanza Popular* noted several unwarranted shootings of Mexicans by Anglos.[38] In 1872, Arizona sheriff T. C. Warden was elected "captain" of the vigilante "Safety Committee" in Phoenix and helped orchestrate the expulsion of Mexicans not deemed to have legitimate business in the region.[39] The violence continued. In July 1873, according to the *Phoenix Herald*, vigilantes hanged alleged outlaw and murderer Mariano Tisnado and eleven of his compatriots over a span of several days.[40] Over the next twelve months, posses and mobs executed another four Mexicans on allegations of murder or theft.[41]

Whether it was economic competition, political tension, or sheer racial hatred that motivated their actions, nearly all of these acts of violence were committed by and against men. Even though rarely threatened directly by lynch mobs, Mexican women nonetheless suffered at their hands when they murdered fathers, husbands, brothers, and sons. When, in 1874, a Brownsville mob hanged two Mexican men for theft and left their bodies on display, the local press reported that female friends and relatives suffered emotional trauma at the sight.[42] The distress caused to women demonstrates the larger injury inflicted by lynch mobs beyond their immediate victims.

———————

The waning of mob violence after the Rabb murders was not as dramatic as was the decline after the Gold Rush or in the 1860s. Mob violence remained a significant problem in the Southwest in the late 1870s and 1880s, but a slow decline followed the government investigations and diplomatic protests of the mid-1870s. The contrast could not be sharper with African Americans who found lynching and mob violence to be a growing threat at the end of the nineteenth century. Yet, once lynching and vigilantism against Mexicans re-emerged after the Mexican Revolution began, it was as potent and extensive as ever, at least in Texas. Unlike previous peak periods, the mob violence of 1915–19 did not build slowly and culminate with riotous violence. Indiscriminate slaying of Mexicans was replete during this period. However, as with previous eras, a single episode of excessive violence did lead to an official investigation that helped close the third and final era of mass lynching of Mexicans.

Two hours past midnight, on January 28, 1918, a band of Texas Rangers and masked ranchers arrived at the home of Manuel Morales in the Presidio County village of Porvenir. A recent Christmas Day raid on the Brite Ranch consumed their thoughts. Mexican outlaws had attacked the ranch, in the process killing several Anglos and Mexicans, robbing the store, and stealing numerous horses. The Rangers and local ranchers believed that residents of Porvenir were acting as spies and informants for Mexican raiders who lived across the border. The investigators rounded up approximately two dozen men and searched their houses. What happened next is a matter of dispute, but a later investigation concluded that the Rangers and ranchers marched fifteen men of Mexican origin to a rock bluff near the village and coolly executed them. As a result of this mass lynching, 140 residents of Porvenir fled to Mexico, leaving the village abandoned. The widows of the slain men carried their bodies to Mexico, where they were buried. A local grand jury returned no indictments in the case, but the Texas legislature would later open an investigation and restructure the Texas Rangers as a result of what happened at Porvenir.

Diplomatic Protest and the Decline of Mob Violence against
Persons of Mexican Descent in the United States

As the data suggest, there are three periods—1852–58, 1873–77, and 1915–19—
where the number of documented lynchings approaches or exceeds twenty
per year. A different type of decline, however, followed each of these peak
periods. The decline after 1858 was quite significant, with the lynching rate
falling by 75 percent from eighteen victims per year to four victims per year.
The second decline was not as rapid, but it was deeper. The lynching rate
remained at ten victims per year for a period of time but eventually declined
to less than one per year. The third decline, however, was the most dramatic,
as it led to the eventual end of public anti-Mexican mob violence. The number of victims fell from over twenty per year to less than one a year in short
order and then disappeared from the historical record altogether.

Two key questions emerge for scholars: (1) how and why did the lynching
of Mexicans decline so dramatically in the late nineteenth century when it
was rising in other parts of the United States, and (2) why did it disappear
altogether in the late 1920s when it persisted until the civil rights era in the
American South?

The answer to both questions, at least in part, is connected to the U.S.-Mexico
border. Most Mexican victims of lynch mobs died in the four American states
that share a border with Mexico, namely, Arizona, California, New Mexico,
and Texas. This is hardly surprising given the concentration of the Mexican-
descent population in those regions of the United States, but the level of violence against Mexicans is not explained solely by demographics. Some regions
of the Southwest were more prone to lynching attacks on Mexicans than were
other regions despite populations of similar size and density. The region around
San Antonio, for example, witnessed fewer episodes of mob violence against
Mexicans than did locations with smaller Mexican populations such as Goliad.
While it is all but impossible to identify all of the reasons that led some localities
to become relatively more lynch prone, the single most important factor was the
attitudes and reactions of local leaders toward lynching episodes.

By the 1880s, Mexican diplomats understood very well the difference in attitudes toward persons of Mexican descent throughout the United States.
They understood that their investigations and protests would be much easier
in those cases where Mexicans were lynched far from the border. Their actions seem to suggest that they prioritized such cases in a conscious effort to
establish precedents that could then be cited and applied in less hospitable
jurisdictions. The lynching of Luciano Padilla in Nebraska is a key example.

On October 2, 1884, the Mexican minister to Washington, Matías Romero,
instructed a New York attorney named E. D. Lawman to open an investiga-

tion into the lynching of a Mexican citizen near Lincoln, Nebraska. Romero was in the middle of what would be a long and illustrious political career.[43] He commanded considerable influence and respect in Washington circles, counting among his personal friends and political allies former secretary of state William H. Seward and former president Ulysses S. Grant. He was a tireless advocate for his country, having lobbied successfully for the support of the United States during the Franco-Mexican War and attempted as the author of numerous works to dispel the negative stereotypes that many Americans had of their southern neighbor. "My experience in dealing with two peoples of different races," he wrote, "speaking different languages and with different social conditions, has shown me that there are prejudices on both sides, growing out of want of sufficient knowledge of each other, which could be dispelled, and by so doing, a better understanding be secured."[44]

Romero probably learned of the Padilla lynching through newspaper coverage, including accounts in the *New York World* and the *New York Times* shortly after the lynching. The details in the press, however, were scant, and Romero decided on an independent investigation headed by Lawman. He offered the attorney $25 per day for up to ten days for his services, a serious financial investment. Romero hoped that the investigation would "ascertain facts" that would allow the "arrest and punishment of the guilty parties." Lawman hired the Pinkerton Detective Agency to travel to Lincoln and then dutifully forwarded Pinkerton's thorough reports to Romero.

Romero's correspondence during 1884 demonstrates that he was well aware of other episodes of mob violence against Mexicans in the United States and that most of those incidents took place much closer to the U.S.-Mexico border than Nebraska. Indeed, his letters indicate concern over the mistreatment and lynching of Mexicans in Texas and Arizona during the same months he is corresponding with Lawman. Yet, Romero prioritized the Nebraska case. Why? Romero understood that the key to preventing lynching in the federal system of the United States lay with local officials. Closer to the border, local sheriffs and law officers had proven to be less than cooperative with Mexican diplomats in the past. Romero, who had and would continue to forge warm relations with Americans in the North, seemed to believe that locations more remote from the border provided him with a better chance for the prosecution of mob members.

While nothing came of the Padilla episode for various reasons, Romero continued to monitor violence against Mexicans and finally found success a decade later with another lynching that took place far from the border. Shortly after midnight on August 26, 1895, a mob of more than two hundred masked men stormed the jailhouse in the mining town of Yreka. Located in the very northern part of California, Yreka was close to the Oregon border but over 750 miles from Mexico. Using sledgehammers to smash the cell doors, the intruders seized four inmates awaiting trial and hauled them to the courthouse square. The mob tied ropes around the necks of the kidnapped men and hanged them one at a time from an iron rail suspended between two locust trees.[45]

The episode may have passed into obscurity, dismissed as another sordid example of frontier lawlessness, were it not for the identity of one of the dead men, a forty-year-old sawmill worker named Luis Moreno. Although Moreno's nationality was initially uncertain, Mexican diplomats led by Romero made immediate inquiries into the lynching.[46] For many months, Romero pressured the State Department to redress the matter. Romero's insistent lobbying finally forced an act of appeasement from the U.S. government. On January 18, 1898, President William McKinley wrote to Congress with a recommendation that it authorize payment of a $2,000 indemnity "out of humane consideration, without any reference to the question of liability" to the family of Luis Moreno.[47]

Romero would successfully utilize the Moreno precedent in other cases much closer to the border. Although he died in 1898, those who followed him pursued an investigation that he had begun into the lynching of Florentino Suaste in Cotulla, Texas. They succeeded, despite much local resistance in Texas, including the burning of court records related to the case, in gaining a similar indemnity for Suaste's family on December 7, 1900.[48]

While Romero's actions could not prevent the return of anti-Mexican violence during the years of the Mexican Revolution, they were foundational. Mexican diplomats would return to making some of the very same arguments in the 1920s, and they would again successfully prevail upon the federal government. These renewed protests finally ended the rise-and-fall cycle of anti-Mexican mob violence in the United States that had begun with the California Gold Rush. While ethnic prejudice against Mexicans and economic factors, especially tensions over the terms of labor, remained strong along the border, the threat of federal intervention decisively altered the mix of factors that had allowed mobs freedom from prosecution for violence against Mexicans. In particular, local government support or indifference to anti-Mexican mob action was no longer a given after the 1920s. Sadly, the cycle of lynching violence was replaced by less public forms of discrimination, intimidation, and killing that have proved much harder to eliminate.

Notes

1. Matías Romero to Señor Secretario, December 31, 1884, including report of William A. Pinkerton to Matías Romero, November 14, 1884, T.342, No.1100, 891–95 Secretaría de Relaciones Exteriores Archives, Mexico City, Mexico (hereafter, SRE); William A. Pinkerton to Matías Romero, November 14, 15, 20, 22, 24, 26, 1884, SRE T.342, No.1100, 891–95; William A. Pinkerton to Matías Romero, November 15, 26, 1884, SRE T.342, No.1100, 891–95; New York Times, August 24, 1884; Jim McKee, "Lancaster County's Only Lynching,"

Lincoln Journal Star, January 6, 2013, accessed July 13, 2015, http://journalstar.com/life styles/misc/jim-mckee-lancaster-county-s-only-lynching/article_a67829c3-33b1-5c7f -a7b7-284dad9e4c12.html. Note that the victim is sometimes identified as "Padillo" in English-language sources, but the authors believe that the victim's name was Padilla based on common spelling in Spanish and on sources in the Mexican records.

2. Manfred Berg and Simon Wendt, eds., *Globalizing Lynching History* (New York: Palgrave Macmillan, 2011); Robert Thurston, *American Mob Murder in Global Perspective* (New York: Routledge, 2011); William D. Carrigan and Christopher Waldrep, eds., *Swift to Wrath: Lynching in Global Historical Perspective* (Charlottesville: University of Virginia Press, 2013); and Michael Pfeifer, *The Roots of Rough Justice: Origins of American Lynching* (Urbana: University of Illinois Press, 2011).

3. This speediness sometimes led to smaller and less brutal executions than might have been the case otherwise. In Tucson, for example, a newspaper lamented the quick execution of a Mexican. "It has just been found out that one of the Mexicans hung at Tucson, some time ago, had a hand in the terrible massacre of the Baker family in which case hanging was too good for him." See *Daily Arizona Miner*, February 9, 1874. One of the differences between the lynching of Blacks and Mexicans is that African Americans were more likely to be lynched by large mobs in spectacle conditions. The border is a likely factor in this divergence.

4. Harold Preece, *Lone Star Man: Ira Aten, Last of the Old Texas Rangers* (New York: Hastings House, 1960), 42. The position of the Texas Rangers can be compared to that of U.S. soldiers who served in Vietnam or, later, in Iraq. In all three instances, linguistic challenges and racial antipathies, combined with hostile and alien surroundings, led these men to abuse innocent and law-abiding citizens.

5. In most cases, it is impossible to verify the nationality and citizenship of lynching victims. This status is one of great significance, as the Mexican government has the ability to investigate and inquire about the murder of Mexican nationals. Nevertheless, the data conflate Mexicans born in the United States with Mexican nationals because the sources upon which the data are built often have nothing to say on the matter or are untrustworthy. The authors believe that most, perhaps two-thirds or more, of lynching victims of Mexican descent were born in Mexico, but such conclusions are based on a combination of limited data and anecdotal evidence. When we use the word "Mexican," we refer to all those of Mexican descent resident in the United States, both U.S. and Mexican nationals.

6. Report of Mr. Green on Mines and Foreign Miners, March 15, 1850, *Journal of the Senate of the State of California First Session* (San José: J. Winchester, 1850), 493–97.

7. *Sacramento Daily Union*, June 12 and 14, 1852; *Nevada Journal*, June 16 and 19, 1852; *Alta California*, June 13, 1852; Hubert Howe Bancroft, "Popular Tribunals—Volume I," in *The Works of Hubert Howe Bancroft* (San Francisco: The History Company, Publisher, 1887), 36:524–25.

8. *Alta California*, January 29, 1853.

9. Edmund Booth, *Forty-Niner: The Life Story of a Deaf Pioneer* (Stockton, CA: San Joaquin Pioneer and Historical Society, 1953), 27; Walter Van Tilburg Clark, ed., *The Journals of Alfred Doten, 1849–1903* (Reno: University of Nevada Press, 1973), 140.

10. Frank W. Johnson, *A History of Texas and Texans* (Chicago: American Historical Society, 1914), 1:515.

11. James Gadsen to William L. Marcy, October 16, 1854, in *Diplomatic Correspondence of the United States*, ed. William R. Manning (Washington, DC: Carnegie Endowment for International Peace, 1937), 734.

12. *Clarksville Northern Standard*, December 25, 1852.

13. *Report of the Committee of Investigation Sent in 1873 by the Mexican Government to the Frontier of Texas* (New York: Baker & Godwin, 1875), 178–92.

14. *San Antonio Herald*, May 29, 1855.

15. H. S. Thrall, *A History of Texas: From the Earliest Settlements to the Year 1876* (New York: University Publishing, 1876), 146.

16. Ronnie C. Tyler, "Slave Owners and Runaway Slaves in Texas" (master's thesis, Texas Christian University, 1966), 68–69; Wendell G. Addington, "Slave Insurrections in Texas," *Journal of Negro History* 35, no. 4 (October 1950): 414–18.

17. *Galveston News*, September 11, 1856, quoted in Olmsted, *A Journey through Texas*, 503.

18. Quoted in *Galveston News*, November 9, 1872.

19. Quoted in *Galveston News*, June 23, 1874.

20. Quoted in *Galveston News*, July 27, 1876.

21. *San Antonio Express*, June 21, 1875.

22. *San Antonio Express*, November 27, 1873.

23. T. C. Warden, Sheriff of Maricopa County, to Governor A. P. K. Safford, June 20, 1872, Secretary of Territory Papers, subject group 10, box 12, folder 171, Arizona State Library and Archives.

24. *Santa Fe New Mexican*, January 2, 1874; Maurice Garland Fulton, *History of the Lincoln County War*, Robert N. Mullin, ed., (Tucson: The University of Arizona Press, 1980), 21–24; Robert N. Mullin, *A Chronology of the Lincoln County War: Scene: Mostly Lincoln County, New Mexico, Time: Mainly 1877–1881* (Santa Fe, NM: Press of the Territorian, 1966), 11; P. J. Rasch, "The Horrell War," *New Mexico Historical Review* 31 (1956): 228; *Old Lincoln County Pioneer Stories: Interviews from the WPA Writer's Project* (Lincoln, NM, 1994), 1–3.

25. Benjamin Heber Johnson, *Revolution in Texas: How a Forgotten Rebellion and Its Bloody Suppression Turned Mexicans into Americans* (New Haven, CT: Yale University Press, 2003), chap. 1.

26. *Dallas Morning News*, September 15, 1915.

27. *Bonham News*, October 22, 1915.

28. Virgil Lott Narrative, pt. 2, 41, Center for American History, University of Texas at Austin.

29. The raiders were alleged to be a band of criminals composed of an Anglo, a Black man, and six to ten Mexicans. *Sacramento Union*, August 10, 1855; *Georgetown News*, August 9, 1855; John Bossenecker, *Gold Dust & Gunsmoke: Tales of Gold Rush Outlaws, Gunfighters, Lawmen, and Vigilantes* (New York: Wiley, 1999), 52–58; Dave Demarest, "Mother Lode Massacre," *Frontier Times* 49, no. 2 (1975): 12–13, 35–36; William B. Secrest, "Revenge of Rancheria," *Frontier Times* (September 1968), 16–19, 59–61.

30. One of the three Mexicans was convicted by the vigilantes on the evidence that an Anglo named Jim Johnson had heard him shout "Viva Mexico" before the killings. After he was hanged, Johnson took over his mining claim. *Alta California*, August 10, 1855; Bossenecker, *Gold Dust & Gunsmoke*, 52–58; Secrest, "Revenge of Rancheria," 16–19, 59–61; Demarest, "Mother Lode Massacre," 12–13, 35–36.

31. *San Francisco Daily Placer Times*, August 10, 1855; *Illustrated London News*, September 29, 1855, in Clipping in California Gold Rush Days, English Clippings, Henry E. Huntington Library; *Georgetown News*, August 16, 1855.

32. *Alta California*, August 13, 1855.

33. William Deverell, *Whitewashed Adobe: The Rise of Los Angeles and the Remaking of Its Mexican Past* (Berkeley: University of California Press, 2004), 15–23. See also *Alta California*, February 14, 1857; *Los Angeles Star*, February 7, 1857; *Sonoma County Journal*, February 20, 1857; *Pacific Sentinel* (Santa Cruz), February 21, 1857; Harris Newmark, *Sixty Years in Southern California, 1853–1913* (New York: Knickerbocker, 1916); Lanier Bartlett, ed., *On the Old West Coast: Being further Reminiscences of a Ranger, Major Horace Bell* (New York: William Morrow, 1930).

34. John J. Linn, *Reminiscences of Fifty Years in Texas* (New York: D. J. Saddler, 1883), 352–54, 353 (quote).

35. Manuel Robles to Lewis Cass, October 14, 1857, Copy of Translation of Letter sent to Lewis Cass, Secretary of State of the United States, Office of the Governor, RG 301, Records of Elisha Marshall Pease, box 301-26, folder 47, Texas State Archives, Austin.

36. See William D. Carrigan and Clive Webb, *Forgotten Dead: Mob Violence against Mexicans in the United States, 1848–1928* (New York: Oxford, 2013), 17–18.

37. Testimony taken by the Committee on Military Affairs in relation to The Texas Border Troubles, H.R., 45th Cong., 2nd Sess. (Washington, DC: Government Printing Office, 1878), Serial Set No. 1820. See also Paul Schuster Taylor, *An American-Mexican Frontier: Nueces County, Texas* (New York: Russell & Russell, 1934); and J. Frank Dobie, *A Vaquero of the Brush Country* (Boston: Little, Brown, 1929, 1957).

38. Cited in *Arizona Citizen* (Tucson), March 25, 1871.

39. T. C. Warden, Sheriff of Maricopa County, to Governor A. P. K. Safford, June 20, 1872, Secretary of Territory Papers, subject group 10, box 12, folder 171, Arizona State Library and Archives; F. Arturo Rosales, *¡Chicano! The History of the Mexican American Civil Rights Movement* (Houston, TX: Arte Público, 1996), 13.

40. *Phoenix Herald*, November 26, 1880.

41. *Arizona Weekly Citizen* (Tucson), September 27, 1873; *Arizona Weekly Citizen* (Tucson), July 25 and December 26, 1874; January 2, 1875.

42. *Galveston Daily News*, December 17, 1874.

43. For more extensive biographical details, see undated newspaper clippings, *Expediente Personal de Matias Romero 1898–1899* (LE 1038), 157–60, SRE.

44. Matías Romero, *Mexico and the United States, A Study of Subjects Affecting Their Political, Commercial, and Social Relations, Made with a View to Their Promotion* (New York: G. P. Putnam's Sons, 1898), I, vii.

45. Warren Franklin Webb, "A History of Lynching in California since 1875" (master's thesis, University of California, Berkeley, 1934), 59–61; *Yreka Journal*, August 27, 30, September 3, 1895; *San Francisco Chronicle*, August 27, 28, 1895.

46. *Yreka Journal*, August 27, 30, 1895; *San Francisco Examiner*, August 28, 1895.

47. "Indemnity to Relatives of Luis Moreno," 1. See also *New York Times*, January 19, 1898; Matías Romero to Ignacio Mariscal, January 18, 1898, SRE T.457 No. 662, p.133; Matías Romero to Ignacio Mariscal, January 19, 1898, SRE T.457, No. 669, p.145; Matías Romero to William R. Day, July 18, 1898, SRE T.455 (1898), No. 54, p. 101.

48. *New York Times*, December 8, 1900; John Hay to Jose F. Godoy, December 30, 1898, *Expediente Personal de Matias Romero 1898–1899*, 177; *New York Times*, December 31, 1898.

Figure 11.1 Clifford K. Berryman cartoon of an irate Uncle Sam pursuing Pancho Villa, who has just raided and torched Columbus, New Mexico; Villa is—very implausibly—shown fleeing barefoot across a cactus-strewn countryside. From the *Washington Evening Star*, March 10, 1916. Courtesy U.S. National Archives.

Chapter 11

Border Violence in Revolutionary Mexico, 1910–1920

ALAN KNIGHT

This chapter analyzes violence on Mexico's northern border during the decade of armed revolution, 1910–20, the most violent decade in the country's
modern history.[1] Since the frontier is long and variegated, while violence is a
protean concept, such an analysis is tricky, the more so because the decade
was also one of rapid change and substantial upheaval, which does not lend
itself to static, freeze-frame analysis. So any account must accommodate
change (which in turn requires a narrative, alias "diachronic," approach),
while at the same time offering conceptual and "synchronic" analysis of what
happened during that decade, in order not to reduce it to "one damn thing
after another."

My analysis therefore involves a simple two-by-two typology: (i) domestic
("civil") war or conflict, as against international; and (ii) "symmetrical" war
(between conventional forces) as against "asymmetrical" (between regular or
conventional forces on the one hand and irregular, guerrilla, or "bandit"
groups on the other).[2] Harking back to an alternative typology, not explicitly
deployed in this chapter, I am chiefly concerned with political violence (macro
and micro), with an admixture of "mercenary" violence.[3]

Combining narrative and analytical approaches works tolerably well, since
the first half of the revolutionary decade (1910–15) was primarily a story of domestic civil conflict in Mexico, which involved a crucial transition from
asymmetrical to symmetrical warfare; during these years, the border played
an important role, but international (U.S./Mexican) conflict was limited, even
inconsequential.[4] In the second half of the decade (1915–20), as the armed Revolution wound down, Mexican domestic conflict diminished, and at the
same time, it reverted to asymmetrical form, as the precarious Carrancista
regime battled to survive in the face of widespread irregular insurgencies,
including the ragtag forces of Pancho Villa in the north.

However, the border now experienced greater violence, including international violence: in particular, Villa's raid on Columbus in March 1916 and recurrent cross-border raiding in the Lower Rio Grande Valley. In response, in
March 1916 the Wilson administration dispatched the Punitive Expedition in
vain pursuit of Villa. Although major, international war was avoided and Carranza survived, pro tem, it was not until the Sonoran faction triumphed in

1920 that Mexico clearly took the path of state-building, economic reconstruction, social reform, and eventually, détente with the United States, which would be the hallmarks of the post-1920 institutional Revolution.

Throughout this violent decade, events along the border were crucial, having consequences far beyond the borderlands. The decade was very nearly framed by the Treaty of Ciudad Juárez (May 1911), which ended the Porfiriato and the Agua Prieta revolt (April 1920), which toppled Carranza and inaugurated the Sonoran dynasty.[5] The two preeminent military leaders of the time, Villa and Obregón, hailed from border states (Villa being a *chihuahuense* by adoption), and their respective armies, even as they swelled to unprecedented size in 1914–15, retained Sonoran and Chihuahuan nuclei.[6] What is more, the winning Sonoran faction—which included not only Obregón, the Revolution's great Napoleonic strategist, but also Calles, the architect of the new regime of the 1920s—was, as Aguilar Camín argued, a quintessential product of the northern frontier.[7]

Indeed, some historians have seen the Revolution as, at root, a triumph of the north, especially the frontier zone, over the rest of Mexico (a triumph that the rest of Mexico often resented).[8] And there is no doubt that some *norteños*—Mexican carpetbaggers, we could call them—saw their victorious southern advance in terms of the go-ahead, progressive, mestizo north grabbing the benighted Indian center and south by the scruff of its grubby brown neck and civilizing it.[9] "Southerners," such as the *oaxaqueño* José Vasconcelos, countered by accusing the northerners, in particular the *fronterizos*, of being *déraciné* "pochos," half-gringo, inadequately Mexican.[10] Some of them, it was further alleged, favored annexation to the United States; twentieth-century Sonora would emulate nineteenth-century Texas.[11] But this was a cheap canard. Norteños and fronterizos were just as "Mexican" as the rest of their compatriots and, as their resistance to U.S. filibusters as well as the Punitive Expedition showed, they had no desire to follow in Texas's footsteps.[12] Indeed, far from seeking secession, the northerners wanted to impose their control on the rest of Mexico, in order to forge a stronger state and society that could better resist the *coloso del norte* (colossus of the north). And that resistance involved emulating elements of North American society—patriotism, education, economic dynamism—which they admired, often on the basis of first-hand experience.

The first half of the revolutionary decade (1910–15) witnessed mounting domestic violence, as asymmetrical (guerrilla/counterinsurgency) warfare gave way to major conventional campaigns: a transition, spanning 1913–14, in which the borderlands played a key role. The first two bouts of civil war (1910–11 and 1913–14) pitted popular insurgents against the old regime; the final bout of civil war (1914–15), which determined who would rule Mexico, involved Carrancistas against Villistas (the latter loosely allied with the Zapatistas of the south).[13] Now, two tried-and-tested revolutionary armies, well armed and substantially similar in both makeup and morale, confronted each other.[14] These armies were disproportionately norteño and even fronterizo; and their maintenance, as large, well-equipped conventional forces, depended heavily on cross-border supply from the United States.[15] Finally, the last five years, from late 1915 through 1920, witnessed the dour struggle of the triumphant but still shaky Carrancista coalition to survive in the face of multiple challenges, both domestic and foreign (the latter including the Punitive Expedition).

This sequence can be schematically presented:

A SCHEMATIC CHRONOLOGY OF THE ARMED REVOLUTION, 1910-20

Porfirian old regime, 1876–1911.
Armed revolution, 1910–15, including:
   Civil war bout 1. Madero Revolution against Díaz, 1910–11: irregular
      popular insurrection(s) against conventional (federal) army. Treaty
      of Ciudad Juárez, May 1911.
   Entr'acte. Madero Government, 1911–13: shaky democracy; continued
      irregular popular insurrection against conventional (federal) army.
   Civil war bout 2. Huerta Government, 1913–14: authoritarian milita-
      rism against renewed irregular popular insurrection, which
      mutates into conventional revolutionary armies, especially in the
      north.
   Civil war bout 3. "War of the Winners," 1914–15: deciding conflict
      between conventional revolutionary armies, each with a northern
      core.
Carranza/Constitutionalist Government, 1915–20: shaky revolutionary
   regime and conventional army faces multiple armed (and other)
   challenges; border insecurity and Punitive Expedition (1916–17).
Revolt of Agua Prieta, April 1920, inaugurates the "Sonoran Dynasty."

————

Now to put flesh on this skeletal outline. The northern border played a key role in the gestation of the armed revolution in 1910–11. We may distinguish basic *causes* and facilitating *conditions*. The first category involves revolutionary grievances; the second includes factors that made revolution possible. Both were important along the northern border, but the second category is particularly crucial.[16] Many of the standard grievances that prompted Mexicans to rise up against Díaz in 1910 can be seen along the border: on the one hand, resentment at the regime's authoritarian and exclusionary ("caciquista") politics; on the other, socioeconomic grievances associated, in particular, with agrarian dispossession (and, to a lesser extent, the oppression and repression of urban labor).[17] To these "structural" grievances should be added "conjunctural" pressures, including the severe recession of 1907–8, which, transmitted from the United States, hit the northern mining and, more broadly, commercial economy, creating unemployment and hardship; in this respect, the north, including the border, was seriously, if temporarily, affected.[18]

However, especially regarding *structural* tensions and grievances, which were arguably more important than *conjunctural* ones, the north in general, or the border zone in particular, was not in the vanguard; agrarian tensions were greater in the center (Morelos being the classic case), while the oppression and repression of labor were just as acute in, for example, Veracruz (e.g., Río Blanco) as in Sonora (e.g., Cananea).[19] The politics of *caciquismo*—"boss politics"—generated sharp resentment in Chihuahua, above all, but Puebla and Yucatán also languished under the long-standing rule of authoritarian political bosses. Meanwhile, Porfirian abuses associated with labor coercion, debt peonage, and associated racism were much weaker in the north than in the center or, a fortiori, the deep south.[20] I would conclude, then, that the border zone became the pioneer of revolution in 1910–11—and again, in 1913–14—less because its inhabitants were more oppressed than because they were more capable of deploying armed resistance to the distant but oppressive "center." They rebelled because they could; and it was, in part, thanks to the presence of the border that they could.

The north's "comparative advantage," when it came to armed revolt, derived from three features. First, the north was farther from the center, thus less easily subject to centralized control.[21] Second, as other chapters in this book show, the north had a long and lively history of local military action,[22] which stretched back to the colonial period, and was reinforced by both continued warfare and deliberate government policy during the turbulent nineteenth century. While playing an important role in the endemic armed conflict of that period, which culminated in the War of the Reform (1857–61) and the liberals' dogged resistance to the French Intervention of 1861–67, the north also had to deal with the so-called *indios bárbaros*: Apaches and Comanches in the northeast, Apaches in the center, Yaquis in the northwest. The *indios bárbaros* were resisted, repressed, and, by the 1880s, largely defeated, though in Sonora the Yaqui wars still rumbled on in the 1900s.

Individual caudillos, like Luis Terrazas of Chihuahua, made their names in these campaigns, while the people of communities like Namiquipa forged reputations as doughty fighters, disdainful of the feeble efforts of the distant "center."[23] These were "self-made" men (and women, and communities) who stood up for their rights and had the guns and mounts, organization and experience, to do so.[24] True, the long years of the Pax Porfiriana (1876–1911) served to attenuate northern autonomy and belligerence, but sporadic revolts— notably in Chihuahua in the 1890s (e.g., San Andrés, Tomóchic)—and the bloody campaigns against the insurgent Yaquis in Sonora maintained the tradition, so that it could swiftly spring back to life in 1910. Thus, the early pioneers of the Revolution were typically products of the rough-and-ready northern frontier: muleteers like Orozco, bandits like Villa, champions of dissident local communities like Toribio Ortega of Cuchillo Parado, some forty miles from the international border.[25]

Third, the proximity of the international border was crucial. During the Porfiriato, the Mexican and United States economies became more tightly connected, as the two railway networks were knitted together, as trade— including cross-border trade—flourished, and American investment poured into northern Mexico.[26] In a sense, the open, shifting, often violent "frontier" of the nineteenth century meshed with the more settled and stable "border" of the twentieth, across which people, goods, and capital flowed in increasing numbers and volumes.[27] Although the border thus filled up, it was still thinly policed: on the eve of the Revolution, only eight U.S. border guards were responsible for the four-hundred-mile sweep of the Big Bend from El Paso to Sanderson; and, while the Revolution compelled the U.S. authorities, both state and federal, to beef up border controls, the latter remained inadequate, at times compromised by interagency squabbles.[28]

As I have said, the major socioeconomic changes of the Porfiriato did not adversely affect the north (or the border) any more than the rest of Mexico; in fact, it could be argued that the north benefited more (or, at least, suffered less). As a result, communications improved and material resources increased; both could be deployed by revolutionary as well as government forces. But to begin with, when revolutionary mobilization involved irregular recruitment and decentralized guerrilla warfare, the government enjoyed great advantages: it controlled the railways, had a loyal and well-armed (if numerically reduced) regular army, and could import arms on a grand scale.[29] The rebels were seriously disadvantaged, but proximity to the border still helped. The border also offered a—more or less—safe haven, where revolutionary leaders like Madero could gather and organize; and it provided a unique means to import arms and ammunition, even if clandestinely.[30]

Initially, the (illegal) cross-border arms traffic was scant:[31] the rebels of 1910–11 were poorly armed, relied heavily on what they could acquire in Mexico, and necessarily fought in hit-and-run style (when they faced the Federals in open battle, where their lack of artillery and machine guns counted, they were liable to lose—and to lose heavily).[32] Similarly, a year later, Pascual

Orozco's insurgent challenge to the Madero government was broken by federal firepower, especially artillery. Lacking heavy weaponry, the rebels improvised, blasting their way through the adobe walls of Ciudad Juárez using homemade dynamite bombs in May 1911; or, a year later at Rellano, sending a dynamite-laden runaway train (a so-called *máquina loca*) against a poorly led federal army, thus winning a notable victory.[33] Arms imports, of course, required hard currency, of which the rebels had relatively little. And, since the Madero revolution ended prematurely after six months, with the Juárez peace treaty of May 1911, they lacked the time, as well as the resources, to exploit the full potential of border arms trafficking.

The Huerta coup of February 1913 changed all that. Madero's shaky democracy ended in treason and bloodshed; Huerta set about creating a fully fledged military regime; and the forces of the Revolution reassembled under the broad aegis of Constitutionalism. Since neither side was disposed to compromise—there would be no repeat of the Ciudad Juárez *transacción*—the revolutionaries now had to make the quantum leap from irregular guerrilla warfare to regular conventional campaigns (that is, from asymmetrical to symmetrical warfare)—which meant defeating the federal army in open battle (as at Tierra Blanca, November 1913), or in more prolonged siege-like set-piece battles (such as Torreón, April 1914). Now, northern resources, exports, and arms imports became crucial to the extensive conventional campaigning of 1913–14, and they explain the greater success of the northern armies—notably Villa's División del Norte and Obregón's División del Noroeste—as compared to Zapata's dogged, but more circumscribed, struggle in Morelos and neighboring states.[34]

For a year following the Huerta coup, the Wilson administration refused to allow the export of arms to the northern rebels. During these crucial months, when the renewed Revolution resisted and gradually took the fight to the federal army, contraband was crucial. The old tradition of cross-border smuggling was revived and amplified in the new context of civil war.[35] Stories of smuggling abound: arms and ammunition were shipped across the border in coffins; individuals—men, women and children—were paid 2 or 3 cents a cartridge to carry small consignments into Mexico, the women taking advantage of billowing skirts; two children were arrested while crossing into Juárez aboard a cart laden with ten thousand rounds.[36] Smuggling was feasible because arms dealers in the American southwest were eager to make a fast buck;[37] because, as already mentioned, the border was long and porous; and because public opinion on the border—which, of course, included a large Hispanic/Mexican population—was overwhelmingly sympathetic to the Revolution.[38]

Why was border opinion revolutionary? First, most Mexicans, particularly northern Mexicans, favored the revolutionary cause, so Mexicans in the United States merely mirrored broader opinion.[39] A small minority of border migrants were political dissidents and exiles, by definition hostile to the Díaz regime. And, perhaps, migrants familiar with the American way of life judged Mexico against a vaguely progressive and democratic yardstick, finding it wanting.[40] Nor were Mexicans in the United States immune to the lure of a fast buck (which, increasingly, meant trading—illegally—with the rebels, not the Huerta regime, whose initial footholds in the north were fast diminishing).

But contraband was costly (illegality pushed up prices), and some consignments did not get through; the porosity of the border was only partial. Artillery and heavy machine guns rarely made it into Mexico.[41] The great achievement of the northern rebels, therefore, was to survive, and to achieve substantial military success, while (relatively) deprived of arms and ammunition during 1913. Gradually, as they gained greater territorial control, they also acquired the material resources whose export would in turn pay for arms imports: the copper of Sonora, the cattle of Chihuahua, and the cotton of the Laguna. When, in February 1914, President Wilson lifted the arms embargo, the hitherto constrained flow of arms and ammunition became a flood, enabling Villa, above all, to equip the División del Norte with the weaponry needed to take the key city of Torreón (April 1914) and to destroy a sizable federal army at Zacatecas (June 1914), thus opening the way to Mexico City.[42] Zapata's slow and partial switch to conventional warfare reflected not only his narrower sociopolitical horizons but also his relative lack of weaponry— hence his need to set up a "primitive munitions factory" at the Atlihuayán Hacienda, where rifle shells were manufactured, using "little pieces of copper cable stolen from Mexico City suburban trolleys and power works."[43]

As the northern rebels built up sizable conventional armies and asymmetrical gave way to symmetrical warfare, the frontier zone served as a crucial base from which those armies could undertake the conquest of central Mexico. In consequence, cross-border trade, which had wilted in 1912–13, now flourished.[44] Meanwhile, only one major battle was fought in this zone: Tierra Blanca (November 1913), which consolidated Villa's control of the state of Chihuahua, obliging federal general Salvador Mercado to evacuate the state capital, along with his army and a bunch of fearful civilians (many of them Spaniards) who, after a miserable month amid the ruins of Ojinaga, crossed the border and sought shelter in an improvised internment camp at Fort Bliss, Texas.[45]

In Sonora, to the west, the incumbent Maderista state government provided the nucleus of the revolutionary force which, with the notable exception of Guaymas, quickly took over the state's towns, mining camps, and border ports.[46] Thereafter, the major clashes occurred farther south—soon, well beyond the frontier states themselves—so the border zone settled down to stable rebel control. Thus, as Villa and others consolidated their power along the border, commerce prospered, mining revived, and American observers—

some of whom had recently considered Villa to be a dangerous desperado—rapidly revised their opinion, seeing him not only as a caudillo with whom they could do business but also as a potential strong man who could satisfactorily govern all Mexico.[47] This process of commercial revival and diplomatic détente brought Villa—and the northern revolutionary authorities more generally—into close, and usually collaborative, relations with American interests: not only consuls and miners, cattle-dealers and arms-suppliers, but also border officials, U.S. army officers, journalists, and movie-makers.[48] But this honeymoon would not last.

During 1914, therefore, the north and the northern frontier were relatively peaceful. Thus far, only the rebels' seizure of Juárez in May 1911 had involved serious fighting near the international line—and Madero, as nominal commander, had sought to avoid even that as I mention below. Two years later, with Madero dead and Huerta the new enemy, the border towns on the Sonora/Arizona border—Naco, Agua Prieta and Nogales—fell quickly and without major encounters in the spring of 1913; Villa mopped up the Chihuahuan/New Mexico/Texas borderlands toward the end of that year; and federal forces held out only along the lower Rio Grande (Piedras Negras and, more important, Nuevo Laredo), where they benefited from the indifferent leadership of revolutionary General Pablo González.[49] Thus, by the spring of 1914, the focus of the fighting had shifted far to the south, where it would remain for a year—until, during 1915, the "War of the Winners" broke out and swiftly spread across the country, including the strategic borderlands.

That final conflict—civil war bout three—involved two similar, closely matched armies, each reasonably well armed and well motivated. It was "symmetrical" in terms not only of conventional warfare but also of rank-and-file morale and social makeup. The biggest and most decisive battles—Celaya, León, and Aguascalientes—were, again, fought far to the south in the Bajío, to the northwest of Mexico City. But there were also lesser theatres of war in the north: in Sonora, where rival revolutionary factions, now redefined as Carrancistas and Villistas, battled for power; and in the northeast, where Villista forces sought to pry Matamoros and Nuevo Laredo from the tenuous control of the Carrancistas. These sideshows did not determine the outcome (as the battles of the Bajío did), but they ruptured the brief peace that had prevailed along the border during 1914.

They also assumed a distinct military pattern, determined by the presence of the border, which is worth mentioning. In general, the battles of the Mexican Revolution were brief and fluid, fought in open country or relatively undefended towns. "Sieges" of a sort occurred (for example, Torreón in April 1914), but they were relatively rare and short.[50] However, as armies acquired better weaponry (notably artillery and machine guns) and as commanders, above all Obregón, acquainted themselves with the defensive tactics of World War I, so it became more feasible and common to defend fixed positions, using trenches, barbed wire, searchlights, machine guns, and artillery.[51] The classic example was the protracted (two-and-a-half-month) siege of El Ebano, on the narrow marshy approaches to the oil port of Tampico; but border ports were also suitable for such defensive tactics, since their northern approaches were off-limits to attackers, and any assault that jeopardized American lives and property risked incurring not only U.S. protests but also U.S. armed reprisals (a dilemma brilliantly captured by that master of irony, the novelist Jorge Ibargüengoitia).[52]

Cautious commanders, like Madero (at Juárez in May 1911) and even Villa (also at Juárez in November 1913), therefore tried to avoid battles in border towns. But Madero failed, and in the subsequent fighting, six Americans were killed, not least because spectators insisted on lining the north bank of the river "as if they were attending a football game."[53] Subsequent border battles—such as Nogales, March 1913—also resulted in shots hitting American territory, eliciting American threats of reprisals.[54]

During the first four years of armed revolution (1910–14), this border-town dilemma affected Mexican military strategy (and tactics) but did not provoke serious (American) losses or American intervention. Indeed, it is the relative *absence* of major bilateral conflict along the border that is striking. However, by 1915, as the Villista cause declined, border battles acquired greater significance, both military and diplomatic; they also signaled a new phase of cross-border tension, which is the theme of the second half of this chapter.

The defense of Agua Prieta by Calles in late 1915 was a key example, since it marked Villa's last throw of the dice, following his decisive defeats in the Bajío and his desperate retreat from Chihuahua across the wintry Sierra Madre into Sonora. The result was another disastrous defeat, as impetuous Villista cavalry charges were cut down by Calles's entrenched defenders, who deployed machine guns, searchlights, and barbed wire.[55] To add insult to injury, the Carrancista forces had been allowed to cross American territory by train to reach Agua Prieta (with U.S. government approval, of course). Coming, as it did, on the heels of American (de facto) recognition of the Carranza administration, this collusion with the Carrancistas at Agua Prieta understandably riled Villa and set him on a new course of virulent anti-Americanism—new because, as already mentioned, Villa's relations with Americans thus far had been generally collaborative, even congenial.

———

Thus, around the turn of 1915–16, halfway through the revolutionary decade, two related trends combined to subvert the relative peace that the border had previously enjoyed. With Villa defeated, at least as a credible contender for national power, organized conventional campaigning gave way to decentralized irregular warfare, with Villa—and a few scattered northern allies—defying the incumbent Carranza administration and its regular army. At the same time, Villa lashed out against the United States, which he believed had betrayed him, had thrown in its lot with Carranza, and was plotting to seize a swath of Mexican territory.[56] Villistas arbitrarily massacred seventeen Americans at Santa Ysabel in January 1916, and two months later, Villa launched his famous raid across the border against Columbus, New Mexico. In response, President Wilson promptly dispatched the Punitive Expedition, which, though it did not prove very punitive, did strain U.S.-Mexican relations to a breaking point, raising the threat of outright war. As a result of these events, the border economy lurched from (relative) boom to bust.[57]

Furthermore, Villa's conversion from collaborative caudillo to vengeful troublemaker roughly coincided with a spate of cross-border raids that are loosely subsumed under the name of the Plan de San Diego (its name taken from the small town of that name in Duval County, Texas). Formally, the Plan espoused a wildly ambitious revanchist goal: the recovery of the territory that Mexico had lost to the United States in 1848. As the indictment of nine captured conspirators put it, they plotted "to steal certain property of the United States . . . to wit, the states of Texas, Oklahoma, New Mexico, Arizona, Colorado and California."[58] However, the Plan also called for violent social revolution in the American Southwest, during which all "white" males would be massacred and the region's Indians, Blacks, and Mexicans would seize control.

Thus, as the second half of the revolutionary decade unfolded, the border saw a distinct shift in the forms and impact of violence. Three analytically distinct phenomena were apparent: the prolonged death-throes of Villismo; heightened politico-ethnic tension and conflict in the United States (especially Texas); and the coercive response of the U.S. government, above all, the Punitive Expedition. Though contemporaneous and closely linked, they are best analyzed separately.

On the Mexican side, irregular Villismo—now virulently anti-American and, many said, reduced to mere mercenary banditry—posed a recurrent threat to both local communities and the overstretched Carrancista army, which now had to switch from conventional "symmetrical" warfare to "asymmetrical" counterinsurgency operations.[59] By now, after five years of costly warfare, most Mexicans were weary of conflict and desired peace; in order to acquire fresh recruits, who would supplement the dwindling hard core of Villista veterans, Villa resorted to the hated *leva*—forced recruitment—even in his heartland of Chihuahua.[60] Local communities were further brutalized by Villista gang rapes, the xenophobic killing of Chinese, and the collective massacre of members of *defensas sociales* (local militias, set up to protect communities against bandits and rebels).[61] Of course, this "moral decline" of Villismo further alienated local people and communities, like Namiquipa, that had once been supportive; and, at the same time, the more respectable, educated, cosmopolitan Villistas (such as Felipe Angeles, Raul, and Emilio Madero, the brothers González Garza) peeled away from the movement, leaving a rump of dedicated fighting Villistas.[62]

One consequence was heightened anti-Americanism. Following his defeat under the searchlights of Agua Prieta, Villa pledged revenge against the gringos who had betrayed him. Two months later, in January 1916, his forces deliberately murdered seventeen American mining company workers at Santa Ysabel;[63] and on March 9, some four hundred Villistas crossed the border and, shortly before dawn, attacked the American garrison town of Columbus, New Mexico. Columbus was unprepared, but the Villista attack was chaotic. Again, seventeen Americans died, while Villista casualties were perhaps six times greater.[64] Not only was this the most serious cross-border raid of the entire revolutionary decade; it was also the biggest foreign attack on the mainland United States between the War of 1812 and the events of 9/11.

Reams have been written about Columbus. I will limit my brief discussion to causes and consequences. Villa's main motive was clearly revenge: to punish the United States for its duplicity, while making life difficult for the precarious Carranza government, which was shown to be incapable of crushing Villa or policing the border.[65] The choice of Columbus may have been influenced by Villa's specific quarrel with a local arms dealer, who allegedly had swindled him out of a promised consignment.[66] As in other cases of U.S.-Mexican conflict in these years, the nefarious hand of imperial Germany has also been detected, but while Germany was clearly keen to see the United States embroiled in a war with Mexico (hence the famous Zimmermann telegram of 1917), there is no good evidence of decisive German incitement.[67] Nor did a man like Villa—proud, macho, violent, and vengeful—need foreign incitement to do what he did.

The Columbus attack led to a rapid U.S. response as President Wilson, facing reelection in November, sent the Punitive Expedition into Mexico to eliminate Villa, as I discuss later. But the expedition failed—in some respects it boosted Villa's fading popularity—and Villa fought on, resorting to hit-and-run raids, while occasionally gathering sizable forces (by means of coercion as well as consent) in order to attack major northern towns: Chihuahua City in September and November 1916, Torreón in December of that year, Juárez in June 1919.[68] The death throes of Villismo were therefore prolonged and violent. And they were not confined to Chihuahua. In Sonora, to the west, Villa's Yaqui allies embarked on freelance operations, not only in their eponymous river valley but also along the border, where they raided, rustled, and clashed with U.S. border forces.[69] In the Lower Rio Grande Valley, too, the detritus of the defeated Villista forces contributed to the endemic violence of the region. Not until 1920, when Carranza fell and Obregón took power, with the backing of the army, did the opportunity arise for Villa—and many others—to broker a deal with the new administration, a deal which, in Villa's case, enabled him to enjoy three final years of peace and prosperity, surrounded by his fellow veterans, on the hacienda which the revolutionary state had gifted him.[70]

Villa's raid on Columbus and the international tension that it provoked formed part of a bigger story of cross-border violence and its consequences. During 1915, the focus of this violence shifted downriver, to the Lower Rio Grande Valley, which witnessed repeated incursions from Mexico into the United States (as well as some U.S. cross-border pursuits).[71] Such incidents were far from unprecedented, as other chapters in this book make clear: the border had witnessed recurrent violence, both politico-revolutionary and criminal, through the later nineteenth century,[72] and the Revolution created conditions in which cross-border clashes and raiding became endemic. Huertista federal troops had seized an American at Palafox, Texas, in February 1914; two months later, sixty "heavily-armed Mexicans, either bandits or revolutionaries," shot up Madero, Texas.[73] But it was in 1915 and after that the raids became serious, persistent, and consequential—especially for the state of Texas.

As already mentioned, raiding acquired a radical political dimension with the publication, in January 1915, of the Plan de San Diego. The Plan called for a mass revolution, involving Tejanos, Mexicans, Native Americans, and Africans Americans, which would wrest the American Southwest from U.S. control and set up an independent republic.[74] Interpretations of the Plan—its origins, authors, and impact—are widely divergent. Very roughly, we can distinguish between versions that stress Mexican agency (that is, direct incitement and organization emanating from south of the border, especially from the Carrancista authorities, including Carranza himself and northeastern military commanders like General Emiliano Nafarrate)[75] and those that place greater emphasis on American—that is, Texan—domestic factors, notably discrimination against Tejanos which in turn produced resentment, rebellion, and, in response to the Plan and raids and rebellions, a violent backlash on the part of the increasingly dominant Anglo community.[76] We can loosely label these the "top-down Mexican" explanation (which stresses Carrancista sponsorship and manipulation) and the "bottom-up Texan" interpretation (which emphasizes ethnic and sociopolitical tensions north of the border).

Clearly these two views are not wholly incompatible; as so often in history, it is a question of interpretative balance. A safe synthesis of the two views might be: mounting ethnic tensions in Texas, exploited by local (Texan) political factions, and further stimulated by events in Mexico (the Revolution's promise of redemption—a promise that did not stop at the border—and the instability and upheaval that the Revolution provoked), revived an old tradition of Tejano armed resistance (recall Catarino Garza et al.). This, in turn, provoked a violent—arguably disproportionate—Anglo response.[77] And the Carrancista authorities perhaps promoted this process in pursuit of their own political and diplomatic ends.

The ideological makeup of the Plan de San Diego plotters was bewilderingly confused. Some, including Plan signatories Basilio Ramos and Agustín Garza, were supposedly supporters of deposed dictator Victoriano Huerta, who in 1915 was engaged in a futile attempt to lead a reactionary counterrevolution from his base in the United States,[78] while other supporters, including prominent figures like Aniceto Pizaña and Luis de la Rosa, were radical Magonistas, followers of the brothers Flores Magón, ergo, exponents of (roughly) anarcho-syndicalism.[79] And the stated goals of the Plan were so extreme and provocative that some considered it to be the work of an agent provocateur.

According to the "top-down Mexican" explanation, the Carranza faction, then in tenuous control of the northeastern Mexican border and engaged in a life-or-death struggle with Villismo, sought to take advantage of this tension, pressuring the United States to grant diplomatic recognition in the hope of restoring stability, while perhaps garnering popular patriotic support in Mexico. The evidence for Carrancista machinations is in part circumstantial: the raids peaked in the autumn of 1915 and then declined (though they did not end) once recognition had been received in early October; they then revived again in 1916, when Carranza was pressing the United States to withdraw the Punitive Expedition from northern Mexico.[80]

On the one hand, Carranza was certainly capable of practicing Realpolitik of this kind, as were subordinates like General Emiliano Nafarrete. On the other hand, his, or their, capacity to control events—to turn the raids on and off like a tap—should not be exaggerated. Harris and Sadler cite evidence that "Carranza might not be able to control all (of his) subordinates"; yet they also bizarrely argue, or rather assert, that he "had a command and control structure [!] that functioned well enough to enable him to dominate [sic] the Mexican revolution from 1913 to 1920."[81] But not well enough to prevent sustained armed opposition by Villistas, Zapatistas, Felicistas, and Pelaecistas, not to mention extensive banditry, labor unrest, congressional opposition, military dissent, the political hijacking of his draft constitution, and his final—remarkably quick and easy—overthrow in 1920.[82]

Much of the evidence of direct Carrancista instigation and manipulation derives from American sources of dubious reliability: spies, agents (and

double agents), fantasists, opportunists, police informants, fearful witnesses, inept forgers, hyperbolic journalists, and the occasional drunk.[83] At
times—perhaps more often than they care to admit—historians who rely on
this sort of questionable evidence are groping their way through a "cloud of
obfuscation."[84] And, as a general historical rule, we should be leery of conspiracy theories that posit Machiavellian central control of highly diverse and
dynamic movements, especially in a context of revolution. Revolutions and
insurgencies are inherently uncontrollable (especially, we might add, when
no "vanguard party" claims to be at the helm), and thus it is entirely possible that Carranza and some of his subordinates sought to take advantage of—
perhaps, here and there, to provoke—violence and subversion along the
border;[85] but to believe that they controlled such processes in the United
States, when they were unable even to control much of Mexico, is stretching
things.

Even this qualified claim, however, runs up against the logic of cui bono.
Would the Carrancista cause be served by allowing mayhem along the Rio
Grande? U.S. recognition depended on the Carrancistas' claim to be a capable
and legitimate government (which is why Villa's raid on Columbus proved such
an embarrassment). And American recognition was granted, as Secretary of
State Lansing cogently argued, because the Carrancistas stood the best chance
of bringing order to Mexico and making U.S. intervention, which Germany
hoped would occur, unnecessary (here, the German factor *was* significant).[86]
There is no clear evidence that the Wilson administration justified recognition
on the grounds that it would stop Carranza from inciting trouble in Texas; indeed, it would have been strange if the administration had believed as much.[87]

As the old Mexican dicho says, "en río revuelto, ganancia de pescadores"
(turbulent river, fishermen's bonanza). Among the fishermen, in this instance,
were common bandits, who certainly took advantage of the prevalent upheaval;
desperate Mexicans (including defeated Villistas), for whom cross-border raiding offered a possible escape from hard times; Carrancista leaders who, for reasons of ideology or profit, may have wanted to make trouble for the Americans;
and—though I think we can largely discard this hypothesis—the devious plotters of the Imperial German government. But, amid the "cloud of obfuscation,"
I do not think we can convincingly claim that the Plan of San Diego and its associated violence were primarily the work of Carranza and his henchmen.

In contrast, the evidence of "domestic" ("bottom-up Texan") motives and
causes is very clear, albeit rather beyond the scope of this chapter, as well as
my own expertise. In short, I would incline to a "bottom-up" rather than "top-
down" explanation, stressing decentralized dynamics within Texas (ethnic
tensions, aggravated by the example of—and spillover from—revolutionary
Mexico). That does not, of course, rule out "top-down" involvement, whether

by Carranza or Nafarrate or other Mexican leaders; but it means that, at most, they took advantage of events that they neither initiated nor controlled. Finally, regarding outcome, the "bottom-up Texan" focus is clearly crucial: the border violence of 1915 led, as mentioned, to over three hundred deaths (many by lynching or summary execution),[88] a "mass exodus" from the valley, especially on the part of fearful Tejanos,[89] and substantial destruction of property. It also left a legacy of ethnic tension and discrimination which lasted long after the Revolution had given way to stability south of the border.

The Punitive Expedition, finally, was the most serious and prolonged American intervention in Mexico during the Revolution. It involved U.S. forces—initially five thousand strong, soon rising to eleven thousand—penetrating 350 miles into northern Mexico, it cost twenty-seven American and up to three hundred Mexican lives, and it brought the United States and Mexico close to outright war.[90] However, neither side wanted war. Wilson had an election to fight in November 1916, so he could hardly sit on his hands when Villista raiders had brazenly shot up Columbus.[91] But, as had been made clear in 1914, Wilson had no desire to launch a full-scale intervention south of the Río Bravo, especially as the European war increasingly absorbed American resources and attention. Carranza, on the other hand, controlled—very shakily and partially—a war-weary country suffering social and economic upheaval; as the Mexican response to the Zimmermann telegram of 1917 showed, a war with the United States was seen (correctly, I would add) as potentially disastrous.[92]

Both leaders therefore wanted to limit the scale of the conflict and instructed their respective commanders accordingly. American and Mexican (Carrancista) representatives continued intermittent negotiations through the spring of 1916. Following clashes at Parral (April 1916) and Carrizal (June 1916)—the latter caused by the gung-ho belligerence of an American officer on the spot—both sides agreed to Pan-American mediation.[93] That mediation failed to find a mutually acceptable solution, but it helped defuse the crisis, thus ensuring that a major war was averted. Wilson now hoped that a continued American military presence in Mexico through the latter part of 1916 would encourage Carranza to curtail Villa's depredations, while inducing the Carrancistas, who were now engaged in drawing up their new Constitution, to adopt moderate policies congenial to American interests. In other words, the expedition's original punitive and policing role now gave way to a more calculated, even cynical, rationale: that of deradicalizing Mexican domestic politics.[94] But in this, the expedition was even more unsuccessful: American pressure failed and the Constitution emerged as a more radical document than even Carranza had planned. In January 1917, the expedition withdrew, and a month later, the new Constitution was promulgated.

Though neither side wanted a war, neither could afford to appear too weak, either. Wilson, facing reelection in November 1916 as well as red-blooded demands for intervention from, among others, the Hearst press,[95] needed a robust response to Columbus (ideally, the capture or killing of Pancho Villa), without precipitating a major confrontation with the Carrancistas, while Carranza, much as he would have liked to see the elimination of Villa, could not allow a sizable American army to roam around Chihuahua as it pleased. Thus, the Carrancistas denied the American forces use of Mexican railways, forcing them to rely on horses and mules, trucks and cars.[96] And, perhaps given his lackluster record when it came to social reform, Carranza had always displayed a stiff-necked nationalism in his dealings with the United States, which he maintained throughout 1916, insisting on the unconditional withdrawal of the expedition.[97] There were, in consequence, several clashes, notably at Parral and Carrizal.

Local Mexican opinion was, in general, hostile, as Pershing regularly complained, although some Mexicans—including the Namiquipenses—did good business providing the Americans with supplies; but Mexicans were hostile more because they resented an American invasion than because they were firmly wedded to the Villista cause.[98] The latter, as already mentioned, was in decline and, as the Punitive Expedition wound its way through Chihuahua, Villa, who had been seriously wounded in the knee and needed crutches, lay low. In fact, having come off worse in initial clashes with American forces, the Villistas avoided contact (the Parral and Carrizal clashes involved Carrancista forces); hence the futility of the expedition became clear. In the end, having secured his own reelection (and discovered that Carranza's government was not amenable to coercive threats), Wilson withdrew the expedition in January 1917, its basic mission unfulfilled. Three months later— as many had foreseen—the United States entered the First World War.

Villa therefore lived to fight another day—in fact, to fight another three years, until, as we have seen, he was amnestied (and paid off with a handsome hacienda) in 1920. During those three years, his hit-and-run raids perturbed Chihuahua and, in 1919, provoked a minor armed American incursion, when U.S. troops briefly occupied Juárez. But this was the last incursion of its kind: thereafter—despite a worrisome war scare in 1927—the United States refrained from coercive measures against Mexico and, quite sensibly and effectively, came to rely on peaceful methods (the so-called diplomacy of ham-and-eggs) to rebuild its relationship with the new Mexico that had arisen from the ashes of the armed revolution.[99]

———

What, to sum up, were the impact and legacy of this violent decade (as regards the border)? The border played a crucial role in the armed revolution, especially in bouts 1 and 2; it would be a plausible, if unprovable, contention that without border resources—commodity exports and arms imports—the Constitutionalist revolution against Huerta might have failed, and certainly would have been much slower and more difficult. The ensuing victory of the norteños/fronterizos, above all the Sonorans, who set their stamp on Mexico in the 1920s and 1930s, was thus in some measure a product of events that took place along the border in 1910–15, as well as reflecting long-standing features of northern/borderland society (notably, resentment of "the center" and a familiarity with violence). Sonoran-style state-building, anticlericalism, labor policy, and (qualified) economic nationalism all flowed from this *fons et origo*. It could be said, therefore, that the norteños/fronterizos' contribution to the armed revolution—the blood and treasure they expended, especially during 1910–15—were well-rewarded.

Like much of Mexico (Yucatán being a notable exception), the northern borderlands suffered heavily from the fighting, material destruction, and economic dislocation.[100] The northern railways, the arteries of conventional warfare, were hard hit; and stock raising took decades to recover.[101] Mining, however, soon revived, helped by wartime demand in the United States; and American demand also boosted the thriving border vice industry (gambling, liquor, and prostitution), especially when army and National Guard units were mobilized along the border.[102] Migration to the United States also took off during this decade, with both "push" and "pull" factors playing their part.

Despite recurrent U.S.-Mexican altercations—and occasional violent confrontations, such as Parral and Carrizal—relations between the two countries were, if anything, strengthened by the Revolution (and the coincidental eclipse of Europe brought on by World War I). Indeed, if we stand back and review the decade, it is less the scale and severity of cross-border violence than its limited and controlled character that is more striking (a conclusion that is all the stronger if we accept the "bottom-up Texan" interpretation of the lower Rio Grande troubles). American investment in Mexico, especially northern Mexico, did not cease and the Sonorans, for all their chippy nationalism, were keen to promote close economic ties to the United States, not least to their own personal benefit. One indicator of the Revolution's positive legacy was demographic: while Morelos—the land of Zapata—suffered a 40 percent fall in its population (the result of constant fighting, harsh repression, disease, and out-migration), the population of Chihuahua, Pancho Villa's stamping ground, remained roughly constant (406,000 in 1910, 402,000 in 1921, the latter figure probably an underestimate). Juárez, for all its revolutionary vicissitudes, grew at over 5 percent a year during the 1910s, its population nearly doubling during the decade, from 10,600 to 19,500.[103] On the other side of the border, the combination of Villista raids, the Plan de San Diego, and the Anglo backlash produced unprecedented levels of violence, as already mentioned, leaving a legacy of ethnic polarization.[104]

As for the Punitive Expedition, it has plausibly been described as the last of the United States' "traditional cavalry" operations of the kind that had won the West, before being deployed in colonial settings in Cuba and the Philippines.[105] But in its pioneering use of airplanes and motor vehicles, it also foreshadowed later armed conflicts, while furthering the careers of future war-leaders like Pershing and Patton. In the short term, it provided the United States, about to enter World War I, with valuable military experience (chiefly in respect of mobilization and logistics: the nature of the fighting was, of course, entirely different). And, given the supposed failures of the U.S. Army in Mexico, the German High Command rashly concluded that it could risk U.S. belligerence by resorting to unrestricted submarine warfare in the North Atlantic, since, taking into account its performance in Mexico, "the US army was not a force to be seriously reckoned with."[106] Indirectly, Mexican border violence thus contributed to violence on a far greater scale in Europe.

Notes

1. Robert McCaa, "The Missing Millions: The Demographic Costs of the Mexican Revolution," *Mexican Studies/Estudios Mexicanos* 19, no. 2 (Summer 2003): 367–400, cogently argues for a very high death toll during the 1910s, with battlefield deaths approaching half a million. I would defend this conclusion against those who downplay the demographic costs, especially those caused by the fighting: see Alan Knight, "Guerra total: México y Europa, 1914," *Historia Mexicana* 64, no. 4 (2015): 1583–1666. International comparisons also confirm the high mortality of the Revolution: D. O. Wilkinson, *Deadly Quarrels: Lewis F. Richardson and the Statistical Study of War* (Berkeley: University of California Press, 1980), 12, 132–33.

2. I put "bandits" in quotation marks because, of course, the distinction between (political) rebels, "social" bandits, and "mercenary" bandits tends to be highly subjective; that said, I think all three categories are "real" and useful, in the sense of denoting actual individuals and their activities.

3. Alan Knight, "War, Violence and Homicide in Modern Mexico," in *Murder and Violence in Latin America*, ed. Eric A. Johnson, Ricardo D. Salvatore, and Pieter Spierenburg (Chichester: John Wiley/BLAR, 2013), 12–48, in which I differentiate (i) "political" violence (incurred in the pursuit of political goals) from (ii) "mercenary" (usually criminal) violence, which is premised on the pursuit of profit, and (iii) "interpersonal" violence, including, for example, violence within families, between neighbors, or in centers of sociability, such as cantinas. The first two are primarily "instrumental" (goal oriented); the third tends to be "affective." I further divide "political" violence into "macro" and "micro," depending on the scale and goals of the conflict. Much of what I discuss in this chapter is "macropo-

litical," because it relates to the conquest and control of state power, rather than low-level skirmishing within an existing state structure (as would occur in Mexico in the 1920s and 1930s). I also mention examples of "mercenary" violence but say nothing about the more elusive—though important—phenomenon of "interpersonal" violence.

4. There were several American troop mobilizations along the border during 1910–14, but the only major armed intervention by the United States—the occupation of the port of Veracruz in April 1914—occurred far away on the Gulf coast; it therefore falls outside my geographical remit. From 1915, as I discuss below, things changed and cross-border violence greatly increased, including a major American invasion of northern Mexico (the Punitive Expedition of 1916–17).

5. Depending on how we choose to define the border (see note 16), we could also include Francisco Madero's Plan of San Luis (October 1910), which signaled the start of the Revolution, since, despite its name, it was promulgated in San Antonio, Texas.

6. Born in Durango, Villa ardently proclaimed his Chihuahuan identity: Friedrich Katz, *The Life and Times of Pancho Villa* (Stanford, CA: Stanford University Press, 1998), 206, 588; on the respective "nuclei," see Katz, *Life and Times of Pancho Villa*, 562; and Knight, "Guerra total," 1631.

7. Héctor Aguilar Camín, *La frontera nómada: Sonora y la Revolución mexicana* (México: Siglo XXI, 1977).

8. Jean Meyer, *The Cristero Rebellion* (Cambridge: Cambridge University Press, 1976); on the northern proconsuls and their often unpopular rule in the south, see Alan Knight, *The Mexican Revolution* (Cambridge: Cambridge University Press, 1986), 2:240–51.

9. For example, Ciro B. Ceballos, a Carrancista intellectual hack, claimed that the *fronterizos* were "summoned to be the rulers of all the inhabitants of the country in the future," even though contact with the lesser breeds of the center and south might lead to "the degeneration . . . of the essential conditions of their present undisputed racial superiority": Knight, *Mexican Revolution*, 2:236, citing a press article from January 1916.

10. On the origins and nature of Vasconcelos's *pochismo* (the allegedly bastard culture of Americanized Mexicans in the borderlands and beyond), see Alejandra Sánchez Valencia, "Nortismo y pochismo: La antimexicanidad según Vasconcelos," *Tema y variaciones de literatura* 33 (2009): 65–76. Though born in Oaxaca, Vasconcelos spent seven formative years on the border, where his father worked in the Piedras Negras customs service and, between the ages of seven and fourteen, José attended school across the border in Eagle Pass, an experience that contributed to his critique of *pochismo* and elevation of Mexican and Latin American values over North American materialism. As Mauricio Tenorio-Trillo forcefully puts it, Vasconcelos's "hatred of gringos and Protestants came from the border": "On *La Frontera* and Cultures of Consumption: An Essay of Images," in Alexis McCrossen, *Land of Necessity: Consumer Culture in the United States–Mexico Borderlands* (Durham, NC: Duke University Press, 2009), 351.

11. Knight, *Mexican Revolution*, 2:17, citing Huertista press reports for March–May 1913.

12. Marco Antonio Samaniego, *Nacionalismo y revolución: Los acontecimientos de 1911 en Baja California* (Tijuana: Centro Cultural Tijuana, 2008) is an excellent recent study of the 1911 revolution in Baja California, which explodes several myths and demonstrates, among other things, a robust nationalist resistance to American filibusters.

13. Apart from a passing comparison, the Zapatistas will not figure in this account, for obvious reasons. For the sake of simplicity, I use the standard (personalized) factional

labels, Villistas versus Carrancistas, without getting involved in alternative labels, such as "Conventionists" and "Constitutionalists."

14. Knight, "Guerra total" analyzes this process in greater detail.

15. For the Villistas, at least. The Carrancistas' arms and ammunition chiefly came by sea to the Gulf coast, though the origin was still the United States.

16. "Along the northern border" is suitably vague: it may be useful to distinguish between, on the one hand, the five (Mexican) "border" states (Sonora, Chihuahua, Coahuila, Nuevo León, and Tamaulipas) plus the federal territory of Baja California Norte and on the other, the "borderlands" or the (international) "frontier," which would denote a narrower strip hugging the border. While it is difficult to define the latter (is the definition political, economic, or cultural?), it is clear that the border towns, from Tijuana in the west to Brownsville in the east, form part of this strip, in demographic and economic terms much the most important part. It should be added that the term *norteño*, while it encompasses all of the above, might for some purposes be stretched (southward) to include, for example, Durango and Sinaloa.

17. I omit "nationalism and xenophobia" because while they played a part, they were significantly less important in the gestation of the Revolution, as was anticlericalism.

18. The relatively new phenomenon of sharp market recession was compounded, in 1908–10, by the ancient scourge of drought, poor harvests, and high food prices: Katz, *Life and Times of Pancho Villa*, 48–49, 58–59.

19. Rodney D. Anderson, *Outcasts in Their Own Land: Mexican Industrial Workers, 1906–1911* (DeKalb: Northern Illinois University Press, 1976), chaps. 3 and 4. As a very rough indicator, we could note that (probably) eighteen workers were killed at Cananea, compared with sixty (or possibly many more) at Río Blanco; Anderson, *Outcasts in Their Own Land*, 111, 167–69.

20. The Yaqui Indians of Sonora are a signal exception: they were not subjected to debt-peonage, but because of their protracted struggle for land and regional autonomy, they incurred severe repression, legitimated by racist discourse: Aguilar Camín, *La frontera nómada*, 46–55.

21. The best example came in early 1913, when the northwestern state of Sonora pioneered the successful Constitutionalist revolt against General Victoriano Huerta, who had just seized power in Mexico City. Sonora was not only far removed from the capital (Hermosillo, the state capital, lay 1,200 miles away); there was also no direct railway connection, so troops had to be sent either overland through the Tepic gap on horseback or by sea. This gave the Sonorenses a crucial window of opportunity in which to organize their forces. Chihuahua and Coahuila, also sites of northern resistance to Huerta, lacked these advantages.

22. A "rich fighting tradition," in the words of Katz, *Life and Times of Pancho Villa*, 96.

23. Katz, *Life and Times of Pancho Villa*, 32–38; Daniel Nugent, *Spent Cartridges of Revolution: An Anthropological Study of Namiquipa, Chihuahua* (Chicago: University of Chicago Press, 1993).

24. President Díaz later opined that "the good breed of the Chihuahua horses" was the key to revolutionary success in 1911 (a somewhat reductionist explanation, not to say excuse). And the best horses were said to be found on the Zuloaga family estate. In addition, rebel leaders like Orozco and Villa were, reputedly, crack shots: see Katz, *Life and Times of Pancho Villa*, 75–76, 81, 96, 288–89, 304.

25. On Ortega's background, see Katz, *Life and Times of Pancho Villa*, 33–34; much of what we know about Ortega and Cuchillo Parado derives from the pioneering work of María Teresa Koreck, only parts of which have been published.

26. Raul A. Fernandez, *The United States–Mexico Border: A Politico-Economic Profile* (Notre Dame, IN: University of Notre Dame Press, 1977), chap. 4, which (p. 90) gives figures showing that by 1902 Sonora and Chihuahua alone had $49 million of U.S. mining investment, a little over half of the total U.S. mining investment in Mexico.

27. Thus, as Katz, *Life and Times of Pancho Villa*, 11, suggests, the Porfiriato witnessed a transition "from the frontier to the border." The same point is made, with "transnationalism" thrown in, by Samuel Truett, "Transnational Warrior: Emilio Kosterlitzky and the Transformation of the U.S.-Mexican Borderlands, 1873–1928," in *Continental Crossroads: Remapping U.S.–Mexican Borderlands History*, ed. Samuel Truett and Elliott Young (Durham, NC: Duke University Press, 2004), 259. This semantic distinction, between the "frontier" as an area of fluid settlement (à la Frederick Jackson Turner) and the "border" as an international line, works in English but not in Spanish, where *frontera* serves for both (though the "the [international] border" could also be rendered as *la línea* [internacional]). For further semantic observations, note Tenorio-Trillo, "On *La Frontera* and Cultures of Consumption," 336–38.

28. In August 1913, U.S. armed forces along the border numbered only four thousand, about one-third the size of the NYPD: Linda B. Hall and Don M. Coerver, *Revolution on the Border: The United States and Mexico, 1910–20* (Albuquerque: University of New Mexico Press, 1988), 50. True, these numbers fluctuated greatly, depending on events in Mexico and reactions in Washington (and Austin). President Taft had briefly mobilized twenty thousand troops for border duties in spring 1911, and as mentioned below, there was a much bigger and more lasting buildup in 1916–17. The celebrated Texas Rangers— "underpaid and under-strength"—were also thin on the ground (numbering barely a dozen in 1910); but the border troubles, especially the interethnic violence that afflicted Texas after 1915, boosted recruitment (up to one thousand), without necessarily improving quality and competence: see Charles H. Harris and Louis R. Sadler, *The Texas Rangers and the Mexican Revolution: The Bloodiest Decade, 1910–20* (Albuquerque: University of New Mexico Press, 2004), 502, 504. On interagency squabbles, which President Wilson appears to have exacerbated, see Hall and Coerver, *Revolution on the Border*, 20, 22, and James A. Sandos, *Rebellion in the Borderlands: Anarchism and the Plan of San Diego, 1904–23* (Norman: University of Oklahoma Press, 1992), 86–87.

29. For a good overview of the Porfirian army in 1910–11, see Santiago Portilla, *Una sociedad en armas: Insurrección antireeleccionista en México, 1910–11* (México: El Colegio de México, 1995), 397–406.

30. The U.S. neutrality laws required that exiles planning armed incursions into Mexico had to be caught in flagrante delicto, that is, crossing into Mexico while under arms. Political activism per se was not illegal. This gave revolutionaries like Madero ample leeway, especially when they enjoyed local support. Porfirian observers—including spies, informers, and private detectives—concluded, often wrongly, that the U.S. authorities were therefore actively sponsoring subversion. It does, however, seem likely that those authorities were more disposed to crack down on radical revolutionary groups—such as the anarcho-syndicalist Magonistas, allies of American leftist groups including the Industrial Workers of the World (IWW)—than on middle-of-the-road activists like Madero. Though

the matter remains hotly debated, I am of the opinion that Taft and Wilson generally played by the letter of law and that up to early 1914, U.S. government informal connivance with Mexican revolutionaries was neither significant nor consequential: see Knight, *Mexican Revolution*, 1:184–86. Of course, by 1914 Wilson had adopted an overtly pro-revolutionary position, and three years later, the neutrality laws were substantially tightened up (as a result of World War I rather than the Mexican Revolution). See Hall and Coerver, *Revolution on the Border*, 17, 19; W. Dirk Raat, *Revoltosos: Mexico's Rebels in the United States, 1903–1923* (College Station: Texas A&M University Press, 1981), chaps. 8 and 9; and P. A. R. Calvert, *The Mexican Revolution: The Diplomacy of Anglo-American Conflict, 1910–14* (Cambridge: Cambridge University Press, 1968), 73–84.

31. "While some arms were smuggled from the United States to the revolutionaries [in 1910–11], the number was small—certainly not sufficient to equip the many men who had rallied to Madero's call for revolt": Katz, *Life and Times of Pancho Villa*, 92. See also Portilla, *Una sociedad en armas*, 323–26.

32. Katz, *Life and Times of Pancho Villa*, 77, 93; Portilla, *Una sociedad en armas*, chap. 5.

33. At Juárez, as Madero related, the rebels had to blast their way through the town, avoiding open fire, until "our hand grenades had become more effective than their cannon, machine guns and Maussers": Katz, *Life and Times of Pancho Villa*, 110–11. The *máquina loca* trick was successfully repeated by Villa in his decisive—and perhaps fortunate—defeat of Huerta's federal army at Tierra Blanca in November 1913: see Katz, *Life and Times of Pancho Villa*, 227–28, and I. Thord-Grey, *Gringo Rebel: Mexico, 1913–14* (Coral Gables, FL: University of Miami Press, 1960), 53. When it came to manufacturing dynamite bombs—and even some primitive artillery—the mining camps of the Mexican north were well provided with workshops, explosives, and skilled workers, most of them sympathetic to the revolutionary cause: Hall and Coerver, *Revolution on the Border*, 120.

34. Zapata's army was the biggest of those raised, in roughly similar circumstances, in central Mexico. At its peak—for example, when attacking Chilpancingo in March 1914—that army (briefly) reached five thousand, although arming them adequately proved difficult and, especially as the rains came and planting began, Zapatista soldiers tended to return to their villages: John Womack Jr., *Zapata and the Mexican Revolution* (New York: Knopf, 1969), 181–82. Villa's División del Norte, at its peak, was some ten times larger; furthermore, Villa was well aware that a wholesale *reparto* (land distribution) might result in the dispersal and disintegration of his army, so unlike Zapata, he stalled on land reform: Katz, *Life and Times of Pancho Villa*, 524, 541.

35. Hall and Coerver, *Revolution on the Border*, 142–43.

36. Hall and Coerver, *Revolution on the Border*, 146, 148; Katz, *Life and Times of Pancho Villa*, 212; Portilla, *Una sociedad en armas*, 324.

37. Including "desperate picaroons . . . with the sporting instinct of skunks," who sold illegal weaponry, cash up front, then tipped off the authorities: Thord-Grey, *Gringo Rebel*, 89.

38. The U.S. secretary of war reckoned, in 1911, that 80 percent of "the Mexican population on both sides of the river" were for the Revolution: Hall and Coerver, *Revolution on the Border*, 145.

39. Regarding opinion in northern Mexico, see Knight, *Mexican Revolution*, 1:182–83, which suggests very high (95 percent) levels of support for the Revolution.

40. It may be objected that firsthand experience of the politics of South Texas—as practiced, for example, by the "notorious" Archie Parr of Duval County—would hardly inspire affection for American-style democracy. However, Parr, like other Texas bosses of his generation, did, of necessity, incorporate Hispanic voters and elites into his political machine, in which respect, it could be said, his brand of bossism foreshadowed that of the Mexican Partido Revolucionario Institucional (the party which ruled Mexico for much of the twentieth century) more than it emulated the contemporary Porfiriato: see Evan Anders, *Boss Rule in South Texas: The Progressive Era* (Austin: University of Texas Press, 1982), chap. 9.

41. During the 1910–11 Maderista revolt, Antonio Villareal managed to make off with a brass cannon from an El Paso public park; though it got to Mexico, there is no evidence that it served any useful purpose. Two years later, in October 1913, when Villa successfully attacked Torreón, he had only two cannon; however, that victory brought a haul of eleven more field-pieces, including "a huge gun known as El Niño," which—"the darling of the army"—accompanied Villa on his subsequent campaigns, transported on a railway flatcar: Knight, *Mexican Revolution*, 1:200; Katz, *Life and Times of Pancho Villa*, 222; John Reed, *Insurgent Mexico* (New York: D. Appleton, 1914), 201, 248, 253.

42. Official figures of U.S. firearms (including ammunition) exports to Mexico show a pronounced increase (in terms of current dollar values): 1913: $269,014; 1914: $488,274; 1915: $1,280,442: Hall and Coerver, *Revolution on the Border*, 157. Apart from excluding contraband, these figures cover all firearms exports to Mexico, to all purchasers and by all routes (i.e., by sea as well as land). Though Villa's campaigns in Chihuahua were the most decisive, Lucio Blanco's seizure of Matamoros, at the mouth of the Rio Grande, in June 1913 also provided a border port through which, especially once the U.S. arms embargo was lifted, arms could flow to the rebels.

43. Womack, *Zapata*, 247–48.

44. Hall and Coerver, *Revolution on the Border*, 154–55.

45. Knight, *Mexican Revolution*, 2:117–18; Reed, *Insurgent Mexico*, 1–8. The camp at Fort Bliss was, incidentally, the closest thing to a "POW camp" witnessed during the Mexican Revolution, even though it was not actually in Mexico.

46. Aguilar Camín, *La frontera nómada*, pt. 3.

47. Katz, *Life and Times of Pancho Villa*, 211, 218, 314–15.

48. Katz, *Life and Times of Pancho Villa*, 318–19, 320–26; Clarence C. Clendenen, *The United States and Pancho Villa: A Study in Unconventional Diplomacy* (Ithaca, NY: Cornell University Press, 1961); Margarita de Orellana, *Filming Pancho Villa: How Hollywood Shaped the Mexican Revolution* (London: Verso, 2009).

49. Charles C. Cumberland, *The Mexican Revolution: The Constitutionalist Years* (Austin: University of Texas Press, 1972), 111–13. González launched an ill-considered assault on Nuevo Laredo on New Year's Day 1914; after it failed, the Federals retained the town until April.

50. Katz, *Life and Times of Pancho Villa*, 307, refers to the battle of Torreón as a "siege," which is correct in that it involved the Division of the North advancing on, investing, and, after some eleven days of fierce fighting, capturing a city whose defenses had been well prepared by a capable Federal commander (see also Cumberland, *Mexican Revolution*, 115–17; and Reed, *Insurgent Mexico*, 220–58). Clearly, it was not a siege comparable to, say, Verdun in 1916; Torreón's defenses and lines of supply were simply too inadequate.

51. Knight, "Guerra total," 1632–33, 1640–41.

52. Jorge Ibargüengoitia, *Los relámpagos de agosto* (México: Joaquín Mortiz, 1998 [1964]), chap. 15, where the inept rebel generals, whose desperate strategy hinges on attacking the border town of "Pacotas," are warned by the U.S. consul that "if a single bullet falls on the other side of the river, the US Government will declare war on Mexico"; unfortunately, recalls our hero/narrator, "our plan of attack presupposed an opening bombardment, such that not just a single bullet, but thousands, would fall on the other side." And for want of an attack, the town and the rebellion were lost.

53. Katz, *Life and Times of Pancho Villa*, 110; Hall and Coerver, *Revolution on the Border*, 20–21. The Baja California revolt of 1911 also drew crowds of American spectators, who were prepared to pay 25 cents to tour the Tijuana battlefield: Rachel St. John, "Selling the Border: Trading Land, Attracting Tourists and Marketing American Consumption on the Baja California Border, 1900–34," in McCrossen, ed., *Land of Necessity*, 120–21.

54. Hall and Coerver, *Revolution on the Border*, 31–32.

55. Katz, *Life and Times of Pancho Villa*, 525–26. Searchlights, which had also been successfully used by the Carrancistas in their defense of El Ebano earlier that year, were important because Villa made a habit of launching night attacks, a tactic he had developed back in the days when the rebels were outgunned by Huerta's federals. But, like many of Villa's tactics, what had worked against Huerta's federal conscripts proved costly when used against well-equipped revolutionary veterans.

56. C. Folsom to R. Lansing, November 29, 1915, SD 812.00/16903, State Department, RG 59, giving details of Villa's proclaimed allegations, which became a staple of Villista rhetoric: for example, Montague, El Paso, to State, October 11, 1916, SD 812.00/19536, describes Villistas haranguing local people thus: "There is no such thing as disagreement of political parties anymore, but just the saving of the country from American intervention." Villa's grievance against the United States is understandable; however, his belief in American territorial ambitions, which seems to have been genuine rather than purely propagandistic, was based on pretty tenuous evidence and certainly did not reflect the policy of the Wilson administration: Katz, *Life and Times of Pancho Villa*, 505–10, 529–32.

57. Hall and Coerver, *Revolution on the Border*, 154–55, which notes that in 1915–16 border trade "dropped almost 50 percent, not recovering to its 1913–14 levels until the end of the decade."

58. Which must surely be the biggest (alleged) theft in criminal history. See Charles H. Harris and Luis R. Sadler, *The Plan de San Diego: Tejano Rebellion, Mexican Intrigue* (Lincoln: University of Nebraska Press, 2013), 1.

59. The Carrancista army had managed to beat the Villistas in major conventional battles during 1915, but between 1916 and 1920, in both Villista Chihuahua and Zapatista Morelos, as well as many other pockets of the country, it was committed to counterinsurgency campaigns that were long, hard, and usually inglorious, involving an elusive enemy who often held the initiative. In consequence, the Carrancista forces came to acquire many of the faults of the old Porfirian army (indeed, we could say, of most armies engaged in such campaigns): low morale, corruption, high desertion rates, and maltreatment of the civilian population. Not that the rump Villista forces were any better.

60. Katz, *Life and Times of Pancho Villa*, 518, 532 (war-weariness); 561, 572, 585, 624, 630 (the *leva*). When Villa briefly occupied Torreón in December 1916, still declaiming against "the gringos [who] . . . are the cause of the present struggles," a crowd of *pelados* (hicks)

gathered to gawk; they were immediately rounded up, and the able-bodied were drafted into his ragtag army: Hanna, Monterrey, to State, January 12, 1917, SD 812.00/20271.

61. Katz, *Life and Times of Pancho Villa*, 634 (gang rape at Namiquipa), 626 (massacre of Chinese), 532 (killing of defensa social of San Pedro de las Cuevas). Hostetter, Hermosillo, to State, December 27, 1916, SD 812.00/17053, reports Villa giving his men the green light for sacking towns in Sonora; at San Pedro de las Cuevas, eighteen men were allegedly shot and many women raped; at the mining town of La Colorada, sixteen Chinese were killed, some (again, allegedly) pulled apart by horses.

62. Katz, *Life and Times of Pancho Villa*, 623 (quote), 517–19 (elite Villista defections). An additional reason for such defections was Villa's increasingly trigger-happy treatment of erstwhile comrades who he felt had let him down in his hour of need (for example, his old bandit sidekick, Tomás Urbina). Of course, while many Villista defectors could seek sanctuary in the United States, even if it meant a life of genteel poverty for the likes of Felipe Angeles and Rafael Buelna, Villa did not have that option, given both the Columbus raid and previous alleged killings, such as that of British rancher William Benton. Thus, when Buffalo Bill's Wild West Show—supposedly—offered Villa a starring role, he was in no position to accept. See Katz, *Life and Times of Pancho Villa*, 522–23 (execution of Urbina), 552 (legacy of the Benton case), 520–21 (Angeles and Buelna), 535 (Buffalo Bill). Regarding Rafael Buelna, it is interesting to note that, his attempt at running a restaurant in El Paso having failed (the "burly former revolutionaries whom [he] employed did not make deferential waiters" and Buelna "did not have it in his heart to refuse meals when exiled revolutionaries with no money asked for food"), Buelna returned to the revolutionary fray in Mexico in 1923 and died in battle. Angeles, too, returned to Mexico in 1918 and was captured, court-martialed, and executed.

63. On the Santa Ysabel massacre, see Katz, *Life and Times of Pancho Villa*, 557–60; and Clarence C. Clendenen, *Blood on the Border: The United States Army and the Mexican Irregulars* (Toronto: Macmillan, 1969), 196–98. According to U.S. military sources, Villa had sworn to "get even" with the Americans; and reports of anti-American declarations and actions came thick and fast from late 1915: report of General Funston, Nogales, November 30, 1915, SD 812.00/16893; Bevan, Tampico, to State and Carothers, El Paso, to State, November 18, 1915, and November 26, 1915, SD 812.00/16857, 16860. While Villista anti-Americanism had some appeal, many northern Mexicans (a) no longer placed their faith in Villa and (b) retained friendly, or at least neutral, feelings toward Americans and American business interests, whose continuance in the Mexican north was economically vital: see Cobb, El Paso, November 27, 1915; Hanna, Monterrey, December 4, 1915, and March 17, 1916; and Blocker, Piedras Negras, April 15, 1916; all to State, SD 812.00/16902, 16945, 17517, 17876.

64. On the events of March 9, 1916, see Katz, *Life and Times of Pancho Villa*, 560–66; Hall and Coerver, *Revolution on the Border*, 59–56; and Clendenen, *Blood on the Border*, 200–209. One mystery that, to my mind, is never satisfactorily explained is how the Villistas, experienced fighters launching a surprise nighttime attack on an unsuspecting town, managed to lose over one hundred dead (Clendenen, 210, suggests as many as 130) out of a total of four hundred, while the American dead amounted to only seventeen, eleven soldiers and six civilians ("surprisingly low," as Clendenen observes, 205). Similar imbalances are evident when we consider the casualties arising during the Punitive Expedition of 1916–17, which were in the ratio of 10(Mexican):1(American): see note 90 below. Were the battle-hardened Villistas that inept or ill-armed, compared with their American opponents? Are the figures reliable?

65. On Villa's motives, see Katz, *Life and Times of Pancho Villa*, 550–57, and Alberto Calzadíaz Barrera, *Porque Villa atacó a Columbus: Intriga internacional* (Mexico: Editores Mexicanos Unidos, 1972).

66. Hence, the attackers sought out the culprit, but he had gone to El Paso for a dentist's appointment: Katz, *Life and Times of Pancho Villa*, 563, 564, 566.

67. James A. Sandos, "German Involvement in Northern Mexico, 1915–16: A New Look at the Columbus Raid," *Hispanic American Historical Review* 50, no. 1 (February 1970): 70–89; Katz, *Life and Times of Pancho Villa*, 555.

68. Katz, *Life and Times of Pancho Villa*, 588–90, 625, 629–33.

69. Hall and Coerver, *Revolution on the Border*, 41–42, who note that, in combating Yaqui raiders in 1918, the U.S. cavalry fought its "last Indian battle." Clendenen, *Blood on the Border*, 349–50, concurs and gives a fuller version.

70. On Villa's deal with Obregón and retirement at the Hacienda Canutillo, see Katz, *Life and Times of Pancho Villa*, 729–44.

71. Charles C. Cumberland, "Border Raids in the Lower Rio Grande Valley—1915," *Southwestern Historical Quarterly* 57, no. 3 (January 1954): 285–311, remains a useful and balanced overview. See also Hall and Coerver, *Revolution on the Border*, 23–24.

72. Alice Baumgartner, "'The Line of Positive Safety': The Violent Formation of the US-Mexican Border on the Rio Grande, 1848–78," M. Phil. thesis, St Antony's College, Oxford, 2013; on the major politico-revolutionary movement associated with Catarino Garza in 1891–93, see Elliott Young, *Catarino Garza's Revolt on the Texas-Mexico Border* (Durham, NC: Duke University Press, 2004).

73. Hall and Coerver, *Revolution on the Border*, 22–23, 53.

74. Harris and Sadler, *Plan de San Diego*, 2–4; Sandos, *Rebellion in the Borderlands*, 80–85. The Plan envisaged the possibility of two new states being set up (one Tejano, one Afro-American), with the proviso that the first might seek annexation to Mexico. Regarding the vexed question of ethnic nomenclature, I am following Johnson's lead in referring to people of Mexican origin or descent who reside in Texas as Tejanos: see Benjamin Heber Johnson, *Revolution in Texas: How a Forgotten Rebellion and Its Bloody Suppression Turned Mexicans into Americans* (New Haven, CT: Yale University Press, 2003), 2.

75. Harris and Sadler, *Plan de San Diego*, would be the best example of this Mexican/international perspective. Friedrich Katz, *The Secret War in Mexico: Europe, the United States, and the Mexican Revolution* (Chicago: University of Chicago Press, 1981), 340, sees the contrasting explanations in similar terms.

76. Johnson, *Revolution in Texas*, represents a recent and forthright version of the Texas/popular interpretation, though Sandos, *Rebellion in the Borderlands*, also stresses domestic (Texas/borderland) social and political factors. That I am not inventing divergent opinions is clear from Harris and Sadler's robust critique of Johnson (see *Plan de San Diego*, 28, 82, 102, 251). "Increasingly dominant" because, during the 1900s, the advent of railways, markets, land enclosure, and Anglo immigration had the effect of squeezing Tejano access to land, while reducing the political and economic status of Tejano ranchers: Johnson, *Revolution in Texas*, 26–37; David Montejano, *Anglos and Mexicans in the Making of Texas, 1836–1986* (Austin: University of Texas Press, 1987), chap. 5.

77. We should recall that in the years 1915–20, amid the backwash of the armed revolution, Mexico itself experienced endemic crime: rustling, robbery, and ("mercenary," i.e.,

distinctly "unsocial") banditry; it is not surprising that this criminal wave would spill over the border. Furthermore, by the later 1910s both Mexico and South Texas were awash with guns: see Knight, *Mexican Revolution*, 2:392–406; Knight, "War, Violence and Homicide," 39–40; and Johnson, *Revolution in Texas*, 38. Most historians agree that the Anglo backlash, including widespread repression by Texas Rangers, was much more deadly (resulting in some three hundred dead) than the original raids and rebellions (which perhaps killed twenty Anglos): Hall and Coerver, *Revolution on the Border*, 24; Johnson, *Revolution in Texas*, 119–20. Harris and Sadler, *Plan de San Diego*, 249–52, offer a review of opinions and estimates (some clearly inflated) and also settle on three hundred "Hispanic" deaths; not, they gratuitously add, a "mini-Holocaust."

78. Katz, *Life and Times of Pancho Villa*, 554; Harris and Sadler, *Plan de San Diego*, 10, 17, 25; however, the authors also suggest that Ramos's alleged Huertismo was "an elaborate cover story," 20. For a résumé of Huerta's abortive conspiracy, which briefly involved the exiled revolutionary caudillo, Pascual Orozco, and ended with Huerta's own death while Huerta was in custody at Fort Bliss, in January 1916, see George J. Rausch Jr., "The Exile and Death of Victoriano Huerta," *Hispanic American Historical Review* 42, no. 2 (1962): 113–15, and Victoria Lerner, "Estados Unidos frente a las conspiraciones fraguadas en su territorio por exiliados de la Revolución: El caso huertista frente al villista (1914–15)," *Estudios de Historia Moderna y Contemporánea* 19 (1999): 85–114. Space does not permit further discussion of these murky events. However, the Huerta and Orozco conspiracy had no chance of success; it was a minor sideshow, involving washed-up politicos who could not reconcile themselves to the dull obscurity of exile.

79. Harris and Sadler, *Plan de San Diego*, chap. 3; Sandos, *Rebellion in the Borderlands*, 80–81, 87–89. As Sandos makes clear (100), Ricardo Flores Magón himself scorned the plan as a "bourgeois invention" designed to distract from class exploitation.

80. In 1915, Carranza adopted a "strategy of creating crisis and chaos on the border so that the United States would recognize his regime in order to end this deplorable state of affairs," a strategy that "succeeded brilliantly." A year later, he sought to "repeat the coup," "reigniting the Texas Revolution" in order to "provide the leverage to secure the Punitive Expedition's withdrawal": Harris and Sadler, *Plan de San Diego*, 83, 124. All along, "Carranza played Woodrow Wilson like a violin" (84). Although the authors state that, with recognition, "the raids into Texas stopped" (85), they then record continued troubles along the Texas border in early 1916 (well before the Punitive Expedition set off), which led Secretary of State Lansing to recommend maintaining troop strength along the border (pages 117–18). We should add that Douglas Richmond, Carranza's charitable biographer, lends credence to this, the "top-down Mexican" explanation of events: Harris and Sadler, *Plan de San Diego*, 85; Douglas W. Richmond, *Venustiano Carranza's Nationalist Struggle, 1893–1920* (Lincoln: University of Nebraska Press, 1983), 201–2.

81. Harris and Sadler, *Plan de San Diego*, 97 and 258, citing U.S. FBI agent Robert Barnes (who, incidentally, is cited a good deal, so is presumably a source to be taken seriously). Nafarrate is a good example of a Carrancista maverick: militarily capable but ideologically radical, anti-American, and, like many of his kind, jealous of his local power, he gave aid and comfort to some border raiders, while promoting anti-American stories in the press; Carranza therefore finessed Nafarrate's removal from Matamoros to Tampico, replacing him by his own (reportedly pro-American) nephew, Alfredo Ricaut. At the same time,

Carranza sugared the pill by promoting Nafarrate to *divisionario* (general of division): Sandos, *Rebellion in the Borderlands*, 117–18, 122–23; Reynolds, El Paso, to State, November 4, 1915, SD 812.00/16820.

82. Given this odd notion of the Mexican Revolution and Carranza's role within it, it is interesting to note that one of Harris and Sadler's many criticisms of Johnson is that "unfortunately, Johnson does not understand the Mexican Revolution": *Plan de San Diego*, 102.

83. Harris and Sadler, *Plan de San Diego*, 46, 48, 96–98, 202, 211, 218.

84. Harris and Sadler, *Plan de San Diego*, 217.

85. Cumberland, "Border Raids," 298.

86. Mark T. Gilderhus, *Pan American Visions: Woodrow Wilson and the Western Hemisphere, 1913–21* (Tucson: University of Arizona Press), 64–65.

87. Katz, *Life and Times of Pancho Villa*, 529–30, while noting that "Wilson never explained why he had recognized Carranza," lists three determining factors: Carranza had "the upper hand" in Mexico; the United States needed "peace and stability" in Mexico in order to have a free hand in Europe; and Carranza had given assurances regarding the protection of American interests. There is no mention of the Texas border troubles, and all three concerns suggest that cross-border Carrancista subversion would have militated against, not in favor of, recognition. In a recent study of Ricardo Flores Magón, Claudio Lomnitz baldly asserts that the San Diego rebellion and its repression "led to U.S. recognition of Carranza": *The Return of Comrade Ricardo Flores Magón* (New York: Zone Books, 2014), 450. It would be truer to say, much more modestly, that Carranza's disposition to rein in border troublemakers like Nafarrate made his recognition by the United States (a recognition premised on quite different considerations) somewhat more palatable.

88. Harris and Sadler, *Plan de San Diego*, 70–71, 77–78, 80, 125; Johnson, *Revolution in Texas*, chap. 5.

89. Cumberland, "Border Raids," 301.

90. Useful overviews of the Punitive Expedition can be found in Hall and Coerver, *Revolution on the Border*, chap. 5, and Clendenen, *Blood on the Border*, chaps. 11–14. I take casualty figures from Major John M. Cyrulik, "A Strategic Examination of the Punitive Expedition into Mexico," master's thesis, Fort Leavenworth, Kansas, 2003, 82, which gives 27 American and 273 Mexican dead (the latter, of course, an approximate estimate). The occupation of Veracruz by American forces in April 1914 was somewhat shorter, was clearly less "penetrative," and caused slightly fewer deaths on both sides (19 American and "at least 200" Mexican): Robert E. Quirk, *An Affair of Honor: Woodrow Wilson and the Occupation of Veracruz* (New York: W. W. Norton, 1967), 103.

91. Joseph P. Tumulty, *Woodrow Wilson as I Know Him* (New York: Doubleday, 1924), 156–57.

92. Thus, Obregón considered Zimmermann's offer to be "absurd": Katz, *Secret War in Mexico*, 364, 366.

93. Hall and Coerver, *Revolution on the Border*, 74–75.

94. T. Edward Haley, *Revolution and Intervention: The Diplomacy of Taft and Wilson with Mexico* (Cambridge, MA: MIT Press, 1970), 236–37. Katz, *Life and Times of Pancho Villa*, 578–79, describes U.S. policy as an attempt to "Cubanize" Mexico: that is, to impose a quasi-protectorate, including a veto on Mexican domestic policy. The tortuous U.S.-Mexican negotiations can be followed in Isidro Fabela, ed., *Historia diplomática de la Revolución mexicana, 1912–17* (Mexico: INEHRM, 2004 [1958/9]), chaps. 7–11.

95. Katz, *Life and Times of Pancho Villa*, 566.

96. The lack of railway transport was, therefore, a severe handicap, all the more galling since the United States had allowed Carrancista troops to travel by train through American territory in order to reinforce and defend Agua Prieta in late 1915: Hall and Coerver, *Revolution on the Border*, 64; Clendenen, *Blood on the Border*, 223–24.

97. The Villista político Roque Gonzalez Garza, representing the cause in Washington, jeered at Carranza for "having played the comedy of being the most nationalistic of Mexicans": Katz, *Life and Times of Pancho Villa*, 530.

98. Regarding Mexican hostility, see Clendenen, *Blood on the Border*, 230, 237–38, 253, 255, 260, 269, and, on Namiquipense collaboration, Clendenen, *Blood on the Border*, 253 and Katz, *Life and Times of Pancho Villa*, 574, 696.

99. Arnaldo Córdova, *La ideología de la Revolución mexicana* (México: Ediciones Era, 2003 [1973]), 379ff.

100. Not least among the problems faced by the Punitive Expedition was that it had to survive in a region that had been "blasted by war": Clendenen, *Blood on the Border*, 249.

101. Manuel A. Machado, *The North Mexican Cattle Industry, 1910–75: Ideology, Conflict and Change* (College Station: Texas A&M Press, 1981).

102. Hall and Coerver, *Revolution on the Border*, 156–57; for illustrative examples of how the border "vice" business grew, especially in Baja California, see Paul J. Vanderwood, *Satan's Playground: Mobsters and Movie Stars at America's Greatest Gaming Resort* (Durham, NC: Duke University Press, 2010), chap. 6, and Eric Michael Schantz, "All Night at the Owl: The Social and Political Relations of Mexicali's Red-Light District, 1909–25," in *On the Border: Society and Culture between the United States and Mexico*, ed. Andrew Grant Wood (Lanham, MD: SR Books, 2001), 91–143.

103. Oscar J. Martínez, *Border Boom Town: Ciudad Juárez since 1848* (Austin: University of Texas Press, 1978). The fact that Juárez, though the largest Mexican border town in 1910, had a population of barely ten thousand reminds us how small these communities were a century ago; today, Juárez has a population of about 1.5 million.

104. Johnson, *Revolution in Texas*; Montejano, *Anglos and Mexicans in the Making of Texas*, 117ff. One side effect was that the Texas Rangers were saved from extinction; however, their violent vigilantism provoked criticism and prompted the 1919 legislative investigation, cataloging the "abuse of power, partisan favoritism, brutality and unprovoked killings" for which they were responsible: Anders, *Boss Rule in South Texas*, 269.

105. Clendenen, *Blood on the Border*, 315.

106. Katz, *Life and Times of Pancho Villa*, 612.

PART IV

Drugs and Migrants

Figure 12.1 South Texas drug seizure by Border Patrol, aerial view, September 26, 2013. Photograph by Donna Burton.

Chapter 12

Narcos and Narcs

Violence and the Transformation of
Drug Trafficking at the Texas-Mexico Border

SANTIAGO IVAN GUERRA

It was December 31, 2003 in the rural border community of El Canton, Texas, when Joker Garcia was preparing to celebrate New Year's Eve alongside his girlfriend and close friends. At the time Joker was twenty-one, and he had been involved in the drug trade since the age of seventeen. He dropped out of high school because severe dyslexia made it impossible for him to continue to the next grade level. Joker had already worked for many years in the drug trade as a marijuana packer and a transporter driving drugs up to *conectas* (connections) in Houston, Texas. However, the majority of his work in the drug trade had centered on being a marijuana packer. At the time, he lived in a small one-room cinderblock building behind my uncle's house, where he compressed marijuana into blocks of various sizes. The purpose of Joker's work was to repackage large one-hundred-pound marijuana bundles into smaller strategically packaged blocks that could be hidden in *clavos*, hidden compartments in automobiles. Joker and some of his associates also tried to devise new ways to package drugs to ship past the Border Patrol checkpoints located within one hundred miles of the South Texas border, in order to reach the lucrative drug markets to the north.[1]

That New Year's Eve as Joker went out to celebrate, he left a large load of marijuana unattended in his *cuartito* (little room). When he returned in the early morning, he found that someone had broken in and taken the marijuana. Later, that afternoon, Joker's bosses picked him up and took him to a secluded ranch; his bosses were in fact former business partners and close relatives of his uncle Juan Garcia. They tortured him and beat him for several hours, expecting that he would own up to the fact that he himself stole the marijuana or at least turn in whomever he suspected of the theft. His bosses also accused Joker's brother Jay of having stolen the shipment, to which Joker replied: "Trayte a es culero pa' ca y si se las robo el, yo mismo me trueno al bastardo."[2] The bosses eventually brought Jay to the ranch, and tortured him as well. However, they could not prove that either Joker or Jay had stolen the pot. The bosses released both Joker and Jay, telling them "Si no hubiera sido tan buen amigo del difunto Blas, aqui me trueno a los dos."[3] Joker, however, was charged with the responsibility of packing marijuana for most of 2004 without pay in order to make up for the "lost" shipment. It was later revealed that Joker's own bosses had taken the "lost" shipment to teach him a lesson. This unfortunate incident served to keep Joker entangled in the complicated web of the drug trade, and furthermore to keep him in a state of constant fear and distrust.

While violence has played a significant role in the history of the U.S.-Mexico border, it has changed, spiking and diminishing, over time. In the case of drug smuggling on the border, violence is intertwined with varied changes in drug policy, border policing, international drug markets, and the growth and consolidation of drug trafficking organizations. For drug smugglers operating along this section of the Texas-Mexico border, violence initially had minimal impact on their contraband activities. However, as drug demand in the United States increased, the modern drug war took shape. Increased policing along the U.S.-Mexico border after Operation Intercept in 1969 generated increased competition for drug routes into the United States. Drug routes along the urban centers of the border generated the growth of well-known drug trafficking organizations in the cities of Juarez, Chihuahua, Tijuana, Baja California, Nuevo Laredo, Tamaulipas, and Matamoros Tamaulipas in Mexico. In the rural South Texas border region between Nuevo Laredo and Matamoros, Tamaulipas, smaller, and lesser known, drug trafficking organizations used their intergenerational history of smuggling to mobilize and profit from the growth of the drug trade. The growth of these drug trafficking organizations resulted in targeted policing initially of the urban strongholds of the border, resulting in further competition and outbursts of violence. This in turn resulted in the subsequent growth of the aforementioned smaller organizations. Violence along the border subsequently intensified with the diversification of smuggling organizations into multidrug trafficking practices, extortion, territorial disputes, and other criminal activities into the present.

Framed around the politically sensitive and obscure issue of "border security," the violence associated with drug trafficking has become a significant force in villainizing Mexico for a whole generation of Americans. In this chapter, I situate the rise of drug-related violence along the Texas-Mexico border within the context of escalating drug policing and the smuggling adaptations that policing engenders. In so doing, I trace the varied manifestations of violence tied to drug smuggling in the South Texas border region, through the stories of the victims of this violence. I demonstrate how drug-related violence, rather than being a certainty of drug trafficking, develops and escalates in response to a variety of forces. As the works of Alberto Barrera-Enderle and Andrew Torget in chapter 1 and Lance Blyth in chapter 3 in this volume demonstrate, the smuggling of goods is a clandestine activity that relies on avoiding detection to be successful. Therefore, violence is to be avoided to ensure the success of smuggling practices. However, if detected and/or intercepted, smugglers often resort to the use of violence in an attempt to ensure evasion and a successful smuggling act. The work of Elaine Carey and José Carlos Cisneros Guzmán presented in chapter 13 in this volume also demonstrates that borderlands violence and smuggling violence in particular impact a larger borderlands community beyond the smugglers themselves. In particular, Carey and Cisneros Guzmán offer insight into the impact of borderlands and drug violence on women beyond this study focused on border Mexicano male drug traffickers. Many other scholars, particularly Peter Andreas and Timothy Dunn, have also demonstrated how the drug war and drug policing have intensified border violence and militarization along the U.S.-Mexico border.[4] More recently, the work of Josiah Heyman, Jeremy Slack, Howard Campbell, Gilberto Rosas, Tony Payan, Kathleen Staudt, and Guadalupe Correa-Cabrera have offered new insights into the ongoing drug war.[5]

The South Texas border as the locus of this history offers a critical vantage point from which to understand the dually constitutive process of borders generating conflict and conflict emphasizing the need for greater enforcement of borders.[6] A second important factor in this history is the recognition of how the perpetrators of violence operate and utilize violence within this aforementioned paradigm. In the case of drug trafficking, states utilize the flow of illicit psychoactive substances as a justification for securitization and border enforcement legitimized through the interest of national security. As such, this process engenders a legitimation of state violence against those perpetrators who undermine national security by transporting illicit psychoactive substances across these borders. As such, increased border policing and enforcement alter the criminal geographies of international drug trafficking. As nation-states make efforts at bordering against illicit flows, they potentially disrupt criminal territories.[7] The disruption of criminal territories results in conflict between drug trafficking organizations and a second level of violence along the border, as drug trafficking organizations challenge each other for control of *las plazas*.[8] Therefore, here I engage with how the South Texas border is subject to these two levels of border violence, state and criminal. The South Texas drug corridor, or the Texas-Tamaulipas border, spanning from Nuevo Laredo, Tamaulipas, Mexico and Laredo, Texas, United States, border cities south to Matamoros, Tamaulipas, Mexico and Brownsville, Texas, United States, offers a unique opportunity from which to examine the history of drug smuggling, and border smuggling more generally. This span of the U.S.-Mexico border is significant as the historic site of the earliest forms of border-making and smuggling, from early instances at cattle rustling and textile smuggling in the mid-1800s through early drug smuggling, including alcohol, in the early twentieth century.[9] Moreover, as part of the specific history of contemporary drug smuggling, the Texas-Tamaulipas border is composed of important drug smuggling sites including three major urban border zones—Laredo/Nuevo Laredo, Reynosa/McAllen, and Brownsville/Matamoros—as well as the interspersed rural communities, like those of Starr County, with a long history of engaging in border smuggling practices.

The international drug trade at the U.S.-Mexico border was an outgrowth of earlier forms of smuggling. Border smugglers, however, were able to diversify their smuggling operations to include several psychoactive substances by the early twentieth century as a result of particular policies targeting the regulation and prohibition of these popular intoxicants. The early twentieth century marked an escalation of domestic and international drug control beginning with the Pure Food and Drug Act of 1906 and the Smoking Opium Exclusion Act of 1909, which was also followed by the International Opium Commission of 1909 and the International Opium Convention of 1912. In 1914, the Harrison Narcotics Tax Act consolidated the United States' targeting and regulation of coca and opiates. The primary function of the Harrison Act was to implement two different taxes on coca and opiates to better control and regulate access to these substances. However, within a short time the act effectively diminished the supply of these substances legally available, resulting in the growth of the illicit market for these substances. Initially, drug enforcement for this particular legislation was carried out by the Department of the Treasury, but in 1930 Congress created the Federal Bureau of Narcotics (FBN) to deal with the drug problem.[10]

While the effective prohibition of coca and opiates as a result of the Harrison Act was a gradual benefit for border smugglers, the prohibition of alcohol in the United States had profound effects on the intensification of border "drug" smuggling.[11] In 1919, the Eighteenth Amendment coupled with the National Prohibition Act banned the manufacture, sale, and prohibition of alcohol in the United States. The prohibition of alcohol, however, could not decrease demand for the substance, and very quickly elaborate criminal networks formed to supply alcohol to this growing illicit market. While most Americans are familiar with the bootleggers in the South and the Chicago organized crime group famously led by Al Capone, border smugglers were a significant part of delivering alcohol to the American market. The Rio Grande valley was a major site of liquor smuggling during prohibition. According to

Maude T. Gilliland's interviews with many of the customs officers charged with policing the Rio Grande valley, three major smuggling routes cut through Starr County, while only one route was identified in each of the neighboring counties. Gilliland states that "their [liquor smugglers'] main crossing strip along the southern part of the border below Laredo was around San Ygnacio, in Zapata County, and on down to about La Grulla, in Starr County, Texas."[12] The practice of liquor smuggling involved "a small band of these Mexicans" who "could load a dozen pack horses with tequila or other Mexican liquor for about one hundred pesos, make a trip into Texas, deliver it to their customers and return to Mexico with at least ten times the amount of money it had cost them. And there was a ready market for it, for during that time there was an influx of rum-runners who came into the border country for the sole purpose of buying liquor from these smugglers."[13]

Once the *tequileros* crossed the Rio Grande/Río Bravo, they rode through the brush country of Starr County, resting a few times before reaching their rendezvous point with rumrunners in South Texas towns of San Diego, Freer, and Benavides, which were at least one hundred miles north of the border. Once in the South Texas ranch country, the *tequileros* could sell their liquor to the rumrunners who would transport the liquor to the urban markets of the interior United States, such as Dallas and Chicago. Unsuccessful smuggling attempts occasionally resulted in firefights between smugglers and law enforcement officers along the South Texas border, as was the case on November 23, 1923 in Zapata County and on January 23, 1926 near Benavides, Texas.[14] Furthermore, the *corrido* (ballad) of "*Los Tequileros*" also recounts the tale of the death of three Mexicano liquor smugglers who were ambushed and killed by *los rinches*, the Texas Rangers.[15]

In 1933, after over a decade of contending with illicit liquor smuggling, manufacture, and sales, the United States repealed the prohibition of alcohol with the passing of the Twenty-first Amendment. The United States continued its prohibitionist drug policies with the implementation of the Marijuana Tax Act of 1937. The act was the culmination and consolidation of several state prohibition measures targeting marijuana beginning with Massachusetts in 1911 and resulting in a total of twenty-one state prohibition measures by 1933. Similar to the Harrison Act, the Marijuana Tax Act was prohibition through taxation; the law effectively made it impossible to be in possession of marijuana without violating the law, resulting in stiff penalties of up to five years in prison and a fine of up to $2,000. Along the Texas-Mexico border, smugglers quickly adapted to the unexpected shift. After having lost revenue through the repeal of alcohol prohibition, drug smugglers solidified the smuggling of the emerging American drug trinity of opiates, cocaine, and marijuana.[16]

Along the South Texas border, Juan Nepomuceno Guerra began a smuggling operation that developed into Mexico's contemporary Gulf cartel.[17] Guerra engaged in the smuggling of several substances and goods including liquor and arms smuggling as well as the drugs prohibited by the Harrison Act. *El Contrabandista* (The Smuggler), a *corrido* of the border region, traces the life of a smuggler in the South Texas region who smuggles cocaine, morphine, and marijuana through the South Texas border towns, including Rio Grande City, Brownsville, and Laredo. Much like Juan Guerra, *el contrabandista* also smuggles liquor across the Mexican border.[18]

In Starr County, another family also began its smuggling tradition at the same time as Juan N. Guerra in the early twentieth century. Blas Garcia was born in the small border community of El Canton, Texas, in 1910. As a result of his father's untimely death and his mother's hospitalization, Blas and his younger brother Salvador were orphans at a young age. In order to survive, Blas and Salvador began working as vaqueros for Anglo and Mexican rancheros in Starr County. By their early teens, the Garcia brothers had been engaged in cattle work throughout the area, and they knew the border terrain well. To supplement their vaquero income, Blas and Salvador began a simultaneous career in smuggling, at first providing their services as rustlers and contrabandistas of mundane goods, but eventually they would transition into becoming part-time tequileros.[19] After the repeal of prohibition, the Garcia brothers continued to rely on smuggling as a supplemental source of income. Through World War II, Blas and Salvador would smuggle rationed goods across the border, continually developing their skills and knowledge of the local geography that was essential to avoiding apprehension. For Blas and Salvador, smuggling was not a malicious criminal enterprise. Rather, the practice of smuggling, as George Diaz has argued, was part of local economic life that was strategically utilized and morally negotiated by border communities.[20] As such, Blas Garcia passed on this invaluable knowledge to his sons as part of an intergenerational process of economic socialization. However, by the time Blas's son, Juan Garcia, came of age in the mid-twentieth century, he utilized this local smugglers' knowledge to become a professional marijuana smuggler. For Blas's son's generation, smuggling became a primary source of income rather than a supplemental one.

By the mid-twentieth century, however, the escalation of prohibitionist drug policies coupled with an increasing demand for these prohibited substances sparked the rise of international drug smuggling along the border. Increasing drug demand in the United States for marijuana, opiates, and cocaine emerged as a result of several factors. After two world wars, many U.S. servicemen returned home with a dependence on opiates, spurring the growth of the existing heroin and morphine market in the United States. Moreover, the post–World War II era ushered in the counterculture movement initiated by the Beat generation, which contributed to the Unites States' growing demand for drugs, especially marijuana, cocaine, and heroin. By the 1960s, drug culture in the United States was revitalized by the emerging Hippie youth movement. The Hippies expanded the drug consumption patterns in the United States to include several other drugs, particularly hallucinogens, but their primary drug of choice was marijuana. The increasing demand for marijuana in the United States had perhaps the most significant effects on drug smuggling practices along the U.S.-Mexico border.

As a result, by the late 1960s, marijuana smuggling became a lucrative smuggling practice along the Texas-Mexico border. Along the South Texas border specifically, drug smugglers rushed to fill the demand in the United States. The *corridos* of the time including *Carga Blanca* (White Load), *Tragedia de los Cargadores* (The Tragedy of the Carriers), and *El Profugo* (The Fugitive) recount the stories of smugglers working along the South Texas border transporting morphine, marijuana, and cocaine.[21] The smugglers chronicled in these ballads were primarily working to satisfy the drug demands of the Beat generation in the 1950s. The Beats generated a counterculture that reconceptualized drug consumption as a form of protest, as well as an activity with positive outcomes for the user particularly with respect to artistic and creative production.[22] By the 1960s, however, the insatiable demand for marijuana in the United States spurred by hippies and other American youth prompted a change in drug smuggling along the South Texas border. In Starr County, some residents have confirmed that many of the individuals who were living in poverty, including some of the farm workers, resorted to marijuana smuggling during this time period as an important source of income. As a result, some of the first drug smugglers in Starr County were farm workers who abandoned the fields for the opportunity to make a lucrative income as marijuana smugglers. Furthermore, farm workers' experiences migrating to other areas of the United States helped to open up drug smuggling routes to drug consumer markets in North Texas, East Texas, and the Midwest.[23]

Andrea Garcia, a longtime female resident of El Canton, one of the small ranch communities in Starr County, believes that the presence of drug trafficking in her *ranchito* (small ranch) can be attributed to a member of the El Canton community, a *compadre* of hers now deceased many years. The practice of drug traffickers required cooperative work between native-born Mexican Americans and Mexican nationals on both sides of the border. The Mexicanos of El Norte often traveled to *el otro lado* (the other side) and worked with Mexican nationals who served as their suppliers. During an interview, Andrea stated, "Because when I moved over here there wasn't any contraband [drug trafficking specifically]. I don't remember and if there was it was very little, I think it was barely starting. And actually I think that the one that started was the compadre [deceased]."[24] Juan Garcia was not the first in his family to smuggle illicit substances across the border. Juan's father, Blas, had spent most of his life supplementing his ranch-hand income with routine smuggling trips through the brush country of South Texas. In his late twenties, Blas worked smuggling liquor across the border, and later during World War II he smuggled sugar and other goods. Juan, and most of his brothers, would carry on the family tradition of smuggling into his generation, with marijuana as their good of choice.

Drug smuggling during the late 1950s and through the 1960s, however, was not the highly elaborate and clandestine operation that it is today. At the time, border policing was not heavily directed at drug interception, and the large expanse of rural land in Starr County made drug interdiction a difficult task, as it remains today. The marijuana smugglers like Juan Garcia and his brothers of the 1950s and 1960s, therefore, had an easier time crossing drugs into the United States than contemporary smugglers. Again, Andrea recalls how her compadre's smuggling operation worked: "I remember that he had a fruit truck, you know the kind you use to transport cantaloupe. And then all of a sudden they would take off to Reynosa I think."[25] In fact, her compadre also smuggled large loads of marijuana into Rio Grande City from Camargo, Tamaulipas. Andrea even remembered a particular instance of interdiction, one day as she was returning from a trip to Camargo and saw her compadre's marijuana smuggling fruit truck detained at the *aduana* on the Mexican side. When I asked Andrea's daughter, Anna, if she remembered her *padrinos* (Juan specifically), she exclaimed, "Uh huh, ellos 'taban ricos" (Uh huh, they were rich). Andrea's compadre's wealth was in stark contrast to the working-class experience of her own family. Anna, however, remembered her padrino fondly: "He used to take us, well since they had money they would take their girls. And so he would take us to Harlingen. And I remember that he always wanted to take us to eat at Burger King. And he would take us over there and he was just joking around with me. He would always kid around with me."[26] Anna and many others from the community remembered Juan as a good man, handsome and wealthy. However, some folks from El Canton did not always view him in the most positive light.

During the 1960s, Juan's brother, Blas Jr. (Andrea's husband and Anna's father), worked in many different occupations as a rancher, painter, and mechanic, and he was a close associate and/or relative of some of the biggest marijuana smugglers in El Canton. Andrea remembered that since Blas Jr. had exceptional mechanic abilities, he was often summoned by Juan and his other brothers to work on vehicles that they were using as part of their marijuana-smuggling operation. She recalled that they would summon him at all hours of the night to perform mechanical rescues when one of their transport vehicles gave them trouble. Juan and his brothers occasionally had trouble with the large trucks that they used to transport marijuana, and so he would have to meet them to perform maintenance on the trucks on site (while loaded with hundreds of pounds of marijuana). However, Blas Jr. was not always happy with his duty as the smugglers' personal mechanic. According to Andrea,

> I'll never forget when we were still living in that house, but I'll never forget one Sunday, the compadre called, and he asked if Junior was there, 'cause they would call him Junior; they wouldn't call him by his name. I told him yes, he's here, and he said, "Let me talk to him. I need to talk to him." He was barely going to sit down to have breakfast. And then when he finished talking, he said, "Damn guys. They think that because they have money that you're their slave." That's what he said.[27]

However, that changed in 1969 with President Nixon's Operation Intercept. On September 21, 1969, the United States engaged in a concentrated large-scale drug interdiction effort that targeted border crossings for increased inspection and surveillance for marijuana smuggling.[28] The operation only lasted until October 2, 1969, but it signaled a new strategy toward dealing with the growing concern of drug consumption in the United States, a strategy now focused on targeting source and transit countries for drug interdiction. However, as Lawrence Gooberman has argued, Operation Intercept also had unintended consequences, especially with respect to the response by drug smugglers. Gooberman suggests that Operation Intercept's drastic surveillance and interdiction strategy effectively prompted the growth of organized illegal drug smuggling along the U.S.-Mexico border. In fact, Operation Intercept was part of the preliminary phase of the contemporary War on Drugs. As a result of the perceived effectiveness of the interdiction tactic, the Nixon administration officially declared the United States' War on Drugs. In fact, these efforts were part of a global policy shift in drug policing escalation that had its roots in the 1912 International Opium Convention and resulted in more sweeping global drug prohibition with the 1961 United Nations Single Convention on Narcotic Drugs and the 1971 United Nations Convention on Psychotropic Substances. It was in the midst of these global drug policy initiatives that the United States' contemporary narcopolitical initiatives took shape. In 1970, the United States passed the Controlled Substances Act to implement its federal drug prohibition strategy in accordance with the UN Single Convention on Narcotic Drugs. In an effort to enforce this new sweeping drug prohibition, the Nixon administration established the Drug Enforcement Administration on July 1, 1973.

Drug smuggling had led to dramatic changes in the ranchito of El Canton, with increases in wealth that were immediately noticeable. According to Anna Garcia, El Canton was not the only ranchito experiencing these changes in wealth as a result of the drug trade. The large span of rural area between Rio Grande City and Roma, the two largest cities in the county, underwent a similar transformation in wealth. Anna elaborated on the transformation that the area experienced:

> And then like going to Roma, to Mexico there was very few houses. There wasn't as many houses back then, *pero todos tenian* [well everyone had] mud houses, and *jacales* [shacks]. Then all of a sudden they all started, *pos* [well] everybody started to get into the *drogas* [drugs] and stuff and the *casas* [houses] started to spread. *Si palla* [yeah over there]. *Si pos alla eran puras casas viejitas, todo eso de alla.* [Yes well over there were a lot of old houses, all of that area]. And then they all started to get *mafiosos* [gangsters]. Like if you drive through there, maybe. . . . *Si ya estaba* [yes, it was already] developed Roma, but like the rich people from Roma like the Guerras lived there. *Pero, all that area eran puras casitas viejitas de tabla y de ladrillo* [they were all old houses made of wood and brick]. *O like mas antes las hacian de tabla y les ponian teja.* [Or like back then they used to make them from wood and they would put thatch]. Like the *teja* [thatch] you put on the ceiling, they would put that around them.[29]

She also provided insight into the experience of witnessing the emergence of drug smuggling as a young person in El Canton. Growing up at a time when many drug smugglers were gaining wealth through their illicit activities and their children reaped the material benefits of this wealth, she continued working through junior high and high school in varying capacities. As a working-class migrant student, Anna worked during the summers and during the school year, as a seasonal farm worker, a convenience store cashier, and a fast food attendant. As migrants, she and her siblings traveled to Oklahoma for two years and West Texas another year to work as farm workers. During the school year and summers, they also worked at the packing sheds for the local agribusiness company—the same packing sheds that only a decade earlier their aunts and uncles had picketed against for better wages. Anna also worked at a local convenience store as a cashier and worked at the local Dairy Queen, while young men her age were beginning to enter the drug trade as a new generation of *mafiosos* in training.

Anna reminisced about her high school experience, and mildly lamented to me the fact that other individuals in her class, whose fathers were drug dealers, had lavish possessions including new vehicles, expensive clothes, and indiscriminate amounts of spending money for "going out." "Yeah 'cause it was open campus and we could go eat at Sonic or wherever you wanted to. And Natalia and I were the ones that usually didn't have money. We would still go with them, but we didn't have money to buy. *Pos no* [well no], they would share with us some of what they bought, but no we wouldn't eat lunch."[30] In the 1970s, many individuals in the community were benefiting from the wealth generated by the drug trade. However, in the 1980s the wealth generated by drug trafficking would increase dramatically as smugglers began to smuggle a more lucrative drug: cocaine.

In Starr County, one of the most important drug trafficking organizations was the one led by Ramon Garcia Rodriguez. He was a native of the small community of Guardados de Abajo located on the south bank of the Rio Grande, next to the Mexican border town of Camargo, Tamaulipas, Rio Grande City's Mexican sister city. In the early 1970s, Ramon Garcia Rodriguez immigrated from Guardados de Abajo to the United States, and by the mid-1970s, he was working as a low-wage factory worker in Chicago, Illinois.[31] By the late 1970s, Garcia Rodriguez had grown tired of his factory job and returned to Starr County, where he began working as a low-level worker in a drug trafficking organization. After he was in the drug trade a few years, Garcia Rodriguez's wealth grew and he was able to lead his own drug trafficking organization with the help of some of his family members. With his newly acquired wealth, he purchased ranches on both sides of the border from which to stage his drug-smuggling operation. According to one news report, "Confidential informants told federal investigators of 'multi-thousand-pound loads' of marijuana moving through the ranches each month," and "one witness told investigators that he once saw 25 tons of marijuana stored at Mr. Garcia's El Tejano Ranch near Camargo, Mexico, across the border from Rio Grande City."[32]

Garcia Rodriguez worked closely with the Martinez drug trafficking organization based out of Hidalgo County, which was led by Ramon Dionicio Martinez and his brothers. In the 1970s, the Martinez organization controlled most of the marijunana smuggling in Hidalgo County, and they had established distribution points to Houston, Dallas, and the Midwest. Then, in the 1980s, the Martinez and the Garcia Rodriguez drug trafficking organizations began cooperating on some drug smuggling efforts. The Martinez organization alone was responsible for "smuggling up to 100 tons of marijuana, valued at $69 million" during the 1980s.[33] Then on "Sept. 18, 1989, a federal grand jury in Houston returned the first of a series of indictments naming Mr. Garcia, Mr. Martinez and his brothers and 27 other defendants as members of a smuggling empire."[34]

Mario Alberto Salinas Trevino was another trafficker who operated another trafficking organization in the Rio Grande valley. Although most of his trafficking activity took place through Hidalgo County, he did conduct some trafficking through Starr County and also worked in close conjunction with Ramon Garcia Rodriguez. Salinas Trevino was originally from Doctor Coss, Nuevo León, a small municipality located on the Tamaulipas–Nuevo León border approximately twenty miles from Roma, Texas. In the mid-1970s, Salinas Trevino immigrated to the United States and began working as a migrant farm worker, making just over $6,000 in 1977.[35] But by the mid-1980s, Salinas Trevino had built up a drug trafficking organization that had allowed him to acquire "businesses, homes and ranches in Starr and Hidalgo counties, San Antonio and California." At the time of his arrest in 1989, federal authorities "seized more than $7 million in assets belonging to Mr. Salinas."[36]

In the mid-1980s, *Time* introduced the world to Starr County in a journalistic exposé. In the article, the author, Richard Woodbury, asserted that "the Rio Grande Valley has emerged as the hot corridor for drug runners," and that "one-third of all the cocaine, marijuana and heroin entering the U.S. from Mexico is believed to come across the valley."[37] Furthermore, he stated that "by one federal estimate, 40% of all the drugs crossing through South Texas move through Starr, sometimes amounting to 15 tons of marijuana and 1,000 lbs. of coke a week."[38] By the mid-1980s, just over one-third of Starr County's population was unemployed. Yet "cocaine [had] given Starr's brown landscape a dash of affluence" and "ornate brick homes protected by iron fences and snarling Rottweilers are popping up along U.S. [highway] 83."[39] As a result of the increased drug traffic coming through Starr County, federal authorities increased interdiction efforts along the South Texas border, as part of the Reagan administration's anti-drug effort "Operation Alliance." The increased efforts resulted in a series of drug busts along the South Texas border including one in November 1986, when "20 federal and state lawmen sporting flak jackets and semi-automatic rifles descended on a secluded bungalow near the Rio Grande in Starr County. All told, 14 Mexicans were charged with drug possession, and 200 lbs of dope were confiscated."[40]

In Starr County, violence also intensified as a result of the drug trade during the 1980s. Drug smugglers engaged in kidnapping, murders, and shootings for a variety of purposes geared at controlling the South Texas drug market. Starr County drug smuggler Ramon Garcia Rodriguez was one of the individuals who employed these violent tactics. A *Dallas Morning News* report stated that "Mr. Garcia controlled his organization with calculated brutality. Beatings, shootings and late-night attacks on family members were designed to keep his workers in line and scare rivals away."[41] These tactics resulted in a growing number of drug-related deaths in Starr County, including the following: "On June 15, 1985, at a horse barn on a ranch near Roma [Texas], the bodies of three men were found face-down and shot in the head."[42] The intensified violence was a result of these interrelated processes of intensified border policing coupled with increased competition for the drug market that was generating significant profits, both actual and perceived, for local smugglers and dealers.

In 1989, a group of Starr County sheriff's deputies were involved in a gunfight with alleged drug traffickers in northern Starr County. Xavier Lopez (Juan Garcia's cousin) was one of the sheriff's deputies involved in the gunfight. One night, in April of 1989, a group of men stormed a home in Roma, Texas, and began opening fire on people inside the home. The violent scene was part of escalating violence in the Starr County region attributed to conflict between drug trafficking organizations. Shortly after shots rang out in the Roma neighborhood, sheriff's deputies were called out to respond. Xavier was on duty that night serving in the Starr County sheriff's department Roma substation. In the late 1980s, only two deputies were on duty for the Roma area overnight. By the time Xavier responded, the shooting suspects had already fled the scene of the shooting, and a high-speed chase ensued down Highway 83 in Starr County. So he sped southeast on Highway 83, in close pursuit of the suspects. After a short chase through Starr County, the suspects lost control of their vehicle, and it came to a screeching halt. Xavier stopped close behind the suspects' disabled vehicle, and he exited the police cruiser. As he exited his vehicle, a gunfight ensued between him and the suspects. Shortly after the gunfight began, another Starr County sheriff's deputy responded to the scene as Xavier's backup. During the exchange of gunfire, Xavier and the other deputy were wounded. Even though they were both down, the deputies continued to exchange gunfire with the suspects. Eventually, more law enforcement units responded to the scene, and authorities were able to arrest the suspects. The damage, however, had already been done. Xavier had been shot a total of six times during the entire exchange. That night, the local evening news covered the story. Images flashed on the screen of a man on a gurney being wheeled into the emergency room. He was covered in blood. and a breathing mask covered his face.

As the 1980s ended, there were approximately fifty drug trafficking organizations "capable of frequent narcotic shipments of many tons each" operating in Starr County and Hidalgo County.[43] There was not one single leader, or capo, that ran the organizations. Rather, the organizations functioned as family-based, independent cells, with some of the larger organizations functioning as suppliers for the smaller organizations. Drug agents concluded that the organizations functioned "much like a narcotics co-op. They buy and sell from each other and at times they even piggyback loads and lend out their distribution networks."[44] However, when interdiction efforts targeted at the area affected the trafficker's success, the groups began competing with one another for their own self-interest and to secure their own profit margins. As a result of the escalation of drug trafficking through the South Texas–Mexico border in the 1980s, drug interdiction efforts were redirected to the region in the 1990s. The decade began with the South Texas region being designated a High Intensity Drug Trafficking Area (HIDTA) in 1990 by the Office of National Drug Control Policy.

The proliferation of cocaine smuggling through the Texas-Mexico border also fueled the American response of border militarization and border policing escalation.[45] Throughout the 1980s and 1990s, the U.S.-Mexico border was the site of intense escalation of police power, and as part of this process local, state, and federal policing agencies began to work more closely with the military and also adopted militaristic tools and tactics. The culmination of this intensification was the Redford shooting of 1997, when a Marine working on a joint task force between the military and the Border Patrol killed Ezequiel Hernandez, an innocent eighteen-year-old man who was killed because of his perceived threat as a possible drug trafficker. The Redford shooting seemed to cause pause, if briefly, with regard to the intensification of policing and the militarization of the border. Oddly enough, the same moment of increased surveillance and attempted closing of the border came at a time of increased legal movement and exchange across the U.S.-Mexico border. On January 1, 1994, the North American Free Trade Agreement went into effect, establishing a free trade zone between Canada, the United States, and Mexico. The free movement of licit trade was a boon for drug traffickers, as they developed the practicing of smuggling drugs through legitimate commerce, a tactic that is still practiced today with great success.

The case of Memito exemplifies the type of violence that smugglers faced from their rivals. Manuel Garcia was one of the few young people in Starr County born into a relatively wealthy family. Manuel's father was a wealthy landowner and a business owner; he owned a small convenience store and gas station on the main highway that passed through the small ranch community of Los Garcias de Abajo. Manuel's mother was an elementary school teacher and one of the few college-educated people in the entire county. Memito, as his friends and family called him, was a smart young man. He excelled in school and was rather gifted. His privilege stood in contrast to most of the other young people growing up in Los Garcias. By the time Memito was graduating high school in the early 1980s, his parents had gifted him a tire-mechanic shop. Memito was set. However, Memito had other plans. He got involved in the drug trade at the exact time that business was booming. By the end of the 1980s, he was already making significant profits as a drug trafficker, dealing in marijuana and cocaine.[46]

By the 1990s, Memito was already on the top of the border drug game. He was running a local organization that smuggled large quantities of marijuana and cocaine across the border into El Canton. His organization then transported the substances to their distributors in Houston, Texas. By 1991, Memito was also recently married, and he had just welcomed his first child, a little girl, into the world; his life was looking great. I consistently visited Memito's home at this time, when I was a young boy, and I would find wads of cash in drawers throughout the kitchen, under the sink in the bathroom, and in the closets.[47]

Memito had participated in the drug trade for nearly a decade without any real negative effects on his life, but that would all change late in the summer of 1991. Late one summer evening, Memito was sitting under his carport, enjoying a cigarette. After finishing his cigarette, he entered his home and proceeded to enjoy his time with his wife and newborn. A short time later, there was a knock at the door. Memito came to the door and stood behind the protective security screen door. Just within sight, but still not completely discernible, stood a man in the darkness not reached by the front porch light. The man was dressed in official uniform of the local county sheriff's department. He called Memito to step outside, stating that he needed to talk to him on official police business. As he stepped outside, two masked men carrying firearms appeared from both sides of the front porch. The two masked men subdued Memito and bound his hands and feet and gagged him with duct tape. A few more men appeared, and they all stormed Memito's house. His wife stood inside holding her newborn, crippled by fear. The men ransacked the house looking for drugs, money, and guns. They found two firearms (a shotgun and a handgun) and a small wad of cash, but no drugs. They came back out threatened Memito and beat him hoping to find more info about his money and merchandise; they threatened his wife. But they were unsuccessful in finding anything else.[48]

Pressed for time, the masked men made their escape. But before leaving, they stood in the front yard, where Memito was now lying still bound, and they made one final statement. One of the masked men held a shotgun to

Memito's head and fired. However, just before firing Memito moved his head, or the gunman jerked his hand, and the shot flew right by his head, leaving a large impression in the front yard next to Memito. After the shot, the men loaded into their vehicles and sped off down the highway. Memito's wife, fearing that her husband had been killed, rushed outside, expecting to find hear husband bloodied and dying on the front porch. Instead, she came out and cut the bindings around Memito's feet, hands, and mouth. Now free, Memito rushed to his pickup and proceeded to try to pursue the group of men that had threatened his life. Unfortunately, he could not make it out of the driveway; the tires to all his vehicles had been slashed. Memito and his family had been the victims of a pseudo-cop home invasion.[49]

After the events of September 11, the United States began to reevaluate the security of its national borders. The U.S.-Mexico border specifically was targeted within political discourse as a porous and unsecured border where terrorists could enter the nation for future attacks. As part of the government's efforts to wage the War on Terror, they began to focus their attention on securing the U.S.-Mexico border. The federal government provided funds to station more Border Patrol agents along the southern border to help with policing efforts. The increased resources provided to the Border Patrol led to the increased surveillance of the border, resulting in increased interception of drugs and immigrants. In 2003, the federal government created the Department of Homeland Security (DHS). The newly created Department of Homeland Security formed a large government entity that now controlled previously independent organizations, such as the Immigration and Naturalization Services (INS) and the U.S. Customs Service.[50] These two organizations were joined in March 2003 to form the largest investigative branch of the Department of Homeland Security: Immigration and Customs Enforcement (ICE). After September 11, the increased surveillance of the border, and increased interception of drug shipments led to a spike in border violence tied to the drug trade.

As the U.S.-Mexico border underwent this increase in drug policing and the intensification of border militarization, the sphere of drug trafficking was considerably altered by a new development. In the early 2000s, the Gulf cartel, with its stronghold along the South Texas–Mexico border, began to employ a paramilitary force as hired protection but also to conduct some trafficking measures. This new paramilitary force, Los Zetas, was initially composed of "31 deserters from the Mexican Army's Airborne Special Forces Group."[51] However, since its original formation in 1997, "the organization has since grown considerably, now consisting of 100–200 men and women, and is distinguished by its advanced training and proficiency in violence."[52] Along the South Texas–Mexico border, Los Zetas became more powerful and initiated heavy recruitment of new members into its organization. This paramilitary organization has established elaborate training camps to train young men in the military tactics and weapons skills necessary to serve as the organization's hitmen. The strategy of employing a paramilitary force, or at least adopting military tactics, was so successful that most drug trafficking organizations began forming their own drug paramilitaries to combat and compete with Los Zetas.[53]

The rapid proliferation of paramilitary drug trafficking practices and organizations sparked significant concern for the United States. The Mexican government made an attempt to deal with this growing threat when President Felipe Calderon assumed the presidency in 2006. Calderon mobilized the Mexican military to combat these new threats, and he deployed troops to drug trafficking and drug violence hotspots to take the fight to *la delincuencia organizada* (organized crime). The result, however, was a long bloody and costly war between drug traffickers and the state. Mexico was at war, but the battling forces on any given day were never certain. The drug war violence was significant along the South Texas–Mexico border, the Gulf Coast, and in southern coastal Mexico, and it quickly spread to other areas of Mexico and the U.S.-Mexico border, reaching its height in 2008 in Juarez, Chihuahua, Mexico. This moment allowed for the establishment of another U.S. drug policy directed at combating drug trafficking, the Merida Initiative, which was signed into law by George W. Bush on June 30, 2008. "The Merida Initiative (colloquially referred to as "Plan Merida" or "Plan Mexico") is a 3-year, $1.4 billion counternarcotics package destined for Mexico and Central American, with Mexico to receive the vast majority of the funds. The central aim of the Merida Initiative is to use U.S. money, training and equipment to strengthen Mexico's military and law enforcement agencies, thereby giving them the capacity to take and hold the initiative in the fight against the cartels."[54]

The increased violence at the border was a result of competition between drug cartels. Furthermore, these changes centralized power within larger transnational criminal organizations that displaced the previous family-operated narco cooperatives. The majority of local smugglers became little more than low-wage, expendable, "contract" laborers for these larger criminal organizations. The young smugglers of the border region became the targets of intensified violence from both drug policing agents and drug trafficking operatives.

The case of Joker, which this chapter opened with, illustrates the new forms of tactical violence used to control the drug trade in Starr County. Joker's experience with drug violence reveals the most recent transformation of power within larger systems of organized crime in Mexico and along the U.S-Mexico border. As part of this process, drug trafficking organizations centralized power into militarized corporate entities that rely on expendable laborers and the "outsourcing" of violence into Mexico.[55] The outsourcing of drug violence along the border relies on impunity in Mexico as well as the targeting of drug workers through tactical violence. By outsourcing, I refer to how, similar to conventional trade relationships, certain activities have been relocated to Mexico in order to avoid the regulations or impositions of the United States' legal oversight.[56] In this case, as a result of impunity in Mexico and the exploitability of the U.S.-Mexico border to discipline drug workers through violence, the use of violence is deployed against workers to a greater extent on the Mexican side of the border. Furthermore, drug workers on the American side are removed (or disappeared) to the Mexican side of the border in order to exploit the transnational nature of drug work, and the differential punishment systems in the United States and Mexico. The story of Adan Garcia highlights the effects of the outsourcing of violence and the corporatization of drug trafficking along the Texas-Mexico border. Adan Garcia was still a teenager when in early 2010 he began working as a mule for a representative of Los Zetas, operating out of the Ciudad Camargo, Tamaulipas–Rio Grande City, Texas, drug corridor. Much like his cousin Joker, Adan was a low-level drug worker, and his expendability was an integral factor in drug trafficking operations along the border. However, Adan would experience a similar system of violence that Joker was subjected to, with some salient distinguishing circumstances. During a smuggling attempt gone wrong, Adan was intercepted by border policing agents. A pursuit ensued. In possession of several hundred pounds of marijuana, Adan made a quick decision to evade the agents and flee to Mexico. In the process, he abandoned the vehicle and the marijuana. When he arrived in Mexico, Adan was *levantado* (abducted) and held hostage for the loss of the marijuana and the vehicle. The members of the organization sent a message to Adan's mother: if she and her family could not pay off Adan's debt from the botched smuggling attempt, Adan would be executed. After a series of bake sales, car washes, and other fund-raising activities, Adan's family was eventually able to gather the funds for his release. In the week that passed, however, Adan was subjected to both physical and psychological torture at the hands of his captors. Adan, much like his cousin Joker, was lucky. He escaped the drug trade with his life. As evident by several recent cases, many of the drug trafficking operatives have not been so fortunate. In the year following Adan's release from captivity, forty-nine decapitated bodies were dumped near Cadereyta-Jimenez, Nuevo León, on the highway leading from Ciudad Miguel Aleman, Tamaulipas, to Monterey,

Nuevo León.[57] The site of the carnage was within a few miles of where Adan was held prior to his release. Perhaps the most egregious example of the visceral and widespread impact of violence on border communities began on February 22, 2010 with what has been termed by Diego Osorno "The Battle for Ciudad Mier." Ciudad Mier, Tamaulipas, often referred to locally as "*El Pueblo Magico*" (the magic town), was among the first of the river communities to be founded, on March 6, 1753. But after the turf war that ensued in 2010 between the Gulf Cartel and Los Zetas, nearly all of the town's residents fled to the neighboring city of Miguel Aleman, Tamaulipas, or to their sister communities on the Texas side of the border. The turf war was a result of the power vacuum that developed as a result of the death of Antonio Cardenas Guillen, the Gulf cartel's leader, and brought public firefights to the small border community after the kidnapping and murder of the town's police forces. The sounds of semiautomatic weapons and high-caliber firearms could be heard across the river in Fronton, Texas, as the battle for Mier took hold.[58]

Violence is a tactical tool of the drug trade but also more broadly of the War on Drugs. The stories of the Garcia family illuminate our understanding of the War on Drugs and its impact on the practice of drug trafficking. The use of violence by *narcos* (drug traffickers) and narcs (drug enforcement officers) has engendered new forms of violence that are replicated and reproduced as part of an escalating militarization of drug policing and the related process of the militarization of drug trafficking. As evidenced by the Garcia family's experiences, drug smuggling along the border has transitioned from a practice involving minimal risk and threats of violence to a dangerous and violent practice that increasingly marks the lives of border residents, smugglers and nonsmugglers alike. The current wave of drug war violence along the border and in Mexico continues to result in innovative and disturbing forms of violent tactics. It is a story that is still being written, and it is a reality that the Garcia smugglers continue to face.

Notes

1. My primary mode of methodological inquiry is ethnography. As such, I have been conducting participant-observation, oral history, and interviews (formal and informal) with members of the border communities of Starr County affected by the border drug war. I rely on this data set in tandem with primary and secondary sources to construct this history of drug trafficking along the South Texas border. Due to human-subject protections, the names of many individuals in this narrative are pseudonyms in order to protect the identity of the individuals who shared their stories.

2. Translated from Spanish by the author. Direct quote from interview: "Bring that asshole here and if he did steal the weed I'll kill him myself."

3. Translated from Spanish by the author. Direct quote from interview: "If I hadn't been such good friends with your deceased grandfather Blas, I'd kill both of you here and now."

4. Timothy Dunn, *The Militarization of the U.S.-Mexico Border: Low-Intensity Conflict Doctrine Comes Home* (Austin: University of Texas Press, 1996); Timothy Dunn, "Border Militarization via Drug and Immigration Enforcement: Human Rights Implications," *Social Justice* 28, no. 2 (2001): 7–30; Peter Andreas, *Border Games: Policing the U.S.-Mexico Divide* (Ithaca, NY: Cornell University Press, 2009).

5. Tony Payan, Kathleen Staudt, and Z. Anthony Kruszewski, eds., *A War That Can't Be Won: Binational Perspectives on the War on Drugs* (Tucson: University of Arizona Press, 2013); Howard Campbell, *Drug War Zone: Frontline Dispatches from the Streets of El Paso and Juarez* (Austin: University of Texas Press, 2009); Gilberto Rosas, *Barrio Libre: Criminalizing States and Delinquent Refusals of the New Frontier* (Durham, NC: Duke University Press, 2012); Guadalupe Correa-Cabrera, *Los Zetas Inc.: Criminal Corporations, Energy, and Civil War in Mexico* (Austin: University of Texas Press, 2017); Jeremy Slack and Howard Campbell, "On Narco-coyotaje: Illicit Regimes and Their Impacts on the US-Mexico Border," *Antipode* 48 (2016): 1380–99; Josiah Heyman and Howard Campbell, "Corruption in the U.S. Borderlands with Mexico: The 'Purity' of Society and the 'Perversity' of Borders," in *Corruption and the Secret of Law: A Legal Anthropological Perspective*, ed. Monique Nuijten and Gerhard Anders (Aldershot, UK: Ashgate, 2007), 191–217; Josiah Heyman, "Guns, Drugs, and Money: Tackling the Real Threats to Border Security" (invited public policy paper). Washington, DC: Immigration Policy Center (2011), https://www.americanimmigrationcouncil.org/research/guns-drugs-and-money-tackling-realthreats-border-security.

6. Gabriel Popescu, *Bordering and Ordering the Twenty-first Century: Understanding Borders* (Lanham, MD: Rowman and Littlefield, 2012).

7. Popescu, *Bordering and Ordering*.

8. Campbell, *Drug War Zone*.

9. George T. Diaz, *Border Contraband: A History of Smuggling across the Rio Grande* (Austin: University of Texas Press, 2015).

10. Bruce Bullington, *Heroin Use in the Barrio* (Lexington, MA: Lexington Books, 1977); David T. Courtwright, *Forces of Habit: Drugs and the Making of the Modern World* (Cambridge, MA: Harvard University Press, 2001).

11. As a prohibited psychoactive substance, alcohol fits into the trajectory of U.S. drug policy and its effects on Mexico–United States drug smuggling.

12. Maude T. Gilliland, *Horsebackers of the Brush Country: A Story of Texas Rangers and Mexican Smugglers* (Brownsville, TX: Springman-King Lithograph Co., 1968), 15.

13. Gilliland, *Horsebackers of the Brush Country*, 15.

14. Gilliland, *Horsebackers of the Brush Country*, 15.

15. James Nicolopulos and Chris Strachwitz, *The Roots of the Narcocorrido* (El Cerrito, CA: Arhoolie Productions, 2004); Diaz, *Border Contraband*.

16. John Hudak, *Marijuana: A Short History* (Washington, DC: Brookings Institution, 2016); Nick Johnson, *Grass Roots: A History of Cannabis in the American West* (Corvallis: Oregon State University Press, 2017); Emily Dufton, *Grass Roots: The Rise and Fall and Rise of Marijuana in America* (New York: Basic Books, 2017).

17. Sam Dillon, "Matamoros Journal: Canaries Sing in Mexico but Uncle Juan Will Not," *New York Times*, February 9, 1996.

18. Nicolopulos and Strachwitz, *The Roots of the Narcocorrido*.

19. Diaz, *Border Contraband*.

20. Diaz, *Border Contraband*.

21. Nicolopulos and Strachwitz, *Roots of the Narcocorrido*.

22. Dufton, *Grass Roots*.

23. David Hanners and David McLemore, "Dealer's Domain Knows No Borders," *Dallas Morning News*, October 14, 1990; Woodbury, Richard, "The Rio Grande's Drug Corridor," *Time*, November 17, 1986.

24. Translated from Spanish by the author. Direct quote from interview: "Porque cuando yo me movi paca no habia el contrabando. Yo no me acuerdo y si habia habia poquito, creo que apenas estaba empezando. Y yo creo que lo empezo fue el difunto."

25. Translated from Spanish by the author. Direct quote from interview: "Yo me acuerdo que tenia un troque frutero, uno desos como pa llevar melon. Y de repente que iban pa Reynosa creo."

26. Translated from Spanish by the author. Direct quote from interview: "He [el compadre] used to take us, pos como ellos tenian dinero, ellos llevaban las guercas. Y el nos llevaba pa Harlingen. Y me acuerdo que siempre nos queria llevar a comer a Burger King. Y nos llevaba pa' ya y nomas iba ahi sonsiando conmigo. He would always kid around with me."

27. Translated from Spanish by the author. Direct quote from interview: "A mi nunca se me olvida cuando estabamos en aquella casa, pero nunca se me olvida un domingo, hablo el compadre, y dijo hay esta Junior porque ellos le decian Junior, no le hablaban por su nombre. Si le dije aqui esta, y dijo dejame hablar con el necesito hablar con el. Apenas se iba a sentar a almorzar. Y cuando acabo de hablar dijo 'pinches pelados, creen que porque tienen dinero que uno es esclavo dellos.' Asi fueron las palabras que dijo."

28. Lawrence Gooberman, *Operation Intercept: The Multiple Consequences of Public Policy* (Elmsford, NY: Pergamon, 1974).

29. Interview by the author. Direct quote as shown.

30. Interview by the author. Direct quote as shown.

31. David Hanners and David McLemore, "Dealer's Domain Knows No Borders," *Dallas Morning News*, October 14, 1990. [The complete citation is in note 23 above]

32. Hanners and McLemore, "Dealer's Domain Knows No Borders."

33. Hanners and McLemore, "Dealer's Domain Knows No Borders."

34. Hanners and McLemore, "Dealer's Domain Knows No Borders."

35. Hanners and McLemore, "Dealer's Domain Knows No Borders."

36. Hanners and McLemore, "Dealer's Domain Knows No Borders."

37. Richard Woodbury, "The Rio Grande's Drug Corridor," *Time*, November 17, 1986.

38. Woodbury, "Rio Grande's Drug Corridor."

39. Woodbury, "Rio Grande's Drug Corridor."

40. Woodbury, "Rio Grande's Drug Corridor."

41. David McLemore and Gayle Reaves, "Alleged Leader of Drug Empire Inspired Fear," *Dallas Morning News*, October 14, 1990.

42. McLemore and Reaves, "Alleged Leader of Drug Empire Inspired Fear."

43. Hanners and McLemore, "Dealer's Domain Knows No Borders."

44. Hanners and McLemore, "Dealer's Domain Knows No Borders."

45. Peter Andreas, *Border Games: Policing the U.S.-Mexico Divide* (Ithaca, NY: Cornell University Press, 2000); Dunn, *The Militarization of the U.S.-Mexico Border*; Dunn, "Border Militarization via Drug and Immigration Enforcement."

46. Memito's story, presented here, is compiled from a range of interviews with Memito and his family and friends during the research period from 2000 to 2011.

47. Some of the information compiled for Memito's story is gathered through autoethnography. As a member of this community, I witnessed many of these events firsthand. As a participant observer and autoethnographer, I also rely on my own recollection of particular events. For further discussion, see Santiago Guerra, "*Entre Los Mafiosos y La Chota*: Ethnography, Drug Trafficking and Policing in the South Texas–Mexico Borderlands," in *Uncharted Terrains: New Directions in Border Research Methods and Ethics*, ed. Anna Ochoa O'Leary, Colin M. Deeds, and Scott Whiteford (Tucson: University of Arizona Press, 2013), 121–139; Santiago Guerra, "Becoming an 'Illegal' Anthropologist," *Anthropology News*, March 2013.

48. "10 'Pseudo-cop' Suspects Arraigned," *Brownsville Herald*, January 21, 2016; Jeanne Russel, "Pseudo Cop Busted," *The Monitor*, February 15, 1997; "Pseudo-cop Suspects Arrested near RGC," *Rio Grande Herald*, August 4, 1994; Randol Contreras, *The Stickup Kids: Race, Drugs, Violence and the American Dream* (Berkeley: University of California Press, 2012). In the *Stickup Kids*, Randol Contreras shows how the disruption of the crack economy in New York City, due to intensified policing, resulted in crack dealers targeting each other in stickups and robbing each other's profits and drugs. This pattern was similarly experienced in the South Texas border region through the pseudo-cop–home invasion practice.

49. I witnessed the aftermath of this event as a young adolescent growing up in close proximity to Memito and his family. I was among the first group of witnesses on the scene after this home invasion. In addition, this story is continuously retold and has become part of Memito's family's oral history.

50. United States Department of Homeland Security, n.d., "Department Subcomponents and Agencies," accessed January 7, 2010, http://www.dhs.gov/xabout/structure/.

51. Hal Brands, *Mexico's Narco-insurgency and U.S. Counterdrug Policy* (Carlisle, PA: Strategic Studies Institute, US Army War College, 2009), 8.

52. Brands, *Mexico's Narco-insurgency and U.S. Counterdrug Policy*, 8.

53. Guadalupe Correa-Cabrera, *Los Zetas Inc.: Criminal Corporations, Energy, and Civil War in Mexico* (Austin: University of Texas Press, 2017).

54. Correa-Cabrera, *Los Zetas Inc.*, 2.

55. Santiago Guerra, "*La Chota y Los Mafiosos*: Mexican American Casualties of the Border Drug War," *Latino Studies* 13, no. 2 (2015): 227–44.

56. As an example, many industrial activities were outsourced to Mexico due to differential environmental policy that permitted greater industrial contamination in Mexico that would not have been permitted in the United States. These activities also benefited from the exploitability and management of workers. See Devon Pena, *The Terror of the Machine: Technology, Work, Gender and Ecology on the U.S.-Mexico Border* (Austin: University of Texas Press, 1997).

57. Dudley Althaus, "Nearly 50 Bodies Recovered from Latest Mexico Massacre," *Houston Chronicle*, May 13, 2012.

58. Diego Osorno, "The Battle for Ciudad Mier," in *Our Lost Border: Essays on Life amid the Narco-Violence*, ed. Sarah Cortez and Sergio Troncoso (Houston: Arte Publico, 2013).

Figure 13.1 "Dessy," Nuevo León, México, 2015. Photograph from authors' personal collection.

Chapter 13

Women, Family, Violence, and Trust

Drugged Lives on the U.S.-Mexico Border, 1950 to the Present

ELAINE CAREY AND JOSÉ CARLOS CISNEROS GUZMÁN

Recently, the analysis of gender, violence, and border drug wars seems more performative than historical, empirical, or even theoretical. Films such as *Traffic* and *The Counselor* and novels such as *La Reina del Sur* and the telenovela it inspired as well as FX's limited docudrama *The Bridge* have tackled the diverse roles of women in the drug trade and the impact of violence.[1] All the films embrace the U.S.-Mexico border, the straits between Spain and Morocco, and the entrepôt of Sinaloa as sites of danger but also sites of lucrative opportunities. In these fictional depictions, the roles and lives of women and their impact on policing and diplomacy are evident, but most historical and popular work has generally ignored the role of women in organized crime or drug trafficking, whether as bosses, partners, mothers, or victims. Moreover, there are few scholarly studies of gender within the drug wars along the U.S.-Mexico border. Media representations historicizing the contemporary drug war have remained almost identical for one hundred years, accentuating a masculine narrative with little analysis of the continuity of the good-versus-evil trope that infuses drug narratives.[2]

When scholars have employed gender as a category of analysis to study the history of narcotics, they have focused on women as victims and addicts. We, as well as other scholars, do not dispute victimhood. Frequently, the partners, husbands, and relatives of women have forced them into the drug trade, whether that consisted of smuggling drugs in suitcases or driving loads across the border, maintaining stash houses, or being forced into dealing and prostitution.[3]

Historical thinking, however, allows us to elaborate on the complexity of gender relations that take place within the trade or within policing it. Not all women are victims of men; some women actively participate in the drug trade, forming their own crews and organized crime families for the pursuit of profit.[4] Men serve as mentors and as partners. Violence, whether in the present or the past, disrupts the pursuit of profit. As Alberto Barrera-Enderle and Andrew Torget in chapter 1, Lance Blyth in chapter 3, and Santiago Guerra in chapter 12 in this volume describe, smuggling and trafficking rely on avoiding detection. For women, their clandestine activities are frequently ignored.

Yet, they are able to thrive in their anonymity, which assists in their success. Women in the past, as well as in the present, navigated the shifts in policy and policing, but they also faced competition from men. Like men, women in the trade confront various forms of violence such as state-sponsored, but women also encounter additional forms of violence such as familial and sexual, which do not tend to be as prevalent in the male experience.

While violence shifts at various points of time depending on diplomacy, policing, and governing officials, the border, which may appear fixed, is also a shifting place of business, control, and policing. The U.S.-Mexico border is a major point of entry for narcotics and drugs from Mexico but also from around the world. The porousness of the border is a historical continuity, and certain people have utilized its expansiveness and openness for illicit trade. Thus, drug trafficking organizations (DTOs) developed transnational networks to meet the demand for drugs in the United States. DTOs operating in Mexico have been connected to global organized crime networks since the 1920s.[5]

Weaving together historical and contemporary case studies of Mexican and Mexican American female drug traffickers challenges the historical and contemporary scholarly argument that little is known about women's involvement in organized crime prior to the 2000s.[6] To demonstrate that the role of women was widely addressed, we play with place and time to demonstrate the complexity of transnational trafficking networks that were multifaceted from production to transportation to distribution. This work also expands the new drug history by closely examining how policing agents perceived and publicly decried women and how their attitudes were influenced by broader concepts of race, class, and gender along the U.S.-Mexico border.[7] The patterns of women's involvement in the drug trade and their uses and perceptions of violence changed over time, impacting the role of the family in drugs and violence. For women in the trade, violence was multidimensional in that it emerges from factional or familial competition and from the state or policing agents. As a contemporary drug trafficker Rosa Vallejo responded when asked why she might not want to be a boss, "Well, I don't know. Perhaps it is because it is easier to be beautiful than it is to have to fucking deal with the men . . . but I don't know. . . . I think you have to have balls and bravado to get in [to the trade].[8]

Using both gender and violence as categories of analysis, we play close attention to the 1955 U.S. Senate Committee on the Judiciary hearings on Illicit Narcotics Traffic. Three case studies in Texas in the 1950s allow for comparison of contemporary women involved in the drug trade. Using the case studies and ethnographic research, we offer a detailed analysis of women in the U.S.-Mexico borderlands in order to demonstrate their historical continuity in the trade that challenges much of the literature of women in organized crime. Put simply, drug trafficking is an organized crime in which women have played critical roles for over a hundred years.[9] More recently, they have been continually "rediscovered" with a sensational, if not fictional, urgency. An analysis of contemporary women's drug traffickers' attitudes toward violence and the trade allows us to draw some conclusions regarding women's historical agency in what has long been perceived as a man's job. As authors in this volume assert, borders are places of violence. These borderland spaces so far from Washington, D.C., and Mexico City have served as sites of economic opportunities for men and women from the nineteenth century to the present. And for that reason, the drug trade lures women for precisely the same reason that it draws men: the opportunities and the potential for wealth promised by drug trafficking that offers the chance for a better life.

Women, Violence, and the Price Daniel Hearings

In 1955, the U.S. Senate Judiciary committee created a subcommittee to undertake a study of drugs and the need to change the federal criminal code. Meetings were held in cities across the United States. In part, the Democratic senator from Texas Price Daniel held these public hearings to bolster legislative changes that ultimately influenced the passage of the 1956 Narcotics Control Act.[10] The hearings in the United States followed similar hearings held in Canada.[11] As in Canada, senators held regional meetings in New York, Pennsylvania, Washington, D.C., Texas, and California.[12] The purpose of the hearings was to establish the extent of drug use and drug trafficking. Much of the concern was associated with "Red China" and its attempts to poison Americans.[13]

The Price Daniel hearings held in September reflected clashes between the medical community and policing agencies over what to do about drug addiction. The New York hearings served as a platform to discuss efforts in the struggle against drug addiction. Those held outside of Washington, D.C., and New York had a regional focus with an emphasis on the growing drug problems in major cities and regions in the United States. In Chicago and Detroit, the hearings highlighted connections to Canada and the role of organized crime families in the major cities of the United States.

During the Texas and California hearings, Mexico emerged as the key supplier of brown heroin but also as a site of transshipment of European and Asian opiate derivatives. H. J. Anslinger, the director of the Federal Bureau of Narcotics (FBN), reported that Mexico accounted for 90 percent of the marijuana in the United States. Because of Mexico's role as a supply country, the Mexican government sent representatives to the hearings in California. In

Texas, Daniel sent an invitation to Óscar Rabasa, the director general of the Mexican diplomatic service, and Carlos Franco Sodi, the attorney general.[14] Both declined, but they outlined their ongoing commitment to the battle against drug trafficking.[15]

A close reading of the 1956 report *Illicit Narcotics Traffic* challenges conclusions common in the drug literature published from the 1970s to the 1990s. Much of the scholarly literature situated Mexico as a minor player in the international narcotics trade.[16] In part, this derived from a lack of appreciation of the strategic geopolitical position of Mexico. Instead, scholars focused on the Asian and European drug trade because the U.S. foreign policy focused on those areas of the world. Ever an astute bureaucrat, Anslinger framed his arguments and rhetoric from the greater foreign policy to ensure the continuation of his bureau. Through the numerous interviews and hearings, policing agents cast Mexico as a major player in heroin and morphine trade in the 1950s throughout the southwestern United States. The Texas and California hearings positioned Mexico not as an upstart in the heroin trade but rather as a historical site of marijuana and heroin supply for years.

In the Texas hearings, men and women appeared as instrumental to the drug trade. Customs agents described how women crossed the international border with their husbands to smuggle marijuana for consumption in Texas. Anslinger recognized that women "obeyed narcotics laws better than men in which men were arrested three times that rate of women.[17] Women from as far away as New York City smuggled marijuana across the U.S.-Mexico border to sell it in Brooklyn and Manhattan. African Americans, Anglo-Americans, and Latinas employed cars, stuffed their clothing, and even used sanitary napkins to smuggle marijuana.[18]

In the Texas hearings, women on both sides of the border were suspect. The celebrated Chicano journalist Rubén Salazar gave testimony about a notorious border boss, Ignacia "La Nacha" Jasso viuda de González, reintroducing her to the U.S. Congress thirteen years after the government attempted to extradite her.[19] Salazar painted the history of a prominent woman in the trade, but his work also provided insight into other women operating on or close to the U.S.-Mexico border in the 1950s. He also exposed ties between drug traffickers and people in power along the border and the conflicts that emerged between different political figures. Salazar's testimony situated La Nacha as a female drug trafficker based along a major port of entry on the U.S.-Mexico border with ties to much of the heroin markets in major U.S. cities. By the mid-1950s, she had been living and working in Ciudad Juárez, where she had trafficked drugs for over twenty years.

Jasso, however, complicates the border vice narrative. Jasso may have lived in Ciudad Juárez, but her poppy fields were in the state of Jalisco, her processing labs were scattered about the nation but mostly based in Guadalajara, and she did not physically move her own product, though she did peddle from her home.[20] The border was a lucrative site, but it was not a fixed place for drug trafficking. While Jasso's husband, Pablote González, was rumored to have murdered competitors and portrayed as vicious, little evidence exists that she used direct forms of violence. While she did not use heroin, she injected others who visited her home. Her heroin was directly linked to overdoses on both sides of the border. On the other side the border, Jasso guaranteed delivery to distributors and dealers in the United States. Salazar's testimony identified that Anglos and Mexicans on both sides of the border took her drugs. And, in some cases, people who consumed her drugs overdosed, such as paratrooper Daniel Barrera.[21] While Jasso did not inject Barrera with the dose of heroin that killed him, he died from heroin that she allegedly supplied to the dealers who sold it to him.

The fact that women like Jasso sold and trafficked to an Anglo market became a growing source of surprise because of low drug use among Mexicans. In the testimony of Captain R. B. Laws of the Criminal Investigation Division of the Austin Police Department and Lieutenant K. R. Herbert, the officer in charge, they outlined their ongoing arrests of male and female addicts in Austin. In Laws and Herbert's testimony, they presented evidence that more Anglo-Americans were addicts compared with Latin Americans or African Americans.[22] Senator Daniel was shocked by this acknowledgment because it contradicted the metanarrative of race, vice, and crime purported by men such as Anslinger. Daniel asked,

This is the first city in which we have held a hearing in which the Anglo Americans are more involved in arrests than the other races. The figures here are considerably higher than in the colored, for instance. In some cities, it is unfortunately the thing, it may be the fault of the way we have taken care of certain races, but we find the arrests among the colored population to be as high as 90 percent of the total arrests. Here, you have just the reverse, not that high a percentage, but there are twice as many Anglo Americans arrested during these years than you have colored.[23]

Captain Laws replied to Daniel's question with an affirmation that in Austin more Anglos were arrested than African Americans and Latinos. Yet evidence that had been gathered by the Bureau of Social Hygiene as early as the 1920s had repeatedly demonstrated that Anglos remained the largest consumers of narcotics whether on the southern or northern border. In El Paso, Texas, Charles E. Terry of the bureau reported that Anglo doctors frequently prescribed narcotics to Mexicans, but Terry argued that most Mexicans preferred traditional healing methods. Thus, pharmacies frequented by Mexicans had one-half the narcotics prescriptions, prescribed by Anglo pharmacists, filled compared with those frequented by Anglos.[24]

In the hearings, the case of Simona Cavazos presents an organization as complicated as that of Jasso but on a smaller scale. Initial testimony described Cavazos as being someone who somehow stumbled onto being an Austin heroin supplier who intoxicated more Anglos than other races. Cavazos's operation and its location created instrumental heroin flows from Mexico to the Texas state capital of Austin, a city more than two hours away by car in the 1950s.[25]

In the testimonies of Lieutenant Herbert and R. C. Scott, an investigator with the Austin Police Department, both worked with Mr. Thomas Bromley of the Federal Bureau of Narcotics. Scott recalled his work with Bromley by describing "a pattern that was handed to me that I had to conform to and I was introduced to these people by a special employee furnished by the Federal Bureau of Narcotics.[26] Scott told the committee about a sting operation in which the "special employee" Bromley participated. Bromley was an FBN informant and a former addict who had just been released from the U. S. Narcotic Farm (a facility for the rehabilitation of addicts) in Lexington, Kentucky.[27]

Scott described visiting Simona and her husband, Alfonso, at a small bar in the "Latin American" district of San Antonio. They ran and likely owned Al's Bar, where Scott met them. After the initial meeting in the bar, the Cavazoses invited him to their home, which was across the street. In the course of their conversation, Simona stated that it was difficult to buy heroin by the ounce because Mexican vendors wanted to sell by *papelito*, or paper. Thirty papers constituted an ounce, and one paper yielded a cost of $25. In Scott's conversation, Simona related that she ordered her drugs in Laredo, but she never crossed the heroin herself across the border; instead, she arranged in Mexico to have it delivered to her in San Antonio.

Simona connected to Mexican drug dealers, like Jasso, who guaranteed delivery on the U.S. side of the border. Other Mexican trafficking organizations offered the same service whether in Tijuana, Nogales, or Nuevo Laredo. When Scott returned for heroin, Simona told him she just received shipment and could sell him two hundred grams for $5,000 (equivalent to $48,550 in 2020). Despite her misgiving about selling an ounce, she now offered to sell him a large amount. Narcotics officers in the 1950s would never have received $5,000 to front a buy.[28] Most likely, Simona offered this amount as a test because she knew that a police officer could not make such a buy, but a drug dealer would have the cash for a large purchase. During their conversation, Scott also reported that Simona had mentioned the hearings. He stated, "She was under the impression you had passed a law that there was going to be a sentence of hanging for anyone who brought back from Mexico, and she was quite disturbed by that." Daniel followed up by asking Scott if he would recite one of her comments regarding the hearing. Scott did not want to say what she had said in mixed company. Daniel replied, "Well I'll ask you if she said this, if this is correct: 'I can't quit selling heroin as long as I can sit on my butt and make $400 to $500[from $3,884 to $4,855 in 2020 dollars] a day.' Did she tell you that?" Scott replied that indeed she did.

Because of Simona's deviance, her ethnic origin, and her posting of a $5,000 bail immediately upon her arrest, Daniel inquired if Simona was a U.S. citizen. Scott assumed so because she and her husband appeared to own Al's Bar. As other people testified to Daniel, Simona and Alfonso's organization became more complex. While many Mexicans trafficked and sold drugs for them, the mother of an Anglo addict testified that she purchased from an Anglo named Raymond Murdock, who worked for Simona. Others testified that Murdock worked with the Cavazoses perhaps as their lieutenant, while a report submitted by narcotics agents in San Antonio reported that Murdock was Simona's lover and partner.[29] Whether Murdock and Simona were lovers or not, he worked closely with her and her extended family in buying and selling drugs and assisting in their operations of fronts to sell stolen goods.[30] More importantly, it was Murdock who sold Simona's heroin in Austin, a town with a far larger Anglo population than San Antonio. Texas and key cities such as San Antonio were nexus points between Mexican heroin and the U.S. market. John Ben Sheppard, the attorney general for the State of Texas, argued that heroin and marijuana moved through his state to neighboring states.[31] Yet the Cavazoses and members of their organization realized that a Mexican distributor might be easily identified and detected in Austin. Thus, Murdock and Cavazos created an alliance that was lucrative. Policing agents saw the actions of Cavazos and Murdock as so criminal and dangerous a harsh punishment was necessary.

Daniel not only showed interest in Simona's citizenship but also followed up with Scott about her opinion of the committee and her reference that a law had been passed to sentence people to hanging for drug trafficking.

In an exchange, *Senator Daniel* asked: Did she say that "G.D. Senate committee recommended hanging"?
Scott: Yes sir.
Senator Daniel: Well, do you think hanging would be too severe for this traffic after having examined what she has done?
Mr. Scott: My personal opinion; it wouldn't.[32]

The exchange between Scott and Daniel reflected the heightened rhetoric that has emerged in a century-long war on drugs that focuses on the criminality of drug trafficking. Significantly, it is an exchange that demonstrates the significance of time and place. Simona was a Mexican woman living in San Antonio, Texas, in 1955. She might have known people or heard stories of Mexican men and women being lynched with the assistance of policing agents such as the Texas Rangers.[33] As William Carrigan and Clive Webb have argued, Mexican women were lynched for forcefully rejecting an Anglo man's sexual overtures, speaking Spanish, or other crimes. Simona's thoughts about hanging and Daniel and Scott's exchange capture the history of violence against women who transgress proper gender roles. Simona, a Mexican American, not only had to fear male competitors who might rob and cheat her but also contended with those in positions of power who questioned whether her crime deserved hanging rather than imprisonment. Her possible status as a Mexican citizen led them to consider lynching, something they did not mention for Anglo or African American women in the drug trade. In the hearing, Daniel and Scott acknowledged that hanging was an appropriate punishment for a Mexican American woman drug trafficker who endangered Anglo men, women, and children.[34]

For much of the hearings, the committee treated certain Mexican American women in the drug trade as hostile such as Purificación (Pura) Rodríguez Pérez, a drug peddler based in Houston. Daniel described her as a hostile witness because of her evasive answers and her refusal to confess her guilt.[35] In a 1955 report prepared by Howard Chappell, a narcotics agent, reported that Rodríguez was believed to sell 100 to 150 grams of heroin per week. She supplied eight to ten other Houston-based heroin dealers. Like many Houston dealers, she received her heroin via San Antonio, but she also bought and smuggled across the border heroin from Monterrey, Mexico.[36] Like Cavazos, Rodríguez worked with her family members and sold from a package store and lounge that she owned as well as from her home. Both women sold to Anglos, and Anglos were the greatest consumers of heroin, on the basis of arrest records in Texas that most likely underreported Anglo drug use compared with that of Mexicans, Asians, and African Americans. Anslinger routinely portrayed drug trafficking and drug addiction as a plague brought to the United States by Asians, Africans, and "Central Americans."[37] And he routinely complained about their proclivities toward addiction and criminality.

Anslinger's heightened rhetoric and the role of women in the drug trade demonstrates multiple historical continuities. In examining the Daniel Committee hearings, Jasso, Cavazos, and Rodríguez's operations were familial, complicated, and vast despite operating out of impoverished neighborhoods in Ciudad Juárez and Latino barrios in San Antonio and Houston. Their drugs addicted young Anglo and Mexican men and women, destroyed families, and contributed to crime and violence. When Daniel interviewed the mother of an Anglo addict, he showed great sympathy for her even when she described buying heroin from Cavazos as well as in Mexico and smuggling it over the border for her addicted son.[38]

While Cavazos and Rodríguez disappeared from the historical record, Jasso remained of interest for years until her death in 1982. Many of her children, nieces, and nephews entered the trade and became professionals, creating a multigeneration trafficking family.

Family and Trust: A Historical Continuity

In the 1950s, a heightened sense that America was under attack, whether from Communists or drug traffickers, reverberates across time. In recent years, these attitudes have emerged again in which women involved in illicit trade have been rediscovered by the media and policing agents. Like all "discoveries," there is a sensational aspect such as when recently Mexican journalists Ioan Grillo and Javier Valdez decried the emergence of women in the drug trade, a business in which men "behave like animals."[39]

The women, whether in the past or present, make rational decisions to enter the trade similar to how Cavazos and Rodriguez did. Jasso, Cavazos, and Rodríguez came from modest backgrounds. They lived in similar poor neighborhoods of small adobe or wooden structures that continue to exist today. The meager evidence available shows that they had modest educational backgrounds, which ensured that they would remain on the economic margins of society.[40] They used their wits to create a livelihood that was more or less successful moving between illicit and licit. Jasso had a small dry goods store and a farm, Cavazos owned a bar with her husband, and Rodríguez owned a lounge with her family. These were Mexican families who gained a liquor license in the 1950s; a costly, and not easy, feat.

While much changed for women in Mexico from the 1950s to the present, women still enter the trade for many of the same reasons. Modern women in the trade demonstrate changes over time but also continuities. Despite more educational and economic opportunities, women continue to work in the drug trade. When asked why she entered the drug trade, modern drug boss Claudia Valenzuela replied, "I was dying of hunger, I needed money, and I had not studied more than secondary school and I did not complete that. My family is from the highlands, and there was no money." Working from the states of Sinaloa and Chihuahua, Valenzuela, like other bosses, had family connections to the drug trade. Her father grew marijuana that he sold to others who then trafficked it across the U.S.-Mexico border. He was not a boss but a farmer who grew marijuana because it paid more than beans and corn, which were difficult to seed and harvest and then sell at a good price. The fact that Valenzuela's father grew marijuana but did not sell or traffic it placed him at the lower economic level of the drug trade. Along with her father, Valenzuela noticed that many of her neighbors and others in her mountain town grew marijuana or poppy. She noted that those who engaged in the poppy trade were wealthier. She realized early on that "goma" paid more, even though less was harvested and sold.[41] Her childhood in the mountains surrounded by others in the drug trade introduced her to drug production and offered her one of few economic opportunities.

Women from states such as Sinaloa have long participated in the drug trade. In the late 1800s and early 1900s, poppy was grown in Sinaloa, Chihuahua, and Durango, and it later spread to Tamaulipas and Veracruz.[42] By the 1870s, poppy also could be found in Michoacán, Nayarit, Oaxaca, Chiapas, and Guerrero.[43] Mexico provided an excellent place for poppy growth due to the soil and full to mostly full sun exposure for much of the year. The Mazatlán port long served as an entry port for Asian opiates, which were then reprocessed and trafficked north. For example, Jasso was originally from the state of Durango. Her heroin most likely came from Sinaloa and Durango, was processed in Jalisco, and was trafficked through Ciudad Juárez. Sinaloa and other drug-producing states are tied to border contraband due to the sophistication of drug and organized crime networks. The border as a fixed place through which contraband flows is part of an intricate commodity chain that extends through Mexico and across the ocean.

The Sinaloan female boss Valenzuela provides a glimpse into the lives of women who enter the drug trade due to personal experiences but also economic analysis. Mexican Americans in the United States and Mexicans from the highlands are portrayed as lazy, as well as violent, which is why they seek to sell drugs: because they do not want to work hard. During the Daniel hearings, Cavazos was portrayed as so lazy that she resorted to drug selling. Despite her work in farming and her dry goods store, the FBI described Jasso as fat, lazy, and sloppily dressed.[44] Valenzuela offers a different interpretation of why women such as her enter into the drug trade. In her small town, she stated there were few businesses and the schools were far from her town. The only industry was growing and selling marijuana and poppy. As she asserted, "In the mountains, we do not know anything else besides narcotrafficking because if we do study we learn there is nothing to do!" What she and her family members and neighbors grew made its way north. Just as Santiago Guerra described in Tamaulipas, drug production and smuggling became a permanent way of life for many families.

Other female drug bosses entered the trade because of family connections or lack of opportunities. Gloria Benítez worked alongside her husband, who transported drugs from Mexico to the United States. They settled in the United States, where initially life was difficult, but they learned the language and made a good living. She recalled, "Living the good life: money, big purchases, and houses in Mexico for the family."[45] That good life ended when her husband was killed in a shoot-out. Having dropped out of secondary school due to pregnancy, she returned to Mexico with her two children. Working with her brother-in-law, she started to move drugs and run crews between Baja California and southern California. Thus, she remained working with her family.

Desireé Guerrero offers a similar story. She too started in the trade with her husband. Originally from Guadalajara, she and her husband operated out of Chihuahua, where her husband was a rancher. With their three children, they vacationed in his home state, Sinaloa, where he and his extended family had business interests. Although Desireé traveled with her husband, she did not see herself as his partner in his drug business because she was not an investor. Instead, she assisted her husband in money laundering, in part because she was more highly educated. After he was kidnapped and killed, she continued to work in the business. She worked closely with his family, first as a "fixer," moving money and paying bribes; later she became more involved. When asked why she did not retire after her husband was killed, she stated, "First, because of my family, and second, I had no idea how I would maintain my life style. Also, I did not want to be maintained asking for money from my brothers-in-law. Furthermore, I learned a lot of things from him (my husband), so I decided and I am still here."[46]

Benítez and Desireé appear very much like the character Helena Ayala in the movie *Traffic* played by Catherine Zeta-Jones. Ayala is a wife left destitute when her husband is implicated in drug trafficking. She turned to his business to make ends meet.[47] Benítez entered the trade to maintain her family, and Desireé continued to work in a business that she had learned from her husband. Both women employed the business and familial networks of their spouses to support their families very similar to Jasso, who had been recognized as an equal trafficker as her husband but expanded the business after his murder.

For many women such as Valenzuela and Benítez, their family members exposed them to the trade. Valenzuela's father's willingness to put her in charge of his business as it grew gave her a skill and an education where there was little available. This too is a historical continuity. For women such as Cavazos and Rodríguez, they too had few opportunities as poorly educated Mexican American women living and working in Texas in the 1950s. Valenzuela did not attempt to look for other work because it would not have paid enough to make a living, as she had little education and few skills. The one skill that she had, her knowledge of marijuana and poppy production and later trafficking, she developed. Her father, like many male family members, brought her into the business because he recognized that she was capable, more capable than some of the male family members. As Carey has discussed and Guerra portrays in this collection, family businesses evolved from small organizations to what sometimes became major organized crime families.[48]

Being a boss or married to a boss, however, did not protect women from violence from their competitors or policing agents. The evidence suggests that Jasso, Cavazos, and Rodríguez had to contend with men who competed with them, stole their drugs, attempted to entrap them, questioned their citizenship or right to be in the United States, and considered harsh punishment for them. Cavazos and Rodríguez demonstrated a keen ability to avoid arrests and, during the hearings, to avoid questioning. Jasso had long avoided attempts by the U.S. government to extradite her, and she avoided arrests despite the testimony regarding her during the Price Daniel hearings.

In part, Rodríguez's evasive answers may be explained by her attempts to protect her family members from the police as well as to not incriminate herself. By being a hostile witness and refusing to answer, she maintained the trust that others had confided in her. Valenzuela adds insight into the significance of family in the distribution of drugs. She described the difficulty of finding people to work with: "In narcotrafficking, trust is a life or death [matter], if you trust someone, they can be very dangerous, but if you do not trust them they can also be! You must know when it is time to trust and when it is not."[49] For her, loyalty is of utmost importance.

The ability to trust explains why so many drug traffickers work closely with family members such as Jasso, Rodríguez, and Cavazos, but women traffickers also trusted and worked with men. Cavazos trusted Murdock, who allowed her to sell drugs in the more lucrative Anglo market of Austin, Texas.[50] Murdock not only worked for the Cavazoses, but the evidence demonstrates that he lived next door to them in the 1950s.[51] Other Mexican male drug dealers also appeared to have been supplied by the Cavazos couple, which means that they built multiple overlapping networks of men whom they trusted. Even in sting operations, policing agents describe having to meet the couple multiple times in order to gain their trust to make a buy or to find a bigger source.[52] For the drug trafficker, the development of trust or even of credentialing of a source is an important part of developing an organized crime network, but it is also a way of avoiding violence.[53]

Women bosses must also fear violence and betrayal from within their organization. Jasso, who also worked with her husband and children, encountered violence and betrayal among men who worked with or for her. That potential for violence within the organization or beyond shifts how women work in the drug trade. For women such as Cavazos and Rodríguez, there is little evidence regarding how their organizations grew. Yet, contemporary female drug traffickers give us insight. Many women work almost exclusively within their family organizations such as Valenzuela and Benítez. It appears that Cavazos and Rodríguez did the same thing, as did La Nacha. However, as organizations grow, women, like men, will have to bring others into the organization. Some women such as Valenzuela prefer to work exclusively with all women because she finds it easier, and she trusts women more than the men. This is something that is unique to women bosses: that they will have all or mostly female lieutenants, workers, mules, and other partners.[54]

Valenzuela also recognized that some women prefer to work exclusively with men. Some women believe that they control the men in their organizations by flirting with them. While men have historically offered women protection, men frequently underestimate the women's power and business acumen. Valenzuela and another female trafficker, Guadalupe Medina, argued that they allowed men to do the "dirty work." And they compensate the men very well for that work. Thus, women have historically distanced and presently distance themselves from actual physical violence.

Valenzuela also mentioned that she once had a business and a romantic relationship. That relationship distracted her from her business, but it taught her something. She argued that men constantly think of "taking." Thus, women have found that men consider taking over their organizations, thinking that the woman might prefer to be a "wife" or "girlfriend" rather than a boss. Frequently, they take by force, so women grow their organizations incrementally, and they maintain a lifestyle that is more moderate to avoid detection from the police. Medina and Valenzuela argued that women, like men, desire money and power. Yet women desire the money to take care of themselves and their family. The money gives women greater control over their lives and those who surround them. They do not have to rely on men in order to support their children.

Both Medina and Valenzuela argue that men desire fame far more than women. That desire to seek fame causes men to grow their businesses too big to control, which contributes to mistakes. Medina noticed that violence leads to fame but is not good for business. She stated, "There are those who are famous but have not money, in a time they die of hunger. They are crude, violent, and conceited."[55] Claudia stated that men enjoyed violence. She highlighted those men who "marked their territory" by bursts of violence at parties or sought fights where none were needed.[56] For women, this type of behavior would jeopardize their business. Both Valenzuela and Guerrero acknowledge that violence has become part of their job, and they must confront it. Thus, they both invest heavily in security and rely on loyalty. That loyalty and familial security extend to their illicit and legitimate businesses. Claudia owns a chain of medical spas in Chihuahua, Sinaloa, and Mexico City which provide Botox and other injectables. These are run by women in her extended family. For Guerrero, she too ensures that her businesses, legal and illicit, are built on loyalty. She is the mother of three adult sons. One works on the illegal side of the family business, while another is an agricultural engineer who tends to her avocado farms. Other family members assist in managing her real estate portfolio that includes hotels, restaurants, and apartment buildings.

Most women in the trade acknowledge that women are more discreet than men.[57] Valenzuela provides an interesting rationale for the discreetness of women and why they build their businesses slowly. Her gendered interpretation asserts that the sexual and gender double standards inform women's decisions. She provided the example that men may sleep with multiple women and have lovers while married and receive little or no public shaming. Women, on the other hand, who have multiple lovers are considered to be whores and are publicly shamed. Men seek to be the center of attention and demonstrate their sexual and financial power with the demonstration of wealth that includes women, jewelry, alcohol consumption, and a narco-presence. These behaviors and characteristics do not translate well for feminine success. Female bosses such as Valenzuela, Medina, Guerrero, and contemporary Ciudad Juárez boss Marimar dress modestly, more like female middle managers than narcos or narco girlfriends.[58] They straddle both lives. Their clothing choices, their avoidance or only modest use of plastic surgery, and their choices to live in middle-class neighborhoods illustrate their lives as comfortable businesswomen. They seek to avoid detection, whether by policing agent, competitors, or even their own bosses.

These characteristics of living a modest life or creating the illusion of a certain station in life also appear to have been maintained by Jasso, Cavazos, and Rodríguez. Despite being able to immediately post bonds of thousands of dollars in the 1950s, they lived modestly and dressed like the women among whom they lived, working-class Mexican and Mexican Americans. Their discreetness and ability to withhold information and to live modest lives despite the wealth that they controlled were to ensure their continued longevity in their business despite the potential for violence. Trust and the ability to maintain the trust of others were essential. They worked with their family members, both male and female. Yet they also attempted to deflect the attention of men, whether policing agents or possible competitors. Mostly, they recognized that violence or threats of violence could erupt at any time, whether from policing agents, competitors in the drug trade, or even their own associates.

Contemporary women encounter greater potential for violence than their predecessors, yet they continue to enter the trade. Modern women bosses such as Valenzuela, Medina, and Guerrero interpret their actions as contrasts to masculine power. They do not sell from their homes or invite potential clients to meet in places that would be identified with them or their family members. What typifies the male narco—at least what is glorified in the media—is a partial and incomplete story of the drug trade. The drug trade presents both men *and* women the promise of a better life through the accumulation of wealth, and so women engage purposefully and willingly in this world for their own and their families' economic betterment. They too thrive in what is often presented and interpreted as a "man's world." To understand gender in the drug trade, we must embrace a broader and more encompassing vision of women at all levels. Female bosses clandestinely operate, toiling in the drug trade while building successful legitimate business for themselves and their children. Their lives tell compelling stories of survival in the drug trade and endurance in times of violence.

Notes

1. Steven Soderbergh, *Traffic*, Bedford Falls Productions, 2000, 147 mins., DVD; Ridley Scott, *The Counselor*, Scott Free Productions, 2013; Arturo Pérez-Reverte, *La reina del sur* (Madrid: Alfaguara, 2002). Pérez-Reverte's book was also adapted into a miniseries of the same title. Maurico Cruz and Walter Doehner, *La reina del sur*, Telemundo Internacional, 2011.

2. Terrence E. Poppa, *Drug Lord: The Life and Death of a Mexican Kingpin—A True Story* (Seattle: Demand Publications, 1999); Ioan Grillo, *El Narco: Inside Mexico's Criminal Insurgency* (New York: Bloomsbury, 2012); Alfredo Corchado, *Midnight in Mexico: A Reporter's Journey through a Country's Descent into Darkness* (New York: Penguin Books, 2013); Charles Bowden, *Murder City: Ciudad Juárez and the Global Economy's New Killing Fields* (New York: Nation Books, 2010).

3. There is a growing literature on women in the Latin American drug trade: Celso Athayde and M. V. Bill, *Falcão, mulheres e o tráfico* (Rio de Janeiro: Objetiva, 2007); Inés Coronado Tinoco, *Causas sociales de la delincuencia femenina por tráfico de drogas* (Lima, Perú: Editorial Gráfica del Perú, 1989); Elaine Costa, Cristina Pimentel, and Ruth Vasconcelos, *Amor bandido: As teias afetivas que envolvem a mulher no tráfico de drogas* (Maceió, Brazil: EDUFAL, Editora da Universidade Federal de Alagoas, 2007); Jennifer Fleetwood, *Drug Mules: Women in the International Cocaine Trade* (New York: Palgrave Macmillan, 2014); Andrés López López and Juan Camilo Ferrand, *Las fantásticas: Las mujeres de el cartel; Un viaje al extraordinario mundo de las mujeres de los narcos* (Doral, FL: Aguilar, 2009); Erika Cecilia Montoya Zavala, *Migrantes, empresarias, políticas, profesionistas y traficantes de drogas: Mujeres en la esfera pública y privada* (Sinaloa, Mexico: Facultad de Estudios Internacionales y Políticas Públicas, Universidad Autónoma de Sinaloa, 2012); Julio Scherer García, *La Reina del Pacífico: La mujer-mito del narco mexicano; Qué significa nacer, crecer y vivir en ese mundo* (México, D.F.: Grijalbo, 2008); Javier Valdez, *Miss Narco: Belleza, poder y violencia; Historias reales de mujeres en el narcotráfico mexicano* (México, D.F.: Aguilar, 2009).

4. Elaine Carey and Andrae Marak, *Smugglers, Brothels, and Twine: Historical Perspectives on Contraband and Vice in North America's Borderlands* (Tucson: University of Arizona Press, 2011); Elaine Carey, *Women Drug Traffickers: Mules, Bosses, and Organized Crime* (Albuquerque: University of New Mexico Press, 2014); José Carlos Cisneros Guzmán, "Tres Jefas " and "Todo se puede terminar en un momento," in *Las Jefas del narco: El ascenso de las mujeres en el crimen organizado*, ed. Arturo Santamaría (Grijalbo, México, D.F: Grijalbo, 2012), and "A la sombra del hombre: La participación de la mujer en el narcotráfico; Su empoderamiento," in Erika Montoya, *"Migrantes, empresarias, políticas y narcos: Una visión internacionalista a la participación de las mujeres en la esfera pública y privada"* (Sinaloa, Mexico: Juan Pablos Editores-UAS, 2013).

5. Elaine Carey, "A History of Mexican Organized Crime," in *Organized Crime: Causes and Consequences*, ed. Robert M. Lombardo (Hauppage, NY: Novo Science Publishers, 2019).

6. Jana Arsovska and Felia Allum, "Introduction: Women and Transnational Organized Crime," *Trends in Organized Crime* 17, no. 1 (2014): 3; Ernest Savona and Gioacchino Nataoli, "Women and Other Mafia-Type Criminal Organizations," in *Women and the Mafia: Female Roles in Organized Crime Structures*, ed. Giavanni Fiandaca (New York: Springer, 2007), 103–7.

7. Paul Gootenberg and Isaac Campos Costero, "Toward a New Drug History of Latin America: A Research Frontier at the Center of Debates," *Hispanic American Historical Review* 95, no. 1 (2015): 1–35.

8. José Carlos Cisneros Guzmán interview with "Rosa Vallejo," Culiacán, Sinaloa, March 2014. All names have been changed to protect the identity of the women and their families.

9. Carey, *Women Drug Traffickers*.

10. Price Daniel was senator from Texas from 1953 to 1957. He then served as governor of the state. During the 1950s, Mexican heroin accounted for 90 percent of the heroin in Texas.

11. U.S. Congress, Hearings before the Subcommittee on Improvements in the Federal Criminal Code of the Committee on the Judiciary, *Illicit Narcotics Traffic*, United States Congress, 84th Cong. (Washington, DC: Government Printing Office, 1956), 2–3. The hearings were held in three of Canada's largest cities. The format was similar to those in the United States in which medical doctors, politicians, policing agents, and addicts appeared before the committee.

12. *Illicit Narcotics Traffic*, 2–3.

13. For a discussion of McCarthyism, see Ellen Schrecker, *Many Are the Crimes: McCarthyism in America* (Boston: Little, Brown, 1998); and Richard M. Fried, *Nightmare in Red: The McCarthy Era in Perspective* (New York: Oxford University Press, 1990).

14. Price Daniel to Óscar Rabasa and Carlos Franco Sodi, October 1, 1955, repr. in *Illicit Narcotics Traffic*.

15. Telegram from consulate of Mexico City to Department of State, December 4, 1959, box 28, file Mexico Border, RG 170, National Archives and Records Administration II (NAII), College Park, MD.

16. While scholars recognized Mexico was involved in the drug trade, they frequently did not account for the extent to which Mexican heroin was the source of heroin for many U.S. cities. See David Musto, *The American Disease: Origins of Narcotics Control* (New

York: Oxford University Press, 1987); and David Musto, *One Hundred Years of Heroin* (Westport, CT: Auburn House, 2002). Also see Eric Schneider, *Smack: Heroin and the American City* (Philadelphia: University of Pennsylvania Press, 2011).

17. *Illicit Narcotics Traffic*, 25. Anslinger also noted that prior to the enforcement of narcotics laws in the United States, women traffickers were four to five times the number of men.

18. The case of Marilyn Grant, a nurse, who smuggled marijuana in a sanitary pad that she made. Her case was sensational. *Illicit Narcotics Traffic*, 2599.

19. The Subcommittee on Improvements in the Federal Criminal Code, part of the Senate Committee on the Judiciary, was composed of Price Daniel (Texas); Joseph O'Mahoney (Wyoming); James O. Eastland (Mississippi); Herman Walker (Idaho); John Marshall Butler (Maryland); C. Aubrey Gasque, general counsel; and W. Lee Speer, chief investigator.

20. For more on La Nacha, see Carey, *Women Drug Traffickers*, 126–57.

21. Carey, *Women Drug Traffickers*, 144–45.

22. *Illicit Narcotics Traffic*, 2391. The numbers of arrested from 1948 to 1955 that Laws provided were "Distribution as to sex: male offenders, 149, female 30, a total of 179. Distribution as to race: Anglo American 81; Latin American, 62; and colored, 36."

23. *Illicit Narcotics Traffic*, 2392.

24. Charles Edward Terry, *A Further Study and Report on the Use of Narcotics under the Provisions of Federal Law in Six Communities in the United States of America for the Period of July 1, 1923 to June 30, 1924* (New York: Bureau of Social Hygiene, 1927). Terry was a medical doctor who practiced in Florida and became the president of the Duval County Medical Society. It was in that role that he became an antidrug crusader, but he also established one of the first maintenance drug programs.

25. *Illicit Narcotics Traffic*, 2397.

26. *Illicit Narcotics Traffic*, 2397.

27. Nancy Campbell, J. P. Olsen, and Luke Walden, *The Narcotics Farm: The Rise and Fall of America's First Prison for Drug Addicts* (New York: Abrams, 2008). Also see their documentary by the same name at http://www.narcoticfarm.com/t2_film.html.

28. As a comparison, in the 1970s, undercover NYPD narcotics officers only received up to $1,500 for a buy in a sting operation.

29. "Narcotics Traffickers—San Antonio, Texas," Daniel's Committee file, box 9, RG 170, Drug Enforcement Administration and Bureau of Narcotics and Dangerous Drugs (DEA-BNDD), National Archives and Records Administration (NARA), College Park, MD.

30. Simona's sister, Victoria Terrazos, ran fronts for stolen goods, and she was a recognized San Antonio crime boss who appears to have played a small role in the drug business. Her brother-in-law, Tony Davila, was a recognized drug supplier and smuggler.

31. *Illicit Traffic in Narcotics*, 2433–35.

32. *Illicit Traffic in Narcotics*, 2401.

33. Richard Delgado, "The Law of the Noose: A History of Latino Lynching," *Harvard Civil Rights-Civil Liberties Law Review* 44: 297–312; and William Carrigan and Clive Webb, *Forgotten Dead: Mob Violence against Mexicans in the United States, 1848–1928* (New York: Oxford University Press, 2013).

34. Carrigan and Webb, *Forgotten Dead*, 70–75.

35. See Carey, *Women Drug Traffickers*, 149–51.

36. Howard Chappell, Narcotics Agents to Ernest M. Gentry, District Supervisor, District 10, Daniel's Committee File, box 9, RG 170 DEA-BNDD, NARAII.

37. See Harry J. Anslinger and William F. Thomkins, *The Traffic in Narcotics* (New York: Funk and Wagnalls, 1953); and with Will Oursler, *The Murderers: The Shocking Story of the Narcotic Gangs* (New York: Farrar, Straus, and Cudahy, 1961).

38. *Illicit Traffic in Narcotics*, 2423–30. The mother was referred to as "an undisclosed witness."

39. Ioan Grillo, "Meet the First Woman to Head a Drug Cartel," *Time*, July 7, 2015; and Javier Valdez, *Miss Narco: Belleza, poder y violencia: Historias reales de mujeres en el narcotráfico mexicano* (México, D.F.: Aguilar, 2011).

40. It appears that Rodríguez entered into the United States at Eagle Pass, Texas, in 1920 when she was around fourteen years old. Her birth date is unknown, but she was born in Muzquiz, Coahuila, "Border Crossings from Mexico to US, 1894–1964," National Archives and Records Administration, RG 85, Records of Immigration and Naturalization Service, microfilm roll 6. There are no records for Simona even under her aliases of Simona Terrazos and Simona Davila. She could have been from a San Antonio family.

41. "Claudia Valenzuela" interview with Jose Carlos Cisneros Guzmán, Mazatlán, Sinaloa, and Delicias, Chihuahua, September 2015.

42. Peter Reuter and David Ronfeldt, "Quest for Integrity: The Mexican-US Drug Issue in the 1980s," *Journal of Interamerican Studies and World Affairs* 34, no. 3, Special Issue: Drug Trafficking Research Update (Autumn 1992): 93.

43. Reuter and Ronfeldt, "Quest for Integrity," 93. Beginning in the 1940s, as Mexico's war on drugs escalated, officials became concerned about trafficking across the southern border. See letter to Manuel Nájera Días, Viceconsul of Mexico in Guatemala from Secretaria de Relaciones Exteriores, Archivo Histórico "Genaro Estrada" Secretaría de Relaciones Exteriores (hereafter, AHSRE), III-1650-2. Poppy was also grown in the southern United States. Mexican customs officials patrolled the southern border for opium from Guatemala.

44. "Ignacia Jasso González W/As La Nacha," Federal Bureau of Investigation, Department of Justice, 64-22536-1, March 25, 1943, obtained under Freedom of Information Act, July 16, 2009.

45. José Carlos Cisneros Guzmán, "Las tres jefas," in *Las Jefas del Narco: El ascenso de las mujeres en crimen organizado*, ed. Arturo Santamaría Gómez (México, D.F.: Grijalbo, 2012), 127.

46. "Desireé Guerrero, interview with Cisneros Guzmán, Monterrey, Tamaulipas, June 2015.

47. Soderbergh, *Traffic*.

48. Carey, *Women Drug Traffickers*.

49. Interview with Valenzuela.

50. For a discussion on the importance of trust in organized crime, see Klaus von Lampe and Per Ole Johansen, "Organized Crime and Trust: On the Conceptualization and Empirical Relevance of Trust in the Context of Criminal Networks," *Global Crime* 6, no. 2 (May 2004): 159–84; Letizia Paoli, "The Paradox of Organized Crime," *Crime, Law and Social Change* 37, no. 1 (2002): 51–97.

51. The Cavazoses lived at 434 Merida Ave. and Murdock lived at 430 Merida. *Illicit Traffic in Narcotics*, 2397, 2426.

52. For a discussion of trust and betrayal, see Carey, *Women Drug Traffickers*, 128–32.

53. Elaine Carey and José Carlos Cisneros Guzmán, "The Daughters of La Nacha: Profiles of Women Traffickers," *NACLA: Report on the Americas*, May/June 2011, vol. 44: 3. For a broad survey of credentialing in organized crime, see Howard Abadinsky, *Organized Crime* (Belmont, CA: Cengage, 2013).

54. Drug bosses such as Griselda Blanco, who worked with the Medellín cartel, and Mery Valencia, who worked for the Cali cartel, had many women in their organizations. Blanco and Valencia, two of the highest-ranking women in their organizations, worked with both men and women, but women frequently had positions of leadership. See Carey, *Women Drug Traffickers*, 177–92, and United States of America v. Mery Valencia, United States District Court Southern District New York, stenographer's report, June 17,18, 21, 22 1999.

55. Cisneros, "Las tres jefas," 137.

56. Claudia interview.

57. Eloise Dunlap, Gabriele Stürzenhofecker, and Bruce D. Johnson, "The Elusive Romance of Motherhood: Drugs, Gender, and Reproduction in Inner-City Distressed Households," *Journal of Ethnicity and Substance Abuse* 5, no. 3 (2006): 1–27; and Eloise Dunlap and Bruce D. Johnson, "Family and Human Resources in the Development of a Female Crack Seller: Case Study of a Hidden Population," *Journal of Drug Issues* 26, no. 1 (1996): 175–98.

58. Cisneros, "Todo lo grande se acaba en un momento," in *Las jefas del narco*, 185–211.

Figure 14.1 The picture shows the author conducting an interview in Palenque with a man from Honduras while he waited for the freight train (*shown on the right*) to depart. Minutes after the picture was taken, the train started moving, and the man jumped on top, leaving the interview abruptly. Photograph from author's personal collection.

Chapter 14

Keep Them Out!

Border Enforcement and Violence since 1986

ALEJANDRA DÍAZ DE LEÓN

The first time that Filadelfo migrated from Honduras to the United States in 1991, it took him five days. He left his house one Wednesday with a change of clothes and 400 lempiras (around $70). He was not scared. He knew he just had to take the train in Mexico and then cross through Tijuana by foot. He did not have to hire a smuggler.[1]

In the summer of 2015, Filadelfo was waiting for a smuggler to pick him up from the Saltillo migrant house. His outlook on migration had completely changed after having experienced the deterrence politics in Mexico firsthand. There were more roadblocks in the southern states of Mexico, so he couldn't take a bus. It was difficult for him to take the train this time because it was going faster. When he managed to take it, members of the Mara, a Central American gang, charged him $100 to stay on it. He didn't have that kind of money, so he got pushed off. He was lucky he did not lose a limb.

This time it took him over a month of walking through the jungle, escaping the gangs, the cartels, the police, and the National Migration Institute (INM in Spanish) officers to even get to the northern border of Mexico. He was scared and tired. "It's too difficult. I wouldn't recommend anyone to come, never never," he told me. Still, he was waiting for the opportunity to cross to the United States. "Now you cannot cross the desert without a coyote [a smuggler]; they say they have sensors, that the Zetas shoot at you in the river if you don't pay them. Some people die in the desert. . . . I need to wait for the coyote my brother sent me because some coyotes can also kidnap you or sell you to the Zetas."[2]

Like Filadelfo, thousands of Mexicans and Central Americans are experiencing the increasingly harsh realities of migrating irregularly to the United States. Many migrants, especially from Central America, are fleeing endemic poverty, violence, and the effects of the climate crisis in their countries and cannot go back. They have been constructed not only as an economic and social threat but also as a danger to national security. By linking migration to crime and terrorism, the media and the U.S. government have created a clear distinction between "good citizens" and "threatening illegal aliens." Protecting the border of the nation-state to keep the threats out has become a task that the United States takes very seriously.

In migration, it might seem that the border is the geographical line where one country ends and the other starts. In practice, however, it is not that simple. William Carrigan and Clive Webb have shown in chapter 10 in this volume the long geographic reach of the U.S.-Mexico border with the lynching of Padillo in Nebraska many miles away from the geographical divide between the United States and Mexico. I define the border as the area where the state tries to exert control over those who "do not belong" and to push them back, regardless of where the actual division of countries lies. In the case of the United States, its border has expanded outside and inside: outside to the southern border of Mexico (over 3,000 km) and inside to comprise up to one hundred miles inside U.S. territory, where the Border Patrol can establish roadblocks and detain migrants.

This "vertical border"[3] has increased the emotional, physical, and economical cost of migrating by enlarging the territory that the migrants have to cross and the institutional and noninstitutional obstacles they have to face. The resources that the United States and later Mexico have used to deter and detain the migrants include military technology, physical obstacles (such as roadblocks or fences), and increased numbers of personnel for the border agencies. These institutional strategies have deviated the flows to more secluded and dangerous routes, increasing the vulnerability of migrants to the elements and to criminals or organized crime.

Borders are violent. The effort of keeping someone out requires pushing against them, deterring them, detaining them out, and returning them. As the United States—with the help of Mexico—expands the border outside and inside its territory, the spaces of struggle and violence increase. More and more people get caught on the effects of the "dissuasion through deterrence" policies.

In this chapter, I show how, since 1986, the United States has expanded its southwestern border to the south, creating a "vertical border" that reaches the southern border of Mexico. Through an analysis of primary sources, literature on border control, and ethnographic research in Mexico and the United States during a total of fifteen months divided between several field trips taken in 2015, 2016, and 2018, I outline how the externalization of the border has affected those whom it has reached. The chapter is divided into two sections. In the first, I provide a brief summary of the strategies that the United States and Mexico have used to stop and deter clandestine migrants. I show how both governments have extended the reach of the border control from the border towns in the United States to the southern states in Mexico. In the second section, I tell four stories based on my ethnographic research on Mexico and the United States that illustrate how migrants experience the effects of border control. The vignettes move from the southern border of Mexico to the Sonoran Desert in the U.S.-Mexico border, like the undocumented migrants themselves. Each story attempts to show different types of violence that migrants commonly face as a consequence of crossing this very long vertical border.

Part One: The Expansion of the Border

Bracero Program, 1942–1964

The first program that started legal migration from Mexico to the United States was the U.S. Bracero Program, which was created in 1942 by the Franklin Roosevelt administration. As the United States became involved in World War II, the demand for workers was higher than the available legal supply, so employers recruited undocumented workers as well. The program continued to thrive until the end of the Korean War when the recession, combined with the paranoia of the McCarthy era, made illegal immigration a political issue again. In response to the opposing pressure from the agricultural employers, who needed migrant workers, and from U.S. citizens who wanted control of the border, the INS launched "Operation Wetback." While the INS increased its migrant apprehensions, it also doubled the bracero visas.[4] Between 1942 and 1964, the program provided two million temporal workers to U.S. farms and ranches; many more were working illegally at the same time.[5]

Although the program ended in 1965, the structural demand for immigrants remained and undocumented migration did not stop. U.S farmers had become reliant on cheap, Mexican labor, and the profession had come to be regarded as "foreign."[6] Consequently, from 1965 to 1985, irregular migration continued to flourish. In 1977, the Silva program (1977–981) expanded Mexican access to U.S. visas by providing 144,946 visas to Mexicans in addition to the hemispheric ceiling of 120,000 per year. The program ended in 1981, reducing the legal channels for Mexican migrants to reach the United States. This fact, added to the rapid population growth and the worsening of the Mexican economy, resulted in a sharp increase in undocumented migration.

Immigration Reform and Control Act, 1986

Since the end of the Bracero and Silva Programs,[7] the U.S. Congress knew a large-scale migratory reform was due. Irregular migrants were more visible because they shifted from working in the fields to working on services. After years of negotiation, the U.S. Congress passed the Immigration Reform and Control Act (IRCA) in 1986. It became the first major revision of America's immigration law in decades.[8]

This law made employment of unauthorized immigrants unlawful, increased the activities of the Border Patrol and other enforcement agencies, boosted the funding for the Border Patrol, and established criminal penalties for illegally transporting people into the United States. At the same time, it offered amnesty to several million irregular immigrants who had lived continuously in the United States since January 1, 1982. The idea was that the act would legalize the population that was already living and working in the United States and, at the same time, prevent new irregular immigration.[9]

It had unintended consequences, however. On one hand, more people than expected applied for legalization. Over three million people applied for temporary residence and nearly 2.7 million people received permanent residence.[10] On the other hand, researchers have found little evidence that the amnesty decreased the number of clandestine entries to the United States. The apprehensions declined immediately after the law was passed, but after six months, they returned to previous levels.[11]

These stricter border controls stopped the circular migration that had been characteristic of Mexican migration to the United States. When crossing the border was easier, migrants would move to the United States when there was work and moved back home when they could not find work or did not need it. Nevertheless, when the border became more difficult to cross, undocumented migrants could not go back home. Most irregular migrants opted to reside permanently in the United States. For those who tried to cross, the price of the coyotes increased because the routes were becoming longer and more dangerous.[12] In 2018 in Nogales, in the northern border of Mexico, I met several middle-aged people who had lived without papers in the United States for decades, after they "got stuck" in 1986. Now their parents, in Mexico, were sick and dying, so some of these "stuck" undocumented migrants who had spent decades in the United States had decided to go back to Mexico to say goodbye in person. Many were finding out that entering the United States clandestinely in 2018 was not as easy as it had been during the 1980s. They were desperate to get back to their spouses, children, and lives but were now stuck in Mexico. Of those who tried, some went missing or died attempting to cross.

Another important influx of immigrants to the United States during the 1980s came from the thousands of people who were fleeing the Central American dictatorships and seeking refuge in Mexico or the United States. Starting in 1973 and continuing throughout the next decade, thousands of people from Nicaragua, Salvador, and Guatemala fled the conflicts in their regions by moving toward Mexico and to the United States.[13] Mexico, although a signatory to the Convention and the Protocol of Refugees of the United Nations, did not have refugee as a legal concept until 1988. The country improvised a response with the first influx of Guatemalan refugees in 1981 to 1983 by letting them stay in the country, close to the southern border.[14]

In 1986, when Mexico joined the GATT,[15] it had attempted to reduce tariffs in trade with the United States. To convince its neighbor of its ability to increase trade but control migration, Mexico also cooperated with the U.S. government to increase their control of the southern border of Mexico. The United States helped with providing information, training of personnel, and funding efforts to stop migration through Mexico.[16] Mexico aligned its migratory policies with the objective of deterring and preventing Central American migration to the United States.[17] The Mexican government established the Beta group in 1990 with the intention of patrolling and preventing crime in the border. The official role of the Beta group was to protect unauthorized crossers on the Mexican side of the boundary. From the U.S. perspective, this was an effort of the Mexican government to curtail illegal migration because the Beta groups targeted smugglers and arrested them. The cooperation between the two agencies and the two countries became evident when the Border Patrol donated radios and equipment to the Beta groups. The two agencies often conjoined in apprehending suspected criminals in the border region.[18] By the beginning of the 1990s, Mexico expelled hundreds of thousands of migrants for the first time (126,440).[19] In my fieldwork, I have seen the contradictory roles of the Beta group in its interactions with the migrants. On the one hand, migrants take the water, food, and rides that the Beta group gives them; on the other, they are certain that Beta group members notice how many migrants are in a certain area and communicate this to other authorities that often come later to detain the migrants. Often, especially in the southern border of Mexico, migrants accepted the help and moved on or hid as soon as the Beta group left, in case they sent some other agency to pick them up.

Putting Control on the Border, 1994

The next push for expanding the border's reach happened in the context of economic liberalization with the signing of the North American Free Trade Agreement (NAFTA) between Mexico, the United States, and Canada, which came into force in 1994.[20] In ten years, it was supposed to eliminate the tariffs to exports and to eliminate nontariff trade barriers. This trade agreement did not directly impact free movement between the countries. However, it did change the economic landscape of Mexico and the United States and the way these countries related to each other.

In 1994, the government of the United States established the strategy of "prevention through deterrence." The strategy for the Border Patrol was to focus on preventing the entry of irregular migrants, not on detaining them

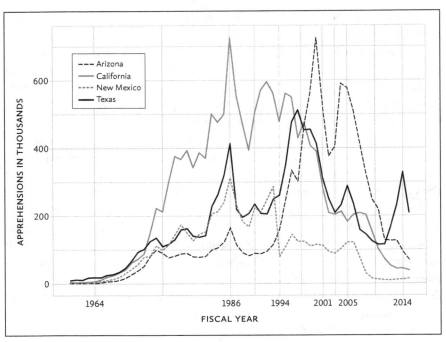

Graph 14.1 Apprehensions in the southwest border of the United States
Source: Immigration and Naturalization Service.

after they had accessed the United States. Several border enforcement operations were put into place. The first one, devised by Silvestre Reyes, the chief
patrol agent of the El Paso Border Patrol Sector, was Operation Hold the Line
(1993). Instead of having the agents conducting raids and looking for undocumented migrants in the border cities, as it had been done until that point,
Reyes moved the officers to the international boundary that had been left virtually unpatrolled until then. The operation effectively built a virtual line of
border agents between El Paso and Ciudad Juarez. With visible agents, helicopters, and a repaired international fence, the operation intended to deter
migrants from crossing in the first place.[21]

Operation Hold the Line was credited with the drop on apprehensions from
285,781 in 1993 to 73,142 in 1994.[22] Border Patrol officers were placed in a visible position to deter immigration. According to experts, the low number of
apprehensions means that fewer migrants tried to cross in that area.[23] At the
same time, there were increased apprehensions in Arizona and California.
This indicates that the migration flow simply shifted from one point of entry
to others,[24] as graph 14.1 shows.

Following the apparent success of Operation Hold the Line, Operation Gatekeeper (1994) in California, Operation Safeguard in Arizona (1995), and Operation Rio Grande in South Texas (1997) were established. As graph 14.1 shows, migrant flows in Arizona were irrelevant until the operations funneled them to that area. As a reaction to the new flows, agents in Arizona were displayed in high-visibility areas. The zone received new surveillance equipment and helicopter surveillance. Between October 1994 and September 2000, the apprehensions at the Arizona border increased from 160,684 to 725,093 (an increase of 351 percent).[25] As table 14.1 shows, the number of migrant deaths increased from 14 in 1994 to 110 in 2014 in the area between Tucson and Yuma.[26]

In general, migrants started taking more dangerous and secluded routes, and this increased the number of migrant deaths. From 1994, the number of deaths in the border started to rise and peaked in 2010, with 252 registered deaths for that year (see table 14.1). The leading causes of death were drowning (most of them in the Rio Grande), motor vehicle accidents, auto-pedestrian accidents, deaths from exposure to heat and cold, and deaths from unknown cases (where only skeletons were found in open areas).[27] The deaths by exposure peaked after 1993, when the migratory flows were deviated. The official figures probably underestimate the number of deaths because bodies decompose quickly in the desert and disappear in the river.[28] I have hiked with and interviewed those who rescue migrants in the Sonoran Desert. As we walked the difficult terrain, they pointed out small wooden crosses where they have found remains. They have told me that they remember when the deaths started increasing, when they went from one or two border crossers a month to up to thirty at their peak. They tell me how overwhelmed the community and the forensic experts were and how their work has not stopped since.[29]

Scholars argue that these border enforcement strategies did not reduce the flow of migrants. In the 1990s, the stock of irregular migrants living in the United States increased (see table 14.1). This was in part because migrants could no longer go back to Mexico and then return to the United States and in part because the migratory flows were only redirected by the various anti-migration operations undertaken by the United States.[30] The Mexican Migration Project evaluated the probability that a migrant had on initiating migration.[31] The probability in 1985 fluctuated between .025 and .030. In 1993 it reached .018, and in 1998, 0.11. This analysis shows that the shifts are minor and not connected to the U.S. border policies.

The shifts in the probability of male migration are more closely connected to the ebbs and flows of the Mexican economy than to U.S. border policies. Hence, they dipped after the onset of the economic crisis in

1982, then rose as the crisis deepened in the mid-1980s, shooting up again during the second round of hyperinflation in 1987 and 1988. Then they fell markedly with the onset of the economic boom of the early 1990s before rising again after the peso devaluation crisis of 1994.[32]

Migration as a National Security Threat, 2001

As tense as the situation was on the border before 9/11, it seemed that Mexico and the United States were going to find a way to improve the conditions of irregular Mexican migrants in the United States. Before the 2001 attacks on the United States, both countries were close to signing a bipartisan framework for a comprehensive immigration agreement. This included "stepped-up border enforcement, a temporary worker program, and legalization of most unauthorized Mexicans in the United States."[33] After 9/11, when immigrants who had legally entered the country attacked the United States, the landscape completely changed; immigration was now linked to national security.

The U.S. government redefined migration as a national security threat. This definition also included "soft security issues" such as cultural differences, social instability, environmental degradation, population growth, social service cutbacks, and loss of jobs. "In short, 'national security' was being redefined to include freedom not only from external threats, but also from fear or anxiety concerning perceived economic and/or cultural damage."[34]

Because of the attacks, the United States created the Department of Homeland Security and passed the USA PATRIOT Act. One of the consequences of the act was the construction of large databases for the collection and analysis of information.[35] These were intended to be used to prevent terrorist attacks by reducing the vulnerability to terrorism in the United States. As part of its immigration objectives, the agency had to achieve effective control of U.S. borders and expand the "zone of security" to Mexico.[36] The Department of Homeland Security also created the Secure Border Initiative (SBI) in 2005. The SBI intended to secure the border with new fencing, ground surveillance radar, infrared cameras, and laser range finders.[37] On December 16, 2005, the U.S. House of Representatives of the 109th Congress passed the Border Protection, Antiterrorism, and Illegal Immigration Control Act (HR 4437).[38] This bill sought to make it a felony to be undocumented and expand border security measures. As Samuel Norton and other have shown, expanding technology to thwart migrants "funnels" illegal border crossers into more dangerous and more difficult areas to traverse. As such, surveillance technology has a direct impact on migrant deaths.[39]

The reach of the U.S.-Mexico border has also expanded inside the United States. Increasingly, for example, U.S. authorities, in the name of national security, are employing Border Patrol checkpoints far in the interior of the United States. This has the effect of "thickening" the territorial boundaries of the United States in terms of its agents and practices of surveillance and social control."[40] On the outskirts of Tucson, Arizona, and San Diego, California, I have seen permanent checkpoints, where Border Patrol agents ask to you stop, look at you and the other passengers, and decide if they need to ask you for your ID or passport. Migrants, even when they are inside U.S. territory, still have to walk through grueling heat in order to avoid checkpoints before they can feel they have made it.

The reinforcement of the southern border of Mexico strategically coincides with the reinforcement of the U.S.-Mexico border by U.S. authorities.[41] In 2001, the National Migratory Institute within Mexico created the "Plan Sur" (Southern Plan) "as part of a Mexican strategy to placate the United States in order to negotiate better conditions for Mexican migrants."[42] In an interview, the commissioner of Mexico's National Migration Institute stated, "We are trying to catch them because it's good for Mexico but I also know very well that our efforts are of great benefit to the U.S."[43] Santiago Creel, Mexico's secretary of the interior, stated, "In exchange for better conditions for Mexicans working in the U.S. our government is prepared to increase measures aiming to arrest foreigners in the country heading for U.S."[44]

The plan had the objective of preventing crimes attributed to Central American migrants crossing Mexico on their way to the United States. It was backed by the U.S. authorities who worked along with Mexico and the Central American governments to implement it.[45] It meant to strengthen the presence of the Mexican state in the combat against organized crime.[46] The idea was to fight the smuggling of migrants and to enforce the human rights protection in the south border in an "environment of respect to the law."[47] Between June 4 and June 17 of 2001, Mexico deported six thousand migrants.[48] In 2012, at a reception hosted by the United States–Mexico Chamber of Commerce, Alan Bersin, the former U.S. acting commissioner of customs and border protection, stated that "the Guatemalan border with Chiapas, Mexico, is now our southern border."[49]

The way the plan was laid out and explained to the press linked migration with crime, and the media provided a sensationalistic portrayal of migrants. This increased the impression that they were a threat to the country.[50] The fact that the army was enforcing the roadblocks also signaled that stopping migration was a matter of national security.

As a consequence of the implementation of the plan and of the stepped-up border enforcement in Mexico, human rights violations and abuses against clandestine migrants in Mexico increased.[51] Since 2002, researchers have documented that migrants in transit experienced extortions, abuses, sexual violence, and kidnappings by criminal bands and traffickers. Some government officials also participated in those crimes. They regularly extorted migrants when they ran into them. Testimonies stated that migrants had observed that their coyotes or *polleros* (smugglers) worked with the criminals or authorities to take advantage of the migrants.[52] Volunteers who helped the migrants were criminalized. I was once stopped for several hours by Mexican authorities for witnessing the violent capture of several Central American men.

Criminal groups and state officials harass human rights activists. They were threatened with being charged with trafficking if they helped migrants. After 2008, Mexico's General Population Law was changed; migration was no longer classified as a crime and helping migrants was no longer criminalized. However, activists[53] and migrants are threatened by members of criminal groups and by state officials constantly, regardless of the legal protections they technically have.

Because of the increasing awareness of the situation of migrants in Mexico and the pressure of the civil society organizations, in 2011 the Mexican government approved the first Migration Act. The basic rights of migrants— regardless of their legal situation—were protected for the first time. According to the law, migrants can access medical services, education, or criminal or civil justice. They should also be informed of their rights and about the possibility of asking for refugee status. Another important change was that the law explicitly stated that people who helped migrants with good will and without the intention of profiting would not be considered guilty of a crime. This, in theory, would protect human rights activists from threats.[54]

Regrettably, the Migration Act has not affected the way migrants are treated in Mexico. Civil society organizations report that the violence has not decreased. Migrants are still victims of robberies, kidnappings, abuses, and murder. State officials continue to work with members of organized crime. Members of civil society organizations are still harassed and threatened.[55] It might take the law some years to start yielding results. Unfortunately, Mexico's recent immigration policies show that the enforcement of the border has just become more restrictive and thus more violent against irregular migrants.

In 2014, the Mexican government approved the "Southern Border Integral Program."[56] The program increased the number of agents and checkpoints in the southern states to detect and detain undocumented migrants. When I went to the southern border in 2015, I counted four checkpoints manned by the federal police and the National Migration Institute in a three-hour bus ride. The government also made it more difficult for migrants to climb on top of the freight trains they frequently use to go across Mexico by making the trains go faster and by building one-meter cement structures along the train tracks that prevented the migrants from running next to the train to catch it.

During my interviews with migrants who had crossed before and after 2014, I learned that the journey had become more dangerous and more expensive since the program was implemented. They told me, and I observed, that they had to walk for many days to move through the territory, as they could not take the train or motor vehicles. They were pushed to more secluded routes in the jungle to avoid the checkpoints and patrols, and they often went thirsty and hungry. They were easier prey for the cartels, the gangs, and opportunistic criminals, too. In 2015, Mexico deported more Central American migrants than the United States.[57] Although the program did not deter the migrants, it did increase the violence they experienced.[58]

While Central American migration persists, Mexican migration to the United States has slowed since 2008. According to the Pew Research Center, in 2015 apprehensions at the U.S.-Mexico border were at their lowest level in nearly fifty years.[59] The top statistical agency of Mexico confirmed this trend by stating that between 2008 and 2014, Mexican international migration (of which most goes to the United States) diminished by 45.5 percent. The main reason is probably the 2008 economic crisis in the United States.[60] It is important to note, however, that although minimal compared with the flows of economic migrants in the last decades, the violence in Mexico, especially in the northern border, has created a new wave of forced migration coming from Mexico.

Another further push to consolidate Mexico as the new externalized border of the United States came shortly after President Donald Trump threatened, in June of 2019, to establish tariffs on Mexican exports if the Mexican president, Andrés Manuel López Obrador, did not stop the flows of undocumented migrants on their way to the United States.[61] After negotiations, the Mexican government agreed to send up six thousand members of the newly consolidated National Guard to eleven municipalities in the southern border of Mexico with the intention of stopping undocumented migration through the country.[62] Although, as this chapter has made explicit, the cooperation between Mexico and the United States to control migration has long existed, this new step reaffirmed the policies of the Mexican government toward the migrants and suggests that their criminalization will not stop with the new president.

Part Two: The Violence of the Border,
from the Jungle to the Desert

In this section, I present four ethnographic vignettes to illustrate some of the different types of violence that migrants experience as they attempt to survive the vertical border that Mexico and the United States have created. I performed ethnographic observation and eighty-one in-depth interviews with migrants from Honduras, Guatemala, El Salvador, Nicaragua, and Mexico in the southern border of Mexico (Palenque, Tenosique, and Tapachula), in the northern border of Mexico (Nogales, Saltillo, and Tijuana), and in the Sonoran Desert in Tucson, in El Paso, and in San Diego where I have hiked the migrant crossing points, observed the surveillance apparatus, and talked to volunteers and border agents. I have also interviewed key activists and journalists who have been covering the border for years. This fieldwork was done between 2015 and 2018.

Southern Border of Mexico: "They Treat Us like Dogs"

This is one of the first things that surprise those new to the southern border of Mexico: the actual line (or river) dividing Mexico and Guatemala is not heavily patrolled. Migrants, day shoppers, and merchandise can cross legally through the crossing points or without permission in big rafts in the Usumacinta and Suchiate Rivers. This is all in the open. The indifference of the police and the military is palpable. This crossing is deceitfully easy and does not set the tone for what happens next. One of the strategies of the Southern Border Plan (2014) was to place three rings of contention inside the southern states of the country, since controlling the border with the jungle and the river required more manpower. The level of cooperation between Mexico and the United States is very strong on border security issues.[63] For example, with the Merida Initiative in 2007, the United States gave a military aid package to Mexico. This included X-ray vans, contraband detection kits, and biometrical kiosks to store facial and retinal information and fingerprints to improve Mexico's border controls.[64] This thick border means that migrants can never relax while in Mexico, as they know more controls are coming even as they overcome some obstacles.

Many migrants cross Mexico by themselves or with their families, without the help of a guide.[65] Before 2001, guides from the community of origin could escort them through Mexico. However, when the routes changed as a consequence of increased border enforcement, the guides did not know the way anymore.[66] Since the paths were more dangerous, the demand for coyotes increased and the prices rose from $1,000 to around $3,500.[67] Now, it costs around $7,000 to pay a smuggler to take you all the way to the United States. Few people can afford it, and most choose to pay for their smuggler in the U.S.-Mexico border. Coyotes have also been known for robbing, abandoning, or killing the migrants they were supposed to lead north.[68]

After crossing the Usumacinta River, the border between Mexico and Guatemala, Juan and Jarvis were forced to walk for a week next to the highway on their way to Palenque, one of the towns in Chiapas with a migrant house next to the train tracks. They could not take *combis*, small passenger vans, because there were too many checkpoints on the highway. "We know how to smell the migrants. They smell like fear, like dirt, like dogs," Jorge told me. Jorge is a National Migration officer who was lauded as one of the best in the Palenque area for detecting migrants by just sight. "Last week we caught eleven in one day. They are very easy to detect. I don't know why they keep taking those *combis*," he observed.[69]

Such checkpoints make a dangerous journey all the more perilous. Juan and Jarvis were forced to walk for seven days instead of taking a three-hour van ride, like the one I took. "What we didn't expect, honestly, were the checkpoints and the *migra* agents" Jarvis told me, "so so many . . . and when you see them, you have to jump to the *monte* [mountain], the jungle, and take a detour that takes days! Look, my sneaker is already broken. Damn jungle."[70] Juan continues, "We were hungry, hot, and thirsty, I swear to you that we were hallucinating food, a good coffee prepared by my wife and chicken, we could barely walk."[71] The detour weakened them. Some migrants have gotten blisters in the sole of the foot that are so big that they cannot walk for days, let alone overcome all the obstacles in Mexico.

Jarvis and Juan were eventually detained by agents of the National Migration Institute (INM in Spanish), or the *migra*, as they call them. They were walking along the highway when they saw the INM van, and they threw themselves to the jungle and started running. They were tired and hungry and Jarvis's sneaker was slowing him down, so Juan decided to stop and be with his friend when they were arrested.

> The *migra* agents are bad people. When they see you, they try to run after you, and they throw things at you to make you stop. The guy who arrested us hit my friend in the head with a stick; here you can see the scar. He also called us "dogs" and was making fun of us. When they stopped us, they stole our sneakers and the last of the pesos we had. I guess we are lucky because this *migra* didn't hand us in to the Maras [Central American gangs] or the *narcos*; they just detained us and were going to deport us.[72]

As the *migra* was driving them in a van (they call it the "doghouse") to the migrant detention center, another migrant who had been caught before them started hitting the mesh windows of the van and managed to make one fall off. "And he jumped off the van and told us: 'Come on!' and then started running," Jarvis told me. "And we were scared, and I thought about it for a second but then I thought, 'I haven't even given Mexico a try yet; they can't deport us so close to the border.' So, I jumped, and Juan jumped, and we ran and ran and ran and here we are; broken but not defeated."[73]

What happened to Juan and Jarvis is so common among migrants that they almost skip it when they narrate their journeys. This is told as a lucky story, a funny tale. But there is violence. By listening to them and all the other migrants in the Palenque migrant house, and by riding the bus to the border, it is obvious that the government of Mexico has designed an obstacle course in its southern states that pushes migrants to more secluded and dangerous areas. By making it impossible for them to take safer and faster transportation routes, they force them to make decisions that will end up with them hurt, disappeared, or killed.

Migrants have to walk for days in uneven terrain in hot and humid conditions. They go hungry and thirsty. Sometimes they get sick and die from drinking water from polluted sources. They twist their ankles, scrape their arms, get sunburns, and get huge blisters that stop them from walking. They get weakened, sad, and desperate. Human predators roam these terrains, too. Some migrants are robbed and assaulted in this "no man's land" terrain; some have gone missing or have been kidnapped. Even though no agent of the state touches the migrant, the state exerts violence over them by forcing them to take that route.

Another type of violence we see in this narrative is the forcefulness of the state agents when they do their job. They dehumanize migrants by calling them "dogs" and calling the van where they put them the "doghouse." They talk about them like animals, and they make them feel like they do not deserve to be treated like a person. "If you could see me when I am at my house, my country, you would see that I am a human; If you could see me after a shower, a good meal . . . I am a human back home; here I am . . . less," another migrant, Rulo, told me about the way the road and the state agents chip away the dignity of the migrants.[74]

When they are caught, migrants suffer from abusive behavior while they are in detention centers before getting deported. In some cases, there are no doctors in the facility, women and men are mixed together, and children are not properly taken care of. Sometimes migrants stay for many days waiting to be repatriated. They do not have access to legal advice, and they are not told about their rights.[75] There are no doctors in the center, they do not cater to special diets, and migrants seldom have contact with lawyers from civil society organizations.[76] Sometimes the agents of the INM take advantage of them. When they are victims of a crime, they are dissuaded from reporting it, or they are deported before they can testify against the perpetrator.[77] They do not have access to justice or redress in the country, even since the 2011 Migration Law was passed.

The violence that Mexico imposes on them is palpable.

Veracruz: Kidnapping and Forced Disappearances

Once migrants overcome the security cordons along the southern border of Mexico, they enter what is perhaps one of the most dangerous states of the migration route, Veracruz. In Veracruz is where the biggest mass grave in Mexico has been found[78] and where people, migrants and nonmigrants, disappear every day.[79] Migrants are vulnerable to organized crime everywhere in Mexico, and antimigrant criminals have occasionally colluded with all levels of authorities. These groups extort, rob, kidnap, kill, and sexually assault the Central American migrants with impunity. Between 2008 and 2009, the National Human Rights Commission of Mexico discovered that 9,758 migrants had been kidnapped.[80] By 2010, 11,333 more victims had been kidnapped.[81] Once they are kidnapped, they are tortured to reveal the number of their family members in the United States. Then they call their relatives and ask them for a ransom. Sometimes the shelters for the migrants get attacked. When migrants report the crimes (which they seldom do), they are sometimes ignored by authorities or sold back to the criminal groups.[82]

Yet the threat of violence has done little to stop the flows of migrants in Mexico toward the United States. During 2012, 75,774 migrants were deported while they attempted cross Mexico.[83] Oxfam, the international confederation of organizations focused on global poverty, estimates that around 140,000 migrants in total tried to cross through Mexico.[84] A great number of migrants are still trying to arrive at the United States despite the increased border security in Mexico.[85] The flows continue because migrants are fleeing what they consider a greater danger in their countries and because the dangers of the road are impossible to comprehend without experiencing them.[86] As Filadelfo stated, "I might die in Mexico, but I might arrive to the United States; if I stay in Honduras I will die for sure; the risk is worth taking."[87] The poverty, the lack of opportunity in their home countries, and their social networks pulling them to the United States are also factors that push their migration. Although kidnappings are common all along the migrant route, it is crossing Veracruz that stuck with most of my interviewees as the place where they could just "disappear." Chaparro, a twenty-seven-year-old migrant from Honduras, barely survived his time in Veracruz:

So, I'm in the train with a bunch of other people, other migrants, and we are ok. I mean, we are hungry and some of them had been beaten badly but we are fine. And then the train stops where it shouldn't, like in the middle of nowhere, and these guys who were all stained [he means they had tattoos] with this swagger [walking confidently] and with guns come on top of the train, force us to come down. . . . We were like 80 people! Some women too. . . . So we came down and they took us all to a security house [where kidnapped people are kept].[88]

Often, the perpetrators of the kidnappings are the various cartels that operate along the country. The cartels that are fighting for the control of Veracruz currently (2019) are the Cartel de Jalisco Nueva Generación and the Zetas. At the same time, migrants report observing gang graffiti and being kidnapped by the Mara Salvatrucha in Veracruz. At the time of my fieldwork, Veracruz was one of the deadliest places for migrants and where more went missing. Migrants whom I interviewed reported that they saw INM or police agents coming into the security houses where they were taken.

Chaparro, for example, knew that a couple of *migra* agents were complicit in his kidnapping: "We saw them come in and have their tacos with the other *malandros* [criminals]."[89] He was kidnapped and held for four months. Since he told the kidnappers (who he believed were from the Mara Salvatrucha) that he did not have any money or family members in Honduras, he had to work off his release. He was forced to go solicit money from tourists and drivers in order to collect $3,000 and pay his own ransom. When I asked him if he really gathered all that money in four months, he replied, "Of course not. I managed to escape when one of them, one of the ones who were 'taking care' of us in the street, had to pee or something. I ran with all my might and hid in a church for a couple of hours."[90] He managed to arrive at a migrant house in the northern border and was hoping that his new look would help him remain undetected.

Northern Border of Mexico: The Wait

The United States intended that the increased difficulty while crossing the border would dissuade people from migrating. The idea, according to the National Strategic Plan (NSP) of 1994, was to force the migrants to take harsher routes, "less suited for crossing and more suited for enforcement."[91] Before, migrants could cross easily and safely through Tijuana. Now, with that zone blocked, migrants have to go through high mountains with very low temperatures in winter or the desert, where they get heat stroke and dehydration, or had to rely on smugglers, or coyotes.[92] Migrants are aware of this. They can see the new fences and the border agents in their ATVs behind them. They hear stories of those who have survived the desert and are being deported. Nahu, a twenty-one-year-old migrant from Honduras, told me, "Everyone knows you have to cross with a coyote, or you die."[93]

The Centro de Apoyo al Trabajador Migrante and the Albergue del Desierto[94] in Mexicali recorded that in 1994 over 60 percent of the migrants reported abuse: 22.5 percent physical abuse, 6 percent verbal abuse, and 27.5 percent abuse of authority (especially destruction of personal documents or clothes). Migrants who are deported from the United States are often dropped in Mexico late at night, when they are more vulnerable to criminals. Families were separated when they were deported, and migrants were not fed when they were detained. The Border Patrol sometimes deported people they caught to the desert, not to border towns. This meant that migrants had to walk back to a city in Mexico to attempt to cross again. Occasionally they had to walk three or four hours. This created more physical and economic hardships.[95]

In the border towns of Mexico, migrants who are stuck waiting for money to pay a smuggler or for an open opportunity to cross the desert by themselves are mixed with Mexican migrants who have been deported all along the border. The new population that has joined them are the Central American asylum seekers who are sent back to Mexico while their cases are heard in the United States, some expecting to be waiting for months.[96] All these immobile but extremely poor populations are vulnerable to the cartels (or mafias, as they call them) that rule the border. An activist told me that "there are some towns that are 'security towns.' What I mean is that migrants can come in, but they cannot go out because they are in effect property of the cartels who come in."[97] As crossing the border becomes more expensive and more dangerous, more and more people are indefinitely trying to survive in the border towns. Many have to live on the streets or move from one migrant house to another. They are beaten, robbed, sexually assaulted, and kidnapped.[98]

When I visited the migrant houses or the canteens set up for the migrants by religious organizations in Nogales, a town that borders with Arizona, one of my contacts pointed out to me some young men standing on rooftops with binoculars: "They are *halcones* [hawks]; they observe who comes in and out; they work for the mafias." My contacts in the border towns have told me that they have documented that the cartels, sometimes with the complicity of the authorities, kidnap the deported or the transit migrants; they make them work for them, or cross drugs in the desert, or they ask their families for ransom. As the border controls grow harsher and the "Remain in Mexico" program (implemented by the Trump administration in 2019) sends more migrants back to wait for their asylum hearings in the United States, more and more vulnerable people have been stuck in the border towns, increasing the number of people vulnerable to organized crime.[99]

Roberto, an Indigenous Guatemalan migrant, was kidnapped in the northern border of Mexico while he was waiting to cross. He did not have any money, so he was sleeping in the streets. "I dropped like a strawberry. I was naive, I guess. I don't know, I met this man who was nice to me and who seemed to know a lot and he told me, 'Come with me to the migrant house and tomorrow we can try to find a smuggler together.'"[100] He ended up being led to a "security house" where he was held with around thirty other migrants from all over Central America for three months. The cartel members called their families to ask for a ransom of between $2,000 and $3,000, and they killed some of them when their families could not pay. The federal police eventually rescued them from the kidnappers and deported them before letting them report the crime or without offering them a humanitarian visa, like they should have.

U.S.-Mexico Border: Death in the Desert

Once migrants find a smuggler or decide to risk the crossing by themselves, they have to survive the U.S.-Mexico border. The southwestern border of the United States extends for 3,201 kilometers. It is separated from Mexico by the Rio Grande, the Sonoran Desert, and some border cities. Until 1994, to reduce the risks for their safety, most unauthorized migrants crossed undocumented in the proximity of the main urban centers. Yet as border control became a priority in the U.S. national security agenda in recent decades, the U.S. Border Patrol officials organized their activities into a three-tiered strategy. First, they reinforced the line watch along the international border; then, they began roving patrols immediately behind this line to arrest those crossing illegally; finally, they set checkpoints farther inside the U.S. territory to catch those who somehow go through undetected.[101] As a consequence, most unauthorized crossings moved away from cities, with undocumented migrants crossing today via the Rio Grande or the Sonoran Desert. One migrant recalled, "We crossed in a group of seven, me, my brother, and five other people. The coyote was guiding us. He made us walk really fast and some could barely keep up. The sun was shining hard and the terrain is rugged; I thought it would be flat and sandy."[102]

This desert extends over most of the border between Mexico and Arizona and consists of a vast territory with hills, ravines, abundant cacti, and temperatures which often rise to up to 50 degrees Celsius (122° F). For this reason, to patrol the area, the Customs and Border Protection (CBP) uses primarily the Remote Video Surveillance System. Border guards also rely on about 250 towers equipped with day and night cameras and Mobile Surveillance Systems (MSSs) such as truck-mounted infrared cameras, radars, planes, helicopters, unmanned aerial vehicles, and a series of databases used to fa-cilitate control at the border.[103]

Pushing migrant streams into more difficult terrain increased the num-ber of migrant deaths. As already stated, from 1994, the number of deaths in the border rose steadily, peaking at 252 registered deaths in 2010.[104] The deaths by exposure peaked after 1993, when the migratory flows began shifting to new routes. In 2018, the remains of 127 dead migrants were recovered from the desert, according to the Pima County Medical Examiner's Office.[105]

Migrants had to rely more on coyotes.[106] The smugglers were not familiar with the new crossing zones. As a consequence of rising demand and the added risk, fares charged by smugglers increased. This made crossing the bor-der even more difficult and more expensive. Migrants who could have once paid the smuggler could no longer afford it.[107] Some, like Ronin, an eighteen-year-old migrant from Honduras, had to acquire debts with the coyote to fi-nance the trip, "I'll be working like a dog for about five years, I think, but at least now I'm in Chicago!" he told me by WhatsApp.[108] Others had to carry drugs to earn money to pay for the journey. There have been reports of mi-grants that have been abandoned in the desert or in locked containers by their coyotes. "Smugglers, and bandits posing as smugglers, prey on migrants and on each other, committing violent crimes such as assault, robbery, kidnap-ping, and homicide."[109]

Enforcement also became harsher along the U.S.-Mexico border, and people who attempted to cross the border were stopped, questioned, and sometimes beaten and harassed by the Border Patrol agents. Unfortunately, like the flows of migrants themselves, these human rights abuses also moved to more re-mote locations and were now mainly targeted to undocumented migrants who could not complain.[110] According to Timothy Dunn, most human rights abuses committed against migrants in the border are directed at those who remain defiant from the point of view of the agents.[111]

Diverting the flow of undocumented migrants to the deserts also promoted a new wave of xenophobic and racist vigilante violence in more rural and de-serted regions of the border. The people who lived in these areas were not used to having large numbers of migrants crossing, and they reacted violently to their increased presence.[112] Vigilante ranchers have gathered in California, Arizona, New Mexico, and Texas.[113] They act in a "legal and moral shade of grey," according to lawyer Peter Yoxall. On the one hand, they act legally by making a "citizen's arrest," but on the other hand, they are motivated by rac-ist and xenophobic agendas and use violent and abusive tactics against the crossers. In interviews, activists in Arizona have described how vigilante groups detain migrants by threatening them with guns. They put them in their SUVs, and they carry them around during the day, without giving water to them or feeding them. Sometimes they beat them before taking them to the Border Patrol agents.[114]

There are organizations that try to help migrants survive the journey; unfortunately, the volunteers are also vulnerable to institutional abuse. Groups like No More Deaths and Humane Borders organize teams of volunteers who help migrants crossing the desert with food, water, and medical care. They also secure water stations and leave water jugs in the desert. "Once, I was volunteering in the migrant house and a migrant came up to me and told me that when they were lost in the desert, they found water jugs, maybe ours, maybe the other group's. And he told me that that's why they lasted so long until the Border Patrol found them. That's why I hike. I'm glad we're saving lives."[115] Volunteers get charged with trafficking, littering, and promoting illegal immigration.[116] More recently, four female volunteers of No More Deaths were found guilty of dropping water in a natural protected area in the Sonoran Desert[117] and a volunteer was tried for smuggling.[118] During the trial of the volunteer, four sets of remains were found in the desert.[119]

———

In this chapter, I have shown how the United States and Mexico have expanded the border enforcement area from the border towns in the United States to the southern states of Mexico. The mix of legislation, physical and technical border enforcement, discrimination, and lack of protection that the countries have created have, at the same time, increased the violence that undocumented migrants face when trying to arrive in the United States and Mexico.

By extending the area that is under surveillance and control, both Mexico and the United States have pushed migrants who are on the move to take more secluded and difficult routes that exhaust and kill them, like the jungle and the desert. State agents of both countries also contribute to the violence against migrants by dehumanizing them, treating them badly, beating and robbing them, and being complicit with criminal organizations. The absence of rule of law and the difficulty of reporting crimes in Mexico for migrants means that they are also incredibly susceptible to the gangs and the cartels that kidnap, disappear, rob, and kill them. The long wait to cross while they are in border cities and towns also increases their vulnerability to criminals.

Filadelfo's journey ended in the Sonoran Desert. After I met him in 2015, he went with four friends to Nogales, Mexico, to wait for an opportunity to cross the Sonoran Desert. It was not the first time he crossed, and he knew he should not do it without help, but he did not have any money to find a smuggler. He and his friends studied maps of the desert, decided on a route, and risked it. They knew they had to walk for at least four days to get to a city, but they were strong and ready, he told me. Some people had made it, he

Table 14.1 Southwest border-sector deaths

Fiscal Year	Big Bend	Del Rio	El Centro	El Paso	Laredo	Rio Grande Valley	San Diego	Tucson	Yuma	Total
2015	4	12	4	2	47	97	6	63	5	240
2014	5	17	6	0	49	116	5	107	3	308
2013	3	18	3	2	56	156	7	194	6	445
2012	1	29	11	1	91	144	5	180	9	471
2011	2	18	5	6	65	66	15	195	3	375
2010	0	23	14	4	35	29	8	251	1	365
2009	3	29	27	5	58	68	15	212	3	420
2008	3	22	20	8	32	92	32	171	5	385
2007	0	20	12	25	52	61	15	202	11	398
2006	4	34	21	33	36	81	36	169	40	454
2005	4	28	30	28	53	55	23	219	52	492
2004	0	21	36	18	22	35	15	142	39	328
2003	0	23	61	10	17	39	29	137	22	338
2002	4	29	64	8	15	30	24	134	12	320
2001	3	41	96	10	28	37	21	80	24	340
2000	3	48	72	26	47	40	34	74	36	380
1999	0	30	56	15	37	36	25	29	21	249
1998	3	28	90	24	20	26	44	11	17	263

Source: U.S. Customs and Border Protection

affirmed. They took two gallons of water each and camouflage backpacks, in order to prevent being detected in the desert. They bought cans of sardines and some peanut butter and hid some dollars in their paints. He was carrying a Bible. One Monday, they left.

For a year, we did not know what had happened to him. I had befriended him on Facebook, but he had not used his account and was not responding to messages. Then, suddenly, while looking at a Facebook page that shows the bodies that have been found in the desert in an attempt to find the families of the dead, I saw his ID next to a body covered by a blanket. Some volunteers had found him. He had huge blisters in his feet and had probably died of dehydration. It is possible that the blisters prevented him from keeping up with the group and that he was left behind. Maybe the *migra* found them and they ran, and he lost his group. It didn't matter; he died after being several days in the desert with just two gallons of water to drink. Filadelfo died because he was poor and he had to migrate; he was weakened by his transit through Mexico and by the wait in the border. When he crossed, he was funneled into one of the most dangerous crossing points in the Sonoran Desert in the middle of the summer because of the border controls elsewhere. He was not rescued because the area is too big and secluded and the volunteers and the Border Patrol could not cover all of it, even if they tried. Since Filadelfo entered Mexico in 2015, his journey took everything away from him, until he died fifteen kilometers from the nearest house in the United States. Like him, thousands of migrants have died or gone missing in the "vertical border" that comprises Mexico and the U.S.-Mexico border.

Notes

1. Thanks to Alan Knight and to everyone from the Violence in the Borderlands Symposium for commenting on both versions of this chapter. This research would not have been possible without the financing of the Consejo Nacional de Ciencia y Tecnología (CONACyT).

2. Interview with Filadelfo, Saltillo, 2015.

3. Tanya Basok, Danièle Bélanger, Martha Luz Rojas Wiesner, and Guillermo Candiz, *Rethinking Transit Migration: Precarity, Mobility, and Self-Making in Mexico* (New York: Palgrave Macmillan, 2015).

4. Kitty Calavita, *Inside the State: The Bracero Program, Immigration, and the INS* (New York: Routledge, 1992).

5. Kelly Lytle Hernández, "The Crimes and Consequences of Illegal Immigration: A Cross-Border Examination of Operation Wetback, 1943 to 1954," *Western Historical Quarterly* 37, no. 4 (2006): 421–44, https://doi.org/10.2307/25443415.

6. Douglas Massey, Jorge Durand, and Nolan J. Malone, *Beyond Smoke and Mirrors: Mexican Immigration in an Era of Economic Integration* (New York: Russell Sage Foundation, 2003).

7. Subsequently, the Immigration Act of 1965 substituted the worldwide limit of 290,000 immigrants per year with a twenty-thousand-person limit per country. In 1976, Congress amended the act to impose a quota of twenty thousand on individual countries of the Americas. Legislators closed a loophole that allowed Mexicans who gave birth to children in the United States to become legal residents.

8. Previous revisions to U.S. immigration law include the Emergency Quota Act of 1921, which established migration quotas; the Immigration and Nationality Act of 1952, which changed the quotas by basing them on the 1920 census; and the Immigration and Nationality Act Amendments of 1965, which abolished national-origin quotas and established a limitation on immigration from countries in the Americas.

9. Migration Policy Institute, "Lessons from the Immigration Reform and Control Act of 1986," Policy Brief: Independent Task Force on Migration and America's Future (Washington, DC: Migration Policy Institute, August 2006).

10. Migration Policy Institute, "Lessons from the Immigration Reform and Control Act of 1986."

11. Pia M. Orrenius and Madeleine Zavodny, "Do Amnesty Programs Encourage Illegal Immigration? Evidence from the Immigration Reform and Control Act (IRCA)," *Federal Reserve Bank of Atlanta*, Working Papers Series, 2001-19 (November 2001).

12. Massey, Durand, and Malone, *Beyond Smoke and Mirrors*.

13. Manuel Ángel Castillo, "Tendencias y Determinantes Estructurales de La Migración Internacional En Centroamérica" (Seminario Internacional sobre la población del Istmo

Centroamericano al fin del milenio, San José de Costa Rica, 1999), http://ccp.ucr.ac.cr/seminario/pdf/castillo.pdf.

14. Castillo, "Tendencias y Determinantes Estructurales de La Migración Internacional En Centroamérica."

15. The General Agreement on Tariffs and Trade was replaced by the World Trade Organization in 1995.

16. Timothy J. Dunn, *The Militarization of the U.S.-Mexico Border, 1978–1992: Low-Intensity Conflict Doctrine Comes Home* (Austin: University of Texas Press, 1996).

17. Carlos Flores, "La Frontera Sur y Las Migraciones Internacionales Ante La Perspectiva Del Tratado de Libre Comercio," *Estudios Demográficos y Urbanos* 8, no. 2 (23) (May 1, 1993): 361–76.

18. Joseph Nevins, *Operation Gatekeeper and beyond: The War on "Illegals" and the Remaking of the U.S.-Mexico Boundary*, 2nd ed. (New York: Routledge, 2010).

19. Castillo, "Tendencias y Determinantes Estructurales de La Migración Internacional En Centroamérica."

20. The president of the United States was Bill Clinton (Democrat) (1993–2001). The presidents of Mexico were Carlos Salinas de Gortari from 1988 to 1994 and Ernesto Zedillo from 1994 to 2000 (both from PRI).

21. Frank D. Bean, Roland Chanove, Robert G. Cushing, Rodolfo de la Garza, Gary Freeman, Charles W. Haynes and David Spener, "Illegal Mexican Migration & the United States/Mexico Border: The Effects of Operation Hold the Line on El Paso/Juárez" (Population Research Center: University of Texas at Austin: U.S. Commission on Immigration Reform, July 1994), http://www.trinity.edu/dspener/publications/imm-jul94.pdf.

22. Immigration and Naturalization Service, "Apprehensions in the Southwest Border" (2015). The official statistics on apprehensions are given in fiscal years, which go from October 1 through September 30 of each year.

23. Bean, Chanove, Cushing, de la Garza, Freeman, Haynes and Spener, "Illegal Mexican Migration & the United States/Mexico Border."

24. Bean, Chanove, Cushing, de la Garza, Freeman, Haynes and Spener, "Illegal Mexican Migration & the United States/Mexico Border"; Timothy J. Dunn, *Blockading the Border and Human Rights: The El Paso Operation That Remade Immigration Enforcement* (Austin: University of Texas Press, 2010).

25. Bill Ong Hing, *Defining America: Through Immigration Policy* (Philadelphia: Temple University Press, 2012).

26. Timothy J. Dunn and Jose Palafox, "Militarization of the Border" (UUA Immigration Study Guide, 2005), http://www.uua.org/sites/live-new.uua.org/files/documents/washington office/immigration/studyguides/handout4.1.pdf.

27. Karl Eschbach, Jacqueline Hagan, and Nestor Rodríguez, "Deaths during Undocumented Migration: Trends and Policy Implications in the New Era of Homeland Security," *The Centre for Migration Studies of New York, Inc.* 26 (2003): 52–57.

28. Eschbach, Hagan, and Rodríguez, "Deaths during Undocumented Migration."

29. Conversations with activists in Nogales and Tucson in 2015 and 2018. These observations were not gathered in the spring of 2019.

30. Eschbach, Hagan, and Rodríguez, "Deaths during Undocumented Migration."

31. They followed men and women (fifteen to thirty-five years old) year by year from 1980 to 1998. If they had never been in the United States in a particular year, they were in

the denominator; if they had migrated in their first undocumented trip that year, they were counted in the numerator. This operation gives them a series of first trip probabilities.

32. Massey, Durand, and Malone, *Beyond Smoke and Mirrors*, 111.

33. Michelle Mittelstadt, Burke Speaker, Doris Meissner, and Muzaffar Chishti, "Through the Prism of National Security: Major Immigration Policy and Program Changes in the Decade since 9/11" (Migration Policy Institute, August 2011), http://migrationpolicy .org/research/post-9-11-immigration-policy-program-changes.

34. Susanne Jonas and Catherine Tactaquin, "Latino Immigrant Rights in the Shadow of the National Security State: Responses to Domestic Preemptive Strikes," *Social Justice* 31, no. 1/2 (2004): 67–91, 69–70.

35. Mittelstadt, Speaker, Meissner, and Chishti, "Through the Prism."

36. Mittelstadt, Speaker, Meissner, and Chishti, "Through the Prism."

37. Yoku Shaw-Taylor, *Immigration, Assimilation, and Border Security* (Lanham, MD: Government Institutes, 2011).

38. Immigration Policy Project, "Border Protection, Antiterrorism and Illegal Immigration Control Act of 2005/H.R. 4437 Co-Sponsors: Representative James Sensenbrenner (R-WI) and Representative Peter King (R-NY)," *National Conference of State Legislatures (NCSL)* (blog), 2015, http://www.ncsl.org/research/immigration/summary -of-the-sensenbrenner-immigration-bill.aspx.

39. Samuel Norton Chambers, Geoffrey Alan Boyce, Sarah Launius, and Alicia Dinsmore, "Mortality, Surveillance and the Tertiary 'Funnel Effect' on the U.S.-Mexico Border: A Geospatial Modeling of the Geography of Deterrence," *Journal of Borderlands Studies* 36, no. 3 (January 31, 2019): 1–26, https://doi.org/10.1080/08865655.2019.1570861.

40. Nevins, *Operation Gatekeeper and Beyond*, 184.

41. Gabriela Rodríguez Pizarro, "Informe presentado por la Relatora Especial, Sra. Gabriela Rodríguez Pizarro, de conformidad con la resolución 2002/62 de la Comisión de Derechos Humanos," Trabajadores Migrantes (ONU, Consejo Económico y Social, October 30, 2002).

42. Lynnaire Maria Sheridan, *"I Know It's Dangerous": Why Mexicans Risk Their Lives to Cross the Border* (Tucson: University of Arizona Press, 2009), 89.

43. Dan Murphy, "Mexico Tightens Own Southern Border," *Christian Science Monitor*, August 24, 2001, http://www.csmonitor.com/2001/0824/p1s3-woam.html.

44. Sheridan, *"I Know It's Dangerous,"* 89.

45. Velia Jaramillo, "Mexico's 'Southern Plan': The Facts: Crackdown Underway on Migration from Central America," *World Press Review*, June 2001, http://worldpress.org /0901feature22.htm.

46. Gabriela Rodríguez Pizarro, "Informe presentado por la Relatora Especial, Sra. Gabriela Rodríguez Pizarro, de conformidad con la resolución 2002/62 de la Comisión de Derechos Humanos."

47. Rodolfo Casillas, "El Plan Sur de México y Sus Efectos Sobre La Migración Internacional (Análisis)," *Ecuador Debate* 56 (2002): 199–210.

48. World Press Review Online, "Mexico's 'Southern Plan': The Facts; Crackdown Underway on Migration from Central America," http://www.worldpress.org/0901feature22 .htm.

49. Steve Taylor, "Our Southern Border Is Now with Guatemala | Latina Lista," *Latina Lista* (blog), September 20, 2012, http://latinalista.com/2012/09/historic-partnership-agreements

-signed; Todd Miller, "OPINION: Mexico: The US Border Patrol's Newest Hire," *Al Jazeera*, April 10, 2014, Al Jazeera America edition, http://america.aljazeera.com/opinions/2014/10/mexico-us-borderpatrolsecurityimmigrants.html.

50. Rodríguez Pizarro, "Informe presentado por la Relatora Especial, Sra. Gabriela Rodríguez Pizarro, de conformidad con la resolución 2002/62 de la Comisión de Derechos Humanos."

51. Sheridan, *"I Know It's Dangerous"*; Casillas, "El Plan Sur de México y Sus Efectos Sobre La Migración Internacional (Análisis)."

52. Rodríguez Pizarro, "Informe presentado por la Relatora Especial, Sra. Gabriela Rodríguez Pizarro, de conformidad con la resolución 2002/62 de la Comisión de Derechos Humanos."

53. On June 5, 2019, the Mexican government arrested two prominent migrant rights advocates, Cristobal Sánchez and Irineo Mujica, for human trafficking. Although a judge eventually dropped both charges, this case shows how human rights defenders are still criminalized and bullied. https://www.jornada.com.mx/ultimas/2019/06/05/detienen-a-activistas-pro-migrantes-cristobal-sanchez-e-irineo-mujica-5079.html.

54. Luisa Gabriela Morales Vega, "Categorías Migratorias En México: Análisis de La Ley de Migración," *Anuario Mexicano de Derecho Internacional* 12 (2012): 929–58.

55. Maria Dolores Pombo, *Violencias y Migraciones Centroamericanas En México* (Mexico: Colegio de la Frontera Norte, 2017), https://libreria.colef.mx/detalle.aspx?id=7649&fbclid=IwAR1DlCC4oxtGJoYYQoPyt8PmFgnagkBSxyuQwtIT_tRmvGw7ctbs6hpq9x0; Rosa Cordelia Landero, "Los Derechos Humanos de Los Inmigrantes de La Frontera Sur de México," *BARATARIA, Revista Castellano-Manchega de Ciencias Sociales* 19 (2015): 139–50; Oxfam, "Oxfam Denuncia Abusos y Violaciones a Derechos Humanos En Contra de Migrantes Forzados de Centroamérica," October 30, 2018, https://reliefweb.int/sites/reliefweb.int/files/resources/Oxfam%20abusos%20y%20violaciones%20migrantes%20centroamericanos%2030102018.pdf.

56. Presidencia de la República, "¿Qué Es El Programa Frontera Sur? México y Guatemala Trabajan Juntos Para Hacer de La Frontera Una Zona Más Segura, Inclusiva y Competitiva," Official Website, December 2014, https://www.gob.mx/presidencia/articulos/que-es-el-programa-frontera-sur.

57. Rodrigo Dominguez Villegas and Victoria Rietig, "Migrants Deported from the United States and Mexico to the Northern Triangle: A Statistical and Socioeconomic Profile" (Washington, DC: Migration Policy Institute, September 2015), http://www.migrationpolicy.org/research/migrants-deported-united-states-and-mexico-northern-triangle-statistical-and-socioeconomic.

58. Alejandra Díaz de León, "Nadie Aprende En Cabeza Ajena: Migración y Violencia En México," *Revista Justicia Posible* 2 (2020): 22–27.

59. Ana González-Barrera, "Apprehensions of Mexican Migrants at U.S. Borders Reach Near-Historic Low," *Pew Research Center*, April 14, 2016, http://www.pewresearch.org/fact-tank/2016/04/14/mexico-us-border-apprehensions/.

60. INEGI, "Información de Migración Internacional Con Datos de La ENOE al Tercer Trimestre de 2015," *Boletín de Prensa* (INEGI, October 28, 2016), http://www.inegi.org.mx/saladeprensa/boletines/2016/especiales/especiales2016_01_10.pdf.

61. Makini Brice, "Trump Threatens More Tariffs on Mexico over Part of Immigration Deal," *Reuters*, June 10, 2019, World News sec., https://www.reuters.com/article/us-usa

-trade-mexico/trump-threatens-more-tariffs-on-mexico-over-part-of-immigration-deal
-idUSKCN1TB182.

62. Roberto Morales, "Trump Suspende Aranceles y México Se Compromete a Parar La 'Marea de Migrantes,'" *El Economista*, June 7, 2019, Relación México-Estados Unidos sec., https://www.eleconomista.com.mx/empresas/Trump-suspende-aranceles-y-Mexico-se -compromete-a-parar-la-marea-de-migrantes-20190607-0073.html.

63. Taylor, "Our Southern Border Is Now with Guatemala | Latina Lista"; Morales, "Trump Suspende Aranceles y México Se Compromete a Parar La 'Marea de Migrantes.'"

64. Miller, "OPINION."

65. Alejandra Díaz de León, "'Transient Communities': How Central American Transit Migrants Form Solidarity without Trust," *Journal of Borderlands Studies*, October 7, 2020, https://www.tandfonline.com/doi/abs/10.1080/08865655.2020.1824683.

66. Casillas, "El Plan Sur de México y Sus Efectos Sobre La Migración Internacional (Análisis)."

67. Murphy, "Mexico Tightens Own Southern Border."

68. Gabriela Rodríguez Pizarro, "Informe presentado por la Relatora Especial, Sra. Gabriela Rodríguez Pizarro, de conformidad con la resolución 2002/62 de la Comisión de Derechos Humanos"; CNDH, "Informe Especial Sobre Secuestro de Migrantes En México" (Mexico, February 22, 2011).

69. Interview with Jorge, Palenque, 2016.

70. Interview with Jarvis, Palenque, 2015.

71. Interview with Juan, Palenque, 2015.

72. Interview with Juan, Palenque, 2015.

73. Interview with Jarvis, Palenque, 2015

74. Interview with Rulo, Saltillo, 2015.

75. Sin Fronteras, "México y su Frontera Sur" (Sin Fronteras, 2005), http://www.sinfronteras .org.mx/attachments/021_México%20y%20su%20Frontera%20sur%202005.pdf.

76. Araceli Ávila Morales, Laura Díaz de León, and Jorge Andrade, "En El Umbral Del Dolor: Acceso a Los Servicios de Salud En Estaciones Migratorias" (Mexico City: Instituto para la Seguridad y la Democracia, Insyde, 2017), http://insyde.org.mx/wp -content/uploads/Acceso_Servicios_Salud_Estaciones_Migratorias-Insyde-Sept2017 .pdf.

77. Loretta Ortiz Ahlf, "Acceso a La Justicia de Los Migrantes Irregulares En México," *Biblioteca Virtual Del Instituto de Investigaciones Jurídicas de La UNAM*, 2012; Ximena Suárez, Andrés Díaz, José Knippen and Maureen Meyer, "El Acceso a La Justicia Para Personas Migrantes En México: Un Derecho Que Existe Sólo En El Papel" (WOLA: La oficina en Washington para asuntos latinoamericanos, July 2017).

78. Edgar Ávila, "Suman 300 Cuerpos Hallados En Fosa Clandestina de Veracruz," *El Universal*, July 24, 2018, Estados sec., https://www.eluniversal.com.mx/estados/suman -300-cuerpos-hallados-en-fosa-clandestina-de-veracruz.

79. Pedro Matías, "Denuncian Desaparición de al Menos 100 Migrantes En Veracruz," *Proceso*, November 5, 2018, https://www.proceso.com.mx/558246/denuncian-desaparicion -de-al-menos-100-migrantes-en-veracruz.

80. CNDH, "Informe Especial Sobre Los Casos de Secuestro En Contra de Migrantes" (Mexico: CNDH, June 15, 2009).

81. CNDH, "Informe Especial Sobre Secuestro de Migrantes En México."

82. Amnesty International, "Invisible Victims: Migrants on the Move in Mexico," Amnesty International Publications (Amnesty International, 2010); Centro Pro Derechos Humanos, "Secuestros a Personas Migrantes Centroamericanas en Tránsito por México," March 22, 2010.

83. Ernesto Rodriguez Chávez and Graciela Martínez Caballero, "Síntesis 2012: Estadística Migratoria" (México: Secretaría de Gobernación/Subsecretaría de Población, Migración y Asuntos Religiosos/Unidad de Política Migratoria/Centro de Estudios Migratorios, 2012), https://docplayer.es/71602001-Sintesis-estadistica-migratoria.html.

84. It is impossible to know how many tried to go through and remained invisible. Oxfam estimated the volume of Central American migration in Mexico in 2011 by adding three groups of data: (1) those detained by migratory authorities (50–55%), (2) those detained by U.S. migratory authorities in the north border (25–35%), and (3) those who managed to access the United States and settled there (15–20%). Ernesto Rodriguez Chávez, Salvador Berumen Sandoval, and Luis Felipe Ramos Martínez, "Apuntes Sobre Migración: Migración Centroamericana de Tránsito Irregular Por México; Estimaciones y Características Generales," *Centro de Estudios Migratorios INM*, July 2011, http://www.oxfammexico.org/wp-content/uploads/2013/06/APUNTES_N1_Jul2011.pdf.

85. Jesús Eduardo González, Rogelio Zapata, and Maria Eugenia Anguiano, "La Situación Demográfica de México," in *Migración Centroamericana En Tránsito Por México 2016*, ed. CONAPO (Mexico City: Consejo Nacional de Población CONAPO, 2017), 221–32, http://www.equidad.org.mx/pdf/Situacion%20Demografica%20Mexico%202016.pdf.

86. Díaz de León, "Nadie Aprende En Cabeza Ajena."

87. Interview with Filadelfo, Saltillo, 2015.

88. Interview with Chaparro, Nogales, 2016.

89. Interview with Chaparro, Nogales, 2016.

90. Interview with Chaparro, Nogales, 2016.

91. U.S. Border Patrol 1994 in Seghetti, 2014, 3.

92. Jason De León, *The Land of Open Graves* (Oakland: University of California Press, 2015), http://www.ucpress.edu/book.php?isbn=9780520282759.

93. Interview with Nahu, Tijuana, 2017.

94. Support Center for Migrant Workers and the Desert Shelter.

95. Martha Guerrero-Ortiz and Martha Cecilia Jaramillo-Cardona, "Deportación y Violación de Los Derechos Del Migrante En Ambas Fronteras," *Convergencia: Revista de Ciencias Sociales* 22, no. 69 (December 2015): 85–106.

96. Camilo Montoya-Galvez and Angel Canales, "More than 10,000 Asylum Seekers Returned under 'Remain in Mexico' as U.S. Set to Expand Policy," *CBS News*, June 8, 2019, https://www.cbsnews.com/news/remain-in-mexico-asylum-seekers-returned-as-us-seeks-to-expand-policy-2019-06-08/.

97. Interview with activist JA: April 20, 2018.

98. Guerrero-Ortiz and Jaramillo-Cardona, "Deportación y Violación de Los Derechos Del Migrante En Ambas Fronteras."

99. Montoya-Galvez and Canales, "More than 10,000 Asylum Seekers."

100. Interview with Roberto, April 2017.

101. Richard M. Stana, *Border Patrol: Checkpoints Contribute to Border Patrol's Mission, but More Consistent Data Collection and Performance Measurement Could Improve Effectiveness* (DIANE Publishing, 2010).

102. Interview with Sandro, Nogales, 2018.

103. Homeland Security, "Testimony of Office of Technology, Innovation, and Acquisition Assistant Commissioner Mark Borkowski, U.S. Border Patrol Chief Michael Fisher, and Office of Air and Marine Assistant Commissioner Michael Kostelnik, Customs and Border Protection, before the United States House Committee on Homeland Security, Subcommittee on Border and Maritime Security, 'After SBInet—the Future of Technology on the Border,'" Testimony (Cannon House Office Building: Homeland Security, March 15, 2016), https://www.dhs.gov/news/2011/03/15/written-testimony-cbp-house-homeland-security-subcommittee-border-and-maritime; Chad C. Haddal, "Border Security: The Role of the U.S. Border Patrol" (Washington, DC: Congressional Research Service, August 11, 2010), http://www.dtic.mil/dtic/tr/fulltext/u2/a530562.pdf.

104. Eschbach, Hagan, and Rodríguez, "Deaths during Undocumented Migration."

105. Daniel González, "The Remains of 127 Dead Migrants Were Recovered in Southern Arizona in 2018," *Arizona Republic*, January 16, 2019, European online edition, https://eu.azcentral.com/story/news/politics/border-issues/2019/01/16/remains-127-dead-migrants-recovered-southern-arizona-2018/2575080002/.

106. Massey, Durand, and Malone, *Beyond Smoke and Mirrors*.

107. Massey, Durand, and Malone, *Beyond Smoke and Mirrors*.

108. Whatsapp communication, Ronin, 2018.

109. Roberto Coronado and Pia M. Orrenius, "Crime on the U.S.-Mexico Border: The Effect of Undocumented Immigration and Border Enforcement," *Migraciones Internacionales* 4, no. 1 (2007), http://www.scielo.org.mx/scielo.php?pid=S1665-89062007000100002&script=sci_arttext&tlng=en.

110. Dunn, *Blockading the Border and Human Rights*.

111. Dunn, *Blockading the Border and Human Rights*.

112. Peter Yoxall, "The Minuteman Project, Gone in a Minute or Here to Stay? The Origin, History and Future of Citizen Activism on the United States–Mexico Border," *University of Miami Inter-American Law Review* 37, no. 3 (April 1, 2006): 517–66, https://doi.org/10.2307/40176628.

113. Arizona is also the state where the SB1070 was enacted. This law made being illegally in Arizona without papers a misdemeanor and established that agents could verify the migratory status of people during any lawful stop and prohibited unauthorized people from applying for work. Most of the most controversial provisions haven't been applied yet.

114. Interview with activist M, Nogales, 2018.

115. Interview with activist R, Nogales, 2017.

116. Julie Whitaker, "Mexican Deaths in the Arizona Desert: The Culpability of Migrants, Humanitarian Workers, Governments and Businesses," *Journal of Business Ethics*, Supplement 2: *Central America and Mexico: Efforts and Obstacles in Creating Ethical Organizations and Ethical Economy* 88, no. 2 (2009): 365–67.

117. Kristine Phillips, "They Left Food and Water for Migrants in the Desert: Now They Might Go to Prison," *Washington Post*, January 20, 2019, National sec., https://www.washingtonpost.com/nation/2019/01/20/they-left-food-water-migrants-desert-now-they-might-go-prison/?noredirect=on&utm_term=.b82b3f3440c7.

118. Miriam Jordan, "An Arizona Teacher Helped Migrants: Jurors Couldn't Decide if It Was a Crime," *New York Times*, June 11, 2019, https://www.nytimes.com/2019/06/11/us /scott-warren-arizona-deaths.html.

119. No More Deaths, "Multiple Remains Recovered This Week," *Abuse Documentation, Local Press Releases, Updates* (blog), May 8, 2019, http://forms.nomoredeaths.org/multiple -remains-recovered-this-week/.

Contributors

Alberto Barrera-Enderle received his PhD in history from the University of California, Irvine in 2013. He is research professor at Centro de Investigaciones y Estudios Superiores en Antropología Social (CIESAS) in Monterrey, Mexico. He is currently completing a book on car smuggling across the U.S.-Mexico borderlands between 1920 and 1960.

Alice L. Baumgartner is assistant professor of history at the University of Southern California. She holds a PhD from Yale University and an MPhil in Latin American Studies from the University of Oxford, where she was a Rhodes Scholar. Her first book, *South to Freedom: Runaway Slaves to Mexico and the Road to Civil War*, was selected as an Editor's Choice by the *New York Times Book Review* and as a finalist for the Gilder Lehrman Lincoln Prize.

Lance R. Blyth is the command historian for the North American Aerospace Defense Command and U.S. Northern Command in Colorado Springs, Colorado. A historian of violence, conflict, and warfare in liminal environments, he is the author of *Chiricahua and Janos: Communities of Violence in the Southwestern Borderlands, 1680–1880* (2015) and is currently researching a history of mountain warfare through the experiences of the U.S. Tenth Mountain Division in World War II.

Timothy Bowman is associate professor and chair of the Department of History at West Texas A&M University in Canyon, Texas. He is the author of *Blood Oranges: Colonialism and Agriculture in the South Texas Borderlands* (2016), and his work focuses on North American borderlands history and the history of the Southern Plains. Bowman is also coeditor of the book series New Directions in Tejano History from the University of Oklahoma Press.

Elaine Carey is dean of the College of Arts and Sciences and professor of history at Oakland University. She is the author of over fifty articles and the books *Plaza of Sacrifices: Gender, Power, and Terror in 1968 Mexico* (2005) and the award-winning *Women Drug Traffickers: Mules, Bosses, and Organized Crime* (2014). As a historian who researches crime and human rights, she has served as an expert witness in courts across the United States and has consulted for radio, podcasts, film, television, archives, libraries, and museums.

William D. Carrigan is professor of history at Rowan University. He earned his BA at the University of Texas at Austin and his PhD from Emory University. He is the author or editor of numerous scholarly articles and four books, including *The Making of a Lynching Culture: Violence and Vigilantism in Central Texas, 1836–1916*. Since 1995, he has been collaborating with Clive Webb and studying the lynching of Mexicans in the United States, and together they have published eight articles and the monograph *Forgotten Dead: Mob Violence against Mexicans in the United States, 1848–1928.*

José Carlos Cisneros Guzmán is a graduate student in the North American Studies master's program in Universidad Autonoma de Sinaloa. His work focuses on ethnography with women inside drug trade organizations. He has authored "Drug Traffickers with Lipstick: An Ethnographic Trip to Sinaloa," published academic chapters in *Las Jefas del Narco* (2012), and coauthored with Elaine Carey "Las Hijas de la Nacha" (2011). As an ethnographer, he has been consulted as an academic adviser for governors. Currently, he works as a mentor at Universidad Tecmilenio Culiacán.

Alejandra Díaz de León is associate professor in sociology at El Colegio de México (COLMEX). She studies social network formation, trust, and bonding between strangers during violent and uncertain situations. Her research focuses on Central American migrants in the transit route through Mexico. She has done ethnographic fieldwork all over Mexico and on both sides of the U.S.-Mexico border.

Miguel Ángel González-Quiroga taught the history of Mexico and the United States at the Universidad Autónoma de Nuevo León in Mexico from 1983 until 2011. He received his bachelor of arts degree at the University of Houston and his master's degree in Latin American History at the University of the Americas in Puebla, Mexico. He has authored, edited, or translated six books and has written numerous articles and book chapters on the Texas-Mexico border region. His latest book, *War and Peace on the Rio Grande Frontier,* was published by Oklahoma University Press in 2020.

Santiago Ivan Guerra currently serves as the W. M. Keck Director of the Hulbert Center for Southwest Studies, the A. E. and Ethel Irene Carlton Professor in the Social Sciences, and associate professor of Southwest studies at Colorado College. He is an interdisciplinary borderlands scholar working at the intersection of anthropology, history, and Chicanx Studies. He is currently completing a book titled *Narcos and Nobodies: Untold Stories of the Border Drug War* that explores the historical and contemporary impact of the border drug war from the perspective of border smugglers and their families.

Gerardo Gurza-Lavalle is professor of history at the Instituto Mora in Mexico City. He is the author of *Una vecindad efímera: Los Estados Confederados de América y su política exterior hacia México, 1861–1865* (2001); with Marcela Terrazas, *Las relaciones México–Estados Unidos 1756–2010,* Volumen I: *Imperios, repúblicas y pueblos en pugna por el territorio: Las relaciones México–Estados Unidos, 1756–1867* (2012); and *Virginia y la reforma de la esclavitud: Los límites del progreso en una sociedad esclavista* (2016).

Sonia Hernández is associate professor of history at Texas A&M University. She is the author of the award-winning *Working Women into the Borderlands* (2014), which was translated and published as *Mujeres, trabajo y región fronteriza* (2017). Her latest book, *For a Just and Better World: Engendering Anarchism in the Mexican Borderlands, 1900–1938,* is forthcoming with the University of Illinois Press. Hernández is currently working on a book on Gregorio Cortez, gender, and transnational state violence.

Alan Knight is emeritus professor of the history of Latin America at Oxford University. He is the author of *The Mexican Revolution* (two volumes), *Revolución, Democracia y Populismo en América Latina*, and *Repensar la Revolución Mexicana* (two volumes), five other books on Latin American—especially Mexican—history, and numerous articles. He has coedited four volumes dealing with petroleum, boss politics, superstition, and the Great Depression. A new volume of his essays on Latin America—*Bandits and Liberals, Saints and Rebels*—came out in 2021.

José Gabriel Martínez-Serna is professor of history in the School of Humanities and Education of the Instituto Tecnológico de Monterrey (Monterrey campus). He holds a PhD in history from Southern Methodist University. He is the author of *Viñedos e indios del desierto: Fundación, auge y secularización de una misión jesuita en la frontera noreste de la Nueva España* (2014) and "Los jesuitas y el desarrollo económico de la frontera sur del imperio hispánico, siglos XVI–XVIII" (2014).

Brandon Morgan holds a PhD in the history of modern Mexico and the American West from the University of New Mexico. Currently, he is chairperson of history, anthropology, economics, political science, and ethnic studies at Central New Mexico Community College in Albuquerque, where he teaches courses on historical thinking, the history of New Mexico, and the history of Latin America. He is working on a book that focuses on the history of violence and community building along the New Mexico–Chihuahua border around the turn of the twentieth century.

Joaquín Rivaya-Martínez is associate professor of history at Texas State University. He holds a PhD in anthropology from UCLA, and was a postdoctoral fellow at Southern Methodist University's Clements Center for Southwestern Studies. He specializes in the history of the Indigenous peoples of the U.S.-Mexico borderlands during the eighteenth and nineteenth centuries. Institutions that have funded his research include the Wenner-Gren Foundation, the American Philosophical Society, the Newberry Library, UC MEXUS, UCLA's Institute of American Cultures, and CONACyT. He has published in the United States, Mexico, Spain, France, Canada, and Ecuador. One of his ongoing projects is a book on the presence of the Plains Indians in Mexico after 1821.

Andrew J. Torget is a historian of nineteenth-century North America at the University of North Texas, where he holds the University Distinguished Teaching Professorship. An award-winning speaker, digital scholarship innovator, and teacher, he is the author and editor of several works on the U.S.-Mexico borderlands. His most recent book, *Seeds of Empire: Cotton, Slavery, and the Transformation of the Texas Borderlands, 1800–1850* (2015), won twelve prizes and awards, including the David J. Weber–Clements Center Prize for Best Non-Fiction Book on Southwestern America from the Western History Association.

Clive Webb is professor of modern American history at the University of Sussex in Brighton, England. His collaboration with William Carrigan led to the book *Forgotten Dead: Mob Violence against Mexicans in the United States, 1848–1928*, and the two authors are now working on a study about the lynching of foreign nationals in the United States.

Index

Page numbers appearing in italics refer to figures, graphs, maps, and tables.

Operation Gatekeeper, 347
Operation Hold the Line, 346, 363n21
Operation Intercept, 298, 305
Operation Rio Grande, 347
Operation Safeguard, 347
Operation Wetback, 343
opiate derivatives, 323
opiates, 300, 301, 302, 330
Opp, Frederick, 228
Ord, Edward O. C., 89–90, 98, 132, 161
Ord Order, 115n3, 161, 165n67
Orozco, Pascual, 269–70, 291n78
Osages, 58–59, 71n41
Osorno, Diego, 315
outsourcing of drug violence, 314, 318n56
Oxfam, 355, 367n84

Pacheco, Macario, 196, 199, 203–4, 206, 207, 212n44
Padilla, Luciano, 241–42, 258–59
Page, Frank, 87
Palacios, Don Antonio, 79–80
Palomas: Customs House raid of, 191, 194–97, 207, 208, 210n9, 212n44; other insurgency activity in, 199, 200–201, 202–3, 204–5, 206
Pantano Ranch, 43
paramilitary organizations, 86–90, 312–13
Paredes, Américo, 216, 223, 225, 235n37
Pariente, Benito, 41
Parr, Archie, 287n40
Pawnees, 58
peelers, hide, 78, 82–83
Penatekas, 53–55, 57, 64
Perales, Macedonio, 57
Perales brothers, 82
Pérez, Rafael M., 191
Pérez, Santana, 14, 192–94, 203, 206, 207–8, 209n5. See also Pérez's insurgency
Pérez's insurgency, 191–208; amnesty and end of, 207–8, 213n58; background and overview of, 122, 191–94; conclusions on, 208; expansion of, 200–202; Mexican government narrative of, 194–97, 202–3, 204, 205–6; Palomas Customs House raid and, 191, 194–95, 199, 211n26; press and,

190, 191–92, 195, 196–97, 200–201, 202–6, 210n9; proclamation of, 197–98, 206, 210n9; Sierra Madre battle of, 205–6; U.S. and, 198–200, 203, 208
Periódico Oficial, 198, 207–8, 224
Peterson del Mar, David, 160
Pew Research Center, 351
Phoenix Herald, 256
Pizaña, Aniceto, 252, 277
Plains Apaches, 49, 64
Plains Indians, 155, 156, 249
Plan de San Diego, 15, 274, 276–79, 282, 290n74, 290–91n77, 292n87
Plan of Tuxtepec, 89, 169, 203
"Plan Restaurador de la Libertad," 170
Plan Sur, 349–50
poppy, 330, 338n43
popular culture, 1–3, 21n5
population growth, 14, 61
Portillo, Antonio, 107, 108, 118n48
Porvenir, 257
Powell, Samuel G., 102
power, state. *See* state power
Powers, Stephen, 108, 126
press: Cortez Incident and, 219, 220, 223–24, 228; Cortina War and, 107–8, 109, 112–13, 126, 127; drug trafficking and, 1, 2–3; Federalist War and, 100, 103, 112–13; on mob violence, 246–47, 250–51, 253; Pérez's insurgency and, *190*, 191–92, 195, 196–97, 200–201, 202–6, 210n9. *See also specific newspapers*
Price Daniel hearings, 323–29, 337n22
prohibition of alcohol, 300–301, 316n11
pseudo cop home invasions, 311–12, 318nn48–49
public lighting, 182, 188n61
Public Security force, 167
Punitive Expedition, 265, 274–75, 277, 279–80, 282, 289n64, 293n100
Punteagudo Ranch, 43
Pure Food and Drug Act of 1906, 300

Quiroga, Miguel, 228
Quiroz, Manuel, 225
quotas, migration, 343, 362nn7–8

National Guard and, 170–71, 184n11; Reyes and, 178–82, 187n49; Rural Forces of the Federation and, 172–74, 185n29

Steele, W. M., 87

Stillman, Charles, 105, 141, 226

sting operations and busts, drug, 296, 308, 326, 332, 337n28

St. John, Rachel, 8–9

stock-raising, 77, 90, 281

"stuck" undocumented migrants, 344

Suaste, Florentino, 260

surveillance, 305, 312, 347, 348–49, 358–59

symmetrical warfare, 265, 266–67, 270, 271, 272, 274

symposiums on U.S.-Mexico border violence, 6, 7

Tamaulipas: about, 45n3, 170; cooperative violence and, 97, 99, 103, 105, 107, 108–9, 112; Cortina War and, 125, 128; drug trafficking and, 298, 299–300, 314–15, 330; government power and, 144, 152; revolt in, 179, 187n50; settlement in, 30–31; state-sanctioned violence in, 170, 173, 174, 179, 180, 181, 187n50; War for Independence and, 36

Tamaulipas National Guard, 105, 107, 109, 112

tariffs, 174, 345, 351

Tatum, H. A., 248

Tejanos: about, 123–24; alliances and, 129–30, 216–17, 222–24; citizenship and, 122–23, 124, 125; Cortez and, 227–28, 231; Cortina War and, 104, 108–9, 112, 118n53, 119n71; Mexican Revolution and, 230; Plan de San Diego and, 276–77, 279, 290n74, 290n76; violence and abuse of, 248, 253. See also mexicanos; specific Tejanos

telegraphs, 145, 177

Tenawas, 53–54

tequileros, 301, 302

Terrazas, Joaquín, 194

Terrazas, Luis, 192, 268

Terrazos, Victoria, 337n30

terrorism, 36–37, 229–30, 312, 341, 348

Terry, Charles E., 325–26, 337n24

Texas: citizenship and, 122, 124–25; European immigration to, 57, 61; Federalist War and, 100–103; fugitive slaves and, 247–49; Mexican War for Independence and, 34–37, 97; mob violence in, 245, 246, 250, 254–56, 257; Native Americans and, 155; Spanish, 29, 30–31, 34–37, 45n3; Treaty of Guadalupe-Hidalgo and, 11; U.S annexation of, 49, 63–64

Texas Historical Commission, 231

Texas Mexicans. See Tejanos

Texas Rangers: cooperative violence and, 107, 108, 109–10, 111, 112; Cortez Incident and, 219, 222, 223; Cortina War and, 127–28, 132, 133; language and, 244, 261n4; liquor smuggling and, 301; during Mexican Revolution, 230, 238n83, 285n28, 293n104; Native Americans and, 155; reconstitution of, 143; state-sanctioned violence and, 229, 238n74, 257

Texas Revolution, 157

Texas-Tamaulipas border, 299–300

theft: of cattle, 145–50, 154–55, 160, 161; of horses, 29, 33, 38–40, 41, 75, 131; ranchers and rancheros and, 76–80, 84, 85. See also lower Rio Grande theft and violence; smuggling

Third Army Zone, 169, 174, 176

33rd Texas Cavalry, 81, 152

Thomas, W. D., 149–50

Thompson, Jerry, 105, 109–10, 134n1

Thompson, William B., 106–7

Thulemeyer, Will A., 217

Thulemeyer Ranch, 215, 217

Tierra Blanca, battle of, 271, 286n33

Tijerina, Antonio, 79, 80

Time, 308

Tisnado, Mariano, 256

Tobin, William Gerard, 107, 127–28

Tomóchic rebellion and massacre, 14, 192–98, 203, 204, 207–8, 209n7

Torreón, 271, 272, 275, 287n41, 287n50, 288–89n60